Critical Issues in Crime and Justice

Second Edition

Mary Maguire: To my colleagues who have dedicated their careers to advancing justice and to my students who are committed to making a difference in the world, this book is for you.

Dan Okada: To the four people who mean the most to me in life: Sharon, Erin, Anny, and Greg Okada. And to all those who are too many to list, from whom I continue to learn and grow, I am grateful for all you give, all you do, and all you are. Namaste.

Critical Issues in Crime and Justice

Thought, Policy, and Practice

Second Edition

Editors

Mary Maguire
California State University, Sacramento

Dan Okada
California State University, Sacramento

Los Angeles | London | New Delhi
Singapore | Washington DC

Los Angeles | London | New Delhi
Singapore | Washington DC

FOR INFORMATION:

SAGE Publications, Inc.
2455 Teller Road
Thousand Oaks, California 91320
E-mail: order@sagepub.com

SAGE Publications Ltd.
1 Oliver's Yard
55 City Road
London EC1Y 1SP
United Kingdom

SAGE Publications India Pvt. Ltd.
B 1/I 1 Mohan Cooperative Industrial Area
Mathura Road, New Delhi 110 044
India

SAGE Publications Asia-Pacific Pte. Ltd.
3 Church Street
#10-04 Samsung Hub
Singapore 049483

Printed in the United States of America

Cataloging-in-publication data is available for this title from the Library of Congress.

ISBN: 978-1-4833-5062-2

This book is printed on acid-free paper.

Acquisitions Editor: Jerry Westby
Editorial Assistant: Laura Kirkhuff
Production Editor: Kelly DeRosa
Copy Editor: Patrice Sutton
Typesetter: C&M Digitals (P) Ltd.
Proofreader: Susan Schon
Indexer: Virgil Diodato
Cover Designer: Candice Harman
Marketing Manager: Terra Schultz

14 15 16 17 18 10 9 8 7 6 5 4 3 2 1

Brief Contents

PART III: Policing and Law Enforcement

PART IV: Policy and Jurisprudence

PART V: Corrections and Societal Response

Detailed Contents

PART II: Offenses and Offenders

PART IV: Policy and Jurisprudence

PART V: Corrections and Societal Response

Preface for the Second Edition

The intent of this volume remains the same as it was in the first edition, to provide provocative material that will stimulate enthusiastic conversation by those who have familiarity with these and other topics that are usually found in a collegiate criminal justice program. The material found in each chapter is not intended to be a comprehensive presentation or examination of that topic. An attempt to do so would be a daunting challenge and entail considerably more heft than was intended here. More to the point, this collection should provide advanced students with reasonable coverage of their academic careers, to include not an abundance of new material, although new material is included, but to remind them to take stock of the lessons their own professors provided and the knowledge that they managed to acquire over their educational experience.

As with other second edition attempts, the opportunity to reinforce the design of our earlier volume was presented to us, and we gave significant consideration to strengthening certain areas and to include some that were not included previously. Again, we are grateful to these new prominent figures in the world of academic criminal justice who contributed their unique voice to the overall statement found in this book. Several chapters were written by different contributors. Given their stature, we are hard pressed to identify them as "new contributors."

In adding this material and recognizing the discussions that this material is likely to stimulate, what becomes glaringly apparent is that there are still areas and material that remain absent. This is the reality of the academic examination of crime and criminal justice. While there may be a basic model on which to develop thoughtful curricula, the dynamics of crime and society along with the needs of the academy result in an abundance of topics that demand attention but have not yet produced adequate scholarship to meet this need.

Our goal has not changed in that we believe that soon-to-be college graduates should be held accountable for the education they received. Not only should they be encouraged, but they should demonstrate and be willing to share as well the knowledge they acquired from the array of sources from which they received it. They must be reminded that given the careers many of them envision for themselves, that they represent the future of criminal justice, and that ultimately, and in spite of any personal misgivings they may have, the application, direction, and fortune of criminal justice rests with them. This affirms the need for providing a strong foundation of the diversity of thought that surrounds the criminal justice enterprise. What is presented here is an attempt to do just that.

It remains the case that many students who enter college with the intent to major in criminal justice have likely done so because of the influence of popular culture. Not only Hollywood movies and television but also popular music and the array of media which they access incessantly have been a constant companion in the lives of these young scholars. For those of us who earn our livings examining both educational practice and scientific inquiry focused on crime and criminal justice, we are rewarded by interacting with those eager to hear what we have to say and engaging our lives in a job we enjoy and an area of inquiry that is unmatched in its significance.

Crime is a very personal matter. While the scholarship of criminal justice can be abstract and makes every attempt to be impersonal, or sterile, we should not forget that the entire criminal justice enterprise is a human service. We appreciate that you are allowing us to provide this information to you on our vision of crime, criminology, and criminal justice. The collective wisdom, perspective, and information possessed by those who have contributed to this volume borders on reverential. That they are sincerely good people is an added bonus. The time you spend here will be well worth your bother.

Mary Maguire
Dan Okada
Sacramento, California

Acknowledgments

Our heartfelt gratitude goes to executive editor, Jerry Westby. Not only is Jerry a pleasure to work with, but his publishing wisdom, encouragement, and guidance made this book a reality. Many thanks also to the tireless efforts of an array of SAGE professionals: MaryAnn Vail, Laura Kirkhuff, and Kelly DeRosa, and copy editor par excellence Patrice Sutton, who all possess the gift of working with recalcitrant egos and issues with appreciated aplomb. Sadly, we report the passing of Olga Storms, creator of our cover art who generously and graciously donated her time, work, and spirit. Our thanks is barely sufficient. In her memory, we maintain her original work on our cover and wash it in blue. We also thank the reviewers, whose efforts and expertise provided insight that helped shape this book into its current form: James Dunn, Bucks New University; Diana R. Grant, Sonoma State University; Robert Mutchnick, Indiana University of Pennsylvania; Melinda D. Schlager, Texas A&M University-Commerce; and Sharon D. Singletary, Winston-Salem State University. This has been a true collaborative effort and we thank all who gave their expertise and effort in producing this effort. We appreciate all of you.

Part I

Criminal Justice and Criminological Paradigms

CHAPTER 1

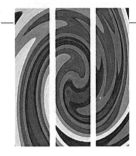

Introduction

The Linearity of Contemporary Criminal Justice Thought: Perspective, Context, and Direction

Dan Okada and Mary Maguire

The lessons of history, while not a favorite journey for everyone, are informative and provide a valuable context for what the present and even the future hold. They also place into a clearer perspective the need for responsible public policy that is tied to reasonable theory construction, that is, the mind meld between science and society. An innovative, contemporary law enforcement strategy arose from a nexus of many buzz terms: Evidence-based practices (EBPs), crime mapping or COMPuter STATistics (CompStat), "hot-spot" analysis, problem-oriented policing, modus operandi investigation, social ecology, and social networking, among an array of other influences, have come together to form what now can be seen as predictive policing. Is it possible for police officers to anticipate where and when a crime will occur before it does? Rather than arrest after the fact, can officers actually be on the scene before the crime occurs and then apprehend a suspect just as s/he breaks the law? That is the intent of this process. In practice, and as a police patrol strategy, this strategy is experiencing implementation in at least two California cities: Santa Cruz and Los Angeles. What is of interest here is that it has its historical roots in Shaw and McKay's (1942) *spot maps*, or cartographic criminology, which itself was an evolution of Park and Burgess's (1925) ambition to turn the city of Chicago into a dynamic social laboratory, which would then establish the University of Chicago's Department of Sociology as the predominant center of social science research.

As a journalist, Robert Park understood that in order to obtain insightful information to better tell a news story, he often had to go to the source of that information, actual witnesses, and hear what they had to say (Rauschenbush, 1979). While he did not use the argot of research methods, he was actually engaged in an early postmodern model of data gathering. His newspaper curiosity to ask the journalistic "5Ws+H"—who, what, when, where, why, and how, in seeking information, allowed him to engage in an early form of self-reporting through face-to-face interviews, although social science methodologies had yet to be created that would catalog this as data collection.

Around this same time, in Berkeley, California, August Vollmer, Berkeley's first police chief, began instituting what was a career-long appetite for innovation as he is credited with establishing such radical innovations in the world of practical policing as the patrol car, the lie detector, forensic investigation, college education for police officers, and crime profiling (the modus operandi method of investigation; Parker, 1972). It is a reasonable assertion to make that he alone is responsible for encouraging the practitioners of academic disciplines as diverse as chemistry, biology, anthropology, psychology, sociology, and economics to turn their creative attention to the problem of crime. To say that Vollmer was a major influence in American policing grossly understates his contributions.

In the mid-1960s, Schwendinger and Schwendinger (1985) interviewed adolescents around the beaches of Los Angeles, asking them to identify their friends and the sorts of activities they engaged in when they were together. In what today would be called social networking, the Schwendingers established that adolescents formed cliques and subcultures around mutually compatible activities and argot that were based on any number of commonalities. The lower class *Eses* were not all that different in character or bonhomie from the upper class *Soces* or the surfer crowd *Hodads*. What tied them together was that each could produce their own quality of mischief. Today, members would have communicated their activities via social media posts to their electronic network of associates, so that the extended networks could vicariously live the adventure but likewise be tracked for the types of crimes committed.

One impetus for Goldstein's (1979) original policing strategy proposal was his dissatisfaction with the benign term *law enforcement* to call the activities he had witnessed as a municipal government employee. Law enforcement and policing were only two of the many activities that police officers were called upon to accomplish when they were at work. Goldstein believed that officers could negotiate the myriad calls for service to which they were dispatched over the course of one day's shift more effectively if they proactively considered their areas of responsibility from a more problem-solving perspective. Officers should be able to recognize the problems occurring in their jurisdictions, determine plausible solutions, implement these solutions based on their ability to coordinate with those who could affect remedies, and then reexamine the positive or negative outcome of their intervention. None of these activities fell into the traditional (i.e., "old school") roles of policing or law enforcement, but if these practices were employed, crime reduction could result. Indeed, police officers needed to be much more problem oriented.

Although there is some controversy as to its actual effectiveness and origins, the acknowledged creator of what is now known as crime mapping was a New York Transit Authority lieutenant, Jack Marple (Martin, 2001). In the early 1990s, Marple mimicked what Shaw and McKay had done in Chicago, in taking a map of the boroughs of New York and through color-coding indicating the locations where various crimes throughout the transit district were reported. He then sent his patrol officers out to those areas having the greatest concentrations of a particular color that identified the crime type, location, time, and suspect descriptions. This practice caught the attention of the newly elected mayor of New York, Rudolph Giuliani, and his appointed police commissioner, William Bratton. When the three municipal police agencies of New York—the Transit Police, the Housing Police, and the police department—were merged into one New York Police Department (NYPD) in 1995, one of Commissioner Bratton's first administrative appointments was to make Marple one of his deputy commissioners. Marple brought his color-coded maps to NYPD and CompStat became hot-spot analysis.

Franklin Zimring (2012) spent over a year going on ride-a-longs, walking the streets, talking to New York City police officers, and becoming intimately familiar with Marple's evolution of cartographic criminology, CompStat (which is also referred to as Comstat in some circles). Based on this research, Zimring concluded that one of the reasons why New York experienced an earlier dramatic decreased crime rate than many other cities and that it has had a longer sustained success rate is because of the heavy implementation of hot-spot policing. Common lore suggests that if police officers showed up at the moment a crime event was about to occur, all that would happen is that that crime would not happen at that place and moment; it would simply move to another location, that is, crime would be displaced. Zimring draws a very different conclusion. He contends that most crimes are typical, predictable, and mostly generated by some conception of opportunity. They occur because of what Cohen and Felson (1979) call "routine activities." A motivated offender, meets a suitable target (victim), absent a capable guardian (no police, no friend, no viewing audience, etc. was present as protection), in a convenient time and place, and crime is committed. At the exact moment of intersection with these three elements present, a crime opportunity manifests itself. What Zimring determined was that if that situation becomes biased with the presence of an officer, say, the crime does not move someplace else—it simply does not happen; the moment is lost. NYPD's implementation and maintenance of CompStat, with the practice of stationing officers in those specific locations, has had a demonstrably positive effect on reducing routine crime and, consequently, all crime.

Santa Cruz (California) Police Department (SCPD) became influenced by the fiscal realities of 21st-century economics, the cry to do "more with less." In attempting to implement this ideal, and based on mathematical projections that were designed to predict earthquake aftershocks, SCPD crime analysts initially loaded in data relevant to three specific crime types—residential and commercial burglaries and motor vehicle thefts—into accessible software. These data then produced not only maps of the city indicating where crimes had occurred but also added a layer of assessment suggesting where these specific crimes would most likely occur next. Over an initial 6-month assessment, over two dozen arrests were made in the targeted locations. An unexpected consequence was a 19% decrease in burglaries in these locations, and officers literally had the increased opportunity to intervene during a crime in progress (Friend, 2013).

The moral to this story becomes the connection between theory, policy, and practice. Responsible theory construction comes from understanding what the problem is that needs attention. Many organizations are now calling for and implementing policies that reflect the insertion of science into the daily activities of criminal justice. EBP is being discussed and becoming the standard from which to consider, install, and operate within many organizations. With these criteria comes the veneer of scientific credibility. Originating in the medical industry's need to come to some consensus as to which procedures and practices would lead to the most favorable patient results, EBP was intended to produce cost savings as well as life savings. The criminal justice enterprise then saw the value of this methodology and has now produced such positive and effective efforts as taking guns off the street and reducing gang violence through Operation Ceasefire (Kennedy, 2011), developing specialty (or boutique) courts to handle such specific behavioral problems as drug use and school-truancy matters (Huddleston & Marlowe, 2011), instituting changes to correctional rehabilitation programs (Smith, Gendreau, & Swartz, 2009), and, perhaps most important, reforming and improving juvenile justice practices (Howell & Lipsey, 2012).

The curse of this field of study is that there is no shortage of real world examples that underscore the relevance of our curiosity. That curse is further underscored by the axiom, "The more we know, the more questions we have." As the study of crime, criminals, and those who work with and within this area evolves, questions persist as to how and what to teach and how and why to learn the material generated with our collective focus. Crime theory, construction, and research; policing and law enforcement; jurisprudence and law; punishment and corrections; and organizations and administration, are the general areas of interest that frame most academic divisions offering criminal justice-related curricula. There is no attempt in this volume to be comprehensive or definitive. Rather, the purpose is to further encourage the lifelong pursuit of learning, of being intellectually curious, by providing enough information so that those who are searching for answers will have their imaginations piqued so that they will take this material and develop it beyond what is presented. Be curious and have an interesting journey.

REFERENCES

Cohen, L., & Felson, M. (1979). Social change and crime rate trends: A routine activity approach. *American Sociological Review, 44*(4), 588–608.

Friend, Z. (2013, April). Predictive policing: Using technology to reduce crime. *FBI Law Enforcement Bulletin.* Washington, DC: U.S. Department of Justice. Retrieved from http://www.fbi.gov/stats-services/publications/law-enforcement-bulletin/2013/April/predictive-policing-using-technology-to-reduce-crime

Goldstein, H. (1979). Improving policing: A problem-oriented approach. *Crime and Delinquency, 25*(2), 236–258.

Howell, J. C., & Lipsey, M. W. (2012). Research-based guidelines for juvenile justice programs. *Justice Research and Policy, 14*(1), 17–34.

Huddleston, W., & Marlowe, D. B. (2011). *Painting the current picture: A national report on drug courts and other problem-solving courts. Programs in the United States.* Washington, DC: National Drug Court Institute.

Kennedy, D. M. (2011). *Don't shoot: One man, a street fellowship, and the end of violence in inner-city America.* New York, NY: Bloomsbury, USA.

Martin, D. A. (2001, August 6). Jack Maple, 48, a designer of city crime control strategies. *The New York Times,* A17.

Park, R. E., & Burgess, E. W. (1925). *The city: Suggestions for investigation of human behavior in the urban environment.* Chicago, IL: University of Chicago Press.

Parker, A. E. (1972). *The Berkeley police story.* Springfield, IL: Charles C Thomas.

Rauschenbush, W. (1979). *Robert E. Park: Biography of a sociologist.* Durham, NC: Duke University Press.

Schwendinger, H., & Schwendinger, J. S. (1985). *Adolescent subcultures and delinquency* (Research ed.). New York, NY: Praeger.

Shaw, C. R., & McKay, H. D. (1942). *Juvenile delinquency and urban areas.* Chicago, IL: University of Chicago Press.

Smith, P., Gendreau, P., & Swartz, K. (2009). Validating the principles of effective intervention: A systematic review of the contributions of meta-analysis in the field of corrections. *Victims and Offenders, 4*(2), 148–169.

Zimring, F. E. (2012). *The city that became safe: New York's lessons for urban crime and its control.* New York, NY: Oxford University Press.

CHAPTER 2

The Importance of Ethics in Criminal Justice

Cyndi Banks

In criminal justice systems, the application of ethical norms has come to be recognized as a crucial part of the process of doing justice. Whether an action is performed by law enforcement, corrections, judges, lawyers, or justice policy makers, we expect that decision making will be ethical, and when it is not, we anticipate that those who violate ethical norms will be held accountable. The field of *normative ethics* sets standards of conduct to assist in determining how to act, and it draws on such sources as religions, natural law, and written law in shaping ethical standards. *Applied ethics* is concerned with resolving issues that raise questions about what is right or wrong and what is good or bad. Criminal justice professionals, who often possess the right to control others through the application of force and coercion, must understand how to act in situations in which ethical dilemmas arise, if they are to avoid accusations of abuse of their powers. Ethical theories about how to act and the rightness or wrongness of acts provide a foundation from which to analyze ethical dilemmas and arrive at a correct conclusion or resolution.

This chapter discusses ethical issues within the justice sector, as well as the theoretical basis from which to make determinations about ethical issues and dilemmas. The aim is to draw attention to the principal normative and applied ethical questions that arise within the sector, to briefly indicate the range and scope of perspectives concerning such questions, and to highlight how disregard for ethical issues and arguments can result in incoherent and irrational policy making and improper and unprincipled conduct.

POLICE ETHICS

Of all the elements in criminal justice systems, policing is the most likely to provoke ethical dilemmas. In the early days of law enforcement in the United States, the police relied unhesitatingly on physical force and coercion to maintain control of the streets and paid little attention to ethical standards. An institutional culture comprising the values, attitudes, and norms of law enforcement developed within policing; this culture encouraged and condoned corruption and the use of force, including lethal force, within the community. Research studies of policing began to identify the nature of policing and developed models of the crime fighter, the emergency operator, the social enforcer, and the social peacekeeper (Kleinig, 1996). Above all, commentators suggested that police developed the notion that the cause of crime fighting was noble and therefore sometimes justified unethical conduct. Police culture supported corruption, the excessive use of force, a cynical and suspicious approach to the community, and the notion that police were themselves victims. Codes of ethics were devised, published, and promoted but were often flouted in favor of the noble cause (Crank & Caldero, 2000). Frequently, police managers reason that police abuse and corruption are caused by the individual acts of "rotten apples" and reject explanations that these acts are indicative of systemic abuse. However, studies have shown that corruption and racism in particular are systemic within law enforcement—particularly the tendency of police to stereotype people in a form known as "racial profiling" (Reiner, 1985; Skolnick, 1966; Walker, Spohn, & DeLone, 2000, p. 95). How do we explain this incidence of noble-cause corruption within law enforcement? To a great extent, it can be linked to the extensive discretionary powers possessed by law enforcement, which can be employed for good or bad ends and purposes. Whereas opponents of broad police discretionary powers contend that the police should be limited by laws and internal rules, regulations, and codes of ethics, others argue that curtailing discretion will impede crime fighting and endanger the community.

Generally, public opinion seems accepting of broad discretionary powers as long as those powers are not directed at the opinion holder. Police misuse of force is a major issue in the exercise of police discretion, and despite codes and rules of ethics that regulate its use, many situations place law enforcement in the position of having to make a determination about the degree and application of force and coercion. Of course, police may be held accountable subsequently for rule violations, but by that time, innocent people may have fatally suffered at their hands. Police culture and the influence of past histories of violence play an important part in determining the level of violence that law enforcement considers acceptable in any given policing situation. As well as force and coercion on the streets, police have powers over individual citizens during interrogation and investigation, and here questions may arise about entrapment, the rights of persons apprehended by police, and such practices as police lying and deception, which tend to be accepted modes of policing. Indeed, some argue that the public has no choice but to accept a certain level of police corruption and abuse in the interests of public safety and in serving the noble cause. Of course, people apprehended by police are normally treated with respect for their dignity and rights; however, sometimes detainees are flagrantly abused, as the following case illustrates.

Case Study: Police Torture in Chicago

On September 11, 2013, Chicago Mayor Rahm Emanuel apologized for what he termed "a stain on the city's reputation," namely, the alleged police torture of two men for whom the city had agreed on a settlement of $12.3 million. Both men had spent 21 years in prison for allegedly murdering two women and three children in 1988, and both had been exonerated and released from prison in 2009. One of the men said in his lawsuit that police beat him with fists, a nightstick, and a telephone.

Former police commander Jon Burge has now cost the city of Chicago about $85 million in settlement payments for torture claims made by an unknown number of African American men. Lawyers say that Burge and other detectives tortured 120 men from 1973 to 1991, used electric shocks, covered suspects' heads with plastic typewriter covers, and conducted mock executions. Although Burge was dismissed from the police department in 1993, no criminal charges have been brought against him. However, he was convicted of lying in civil proceedings brought by victims in 2010 and sentenced to four and a half years imprisonment in 2011.

Source: Wisniewski (2013).

DISCRIMINATION

There is a consistent belief among minorities that racism exists in multiple forms within the justice system at certain decision-making points, for example, in police decisions about arrest, in granting alleged offenders bail, in jury selection, and in conviction and sentencing. Numerous studies have shown that, although there may be no systemic racism, individual acts of discrimination do take place at certain points within the criminal justice system where decisions are made and also that racism may be present in complex forms hidden from obvious view (Georges-Abeyie, as cited in Russell, 1998, p. 32; Pope & Feyerherm, 1990a, b). This means that all those who exercise decision-making powers within the system should always act ethically and must deliver decisions that are free from explicit or implicit racial bias and discrimination. The following case demonstrates how police can target and scapegoat minorities.

Case Study: "Looking Mexican"

In July 1997, the city of Chandler, a suburb of Phoenix, Arizona, with a population of 143,000, began Operation Restoration, which was intended to construct a new civic center, including police headquarters, municipal court, and library, and to revitalize the town. Since its founding in 1912, Chandler had become two cities: one affluent, the other the old, impoverished, downtown area.

(Continued)

(Continued)

Seeking a cause for the city center's decay, city officials fixed on illegal immigration and focused on alleged criminal activity by illegal immigrants. The city police and the Border Patrol collaborated on a plan linked to Operation Restoration, and on the first day of the operation, two dozen police officers and five Border Patrol agents moved through the downtown area, chasing suspected illegal immigrants from work sites and filling up buses with those they captured. In all, police eventually removed 432 illegal immigrants, all but 3 from Mexico.

However, the illegal immigrants in Chandler coexist with a large, well-established Mexican American community in which Latinos make up about 15% of the population. As police questioned those leaving markets favored by Latinos, they encountered U.S. citizens, from whom they also demanded identification and immigration papers. The police operations targeted legal residents and U.S. citizens who "looked Mexican."

Four months later, the Arizona attorney general revealed the results of his inquiry into this raid. These included that Chandler police had stopped residents, questioned them, and entered their homes without warrants, relying only on skin color, Mexican appearance, or use of the Spanish language to identify the residents as suspected illegal immigrants. Moreover, the city officials had not requested formal permission from the U.S. attorney general to act against illegal immigrants, as is required by federal law.

The city manager officially reprimanded the police chief for the raid, and a group of Latinos launched a $35 million lawsuit against the city. Latinos commented that it would take 10 or 15 years for people to feel comfortable again in the town.

Source: Tobar (1998).

LEGAL ETHICS

As professionals, lawyers are subject to detailed rules and codes that govern their actions in relation to their clients and to the justice system in general. An instance of this is the *American Bar Association Model Rules of Professional Conduct* (1983). Lawyers' duty to the court is specified in such texts, and there are rules governing the conduct of prosecutions and the tactics and strategies defense lawyers may or may not employ in representing their clients. Ethical norms are therefore highly developed within the legal profession, and accountability for violations is ensured through professional associations and the courts, both of which have the power to discipline and even disbar lawyers for unethical conduct. In cases where an ethical rule is unclear, a lawyer can seek advice from within the profession, and this facilitates the task of keeping within the boundaries regulating a lawyer's conduct and practice. Among the general public, however, there is only very limited awareness of professional ethical rules; significant misunderstandings exist about the operation of the common-law adversarial system of justice, a system that gives lawyers a good deal of control over the court process. For example, the public routinely faults defense lawyers for "defending persons they know to be guilty," based on a lack of understanding of the link between the protection of an accused person's rights and the role of the defense lawyer in ensuring that those protections are enforced. Lawyers are required to adhere to the principles of partisanship and neutrality. They must put the interests of the client above the public good and, in representing a client, must disregard questions of personal morality so that the client's interests always take precedence over those of the lawyer.

The primary duty of a prosecutor is not merely to secure a conviction but to ensure that justice is done. Prosecutorial work brings into play a special set of ethical issues that result from the wide discretion that prosecutors (like police) enjoy in the operation of certain functions such as deciding what crime to indict a person with and those relating to the practice of plea bargaining. As well, the right of the prosecutor to determine, within a limited framework of rules, what evidence is to be put before the court and what evidence is to be made available to the defense can give rise to serious ethical conflicts. In the United States, many prosecutors are elected officials, and this gives rise to a further set of ethical issues, including community pressures about how the prosecutorial function is exercised in the context of promises made and expectations raised during the election process. Whether the primary concern is for the victim, the community, reelection, or discovering "the truth," prosecutors must make choices and decide their constituency, either generally or in a particular case. The likelihood that judges and prosecutors may become corrupt or act unethically increases according to the extent to which they are allowed wide discretionary powers. However, because judges generally perform their functions transparently and in public, the risks of impropriety are reduced. The same cannot be said about prosecutors, who conduct much of their business behind closed doors and who do not open to public scrutiny such processes as plea bargaining. Sometimes, judges are so blatantly corrupt that they actually manipulate the judicial system to enrich themselves, as can be seen in the following case study.

Case Study: "Pennsylvania Rocked by 'Jailing Kids for Cash' Scandal"

Luzerne County, Pennsylvania, has been shocked by a scandal involving two elected judges, Mark Ciavarella and Michael Conahan, who received more than $2.6 million in kickbacks for jailing juveniles. The two judges have been disbarred and have also resigned from their elected positions. They will serve 87 months' imprisonment under plea bargains for fraud and tax charges. The corruption began in 2002, when Conahan shut down the state juvenile facility and used funds from the county budget to fund a private facility. The federal government began an investigation in 2006.

The two judges engaged in the practice of sending children to private juvenile detention centers owned by Mid-Atlantic Youth Services Corporation under a contract with the court; in return for this, the two judges were paid kickbacks. The private detention

(Continued)

(Continued)

center operator is still in business, and the owner denies any involvement or knowledge of the scheme practiced by the two judges. Records indicate that two people paid the judges, one of whom was the former owner of Mid-Atlantic, who claims he was pressured to pay by the judges.

Of the hundreds of children appearing before the judges, many had no lawyers, and about half of those who appeared before Ciavarella were sent to a placement, as compared to only 8.4% across the state. Records showed that numerous minors charged with nonviolent crimes were given harsher sentences than recommended by probation reports.

Pennsylvania has the second-highest number of privatized juvenile detention facilities after Florida and accounts for about 11% of all such private facilities in the United States. Critics say that these private facilities are able to hide illegal and improper activities because they are not subjected to the same inspection and audit requirements as state facilities.

Source: Stephanie Chen. February 24, 2009. CNN.com Edition.

PUNISHMENT

What is the ethical rationale for punishment, and how do we justify its imposition? The sociological approach to understanding why we punish focuses on how the currents and modes of thinking in society affect the climates of tolerance and intolerance. Social theories about punishment treat it as a social phenomenon and explore relations between punishment and society. Philosophical theories apply utilitarian and retributive theories, asking questions about the goals of punishment and its overall purpose. According to these theories, punishment is justified according to theories of deterrence, retribution, *just deserts*, rehabilitation, incapacitation, and restorative justice. Many believe that punishment deters the crimes of both repeat offenders and potential offenders. Deterrence theory was first proposed by utilitarian philosophers, who contended that it is the fear of the consequences of criminal actions that deters crime. However, numerous research studies have failed to show conclusively that deterrence works, partly because the commission of much crime does not appear to be based upon rational decisions that weigh the potential consequences (Beyleveld, 1979, as cited in Hudson, 1996, p. 23; Blumstein, Cohen, & Nagin, 1978, p. 66; Ten, 1987, p. 9).

The theory of retribution contends that punishment can be justified because it is deserved and that persons ought to be held accountable for acts that harm society. Retributionists argue that the punishment imposed should always be proportionate to the wrongdoing, a standpoint known as *just deserts;* further, that retribution is considered justified in terms of criminals owing and paying a debt to society; that society ought to censure those who break its norms and rules; and that punishment has an expressive function (in that society is expressing its condemnation of an offender) that ought to be communicated to an offender. Retribution or just deserts theory began to gain ground over alternative versions of the purpose and justification of punishment in the 1980s. It has emerged as the premier rationale for punishment and, consistent with its emphasis on proportionality, has led to the development of sentencing guidelines and sentencing commissions charged with determining the extent of punishment that ought to be imposed for particular crimes. Just deserts theory focuses only on the harm involved in the crime and on the culpability of the offender. Its critics argue that it lacks any principled basis for determining commensurate sentences for crimes and completely ignores social and other factors that ought to be taken into account in arriving at an appropriate sentence (Hudson, 1996, p. 46; Tonry, 1994, p. 153). Critics of retribution argue that it is nothing more than vengeance, but Nozick (1981, p. 366) points out that, unlike retribution, revenge possesses no limits and may be inflicted on an innocent person, perhaps a relative, and not necessarily on the offender.

The concept of rehabilitation is that punishment ought to be concerned with healing the offender so that he or she may return to society after punishment with little or no chance of becoming a repeat offender. Crime is regarded as a social disease to be treated and cured. To determine the appropriate punishment, the offender's social and economic background must be fully taken into consideration. Previously, indeterminate sentences were imposed that made the release of the offender contingent on the successful completion of rehabilitation programs. The decision to release was exercised by boards, based on their assessment of an individual's progress through rehabilitation, and was not determined exclusively by the court. In the 1970s, opinion turned against rehabilitation as the proper rationale and basis for determining punishment when meta-studies of rehabilitation programs purported to show that "nothing works" (Martinson, 1974). The discredited rationale of rehabilitation has been replaced by the now-dominant theories of just deserts and incapacitation.

Incapacitation theorists argue that the public ought to be protected from the chance of future offenses committed by those who are already convicted criminals and that placing offenders in custody for long periods of time is justified in the pursuit of this end. Opponents of incapacitation contend that offenders are therefore being punished on the basis of predictions of their likely future conduct and that this is arbitrary, unfair, and entirely speculative (Morris, 1974, p. 241). They question the ethics of punishing people for crimes they have yet to commit.

Restorative justice proponents emphasize community involvement in determining an appropriate punishment and maintain that a process through which a victim confronts the offender with the harm suffered will help restore that offender to the community with an enhanced capacity to support social cohesion and not reoffend. Restorative justice calls for a return to community punishment practices that disappeared with the emergence of the state as the exclusive authority for administering punishment and providing solutions to crime. This form of justice has generally been employed to deal with minor offenses but has been accepted in some jurisdictions as the most appropriate means of punishing juvenile delinquency.

CORRECTIONAL ETHICS

Over the last two decades, criminal justice policies focusing on crime control—including so-called zero-tolerance practices and incapacitating offenders for very long periods of time under laws, such as "three strikes, you're out"—have caused an explosion in the size of the prison population (Harrison & Beck, 2003). Commentators now regularly describe U.S. policy as favoring "mass imprisonment" (Christie, 2000). Within justice systems, police and corrections officers have always been empowered to exercise a degree of physical control over citizens; now, contemporary crime-control strategies bring even greater numbers of citizens into direct contact with law enforcement and corrections staff. Heightened tensions between the public and criminal justice officials, arising from policies of mass imprisonment, make it essential that ethical standards of treatment and conduct be observed in prisons and jails.

Like law enforcement, corrections work possesses an institutional culture that has developed over time in conjunction with changes in prison operations, staffing, and disciplinary regimes. An understanding of that culture is vital to an appreciation of the ethical challenges faced by corrections staff. The organization and management of corrections developed from early individualistic methods of controlling people in custody into full-fledged bureaucratic and managerialist regimes of control, with detailed rules and procedures that covered both prison staff and those incarcerated as well as the permitted interactions between them. Historically, prisoners had few rights and were treated harshly and with high levels of brutality; more recently, prisoners regularly test the scope and content of their rights in the courts. How does ethics relate to corrections when prisoners are in custody, sometimes under maximum security conditions and sometimes within lightly guarded facilities? Commentators argue that a person is sent to prison *as* punishment and not *for* punishment; therefore, such practices as highly controlled visitation, strip searches, and punishment of prisoners through removal of so-called privileges should be prohibited because they amount to the imposition of additional and unauthorized sanctions (Kleinig, 2001, p. 7). Adopting an ethical standard would therefore mean respecting the dignity, humanity, and rights of prisoners as well as refraining from imposing any further forms of punishment.

The nature of the relationship between guards and prisoners and between guards and their coworkers also raises questions about normative conduct. Obviously, there is a significant power dynamic between inmates and guards, and the guards, in the absence of rules that incorporate ethical standards and norms, potentially have the power to seriously abuse prisoners (Kleinig, 2001, p. 10). Guards are required to demonstrate the ability to manage prisoners but must also accept that they are dependent on good relations with prisoners to protect their personal safety. Guards possess a personal authority derived from character and personality, as well as a legal authority, the source of which is the prison rules and regulations. Therefore, an ethical framework that regulates these interactions is required. One extreme school of thought argues, however, that the nature of incarceration makes it virtually impossible to apply ethical standards of conduct and that degradation and brutality are inescapable (Smith, 2001, p. 30).

Research has revealed the prison guard code and the "gray wall of silence," which incorporate key tenets of the business of guarding, including "Always aid an officer in distress," "Don't rat," and "Never make a fellow officer look bad in front of inmates" (Kauffman, 1988, pp. 86–117). The institutional culture of corrections valorizes the dangers and tensions of incarceration and the way these elements combine to engender a sense of suspicion about events in a facility that are out of the ordinary or seem to be violations of prison rules. However, research studies have revealed that guards, despite their apparent absolute dominance, in fact must negotiate the extent of their domination with inmates through a process of contestation (Lombardo, 1989, p. 94). This process can result in the "corruption of authority" and means that rule books are often jettisoned in the interests of flexibility and of establishing a modus vivendi. Similar to law enforcement, individual discretion and its exercise are an important part of being a guard and are influenced by the guard culture, relevant rules, and the overall prison disciplinary regime. Studies of this culture have revealed that recruits into the corrections industry are socialized to adhere to the elements of the prison guard code that focus on solidarity between coworkers against inmates (Kauffman, 1988, p. 198).

The use of force by corrections staff is a major ethical issue within corrections. In the past, violence was prevalent and expected. Nowadays, despite rules regulating the application of force and accountability (including actions in the courts), some prison systems continue to permit extralegal levels of coercion and force against inmates. The guard culture contends that force is always justified because only the threat of violence or violence itself will ensure control within the facility, and violence deters inmate attacks on guards (Kauffman, 1988, p. 141). Reprisals for attacks by inmates are considered essential and entirely appropriate within the guard culture. Nevertheless, there is also an appreciation within corrections that violence begets more violence and that inmate resistance cannot be repressed by the constant application of force (Kauffman, 1988, p. 71). Nowadays, the use of force is regulated by rules and by the courts, the state, and the federal government. Other forms of conduct that violate ethical norms include institutional and guard attitudes toward rape in prison and the promotion of corruption through smuggling, drug trafficking, and similar activity. The following is a case of male prison rape.

Case Study: Rape in Prison—A Survivor's Story

Kerry Max Cook entered the Texas prison system at age 19 and was released aged 46 from Texas's death row after getting a new trial. During his time in prison, he says he was gang raped by other inmates. The first attack came soon after he was incarcerated. Inmates forced him to take his clothes off, bent him over a concrete embankment in the yard, raped him, and carved obscenities on his backside. Cook says he was repeatedly assaulted over the next 2 years.

Johnny Vasquez, a former Texas prison guard, agrees with inmates who claim the Texas prison system is indifferent to claims of rape. He says he can recall hearing responses to such claims as, "You need to grow some and defend yourself. Quit coming in here crying. Get out of my office. Don't bring this to me" (Harris, 2013, p. 1).

Source: Human Rights Watch (2001: 148–149).

Probation and parole were originally linked to plans for the individualized treatment of prisoners, but in their contemporary form, they are focused almost exclusively on punishment and the enforcement of court sanctions (Petersilia, 1999, p. 480). Parole officers have always been closer to law enforcement. Now, probation officers adopt a policing posture toward probationers, are armed, and often collaborate with law enforcement officers in raiding premises. Accordingly, both probation and parole officers now exercise substantial degrees of control over probationers and parolees and face ethical concerns like those in corrections and law enforcement.

ETHICAL CRIMINAL JUSTICE POLICY MAKING

Crime control and how to punish offenders are key elements of justice policy making. For example, the development of private prisons as a policy option for punishment is an important issue in criminal justice policy and raises significant ethical issues, such as whether the state or government should ever permit outside agencies to punish citizens, whether the profit motive is compatible with the exercise of the right to inflict punishment through incarceration, and how private prisons resolve issues connected with the use of force.

Ethical considerations ought to play a significant role in criminal justice policy making; however, since the 1970s, policy making has typically been more concerned with formulating punitive policies than with examining alternative options for punishment and exploring the ethical basis of certain policy approaches. Most policy making is the outcome of cost-benefit analysis, and that process does not usually incorporate ethical models or arguments. Normally, it is essential in designing policies to advance a justification for a particular approach to a policy issue. Policies may be justified on ideological, empirical, or ethical grounds. Policies grounded in an ethical approach are analyzed under a process that has determined the rightness or wrongness, or the "good or bad," of a particular approach. There are two central concerns. First, it is necessary that policy makers always act ethically in formulating policies; second, there exists an ethical responsibility in making policy about subjects like punishment that have inherently ethical requirements. This latter kind of policy making can be termed *morality policy making*. In contemporary policy making, there is a clear link between morality policy making and so-called moral panics (Mooney, 2001, p. 16). A moral panic arises when an event is constructed and portrayed as a danger or menace to society and its values. Good examples are the various "wars" declared by different administrations, for example, the war on poverty, the war on drugs, and the war on terrorism. Media, and therefore public, attention to particular forms of criminality has resulted in mandatory minimum sentencing, the war on drugs, truth-in-sentencing laws, and legislation designed to combat sexual predators and superpredators. The media frequently construct issues like drug abuse as moral panics, and the outcome is often badly conceived laws that are fundamentally unethical. The present mass incarceration of offenders is the result of policy choices based on converging policies and decisions that do not represent a rational, coherent response to crime. What standards and conditions should be applied to imprisonment? Periodically, the topic of the level of amenities to be supplied to prisoners resurfaces in the media. Politicians who wish to demonstrate a "tough on crime" approach protest that prisoners are given access to weight-lifting equipment, televisions, radios, and "good" food (Banks, 2005, p. 137). The following case reveals one sheriff's view of the standard of amenities to be applied to prisoners.

Case Study: Prison and Amenities

In Maricopa County, Arizona, Sheriff Joe Arpaio's policies of housing inmates in tents without air conditioning in the more than 110°F summer weather, clothing inmates in pink underwear and striped uniforms, instituting chain gangs for both men and women, and providing basic and unappealing food such as bologna on dry bread exemplify his attitude [toward punishment]. Some politicians argue that if prisoners have standards of incarceration that are superior to the standard of living of the man on the street, then they cannot be said to be suffering punishment. The media fuel this debate by reporting that prisons are "holiday resorts" where prisoners enjoy extravagant amenities and conditions (see Lenz, 2002). In response to this political discourse, the No Frills Prison Act was passed in 1996; it bans televisions, coffeepots, and hot plates in the cells of federal prisoners. It also prohibits computers, electronic instruments, certain movies rated above PG, and unmonitored phone calls (Lenz, 2002).

The assumption underpinning this legislation is that a deterrent effect will be achieved "by making a sentence more punitive, that is, making the inmate suffer more" (Banks, 2005, p. 138). Thus, it is assumed that an inmate will be "less inclined to reoffend knowing

(Continued)

(Continued)

the harsh conditions in prison" (p. 138). The problem is that no research exists to support this assumption. Some have argued that there are cost savings to the prison system and to the taxpayers through this approach, but, again, this is not supported, given that the 31 states that allow inmates televisions in their cells do not pay for them (prisoners or their relatives pay for them), and cablevision is paid for out of profits from the prison commissary, vending machines, and long-distance telephone charges (Finn, 1996, pp. 36–37).

Interestingly, prison administrators are often in favor of permitting amenities in the prisons because staffs rely heavily on a system of rewards and punishments to maintain control in their institutions (Lenz, 2002, p. 506). They recognize that keeping inmates busy provides important benefits to inmate order and inmate activities. In other words, bored and unhappy prisoners are more likely to cause security problems to which staff, who are in short supply, will have to respond.

Source: From Banks, C. *Criminal Justice Ethics: Theory and Practice 2/1.* © Copyright SAGE Publications.

Policy is usually formulated by elected officials and representatives who react hastily to perceived constituency concerns and to the views of the general public, which are heavily influenced by media representation of an issue as a moral panic. Surveys have revealed that the public has a general tendency toward favoring punitive measures toward offenders. In the United States, imprisonment is generally regarded as the appropriate form of punishment for most criminality, but this is not so in other Western countries where minor crimes are punished much more leniently. As for the ultimate penalty of capital punishment, which is a major issue of morality for many citizens, it has found steady support since the 1970s, and this is usually reflected in political platforms and in legislative approaches to punishment.

An ethical responsibility includes an obligation to act with integrity. For example, a legislator can be said to act unethically when he or she proposes changes in legislation in the expectation that such action will ensure his or her reelection, knowing that it is unlikely to achieve its aims and might even cause fresh injustice. Other acts of policy making that could be considered unethical include responding to a particular event or series of events by formulating policies that are arbitrary, lack reason or good judgment, and have failed to take account of relevant ethical considerations.

Case Study: Airline and FBI Sued for Racial Profiling

Shoshana Hebshi, a 36 year old half Jewish and half Arab woman from Ohio, has filed a lawsuit claiming she was taken off an airplane in Detroit on the 10th anniversary of the September 11 attacks, strip searched, and kept in custody for more than 4 hours in a cell because of her ethnicity. She said no one told her what was happening and why she was being taken into custody.

The American Civil Liberties Union (ACLU) filed the lawsuit on her behalf, claiming that she and two Indian American [of India, South Asia, descent] men she was sitting next to were targeted by federal agents who entered the plane, ordered them off, and took them into custody. Hebshi said she was placed in a cell, ordered to strip naked, squat, and cough while an officer scrutinized her and that she was both frightened and humiliated. She and the two men were detained in response to reports from other passengers to the flight attendants that two of them were going to the restroom. The flight attendants told the pilot that the men using the restroom were "possibly of Arab descent."

Source: Warikoo (2013).

The war on terrorism provokes significant ethical questions and issues. A central issue concerns the normative considerations applicable to this program. Questions include why the United States declared a war on terrorism after 9/11 and why it created a special prosecution and detention regime for alleged terrorists instead of giving the criminal justice system the responsibility for responding to terrorist acts. After all, terrorist acts normally constitute offenses under the criminal law and can be prosecuted and punished as such. Another issue concerns the extent to which, if at all, torture or so-called enhanced interrogation can be applied to alleged terrorists in custody, even in the cause of averting further acts of terrorism. Third, there is the question of the extent to which rights and freedoms ought to be restricted within the United States in order to fight the war on terrorism. The argument in this case is that we ought to be prepared to surrender some or even all of those rights and freedoms in the interest of reducing the risk of further terrorist acts. Those rights include privacy and freedom from intrusive surveillance. In addition, pursuing the war on terrorism is said to require the establishment of specially constituted courts or military commissions to undertake the trials of alleged terrorists, raising the further question of what legal protections and rights those accused should enjoy before such courts or commissions. These are complex issues that impact fundamental values and ethical norms.

The difficulties of ethical policy making in this field are compounded by questions concerning the fact that there is no single "correct" definition of terrorism and that the nature of the war on terrorism has been shaped almost entirely by the events of 9/11. It is clear that, although termed a *war* in the same way that previous campaigns have been described as a war on crime or a war on drugs, the war on terrorism is much more like a conventional war but lacks the attributes of one. Policy makers have constructed the war on terrorism not as an issue of crime control but as involving issues of national security. In so doing, they have sought to justify exceptional measures, such as illegal international rendition and techniques that some have termed *torture* (Ackerman, 2004). By defining the campaign against terrorists as a war, the Bush administration justified measures, like the Patriot Act, that have significantly increased surveillance powers over citizens and diminished rights and freedoms. The debate is concerned with whether such measures are ethically appropriate in all the circumstances. Some argue that such measures are immoral simply because they disregard customary and international rules governing the treatment of detainees (by categorizing them as "unlawful combatants"), the rules of war, humanitarian laws of war, and prohibitions against torture and degrading treatment (Emcke, 2005, p. 237).

It has also been argued that depicting a counterterrorist strategy as warfare has the effect of portraying a level of activity inferior to that normally required by actual conventional warfare, as if it were a conventional war between states. Thus, through this process of categorization, the United States has somehow been empowered to conduct "battles" within the ambit of a never-ending war on terrorism. For example, in the pursuit of the war on terrorism, the United States deploys unmanned aircraft, or drones, in the airspace of other states' territories, without their knowledge, in order to conduct assassinations of "known" terrorists. Sometimes, these attacks cause so-called collateral damage to civilians, and some ask whether it is ethically correct to cause injury and death to innocent civilians in this way and whether the effects of this strategy actually mimic the acts of the terrorists themselves (Wilkinson, 2001, p. 23). Therefore, some argue that the war on terrorism might in fact constitute a greater evil than terrorism itself (Wilkinson, 2001, p. 115). In defending the war and its actions, some have suggested that so long as citizens can rely on the legislature and the courts for oversight, there is sufficient protection against excesses (Ignatieff, 2004, p. 8). Yet others point to the lack of executive transparency and the administration's active concealment of surveillance activities that have come to light only through the activities of whistle-blowers. In other words, the modern state has the capacity, if it possesses the will, to conduct a wide range of activities in pursuit of a goal that it alone deems critical to public interest and that many would judge illegal and certainly immoral or unethical.

ANALYZING ETHICAL DILEMMAS

Ethical theories attempt to provide a means to respond to such critical ethical questions as, How ought I to act in this situation? Thus, for criminal justice professionals, ethical theories provide a foundation and a source of knowledge about how to go about the business of acting ethically in everyday situations. They help provide structure in an otherwise complex environment. A number of ethical theories exist, each offering a varying perspective and approach to ethical dilemmas. It is necessary, therefore, to be aware of the various arguments and perspectives to fully engage with the analysis and resolution of ethical issues. The principal ethical theories are *deontology* and *consequentialism* (also called *utilitarianism*). However, more recently, *virtue ethics* has gained a strong footing in ethical theorizing. Less significant theories include the Greek theories of *hedonism, stoicism,* and *ethical egoism.* Contemporary ethical theorists, such as John Rawls (1973) and Carol Gilligan (1982), have added *social justice* and *feminist ethics* (also called the *ethic of care*) to the theoretical framework.

Principles, Consequences, or Character?

The principal theories of deontology and consequentialism take contrasting positions on the question of how we ought to conduct ourselves in varying situations when faced with the question, How ought I to act? Consequentialists believe that the task of identifying the right way to act in a given situation always depends on the goodness, for everyone affected, of the consequences of acting in a particular way. Therefore, consequentialism always looks at outcomes in determining the proper course of action. In contrast, deontology rejects consequentialism and argues that rules and principles that place limits on our activities and actions ought to guide us in making ethical decisions. Thus, they argue that certain acts are always wrong in themselves, lack moral support, and cannot be employed to justify pursuing any ends, even morally good ones. For example, deontologists absolutely reject the act of lying and argue that lies are wrong because of their nature, even if they result in good consequences. Deontologists emphasize notions of obligation and duty and believe, for example, that it is right to keep promises, regardless of the effects of carrying them out. Often, applying the primary theories will result in similar moral outcomes. For example, a deontologist will argue that stealing goods or breaking promises is always wrong; a consequentialist would come to the same conclusion but for different reasons, arguing that it is the consequences of such acts to the public welfare that renders them wrong, not their inherent wrongness. Conflicts will arise between these theories, however, when performance of an act normally considered unethical results in an increase in the utility achieved by the result.

Aristotle's virtue ethics has enjoyed resurgence in ethical theorizing, partly because the two principal theories seem to offer little except a choice between a focus on the consequences or a set of absolute rules about how to act. Virtue theories aim to provide us with a picture of the good life and how it can be realized. The good life, in Aristotle's time, was seen as one in which one's full potential as a human person is satisfied. This contrasts with modern ethical theories, which see the good life and morality as separate notions. To the ancient Greek virtue theorists, the chief goal was to achieve a good life and realize our true nature; to them, satisfying this aim was the test of the moral worth of a particular act. From the 16th century on, these concepts were abandoned; modern ethical thinking has discouraged notions of final ends and purposes and the concept of the good life. *Postmodernism* has also impacted ethical thinking; Bauman (1993), for example, argues that few ethical choices can be considered absolutely good or correct and that such choices are largely based on the application of impulses. He argues that uncertainty and ambivalence, which are the characteristics of postmodernism, apply equally to morality (itself diverse in nature, irrational, and subject to the exercise of power relations), so moral codes are often the outcome of political claims of universalism. Richard Rorty goes further, arguing that philosophy itself is dead in the sense that claims to universal rules and principles are no longer possible or accepted in contemporary societies (Rumana, 2000, p. 4).

A Matter of Principle

Immanuel Kant is regarded as one of the greatest modern philosophers and as the one most responsible for shaping and explaining deontology. In answering the question, What ought I to do? Kant believed that a person should categorically act in a rational manner, in accordance with duty and obligation, and take no account of the consequences (Benn, 1998, p. 172). Kant called this idea the *categorical imperative* and contended that all other considerations were irrelevant. This notion gives rise to the question of how to determine the nature and extent of a duty or obligation. In response, Kant stated that this could be determined by applying the test of whether an individual is willing that a particular act be followed by *all* persons at all times. If so, this gives the act the status of a rule, and it withstands the test of a universal law. Although this seems straightforward, it can pose difficulties. For example, Kant stated that the rule prohibiting lying was a categorical imperative; therefore, it was wrong to lie under any circumstances (Rachels, 1999a, p. 125). In reality, however, a person may lie when faced with moral choices, such as when it is both wrong to lie and wrong to allow innocent people to be murdered. Thus, two categorical imperatives may conflict with each other. How, then, should this conflict be resolved? One suggestion is to treat moral rules not as absolute categorical rules but as generalizations. Therefore, although we should generally always refrain from telling lies, we may abrogate this rule if factors exist that ought to override this imperative.

Kant advanced the important notion that we should always respect others because they are rational human beings with dignity (Hill, 2000, p. 64). Thus, a person should not be treated as a means to an end but as an end in himself or herself. Thus, we ought not to use people to satisfy our own ends; we should always respect others' rights, promote their welfare, and avoid causing them harm. In this way, we will be promoting the worth and dignity of every person—as, for example, in the criminal justice process, in which the right to a fair trial is afforded. This rule would also require that prisoners be treated with dignity, compassion, and humanity.

Considering the Consequences

Consequentialists, or utilitarians, look to the consequences of an act to determine its rightness or wrongness and disregard all other considerations. The question to ask when faced with an ethical question or dilemma is, therefore, Which action will bring about the best possible consequences for everyone affected? This principle is known as the *principle of utility,* and it imposes a duty to act in ways that produce the greatest happiness for everyone affected. Underlying this theory is the thinking of the classical utilitarians, Jeremy Bentham and John Stuart Mill, who regarded happiness as equivalent to pleasure and believed that humans look for pleasure and try to avoid pain and that this explains how we make choices about how to act (Rachels, 1999b, p. 65). More recent thinking substitutes the idea of preference satisfaction for happiness; therefore, we should not aim for pleasure over pain but instead should determine how we can best satisfy human preferences, interests, or desires. Utilitarians can be categorized as either *act utilitarians* or *rule utilitarians*. The former argue that it is possible to measure whether an act causes more pleasure than pain and therefore whether it has more "utility." Given the complications of applying such a rule, act utilitarians follow rules of thumb that rely on past experience. Rule utilitarians, on the other hand, link consequentialism with moral rules and contend that following specific moral rules will result in better consequences. Thus, rule consequentialism aligns to an extent with deontology. An example of rule utilitarianism is that it is generally better to follow the rule that one should speak the truth even when it means that doing so in a specific instance would cause more pain than pleasure, because in the long term, telling the truth produces greater benefits overall. Consequentialism is criticized for placing the outcome of an action above the ideals of justice. Also, critics argue that it would require us to give all our resources to others because such an act would promote the general welfare and pleasure of others.

It can be seen that the choice between duty and consequences involves evaluating absolute rules about conduct by calculating which act will provide the most pleasure for the greatest number of people. Consequentialism enjoys a primary role in punishment policy making in the form of the theory that punishment deters crime. It is claimed that everyone benefits by the imposition of severer penalties for certain crimes to deter others from committing similar crimes.

A Question of Character

Virtue ethics does not ask, What ought I to do? but, What kind of person should I become? According to virtue theorists, the correct course of action can be determined only when that question has been answered. Virtue comprises those personal qualities that we develop through habitual action and that aid us to become persons of excellent character during our lives. Virtues are both natural and acquired qualities, such as intelligence, honesty, generosity, loyalty, integrity, dignity, and self-control. In contrast to deontology's absolute prohibition on lying and consequentialism's acquiescence to lying if the consequences are beneficial, virtue ethics takes the position that lying is dishonest and that dishonesty is a vice, not a virtue. Virtue ethics can be problematic, however. For example, is a suicide bomber acting courageously by dying for a cause he or she believes in? If being generous is a virtue, how generous should one be? Aristotle believed that a good life included happiness in the form of well-being or flourishing and that virtues promote such happiness (Tessitore, 1996, p. 20). Aristotle thought that we should always act in ways that will bring about flourishing, and he advanced the notion of the golden mean: When required to make decisions, we should seek the mean, or the average between extremes. An example is to be neither stingy nor lavish but generous—that is, to aim for the golden mean. It is easy to see how this idea can be applied to everyday ethical behavior. When applied to questions of conduct, the golden mean would be the middle course between forms of radical action.

Aristotle also advocated the notion of practical wisdom: thinking about the circumstances, reasoning correctly, and making the right choices. Those who live with practical wisdom are said to have a kind of insight or perception that guides them in making right decisions (Darwall, 1998, p. 213). Critics argue that virtue ethics must be regarded as contextually and historically tied to an ancient time period, namely, Athenian society of the 5th century, which took it for granted that virtues were possessed only by those with great wealth and high social status (MacIntyre, 1984, p. 11). Women and slaves were not considered human; therefore, virtue ethics could not apply to them. Even so, modern philosophers attracted by virtue ethics and its focus on character link it to modern-day social life and the community, emphasizing the need to learn virtues within the family and the community (Blum, 1996, pp. 232–233). As for Aristotle's list of virtues, while some see it as arbitrary, others argue for the universality of virtue whatever the nature of a society or its culture (Hinman, 1998, pp. 334–335). A major criticism of virtue ethics is that it gives us no guidance about how to act in relation to ethical issues. For example, it provides no assistance about such ethical questions as the imposition of capital punishment. However, in favor of virtue ethics, it can be argued that it fulfills an essential role in supplementing other ethical approaches that have provided guidance in deciding how to act (Rachels, 1999a, p. 189). It is also claimed that developing and possessing a virtuous character or a moral self is a prerequisite for resolving ethical dilemmas. Some modern philosophers argue that virtue ethics can stand alone as the ethical basis for ethical action because an action will be correct and moral if performed by a virtuous person acting in character in particular circumstances (Hursthouse, 1999, p. 26). Of course, virtue ethics seems very relevant to the criminal justice system, in which power and authority are susceptible to abuse.

Indifference, Pleasure, or Selfishness?

The ethical theories of stoicism, ethical egoism, and hedonism do not enjoy much support among moral philosophers despite the fact that egoism and hedonism, in their celebration of self-gratification, might be said to resonate with the values of our modern consumer society. Stoicism, like virtue ethics, is historically specific and contends that the path to virtue lies in adopting an attitude of indifference toward external differences, cultivating a life of indifference, and accepting that while some things are within our power to change and influence, others are not (Prior, 1991, p. 209). Stoics believe in predestiny and the notion that whatever happens has a rational explanation and is always for the best. In some respects, stoicism echoes the claims of virtue ethics about individual character because stoics argue that developing the appropriately stoic frame of mind leads to virtue.

Hedonism comes in the forms of *psychological hedonism* and *ethical hedonism*. The former imagines a life devoted to the pursuit of pleasure and assumes that all action aims to achieve pleasure and avoid pain. Ethical hedonism is a moral version of hedonism and asserts that seeking pleasure is right conduct because pleasure alone is good (Feldman, 1997, p. 109). In this sense, hedonism seems unsatisfactory because it is difficult to accept that seeking pleasure can constitute the sole basis for deciding ethical issues. The theory of ethical egoism contends that right action is action that promotes one's own self-interest, regardless of the interests or concerns of others.

Egoism is separated into two categories, *psychological egoism* and *ethical egoism*. The former holds that all persons are motivated by, and act according to, egoistic concerns. It rejects all altruistic explanations of behavior and argues that acts that may seem unselfish are always performed for egotistical reasons. An ethical egoist argues similarly that morality and reason are satisfied by promoting one's own greatest good and self-interest before anyone else's. The focus on self-interest does not exclude action that might help others, as long as the primary goal is our own interests. Ethical egoism as a theory seems to lack a principled foundation, and some argue that it resembles racism in its focus on the interests of one group alone (Rachels, 1999a, p. 94). Others suggest that it precludes any development of sustained relations between persons, because an ethical egoist is so focused on his or her own good that certain acts are precluded, such as assisting those in need, unless such action first serves a self-interest (Hinman, 1998, p. 154). In terms of criminal justice, ethical egoism would seem to supply justification for acts that are corrupt or inhumane.

Social Justice

John Rawls's theories seek to fix fundamental principles that would govern a morally good society, and in this sense, his search for a set of rules is Kantian. His concern is not with the individual ethical actor so much as with justice, in the sense of fairness, and he regards justice as a founding principle capable of providing guidance concerning how a society ought to conduct itself (Rawls, 1973, pp. 50–51). According to Rawls, a moral person is one who possesses a sense of justice and the potential to pursue a conception of the good (p. 121). Achieving this potential requires us to create a just society and to agree on its governing principles. Rawls imagines a group of persons who collectively agree on the nature of this society from a position of ignorance about their class or social position and without taking account of any natural assets or abilities. His argument is that they would choose two principles of justice, one concerned with the equal right to basic liberties and the other with social and economic inequalities (p. 60). The first principle would provide personal liberties, such as the right to vote and to stand for public office and freedom of speech and assembly. The second principle, part of which is known as the *difference principle,* would comprise the equal distribution of primary goods and services as well as burdens and responsibilities. However, certain inequalities would be considered just if they benefited everyone, especially the least advantaged (p. 75). Thus, there would be no injustice if the least advantaged were better off in an unequal situation than they would be with equality. Consequently, a just society that desires to treat all with equality would give more attention to those victimized by injustice or to those who enjoy a less favorable position because of unfair treatment. This echoes the Kantian principle that people should always be treated as ends in themselves and not as means to an end.

Rawls sees his principles as purely hypothetical but nevertheless argues that they would be accepted by free and rational people and would make explicit his notion of "justice as fairness" (1973, p. 11). Rawls describes three stages of moral development in a life: the *morality of authority,* developed by parents; the *morality of association,* which arises through contact with the school and the neighborhood; and finally the *morality of principles,* wherein individuals follow moral positions as a result of earlier moral development and because they seek the approval of the wider society (pp. 476–473). Rawls suggests that, in a society that seeks to achieve social justice, his principles will create harmony and cooperation and reduce injustice. In terms of relevance to the criminal justice system and its institutions, Rawlsian notions of social justice can assist in overcoming not only inequalities in access to justice but also forms of discrimination within the system.

The Ethic of Care

Feminist ethical theories focus on the centrality of gender and are critical of other established theoretical approaches for giving too much prominence to the individual, to impartiality, and to universality (Hinman, 1998, pp. 367–369). Feminist theories give importance to relationships, care, and connectiveness. Seminal research by Carol Gilligan (1982) and Lawrence Kohlberg (1966) has revealed that moral development varies according to gender and that gender shapes the nature of moral inquiry. Gilligan contends that women tend to see moral life in terms of care and responsibility, asking if relationships would be maintained or harm suffered because of an intended action, whereas men see the application of rules in a fair, impartial, and equal manner as the prime consideration (Flanagan & Jackson, 1993, p. 70). Men also show a concern for individual rights and autonomy, but women are more likely to resolve ethical issues by applying solutions that affirm relationships and minimize harm. This does not mean that women should be regarded as inherently emotional beings entirely lacking rational attributes. Both men and women are the products of social conditioning, and gender is socially constructed; men, too, may follow an ethic of care rather than an individualistic ethical approach (Rachels, 1999a, p. 168).

Some question whether the ethic of care possesses enough weight and dimension for an ethical theory and suggest that it is best viewed as complementing virtue ethics (Blum, 1994, p. 208). Also problematic is the scope of the care ethic itself, because, although it is obvious that the ethic of care applies in close family relationships, the question is, To what extent does it (for example) apply to the needy throughout the world? While some regard the familial obligation as absolute and other obligations as secondary, others emphasize the depth of a relationship outside the family circle. Still others argue that our duty can be broad enough to include a communal identity, such as membership of an ethnic group (p. 249). Robin West advocates linking the ethic of care with the ethic of justice so that public institutions would be obliged to exercise compassion or care when dispensing justice (West, 1997, p. 9). She contends that a combined project of care and justice would mean reading and interpreting the law compassionately, for example, taking account of the life circumstances of an accused in a death penalty case. The notion of *peacemaking* has close links with the ethic of care but represents a distinct ethical philosophy variously termed *peacemaking, peacekeeping,* and *peacemaking criminology* (Braswell & Gold, 1998, p. 26). Peacemaking also calls attention to relationships, caring, and mindfulness (thinking about our actions and the needs of others in the long term). In terms of criminal justice policy making, peacemaking claims nonviolence as a fundamental principle and argues that violence and coercion, in such forms as capital punishment and the excess use of force in policing, should be rejected.

CONCLUSION

This exploration of ethics in criminal justice has highlighted the importance of the theoretical underpinnings of normative and applied ethics to the resolution of ethical issues and dilemmas, and it has revealed the nature and scope of the multiple ethical questions that can arise in "doing justice." In law enforcement and corrections in particular, where there is daily direct interaction with suspected offenders and inmates, the level of ethical practice of an agency is greatly influenced by its institutional culture. Codes of ethics and accountability mechanisms, such as civilian oversight and the courts, can resolve individual cases of improper conduct; but systemic racism, corruption, and abusive conduct have proved difficult to eradicate. Sometimes, as in the case of terrorism, questions about how one ought to act are fundamentally about human rights and human dignity. Theoretical approaches to ethical dilemmas and issues apply various mechanisms to evaluate and test the questions that arise, and fresh postmodern perspectives now challenge long-established theories. Shifts in both ethical practice and theory congruent with shifts in the social order ensure that the incorporation of ethical norms and standards will continue to be a testing and challenging field of endeavor in criminal justice.

DISCUSSION QUESTIONS

1. Is there any relationship between the style of policing chosen by a department and the ethical practices it feels are legitimate for its officers to use in carrying out their duties? Which style of policing would support racial profiling, and why?

2. In an ethical correctional system, all prisoners would be treated with humanity. Explain how prisoner humanity would be respected in the use of force to deal with violence, including prisoner rape, and in the conditions of confinement.

3. One criminal justice policy that many states have supported is prisoner disenfranchisement. Comment on this policy in light of the fact that, for example, if

disenfranchisement is permanent, more than 40% of the African American male population will have no say in the policies and laws that have a significant effect on them and on their communities.

4. Is it ever ethically acceptable to torture a person in the war on terrorism? Support your argument by referring to the criteria of at least one ethical philosophy.

5. Why do modern philosophers regard virtue ethics as an alternative to deontological and consequentialist ethical decision-making approaches? Explain with examples.

REFERENCES

Ackerman, B. (2004, June). This is not a war. *Yale Law Journal, 113,* 1871–1908.

American Bar Association (ABA). (1983). *American Bar Association model rules of professional conduct.* Chicago, IL: American Bar Association.

Banks, C. (2005). *Punishment in America: A reference handbook.* Santa Barbara, CA: ABC-CLIO.

Bauman, Z. (1993). *Postmodern ethics.* Oxford, United Kingdom: Blackwell.

Benn, P. (1998). *Ethics: Fundamentals of philosophy.* Montreal, Quebec, Canada: McGill-Queen's University Press.

Blum, L. (1994). *Moral perception and particularity.* Cambridge, United Kingdom: Cambridge University Press.

Blum, L. (1996). Community and virtue. In R. Crisp (Ed.), *How should one live? Essays on the virtues* (pp. 231–250). Oxford, United Kingdom: Clarendon Press.

Blumstein, A., Cohen, J., & Nagin, D. (Eds.). (1978). *Deterrence and incapacitation: Estimating the effects of criminal sanctions on crime rates.* Washington, DC: Panel on Research on Deterrent and Incapacitative Effects.

Braswell, M., & Gold, J. (1998). Peacemaking, justice and ethics. In M. Braswell, B. McCarthy, & B. McCarthy, *Justice, crime and ethics* (3rd ed., pp. 25–39). Cincinnati, OH: Anderson.

Chen, S. (2009, February 24). Pennsylvania rocked by "jailing kids for cash" scandal. *CNN.com (International ed.).* Retrieved February 24, 2009, from http://www.cnn.com/2009/CRIME/02/23/pennsylvania.corrupt.judges/index.html

Christie, N. (2000). *Crime control as industry: Towards gulags, western style?* London, United Kingdom: Routledge.

Crank, J., & Caldero, M. (2000). *Police ethics: The corruption of noble cause.* Cincinnati, OH: Anderson.

Darwall, S. (1998). *Philosophical ethics.* Boulder, CO: Westview Press.

Emcke, C. (2005). War on terrorism and the crises of the political. In G. Meggle (Ed.), *Ethics of terrorism and counter-terrorism* (pp. 227–244). Frankfurt, Germany: Ontos.

Feldman, F. (1997). *Utilitarianism, hedonism, and desert: Essays in moral philosophy.* New York, NY: Cambridge University Press.

Finn, P. (1996). No-frills prisons and jails: A movement in flux. *Federal Probation, 60*(3), 35–44.

Flanagan, O., & Jackson, K. (1993). Justice, care, and gender: The Kohlberg–Gilligan debate revisited. In M. J. Larrabee (Ed.), *An ethic of care: Feminist and interdisciplinary perspectives* (pp. 69–86). New York, NY: Routledge.

Gilligan, C. (1982). *In a different voice: Psychological theory and women's development.* Cambridge, MA: Harvard University Press.

Harris, D. (2013, April 16). Prison rape widely ignored by authorities. *ABC News.* Retrieved from http://abcnews.go.com/WNT/story?id=131113&page=1

Harrison, P., & Beck, A. (2003, July). *Prisoners in 2002* (Bureau of Justice Statistics Bulletin NCJ 200248). Washington, DC: U.S. Department of Justice.

Hill, T. E. (2000). *Respect, pluralism, and justice: Kantian perspectives.* Oxford, United Kingdom: Oxford University Press.

Hinman, L. (1998). *Ethics: A pluralistic approach to moral theory.* Fort Worth, TX: Harcourt Brace.

Hudson, B. (1996). *Understanding justice: An introduction to ideas, perspectives and controversies in modern penal theory.* Buckingham, United Kingdom: Open University Press.

Hursthouse, R. (1999). *On virtue ethics.* Oxford, United Kingdom: Oxford University Press.

Ignatieff, M. (2004). *The lesser evil: Political ethics in an age of terror: The Gifford Lectures.* Princeton, NJ: Princeton University Press.

Kauffman, K. (1988). *Prison officers and their world.* Cambridge, MA: Harvard University Press.

Kleinig, J. (1996). *The ethics of policing.* New York, NY: Cambridge University Press.

Kleinig, J. (2001). Professionalizing incarceration. In J. Kleinig & M. L. Smith (Eds.), *Discretion, community, and correctional ethics* (pp. 1–15). Lanham, MA: Rowman & Littlefield.

Kohlberg, L. (1966). A cognitive-developmental analysis of children's sex-role concepts and attitudes. In E. E. Maccody (Ed.), *The development of sex differences* (pp. 82–172). Stanford, CA: Stanford University Press.

Lenz, N. (2002). "Luxuries" in prison: The relationship between amenity funding and public support. *Crime and Delinquency, 48*(4), 499–525.

Lombardo, L. (1989). *Guards imprisoned: Correctional officers at work* (2nd ed.). Cincinnati, OH: Anderson.

MacIntyre, A. (1984). *After virtue: A study in moral theory.* Notre Dame, IN: University of Notre Dame Press.

Martinson, R. (1974, Spring). What works? Questions and answers about prison reform. *The Public Interest, 35,* 22–54.

Mooney, C. (2001). Introduction: The public clash of private values: The politics of morality policy. In C. Mooney (Ed.), *The public clash of private values: The politics of morality policy* (pp. 3–18). New York, NY: Chatham House.

Morris, N. (1974). *The future of imprisonment.* Chicago, IL: University of Chicago Press.

Nozick, R. (1981). *Philosophical explanations.* Cambridge, MA: Harvard University Press.

Petersilia, J. (1999). Parole and prisoner reentry in the United States. In M. Tonry & J. Petersilia (Eds.), *Prisons* (pp. 479–529). Chicago, IL: University of Chicago Press.

Pope, C., & Feyerherm, W. (1990a, June). Minority status and juvenile justice processing: An assessment of the research literature (Part 1). *Criminal Justice Abstracts, 22*(2), 327–335.

Pope, C., & Feyerherm, W. (1990b, September). Minority status and juvenile justice processing: An assessment of the research literature (Part 2). *Criminal Justice Abstracts, 22,* 527–542.

Prior, W. (1991). *Virtue and knowledge: An introduction to ancient Greek ethics.* London, United Kingdom: Routledge.

Rachels, J. (1999a). *The elements of moral philosophy* (3rd ed.). Boston, MA: McGraw-Hill.

Rachels, J. (1999b). *The right thing to do: Basic readings in moral philosophy* (2nd ed.). Boston, MA: McGraw-Hill.

Rawls, J. (1973). *A theory of justice*. Oxford, United Kingdom: Oxford University Press.

Reiner, R. (1985). The police and race relations. In J. Baxter & L. Koffman (Eds.), *Police: The constitution and the community* (pp. 149–187). London, United Kingdom: Professional Books.

Rumana, R. (2000). *On Rorty*. Belmont, CA: Wadsworth.

Russell, K. (1998). *The color of crime: Racial hoaxes, White fear, Black protectionism, police harassment, and other macro aggressions*. New York: New York University Press.

Skolnick, J. (1966). *Justice without trial*. New York, NY: Wiley.

Smith, M. L. (2001). The shimmer of reform: Prospects for a correctional ethic. In J. Kleinig & M. L. Smith (Eds.), *Discretion, community, and correctional ethics* (pp. 17–37). Lanham, MA: Rowman & Littlefield.

Ten, C. L. (1987). *Crime, guilt, and punishment: A philosophical introduction*. Oxford, United Kingdom: Clarendon Press.

Tessitore, A. (1996). *Reading Aristotle's ethics: Virtue, rhetoric, and political philosophy*. Albany: State University of New York Press.

Tobar, H. (1998, December 28). An ugly stain on a city's bright and shining plan. *Los Angeles Times*, p. A1.

Tonry, M. (1994). Proportionality, parsimony, and interchangeability of punishments. In A. Duff & D. Garland (Eds.), *A reader on punishment* (pp. 133–160). Oxford, United Kingdom: Oxford University Press.

Walker, S., Spohn, C., & DeLone, M. (2000). *The color of justice: Race, ethnicity, and crime in America*. Belmont, CA: Wadsworth.

Warikoo, N. (2013, January 22). Ohio woman sues, FBI, airline for racial profiling: A half-Jewish half-Arab woman was removed from a plane with two others on 10th anniversary of Sept. 11. *Detroit Free Press*. Retrieved from http://www.usatoday.com/story/news/nation/2013/01/22/racial-profiling-lawsuit/1856619/

West, R. (1997). *Caring for justice*. New York: New York University Press.

Wilkinson, P. (2001). *Terrorism versus democracy: The liberal state response*. Portland, OR: Frank Cass.

Wisniewski, M. (2013, September 12). Chicago police torture: Mayor Rahm Emanuel apologizes, says "Let us now move on." *Huffington Post*. Retrieved from http://www.huffington post.com/2013/09/12/chicago-police-torture-mayor_n_3910197.html

CHAPTER 3

Criminological Theory and Crime Explanation

Dan Okada

SCIENCE/SOCIETY/LAW/CRIME/CRIMINOLOGY

In studying crime, or examining the various constructs that provide the structure from which to study crime scientifically, what is sometimes overlooked is that process, although important, is nonetheless an academic exercise. The canons of science demand *value-free* investigation and consideration. This can be understood against the political incrimination of "flip-flopping," which has no relevance in scientific inquiry. The aim is to gather as much useful information as possible, that is, to collect data and then to competently assess what has been collected. It is not until this analysis has been completed that any sort of determination, one way or another, can be made. Scientists must be constitutionally willing to change their minds because their minds can be made up based solely on what they find. This same reminder is provided to criminology students who are regularly frustrated when they realize that these explanations that they have painstakingly committed to memory are *only theories*. Scientific theories are constructed to fail as well as to succeed. A good theory is intended to be controversial, to stimulate investigation, and to be tested and examined and ultimately may indeed be discredited based exclusively on the data collected in testing it.

The outcome of theory construction and testing provides understanding, even enlightenment. Because this discussion comes in conjunction with lessons in investigation and jurisprudence, a context must be provided. There is only modest interest in turning these explanations into courtroom legal defenses or prosecution strategies. Criminological theories attempt to explain what is often inexplicable and to examine what is often the cruelty, oppression, or even evil some visit on others. They are scientific examinations of a particular social phenomenon. This said, there is no attempt in this presentation to be comprehensive in either the discussion of individual theories or their number but rather to highlight them, to pique the curiosity of those who become interested, and to thus stimulate greater subsequent exploration.

Akers (1994) noted that the criteria for determining the value of any theory are their logic, testability, empirical support, and utility. The hope is that upon constructing reasonable explanations and then testing their fit, the enterprise will influence reasonable and effective enactment of public policy that will minimize levels of victimization and reduce instances of crime. Thus, criminological theories are created so that we can better understand why people behave as they do and that in understanding the *why*, we can respond more effectively to these actions and actors.

Criminology focuses on crime as the question, Why? This differs from the criminal justice question, which asks, What now? Answering the why question offers a range of challenges and opportunities from many perspectives and disciplines. In this endeavor there are many "right" answers. For instance, introductory criminology and criminal justice students learn that the earliest explanations of criminal behavior were theological in orientation. Demonic possession, for instance, was once believed to be the sole answer to the question, Why? (Vold & Bernard, 1979). As technology and the scientific method evolved and influenced scholars, theories likewise increased. It is important to appreciate this evolution so that we can better understand and assess contemporary theories.

A theory is a series of statements that seek to explain or understand a particular phenomenon. Merton (1968, pp. 59–60) suggested that those with a more practical orientation should focus their attention on what he called "theories of the midrange," that is, specific explanations of specific behaviors—rather than look for one broad-based theory, or what Babbie (2013) identified as a nomothetic, comprehensive, all-inclusive explanation that in this sense addresses all forms of crime. This exercise, naturally, would be fraught with frustration because of the nature, breadth, and complexity of crime. A concentrated, more uniquely directed, that is, idiographic, theory that seeks to explain specific crime typologies would serve end users and students more effectively.

The professoriat is often guilty of passing along the myriad explanations, what are called here "named theories," through lectures that pass as academic erudition but that are often interpreted by rote and less so by conviction. It is no wonder that because of their abundance, these explanations are discouragingly seen as superfluous or even worse, irrelevant. A legitimate criticism is that if everything is important, then what is truly important? From a student's perspective, the question remains, What is the relevance of studying theories? The abstract reasoning necessary to consider scientific theories from a particular academic perspective often holds little attraction for the student who is more interested in the practice and application of criminal justice. While examinations that focus on *why* may not compete favorably against interest focusing on *how*, or *who*, or *what now*, the why is the focus of this examination. A lengthy discussion could be had defining criminology and its parameters, but that is not the intent here. Criminology is the study of crime; specifically, the focus here will be on the causes of crime by those who engage in it.

MICRO-LEVEL ANALYSES

Biological Explanation

While it is true that many criminal justice students believe that the answers to crime understanding can be found in the social sciences, many others gravitate to these disciplines because of their previous inconsistent or modest academic success in what some perceive to be the harder, that is, more rigorous, sciences: biology, chemistry, physics, and math, believing that a less arduous journey to a college degree can be found in a "practical" major. The history of criminal justice program acceptance has met a complementary bias as colleagues in the natural sciences have been quick to discredit their social science brothers and sisters. It can be argued that this has also led to the infusion of sophisticated methodological designs and analyses as a response to charges of lack of scientific rigor.

Students are compelled to enroll in a required criminology theory class and, as a typical starting point, are thrust headfirst into the criminal justice/criminology-catechism and exposed to the father of modern criminology, Cesare Lombroso. Atavism and the *born criminal* now enter their vocabulary as they listen to how the scientific method was first introduced to the study of criminal behavior along with data collection, hypotheses testing, and ultimately statistical analysis. Eyes roll, shoulders tense, and teeth grit.

Lombroso's education and training led to his securing the role of chief pathologist of the Italian penal system (Sellin, 1937). His lasting contribution to criminology was in being the first to ask the question, Why? Why did those convicts to whom he had access, and on whom he performed autopsies, commit the crimes for which they were convicted? Given the technology and research methods of this day, Lombroso offered cutting-edge analysis. The answer had to lie in each individual's physiology. Since all these criminals were male and possessed similar physical characteristics that were pronounced and obvious, the traits that each carried from birth had to provide the answer to the question why.

Although the notion that criminals are born and not made is often found to be incredible by today's student, that certain innate behaviors and characteristics seem to dispose those who exhibit them with tendencies that may lead to criminal behavior is not likely. Having an abundance of body hair or an asymmetrical face, such as Lombroso proposed in his early work (1876), may be disputed links to criminal behavior, but on the other hand, irritability and impatience that are only occasionally controlled through overt effort are part of an individual's makeup that given the proper catalyst, need, situation, or encouragement can coalesce in a meaningful way as criminal behavior.

Lombroso never imagined that his findings would or could be turned into public policy that discriminates against those particular social members possessing particular physiological characteristics that he identified. Rather, he was performing science by assessing his data; these "stigmata" helped identify those social members who were "predisposed" to engage in criminal behavior. As an investigatory tool, these characteristics simplified detection. It can be seen how his broad-based generalizations, based on the body type, physicality, and even genetics, turned into such controversial contemporary law enforcement techniques as racial profiling or even the internment of Japanese Americans during World War II.

Brain Development

One of the more fascinating directions the study of human biology and neuroscience has taken in the study of crime is with the emerging research regarding the brain's prefrontal cortex. Raine (2013) argued that the brains of violent criminals function differently from others. Murderers can be identified as falling into one of two categories, reactive or proactive killers. Reactive killers can be observed as tending to have measurably reduced activity in their prefrontal cortex, the part of the brain responsible for decision making and impulse control. Reactive killers are unable to, or even uninterested in, controlling their urge to act out. On the other hand, proactive killers are manipulative, calculating, and can deliberately target and plan their attack. Their prefrontal cortex glows under brain scans as does their limbic system, the brain's center of emotion.

At different times and to varying degrees in anyone's physical and mental development, the prefrontal cortex is virtually encased in dopamine, the brain's motivation, reward, and pleasure-producing neurotransmitter chemical. This substance is also related to both the inhibition of rational processing of consequences and delaying gratification. An abundance of dopamine virtually prohibits the consideration of potential repercussions of behavior, which can be seen as its link to crime as it limits the prefrontal cortex's ability to control. Because we all develop at different rates, from infancy through adolescence, as we mature, some can be found to be incapable of making rational choices or understanding the consequences of their actions even into young adulthood while others seem to be wise beyond their years. Although the results of this research are not absolute, the potential for greater understanding is significant.

Psychology

The field of psychology has routinely lent itself to analysis involving aberrant or antisocial behavior. One controversy that reigns is with the release of each new edition of the American Psychiatric Association's guidebook, the *Diagnostic and Statistical Manual of Mental Disorders (DSM)*. Since the *DSM* includes treatment protocols along with its descriptions of symptomology and effects, the value and use of psychotropic drugs as control mechanisms for mental disorders is only one of the debates raging among *DSM* subscribers. One issue is the *over*-diagnosis of mental illnesses that could or should be chemically treated. Longtime psychiatric gainsayer Thomas Szasz (1974) argued that aside from specific brain diseases that produce outcomes such as autism or Alzheimer's disease, that mental illnesses are more theoretically constructed than they are organic.

In spite of this criticism, the connection between psychology, mental illness, and crime is prominent as many concepts or constructs generated by investigators promote examination of cognitive processing, personality disorders, and even levels of intelligence as personality characteristics possessed by the criminal. In this regard, impulsiveness, egoism, incorrigibility, and temperament are discussed as psychological states that foster criminality (Agnew, 2005; Lanier & Henry, 1998). According to cognitive psychology, when those who possess these characteristics interact with influences existing in their social environments, they are more likely to engage in criminality than those not so ably equipped (Walters, 1989). Because of what are seen as intrinsic compulsions, when faced with temptation, frustration, anger, or lust, those individuals are more likely to behave aberrantly. Lacking the desire to control his/her urges, short-term hedonism wins out over prosocial behavior. Obviously, the journey to crime is not as simple or linear as this, but cognitive psychologists argue that these traits are linked to crime.

Yochelson and Samenow (1976) conducted a case study of over 200 inmates at Washington, D.C.'s St. Elizabeth's Hospital for the Criminally Insane. Through interviews, self-reflections, and group discussions with their patients, they concluded that the common thread running through all of these criminals was an inherent "criminal personality." Criminals think differently than noncriminals. Through an integration of rational choice, free will, and antisocial decision making, criminals "chose to be" criminals. But this is closest to the suggestion that criminals have some sort of identifiable personality characteristic.

Kohlberg (1984) added to the discussion, suggesting that individual morality can be examined along a continuum. As we age, we also grow morally. Developmental psychology, behaviorism, and Freudian psychoanalysis all find their way into Kohlberg's model. Moral development can be measured, does not occur at the same rate in everyone, and does not emerge consistently; but until morality is mastered through the various developmental stages identified by Kohlberg, moral behavior is improbable. Kohlberg takes overt behavior and loops it back to the basic philosophy of the existence of crime, that is, that crime is a violation of morality.

Such areas of examination as offender typologies and profiles, such as those constructed to identify serial killers; the effect of post-traumatic stress disorder and antisocial behavior; and the development of various intervention methodologies seeking to rehabilitate criminals are demonstrations of the link between psychology and crime. Because of the plethora of media portrayals, areas of abnormal psychology often are the gateway for students becoming interested in careers in criminal justice.

Gender

When asked to describe a criminal, the first characteristic most respondents would identify is "male." Other sociodemographic characteristics may emerge, but maleness is generally the first. Aside from popular culture depictions, a cursory look at the data produced by any criminal justice agency show that males commit the vast majority of all crime. The Bureau of Justice Statistics (2012) reported that in 2011, women made up 24% of all arrests that year, while contributing over 50% of the total U.S. population. While the number of female offenders has been steadily increasing over the past few decades, few would argue that females are more criminal than males.

The scholarship that addresses female criminality is often couched in terms of offender oppression, discrimination, conflict, and economic disadvantage. Using traditional criminological explanations, just as it can be postulated that men feel strain and anomie in their attempts to secure social capital, so a social reality is that women face greater distress. Just as men engage in neutralization as they appeal to higher loyalties, such as their gangs or their neighborhoods, so women feel the same about their families and friends.

Interest in female criminality has grown proportionately: matching their increase in criminality as well as the changing demographics of the researchers and academics. In a not too distant past, women had difficulty in finding a place in any area of criminal justice. Along with an increase in offenders, women have increased their numbers in virtually every arena of practical and administrative criminal justice. Along with the raw numbers of women engaged in the criminal justice enterprise has emerged a criminology devoted to their crime activity (see Chesney-Lind, Chapter 7, in this volume). While the context of feminism has taken a place in academic examination, a review of crime explanations asks, Do women commit crimes for reasons different from men's? The scholarship responding to this question answers yes.

Cohen and Felson's (1979) routine activities theory, aside from its modest attempt at explaining crime causation, highlights crime as the often random intersection of a motivated offender meeting a target of opportunity. No attempt is made to explain why this motivated offender became motivated. Under this same construct, the increased number of women engaged in activities outside their domiciles, provides more women with the opportunity to both engage in and be victimized by crime. While this does not provide the sole explanation for their behavior, it does provide a perspective to understand the influences that women in an earlier historical epoch might not have considered. If you are out in public, you have a greater chance of engaging in a range of human contact.

The feminist perspective argues that women face a number of social obstacles that men do not. While men may feign understanding, or even sympathy, one challenge they are unlikely to truly understand is the existence of rampant cultural sexism. To say that criminal justice is a male-dominated enterprise is a gross understatement. There is no area in the crime arena in which men do not prevail. To suggest that this overt, institutional, and systemic discriminatory interaction would not have a dilatory response on those facing it would be disingenuous. The suggestion that women might be better equipped to "take it" because of some genetic predisposition to tolerance is itself discriminatory. The social pressure felt by a constant and insidious prejudice may be grounds enough for an aberrant response.

The complement to sexism is paternalism. Chesney-Lind and Shelden (1992) contended that a reason provided for why girls are often taken into custody is, "for their own good." The protective father in the form of the criminal justice practitioner is exercising his nurturing nature by taking care of his (even though the law enforcement practitioner may be a woman) wayward offspring. The underlying suggestion is that female offenders obviously cannot take care of themselves. Language comes into play here as derogatory terms, such as *sluts, hoes,* and *bitches,* do not have similar masculine counterparts.

Messerschmidt (1993) goes in a different direction as he addresses the gender inequality existing in criminal justice. He argued that crime is simply one of the resources men have at their disposal to fulfill their male-dominance (i.e., hegemonic) destiny. Males exist in a state of privilege. Their wants, needs, desires, motivations, and expressions are accepted, even expected, as universal. To question male superiority is irrelevant; men simply are. All their activity supports this basic contention. Thus, the more aggressive, the more violent, more clever, the more insidious the crime, the greater the thrill and reward. This is what men do. To not act in this fashion is to be thought of as less manly, that is, to be womanly.

It should be recognized that gender, both masculinity and femininity, is as critical to social behavior as is class or race and ethnicity. Societies, for good or ill, differentiate resources, opportunities, and even perspective based on these sociodemographic characteristics. One unfortunate artifact of this discrimination can be seen in correctional settings where programs and opportunities for rehabilitation or reentry for women are dramatically fewer in number and kind than are male-oriented programs. Those that do exist seem to focus on female "trades," like cosmetology or data entry, if they exist at all.

More and more females are gaining entry into all facets of the crime enterprise. Scholars such as Chesney-Lind, Daly, Miller, Belknap, Wonders, Adler, Morash, Danner, Cook, and many others are now as prominent in the criminological literature as are Merton, Sutherland, Cressey, Cohen, Hirschi, and other male scholars cited in this chapter. In criminal justice terms, women have now become the majority of first-year law students and are increasing in critical mass across all practical areas of criminal justice. It is no surprise that their activity in crime creation has also become recognized. While not dominant, at least the recognition that gender matters has taken root in both the study and practice of crime.

MACRO-LEVEL ANALYSES

Social Learning

Edwin Sutherland was attempting to provide a reasonable explanation for the behavior of a particular kind of criminal. Chic Conwell, the thief in Sutherland's *The Professional Thief* (1937), grew up in a comfortable environment but fell into crime after getting involved in drug use and a misguided relationship with a "showgirl."

This relationship led to contacts with an underworld that enticed him and provided what Katz (1988) might later call "sneaky thrills." Conwell became a thief. It was a profession that required him to acquire techniques, mores, and ethics and learn the culture of thieving.

Sutherland later interviewed other thieves who were far more unscrupulous and dangerous. These criminals also happened to hold prestigious positions in American business and industry. They were chairmen (for there were no women in these positions at that time) of the boards of directors of many of the major corporations of the early to mid-20th-century corporate America. They practiced collusion, fraud, and larceny against the public and the federal government. These men passed their trade secrets and practices around in a similar fashion as did Chic Conwell and his associates. Because of the stature and position of these previously unrecognized offenders, Sutherland (1983) coined a new term to describe them: They collectively became the "white collar criminal."

The common thread running through the professional and white-collar thief culture was their criminal activities. After matriculating through an apprenticeship where they were initially naïve, which then led to interaction with skilled others, they learned how to become criminal. In creating his explanation, the critical components of Sutherland's explanation consisted of the intensity and frequency with which these associates interacted, as well as the knowledge they exchanged and the quality of their interactions. These gentlemen engaged in *differential association,* which was offered up as the explanation as to why these criminals did what they did. Sutherland wedded nascent American sociology to a more polished political economic perspective to develop his understanding of the cause of these crimes. As one of the first scholars to write in the field of criminology, he used techniques that contemporary methodologists now recognize as grounded theory and ethnographic data collection.

Sutherland's explanation was a deductive process where his original seven propositions (1939) eventually grew to nine (Sutherland & Cressey, 1947; in the 3rd, or 1939, edition of Sutherland's *Principles of Criminology* there are six propositions of his theory; in the 4th edition, the 1947 redo of this book, with coauthor Cressey, there are now nine) and evolved from the explanation of a particular kind of behavior into one of the most popular criminological theories ever formulated as it has been used to explain behaviors as diverse as juvenile delinquency (Smith & Braeme, 1994) and computer crime (Skinner & Fream, 1997).

If it is so, that nascent criminals can become more accomplished criminals by closely, differentially associating themselves with those who know how to be better criminals, then the connection between science and society generates this uncomfortable question, Why do we send those young criminals who we capture and prosecute to prison to associate with more veteran offenders? If differential association makes sense, then incarceration is an illogical response to crime reduction. Herein lies the social science quandary; after constructing reasonable explanations about a phenomenon (i.e., crime), acquiring reliable, relevant support from methodologically sound research, what should be done with the information produced? Advocacy is not the responsibility of science.

Anomie/Strain

Anomie, according to Durkheim (1893), is a psychological state of confusion caused by rapidly changing industrial evolution and an accompanying societal dislocation and the effect this change has on people. This state is popularly conceptualized as "normlessness." It is a feeling, an attitude, a psychological perspective that causes those who experience it to feel confused, frustrated, annoyed, angry, hostile, embarrassed, and even resigned or doomed. Angst lingers as they adjust their thinking and behavior to deal with it. This onus can be debilitating or just uncomfortable, but it exists in reality. Durkheim (1951) contended that those who feel this way may attempt to relieve themselves by committing deviant acts while others may resort to an extreme aggravated resolution and commit suicide. Either may be considered an overreaction, but many are ill equipped to deal with the pushes and pulls they face, and for some, those extreme measures described by Durkheim may have been the only viable solution.

The American version of anomie comes from Merton (1968) who saw that psychological stress results from a perceived inability to successfully compete for social capital. On a continuum, those who have access, or can successfully compete for social capital (money), are more content (have less anomie), whereas those who do not are less satisfied and thus experience more anomie. While Merton believed that the dream to be successful is universal, the ability to achieve that dream is not. The causes of this inequality may be structural: education, training, social status, and so on, but they are aspirations shared by everyone.

Merton suggested that those feeling anomie were likely to respond through one of five modalities: *conformity* (dealing with it); *innovation* (creatively circumventing it); *ritualism* (recognizing that success was unlikely but beyond complaining about it, accepting the reality that they had done all they could); *retreatism* (dropping out typically through substance abuse, homelessness, etc.); or *rebellion* (creating alternative processes to achieve the rewards that are impossible through mainstream or traditional means; i.e., becoming involved with gangs, organized crime, etc.). The universality of this theory is that everyone at one time or another faces anomie. We may be frustrated at life; our work efforts go unrecognized or are poorly rewarded; incompetent motorists continually confound us; and so on—we are hassled. While these experiences are all unnerving, as they happen or in their totality, Merton contended that we adapt. This version of anomie has been recontextualized by others and been fashioned into social strain and hence social strain theories.

A complaint students often voice as they learn criminological theories is the seeming disconnect they have with real-world public policy. That is, as they learn about the assumptions, propositions, hypotheses, and so on that come from constructing and testing theories, students rightly ask, Now what? With social strain comes the recognition that at least these theories had a direct effect on actual public policy.

Collectively, social strain theories suggest that when confronted with the inability to achieve success and when faced with the strain that ensues following the realization that personal talents, training, or desires cannot achieve that which is desired, criminal behavior may result. Obviously, there are those who elect not to become criminals, which adds to the frustration in accepting strain theory's basic premise; however, strain theory suggests that a plausible outcome to those who do not possess patience or who cannot handle stress (i.e., anomie or strain) well is crime.

The fathers of strain theory are Cohen (1955) and Cloward and Ohlin (1960). Cohen believed that juveniles joined gangs because they seek traditional social status but do not possess the wherewithal to achieve it legitimately. This inability is exacerbated by the reality that culture dictates upward mobility, which divines a "middle-class measuring rod" as the status-defining standard. We are naturally competitive, so when Cohen's low-income juveniles compete with others of the same class, they see themselves as more or less equal players in the same game. However, when they compare themselves to a middle or higher status, they recognize the inequality of their lives and that while their relative status was not problematic when compared with their gang friends, when juxtaposed to those having greater resources, strain ensues. In fact, antagonism may arise and crime is committed to assuage the strain.

Popular culture also influences some (see Swan, Chapter 9, this volume). Television commercials, print ads, product placement in movies, and so on identifies to the masses what is cool, what products are "hot," and, conversely, defines what is not. Having that which has been identified as the "in" thing but which can only be attained with enough social capital (money) establishes the standard from which many recognize their depraved status. Their wants cannot be satisfied through prosocial activity. Nefarious, deceitful, criminal means and associations are necessary to achieve success.

In trying to understand juvenile criminality, Cloward and Ohlin believed that equal *opportunity* to achieve social capital would reduce the desire to become delinquent. Those living in urban areas experience poverty and low-quality education delivered in often blighted schools; they face all the failings associated with the social disorganization found in the "inner city" (Shaw & McKay, 1942). They are more likely to make life choices that include crime. Thus, if greater opportunities were available to mitigate the influence of society's neglect, their lives would improve, or at least the opportunity to become criminal would be less profound and crime would be reduced.

Strain and opportunity theories have been credited with influencing the presidential efforts of President Kennedy's creation of the Department of Health, Education, and Welfare (HEW) and President Johnson's war on poverty and the Mobilization for Youth program (Short, 1975). The foundation for HEW and the war on poverty was that social problems found in urban areas are the product of the unequal distribution of wealth and access that many experience. Social programs that provide access to medical and/or psychological treatment, better educational opportunities, and job training and placement could positively affect society. The point strain theory makes is that if access to social capital was normalized, prosocial behavior would ensue. Much social science research and the contemporary movement to evidence-based programming are tangible outcomes of social strain theory.

Conflict

The social upheavals of the 1960s and 1970s caused a reassessment of crime causation explanations in the academic criminology world. With the increased cultural and social awareness that was taking place via the civil rights movement, the war in Vietnam, assassinations of popular political and social icons, Kent State, and Watergate, this was a time of turmoil. Liberal positivist criminology was not prepared, was inadequate, and even thought to be inappropriate to explain or understand crime in this era. The state and the ruling moneyed classes, the age old battle between the haves and have-nots, and a generation of adolescent immaturity were seen as the genesis of much social unrest and certainly crime. The generation of scholars who came of age at this time, questioned authority and focused their inquiry on the inequity, oppression, discrimination, and rage that existed throughout society. Explanations of criminal behavior were found in the creation of law, the war between the classes, and a culture that nurtured exploitation. Controversy exists but various descriptors were used to identify this perspective: *radical criminology* (Platt, 1974), *new criminology* (Taylor, Walton, & Young, 1973), *Marxist criminology* (Schwendinger & Schwendinger, 1970), *critical criminology* (Quinney, 1973), and *anarchist criminology* (Tifft, 1979; Meltzer, 1996), but now this discussion is carried under the mantle of *conflict criminology*.

The conflict perspective is broken down into three areas: conflict between groups (cultures, societies, ethnicities, races, genders, etc.); conflict between classes (bourgeois vs. the proletariats, haves vs. the have-nots); and economic conflict caused by the unequal distribution and control of social resources. The struggle to attain limited social access to money, services, employment, education, and so on was seen as the genesis of that era's social upheavals. Social justice could be achieved only when all societal members had equal access to all social resources. Until equity was achieved, conflict and thus crime would continue to exist.

The controversy surrounding the basic premises of conflict criminology focus on a lingering shortcoming: the difficulty faced when attempting to scientifically test its propositions. Although status equity might reduce crimes of exploitation, there is little evidence suggesting that crimes of violence are fewer in those societies professing no class distinctions. In fact, uncovering existing societies that are classless is impossible. Access to crucial goods and services is distinctly class related. Thus, conflict theories become statements of belief rather than scientific explanations. In spite of the dissonance that surrounds it, conflict theory exists and demands consideration and thus fulfills one proposition needed in determining a "good" theory: It stimulates critical thought and demands efforts to discredit it. Few would argue that conflict does not contribute to crime. Defining conflict becomes the problem.

Labeling

Tannenbaum's (1938) "dramatization of evil," Merton's (1968) self-fulfilling prophecy, and Becker's (1963) deviant behavior as an outcome of individual self-definition and society's response to that behavior provide the foundation for labeling theory. Lemert (1951) suggests that those stigmatized with the label of criminal are destined to live their lives dictated by that label and would therefore comport themselves as such. The theory, however, is even more insidious than that.

Under Merton's gaze, many of us live up or down to the expectations placed on us by others. This is old school University of Chicago, Department of Sociology symbolic interactionism. In the framework of labeling theory, the actor has engaged in criminal behavior (labeling theory does not address the original act) and once detected is adjudicated criminal through a successful degradation ceremony (Garfinkel, 1965); thus, s/he has been certified with a state-endorsed label. The actor then succumbs and internalizes the label believing him/herself to be the essence of that label. Whether or not s/he is sentenced and incarcerated and then eventually reforms or not is irrelevant. Labeling theory is classified as a conflict theory because of the process it describes, that is, designation by the state.

Upon release, that individual now bears the accursed label *ex-convict*, and it now matters not what s/he feels that s/he is; the state and his/her community now recognize the label and not the individual and believe him/her to be dangerous, suspicious, and contemptible. Employment, housing, and services are denied or grudgingly provided making reintegration back into society at best challenging and at worst impossible. To say that the effect of labeling has little to do with the way this actor may behave is disingenuous.

Social Control

It is the province of crime theories to answer the question, Why did that individual become a criminal? Social control theories turn this inquiry around by asking its converse, Why didn't that individual become a criminal (Hirschi, 1969)? Since the potential to become a criminal is ubiquitous, as opportunities are readily available to anyone, why isn't everyone criminal? For social control theorists, the answer is simple: because we are controlled. The method of control then becomes the interest of control theory. As is the case in all theory construction, control theories include vestiges of many other theoretical conventions.

Reiss (1951) established the foundation for control theories by arguing a psychological perspective that when an individual lacks sufficient "inner controls," what some might call morality or Freud might call the super ego, and this deficit is juxtaposed to an absence of effective social controls, like prosocial significant others, effective schools, or family, the outcome could easily be crime commission. Reckless (1955) followed by adding his own interpretation of control, calling it "containment." Containment theory stipulates that the self, identified by such diverse psychological concepts as self-concept and super ego, is responsible for maintaining a social equilibrium that balances potential to do crime with the realization that crime is inappropriate. A healthy, prosocial, contained self, can "insulate" the individual from antisocial influences (Reckless, Dinitz, & Murray, 1956).

Although not typically thought of as a control theory, Sykes and Matza's (1957) *techniques of neutralization* resides in this domain. Neutralization is not a theory in the scientific testing sense but rather an approach at understanding a criminal's mind-set. It spins the control question and asks, Why do good people do bad things? When faced with the choice or opportunity to commit a crime, or not, neutralization surmises that individuals "drift" (where Matza, 1964, eventually took this perspective), allowing the actor to *neutralize*, that is, rationalize his/her decision. Martyrs, victims of wrong place at the wrong time, or those who may believe they were coerced into crime commission may claim *denial of responsibility*. Those who believe that their actions are so insignificant that they would not be noticed or indeed cause little harm may neutralize a *denial of injury*. Sometimes, offenders even claim that their victims got what they deserved. Through a mental mind switch that depersonalizes the recipient of a criminal act, these offenders neutralize a *denial of the victim*. Other offenders believe that their victim was some sort of miscreant and therefore "had it coming," for whatever that reason is, and thus these offenders neutralize by *condemning the condemners*. One of the most likely, and even understandable, techniques rationalizes crime as an act to support or even protect significant others, the gang, the family, even the state and thus neutralization is caused by an *appeal to higher loyalties*. The actor understands what s/he has done and does not deny the action s/he has taken but feels that there was good reason for what s/he did and therefore is not culpable. A broader interpretation of control theory might suggest that if this offender had been better controlled, s/he would not have had to neutralize.

One of the most popular control constructs, and one of the most widely tested criminological theories in the literature, followed the strategy of Reckless. Hirschi (1969) continued the integration of various theories: anomie, social disorganization, differential association, labeling, and containment in proposing *elements of the social bond*. *Bond* consists of four elements: attachment, commitment, involvement, and belief and when wedded together form a bond to the conventional order.

Hirschi postulates that the stronger the bond, the greater the chances of prosocial activity. Conversely, the weaker the bond, the more likely crime will ensue. Conventional behavior was instilled through close interaction with school, work, family, community, and friends. Alienation or dissonance with these elements, that is, weaker bonds will more likely result in crime. Unfortunately, Hirschi never addressed associations that were made with institutions or significant others who were already criminal, such as felonious parents or friends, gangs, or various other threat groups. The key to Hirschi's bond is the interaction anyone has with those who are important to his/her life.

Social Ecology

Social disorganization theories are the legacy of the University of Chicago. Its Department of Sociology is hallowed ground for American criminology. Using the city of Chicago as a starting point, faculty set out to examine the urban setting as a social science laboratory. Chicago sociologists collected data from those urban entities that interested them, people and the places and things with which and where people interacted. Today's students take these dicta as common sense, as they blithely disregard the fact that all of these explorations were novel for the Chicago alliance—this was innovative.

That ethnic, cultural, and economic kin shared similar environments generated theories that examined the "inner city" with its "concentric zones" (Park & Burgess, 1924), its prevalent "social disorganization" (Shaw & McKay, 1942), and existent "culture conflict" (Sellin, 1938) that those groups living in these environments shared. Cities stimulated misbehavior. Human interaction happened in cities, and while people were usually cordial, sometimes they acted criminally, even violently. There was a distinct absence of "collective efficacy," ties among community residents that provide a sense of symbiosis (Sampson, Raudenbush, & Earls, 1997).

From the family interactions that occur in the confines of any home to the streets where unsupervised youth might congregate and turn boasts and posturing into conflict or dangerous interaction, the specific geographic location of those interactions, the street or block or corner where people live and spend time is related to the types of activities in which those actors engaged. Language, words, gestures, and symbols that are exchanged, interpreted, or misinterpreted, even the clothing that is worn, can be provocative. Who a particular person is, his/her stature in the community or gang, or his/her influence, or the way that influence is interpreted is information that can be substantively assessed. In the infancy of criminology—what is now commonplace—these parameters were first examined. "Hot-spot analysis," the "hood," CompStat, "broken windows," "turf wars," and "gang" examinations of today, as well as one of the most esteemed scholarly publishing houses in the social sciences, are the contemporary progeny of the Chicago school parent.

General Theory

Two versions of a diverse crime explanation, coincidentally calling themselves by the same name, have recently emerged. Gottfredson and Hirschi (1990) expanded on Hirschi's social bond to create an extended control theory they call the general theory of crime. At its center is the recognition that the most reasonable and effective form of crime prevention is individual self-control. The failure to exhibit better control over one's impulses leads to crime. Controversy is sparked over the quality of parenting strategies, which were highlighted as the root cause of effective or ineffective self-control. Gottfredson and Hirschi suggested that if parents were more effective at instilling delayed gratification skills in their children, crime and delinquency could be prevented.

In Agnew's (2005) vision of a general theory of crime causation, various life influences intersect to form a "web of crime." These influences, or domains, comprise the self, family, school, peers, and work. Each domain ebbs and flows in its influence over the others, prosocially at times and antisocially at others. Agnew argued that when an impulsive individual, who has ineffective parents, finds him/herself in a poor school experience, which encourages interactions with other disinterested, confused, or frustrated peers, which then leads to under or unemployment, a web or nexus is created that results in crime. This web is affected by either low constraints and/or high motivation to commit crime.

These general theories suggest that more effective parenting strategies along with greater accountability placed on individuals by all social enterprises, because we would all pay greater attention to those in need, would influence those individuals at society's margins to disassociate themselves with criminality. We are truly all responsible for each other.

CONCLUSION

Other named theories than those presented here can be found throughout the literature, enough to encourage some to continue to exercise their curiosity and seek their own answers to the why crime question. We remain intrigued by those unknowns that tempt, confuse, confound, and frighten us. Crime is one of the most curious of all human activities. Criminology is the scholarly attempt to understand crime. While the criminal is an enigma, being his/her potential victim is what concerns us. We understand that the criminal justice mechanism is reactive; it is unlikely to adequately protect any one of us from harm. Our hope is that criminology, in spite its foibles, has the ability to help us understand, to predict who among us, given his or her constitution and situation, will commit crimes against us. That will be our protection. Alas, that is also our frustration: that a plausible explanation may successfully increase our awareness of the conditions that could affect a crime's commission but that this only intellectually affects us. Ultimately, we want to understand the motivation to commit crime and how to discourage this. As we become more sophisticated in our endeavors, what we must understand is that in our efforts to study crime, there are not too many theories; there are not enough.

DISCUSSION QUESTIONS

1. What perspective, sociology, psychology, anthropology, economics, political science, biology, or others, is best equipped to explain crime?

2. If reducing crime is the goal, what is the role of science in achieving that goal? What is the role of the state or society?

3. Are there areas of investigation that have not yet been tapped in trying to understand the causes of crime? If the role of science is to ask questions and provide answers, what questions have not yet been asked?

4. What is the value of constructing theories reflecting crime causation? Is there an identifiable end product that this activity is intended to produce?

5. What are the major considerations or variables necessary in constructing a reasonable crime causation explanation? What factors are likely to increase the probability of crime, and what factors are likely to decrease the probability? Do we actually know?

REFERENCES

Agnew, R. (2005). *Why criminals offend: A general theory of crime and delinquency.* Los Angeles, CA: Roxbury.

Akers, R. L. (1994). *Criminological theories: Introduction and evaluation.* Los Angeles, CA: Roxbury.

Babbie, E. (2013). *The practice of social research* (13th ed.). Belmont, CA: Wadsworth/Thomson Learning.

Becker, H. S. (1963). *Outsiders: Studies in the sociology of deviance.* New York, NY: The Free Press.

Bureau of Justice Statistics. (2012). Arrests: By offense charged and sex, 2011 [Table 4.8.2011]. *Sourcebook of criminal justice statistics online.* U.S. Department of Justice, Office of Justice Programs. Retrieved from http://www.albany.edu/sourcebook/pdf/t482011.pdf

Chesney-Lind, M., & Shelden, R. G. (1992). *Girls, delinquency, and juvenile justice.* Belmont, CA: Wadsworth.

Cloward, R. A., & Ohlin, L. E. (1960). *Delinquency and opportunity: A theory of delinquent gangs.* New York, NY: The Free Press.

Cohen, A. K. (1955). *Delinquent boys: The culture of the gang.* New York, NY: The Free Press.

Cohen, L. E., & Felson, M. (1979, August). Social change and crime rate trends: A routine activity approach. *American Sociological Review, 44*(4), 588–608.

Durkheim, É. (1893). *The division of labor in society* (G. Simpson, trans.). New York, NY: The Free Press.

Durkheim, É. (1951). *Suicide: A study of sociology* (J. A. Spaulding & G. Simpson, trans.). New York, NY: The Free Press.

Garfinkel, H. K. (1965). Conditions of successful degradation ceremonies. *American Journal of Sociology, 61*(5), 420–424.

Gottfredson, M. R., & Hirschi, T. (1990). *A general theory of crime.* Stanford, CA: Stanford University Press.

Hirschi, T. (1969). *Causes of delinquency.* Berkeley: University of California Press.

Katz, J. (1988). *Seductions of crime: Moral and sensual attractions in doing evil.* New York, NY: Basic Books.

Kohlberg, L. (1984). *The psychology of moral development: The nature and validity of moral stages.* San Francisco, CA: Harper & Row.

Lanier, M. M., & Henry, S. (1998). *Essential criminology.* Boulder, CO: Westview Press.

Lemert, E. M. (1951). *Social pathology*. New York, NY: McGraw-Hill.

Lombroso, C. (1876). *L'Uomo Delinquente* [The criminal man]. Milan, Italy: Hoepli.

Matza, D. (1964). *Delinquency and drift*. New York, NY: Wiley & Sons.

Meltzer, A. (1996). *Anarchism: Arguments for and against*. Sanday, Orkneys: Cienfuegos Press.

Merton, R. K. (1968). *Social theory and social structure* (Rev. & enlarged ed.). Glencoe, IL: The Free Press.

Messerschmidt, J. W. (1993). *Masculinities and crime: Critique and reconceptualization of theory*. Lanham, MD: Rowman & Littlefield.

Park, R. E., & Burgess, E. W. (1924). *Introduction to the science of sociology* (2nd ed.). Chicago, IL: University of Chicago Press.

Platt, T. (1974). Prospects for a radical criminology in the United States. *Crime and Social Justice, 1*(Spring–Summer), 2–6.

Quinney, R. (1973). *Critique of legal order: Crime control in a capitalist society*. Boston, MA: Little, Brown.

Raine, A. (2013). *The anatomy of violence: The biological roots of crime*. New York NY: Random House.

Reckless, W. C. (1955). *The crime problem*. New York, NY: Appleton-Century-Crofts.

Reckless, W. C., Dinitz, S., & Murray, E. (1956). Self-concept as an insulator against delinquency. *American Sociological Review, 21*(5), 744–756.

Reiss, A. J. (1951). Delinquency as the failure of personal and social controls. *American Sociological Review, 16*(2), 196–207.

Sampson, R. J., Raudenbush, S. W., & Earls, F. (1997). Neighborhoods and violent crime: A multilevel study of collective efficacy. *Science, 277*(5328), 918–924.

Schwendinger, H., & Schwendinger, J. (1970). Defenders of order or guardians of human rights? *Issues in Criminology, 5*(2), 113–146.

Sellin, T. (1937). Letters to the editor: The Lombrosian myth in criminology. *American Journal of Sociology, 42*(6), 895–901.

Sellin, T. (1938). *Culture conflict and crime*. New York, NY: Social Science Research Council.

Shaw, C. R., & McKay, H. D. (1942). *Juvenile delinquency in urban areas*. Chicago, IL: University of Chicago Press.

Short, J. (1975). The natural history of an applied theory: Differential opportunity and "Mobilization for youth." In N. Dermerath, O. Larsen, & K. Schuessler (Eds.), *Social policy and sociology* (pp. 193–210). New York, NY: Academic Press.

Skinner, W. F., & Fream, A. M. (1997). A social learning theory analysis of computer crime among college students. *Journal of Research in Crime and Delinquency, 34*(4), 495–518.

Smith, D. A., & Brame, R. (1994). On the initiation and continuation of delinquency. *Criminology, 32*(4), 607–629.

Sutherland, E. H. (1937). *The professional thief: By a professional thief*. Chicago, IL: The University of Chicago Press.

Sutherland, E. H. (1939). *Principles of criminology* (3rd ed.). Philadelphia, PA: J. B. Lippincott.

Sutherland, E. H. (1983). *White collar crime: The uncut version*. New Haven, CT: Yale University Press.

Sutherland, E. H., & Cressey, D. R. (1947). *Principles of criminology* (4th ed.). Philadelphia, PA: J. B. Lippincott.

Sykes, G. M., & Matza, D. (1957). Techniques of neutralization: A theory of delinquency. *American Sociological Review, 22*(6), 664–670.

Szasz, T. S. (1974). *The myth of mental illness: Foundations of a theory of personal conduct* (Rev. ed.). New York, NY: Harper & Row.

Tannenbaum, F. (1938). *Crime and the community*. Boston, MA: Ginn.

Taylor, I., Walton, P., & Young, J. (1973). *The new criminology: For a social theory of deviance*. London, United Kingdom: Routledge and Kegan Paul.

Tifft, L. L. (1979). The coming redefinitions of crime: An anarchist perspective. *Social Problems, 26*(4), 392–402.

Vold, G. B., & Bernard, T. J. (1979). *Theoretical criminology* (2nd ed.). New York, NY: Oxford University Press.

Walters, G. D. (1989). Putting more thought into criminology. *International Journal of Offender Therapy and Comparative Criminology, 33*(3), v–vii.

Yochelson, S., & Samenow, S. (1976). *The criminal personality: Vol. 1. A profile for change*. New York, NY: Jason Aronson.

CHAPTER 4

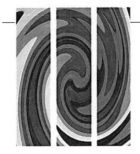

Unleashing the Power of Criminal Justice Theory

Peter B. Kraska

Three serious concerns about how our field of study, criminology and criminal justice, approaches theory are addressed. First, although theorizing about the why of crime is a recognized and institutionalized endeavor, theorizing about criminal justice is unrecognized, underdeveloped, and in need of an infrastructure and legitimation. Second, due to the dominance of the positivist social science model, the power of theory has been severely diminished as an educational tool. Criminal justice theory harbors tremendous transformative powers when used to cultivate critical thinking skills and as a means to raise consciousness. This classic role of academic theorizing, however, has been displaced more often than not by the assumption that the single, ultimate goal of theory is to develop universal causal laws. Third, the academy has taken exclusive ownership of theory and, in doing so, has inappropriately tended to define any theorizing that occurs in the public sphere as mere ideology or pointless rhetoric. The assumption that theorizing is an activity conducted by academics for other academics seriously diminishes its educative power in public discourse and hence its ability to affect how we collectively make theoretical sense of crime and justice issues.

THE POWER OF CRIMINAL JUSTICE THEORY FOR OUR DISCIPLINE

As a graduate student, I was required to take numerous theory courses. At the same time, I became keenly interested in the intensely punitive turn taken by the American criminal justice system (i.e., the war on crime and the war on drugs). What I noticed was that all of the *theory* instruction I was receiving focused on the why of *crime*—and paid very little explanatory attention to the why of *criminal justice*. My experiences were typical of our field, and I made an early and unsettling observation: The only recognized theoretical infrastructure and theoretical project we acknowledge in crime and justice studies is crime theory.

Over the years, I have come to recognize this as a serious disciplinary defi-ciency—one that some of us are attempting to remedy (Bernard & Engel, 2001; Duffee & Maguire, 2007; Kraska, 2006, 2004; Kraska & Brent, 2011). Our disci-pline assumes that theory work is reserved for the why of crime and crime rates. Within our leading scholarly journals, theory development and testing is targeted primarily at explaining crime. Our theory textbooks focus almost exclusively on the why of deviance, crime, and delinquency. Even the majority of our introductory criminal justice textbooks, which have the criminal justice system as their explicit object of study, dedicate nearly all their discussion of theory to theories of criminal behavior. Our undergraduate and graduate degree programs assume that the theory component of their curriculum should concentrate almost exclusively on the why of crime. And teaching theory, as part of these curricula, refers universally to teaching crime theory.

Overall, then, it is taken for granted that the central object of our theorizing in crime and justice studies is crime. Pursuing a recognized and usable theoretical infra-structure about criminal justice—despite the frustration with this state of affairs voiced by some leading scholars in the field over the last three decades—has not been an acknowledged priority and certainly does not constitute a recognized theo-retical project (Bernard & Engel, 2001; Duffee & Maguire, 2007; Hagan, 1989; Kraska, 2006; Kraska & Brent, 2004; Marenin & Worrall, 1998).

In fact, to make matters worse, studying criminal justice is usually framed as merely a practical endeavor, with little concern for theory development or high-level intellectualism. Theory work is relevant to criminal justice only insofar as theories of crime causation lead to more effective crime control policies and tactics (again, criminal justice behavior is treated as simply the independent variable that affects crime). Embedded in this thinking is the presumption that studying crime control and criminal justice is strictly a "practical," as opposed to a theoretical, endeavor concerned only with what works and the how-to of crime control.

Many criminologists, therefore, see no need for criminal justice theory, since for them, crime theory already provides the theoretical foundation for what the crimi-nal justice system should and should not do about crime. Of course, distinguishing between theorizing crime and theorizing criminal justice is not difficult; most crime and justice scholars can appreciate the qualitative difference between explaining crime and explaining crime control. The latter concentrates on making theoretical sense of criminal justice and crime-control phenomena, such as the behavior of the state, the behavior of criminal justice organizations (police, courts, corrections, and juvenile justice organizations), overall trends in the entire criminal justice apparatus, and the private sector's crime-control activities.

Clearly, then, we need different theoretical infrastructures for understanding the nature of crime behavior versus the nature of crime-*control* behavior. And although the two no doubt intersect (see Figure 4.1) in the realm of law creation, the study of criminal justice behavior and crime behavior will require quite different theoretical tools.

The thinking that crime theory constitutes our intellectual core is so reified that many bright and capable academics have difficulty understanding that there is even

| Figure 4.1 | Venn Diagram of Criminal Justice Theory and Crime Theory |

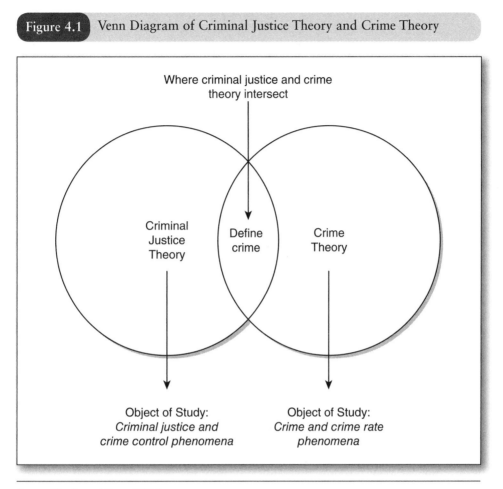

Where criminal justice and crime
theory intersect

Criminal
Justice
Theory

Define
crime

Crime
Theory

Object of Study:
*Criminal justice and
crime control phenomena*

Object of Study:
*Crime and crime rate
phenomena*

Source: Kraska and Brent (2004).

a need for criminal justice theory. One reason is that theorizing criminal justice is inherently a more critical endeavor than theorizing crime. When our object of study shifts from crime to criminal justice and we are forced to examine, for example, the why of the drug war as opposed to drug use, or the why of the war on terrorism as opposed to terrorism itself, or the why of police behavior as opposed to the commission of crime—we are essentially problematizing crime-control activities and the criminal justice institution as opposed to crime itself. Doing so necessitates the scrutiny of state behavior, of private-sector crime-control activities, and of societal shifts in criminal justice punitiveness.

This is precisely why the "critical" theories found in traditional crime theory textbooks are an odd fit, if not conspicuously misplaced. In examining the state's oppression of marginalized groups (women, the poor, racial minorities, homosexuals) via the criminal justice system, the truth is that the theories do not belong—because their explanatory gaze is directed less at crime than at the state's creation of and reaction to crime.

CRIMINAL JUSTICE: A WORTHY OBJECT OF THEORIZING

Another difficulty is, when we theorize criminal justice, our central object of study is even more complex than it is for crime. The terrain of possible foci is vast, ranging from explaining individual practitioner behavior to explaining the growth of the criminal justice system over the last 100 years. Such foci might include theorizing criminal justice practitioner behavior, the system's subcomponents or its historical development, or perhaps explaining the system's steep growth in power and size over the last 30 years, a central objective of Garland's (2001) well-regarded book, *The Culture of Control*. Theorizing could also focus on contemporary trends and issues in crime-control practices, such as privatization, militarization, federalization, the expansion of surveillance, racial profiling, erosion of constitutional safeguards, or trends and issues related to the "wars" on terrorism and drugs. More conventionally, criminal justice theory could seek to explain the behavior of criminal justice policy, agency behavior, and the why of practitioner and organizational decision making.

These varied and important objects of explanation should demonstrate that explanatory frameworks, other than those provided by crime theories, are not only possible but needed. Traditional criminological theories, despite their obvious interconnection with criminal justice practice, are not designed to function as explanations for criminal justice system or crime-control behavior.

Please note that the claim here is not necessarily a lack of theorizing about the criminal justice system and crime-control activities but rather the lack of a recognized infrastructure, the lack of recognition that a body of theory separate from crime theory even exists, the lack of desire to articulate, let alone teach, criminal justice theory, and due to all of these, lack of access to these theories for students and academics alike.

DEVELOPING A USEFUL THEORETICAL INFRASTRUCTURE

To begin the large task of remedying this situation, an avenue is presented for developing an infrastructure (Kraska, 2004; Kraska & Brent, 2011). The approach is fairly straightforward: A large volume of existing theoretical scholarship about our reaction to crime is organized around eight explanatory constructs called *theoretical orientations*. These orientations are a type of theoretical lens, framed as metaphors, through which criminologists view and make sense of criminal justice and crime-control phenomena. Formally defined, a theoretical orientation is an interpretive construct that includes a logically coherent set of organizing concepts, causal preferences, value clusters, and assumptions that work to orient our interpretations and understanding of criminal justice phenomena (similar to a paradigm).

The goal is not to develop a single, testable criminal justice theory; on the contrary, the objective is to illuminate the multiple theoretical lenses crime and justice scholars can employ to help us understand the behavior of the criminal justice system and trends in crime control. Figure 4.2 provides a schematic of the eight theoretical orientations.

These metaphors are routinely employed in our field of study. They include criminal justice as (a) rational legalism, (b) system, (c) crime control versus due process, (d) politics, (e) the social construction of reality, (f) growth complex, (g) oppression, and (h) late modernity. The features of each theoretical orientation are noted beneath it.

Several theoretical orientations in our field are easily identified; the systems are the most obvious. Most academics would agree that the system's framework has dominated our field's thinking and research about criminal justice. The network of governmental agencies responding to our crime problem is universally known as the criminal justice *system*. The system's framework is derived from the biological sciences, Parson's structural functionalism, and organizational studies. It has a strong reformist element, emphasizing the importance of enhancing criminal justice coordination, efficiency, rational decision making, and technology.

Another not-so-common explanatory framework is termed here the *late-modern* theoretical orientation. This theoretical lens situates the criminal justice apparatus (broadly defined) within macroshifts associated with the current era of social history labeled *late modernity*. Criminal justice and crime-control phenomena are best explained as adaptations to late-modern social conditions. An impressive body of scholarship has emerged in this area (a few examples include Garland, 2001; O'Malley, 1999; Simon, 2007; and Young, 1999). Five late-modern conditions frame this orientation:

- The rise of actuarial justice and the influence of the risk society
- The neoliberal shift in macropolitics
- Increasing contradictions and incoherence in crime-control policy
- The decline of the sovereign state's legitimacy
- The ascendance of an exclusion paradigm for managing those perceived to pose a safety threat in an increasingly security-conscious society

The late-modern orientation is probably the most theoretically vigorous pursuit of criminal justice and crime-control phenomena in the literature today. As shown in Figure 4.2, there are many other possible theoretical lenses through which to view criminal justice behavior. Space limitations inhibit a more detailed examination; further elaboration can be found in Kraska and Brent (2011).

THE POWER OF THEORY TO TRANSFORM CONSCIOUSNESS

As a result of constructing this infrastructure, I have been teaching criminal justice theory, instead of crime theory proper, to students for the last 10 years. And I have come to realize the very real power of theory, and particularly criminal justice theory, to affect students' thinking. Theory work, if approached in the right spirit,

Figure 4.2   Criminal Justice Theoretical Orientations

Major Features	Rational/ Legal	System	Packer's Crime Control vs. Due Process	Politics	Social Construction	Growth Complex	Oppression	Late Modernity
Intellectual Tradition	neoclassical; legal formalism	structural–functionalism; biological sciences; organizational studies	liberal legal jurisprudence; legal realism; sociolegal studies	political science; public administration	interpretive school; symbolic interaction; social construction	Weber; Frankfurt School; critical public administration	Marx; feminism; critical sociology; race studies	Foucault; governmentality literature; postmodernism
Approaches to Knowledge Production	technical legal research; status quo positivism	mainstream positivist social science (critical and status quo focus)	academic legal research; sometime positivist	historical; comparative; positivist social science; theoretical synthesis research	interpretive social science; critical social science; content analysis	critical social science; theoretical synthesis research	critical social science; critical ethnography; feminist approaches	critical social science; theoretical synthesis research; minimal interpretive social science and positive social science
Key Concepts Employed	rational–legalistic; rulebound; taken for granted	functional; equilibrium; efficiency; technology; external forces; open system; closed system	value-cluster; efficiency, crime control values; due process values; needs-based values	ideology; conflict; symbolic politics; policymaking/ implementing; state, community	myth; reality; culture; symbols; legitimacy; moral panic; impression management institutional theory	bureaucracy building; privatization profit; complex; technical rationality; merging complexes	dangerous classes; gender; patriarchy; racism; class bias; conflict model; structural thinking; dialectics; praxis	actuarial justice; neoliberal politics; exclusive society; safety norm; incoherence in criminal justice policy

Major Features	Rational/ Legal	System	Packer's Crime Control vs. Due Process	Politics	Social Construction	Growth Complex	Oppression	Late Modernity
Reasons for Rapid Criminal Justice Expansion in Last 30 Years	legal reaction to increased law-breaking (forced reaction theory)	criminal justice system reacting to increases in crime (forced reaction theory)	pendulum swing toward crime control values; choosing punitiveness	politicians exploiting problem; politicized drug war; shift in ideology	moral panics; media exploitation; runaway cultural process; crime as scapegoat	dynasty building; growth complex; merging private with public, criminal justice with military	control of threatening groups; marginalized used as scapegoats; crisis in state legitimacy	crisis in state sovereignty; risk-aversive society; growth complex; moral indifference; social exclusivity paradigm
Assumptions About Agency and Practitioner Motives	well-intended; protecting; serving; rule following; law abiding; professionalism	rational decision makers; efficient; adapting to external forces	role/goal conflict; mixed messages; mimic the value messages provided from public	responsive to politics; interestbased; ideological pulls; powerplayers	constructing problems for existing solutions; reacting to moral panics; culturally bound; managing appearances	self-serving; power building; quest for immortality; means over ends; bureaucratic survival; technical over moral thinking	institutional racism, sexism, classism; often unaware of oppressive end result of their own activities	navigating through massive transformations, late-modern forces; good intentions, disturbing results
Issues of Concern	deterrence; defending the virtues and honor of the criminal justice system	abuse of discretion; cutting-edge technology; streamline/ centralize operations	erosion of constitutional rights; governmental intrusiveness	federalization; symbolic politics; ideological intensification	media/ bureaucrat/ political exploitation; mythology	exponential growth; private/ public, military/ police blur	violence against women; drug war's impact on marginalized; racial profiling	growth of system; changes in social control; rise of surveillance society

Sources: Kraska (2004); Kraska & Brent (2011).

harbors tremendous transformative powers through cultivation of critical thinking skills and as a means to raise consciousness.

To fully appreciate its potential, we have to recognize the integral part theory plays, not just in such journals as *Criminology* but in our everyday lives. When my 8-year-old daughter Cora was only 3, she asked me, completely out of the blue, "How does a butterfly get the dust on its wings?" After I recovered, and made a feeble attempt to cultivate her theoretical skills, I asked her what she thought. She responded first by positing that "the butterflies are just born that way" (i.e., an inherent part of their biological makeup). I told her that was correct—but then she demonstrated the early signs of a keen theoretical and creative mind. She said, "Daddy, I knew that was the right answer, but I was hoping it was because they pick up different colors of dust from the flowers."

This anecdote demonstrates that the activity of theorizing is essential to everything we think and do, beginning in our earliest years. We craft theory throughout our lives as a way to make sense of our surroundings. The way in which we make theoretical sense of things guides the decisions we make, so that we can navigate those surroundings competently and decently—to solve problems, to think through complex phenomena, to make accurate predictions, to understand others and feel compassion or anger, and to make sense of our workplaces and organizational environments. Thousands of times a day, we either assume or assess the why of things, and these assumptions and assessments frame our thinking and actions. Theory is integral not only in everyday life but also to all those who work in organizations that deal with criminal or social justice.

Our field's traditional approach to teaching theory diminishes its pedagogical power and practical strength. Overall, the accepted approach involves (a) empirically testing existing crime theories, making minor modifications along the way; and (b) teaching students about these crime theories and examining the evidence that supports and/or refutes them.

Theory is something therefore owned by academics for academics, for the exclusive purpose of developing universal causal laws for the explanation of crime through testing relationships between clearly operationalized independent and dependent variables. Of course, this critique is not meant to diminish the importance of this activity; those of us who do this kind of work are a great asset to our field. What I question is whether this approach *alone* is the most efficacious for teaching and educating our students.

I have learned a lot about teaching theory in the last 12 years that I did not really recognize for the 12 years before. I now concentrate on teaching criminal justice theory in a way that enhances student's theoretical skills, sensitivities, and lenses and that cultivates their critical thinking abilities. My views about theory have matured while teaching graduate students in an in-service leadership program to police administrators and in another, similar in-service program teaching air force officers who work as military police.

I have taught these nontraditional students theory by exposing them to some of the major theoretical orientations in our field that help make sense of criminal justice phenomena. I present each of these theoretical orientations as lenses, or theoretical filters, which provide ideas and organizing concepts that allow students to view their objects of theorizing in a different theoretical light. We talk about how they each harbor a personal theoretical framework that has developed over their lifetime based on what they have learned through direct experience, entertainment, news media, significant others, and the educational system.

They come to realize that their personal theoretical frameworks are always under construction and that the process of learning to interpret their surroundings through differing theoretical filters is a vital part of their educational experience. I concentrate on the eight theoretical lenses noted earlier. The idea is for students to read, think deeply about, and apply, through numerous engagement-oriented exercises, these varying theoretical lenses. The objective is to develop critical theoreticians who can

- raise vital questions and problems, formulating them clearly and precisely;
- gather and assess relevant information;
- use abstract ideas to make theoretical sense of things effectively;
- come to well-reasoned, explanatory-based conclusions and solutions, and test them against relevant criteria and standards;
- think open-mindedly, reflectively, and creatively, with an ability to view their objects of theorizing with multiple theoretical lenses;
- communicate effectively with others in figuring out explanations and solutions to complex problems; and
- more competently navigate their way through an increasingly complex social and criminal justice environment.

I have found that these in-service police and military students have a tremendous capacity for developing their own personal theoretical frameworks. One explanatory framework I have found particularly enlightening for these students is the metaphor of a *growth complex*. The growth complex theoretical orientation illuminates the possibility that organizations (or entire institutional systems) can devolve into entities more motivated by their own bureaucratic interests than by the public good. The underlying assumption is that *any bureaucracy's most basic instinct is to survive and grow*, to survive. Growth complex thinking, therefore, casts the criminal justice apparatus in an intensely critical light.

The criminal justice growth complex is an entity comprising numerous interrelated and interdependent parts—an intricate structural matrix of criminal justice and non-criminal justice governmental bureaucracies, politicians, private companies, media agencies, academic institutions, and myriad interests. Although not operating in harmony necessarily by design or even by intent, the net effect is nonetheless a complex of loosely and tightly connected organizations and interests that generate a synergy ideal for expansion.

In the quest for survival, growth, and influence building, the overall goal of pursuing the public interest through democratic processes and values (participation, accountability, fairness, and a concern for human dignity) is relegated to the back burner. The growth complex orientation views the criminal justice apparatus as an entity that seeks out and constructs new problems for its solution, that actively pursues its own self-serving agenda as opposed to working toward the public good, and that is increasingly influenced by the private-sector objectives of profit and growth. In its simplest terms, garnering power and size becomes not a means to a laudable end but an end in itself. (Please recall that this is only one lens and therefore only illuminates one potential dimension of criminal justice functioning.)

I have found that the reason this theoretical orientation resonates with military and police practitioners is that its theoretical premises coincide with their real-world experiences (data and theory are consistent). The growth complex lens influenced one police administrator in dramatic fashion. He was in charge of securing grants for his department and apparently good at his job. He wrote an excellent paper during the semester, applying growth complex thinking to his job. A year or so after the class was over, he e-mailed me, wanting me to know that he was under a lot of pressure in his department from other administrators to renew a federal grant that the department had secured based on false premises (I'm being purposely vague). He argued against renewal, won the battle, and attributed his action to the new theoretical lenses he had recently adopted. Modifying his personal theoretical framework, of course, affected his values and his value choices. He acted against what he called "mindless bureaucracy building."

This example demonstrates that it is vital to value the everyday and real-world relevance of theory and not approach it merely as a body of scientific work found in books and articles. It is indeed an activity, something we do. Theorizing is part of what ought to be happening in a theory class: the application and even crafting of theory—approaching it as an activity, as opposed to simply learning a body of work (Frauley, 2005). Remember, we have been crafting theory since the day we were born. We have tested our theories in the real world. Some of us have done a good job, others not as good. The key is to not just have students learn about theory and famous theorists but to apply what they have learned to differing objects of study—like the way many of us conduct a research methods class—we ask them to conduct research.

The overall point here is that we should not limit the power of theory. It has the potential to foster creativity, empathy, the expansion of our cognitive gaze, a rethinking or at least a clarification of value preferences, and a serious questioning of and introspection about our taken-for-granted reality. Learning theory should be replete with aha! experiences. The purposes of learning theory should include enabling individuals to know themselves and their situation through retrospection and a raising of their consciousness about our complex social world.

THE POWER OF THEORY TO AFFECT PUBLIC EXPLANATIONS

My third and final concern is directly related to the second: Academe has taken complete ownership of theory and, as a result, has diminished its significant potential to shape public discourse. I fully realized the gravity of this concern while watching the Hurricane Katrina disaster unfold.

Catastrophic natural disasters, despite all the suffering and pain they inflict, often play out ultimately as stories of human triumph, heroism, and community solidarity. We construct them as testaments to the true decency of humankind. The urgent task at hand, to take care of each other's most basic needs, trumps at least temporarily some of our uglier societal faults, such as class, race, and gender divisions and prejudices, self-centeredness, entrenched political conflict, and a lack of social caring.

Hurricane Katrina, which hit the coasts of Alabama, Louisiana, and Mississippi on August 29, 2005, was different. While human triumph and decency were evident, the lasting legacy of Katrina will be that it washed away the veil of denial and neglect and laid bare the ugly societal faults that are usually pushed to the periphery. It seemed to stir up and inflame some of our deepest contemporary fears: poor racial minorities free to loot and victimize others, a sign of things to come as the result of global warming, and a government so inept in homeland security matters that it failed on almost all accounts.

Just as with the terrorist attack of September 11, 2001, we have a strong collective desire to make sense of these types of catastrophic events, both for therapeutic reasons and to prevent or minimize the harm they cause. What exactly does *making sense* mean, though? Making sense, for some people, means resorting to religious explanations (e.g., "It must be God's will"); for others, it means filtering the event through a rigid ideology in order to reaffirm the truth of that ideology (e.g., "It's the fault of our welfare system; only those dependent on welfare would be unable to get out of New Orleans"). For the social scientist, it means using theory and research to examine rigorously the many unanswered questions.

Each of these endeavors seeks explanation, or a theoretically based narrative—an attempt to construct and find meaning in a highly complex and unsettling event. Traumatic events such as 9/11 and Katrina bring about a state of collective cognitive dissonance in which reality as previously constructed and perceived comes into serious question. Comfortable ideas, expectations, and assumptions are shattered, creating what Garfinkel called a temporary state of "meaninglessness." Theory helps us to put the pieces back together (Kraska & Neuman, 2008, p. 65).

Kishonna Gray and I examined real-world theorizing found in the public sphere after Hurricane Katrina (Gray & Kraska, 2006). Examining this catastrophe provided a valuable opportunity to study how theory operates in the real world. Katrina exposed a host of theoretical questions that are rarely examined, at least outside of academe, and generated an incisive public discourse about power structures, economic inequalities, racial injustice, governmental ineptitude and corruption, and accountability. Contrast this rich, contextualized coverage during Katrina with the public theorizing following 9/11, an insular and uncritical discourse emphasizing themes of xenophobia and evildoers.

Many regarded as unpatriotic any theorizing that fell outside these narrow parameters. The unique example of real-world theorizing found in the post-Katrina public sphere was essential to study, both for theoretical and practical reasons. Unfortunately, the social science community has constructed a disciplinary straitjacket around the notion of theory, limiting theory to testing the relationship between measurable variables by academics and generally for other academics. Academics have unwisely taken exclusive ownership of theory, rendering it an entity separate from everyday thinking. Not only is this an untenable position, for most if not all social science theory emanates from real-world thinking and ideas, but it ignores as well the fact that *public theorizing* is of far greater consequence than what we do in academe. Indeed, the field of crime and justice studies tends to lose sight of what ought to be the premier goal of academic theory: the influencing and shaping of public thinking (i.e., public theory).

One particularly revealing theoretical moment emerged soon after Katrina hit. Kanye West, a music industry star, was standing next to comedian Mike Myers and said the following on live national television during a post-Katrina fund-raising event:

> I hate the way they portray us in the media. You see a black family, it says, "They're looting." You see a white family, it says, "They're looking for food." It's been five days waiting for federal help because most of the people are black. . . . So anybody out there that wants to do anything to help . . . please.

After Myers made another comment, West concluded his analysis by saying, "George Bush doesn't care about black people."

West's comments instantly became the cultural flash point for those who agreed and disagreed with his assertion. It is critical to note that West never said (despite the assertions of many reactionaries and some in the mainstream media) that George Bush *hated* Black people. Several news reports even misquoted West by using the word *hate.* This popular culture moment highlighted the prominent role that race-based explanations played in public dialogue about the Katrina disaster. It would be a mistake to discount West's narrative as mere "sounding off" with little theoretical significance.

Of course, had he said *hate,* it would have implied a type of overt prejudice, a type of intentional racism that most would agree has diminished significantly in the last 50 years and is widely condemned as illegitimate in mainstream society. Framing and interpreting West's assertion, therefore, as one of overt bigotry made it easy to delegitimize.

The phrase, *doesn't care about black people,* however, connotes something entirely different. It is the essence of what is called *structural racism*—in which, even though intentional bigotry is not evident, the historical patterns and arrangements of race-based exclusion continue. Long after the bulk of White people have ceased to actively hate and consciously discriminate against racial minorities, there still exists an array of social and economic arrangements, constructed during a time of explicit hatred, that work to the disadvantage of racial minorities.

Where racial prejudice is kept alive by hate, structural racism thrives under conditions of indifference. West emphasized a lack of caring, positing that the abysmal response to the disaster was due to a lack of concern for African Americans. He captured succinctly an important theoretical organizing concept: that the enduring legacy of hate-based racism is a new form of racism, one based in conscious and unconscious indifference, neglect, apathy, and uncaring. It took indifference for our government at many levels to ignore a federally funded task force of scientists who since 2002 have predicted exactly this fate for the population of poor African Americans in New Orleans if a hurricane the magnitude of Katrina were to hit. It took indifference for Chertoff, the director of Homeland Security, to go to a conference the day after the disaster and not attend to a single detail of the relief operation (and for President Bush to remain on vacation). It took indifference to wait 5 days to provide any type of substantive humanitarian relief to those stuck in New Orleans, while in the meantime the area was being "secured" by military and police forces.

The purpose of this example is to illustrate that our field of study needs to broaden our notion of theory and to recognize that we should not divorce our academic theorizing from public theory. The aftermath of Katrina gave a small glimpse of the potential of theoretical discourse within the public sphere to make a difference—a difference brought about by cracking the veneer of taken-for-granted ideology to reveal other possible explanations and richer theoretical narratives.

CONCLUSION: EMBRACING CRIMINAL JUSTICE THEORY

The transformative powers of theory, both in our private lives and in the public sphere, should be acknowledged and cultivated. We should find ways to encourage our theoretical curiosity and the creation of multiple theoretical lenses. This can assist us in seeing through reified and counterproductive dominant explanations, not just about terrorism but the war on terrorism, not just about drugs but the war on drugs—explanations that will help us discuss the undiscussable, confront the uncomfortable, and reveal the taken for granted. Competent, meaningful, accurate, and deep theorizing is an essential precursor for thoughtful, substantive, humane solutions.

Marenin & Worrall (1998, p. 465) asserted that "criminal justice is an academic discipline in practice but not yet in theory." Our field has not placed high value on this endeavor for two primary reasons. The first has already been discussed: Crime theory suffices. The second is more difficult to overcome: While exploring the why of crime has prima facie importance, our field has neither articulated nor acknowledged the value provided us by theorizing criminal justice. Some assume, in fact, that studying criminal justice is inherently and necessarily atheoretical because it concentrates on practice. The notion that practice can somehow be severed from theory has been thoroughly debunked in most other major fields of study. Theory and practice are implied in one another; no policy analysis, implementation, strategic plan, or practitioner action is devoid of theory. To deny the integral role theory plays in all these instances is to remain ignorant of its influence.

As noted, theorizing criminal justice is an inherently critical endeavor providing important insights into the system's irrationalities, missteps, and disconcerting implications. Theoretically based scrutiny focused on criminal justice and crime control should not be misconstrued as inappropriately critical. It simply approaches criminal justice as a research problem—similar to the way we study crime.

Nor should theorizing criminal justice phenomena be viewed as an endeavor intended exclusively for practical change. Numerous scholars in our field find studying our society's reaction to crime intellectually stimulating in and of itself, much like biologists who study the animal kingdom or astronomers who study the solar system. Studying humans and organizations that attempt to control wrongdoing (and that sometimes engage in wrongdoing in the attempt) yields intriguing insights about the nature of society, our political landscape, and cutting-edge cultural trends. In short, how we react to crime tells us a lot about ourselves and where our society might be headed.

I am certain criminal justice theory will eventually become a normalized presence in our criminal justice and criminology degree programs, our textbooks, and our doctoral training. The realization is growing that nothing less than our disciplinary integrity is at stake. However, as this process unfolds, it is critical to avoid the short-comings evident in the development of crime theory. In order for criminal justice theory to reach its full potential, we must (a) develop its infrastructure in a manner that renders it both intellectually stimulating and accessible, (b) teach it in a way that acknowledges our positivist tradition yet allows space for the classic function of transforming consciousness, and (c) apply it to the real world through policy prescriptions based on research findings, yet attempt as well to actively influence public theories about criminal justice issues. Criminal justice theory holds significant potential power; let us hope it is wielded constructively.

DISCUSSION QUESTIONS

1. Is it really possible for criminal justice students to theorize? Or is it more appropriate that they read and learn about preexisting theories and the research that tests their veracity?

2. Why is it likely that the field of criminal justice will proceed slowly and with many obstacles in developing the idea of criminal justice theory?

3. What types of *public theorizing* typify such major criminal justice efforts as the war on terror or the war on drugs?

4. What is structural racism, and how is it still relevant to the operations of the criminal justice system today?

REFERENCES

Bernard, T., & Engel, R. (2001). Conceptualizing criminal justice theory. *Justice Quarterly, 18*(1), 1–30.

Duffee, D. E., & Maguire, E. R. (2007). *Criminal justice theory: Explaining the nature and behavior of criminal justice*. New York, NY: Routledge.

Frauley, J. (2005). Representing theory and theorising in criminal justice studies: Practising theory considered. *Critical Criminology, 13*(3), 245–265.

Garland, D. (2001). *The culture of control: Crime and social order in contemporary society.* Chicago, IL: University of Chicago Press.

Gray, K., & Kraska, P. B. (2006, February). *Hurricane Katrina meltdown: Examining the relevance of everyday theory.* Paper presented at the meeting of the Academy of Criminal Justice Sciences, Baltimore, MD.

Hagan, J. (1989). Why is there so little criminal justice theory? Neglected macro- and micro-level links between organizations and power. *Journal of Research in Crime and Delinquency, 26*(2), 116–135.

Kraska, P. B. (2006). Criminal justice theory: Toward legitimacy and an infrastructure. *Justice Quarterly, 23*(2), 167–185.

Kraska, P. B. (2011). *Theorizing criminal justice: Eight essential orientations* (2nd ed.). Prospect Heights, IL: Waveland Press.

Kraska, P. B., & Brent, J. (2004). *Theorizing criminal justice: Eight essential orientations* (1st ed.). Prospect Heights, IL: Waveland Press.

Kraska, P. B., & Neuman, L. (2008). *Criminal justice and criminology research methods.* Boston, MA: Pearson.

Marenin, O., & Worrall, J. (1998). Criminal justice: Portrait of a discipline in progress. *Journal of Criminal Justice, 26*(6), 465–480.

O'Malley, P. (1999). Volatile and contradictory punishment. *Theoretical Criminology, 3*(2), 175–196.

Simon, J. (2007). *Governing through crime.* Boston, MA: Oxford University Press.

Young, J. (1999). *The exclusive society: Social exclusion, crime and difference in late modernity.* London, United Kingdom: SAGE.

CHAPTER 5

Victimology

Leah E. Daigle

INTRODUCTION

Victimology includes the *etiology* (or causes) of victimization, the consequences of victimization, how the criminal justice system accommodates and assists victims, and how other elements of society, such as the media, deal with crime victims. Victimology is the study of victims. For example, instead of simply wondering or hypothesizing why younger people are more likely to be victims than older people, victimologists examine why younger people appear to be more vulnerable than the elderly.

Each year, the Bureau of Justice Statistics publishes *Criminal Victimization in the United States* (Bureau of Justice Statistics [BJS], 2006a). In 2012, 26.5 million victimizations were experienced (Truman, Langton, & Planty, 2013). Of these, 6.8 million violent crime victimizations were experienced; however, 19.6 million property crime victimizations were reported. The most common type of property crime experienced was theft, while simple assault was the most common violent crime.

THE TYPICAL VICTIMIZATION AND VICTIM

Of some concern was the realization that most often victims identified their attacker as a friend or acquaintance. Strangers accounted for only about one third of all violent victimizations in the National Crime Victimization Survey (NCVS; BJS, 2006b). In only 1 in 5 incidents did the offender have a weapon (BJS, 2006b), and in fewer than 7% of all incidents was a firearm involved (Truman et al., 2013). This may be one of the reasons why most victimizations do not result in physical harm—about one fourth of assaults result in physical injury, while 35% of robbery victims suffer a physical injury (BJS, 2006b).

Gender. The NCVS has shown that for all violent victimizations, except for rape and sexual assaults, males are more likely to be victimized than females. On the other hand, females are more likely than males to be victimized by an intimate partner. In 2010, 22% of all violent victimizations against females were perpetrated by an intimate partner compared to only 5% of incidents involving male victims (Truman, 2010).

Race and ethnicity. Respondents who are non-Hispanic Blacks have higher victimization rates than persons who are White or Hispanic (34.8 per 1,000 persons compared to 25.2 per 1,000 and 24.5 per 1,000 respectively; Truman et al., 2013). Persons who reported being of two or more races (42.8 per 1,000) or who are American Indian or Alaskan Natives (46.9 per 1000), however, had the highest rates of violent victimization in 2010 (Truman, 2010).

Age. Respondents who are young face the greatest risk of becoming a victim of violent crime. Those between the ages of 12 to 17 years of age have the highest violent victimization rate, followed by 18 to 24 year olds and 25 to 34 year olds. Those 65 and older have the lowest rate of victimization (Truman et al., 2013).

Household characteristics. Households having low income are more likely to experience a property victimization. Households in the lowest income categories—those earning less than $7,500 or between $7,500 and $14,999 annually—faced the greatest risk of burglary and theft. Households earning less than $7,500 had a burglary victimization rate that was twice the rate of households with incomes $75,000 per year or higher (Truman, 2010). It was also reported that the greater the number of occupants per household, the greater the property crime victimization rate. In fact, households with six or more occupants had a property crime victimization rate that was almost 2.5 times higher than single-headed households (Truman, 2010).

THE COSTS OF VICTIMIZATION

Victimization is a public health issue. Economic costs can result from property losses; costs associated with medical care; time lost from work, school, and housework; physical and emotional pain, suffering, and reduced quality of life; and legal costs. In 2008, the total economic loss from crimes was estimated to be $17,397 billion as reported by the NCVS (BJS, 2008).

Direct property losses. Generally when determining property losses, the value of property that is damaged or taken and not recovered, as well as insurance claims administration costs, are taken into consideration. According to the 2008 NCVS, 94% of all property crimes resulted in economic losses (BJS, 2008). Miller, Cohen, and Wiersema (1996) estimated the property loss or damage experienced per crime victimization event and concluded that arson victimizations resulted in an estimated $15,500 per event. Motor vehicle thefts cost approximately $3,300 for each incident. It is rare for a victim of a violent or property offense to recover even some of his/her losses. In only about 1 in 10 instances do victims recover all or some property (BJS, 2008).

Medical care. Results from the 2008 NCVS indicate that 542,280 violent crime victims received some type of medical care (BJS, 2008). Of those victims, slightly over one third received care at a hospital emergency room or an emergency clinic, while 9% were hospitalized. Receiving medical care oftentimes results in victims incurring additional medical expenses. Almost 6% of victims of violent crimes reported having medical expenses as a result of their victimization. About 63% of injured victims report having health insurance or eligibility for public medical services.

Although crime victims often do not require hospitalization, even if they are treated in the emergency room, the Office for Victims of Crime (Bonderman, 2001), showed that gunshot victims make up one third of those requiring hospitalization. Victims who are shot and admitted to a hospital, are likely to face numerous rehospitalizations and incur medical costs across their lifetime. In 1994, for all victims of firearm injuries, the lifetime medical costs totaled $1.7 billion.

Mental health care costs. It is estimated that between 10% and 20% of all total mental health care costs in the United States are related to crime (Miller et al., 1996). Most of this cost is a result of crime victims seeking treatment to deal with the effects of their victimization. Between one quarter and one half of all rape and child sexual-abuse victims receive mental health care (Miller et al., 1996). Sexual victimizations, of both adults and children, result in some of the largest mental health care costs for victims.

Pain, suffering, and lost quality of life. The most difficult cost to quantify is the pain, suffering, and loss of quality of life that crime victims experience. This cost is the largest that crime victims sustain. For example, Miller et al. (1996) estimated the cost of rape to victims in out-of-pocket expenses to be slightly less than $5,100 per incident.

Another cost that crime victims may experience is a change in their daily routine and lifestyle. To illustrate, victims of stalking may change their phone number, move, or change their normal routine. Some may stop going out alone or start carrying a weapon when they do so. Although these changes may reduce risk of being victimized again, for victims to bear the cost of crime is unjust.

SYSTEM COSTS

When including costs for law enforcement, juridical processing, and corrections, the direct expenditures of the criminal justice system are over $214 billion annually (BJS, 2006). The criminal justice system employs over 2.4 million, with a payroll over $9 billion a year.

Insurance companies pay approximately $45 billion annually due to crime ("Guns, Money, & Medicine," 1996). Additionally, the federal government pays $8 billion annually for restorative and emergency services to crime victims ("Guns, Money, & Medicine," 1996). Gunshot victims alone cost taxpayers over $4.5 billion dollars annually ("Guns, Money, & Medicine," 1996). These costs are not distributed equally across society. Some communities have been hit particularly hard by violence and gun violence in particular. Some 96% of all hospital expenses associated with gun violence at King Drew Medical Center in Los Angeles, California (the city emergency care facility located in what the media calls "South Central"), are paid with by public funds (Bonderman, 2001).

MENTAL HEALTH CONSEQUENCES AND COSTS

It is likely that the way people deal with victimization is tied to their biological makeup, their interactional style, their personal coping style and resources, and the context in which the incident occurs. Some of responses can be quite serious and long term while others are more transitory.

Three affective responses that are common among crime victims are depression, reduction in self-esteem, and anxiety. The way in which depression manifests itself can include sleep disturbances, changes in eating habits, feelings of guilt and worthlessness, and irritability. Generally, those who are depressed will have a general decline in interest in activities they once enjoyed, feelings of distress, or both. Victimization may be powerful enough to alter the way in which a crime victim views him/herself. Self-esteem and self-worth are reduced in some crime victims, particularly females. There may also be a difference in crime's impact on self-appraisal based on the type of victimization experienced. For example, victims of both child and adult sexual abuse are likely to suffer long-term negative impacts to their self-esteem (Cutler & Nolen-Hoeksema, 1991, Turner, Finkelhor, & Ormrod, 2006).

Post-Traumatic Stress Disorder. One of the recognized disorders associated with a patterned response to victimization is post-traumatic stress disorder (PTSD). Commonly associated with returning war and combat veterans, PTSD is a psychiatric condition that has been recognized as a possible consequence of other traumatic events, such as criminal victimization. To be diagnosed with PTSD, a victim must have experienced or witnessed a traumatic event involving actual or threatened death or serious injury, or threat to the physical integrity. The victim must have experienced fear, helplessness, or horror in response to the event then reexperienced the trauma over time via flashbacks, nightmares, images, and/or reliving the event. Finally, PTSD is characterized by hyperarousal (American Psychiatric Association [APA], 2000). PTSD can be debilitating and can impact a victim's ability to heal, move on, or thrive after being victimized. Depression also commonly co-occurs in victims who suffer PTSD (Kilpatrick & Acierno, 2003). The occurrence of PTSD in rape victims has been estimated to be almost 1 in 3 (Kilpatrick, Edmunds, & Seymour, 1992).

Self-blame and learned helplessness. After victimization, the victim may blame him/herself for his/her victimization. One type of self-blame, *characterological self-blame,* occurs when the victim ascribes blame to a nonmodifiable source such as his/her own character (Janoff-Bulman, 1979). Characterological self-blame involves believing that the victimization was deserved. *Behavioral self-blame* occurs when a modifiable source—behavior—is ascribed (Janoff-Bulman, 1979). When a person turns to behavioral self-blame, future victimization can be avoided, so long as his/her behavior changes. Victims can learn that responding is futile and become passive and numb (Seligman, 1975). Thus, victims may not take appropriate defensive action in the face of danger and, instead, risk subsequent victimization.

FEAR OF CRIME

Fear is an emotional response to a perceived threat (Ferraro & LaGrange, 1987). Victimization is not a requirement for being fearful. For example, females (Ferraro, 1995, 1996; Haynie, 1998; May, Rader, & Goodrum, 2010; Rountree, 1998) and the elderly (Ferraro, 1995) have higher levels of fear of crime than do males and those who are younger. For females, this elevated fear of crime has been attributed to their overarching fear of sexual assault. In what is known as the *shadow hypothesis*, the fear of sexual assault actually serves to increase females' fears of other types of crimes (Warr, 1984, 1985; Ferraro, 1995, 1996).

In response to fear of crime, some may engage in proactive behavior modification to prevent harm. *Avoidance behaviors* are restrictions that are placed on behavior as protection from harm, for example, staying home at night. Others may engage in *defensive or protective behaviors* to guard themselves from victimization, such as purchasing a gun or installing security lights (Ferraro & LaGrange, 1987).

RECURRING VICTIMIZATION

Unfortunately, those who are victimized once are at greater risk of being victimized again. In fact, any victim is *more* likely than nonvictims to be victimized again.

Extent of recurring victimization. *Recurring victimization* occurs when a person or place is victimized with any type of victimization more than once. *Repeat victimization* occurs when a person or place is victimized more than once by the same type of offense. *Revictimization* refers to a recurring victim across a relatively wide span of time—like from childhood to adulthood.

The British Crime Survey, a victimization survey similar to the NCVS, revealed that of those who were victimized, 28% experienced two or more incidents during the same year (Crime in England and Wales, 2004/05; see Nicholas, Povey, Walker, & Kershaw, 2005). Victims of intimate partner violence, rape, and assault are all at risk of experiencing a subsequent incident following their initial victimization.

These recurring victims experience a disproportionate share of all victimization events. Daigle, Fisher, and Cullen (2008) found that 7% of college women they surveyed had experienced more than one different sexual victimization incident during the previous academic year, and these women experienced almost three fourths of all sexual victimizations reported.

Characteristics of recurring victimization. For recurring victims, it is likely that their next incident will happen quickly. For college sexual victims, Daigle et al. (2008) found that most subsequent incidents happen within the same month or one month after the initial incident. Fortunately, over time, the risk of experiencing another victimization wanes. Reiss (1980) found that when a person is victimized a subsequent time, s/he is likely to experience the exact same type of victimization. For example, a theft victim is likely to revisit that theft experience a second time.

Theoretical explanations of recurring victimization. While painting a picture of what recurring victimization "looks" like, the literature does not address why some people are victimized a single time and others find themselves victimized again.

There are two theoretical explanations that have been proffered to explain recurring victimization. The first is *risk heterogeneity*. This explanation focuses on the qualities or characteristics of the victim. Those qualities or characteristics that place a victim at risk of being a victim, initially, will keep him/her at risk of experiencing a subsequent victimization if s/he does not change.

The second theoretical explanation of recurring victimization is known as *state dependence*. This suggests that it is not the qualities or characteristics of a victim that are important for recurring victimization so much as what happens during and after the victimization. How the victim acts and reacts during and after the incident and the information gleaned during and after the incident will influence the likelihood of revictimization. For example, a burglar who successfully enters a home and steals a television has learned that the home does not have a security system, how to enter and leave the home, and that the home has a nice television. This information may lead to an increased likelihood of the burglar returning to the home in hopes of stealing a replacement television. To be clear, neither of these explanations should be used to blame or hold responsible the victim or place for the victimization. The offender is solely responsible for his/her actions. These explanations are, however, tools to help understand why some people are targeted over and over again.

THEORIES OF VICTIMIZATION

The Role of the Victim in Crime: Victim Precipitation, Victim Facilitation, and Victim Provocation

The first studies of crime victims did not perceive victims to be innocents who were wronged at the hands of an offender. Rather, concepts such as *victim precipitation, victim facilitation*, and *victim provocation* were developed from these investigations. Victim precipitation is the extent to which a victim is responsible for his/her own victimization. The concept of victim precipitation is rooted in the notion that although some victims may not be responsible at all for their victimization, others are in fact responsible. In this way, victim precipitation acknowledges that a victimization involves at least two people—an offender and a victim—and that both are acting and oftentimes reacting before, during, and after the incident. Identifying victim precipitation does not necessarily lead to negative outcomes. It is problematic, however, when it blames the victim while ignoring the offender.

Victim facilitation occurs when a victim makes it, unintentionally so, easier for an offender to commit the crime. A victim may, in this way, be a catalyst for victimization. Facilitation helps explain why a one person may be victimized over another, but it does not affix blame or responsibility.

Victim provocation occurs when someone actually does something to incite someone else to commit a crime. Provocation suggests that without the victim, the crime would not have occurred. Provocation, then, most certainly connotes blame. In fact, the offender bares little responsibility.

Hans von Hentig. Von Hentig (1948) looked at the criminal-victim dyad, recognizing the importance of considering the victim and the criminal not in isolation but together. He attempted to identify the characteristics of a victim that might effectively influence victimization risk. He argued that crime victims could be placed into one of 13 categories based on their propensity for victimization: (a) young, (b) female, (c) old, (d) immigrant, (e) depressed, (f) mentally defective or deranged, (g) the acquisitive, (h) dull normal, (i) minority, (j) wanton, (k) the lonesome and heartbroken, (l) tormentor, and (m) the blocked, exempted, and fighting. Each of these types of victims is targeted and contributes to his/her own victimization because of his/her characteristics.

Benjamin Mendelsohn. Known as the father of victimology, Benjamin Mendelsohn (1968) coined the term "victimology" in the 1940s. He created a classification scheme based on culpability or the degree of victim blame. His classification entailed these features:

1. *Completely innocent victim:* a victim who bears no responsibility at all for his/her victimization; becomes a victim simply because of his/her nature such as being a child

2. *Victim with minor guilt:* a victim who is victimized due to ignorance; a victim who inadvertently places him/herself in harm's way

3. *Victim as guilty as offender or a voluntary victim:* a victim who bears as much responsibility as the offender; a person who, for example, enters into a suicide pact

4. *Victim more guilty than offender:* a victim who instigates or provokes his/her own victimization

5. *Most guilty victim:* a victim who is victimized during the perpetration of a crime or as a result of crime

6. *Simulating or imaginary victim:* a victim who actually was not victimized at all but instead fabricates his/her victimization event

Stephen Schafer. One of the earliest victimologists, Schafer, in his (1968) *The Victim and His Criminal: A Study in Functional Responsibility,* located victims in groups based on how responsible they were for their own victimization using social characteristics and behaviors. He argued that victims have a functional responsibility to not provoke others into victimizing or harming them and that they also should actively attempt to prevent victimization from occurring. He based groups on these seven categories and responsibilities:

1. Unrelated victims—no responsibility

2. Provocative victims—share responsibility

3. Precipitative victims—some degree of victim responsibility

4. Biologically weak victims—no responsibility

5. Socially weak victims—no responsibility

6. Self-victimizing—total responsibility

7. Political victims—no responsibility

Menachem Amir. The crime of rape is not immune from victim blaming either today or in its history. Amir (1971) conducted an empirical investigation on rape incidents reported to the police. He examined the extent to which victims precipitated their own rapes and also identified commonalities to that type of rape. He concluded that almost 1 in 5 rapes were victim precipitated. He determined that these rapes likely involved alcohol, the victim likely engaged in seductive behavior, she [in this era, statute mandated that males could not be raped] likely wore revealing clothing, likely used risqué language, and likely had a peccant reputation.

Amir also determined that the offender's interpretation of the victim's actions was important rather than what the victim actually did. The offender may view the victim—her actions, words, and clothing—as immodest, against his perception of appropriate female behavior. In this way, the victim is viewed as salacious, provocative. He may then rape her (or him) because of his misguided view of appropriate feminine behavior; she/he then deserves it, she/he had it coming. Amir's research was quite controversial—and was attacked for blaming victims for their own victimization.

ROUTINE ACTIVITIES AND LIFESTYLES THEORIES

Victimization theory is a set of testable propositions designed to explain why anyone is victimized. Both routine activities and lifestyles theories propose that victimization risk can best be understood by the extent to which the victim's routine activities or lifestyle creates opportunities for a motivated offender to offend.

In developing routine activities theory, Cohen and Felson (1979) argued that a person's daily routines impacted his/her risk of being a crime victim. In so much as anyone's routine activities brings him/her into contact with *motivated offenders,* victimization risk abounds. Cohen and Felson believed that motivated offenders are plentiful and their motivation to offend does not need explaining. Rather, their selection of particular victims is more interesting. Cohen and Felson noted that some factor of an individual or place encourages selection by a motivated offender. In fact, *suitable targets* are based on their attractiveness by the motivated offender. Attractiveness relates to qualities about the target, such as ease of transport, which is why a burglar may break into a home and leave with an iPod or laptop computer rather than a couch. Attractiveness is further evident when the target does not have *capable guardianship*, that is, the means by which a target can be effectively guarded so that a victimization is prevented. Guardianship is considered to be *social,* when the presence of another person makes the potential victim a less attractive target. Guardianship can also be provided through *physical* means, such as a home equipped with a burglar alarm or a person who carries a weapon for self-protection. When these three elements—motivated offenders, suitable targets, and lack of capable guardianship—coalesce in time and space, victimization is likely to occur.

When Cohen and Felson originally developed their theory, they focused on predatory crimes and were originally interested in explaining changes in rates of these types of crimes over time. As people spent more time interacting with others, they were more likely to come into contact with motivated offenders. They also linked the increase in crime to the production of durable goods. Electronics began to be produced in sizes that were portable, making them easier to steal. Similarly, cars and other expensive items that could be stolen, reused, and resold became targets. As Cohen and Felson saw it, social prosperity produces an increase in criminal victimization.

Hindelang, Gottfredson, and Garofalo (1978) posited that certain lifestyles or behaviors place people in situations in which victimization is likely to occur. A lifestyle that includes going to bars or working late at night in relative seclusion, increases risk of victimization. As a person comes into contact—via lifestyle and behavior—with potential offenders, s/he is creating opportunities for crime victimization. Probability of victimization comes from associates, working outside of the home, and engaging in leisure activities. In this way, a person who associates with criminals, who works outside of the home, and who participates in activities, particularly at night, away from home and with nonfamily members, is a more likely target for personal victimization than others. Hindelang and his colleagues used the *principle of homogamy*, in which the more frequently a person comes into contact with persons in demographic groups with likely offenders, the more likely victimization will occur. This frequency may be a function of demographics or lifestyle.

One of the reasons that routine activities and lifestyles theories have been the prevailing theories of victimization for over thirty years is because of the wide empirical support found when testing them. It has been shown that a person's routine activities and lifestyles impact risk of being sexually victimized (Cass, 2007; Fisher, Daigle, & Cullen, 2010; Mustaine & Tewksbury, 1999, 2007; Schwartz & Pitts, 1995); auto theft (Rice & Smith, 2002); stalking (Mustaine & Tewksbury, 1999);

cybercrime victimization (Holt & Bossler, 2009); adolescent violent victimization (Lauritsen, Laub, & Sampson, 1992); theft (Mustaine & Tewksbury, 1998); victimization at work (Lynch, 1997); and street robbery (Groff, 2007).

STRUCTURAL CAUSES OF VICTIMIZATION

Some areas are so crime prone that they are considered to be "hot spots" for crime. First identified by Sherman, Gartin, and Buerger (1989), hot spots are areas that have a concentrated amount of crime. He found through examining police call data in Minneapolis, that only 3% of all locations made up most calls to the police. If a person lived in or frequented a hot spot, s/he would be putting him/herself in danger. The features of these hot spots and other high-risk areas create opportunities for victimization that, independent of a person's lifestyle or demographic characteristics, enhance his/her chances of being victimized.

What is it about certain areas that make them related to victimization? A body of recent research has identified many features, particularly of neighborhoods. One factor that is related to victimization is *family structure*. Sampson (1985), in his seminal piece on neighborhoods and crime, found that neighborhoods that have a large percentage of female-headed households have higher rates of theft and violent victimization. He also found that *structural density*, as measured by the percentage of units in structures with five or more units, is positively related to victimization. *Residential mobility*, or the percentage of persons 5 years and older living in a different house from 5 years earlier, also predicted victimization.

Living in a neighborhood that is disadvantaged places individuals at risk of being victimized, even if they do not have risky lifestyles or other characteristics related to victimization (Browning & Erickson, 2009). Using collective efficacy, it makes sense that neighborhoods that are disadvantaged are less able to mobilize effective sources of informal social control (Sampson, Raudenbush, & Earls, 1997). Informal social controls are oftentimes used as mechanisms to maintain order, stability, and safety in neighborhoods. When communities do not have strong informal mechanisms in place, violence and other deviancy are likely to abound. Such communities are less safe; hence, its residents are more likely to be victimized than residents of more socially organized areas.

CARING FOR THE VICTIM

Victim's Rights

Once essentially ignored by the criminal justice system and the law, victims are now granted a range of rights. The first such law guaranteeing victims' rights and protections was passed in Wisconsin in 1979; now every state has some form of victims' rights legislation (Davis & Mulford, 2008). Despite each state having laws that afford victims' rights, each differs according to whom the law applies, when the rights begin, what rights victims have, and how these rights can be enforced. Common, however, is the goal of victims' rights—to enhance victim privacy, protection, and participation (Garvin, 2010).

Slightly less than half of all states grant [some] rights to *all* victims (Howley & Dorris, 2007). In all states, the right to compensation, notification of rights, notification of court appearances, and ability to submit *victim impact statements* (VISs) before sentencing is granted to at least some class of victims (Dees, 1999). Other common rights given to victims in the majority of states are the right to restitution, to be treated with dignity and respect, to attend court and sentencing hearings, and to consult with court personnel before plea bargains are offered or defendants released from custody (Davis & Mulford, 2008).

VICTIM REMEDIES AND SERVICES

Victim compensation. One way that victims receive financial compensation for their economic losses is through state-run victim compensation programs. First begun in 1965 in California, victim compensation programs now exist in every state. Funding for compensation comes from a variety of sources. A large portion derives from criminals themselves—fees and fines imposed on those charged with criminal offenses. These fees are attached to the normal court fees that offenders are expected to pay. In addition, the Victim of Crime Act of 1984 (VOCA) authorized funding for state compensation and assistance programs. Today, the VOCA Crime Victims Fund provides over $700 million annually to states to assist victims and constitutes about one third of each program's funding (National Association of Crime Victim Compensation Boards, 2009). Not only did VOCA increase funding for state programs, but it also required states to cover all U.S. citizens victimized within the state's borders, regardless of the victim's residency.

Not all victims, however, are eligible for compensation from the Crime Victims Fund. Only victims of rape, assault, child sexual abuse, drunk driving, domestic violence, and homicide are eligible, since these crimes are known to create an undue hardship on victims (Klein, 2010). In addition to the type of victimization, victims must meet other requirements to be eligible:

- Must report the victimization promptly to law enforcement; usually within 72 hours unless "good cause" can be shown such as being a child or incarcerated or otherwise incapacitated
- Must cooperate with law enforcement and prosecutors in the investigation and prosecution of the case
- Must submit application for compensation within a specified time, generally 1 year from the date of the crime that includes evidence of expenses
- Must show that costs have not been compensated from other sources such as insurance or other programs
- Must not have participated in criminal conduct or significant misconduct that caused or contributed to the victimization

Victims can be compensated for a wide variety of expenses including medical care costs, mental health treatment costs, funeral costs, and lost wages. Other expenses for which victims may be able to be compensated include the replacement or repair of eyeglasses or corrective lenses, dental care, prosthetic devices, and forensic sexual assault exams. Note that property damage and loss are not compensable expenses (Office for Victims of Crime, 2010), and only three states currently pay for pain and suffering (Klein, 2010).

Of some import is that there is little evidence that persons who receive compensation are any more satisfied than others (Elias, 1984) or that they are more likely to participate in the criminal justice process (Klein, 2010).

Victim impact statements. As previously discussed, criminal trials involve two parties in an adversarial system that reflects that a crime is a harm against the state. As such, victims seldom play more than the role of witness in the trial. It was not until the 1970s that victims received rights that guaranteed them at least some voice in the criminal trial process. One of these rights was first adopted in 1976 in Fresno, California, giving victims an opportunity to address the court through a victim impact statement (VIS).

The VIS can be submitted by direct victims or by those who are indirectly impacted by the crime, such as family members. The VIS can be submitted in writing or presented orally (victim allocution).

Victim/Witness Assistance Program. Victim/Witness Assistance Programs (VWAPs) provide victims with assistance as they navigate the criminal justice system. These programs are designed to ensure that victims know their rights and have the resources necessary to exercise them. At its heart, however, is a goal to increase victim and witness participation in the criminal justice process particularly by being witnesses, with the notion that victims who have criminal justice personnel assisting them will be more willing to participate in and be satisfied with their experience.

In the *President's Task Force on Victims of Crime: Final report* (Office of Justice Programs, 1982), the Task Force recommended that prosecutors better serve victims. Specifically, the Task Force noted that prosecutors should work more closely with crime victims and receive their input as their cases are processed. It also noted that victims needed protection and their contribution should be valued—prosecutors should honor scheduled case appearances and return personal property as soon as possible. To this end, VWAPs have been developed, most commonly administrated through prosecutors' offices, but some also run through law enforcement agencies. At the federal level, each U.S. Attorney Office has a victim witness coordinator to help victims of federal crimes.

Today, these programs most commonly provide victims with background information regarding the court procedure and their basic rights as crime victims. Notification about court dates and changes to those dates is also made. Information regarding victim compensation and aid for victims in applying for compensation if eligible is also provided. A victim who wishes to make a VIS can receive assistance from the VWAP. Another service offered by a VWAP is making sure the victims and witnesses have separate waiting areas in the courthouse so that they have privacy. In some instances, VWAP personnel will attend court proceedings and trials with the victim and his/her family.

Despite the effort of VWAP programs, research shows that some of the first of these programs did little to improve victim participation. The Vera Institute of Justice's Victim/Witness Assistance Project that ran in the 1970s provided victims with a wide range of services—day care for children while parents went to court, counseling for victims, assistance with victim compensation, notification of all court dates, and a program that allowed victims to stay at work rather than come to court if their testimony was not needed—to little "success" (Herman, 2004). Herman (2004) showed that victims were no more likely to show up at court. It was not until the Vera Institute developed a program that used victim advocates to go to court with victims that positive outcomes emerged. Few programs provide services that have been identified as most critical in the research literature; instead, VWAPs are largely oriented toward ensuring that witnesses cooperate and participate in court proceedings rather than ensuring that crime victims receive needed services (Jerin, Moriarty, & Gibson, 1996).

Family justice centers. Because crime victims often need a variety of services, family justice centers (http://www.familyjusticecenter.org/) are designed to provide many "one stop" services. These centers provide counseling, advocacy, legal services, health care, financial services, housing assistance, employment referrals, and other services (see also National Coalition Against Domestic Violence, n.d.). The advantages to doing so are many—victims can receive a plethora of services without having to navigate the maze of health and social service agencies throughout their jurisdiction. Instead, these services can be found in one central location.

Victim-offender mediation programs. Some victims may not wish to sit in the background and only interact on the periphery of the criminal justice system. Instead, they may want to have face-to-face meetings with their offender. As a way to allow such a dialogue between victims and offenders, victim-offender mediation (VOM) programs have sprouted up throughout the United States, with over 300 such programs in operation today (Umbreit & Greenwood, 2000). With the American Bar Association endorsing the use of VOM and what appears to be widespread public support for these programs, victim-offender mediation has become almost commonplace in U.S. courts (Umbreit & Greenwood, 2000). Victim-offender mediation is already widely used internationally, with more than 700 programs in operation in Europe (Umbreit & Greenwood, 2000).

Mediation in criminal justice cases most commonly occurs as a *diversion* from prosecution. This means that if an offender and victim agree and complete mediation and if the offender completes any requirements set forth in the mediation agreement, then the offender will not be formally prosecuted in the criminal justice system. Mediation can also take place as a condition of probation. For some offenders, if they formally admit guilt and are adjudicated, they may be placed on probation by the judge with the stipulation that they participate in mediation. In all instances, it is up to the victim to ultimately participate in VOM programs (Umbreit & Greenwood, 2000). Most victims who are given the opportunity to participate in victim-offender mediation do so (Umbreit & Greenwood, 2000); it is the offender who is more likely to be reluctant.

Victim-offender mediation programs are designed to provide victims—usually property and minor assault victims—a chance to meet their offenders in a structured environment. Sessions are led by a third-party mediator whose job it is to facilitate a dialogue through which victims are able to directly address their offenders and tell them how the crime impacted their lives. The victim may also question the offender. To achieve the objectives of restorative justice, mediation programs use humanistic mediation, dialogue rather than settlement driven (Umbreit, 2000). The mediator is there to be impartial and to provide unconditional positive concern and regard for both parties, with minimal interruption. As noted by Umbreit (2000), humanistic mediation emphasizes healing and peacemaking over problem solving and resolution. One tangible product often but not always created from VOM is a restitution plan for the offender that the victim plays a central role in developing. This agreement becomes enforceable with the court, whereby when an offender does not meet his/her requirements, s/he can be remanded to court.

What happens after an offender and victim meet? Do offenders and victims both receive a benefit? What about the community? Collectively, research shows that there are many benefits to VOM programs. Participation has shown a reduction in fear and anxiety among crime victims (Umbreit, Coates, & Kalanj, 1994) including PTSD symptoms (Angel, 2005) and a desire to seek revenge against or harm offenders (Sherman et al., 2005; Strang, 2002). In addition, both offenders and victims report high levels of satisfaction with the VOM process (McCold & Wachtel, 1998; see Umbreit & Greenwood, 2000). Victims who meet their offenders report higher levels of satisfaction with their results than do victims of similar crimes who have their cases formally processed (Umbreit, 1994a). In addition to satisfaction, research shows that offenders are more likely to complete restitution required through VOM (Umbreit et al., 1994). More than 90% of restitution agreements from VOM programs are completed within one year (Victim-Offender Reconciliation Program Information and Resource Center, 2006). Reduction in recidivism rates for offenders has also been found (Nugent & Paddock, 1995; Umbreit, 1994b).

SUMMARY

The field of victimology emerged during the mid-1900s. Similar to criminology, victimology studies the causes and consequences of victimization and of how the criminal justice system and other social service agencies respond to crime victims.

We know from official data sources and victimization surveys that the victimization rate had been steadily declining since 1994 until a slight increase from 2010 to

2013. We also know who faces the greatest risk of being a crime victim. Young, Black males have the highest violent victimization rates (Truman et al., 2013). We also know that households that are low income and those having a greater number of occupants living in them are more likely to experience a property victimization than lesser populated households (Truman, 2010).

Once a person is victimized, s/he often experiences a range of consequences. For some victims, there are economic costs associated with victimization. These economic costs can result from property losses; from money spent on necessary medical or mental health care; from costs associated with losses in productivity or time lost from work, school, or housework; from pain and suffering; from reduced quality of life; and from legal costs. In 2008, the total economic loss from crimes was estimated to be $17,297 billion. Victimization also impacts other entities. In the United States, direct expenditures of the criminal justice system are over $214 billion annually (BJS, 2006a). Insurance companies also pay claims associated with crime—annually these costs top $45 billion ("Guns, Money & Medicine," 1996). When uninsured individuals are injured from crime and seek medical attention, society absorbs the cost.

Economic costs are not the only expenses incurred by crime victims. Many victims experience affective responses to victimization. The most common are depression, reductions in self-esteem, and anxiety. More recently, PTSD has been recognized as a possible outcome to severe trauma, including victimization. PTSD is characterized by fear, helplessness, or horror in response to the event; reexperience of the trauma over time via flashbacks, nightmares, images, and/or reliving the event; avoidance of stimuli associated with the traumatic event; numbness of responses and hyperarousal (APA, 2000).

Many victims blame themselves for their own victimization or experience learned helplessness, whereby they have learned that responding to victimization is futile and so become passive and numb (Seligman, 1975). Another potential cost of victimization is fear. Women and the elderly are fearful, although their actual victimization risks are low (Ferraro, 1995).

Victims face the real risk of being victimized again. Although most who are victimized will not experience another victimization, there is a sizable portion who do, and they are most at risk in the time period immediately following their initial incident. Two competing explanations have been offered to explain this phenomenon: risk heterogeneity and state dependence (Pease, 1998). According to this perspective, characteristics that place an individual at risk, if left unchanged, will continue to keep a victim at risk for subsequent incidents. State dependence, on the other hand, argues that it is what happens during and after an incident that impacts risk. What the victim and offender do and learn during and after an incident will shape future risk.

Early explorations in the field of victimology were centered on determining how much a victim contributes to his/her own victimization. In this way, early researchers were interested in victim precipitation—the extent to which victims are responsible for their own victimization. They studied victim facilitation that makes it easier for an offender to commit a crime. Finally, victim provocation, which occurs when a person incites another person to commit a crime against him, was also examined. Early publications by von Hentig (1948), Mendelsohn (1968), and Schafer (1968) involved developing victim typologies based on the degree to which they were responsible for their own victimization. Empirical studies of victim precipitation were conducted by Amir (1971) who found that almost 1 in 5 rapes were victim precipitated.

The most widely used theories to explain victimization are routine activities and lifestyles theories. According to routine activities theory, when a person's daily routine activities bring him/her into contact with motivated offenders, without capable guardianship, victimization risk is high. Cohen and Felson (1979) argued that it is the coalescence of time and space of motivated offenders and suitable targets without capable guardianship that predict victimization. Hindelang, Gottfredson, and Garofalo's (1978) lifestyles theory is closely related to routine activities theory. Accordingly, it is a person's lifestyle that shapes victimization risk. Lifestyles that involve spending time outside of the home, especially at night away from the family, are risky in that people come into greater contact with potential offenders.

Others have suggested that place characteristics make certain areas ripe for victimization. Some areas, known as "hot spots," are particularly crime prone. Sampson (1985) argued that certain features of neighborhoods impact their risk: family structure, structural density, and residential mobility.

Given the interest in crime victims, it is not surprising to learn that victims now have many rights. Commonly, victims have the right to compensation, the right to notification, the right to attend court hearings, and the right to submit a VIS. Some states also provide the right to restitution, the right to be treated with dignity and respect, the right to consult with court personnel before bond hearings and plea bargaining decisions, the right to protection, and the right to a speedy trial (Davis & Mulford, 2008).

Victim compensation is financial compensation for victims, which is administered through the state. Often, these funds are paid through charges attached to court fees along with Victim of Crime Act funding from the federal government (National Association of Crime Victim Compensation Boards, 2009). To be eligible for compensation, in many states, victims must report the incident to the police in a timely fashion, cooperate with criminal justice personnel in the investigation and prosecution process, submit an application within a specified time, document actual costs and show that these costs have not been paid from other sources, and not have participated in criminal conduct that contributed to the victimization.

Victims (and those indirectly impacted by the crime) may also have the right to make a VIS, which is written or given orally. The VIS details the effects of being victimized and often includes the victim's recommendation for sentence or release (National Center for Victims of Crime, 1999; see also National Center for Victims of Crime, 2009).

Many of the rights that victims have are exercised through their work with Victim-Witness Assistance Programs (VWAPs). VWAPs are designed to assist victims in knowing their rights and making sure they have the ability to exercise these rights. Often through prosecutors' offices, VWAPs most commonly provide victims with information about court processes and their basic rights as crime victims. Newer programs to assist crime victims where victims receive a range of services in one place have developed. These family justice centers provide counseling, advocacy, legal services, health care, financial services, housing assistance, employment referrals, and other centrally located services (see also National Coalition Against Domestic Violence, n.d.).

Some programs provided to victims allow them to play a more direct role with the criminal justice process. Victim-offender mediation involves face-to-face meetings between the victim and offender and a neutral, third-party mediator. During mediation sessions, the victim is allowed to tell the offender how the victimization impacted his/her life and ask the offender questions. Similarly, the offender is provided an opportunity to apologize and to explain his/her behavior. Sometimes, mediation results in agreed-upon outcomes for the offender, such as restitution to be paid to the victim, that are enforceable by the court.

DISCUSSION QUESTIONS

1. Who is the "typical" crime victim? Given the characteristics of the typical crime victim, why do you think that these persons are more at risk than others of being victimized?

2. Have you been the victim of a crime? Has anyone you know been a victim of a crime? If so, think about the costs associated with your or his/her victimization. Had you considered all of these costs before? How did you or him/her deal with the costs of being victimized? How should the criminal justice system deal with victim costs?

3. Using routine activities and lifestyles theories, evaluate your own risk of becoming a crime victim. What measures do you already take to avoid victimization? What could you do but do not? Why do you not do these things? Is it fair to ask victims to change their habits and behavior to reduce victimization? Why or why not?

4. What other factors beside routine activities and lifestyles do you think increase victimization risk? Why would these factors increase victimization?

5. What do you think is the most important right given to crime victims? Why is this the most important?

6. Investigate the rights given to crime victims in your home state. Is it clear what rights are given to victims? Who is responsible for notifying victims of their rights? What remedy do victims have in your home state if their rights are not being met?

REFERENCES

American Psychiatric Association (APA). (2000). *Diagnostic and statistical manual of mental disorders* (4th ed., text rev.). Washington, DC: Author.

Amir, M. (1971). *Patterns of forcible rape*. Chicago, IL: University of Chicago Press.

Angel, C. (2005). *Crime victims meet their offenders: Testing the impact of restorative justice conferences on victims' post-traumatic stress symptoms* (Unpublished doctoral dissertation). University of Pennsylvania, Philadelphia.

Bonderman, J. (2001). *Working with victims of gun violence*. Washington, DC: U.S. Department of Justice, Office of Victims of Crime.

Browning, S., & Erickson, P. (2009). Neighborhood disadvantage, alcohol use, and violent victimization. *Youth Violence and Juvenile Justice, 7*(4), 331–349.

Bureau of Justice Statistics (BJS). (2006a). *Criminal victimization in the United States: Statistical tables*. Washington, DC: U.S. Department of Justice.

Bureau of Justice Statistics (BJS). (2008). *National Crime Victimization Survey, 2005*. Ann Arbor, MI: Inter-University Consortium for Political and Social Research. Retrieved from http://www.ICPSR.umich.edu/icpsrweb/NACJD/studies/22746

Cass, A. I. (2007). Routine activities and sexual victimization: An analysis of individual and school level factors. *Violence and Victims, 22*(3), 350–366.

Cohen, L. E., & Felson, M. (1979). Social change and crime rate trends: A routine activities approach. *American Sociological Review, 44*(4), 588–608.

Cutler, S., & Nolen-Hoeksema, S. (2006). Accounting for sex differences in depression through female victimization: Childhood sexual abuse. *Sex Roles, 24*, 425–438.

Daigle, L. E., Fisher, B. S., & Cullen, F. T. (2008). The violent and sexual victimization of college women: Is repeat victimization a problem? *Journal of Interpersonal Violence, 23*(9), 1296–1313.

Davis, R. C., & Mulford, C. (2008). Victim rights and new remedies: Finally getting victims their due. *Journal of Contemporary Criminal Justice, 24*(2), 198–208.

Dees, P. (1999). *Victims' rights: Notification, consultation, participation, services, compensation, and remedies in the criminal justice process*. New York, NY: Vera Institute of Justice.

Elias, R. (1984). Alienating the victim: Compensation and victim attitudes. *Journal of Social Issues, 40*(1), 103–116.

Ferraro, K. (1996). Women's fear of victimization: Shadow of sexual assault? *Social Forces, 75*(2), 667–690.

Ferraro, K. F. (1995). *Fear of crime: Interpreting victimization risk*. Albany: State University of New York Press.

Ferraro, K., & LaGrange, R. L. (1987). The measurement of fear of crime. *Sociological Inquiry, 5*(7), 70–101.

Fisher, B. S., Daigle, L. E., Cullen, F. T. (2010). What distinguishes single from recurrent sexual victims? The role of lifestyle-routine activities and first incident characteristics. *Justice Quarterly, 27*(1), 102–129.

Garvin, M. (2010). Victim's rights movement, United States. In B. S. Fisher & S. P. Lab (Eds.), *Encyclopedia of victimology and crime prevention* (Vol. 2, pp. 1019–1020). Los Angeles, CA: SAGE.

Groff, E. R. (2007). Simulation for theory testing and experimentation: An example using routine activity theory and street robbery. *Journal of Quantitative Criminology, 23*(2), 75–103.

Guns, money & medicine. (1996, July 1). *U.S. News & World Report*, pp. 31–40.

Haynie, D. L. (1998). Explaining the gender gap in fear of crime over time, 1970–1995: A methodological approach. *Criminal Justice Review, 23*(1), 29–50.

Herman, S. (2004, April 28). *Supporting and protecting victims: Making it happen.* Keynote address at the National Victims Conference, London. Retrieved from http://www.ncvc .org/NCVC/main.aspx?dbName=DocumentViewr&DocumentI=38044

Hindelang, M. J., Gottfredson, M. R., & Garofalo, J. (1978). *Victims of personal crime: An empirical foundation for a theory of personal victimization.* Cambridge, MA: Ballinger.

Holt, T. J., & Bossler, A. M. (2009). Examining the applicability of lifestyle-routine activities theory for cybercrime victimization. *Deviant Behavior, 30*(1), 1–25.

Howley, S., & Dorris, C. (2007). Legal rights for crime victims in the criminal justice system. In R. C. Davis, A. J. Lurigio, & S. Herman (Eds.), *Victims of crime* (3rd ed., pp. 299–314). Thousand Oaks, CA: SAGE.

Janoff-Bulman, R. (1979). Characterological versus behavioral self-blame: Inquiries into depression and rape. *Journal of Personality and Social Psychology, 37*(10), 1798–1809.

Jerin, R. A., Moriarty, L. J., & Gibson, M. A. (1996). Victim service or self-service: An analysis of prosecution-based victim-witness assistance programs and services. *Criminal Justice Policy Review, 7*(2), 142–154.

Kilpatrick, D. G., & Acierno, R. (2003). Mental health needs of crime victims: Epidemiology and outcomes. *Journal of Traumatic Stress, 16*(2), 119–132.

Kilpatrick, D. G., Edmunds, C. N., & Seymour, A. K. (1992). *Rape in America: A report to the nation.* Arlington, VA: National Victim Center & Medical University of South Carolina.

Klein, L. (2010). Victim compensation. In B. S. Fisher & S. P. Lab (Eds.), *Encyclopedia of victimology and crime prevention* (Vol. 2, pp. 971–974). Los Angeles, CA: SAGE.

Lauritsen, J. L., Laub, J. H., & Sampson, R. J. (1992). Conventional and delinquent activities: Implications for the prevention of violent victimization among adolescents. *Violence and Victims, 7*(2), 91–108.

Lynch, D. R. (1997). The nature of occupational stress among public defenders. *Justice System Journal, 19*(1), 17–35.

May, D. C., Rader, N. E., & Goodrum, S. (2010). A gendered assessment of the "threat of victimization": Examining gender differences in fear of crime, perceived risk, avoidance, and defensive behaviors. *Criminal Justice Review, 35,* 159–182.

McCold, P., & Wachtel, B. (1998). *Restorative policing experiment: The Bethlehem Pennsylvania Police Family Group Conferencing Project.* Pipersville, PA: Community Service Foundation.

Mendelsohn, B. (1968). Rape in criminology. In S. Schafer (Ed.), *The victim and his criminal.* New York, NY: Random House.

Miller, T. R., Cohen, M. A., & Wiersema, B. (1996). *Victim costs and consequence: A new look.* Washington, DC: U.S. National Institute of Justice.

Mustaine, E. E., & Tewksbury, R. (1998). Predicting risks of larceny theft victimization: A routine activity analysis using refined lifestyle measures. *Criminology, 36*(4), 829–857.

Mustaine, E. E., & Tewksbury, R. (1999). A routine activity theory explanation for women's stalking victimizations. *Violence Against Women, 5*(1), 43–62.

Mustaine, E. E., & Tewksbury, R. (2007). The routine activities and criminal victimization of students: Lifestyle and related factors. In B. S. Fisher & J. J. Sloan (Eds.), *Campus crime: Legal, social, and policy perspectives* (pp. 147–166). Springfield, IL: Charles C Thomas.

National Association of Crime Victim Compensation Boards. (2009). National conference to mark 25 years of VOCA grants to states. *Crime Victim Compensation Quarterly, 2*, 1. Retrieved from http://www.nacvcb.org/NACVCB/files/ccLibraryFiles/Filename/000000000 024/20093.pdf

National Center for Victims of Crime. (1999). *Victim impact statements.* Retrieved from http://www.ncvc.org/ncvc/main.aspx?dbName=documentID=32347

National Center for Victims of Crime. (2009). *About victims' rights.* Retrieved from http://www.victimlaw.ifo/victimlaw/pages/victimsRights.jsp

National Coalition Against Domestic Violence. (n.d.). *Domestic violence facts.* Retrieved from http://www.ncadv.org/files/DomesticViolenceFactSheet(National).pdf

Nicholas, S., Povey, D., Walker, A., & Kershaw, C. (2005). *Crime in England and Wales 2004/2005.* United Kingdom: Great Britain Home Office Research Development and Statistics Directorate. Retrieved from http://webarchive.nationalarchives.gov.uk/2013 0128103514/http://www.homeoffice.gov.uk/science-research/research-statistics/crime/crime-statistics/british-crime-survey/

Nugent, W. R., & Paddock, J. B. (1995). The effect of victim offender mediation on severity of re-offense. *Mediation Quarterly, 12*(4), 353–367.

Office for Victims of Crime. (2010, April). *Crime Victims Fund: OVC fact sheet.* Retrieved from http://ovc.ncjrs.gov/Publications.aspx?SeriesID=70

Office of Justice Programs. (1982). *President's Task Force on Victims of Crime: Final report.* (1982). http://ojp.gov/ovc/publications/presdntstskforcrprt/welcome.html

Pease, K. (1998). *Repeat victimisation: Taking stock.* London, United Kingdom: Home Office, Police Research Group.

Reiss, A. (1980). Victim proneness in repeat victimization by type of crime. In S. Fienberg & A. Reiss (Eds.). *Indicators of crime and criminal justice: Quantitative studies* (pp. 41–53). Washington, DC: U.S. Department of Justice.

Rice, K. J., & Smith, W. R. (2002). Sociological models of automotive theft: Integrating routine activity and social disorganization approaches. *Journal in Research in Crime and Delinquency, 39*(3), 304–336.

Rountree, P. W. (1998). A reexamination of the crime-fear linkage. *Journal of Research in Crime and Delinquency, 35*(3), 341–372.

Sampson, R. J. (1985). Neighborhood and crime: The structural determinants of personal victimization. *Journal of Research in Crime and Delinquency, 22*(1), 7–40.

Sampson, R. J., Raudenbush, S. W., & Earls, F. (1997). Neighborhoods and violent crime: A multilevel study of collective efficacy. *Science, 277*(5328), 918–924.

Schafer, S. (1968). *The victim and his criminal: A study in functional responsibility.* New York, NY: Random House.

Schwartz, M. D., & Pitts, V. L. (1995). Exploring a feminist routine activities approach to explaining sexual assault. *Justice Quarterly, 12*(1), 9–31.

Seligman, M. (1975). *Helplessness.* San Francisco, CA: Freeman.

Sherman, L. W., Gartin, P. R., & Buerger, M. E. (1989). Hot spots of predatory crime: Routine activities and the criminology of place. *Criminology, 27*(1), 27–55.

Sherman, L. W., Strang, H., Angel, C., Woods, D., Barnes, G. C., Bennett, S., & Inkpen, N. (2005). Effects of face-to-face restorative justice on victims of crime in four randomized, controlled trials. *Journal of Experimental Criminology, 1*(3), 367–395.

Strang, H. (2002). *Repair or revenge: Victims and restorative justice.* Oxford, United Kingdom: Clarendon.

Truman, J. L. (2010). *Criminal victimization, 2010.* Bureau of Justice Statistics. Retrieved from www.bjs.gov

Truman, J., Langton, L., & Planty, M. (2013). *Criminal victimization, 2012*. Washington, DC: U.S. Department of Justice, Bureau of Justice Statistics.

Turner, H. A., Finkelhor, D., & Ormrod, R. K. (2006). The effect of lifetime victimization on the mental health of children and adolescents. *Social Science & Medicine, 62*, 13–27.

Umbreit, M. S. (1994a). Crime victims confront their offenders: The impact of a Minneapolis mediation program. *Research on Social Work Practice*, 4(4), 436–447.

Umbreit, M. S. (1994b). *Victim meets offender: The impact of restorative justice and mediation*. Monsey, NY: Criminal Justice Press.

Umbreit, M. S. (2000). *Peacemaking and spirituality: A journey toward healing and strength*. Saint Paul: Center for Restorative Justice and Peacemaking, University of Minnesota. Retrieved from http://www.cehd.umn.edu/ssw/rjp/Resources/Forgiveness/Peacemaking_and_Spirituality_Journey_Toward_Healing.pdf

Umbreit, M. S., Coates, R., & Kalanj, B. (1994). *Victim meets offender: The impact of restorative justice and mediation*. Monsey, NY: Criminal Justice Press.

Umbreit, M. S., & Greenwood, J. (2000). *Guidelines for victim-sensitive victim offender mediation: Restorative justice through dialogue*. Washington, DC: Office for Victims of Crime, Office of Justice Programs.

Victim-Offender Reconciliation Program Information and Resource Center. (2006). *About victim offender mediation and reconciliation*. Retrieved from http;//www.vorp.com/

von Hentig, H. (1948). *The criminal and his victim: Studies in the sociobiology of crime*. New Haven, CT: Yale University Press.

Warr, M. (1984, September). Fear of victimization: Why are women and the elderly more afraid? *Social Science Quarterly, 65*, 681–702.

Warr, M. (1985). Fear of rape among urban women. *Social Problems, 32*, 238–250.

Part II

Offenses and Offenders

CHAPTER 6

Juvenile Delinquency

David L. Parry

Available statistics reveal that persons under 18 years of age accounted for approximately 11.8% of all arrests in the United States in 2011, a percentage that has declined steadily since reaching its peak level of 19% in 1996 (Federal Bureau of Investigation, 1996–2011, 2012). As in previous years, most arrested youth fell within the delinquency-prone 15 to 17 aged group, and the vast majority were charged with theft, minor assaults, vandalism, drug offenses, liquor law violations, disorderly conduct, or status offenses, such as curfew violations and loitering. Contrary to the overblown myths and hysterical rhetoric fueling what Howell (2009) has dubbed a "moral panic" over supposedly escalating juvenile violence, Columbine-style school shootings, and a wave of juvenile superpredators, less than 1 in 20 juveniles arrested in 2011 was charged with a serious violent crime, and the total number of juvenile arrests in that year—estimated at roughly 1.47 million—had decreased 31% in the preceding 10 years (Puzzanchera, 2013).

So who are these delinquents? Where do they come from, and why do they do it? What pathways do they follow into delinquency and—for most—back out as they mature into young adults? What is *delinquency* anyway, and how much of it *really* occurs? These are among the many questions raised in this chapter. The answers are elusive, and the literature exploring them is voluminous. The goal, therefore, is not to present an exhaustive review but rather to selectively examine several key aspects of the delinquency problem, highlighting exemplary statistics and research findings as a vehicle for exploring some of the central issues that must be confronted if we are to better understand and more effectively respond to the delinquency around us and the young people engaged in it.

WHAT IS DELINQUENCY?

Let's begin by taking a look at the meaning of the term *juvenile delinquency*. Traditionally, juvenile courts have exercised jurisdiction in three distinct types of cases. Although statutory language varies, the *delinquency jurisdiction* of these courts generally authorizes intervention in any case involving a minor charged with an act which would be a crime if committed by an adult. It is thus differentiated from their jurisdiction over *status offenders* (youth who engage in activities that would be permissible for an adult but are prohibited for children) and *neglected or dependent* youth (those who have no parent or are the victims of parental neglect or abuse).

This deceptively straightforward definition of juvenile delinquency as a legal category masks significant state-by-state variations that make it exceedingly difficult to pin down exactly who and what we are studying when we try to *understand* delinquency. First, who falls within the delinquency jurisdiction of the juvenile court varies tremendously across states. The Illinois statute commonly heralded as the first anywhere in the world to authorize creation of a separate court for juveniles, for example, limited the delinquency jurisdiction of juvenile courts to "any child under the age of 16 years who violates any law of this State or any city or village ordinance" (An Act to Regulate the Treatment and Control of Dependent, Neglected and Delinquent Children, 1899; see Illinois Juvenile Court Act § 5 [1899]). Today, however, only two states continue to restrict delinquency jurisdiction so severely. Most now cap it at the 18th birthday, while 10 states limit it to youth under 17 (Griffin, 2012; Office of Juvenile Justice and Delinquency Prevention, 2012).

Further complicating matters, juvenile courts have almost universally retained authority to transfer youth under the age cap to criminal court for prosecution as adults if the judge deems the child unamenable to effective treatment within the juvenile justice system, and many states also automatically (i.e., by statute) exclude certain categories of youth (usually those above a specified age) who are charged with very serious offenses from juvenile court jurisdiction and/or grant prosecutors discretion to file such cases directly in criminal court if they choose to do so (see discussion in Griffin, Addie, Adams, & Firestine, 2011). At the other extreme, statutes in most states allow for extended juvenile court jurisdiction over adjudicated delinquents placed on probation or committed to a juvenile correctional facility until well beyond the age at which original jurisdiction ends—most commonly until the youth turns 21 or even, in a handful of states, to age 25 (Snyder & Sickmund, 2006). The term—the label—thus applies not only to the *act* but also to the *person* (the teenager or, occasionally, the child) who committed it, and even to the young adult still under juvenile court jurisdiction despite advancing age.

The definition of juvenile delinquency gets even murkier when we consider the offenses that underlie the delinquency label. For example, underage drinking is regarded by many as a status offense because it is prohibited only for those under 21 years of age. In most states, however, it is prosecutable as a misdemeanor for "minors" who are younger than 21 but above the maximum age for juvenile court jurisdiction, rendering it a delinquent act for those under that age. A similar dilemma confronts us regarding possession of both medicinal and recreational marijuana, a misdemeanor under federal law and the laws of most states and therefore a delinquent offense for juveniles in those jurisdictions. But two states have recently legalized possession of small amounts of the drug by adults over 21, while in several others, marijuana possession has been reclassified as a noncriminal infraction subject only to a monetary fine, and initiatives elsewhere suggest that sentiment favoring elimination of criminal penalties is gaining traction in still more states across the country (see discussions in Lyman, 2014; Office of National Drug Control Policy, n.d.; Walsh, 2013).

These and other variations in statutory provisions applicable to the delinquency jurisdiction of juvenile courts have significant implications for efforts to understand delinquency as a *social* problem. We saw, for example, that even preteens may sometimes be convicted and punished as adult criminals in the eyes of the law, whereas other young people may technically remain "juvenile delinquents" until their mid-20s. Does this mean researchers seeking to gauge the extent of delinquency or to understand its causes should rely on after-the-fact decisions by juvenile justice system officials or on legislatively established age caps for juvenile court jurisdiction, in determining whether to regard particular behaviors as delinquency or as adult crime? Similarly, do variations in state laws mean we should consider teenaged marijuana smokers to be delinquent if they live in California but not if they live in Massachusetts? What about underage drinking—delinquency or not?

HOW MUCH DELINQUENCY?

These definitional challenges become especially problematic in any effort to gauge the extent of juvenile delinquency and the characteristics of juvenile offenders, even more so given the monumental obstacles to accurate measurement. Nonetheless, we can gain at least a general sense of the frequency and distribution of juvenile offenses by examining data derived from official arrest records, and we can further flesh out the picture by examining additional information gleaned from unofficial sources based on surveys tapping self-reported delinquency.

Arrest Data

Frequency and rate estimates for arrests of persons under 18 years of age—the closest feasible approximation of youth whose delinquent behavior actually falls within the jurisdiction of juvenile courts in their respective home states—are developed annually by researchers at the National Center for Juvenile Justice (NCJJ), based on Uniform Crime Reports (UCR) data compiled by the Federal Bureau of Investigation and distributed in its *Crime in the United States* series. Prepared under a cooperative agreement with the U.S. Justice Department's Office of Juvenile Justice and Delinquency Prevention (OJJDP), the NCJJ estimates for 2011 peg nationwide arrests of juveniles as thus defined at 1.47 million that year (Puzzanchera, 2013). Among the eight "Part I" offenses (formerly the "Crime Index"), the comparative infrequency of violent offenses is striking. These four offenses (murder, forcible rape, robbery, and aggravated assault) together accounted for less than 5% of all arrests of juveniles in 2011; arrests of juveniles for murder, despite their prominence in news reports and in popular culture, occurred just once in every 1,750 juvenile arrests. Part I property offenses (burglary, larceny-theft, motor vehicle theft, and arson) constituted a much greater share of juvenile arrests—nearly 23%—with the large assortment of generally less serious Part II offenses making up the remainder. Representation of juveniles among *all* persons arrested in 2011 ranged as high as 42% for arson, 29% for vandalism, and 28% for disorderly conduct. But for other offenses, it was considerably lower: 20% to 21% for most Part I property offenses, 22% for robbery, just 8% for murder, and 10% to 14% for the remaining Part I violent offenses, with their representation among arrestees for other offenses ranging widely, from a high of 18% for weapons violations to less than 5% for drunkenness, fraud, prostitution, and driving under the influence (Federal Bureau of Investigation, 2012; Puzzanchera, 2013).

Females accounted for 29% of all juvenile arrests in 2011 and for 36% of arrests for property offenses, but their representation dropped to just 18% for violent offenses (Federal Bureau of Investigation, 2012; Puzzanchera, 2013). In contrast with the underrepresentation of females, African American youth, representing about 17% of the under-18 aged population, were substantially overrepresented, both among juveniles arrested for property offenses (35%) and, even more so, among those arrested for violent offenses (51%), with their representation spiking to fully two thirds (68%) of all juveniles arrested for robbery and 54% of those arrested for murder.

Turning briefly to trends over time, juvenile arrests declined by 31% overall between 2002 and 2011 (Federal Bureau of Investigation, 2012; Puzzanchera, 2013). Arrests for specific offenses fell by at least 34 percentage points for every Part I offense except robbery—which decreased by just 3%, compared to a slight *increase* among adults—and by comparably large amounts for most Part II offenses as well. In contrast, the number of adults arrested for violent offenses fell just 12% over the 10-year span, less than half as much as the 27% decline for juveniles. Arrests for property offenses similarly declined just half as much for adults (15%) as for juveniles (30%). The differences were especially noteworthy for motor vehicle theft, which declined by an astounding 69% for juveniles compared to a less precipitous decline of 49% for adults, and for burglary and larceny-theft, both of which declined by 25% or more for juveniles while *increasing* substantially among adults (16% for burglary and 23% for larceny-theft).

Comparing trends by gender, arrests for violent offenses declined by similar amounts for males (26%) and females (28%) between 2002 and 2011, whereas the gender gap in arrests for property offenses narrowed considerably during this period, with arrests falling by 35% for males compared with a decline of just 19% among females. Comparing racial trends in terms of changes in rates per 100,000 youth rather than in the frequency of arrests, Puzzanchera (2013) reported 10-year declines of 35% or more in rates of arrest for both violent and property offenses among White, Asian, and American Indian youth, while African American youth experienced declines of just 13% for property offenses and 15% for violent offenses during the same period.

Self-Report Surveys

Although arrest data offer important insights about delinquency patterns and trends, they are of questionable reliability as barometers of the frequency with which young people actually engage in delinquent behavior (see discussions in Brame, Fagan, Piquero, Schubert, & Steinberg, 2004; McCord, Widom, & Crowell, 2001; Puzzanchera, 2013; Snyder & Sickmund, 2006). Alternative measures—especially those based on surveys tapping participants' self-reported involvement in unlawful behaviors—have therefore become an essential adjunct to official records in assessing the extent of delinquency.[1] Self-report data reveal levels of participation in at least minor forms of delinquency that in some studies approach or even exceed 90% (see Moffitt, 1993; Thornberry, Huizinga, & Loeber, 2004), and the cumulative prevalence of self-reported involvement (i.e., the proportion of youth admitting *any* past engagement) in acts characterized as serious violence runs as high as 30% to 40% of males and 16% to 32% of females in some accounts (see discussion in Office of the Surgeon General, 2001). Self-report data also tend to indicate smaller race and gender differences in rates of juvenile offending from arrest statistics, although the extent of such differences varies tremendously across studies, with some researchers finding no differences at all and others reporting even wider gaps than those found in officially recorded arrests (see discussions in Jensen & Rojek, 2009; Lauritsen, 2005; Zahn et al., 2008).

ADOLESCENT DEVELOPMENT, RISK FACTORS, AND PATHWAYS TO DELINQUENCY

Systematic assessment of the underlying causes of juvenile delinquency falls well outside the scope of this chapter and, in any event, would carry us into territory addressed in Okada's discussion of criminological theory and crime explanations in Chapter 3 of this book. But several strands in contemporary delinquency research warrant our attention here insofar as they offer valuable insights about ways in which delinquency is conditioned by the nature of adolescent development, risk factors that increase the likelihood of escalating antisocial behavior, and pathways leading toward increasingly serious delinquency that carry important practical implications for delinquency prevention and juvenile justice policy.

Moffitt's (1993) well-known distinction between adolescence-limited and life-course-persistent offenders provides a useful starting point for discussing the place of delinquency in the life-course trajectories of youth. While large proportions of youth engage in delinquent behavior during adolescence, only a small minority continue their antisocial behavior into adulthood. Even fewer develop into career offenders, cycling in and out of jails and prisons while most of their peers "grow out of it" as they mature and take on law abiding adult social roles. In contrast with the *discontinuity* displayed in the transitory delinquency of adolescence-limited offenders, who commit their first offenses as young teenagers and then *desist* as they enter adulthood, Moffitt describes a pattern of striking *continuity* across the entire life span in the antisocial behavior of life-course-persistent offenders. These offenders—estimated at roughly 5% to 6% of the population[2]—are likely to exhibit "difficult" temperaments and aggressive tendencies even in infancy, have their first police contacts for delinquency before reaching puberty, become immersed in delinquency as teenagers, and develop into career offenders in adulthood.

Normal Adolescent Behavior?

Many delinquency researchers share Moffitt's belief that some level of engagement in delinquent or otherwise antisocial behavior is an entirely normal part of adolescent development. Some, like Moffitt, view adolescence-limited offending through a social learning lens, as a self-reinforcing way for adolescents to cope with the uncomfortable paradox of attaining biological maturity years before the autonomy and privileges of adult status are extended to them, a temporary digression that is soon cast off as the transition to young adulthood brings new opportunities and altered contingencies that make desistance increasingly rewarding (Moffitt, 1993).

Others, looking to the lessons of developmental psychology for answers, have sought an explanation in the still-developing decision-making capabilities of adolescents (see discussions in Bonnie, Johnson, Chemers, & Schuck, 2013; Scott & Steinberg, 2008). In one such approach reflecting broadly shared insights, researchers examining the impact of psychosocial immaturity on adolescents' competence to stand trial (an initiative of the MacArthur Foundation Research Network on Adolescent Development and Juvenile Justice) have systematically explored the ways in which teenagers differ from adults in cognitive capacity (reasoning ability) and judgment (common sense). Their findings indicate that, although the cognitive abilities of most youth appear to approximate those of adults by mid-adolescence, their decision making is still deeply impacted by heightened sensitivity to peer influence, comparatively cavalier attitudes toward risk, and a temporal perspective emphasizing short-term benefits over longer-term consequences (Grisso et al., 2003; Scott & Grisso, 1997; Steinberg & Scott, 2003; see also Grisso & Schwartz, 2000; Scott & Steinberg, 2008). This cluster of psychosocial factors is argued to affect adolescents' judgment in ways that lead them to use information differently, deploy their reasoning skills differently or less reliably, and weigh costs and benefits of their actions differently from an adult in a comparable situation, thus, increasing their vulnerability to external pressures supporting delinquent behavior (Scott & Grisso, 1997; see also Bonnie et al., 2013; Scott & Steinberg, 2008).

Risk and Protective Factors

The efforts of Moffitt (1993) and others to isolate characteristics that can help predict the direction a young offender's life will take—toward persistent offending in adulthood or toward desistance as he or she matures—have spawned extensive research seeking to identify *risk factors* that are predictive of later patterns of serious, violent and/or chronic offending, and the *pathways* leading toward escalating antisocial behavior.

A sense of the wide variety of factors that have been found to place a child at increased risk for later involvement in such behavior can be gathered from the following enumeration of individual, family, school, peer, and community characteristics that researchers participating in the Office of Juvenile Justice and Delinquency Prevention's Study Group on Serious and Violent Juvenile Offenders determined to be at least somewhat predictive of later violence, based on their findings in a groundbreaking and at the time exhaustive meta-analysis of 66 rigorous, separately conducted longitudinal studies published between 1959 and 1997:

- **Individual factors:** Pregnancy and delivery complications; low resting heart rate; internalizing disorders; hyperactivity, concentration problems, restlessness, and risk taking; aggressiveness; early initiation of violent behavior; involvement in other forms of antisocial behavior; beliefs and attitudes favorable to deviant or antisocial behavior.
- **Family factors:** Parental criminality; child maltreatment; poor family management practices; low levels of parental involvement; poor family bonding and family conflict; parental attitudes favorable to substance use and violence; parent-child separation.
- **School factors:** Academic failure; low bonding to school; truancy and dropping out of school; frequent school transitions.
- **Peer-related factors:** Delinquent siblings; delinquent peers; gang membership.
- **Community and neighborhood factors:** Poverty; community disorganization; availability of drugs and firearms; neighborhood adults involved in crime; exposure to violence and racial prejudice. (J. D. Hawkins et al., 2000, p. 2; see also J. D. Hawkins et al., 1998)

Not surprisingly, risk factors have been found to differ substantially in their predictive value, and research has shown that particular factors may be stronger— or weaker—predictors of later behavior when observed in young children as compared to adolescents. In another pioneering meta-analysis by members of the Study Group on Serious and Violent Juvenile Offenders, Lipsey and Derzon (1998) found that the predictive value of particular factors differed considerably for young children as compared with adolescents. For children aged 6 to 11, commission of a general juvenile offense (i.e., *any* juvenile offense committed by a child in this age group) was found to be the single strongest predictor of serious or violent behavior at ages 15 to 25, followed by substance abuse and, in a second rank of predictive variables, gender (i.e., being male), family socioeconomic status (SES), and antisocial parents. For 12 to 14 year olds, the strongest predictors were weak social ties and antisocial peers, with commission of general offenses following in the second rank, but having noticeably less predictive value than was observed for the younger group. By contrast, antisocial peers had very little impact on later behavior for 6 to 11 year olds, while substance abuse and family SES carried only minimal predictive value for the older group. Curiously, broken homes and abusive parents were ranked among the weakest predictors for both groups, although later research has emphasized the importance of child maltreatment as a predictor of various forms of violence and other antisocial behavior—especially if it occurs during adolescence (Maas, Herrenkohl, & Sousa, 2008; Thornberry et al., 2004).

Many of the risk factors identified here have found additional support in more recent studies, and other factors not specifically examined in the earlier studies have also been identified (see Loeber & Farrington, 2012). Researchers have also observed a *cumulative* effect of risk factors, such that exposure to multiple risk factors increases the likelihood of later antisocial behavior (Farrington, 1997; Herrenkohl et al., 2000). Other research has shown that the deleterious effects of exposure to one or more risk factors may be mitigated by the presence of *protective* factors that help insulate the child from negative influences—for example, intolerant attitudes toward deviance, supportive relationships with parents or other adults, or a strong commitment to school (see discussions in Loeber & Farrington, 2012; Office of the Surgeon General, 2001).

Pathways to Delinquency

Considerable attention has been paid in recent years to the developmental "pathways" followed by adolescents as they progress toward deeper involvement in delinquency. The most ambitious research to date in this regard has taken place within the broader context of three coordinated longitudinal studies undertaken in furtherance of yet another major Office of Juvenile Justice and Delinquency Prevention initiative—the Program of Research on the Causes and Correlates of Delinquency. Based on an initial analysis of the offense trajectories of boys tracked over an extended period in the Pittsburgh Youth Study, project director Rolf Loeber and his associates identified three distinct patterns of escalating delinquency (Kelley, Loeber, Keenan, & DeLamatre, 1997):

- **Authority conflict** is the first and earliest pathway. The pathway begins with stubborn behavior (Stage 1) and can be followed by defiance (Stage 2), such as refusal and disobedience. This, in turn, can be followed by authority avoidance (Stage 3), such as truancy and running away from home. The authority conflict pathway applies to boys prior to age 12, because after that age, some youth are likely to enter the pathway at the highest levels with behaviors such as truancy and staying out late at night.
- **Covert** acts and their escalation are addressed in the second pathway. This pathway tends to start with minor covert behaviors (Stage 1), such as lying and shoplifting, and can be followed by property damage (Stage 2), including

vandalism and fire setting, and later by more serious forms of property crimes (Stage 3), such as burglary.

- **Overt** or increasingly aggressive acts make up the third pathway. This sequence starts with minor aggression (Stage 1), such as annoying others and bullying. This can be followed by physical fighting (Stage 2), including gang fighting, and then by violence (Stage 3), such as attacking someone, strong-arming, and raping. (pp. 8–9)

The three-pathway model has been replicated in a variety of contexts, including various subsets of the Pittsburgh sample and in both the Rochester Youth Development Study and the Denver Youth Survey. Summarizing their findings in a later report, the project directors of the three causes and correlates studies reiterated the conclusion that youth tend to follow an orderly sequence as they move from less serious to more serious delinquency, even in those instances where they progress on multiple pathways, engaging in a wider variety of delinquent behaviors as they get older (Thornberry et al., 2004). Referencing related aspects of the studies, they emphasized the predictive importance of early onset (i.e., childhood aggression beginning before age 13), child maltreatment, and gang membership as precursors of escalating involvement in delinquent behavior. But they also cautioned that accurate differentiation between those whose behavior persists and escalates over time and those who desist following a period of experimentation remains distressingly elusive.

Different for Girls?

Seeking to remedy the general dearth of attention paid to delinquent girls even as the gender gap in arrest rates narrows (see Chapter 7 of this book; Puzzanchera, 2013; Zahn et al., 2008), researchers have begun compiling an empirical record addressing the developmental pathways girls follow and the risk and protective factors that influence their delinquent involvement. While some have concluded that girls tend to follow the same developmental pathways as boys and that the risk factors for male and female delinquency are similar, others have found girls to follow distinctive routes and to respond differently to particular risk factors and protective factors (see discussions in S. R. Hawkins, Graham, Williams, & Zahn, 2009; Howell, 2009; Huizinga et al., 2013; Zahn et al., 2010).

With remarkable consistency, research on female delinquency points to a cluster of life circumstances shared by large proportions of delinquent girls. For example, in one study of girls in the California juvenile justice system, 92% of offenders reported a history of physical, emotional, and/or sexual abuse; 95% lacked a stable home environment; 91% had experienced some form of school failure; and 75% had a history of drug or alcohol abuse (Acoca & Dedel, 1998; see also Acoca, 1999). In another study, focus groups with system-involved girls in 10 California counties revealed a set of risk factors for delinquency including family issues (family conflict, parental absence, parental criminality or drug abuse, poor communication); sexual, physical, and emotional abuse; running away from home; substance abuse; gang involvement and fighting; school difficulties and negative attitudes toward school; and early and inappropriate sexual behavior (Bloom, Owen, Rosenbaum, & Deschenes, 2003). The themes of sexual victimization, family disruption, educational failure, substance abuse, and running away also permeate Chesney-Lind's examinations of the lives of female delinquents and the ways in which gender stratification and its consequences condition not only their delinquency but also their "invisibility" once drawn into the juvenile justice system (see especially Chesney-Lind, Morash, & Stevens, 2008; Chesney-Lind & Shelden, 2004). These themes appear as well in Howell's (2009) discussion of girls' delinquent careers. Linking together findings from numerous studies of female delinquents, OJJDP's former deputy administrator and long-time director of research and program development built the case for a sequence of six "stepping-stones" for girls following a pathway toward serious, chronic, and/or violent delinquency. Describing a process grounded in the notion that the "gendered" nature of risk factors that girls experience in common with boys may exacerbate the impact on girls, Howell traced a pathway leading from physical and/or sexual child abuse to mental health problems, drug abuse, running away from home, youth gang activity and, finally, juvenile justice system involvement.

CONCLUSION

This brief overview has taken a highly selective look at several aspects of the delinquency problem that have recently drawn the attention of delinquency researchers. As indicated at the outset, the goal has been to highlight statistics and research findings that help point the way toward more effective ways of preventing and responding to delinquency. But the lessons of research are not always straightforward, and the policy implications of studies addressing one aspect of research may lead us in very different directions from those emerging from a different line of research, or point us in different directions depending upon other considerations.

We have learned, for example, that delinquency is "normal" in adolescence but that most of us desist from illegal activity as we enter adulthood. In fact, age consistently ranks among the strongest correlates of criminal behavior (Farrington, 1986; Federal Bureau of Investigation, 2012; Hirschi & Gottfredson, 1983), and the pervasiveness of delinquent involvement during adolescence followed by desistance in early adulthood is now well documented (see Moffitt, 1993; Thornberry et al., 2004). Even among serious juvenile offenders, a life-course trajectory leading toward desistance in adulthood appears to be the norm rather than the exception (MacArthur Foundation Research Network on Adolescent Development and Juvenile Justice, n.d.; Mulvey et al., 2004; Sampson & Laub, 2003).

These patterns offer at least a modicum of support for the arguments of labeling theorists that juvenile court intervention is unnecessary or even counterproductive for most youthful law violators (Lemert, 1967; Schur, 1973). Does this mean we should follow their advice and avoid intervention altogether or intervene only if it is absolutely essential in order to protect public safety? Or does it direct us to heed the findings of research on risk factors and pathways to escalating delinquency, doing our best to identify potential life-course-persistent offenders as early as possible, so we can steer them in a different direction while leaving the adolescence-limited offenders alone as much as possible?

As the researchers involved in the causes and correlates studies discovered, early intervention is crucial to the success of efforts to divert youth from pathways leading to increasingly serious and persistent delinquency; so a this too will pass approach risks waiting until the opportunity to intervene effectively is long past (Kelley et al., 1997, p. 17; see also Thornberry et al., 2004). But categorizing young offenders based on the presence of known risk factors is not a panacea either. Aside from questions about the fairness of treating youth differently based on personal characteristics rather than on the nature of the offense, even the most sophisticated research still lacks the ability to accurately distinguish "persisters" from "experimenters" (Kelley et al., 1997). Statistical association between a particular characteristic and later antisocial behavior cannot be taken as an indication that a youth exposed to that risk factor, or even to a constellation of factors, will necessarily become a serious or chronic offender later in life. It also bears emphasis that the findings of individual studies, or even of a combination of studies, cannot be taken as definitive with respect to factors that predict later delinquent behavior. Aside from variations in the overall quality of study design and execution that impact results, the focus of research varies considerably from one study to the next. Some studies investigate predictors of *violent* behavior, while others expand the focus to encompass predictors of *serious* delinquency, whether violent or otherwise, or even to *any* delinquent involvement. Yet others investigate predictors of *chronic* antisocial behavior continuing into adulthood, or narrow the focus to risk factors for engagement in particular *types* of delinquent activity or other antisocial behavior (e.g., gang membership, sex offenses, or intimate partner violence). Likewise, the independent variables that are tested differ across studies, and study samples differ in ways that greatly affect results (e.g., risk factors may be very different for males and females or for youth of different racial groups, so findings based on a study of one group cannot be generalized to others). Even the measures of delinquency (arrest data, self-reports, etc.) differ tremendously from one study to the next in ways that impact results.

These observations offer just a hint of the many ways in which delinquency research can be used to stimulate consideration of policy innovations carrying the potential to divert youth from deeper involvement in delinquent behavior. But they should also serve as a caution against thoughtlessly translating research into policy without recognizing the probabilistic nature of the findings and the potentially conflicting implications for preventing or responding to delinquency arising from different lines of research.

DISCUSSION QUESTIONS

1. If delinquent behavior is really a normal part of adolescent development that most youth engage in to some degree, what should be done about those who are caught, and what characteristics of the offense and the offender do you think should be taken into consideration in deciding how to respond in a particular case?

2. In light of what we know about adolescent development, the pervasiveness of adolescence-limited delinquency, and the distribution of crime across age groups (i.e., the correlation between age and crime), what maximum age for juvenile court jurisdiction would you consider most appropriate?

3. Given the importance of early onset as a risk factor for later involvement in serious, violent, and chronic offending, should young children who are caught committing delinquent acts be treated differently from adolescents who commit comparable offenses?

4. Based on what we know about risk factors and pathways to delinquency, what elements would you recommend including in a prevention program in order to maximize its effectiveness in steering young people away from delinquency? What differences would you recommend in prevention programs targeting the following groups?

   - Adolescents versus preteens
   - Males versus females
   - Youth at high risk to become life-course-persistent offenders versus those likely to remain adolescence-limited offenders

5. How might research on adolescent development, risk factors, and pathways to delinquency be used to facilitate correctional intervention with youth who have been caught committing delinquent acts?

NOTES

1. Although the many shortcomings of early self-report studies have not been entirely alleviated, increasing sophistication of the sampling frames, measures of delinquency, and question formats employed in contemporary survey instruments has greatly enhanced their utility as indicators of delinquent behavior (Brame et al., 2004; Hindelang, Hirschi, & Weis, 1981; Huizinga & Elliott, 1986; Thornberry & Krohn, 2000).

2. This figure is commonly traced to Wolfgang, Figlio, and Sellin's (1972) seminal finding that about 6% of boys born in Philadelphia in 1945 were responsible for over half of all offenses committed by youth in the "birth cohort." Moffitt (1993) cites a broad array of subsequent studies that have obtained comparable results with respect to various measures of serious and chronic antisocial behavior among children, adolescents, and adults.

REFERENCES

Acoca, L. (1999). Investing in girls: A 21st century strategy. *Juvenile Justice, 6*(1), 3–13. Retrieved from https://www.ncjrs.gov/pdffiles1/ojjdp/178254.pdf

Acoca, L., & Dedel, K. (1998). *No place to hide: Understanding and meeting the needs of girls in the California juvenile justice system.* San Francisco, CA: National Council on Crime and Delinquency.

Bloom, B., Owen, B., Rosenbaum, J., & Deschenes, E. P. (2003). Focusing on girls and young women: A gendered perspective on female delinquency. *Women & Criminal Justice, 14*(2/3), 117–136.

Bonnie, R. J., Johnson, R. L., Chemers, B. M., & Schuck, J. (Eds.). (2013). *Reforming juvenile justice: A developmental approach.* Washington, DC: National Academies Press.

Brame, R., Fagan, J., Piquero, A. R., Schubert, C. A., & Steinberg, L. (2004). Criminal careers of serious delinquents in two cities. *Youth Violence and Juvenile Justice, 2*(3), 256–272.

Chesney-Lind, M., Morash, M., & Stevens, T. (2008). Girls' troubles, girls' delinquency, and gender responsive programming: A review. *The Australian and New Zealand Journal of Criminology, 41*(1), 162–189.

Chesney-Lind, M., & Shelden, R. G. (2004). *Girls, delinquency and juvenile justice* (3rd ed.). Belmont, CA: Wadsworth.

Farrington, D. P. (1986). Age and crime. In M. Tonry & N. Morris (Eds.), *Crime and justice: An annual review of research* (Vol. 7, pp. 189–250). Chicago, IL: University of Chicago Press.

Farrington, D. P. (1997). Early prevention of violent and nonviolent youthful offending. *European Journal on Criminal Policy and Research, 5,* 51–66.

Federal Bureau of Investigation. (1996–2011). *Crime in the United States, 1995–2010.* Retrieved from http://www.fbi.gov/about-us/cjis/ucr/ucr

Federal Bureau of Investigation. (2012). *Crime in the United States, 2011.* Retrieved from http://www.fbi.gov/about-us/cjis/ucr/crime-in-the-u.s/2011/crime-in-the-u.s.-2011

Griffin, P. (2012). Legal boundaries between the juvenile and criminal justice systems in the United States. In R. Loeber & D. P. Farrington (Eds.), *From juvenile delinquency to adult crime: Criminal careers, justice policy and prevention* (pp. 184–199). New York, NY: Oxford University Press.

Griffin, P., Addie, S., Adams, B., & Firestine, K. (2011). *Trying juveniles as adults: An analysis of state transfer laws and reporting.* Washington, DC: Office of Juvenile Justice and Delinquency Prevention. Retrieved from https://www.ncjrs.gov/pdffiles1/ojjdp/232434.pdf

Grisso, T., & Schwartz, R. G. (Eds.). (2000). *Youth on trial: A developmental perspective on juvenile justice.* Chicago, IL: University of Chicago Press.

Grisso, T., Steinberg, L., Woolard, J., Cauffman, E., Scott, E., Graham, S., . . . Schwartz, R. (2003). Juveniles' competence to stand trial: A comparison of adolescents' and adults' capacities as trial defendants. *Law and Human Behavior, 27*(4), 333–363.

Hawkins, J. D., Herrenkohl, T., Farrington, D. P., Brewer, D., Catalano, R. F., & Harachi, T. W. (1998). A review of predictors of youth violence. In R. Loeber & D. P. Farrington (Eds.), *Serious and violent juvenile offenders: Risk factors and successful interventions* (pp. 106–146). Thousand Oaks, CA: SAGE.

Hawkins, J. D., Herrenkohl, T. I., Farrington, D. P., Brewer, D., Catalano, R. F., Harachi, T. W., & Cothern, L. (2000, April). *Predictors of youth violence* [Bulletin]. Washington, DC: Office of Juvenile Justice and Delinquency Prevention. Retrieved from http://www.ncjrs.gov/pdffiles1/ojjdp/179065.pdf

Hawkins, S. R., Graham, P. W., Williams, J., & Zahn, M. A. (2009). *Resilient girls—Factors that protect against delinquency.* Washington, DC: Office of Juvenile Justice and Delinquency Prevention. Retrieved from https://www.ncjrs.gov/pdffiles1/ojjdp/220124.pdf

Herrenkohl, T. I., Maguin, E., Hill, K. G., Hawkins, J. D., Abbott, R. D., & Catalano, R. F. (2000). Developmental risk factors for youth violence. *Journal of Adolescent Health, 26*(7), 176–186.

Hindelang, M. J., Hirschi, T., & Weiss, J. G. (1981). *Measuring delinquency.* Beverly Hills, CA: SAGE.

Hirschi, T., & Gottfredson, M. R., (1983). Age and the explanation of crime. *American Journal of Sociology, 89*(3), 552–584.

Howell, J. C. (2009). *Preventing and reducing delinquency: A comprehensive framework* (2nd ed.). Thousand Oaks, CA: SAGE.

Huizinga, D., & Elliott, D. S. (1986). Reassessing the reliability and validity of self-reported data. *Journal of Quantitative Criminology, 2*(4), 293–327.

Huizinga, D., Miller, S., & the Conduct Problems Prevention Research Group. (2013). *Developmental sequences of girls' delinquent behavior.* Washington, DC: Office of Juvenile Justice and Delinquency Prevention. Retrieved from http://ojjdp.gov/pubs/238276.pdf

Illinois Juvenile Court Act § 5 (1899) Ill. Laws 133. 33.

Jensen, G. F., & Rojek, D. G. (2009). *Delinquency and youth crime* (4th ed.). Long Grove, IL: Waveland Press.

Kelley, B. T., Loeber, R., Keenan, K., & DeLamatre, M. (1997). *Developmental pathways in boys' disruptive and delinquent behavior.* Washington, DC: Office of Juvenile Justice and Delinquency Prevention. Retrieved from http://www.ncjrs.gov/pdffiles/165692.pdf

Lauritsen, J. L. (2005). Racial and ethnic differences in juvenile offending. In D. Hawkins & K. Kempf-Leonard (Eds.), *Our children, their children: Confronting race and ethnic differences in American criminal justice* (pp. 83–104). Chicago, IL: University of Chicago Press.

Lemert, E. M. (1967). Appendix D: The juvenile court: Quest and realities. In *Task force report: Juvenile delinquency and youth crime—Report on juvenile justice and consultants' papers* (Vol. 36, pp. 91–106). Washington, DC: U.S. Government Printing Office.

Lipsey, M. W., & Derzon, J. H. (1998). Predictors of violent or serious delinquency in adolescence and early adulthood: A synthesis of longitudinal research. In R. Loeber & D. P. Farrington (Eds.), *Serious and violent juvenile offenders: Risk factors and successful interventions* (pp. 86–105). Thousand Oaks, CA: SAGE.

Loeber, R., & Farrington, D. P. (Eds.). (2012). *From juvenile delinquency to adult crime: Criminal careers, justice policy and prevention.* New York, NY: Oxford University Press.

Lyman, R. (2014, February 27). Pivotal point is seen on legalizing marijuana. *The New York Times,* pp. A1, A3.

Maas, C., Herrenkohl, T. I., & Sousa, C. (2008). Review of research on child maltreatment and violence in youth. *Trauma, Violence, & Abuse: A Review Journal, 9*(1), 56–67.

MacArthur Foundation Research Network on Adolescent Development and Juvenile Justice. (n.d.). *Creating turning points for serious adolescent offenders: Research on pathways to desistance* (Issue Brief 2). Retrieved from http://www.adjj.org/downloads/7230issue_brief_2.pdf

McCord, J., Widom, C. S., & Crowell, N. A. (Eds.). (2001). *Juvenile crime, juvenile justice.* Washington, DC: National Academy Press. Retrieved from http://www.nap.edu/catalog.php?record_id=9747

Moffitt, T. E. (1993). Adolescence-limited and life-course-persistent antisocial behavior: A developmental taxonomy. *Psychological Review, 100*(4), 674–701.

Mulvey, E. P., Steinberg, L., Fagan, J., Cauffman, E., Hecker, T., Piquero, A., . . . Losoya, S. H. (2004). Theory and research on desistance from antisocial activity among adolescent serious offenders. *Youth Violence and Juvenile Justice, 2*(3), pp. 213–236.

Office of Juvenile Justice and Delinquency Prevention. (2012). *OJJDP statistical briefing book.* Retrieved from http://www.ojjdp.gov/ojstatbb/structure_process/qa04101.asp? qaDate=2011

Office of National Drug Control Policy. (n.d.). *Marijuana Resource Center: State laws related to marijuana.* Washington, DC: The White House, Office of National Drug Control Policy. Retrieved from http://www.whitehouse.gov/ondcp/state-laws-related-to-marijuana

Office of the Surgeon General. (2001). *Youth violence: A report of the surgeon general.* Washington, DC: U.S. Department of Health and Human Services, Office of Public Health and Science, Office of the Surgeon General. Retrieved from http://www.ncbi.nlm .nih.gov/books/NBK44294/

Puzzanchera, C. (2013). *Juvenile arrests 2011.* Washington, DC: Office of Juvenile Justice and Delinquency Prevention. Retrieved from http://www.ojjdp.gov/pubs/244476.pdf

Sampson, R. J., & Laub, J. H. (2003). Life-course desisters? Trajectories of crime among delinquent boys followed to age 70. *Criminology, 41*(3), 555–592.

Schur, E. M. (1973). *Radical nonintervention: Rethinking the delinquency problem.* Englewood Cliffs, NJ: Prentice Hall.

Scott, E. S., & Grisso, T. (1997). The evolution of adolescence: A developmental perspective on juvenile justice reform. *Journal of Criminal Law and Criminology, 88*(1), 137–189.

Scott, E. S., & Steinberg, L. (2008). *Rethinking juvenile justice.* Cambridge, MA: Harvard University Press.

Snyder, H. N., & Sickmund, M. (2006). *Juvenile offenders and victims: 2006 national report.* Washington, DC: Office of Juvenile Justice and Delinquency Prevention. Retrieved from http://www.ojjdp.gov/ojstatbb/nr2006/

Steinberg, L., & Scott, E. (2003). Less guilty by reason of adolescence: Developmental immaturity, diminished responsibility, and the juvenile death penalty. *American Psychologist, 58*(12), 1009–1018.

Thornberry, T. P., Huizinga, D., & Loeber, R. (2004). The causes and correlates studies: Findings and policy implications. *Juvenile Justice Journal, 9*(1), 3–19. Retrieved from http://www.ncjrs.gov/pdffiles1/ojjdp/203555.pdf

Thornberry, T. P., & Krohn, M. D. (2000). The self-report method for measuring delinquency and crime. In D. Duffee (Ed.), *Criminal justice 2000: Vol. 4. Measurement and analysis of crime and justice* (pp. 33–84). Washington, DC: National Institute of Justice. Retrieved from http://www.ncjrs.gov/criminal_justice2000/vol_4/04b.pdf

Walsh, J. (Ed.). (2013). *Q&A: Legal marijuana in Colorado and Washington.* Washington, DC: The Brookings Institution. Retrieved from http://www.brookings.edu/research/ papers/2013/05/21-legal-marijuana-colorado-washington

Wolfgang, M. E., Figlio, R. M., & Sellin, T. (1972). *Delinquency in a birth cohort.* Chicago, IL: University of Chicago Press.

Zahn, M. A., Agnew, R., Fishbein, D., Miller, S., Winn, D., Dakoff, G., . . . Chesney-Lind, M. (2010). *Causes and correlates of girls' delinquency.* Washington, DC: Office of Juvenile Justice and Delinquency Prevention. Retrieved from https://www.ncjrs.gov/pdffiles1/ ojjdp/226358.pdf

Zahn, M. A., Brumbaugh, S., Steffensmeier, D., Feld, B. C., Morash, M., Chesney-Lind, M., . . . Kruttschnitt, C. (2008). *Violence by teenage girls: Trends and context.* Washington, DC: Office of Juvenile Justice and Delinquency Prevention. Retrieved from http://www .ncjrs.gov/pdffiles1/ojjdp/218905.pdf

CHAPTER 7

Gender Matters

Trends in Girls' Criminality

Meda Chesney-Lind

In 2006, girls accounted for nearly a third (29.1%) of juvenile arrests (Federal Bureau of Investigation [FBI], 2007). From the 1960s to the 1980s, girls accounted for between 17% and 22% of juvenile arrests, one fifth of the total (Chesney-Lind & Shelden, 2004, pp. 9–11). This is a remarkable increase in their "share" of official delinquency and one that requires exploration.

The forces that create criminal behavior may be different for adolescents, and we now suspect that this has been particularly the case for the last two decades. If one were to use arrests as a gauge of delinquency trends, female activity has been trending differently from that of their male counterparts. The much discussed "crime drop" in juvenile delinquency in the 1990s was more correctly a *boy* crime drop, fueled by a decline in gun- and drug-related violence among boys and young men (Blumstein & Wallman, 2000).

Looking specifically at arrest data, it appears that boys' arrests peaked in 1993 and then began dropping, but during the same decade, girls' arrests continued to climb. According to FBI reports (FBI, 2004, p. 275, Table 33), between 1993 and 2002 girls' arrests increased 6.4%, whereas boys' arrests decreased by 16.4%. Between 1997 and 2006, the data do not show a stark increase in female offenses; nonetheless, their arrests decreased by a far smaller percentage than boys', 17.6% compared to 26.4% (FBI, 2007, Table 33). This said, in the most recent year for which we have data, girls' arrests seem finally to have leveled off (decreasing by 1.7% between 2005 and 2006), whereas arrests of boys began to move up, particularly serious violent crime.

Juvenile delinquency has long been assumed to be a male problem, and girls were either ignored or excluded from consideration, particularly by researchers who worked during the formative years of criminological theory building. Hirschi (1969) excluded self-report data on females from analysis in his classic *Causes of Delinquency*. Others regarded delinquency as quintessentially male; the delinquent was the "rogue male," according to Cohen's (1955) classic book on gangs.

107

Seminal criminological theories assumed delinquency to be male and therefore focused on male offenders; research settings were used to access boys and young men involved in these typically male offenses (see Chesney-Lind & Shelden, 2004). As a result, programs were aimed at male delinquency prevention and intervention (see Girls Incorporated, 1996; Lipsey, 1992). Yet at virtually all levels within the juvenile justice system, there are more girls than ever. The academic, policy, and programmatic neglect of girls' issues, coupled with recent arrest trends, suggest that it is clearly time to consider female delinquency in its own right, not as an afterthought to boys' delinquency.

DELINQUENCY: GENDER MATTERS

The picture of female delinquency that emerges from the available data reflects the existence of substantial gender differences in both self-reported and official delinquency. For starters, girls are less "serious" delinquents than boys. If one examines gender differences in court populations around the country, for example, girls' delinquency differs from boys' in that it is less chronic and less serious. Based on an in-depth study of one large, urban court system, Snyder and Sickmund (1999, p. 80) found that 73% of females (compared to 54% of males) who enter the juvenile justice system never return to court on a new referral. They also noted that, of the youth who came to court for delinquency offenses, only 3% of females had committed a violent offense by the age of 18, compared to 10% of boys; likewise, only 5.5% of girls, compared to 18.8% of boys, had more than four referrals to court (p. 81).

The significant role played by minor offenses in girls' delinquency also emerged in the Annie E. Casey Foundation study of youth in detention in several cities. Researchers found that many more girls than boys were detained for "minor" offenses, such as public disorder, probation violations, status offenses, and traffic offenses. Finally, it was also learned that "rather than histories of violence, detained girls had more status offenses and misdemeanors in their histories" (American Bar Association & National Bar Association [ABA & NBA], 2001, pp. 18–19). This research documented that race as well as gender matters in girls' detentions; African American girls make up half of those in secure detention, according to this study, and Latinas, 13% (ABA & NBA, 2001, pp. 20–21).

The American Correctional Association's (ACA, 1990) earlier study of girls held in state training schools found that substantial numbers of girls were incarcerated for probation or parole violation (15%), followed by aggravated assault (9.5%), larceny-theft (9%), and runaway (6.5%). Roughly half the girls were White (50.5%), nearly a third were Black or partly Black (31.7%), 6.2% were Hispanic, and 7.7% were Native American (p. 47). Most were between 16 and 17 years of age, and 18.6% were mothers at the time of their incarceration.

That same study found disconcertingly high rates of sexual abuse among incarcerated girls; over 60% had been the victim of some form of physical abuse, and 54% reported being the victim of sexual abuse. This finding may or may not explain why over 80% of the girls in training schools report that they have run away from home at least once, and a staggering 50% have run away from home six or more times.

The ACA (1990) study also found that 60% of this population needed substance-abuse treatment at intake and that over half were multiply addicted. They also reported that many of these girls took drugs (34.4%) or drank alcohol (11.4%) as a form of self-medication to make themselves feel better. In addition, a majority stated that they used alcohol (50%) and marijuana (64%) regularly. Of the girls who were substance dependent, most started using between the ages of 12 and 15 (pp. 59–60). Although models that delineate the relationship between delinquency and substance abuse have largely involved adolescent males, evidence for females also indicates that substance abuse is highly correlated with disruptive behavior (Girls Incorporated, 1996).

These portraits of officially delinquent girls, particularly the ACA study, point out two important themes in girls' delinquency, particularly the form that brings girls into the juvenile justice system. First, although most girls' delinquency involves offenses that are not as legally serious as those committed by boys, this does not mean that they do not have serious problems, particularly those who stay in the system. Just because girls are arrested and referred to juvenile courts for legally less serious offenses gives a false impression; these "trivial" offenses often mask significant and ongoing problems, like sexual abuse, for which gender-responsive programming might well be appropriate.

GIRLS' CRIME, GIRLS' OFFENSES

An overview of girls' arrest patterns reflects and amplifies the themes found in the portraits of official delinquents (see Table 7.1) and seems a logical starting point in discussing key themes in female delinquency. In 2006, girls were most frequently arrested for larceny-theft, a property offense which, as we shall see, for girls means shoplifting (Campbell & Harrington, 2000; Chesney-Lind & Shelden, 2004).

Girls were also arrested in large numbers for running away from home, an offense for which only juveniles can be taken into custody. Finally, large numbers of girls, particularly in recent years, were arrested for the seemingly nontraditional offenses of simple assault and disorderly conduct. Boys' arrests are more diffuse, meaning that the top offenses account for slightly over half of all boys' arrests (58.9%), whereas for girls over two thirds (68.4%) of their arrests are accounted for by these five offense categories. The data also indicate that girls' arrests for simple assault have replaced runaway arrests as a key theme in girls' official delinquency.

GIRLS' VIOLENCE: WHEN SHE WAS BAD

Female aggression and violence have been much in the news in recent decades. Whether it was the female revolutionary of the 1970s, the girl gangbanger of the

Table 7.1	Rank Order of Arrests for Juveniles, 1997 and 2006 (figures based on % distribution within each gender cohort)

Male		Female	
1997	2006	1997	2006
(1) All Others (17.3)[1]	All Others (18.4)	Larceny-Theft (22.9)	Larceny-Theft (18.3)
(2) Larceny-Theft (16.3)	Larceny-Theft (10.9)	Runaways (16.2)	All Others (16.1)
(3) Drug Abuse (8.6)	Other Assaults (10.5)	All Others (15.3)	Other Assaults (12.9)
(4) Other Assaults (8.1)	Drug Abuse (10.4)	Other Assaults (8.9)	Disorderly Conduct (10.7)
(5) Curfew (6.6)	Disorderly Conduct (8.7)	Disorderly Conduct (6.6)	Runaway (10.4)

	Male		Female	
	2006	1997	2006	1997
Arrests for Serious Violent Offenses	4.9	5.2	2.5	2.7
Arrests for All Violent Offenses	12.9	15.7	11.1	15.6
Arrests for Status Offenses	10.9	9.5	23.9	17.1

Source: FBI, *Uniform Crime Reports: 2006 Crime in the United States* (2006, Table 33, "Ten-Year Arrest Trends"). Retrieved from http://www.fbi.gov/about-us/cjis/ucr/crime-in-the-u.s/2006

[1]"All Others" refers to a variety of offenses, usually against state and local ordinances. Among the most common are public nuisance, trespassing, failure to appear on warrants, contempt of court, and, for juveniles especially, violation of various court orders (e.g., probation, parole) and certain status offenses. This category does not include traffic offenses. Status offenses other than runaway and curfew also account for a large proportion of girls' arrests for other offenses (Chesney-Lind & Shelden, 2004).

1980s, the *violent girl* of the 1990s, or the mean girls who ushered in the new millennia, the last few decades have seen a cavalcade of girls' acting out in ways that seem far worse than merely unfeminine (see Chesney-Lind & Irwin, 2008). Quite often, the media frame is one that juxtaposes girls' aggression or violence with stereotypical images of a girlhood devoid of behavior of this sort. The 1993 *Newsweek* issue on youth violence, as an example, included an insert on girls' violence complete with a picture of an African American girl wearing a bandanna over her face, peering at the camera over the barrel of a gun, with the headline "Girls Will Be Girls" (Leslie, Biddle, Rosenberg, & Wayne, 1993, p. 44). In many ways, this gender juxtaposition makes sense in a country that grew up reading Longfellow's

(1992, p. 513) poem about his daughter: "When she was good, she was very, very good, but when she was bad she was horrid."

Of course, the reality is much more complex. First, it turns out that self-report data routinely show that girls act out violently and have been since the earliest self-report data were published (Elliot & Voss, 1974). Second, there appears to be very little evidence that these patterns have changed in the last decade, despite the media frenzy on the topic. The Centers for Disease Control and Prevention (CDC) in Atlanta has monitored youthful behavior in a national sample of school-aged youth in a number of domains (including violence) at regular intervals since 1991 in a biennial survey titled the Youth Risk Behavior Survey. As an example, a review of the data collected over the 1990s and into this century reveals that although 34.4% of girls surveyed in 1991 said that they had been in a physical fight in the previous year, by 2001 that figure had dropped to 23.9%, a 30.5% decrease in girls' fighting; boys' violence also decreased during the same period but less dramatically—from 50.2% to 43.1%, a 14.1% drop (Centers for Disease Control and Prevention [CDC], 1992–2004).

While girls had long reported that they were acting out violently, their arrests, particularly in the 1960s and 1970s, did not necessarily reflect that reality. Instead, girls' arrests tended to emphasize petty and status offenses; by the 1990s, that had changed dramatically, as more girls were arrested, particularly for such seemingly "masculine" offenses as simple assault. Between 1997 and 2006, despite an overall decrease in girls' arrests, girls' arrests for simple assault continued to climb, increasing by 18.7%, while boys' arrests for the same offense declined by 4.3%.

Research increasingly suggests that these shifts in girls' arrests are not products of a change in behavior, with girls getting "more" violent. Not only do other measures of girls' criminality fail to show an increase in girls' violence, but there is ample evidence also that girls are being more heavily policed, particularly at home and in school (see Chesney-Lind & Irwin, 2008). Specifically, girls are being arrested for assault because of arguments with their parents, often their mothers (see Buzawa & Hotaling, 2006), or for "other assault" for fighting in school because of new zero-tolerance policies enacted after the Columbine shootings (see New York Civil Liberties Union [NYCLU], 2007). In decades past, this violence would have been ignored or labeled a status offense, like being "incorrigible" or a "person in need of supervision." Now, an arrest is made.

Girls are also staying in the system after being arrested for these new "violent" offenses. Between 1985 and 2002, the number of girls' delinquency cases referred to juvenile courts increased by 92%, compared to a 29% increase for males (Snyder & Sickmund, 2006). Arrests of girls for crimes of violence clearly played a role in this pattern: "For females, the largest 1985–2002 increase was in person offense cases (20%)." Finally, like the pattern seen in girls' arrests, girls have proportionately more person offense referrals than boys: 26% compared to 23% (Snyder & Sickmund, 2006, p. 160).

Girls' arrests for crimes of violence have also ushered in a dramatic increase in the incarceration of girls. Between 1991 and 2003, girls' detentions rose by 98%, compared to a 29% expansion by boys (Snyder & Sickmund, 2006, p. 210). Girls detained for violent offenses were far more likely to be held on other person offenses, like simple assault. Well over half (57.3%) of the girls but less than a third of the boys (32.4 %) were held for these minor forms of violence (Sickmund, Sladky, & Kang, 2004). Likewise, girls' commitments to facilities increased by an alarming 88% between 1991 and 2003, while boys' commitments increased by only 23% (Snyder & Sickmund, 2006, p. 210).

Media sensationalism aside, girls' behavior, including violence, needs to be placed within a larger discussion of girls' place in a society that expects and normalizes aggression and violence from boys while encouraging girls and women to be nice, pretty, and feminine. It is important to chart the contexts that produce violence in girls (see Morash & Chesney-Lind, 2008).

Some hints of these issues can be found in the backgrounds of girls who act out violently. In her analysis of self-reported violence in girls in Canada, Artz (1998) noted that girls who reported problems with violence reported significantly greater rates of victimization and abuse than their nonviolent counterparts, and girls who were violent reported greater fear of sexual assault, especially from their boyfriends. Specifically, 20% of violent girls stated they were physically abused at home, compared to 10% of violent males and 6.3% of nonviolent girls. Patterns for sexual abuse were even starker; roughly 1 out of 4 violent girls had been sexually abused compared to 1 in 10 nonviolent girls (Artz, 1998). Follow-up interviews with a small group of violent girls found that they had learned at home that might makes right and had engaged in *horizontal violence* directed at other powerless girls. Certainly, these findings provide little ammunition for those who would contend that the *new* violent girl is a product of any form of "emancipation." Histories of physical and sexual abuse, then, may be a theme in girls' physical aggression, just as it is in their runaway behavior.

Aggressive and violent girls are, ironically, often quite committed to the "ideology of familial patriarchy . . . [which] supports the abuse of women who violate the ideals of male power and control over women" (DeKeseredy, 2000, p. 46). This ideology is acted out by those males and females who insist that women be obedient, respectful, loyal, dependent, sexually accessible, and sexually faithful to males. Artz (1998) builds upon that point by suggesting that violent girls, more often than not, buy into these beliefs and "police" other girls' behaviors thus preserving the status quo, including their own continued oppression.

Such themes are particularly pronounced among girls who have the most serious problems with delinquency. Artz, Blais, and Nicholson (2000, p. 31) found that the majority of their girl respondents were also male focused, expressed hostility to other girls, and wanted very much to have boyfriends—always making sure that they had at least one, both in and out of jail. One girl strongly identified with the boys and saw herself as "one of the guys," also admitting that she had "always wanted to be a boy." Only one girl spoke little about boys—at 18 years of age, she was the oldest girl in the center. All the girls used derogatory terms to describe other girls, and when they spoke about girls, their words reflected views of females as "other." Many saw other girls as threats, particularly if they were pretty or "didn't know their place." A "pretty" girl, or a girl that the boys paid attention to, was a primary target for girl-to-girl victimization because she had the potential to unseat those who occupied the top rung on the "pretty power hierarchy" (Artz et al., 2000, p. 124). An "ugly" or "dirty" girl (a girl designated a slut) was also a primary target for girl-to-girl victimization because she "deserved" to be beaten for her unappealing looks and for her "unacceptable" behavior (Artz et al., 2000).

Such a perspective is puzzling, but the sad reality is that marginalized girls who have been the victims of male power often see that sort of agency as the only source of power available to them. Most of these girls regarded their victims as "responsible" for the violence that they committed, since they were acting as "sluts," "total bitches," or "assholes" (Artz et al., 2000, p. 189). Clearly, where these girls live, "you've gotta watch your back" because "the world is a piece of shit" (p. 189). Those girls who have problems with violence suggest that both girls' and women's victimization, as well as girls' violence toward other girls, are really twin products of a system of sexual inequality that valorizes male violence as agency and has girls growing up "seeing themselves through the eyes of males" (Artz, 1998, p. 204).

RUNNING AWAY: GIRLS COPING WITH TRAUMA AND ABUSE

Running away from home and prostitution remain the only two arrest categories in which more girls than boys are arrested. Many more girls are arrested for running away than for prostitution, despite the public fascination with the latter. In 2006, there were 38,461 girls arrested for running away, whereas less than 1,000 were arrested for prostitution. In 2006, girls constituted over half (56.4%) of those arrested for this one status offense. This means that, despite the intention of the Juvenile Justice and Delinquency Prevention Act of 1974, which, among other things, encouraged jurisdictions to divert and deinstitutionalize youth charged with status offenses, arrests for these offenses remained substantial. Having said this, it should be noted that the arrest rates for runaways have been decreasing significantly for both girls and boys; from 1997 to 2006, these arrests decreased by 47.1% for girls during the same period that arrests of girls for simple assault increased by 18.7% (FBI, 2007, Table 33).

For many years, statistics showing large numbers of girls arrested and referred to court for status offenses were taken as representative of the different types of male and female delinquency. Yet studies of actual delinquency show that girls and boys run away from home about equally. As an example, Canter (1982) found in the National Youth Survey that there was no evidence of greater female involvement, compared to males, in any category of delinquent behavior. Indeed, males were significantly more likely than females to commit status offenses. A study of inner-city adolescents who had been referred to a diversion program found that, while youth showed considerable, and expected, gender differences in official arrests, with males being referred for law violations and girls being referred for status offenses and "personal problems," self-report data from the same group "found that girls did not actually commit more status offenses than boys" (Rhodes & Fischer, 1993, p. 884). National self-report data collected from youth aged 12 to 16 also showed no gender difference in runaway behavior; roughly 10% of both boys and girls reported that they had "ever" run away from home (Snyder & Sickmund, 1999, p. 54).

Thorne (1994), in her ethnography of gender in grade school, found that girls used "cosmetics, discussions of boyfriends, dressing sexually, and other forms of exaggerated 'teen' femininity to challenge adult, and class- and race-based authority in schools." She also found that "the double standard persists, and girls who are overtly sexual run the risk of being labeled sluts" (p. 156).

Contemporary ethnographies of school life echo the validity of these parental perceptions. Orenstein's (cited in Thorne, 1994) observations also point to the durability of the sexual double standard; at the schools, she observed that sex "ruins girls" but "enhance[s] boys" (p. 57). Parents, too, according to Thorne (1994), have valid reasons to enforce the time-honored sexual double standard. Concern about sexual harassment and rape, to say nothing of HIV/AIDS, if their daughters are heterosexually active, have caused "parents in gestures that mix protection with punishment, (to) often tighten control of girls when they become adolescents, and sexuality becomes a terrain of struggle between the generations" (Thorne, 1994, p. 156; see also Lamb, 2003). Finally, Thorne notes that, sadly and ironically, as girls use sexuality as a proxy for independence, they reinforce their status as sexual objects seeking male approval—ultimately ratifying their status as the subordinate sex. Whatever the reason, parental attempts to adhere to and enforce the sexual double standard will continue to be a source of conflict between parents and their daughters.

Another reason for different responses to running away from home speaks to differences in boys' and girls' reasons for running away. Girls are, for example, much more likely than boys to be the victims of child sexual abuse. According to the *Executive Summary of the Third National Incidence Study,* girls are sexually abused 3 times more often than boys (Sedlak & Broadhurst, 1996). Sexual abuse typically starts early; both boys and girls are most vulnerable to abuse between the ages of 7 and 13 (Finkelhor, 1994). Not surprisingly, the evidence also suggests a link between this problem and girl delinquency—particularly running away from home, since girls are more likely to be the victims of intrafamilial abuse (Finkelhor, 1994). Moreover, this abuse lasts longer and has more serious consequences than stranger abuse (Finkelhor, 1994).

Widom (1995) found that victims of child sexual abuse are 27.7 times more likely than nonvictims to be arrested for prostitution as adults; it is speculated that some victims become prostitutes (if female) or abusers (if male) because they have a difficult time relating to others except on sexual terms. Not all studies find a link between sexual abuse, running away, and prostitution, however. In a comparison of prostitute and nonprostitute youth, Nadon, Koverola, and Schludeermann (1998) found that prostitute youth were not significantly more likely than an appropriate comparison group to report sexual abuse. However, adolescent prostitutes ran away from home significantly more often than adolescent nonprostitutes. Nadon and colleagues state that "it was determined prostitution may be a particular survival strategy for girls in very difficult circumstances" (p. 206).

Another study that tracked the gendered consequences of running away for girls and boys (Tyler, Hoyt, Whitbeck, & Cauce, 2004) showed that, for females, running away from home for the first time was associated with engaging in deviant subsistence strategies, survival sex, and victimization by a "friend or acquaintance." For boys, survival sex was associated with stranger victimization; for homosexual boys, though, victimization came at the hands of an acquaintance or friend (Tyler et al., 2004, p. 153).

Most girl runaways have fled homes where abuse, including sexual abuse, was a prominent theme. Yet, ironically and tragically, their lives on the streets are almost always even more abusive because, like all other aspects of life, the streets are gendered. Once on the streets, girls quickly discover both the dangers involved in street life and the narrow range of survival options available to them. They also discover that they are in possession of a form of sexual capital that they can access, whereas boys tend to engage in a wider variety of survival strategies.

The tragedy here is that a girl who runs from physical and sexual abuse is forced to confront terrible choices: She does not want to return to an intolerable home, yet she cannot legally go to school, get employment, or find housing without risking return. In short, her legal options are criminalized by a system that has traditionally encouraged her to return home and obey her parents. Even systems that want to explore other sorts of placement possibilities face numerous challenges, not the least of which is a shortage of programs for girls (Freitas & Chesney-Lind, 2001). Faced with abysmal choices, some girls turn to survival sex, which they may not even recognize as sexual exploitation (Beyette, 1988), or some other form of sex work, like prostitution. For some, but not necessarily all, girl runaways, survival sex and possibly prostitution become a way to survive in the absence of few other earning skills (Campagna & Poffenberger, 1988; Miller, 1986).

WILD IN THE STREETS: GIRLS, DRUGS, AND ALCOHOL

A review of trends in girls' arrests for substance abuse also reveals a gendered pattern. Specifically, girls' arrests tended to increase for most offenses during the last decade, whereas boys' arrests decreased. As an example, the FBI (FBI, 2007, Table 33), reports that girls' arrests for disorderly conduct increased by 19.0%, while boys' arrests decreased by 22.1%. Likewise, girls' arrests for driving under the influence showed a 39.3% increase, as compared to a 6.4% decrease seen in boys' arrests.

Reviews of self-reported drug use, like the Youth Risk Behavior Surveillance System, indicate that male and female use of alcohol has actually declined in the most recent decade for which data are available (1991–2004), while marijuana and cocaine use has actually increased slightly among respondents. Moreover, there is an apparent gender convergence. In 1993, 50.1% of boys reported "current alcohol use," whereas 45.9% of girls did; in 2003, only 43.8% of boys and 45.8% of girls reported use. With marijuana, 20.6% of boys reported use in 1993, compared to 25.1% in 2003; for girls, 14.6 % reported use in 1993, compared to 19.3% in 2003 (CDC, 1992–2004).

In the area of drug use, at the point of arrest, in 1997, 29% of arrested girls tested positive for one or more illegal drugs, compared to 57% of boys, largely due to marijuana use (Belenko, Sprott, & Petersen, 2004, p. 6). In subsequent interviews with arrested youth, 33% of arrested and detained girls and 34% of boys reported some alcohol use, and 61% of girls, compared to 75% of boys, were drug involved (Belenko et al., 2004, p. 6).

In delinquent girls, depression is a major problem, whether we are discussing runaway youth, aggressive youth, or youth with substance abuse issues. In fact, girls in general are more likely to report problems of depression and anxiety than boys, and these trends are magnified among girls in the juvenile justice system (Belenko et al., 2004, p. 21).

Kataoka and colleagues (2001) found that female juvenile offenders were 3 times more likely than girls who were not in the system to show clinical symptoms of anxiety and depression. As mentioned earlier, many of the girls in the justice system have extensive histories of abuse, which can explain their choices to self-medicate in response to that traumatic history. The links between post-traumatic stress disorder (PTSD) and drug use are certainly more pronounced in girls than in boys. Deykin and Buka (1997) found that almost half (40%) of reported substance-abusing girls showed current prevalence of PTSD, compared to slightly more than one tenth of boys (12.3%).

SHOPLIFTING: YOU SHOPLIFT AS YOU SHOP

Property crimes, particularly larceny-theft, accounted for 1 out of 5 girls' arrests in 2006; in contrast, this offense accounted for only 1 in 10 boys' arrests. There is evidence that this offense is gendered, with the bulk of girls' larceny-thefts involving shoplifting, while boys are more involved in buying stolen goods and thefts from cars or bicycle theft (Campbell & Harrington, 2000; Chesney-Lind & Shelden, 2004). Girls' "share" of this offense has also increased over time, from 34.1% to 40.8% (FBI, 2007).

Such a gender shift is also apparent in the self-report data. Data collected from high school seniors suggest that while roughly a quarter (25.9%) of girls said they had taken something from a store without paying for it at least once in the past year, that this was about the same as a decade earlier (25.2%); for boys, the comparable figures were 30% in 2002 and 36% in 1994. Thus, although male shoplifting has been dropping, these data suggest that female involvement has stayed about the same (Bureau of Justice Statistics, 2003, Table 3.47). These data show that larceny-theft committed by boys has declined over time, possibly as a result of increased surveillance in malls (Hayward, 2004, p. 189), though it is not clear why this would have affected boys' but not girls' levels of shoplifting.

Increasingly, discussions of women's crime and changes in the volume of female offending have focused on the role played by economic marginalization and patterns of women's employment in property crimes (see English, 1993; Heimer, 2000). Specifically, females have experience as employees in retail settings and, as a consequence, often know the routines that characterize security in these establishments, even if they do not work there (English, 1993). As retail employees, they are also likely to augment often-meager salaries by stealing or shoplifting where they work (Franklin, 1979). Men, if they steal from the workplace, tend to be employed in higher level positions; if they steal, they are less likely to be caught (because they are less heavily supervised), they steal larger amounts, and they are often not prosecuted (Franklin, 1979).

According to self-report studies, however, males are more likely to shoplift. An English study found that males outnumbered females by a 2:1 ratio. Recall though, that recent U.S. data show that, while the gender gap has closed, that is because boys report doing less shoplifting. Another study found males to be more likely than females to shoplift, but the male-female ratio for youths "cautioned by the police" or actually sentenced was only 1.7:1 (Morris, 1987, p. 31). Morris (1987) suggests that females are more often detected by store personnel because the latter expect women to shoplift more than men and therefore watch women more.

Explanations of male and female shoplifting have generally been simplistic and gender biased. A common explanation for female shoplifting, according to Morris (1987, p. 65), is that it is "a result of subconscious motivations (kleptomania), depression (for example, resulting from the menopause), or poverty (for example, mothers on welfare who steal food)." A common explanation of male shoplifting is that it results from "peer-group pressure and the search for excitement" (p. 65).

One consideration that rarely appears in work on shoplifting is that young people, especially girls, may be inordinately sensitive to the consumer culture: They steal things they feel they need or indeed may actually need but cannot afford. For example, Campbell (1981) notes that women—young and old—are the targets of enormously expensive advertising campaigns for a vast array of personal products. They also constitute a large proportion of those who shop, spend more time doing so as a pastime, and consequently are exposed to greater temptation (Campbell, 1981, pp. 122–123). Temptation is probably most pronounced for girls, whose popularity is tied very closely to physical appearance and participation in fashions and fads (see Adler & Adler, 1998).

Participation in the teen consumer subculture is costly, and if a young woman cannot afford participation, she is likely to steal her way in. It is no surprise, then, that girls are more likely than boys to shoplift cosmetics and clothes (Campbell, 1981, pp. 122–123). Moreover, because girls spend more time shopping, they undergo more scrutiny by store detectives, who report they are suspicious of young people in groups, particularly if they are not dressed well (May, 1978). In short, girl subculture, where popularity is based on an appearance that includes "expensive clothing" and other "material possessions" (Adler & Adler, 1998, p. 47), may be particularly hard on girls from poor families. They are bombarded daily with the message that they are acceptable only if they look a particular way, and yet they do not have the money necessary to purchase that look.

In general, shoplifting by girls must be placed within the context of girls' lives in a youth- and consumer-oriented culture. Here, the drawbacks of not having money are evident, and for girls there are few avenues to success. Shoplifting, then, is a social cost attributable to goods attainable only with money that many of them do not have.

CONCLUSION

Girls are an increasingly large proportion of those being arrested. The arrest data show large numbers of girls arrested for assault, yet there are reasons to suspect that the increases seen in the arrest data are reflective not of actual behavior but rather of changes in the policing of girls. That said, girls' aggression and violence are best understood from within the context of their situations in their families, in their schools, and on the streets. Research on girls engaging in physical violence suggests that violent girls are often themselves the victims as well as the victimizers.

Initially, arrests for running away were actually proxies for suspected sexual activity in girls, and there is still some evidence that the gender difference in girls' and boys' arrests for these offenses are products not of their behavior but rather of their parents', who report their daughters' running away but not their sons'. Girls on the run are often forced by current laws to live like escaped convicts. Unable to attend school, get a job, or even live apart from their abusive families, girls are forced into criminal behavior simply to survive. Sometimes, that behavior further criminalizes them and involves them in other risky behaviors, like survival sex, prostitution, and/or drug use.

Shoplifting accounts for many juvenile female arrests, and studies indicate that girls may well shoplift for reasons that are very much a product of a youth culture that, particularly for girls, stresses the importance of appearance.

What forces will shape the female delinquency of the new millennia? Those who study and work with these offenders must consider not only class but also gender and race when crafting their theories. Those who hope to effectively prevent and intervene in this behavior would do well to consider the gendered way in which youth experience adolescence. In short, delinquency theory, which has long focused (uncritically) on boys' delinquency with a particular emphasis on the role of class, would do well to consider gender both in crafting an approach to the problem and in developing responses that will help rather than further stigmatize and victimize.

The need to focus on the unique forces that bring girls into the justice system is very clear, as girl incarcerations are soaring at a time when no such dramatic increase is seen in the incarceration of boys. These trends, driven largely by the arrest and referral of girls for simple assault, threaten to undo more than 30 years of efforts to remove youth from institutional settings. It also means that the mass incarceration that has so heavily impacted adult women, particularly women of color, might well be visited upon their younger sisters unless a vigorous campaign of education and advocacy is not launched.

DISCUSSION QUESTIONS

1. Do females engage in crime for reasons different from their male counterparts and therefore require justice system treatment that is also different? Does this also cause them to engage in different sorts of crime activities?

2. Are girls subject to situations and conflict in their homes from which their brothers are excluded?

3. Must the justice system amend its previous practices to account for the influx of gender differences that were not present in previous decades? What should the justice system do?

4. What is the role of social patriarchy in the handling of female offenders versus male offenders? Are girls subjected to judicial treatment that is different from that faced by their brothers or other male offenders? Is there a remedy for this discrepancy?

REFERENCES

Adler, P., & Adler, P. (1998). *Peer power: Preadolescent culture and identity.* New Brunswick, NJ: Rutgers University Press.

American Bar Association and the National Bar Association (ABA & NBA). (2001). *Justice by gender: The lack of appropriate prevention, diversion and treatment alternatives for girls in the justice system.* Chicago, IL: American Bar Association.

American Correctional Association (ACA). (1990). *The female offender: What does the future hold?* Washington, DC: Author.

Artz, S. (1998). *Sex, power and the violent school girl.* Toronto, Ontario, Canada: Trifolium Books.

Artz, S., Blais, M., & Nicholson, D. (2000). *Developing girls' custody units.* Unpublished report.

Belenko, S., Sprott, J. B., & Petersen, C. (2004, March). Drug and alcohol involvement among minority and female juvenile offenders: Treatment and policy issues. *Criminal Justice Policy Review, 15*(1), 3–36.

Beyette, B. (1988, August 21). Hollywood's teen-age prostitutes turn tricks for shelter, food. *Las Vegas Review-Journal.*

Blumstein, A., & Wallman, J. (2000). *The crime drop in America.* Cambridge, United Kingdom: Cambridge University Press.

Bureau of Justice Statistics. (2003). *Sourcebook on criminal justice statistics.* Washington DC: Author. Retrieved February 14, 2008, from http://www.albany.edu/sourcebook/pdf/t347.pdf

Buzawa, E. S., & Hotaling, G. T. (2006). The impact of relationship status, gender, and minor status in the police response to domestic assaults. *Victims and Offenders, 1,* 323–360.

Campagna, D. S., & Poffenberger, D. L. (1988). *The sexual trafficking in children.* Dover, MA: Auburn House.

Campbell, A. (1981). *Girl delinquents.* New York, NY: St. Martin's Press.

Campbell, S., & Harrington, V. (2000). *Youth crime: Findings from the 1998/1999 youth lifestyles survey* (Home Office Research Findings 126). London, United Kingdom: Home Office.

Canter, R. J. (1982). Sex differences in self-report delinquency. *Criminology, 20*(3–4), 373–393.

Centers for Disease Control and Prevention (CDC). (1992–2004). *Youth risk behavior surveillance—United States, 1991–2004* (CDC Surveillance Summaries). U.S. Department of Health and Human Services. Atlanta, GA: Author.

Chesney-Lind, M., & Irwin, K. (2008). *Beyond bad girls: Gender, violence, and hype.* New York, NY: Routledge.

Chesney-Lind, M., & Shelden, R. (2004). *Girls, delinquency, and juvenile justice* (2nd ed.). Belmont, CA: Thompson/Wadsworth.

Cohen, A. K. (1955). *Delinquent boys: The culture of the gang.* New York, NY: The Free Press.

DeKeseredy, W. (2000). *Women, crime, and the Canadian criminal justice system.* Cincinnati, OH: Anderson.

Deyken, E. Y., & Buka, S. L. (1997). Prevalence and risk factors for posttraumatic stress disorder among chemically dependent adolescents. *American Journal of Psychiatry, 154*(6), 752–757.

Elliot, D., & Voss, H. (1974). *Delinquency and dropout.* Lexington, MA: D. C. Heath.

English, K. (1993). Self-reported crime rates of women prisoners. *Journal of Quantitative Criminology, 9*(4), 357–382.

Federal Bureau of Investigation (FBI). (2004). *Crime in the United States, 2003.* Table 33, Ten-year arrest trends. Washington, DC: U.S. Government Printing Office. Retrieved from http://www.fbi.gov/about-us/cjis/ucr/crime-in-the-u.s/2003/03sec4.pdf

Federal Bureau of Investigation (FBI). (2007). *Crime in the United States, 2006.* Table 33, Ten-year arrest trends. Washington, DC: U.S. Government Printing Office.

Finkelhor, D. (1994). Current information on the scope and nature of child sexual abuse. *The Future of Children, 4*(2), 31–53.

Franklin, A. (1979). Criminality in the workplace: A comparison of male and female offenders. In F. Adler & R. Simon (Eds.), *The criminality of deviant women.* Boston, MA: Houghton Mifflin.

Freitas, K., & Chesney-Lind, M. (2001, August/September). Difference doesn't mean difficult: Workers talk about working with girls. *Women, Girls, & Criminal Justice, 2*(5), 65–78.

Girls Incorporated. (1996). *Prevention and parity: Girls in juvenile justice.* Indianapolis, IN: Girls Incorporated National Resource Center.

Hayward, K. J. (2004). *City limits: Crime, consumer culture, and the urban experience.* London, United Kingdom: Glasshouse Press.

Heimer, K. (2000). Changes in the gender gap in crime and women's economic marginalization. In G. Lafree (Ed.), *Criminal justice 2000: Vol. 1. The nature of crime: Continuity and change* (pp. 427–483). Washington, DC: National Institute of Justice.

Hirschi, T. (1969). *Causes of delinquency.* Berkeley: University of California Press.

Kataoka, S., Zima, B., Dupre, D., Moreno, K., Yang, X., & McCracken, J. (2001). Mental health problems and service use among female juvenile offenders. *Journal of the American Academy of Child and Adolescent Psychiatry, 40*(5), 549–555.

Lamb, S. (2003, May–June). Not with my daughter: Parents still have trouble acknowledging teenage sexuality. *Psychotherapy Networker, 27* (May/June), 44–49.

Leslie, C., Biddle, N., Rosenberg, D., & Wayne, J. (1993, August 2). Girls will be girls. *Newsweek,* p. 44.

Lipsey, M. (1992). Juvenile delinquency treatment: A meta-analytic inquiry in the variability of effects. In T. A. Cook, H. Cooper, D. S. Cordray, H. Hartmann, L. V. Hedges, & R. J. Light (Eds.), *Meta-analysis for explanation: A casebook* (pp. 83–127). New York, NY: Russell Sage.

Longfellow, H. W. (1992). "There was a little girl." In J. Bartlett & J. Kaplan (Eds.), *Familiar quotations* (16th ed., p. 513). Boston, MA: Little, Brown.

May, D. (1978, May). Juvenile shoplifters and the organization of store security: A case study in the social construction of delinquency. *International Journal of Criminology and Penology, 6*(2), 137–160.

Miller, E. M. (1986). *Street woman.* Philadelphia, PA: Temple University Press.

Morash, M., & Chesney-Lind, M. (2008). Girls' violence in context. In M. Zahn (Ed.), *The Delinquent Girl* (pp. 182–206). Philadelphia, PA: Temple University Press.

Morris, A. (1987). *Women, crime, and criminal justice.* New York, NY: Blackwell.

Nadon, S., Koverola, C., & Schludeermann, E. (1998). Antecedents to prostitution: Childhood victimization. *Journal of Interpersonal Violence, 13,* 206–221.

New York Civil Liberties Union (NYCLU). (2007). *Criminalizing the classroom: The over-policing of New York City schools.* New York: NYCLU.

Rhodes, J. E., & Fischer, K. (1993). Spanning the gender gap: Gender differences in delinquency among inner-city adolescents. *Adolescence, 28*(112), 879–889.

Sedlak, A., & Broadhurst, D. (1996). *Executive summary of the Third National Incidence Study of Child Abuse and Neglect.* Washington, DC: National Center on Child Abuse and Neglect, U.S. Department of Health and Human Services.

Sickmund, M., Sladky, T. J., & Kang, W. (2004). *Census of juveniles in residential placement databook.* Washington, DC: U.S. Department of Justice. Retrieved February 14, 2008, from http://www.ojjdp.ncjrs.org/ojstabb/cjrp/

Snyder, H. N., & Sickmund, M. (1999). *Juvenile offenders and victims: 1999 national report.* Washington, DC: Office of Juvenile Justice and Delinquency Prevention: National Center for Juvenile Justice.

Snyder, H. N., & Sickmund, M. (2006). *Juvenile offenders and victims: 2006 national report* (NCJ 178257). Washington, DC: U.S. Department of Justice, Office of Justice Programs, Office of Juvenile Justice and Delinquency Prevention.

Thorne, B. (1994). *Gender play: Girls and boys in school.* New Brunswick, NJ: Rutgers University Press.

Tyler, K., Hoyt, D., Whitbeck, L., & Cauce, A. (2004). The impact of childhood sexual abuse on later sexual victimization among runaway youth. *Journal of Research on Adolescence, 11*(2), 151–176.

Widom, C. S. (1995). *Victims of childhood sexual abuse: Later criminal consequences.* Washington, DC: National Institute of Justice, U.S. Department of Justice.

CHAPTER 8

Race and Crime

Helen Taylor Greene

The concepts of race and crime have been inextricably linked in the study of criminology and criminal justice since the late 19th century. Today, many colleges and universities that offer undergraduate and graduate degrees in criminology/criminal justice have either a required or elective course on race and crime. Usually, such courses explore the economic, historical, political, and sociological contexts of race and crime. Some courses also include analyses of ethnicity, class, gender, and comparative perspectives. Most examine historical and contemporary issues including race and the extent of crime, police, courts, corrections, juvenile justice, disproportionate minority confinement and contact, bias and hate crimes, immigration and crime, racial profiling, and sentencing disparities.

DEFINITIONAL ISSUES

The definition of race is complex. Historically, race was conceptualized biologically and primarily based on one's physical characteristics. Beliefs about the superiority of Whites and inferiority of others, especially people of color, prevailed. Over time, according to the American Anthropological Association (1997), the concept of race acquired a cultural and ideological context in the United States and elsewhere in the world that

> magnified the differences among Europeans, Africans, and Indians, established a rigid hierarchy of socially exclusive categories, underscored and bolstered unequal rank and status differences, and provided the rationalization that the inequality was natural or God-given. (p. 1)

Biological differences between individuals, especially color and hue, provide the foundation for what many refer to as the social construction of race (Aguirre & Turner, 2011). Are individuals that look different on the outside different on the

123

inside? If not, why are race and ethnicity (used here interchangeably with minorities) at the center of so many controversies nationally and internationally?

In 2000, the U.S. Bureau of the Census noted that racial categories were sociopolitical constructs and not scientific or anthropological in nature (Gabbidon & Greene, 2009). The U.S. Census Bureau recognizes five racial categories including American Indian, or Alaskan native, Black or African American, Native Hawaiian or other Pacific Islanders, and White; Latino or Hispanic origin is recognized as an ethnic category. A category for "some other race" with numerous combinations to choose from was added in 2000 as well. In 2010, "more than 9 million Americans considered themselves multiracial and self-identified with two or more races" (Gabbidon & Greene, 2013, p. 7). Persons of Hispanic or Latino ethnicity, the largest minority group in the population, also are of very diverse origins (Gabbidon & Greene, 2013). In spite of more categories, race does not capture heterogeneity, that is, differences within racial and ethnic groups. All members of a racial/ethnic-minority group are not the same; there are cultural, subcultural, and class differences not only between but also within racial and ethnic groups.

The complexities of race in America were an important topic during the election of President Barack Hussein Obama in 2008. His mother was White, his father was African, and he was raised for many years by his White grandparents in Honolulu, Hawaii. Does that make him White? African? African American? In March 2008 in a speech on race, President Obama stated that "I have brothers, sisters, nieces, nephews, uncles and cousins, of every race and every hue, scattered across three continents" ("Barack Obama's Speech," 2008, para. 8). His race, and that of many other Americans, is not easily categorized as either Black or White. At an earlier time in our country, President Obama would be classified as Black and, depending on the time period, referred to as either mixed, mulatto, colored, Negro, or African American, because of his skin color. In the past, Americans with any African blood, especially if they did not look White, were considered Black.

Unlike race (and ethnicity), crime is easier to define. In the early 20th century, Paul Tappan (1947) defined crime as "an intentional act in violation of the criminal law (statutory law and case law) committed without defense or excuse, and penalized by the state as a felony or misdemeanor" (p. 99). Over time, behaviors that are labeled as crimes change, although some including murder, rape, burglary, and theft always have been considered crimes. In the past and present, many factors including values, industrialization, immigration, and technological developments have led to both the criminalization and decriminalization of many behaviors. For example, when legislative efforts to outlaw the sale and use of alcohol failed (the Volstead Act), it was decriminalized. Decades later, as the use of automobiles increased, so did the problem of driving under the influence of alcohol or drugs. Due to increased attention, especially from Mothers Against Drunk Driving (MADD), penalties for vehicular homicides by drunk drivers have increased. Today, 20 states and the District of Columbia have legalized medical marijuana, and in two, Colorado and Washington, recreational use of marijuana is legal. Since the late 20th century, the prevalence of computers has led to increases in cybercrimes, and many crimes such as child pornography, bullying, fraud, and identity theft have moved to the Internet.

Even though Whites commit numerous crimes, the study of race and crime has been concerned primarily with crimes committed by Blacks and other minorities. In the past, acts considered criminal for Blacks were not necessarily viewed as such when committed by Whites. For example, prior to the Civil War, slave owners were rarely punished for beating, branding, raping, and killing their slaves. According to Kennedy (1997), the law protected Whites in order to maintain their supremacy. Both before and after the Civil War, the law was used to maintain social control and "keep the Negro in his place" (Work, 1937, p. 111) as well as to control immigrant Whites and other minorities.

Some of the focus on minorities in the study of criminology/criminal justice, evolves from their disproportionate involvement in crime, especially violent personal crimes. According to Young (1996, p. 74),

> The concept of disproportionality, has become the mainstay of discussions of race and crime. . . . (W)hen authors review trends and patterns of crime and introduce the "variable" race the comparisons are between Blacks, whites and others and the emphasis is on the disproportionate involvement of nonwhites, in particular Blacks.

Even though Whites commit violent crimes, especially bias or hate crimes, they do not receive as much attention as Blacks and other minorities. Corporate and other white-collar crimes committed by Whites don't receive much attention either. This fixation on *Black crime*, contributes to the racialization of crime (Covington, 1995), a belief that the majority of Blacks (and perhaps other minorities) commit crimes.

The overreliance on official statistics such as the Federal Bureau of Investigation's Uniform Crime Reports (UCR) contributes to misperceptions about race and crime in the United States. For example, most students are often surprised to learn that (a) most Americans, regardless of race, are not arrested and that (b) even though Blacks are vastly overrepresented in arrest statistics, most persons arrested are White. Crime and victimization statistics in the study of race and crime are discussed next.

Race, Crime, and Victimization

The two major sources of statistics on crime and victimization are the UCR, collected and compiled by the Federal Bureau of Investigation (FBI), and the National Crime Victimization Survey (NCVS), compiled for the Bureau of Justice Statistics (BJS) by the U.S. Bureau of the Census. Both the UCR and NCVS collect and report information on race although they do so differently. The BJS (see www.ojp.usdoj .gov/bjs/) provides statistics about many aspects of crime and criminal justice that include race and provides users with the capability to analyze some crime and justice data online (see http://bjsdata.ojp.usdoj.gov/dataonline/index.cfm). There are other governmental and nongovernmental sources of information on crime and victimization that permit analyses by race as well, such as the Death Penalty Information Center (www.deathpenaltyinfo.org) and The Sentencing Project (www .sentencingproject.org/). What do the two major sources tell us about race, crime, and victimization?

FBI Uniform Crime Reports

In the Crimes Reported section of the 2012 FBI UCR, the estimated size of the United States population was 313,914,049. An estimated 1,214,462 violent crimes were reported in 2012, about 386.9 violent crimes per 100,000 inhabitants. There were an estimated 8,975,438 property crime offenses reported in 2012, a rate of about 2,859.2 offenses per 100,000 inhabitants. Larceny-theft offenses accounted for over two thirds (68.5%) of all property crimes in 2012. Between 2006 (1,435,123) and 2011 (1,206,005), estimated violent crimes reported steadily decreased and increased slightly in 2012. Property crimes continued to decline between 2006 and 2012. (Federal Bureau of Investigation [FBI], 2013).

In the Persons Arrested section of the UCR, information is provided by race in four categories: (1) Whites, (2) Blacks, (3) American Indian or Alaskan Native, and (4) Asian or Pacific Islander. In this section the population is estimated to be 242,925,157. There were 9,390,473 reported arrests, including 6,502,919 Whites, 2,640,067 Blacks, 135,165 American Indian or Alaskan Natives, and 112,322 Asian or Pacific Islanders. For the traditional Part I offenses (murder/non-negligent manslaughter, aggravated assault, robbery, forcible rape, burglary, larceny-theft, motor vehicle theft, and arson), most persons were arrested for larceny-theft, regardless of race, followed by arrests for aggravated assault and burglary. When examining the percentage distribution by race, Blacks are overrepresented in reported arrests for all Part I crimes, and Whites for arson (see Table 8.1). Though not shown in Table 8.1, Whites also are overrepresented in several of the Part II offenses including vandalism, sex offenses, and driving under the influence. Blacks are overrepresented for many Part II offenses including suspicion, gambling, and prostitution (FBI, 2013).

How do the UCR arrest data contribute to understanding race and crime? The answer to this question is unclear and requires taking the following weaknesses of the UCR data into consideration:

- Arrests of Hispanics and/or Latinos usually are included in the White category.
- Many (crimes and) arrests are not reported (often referred to as the dark figure of crime), and others are not recorded by the police.
- The UCR utilize estimates of the total population, crimes reported, and persons arrested that might be inaccurate.
- Police biases can result in different racial and class arrest decisions.

Table 8.1 Persons Arrested by Race for Part I Crimes, 2011

Offense charged	Total arrests					Percent distribution[1]				
	Total	White	Black	American Indian or Alaskan Native	Asian or Pacific Islander	Total	White	Black	American Indian or Alaskan native	Asian or Pacific Islander
TOTAL	9,390,473	6,502,919	2,640,067	135,165	112,322	100.0	69.3	28.1	1.4	1.2
Murder and nonnegligent manslaughter	8,506	4,101	4,203	102	100	100.0	48.2	49.4	1.2	1.2
Forcible rape	13,886	9,027	4,512	183	164	100.0	65.0	32.5	1.3	1.2
Robbery	80,135	34,761	44,002	601	771	100.0	43.4	54.9	0.7	1.0
Aggravated assault	299,943	188,505	102,371	4,312	4,755	100.0	62.8	34.1	1.4	1.6
Burglary	219,232	147,156	67,554	1,966	2,556	100.0	67.1	30.8	0.9	1.2
Larceny-theft	994,304	677,895	288,025	15,052	13,332	100.0	68.2	29.0	1.5	1.3
Motor vehicle theft	52,952	35,252	16,301	645	755	100.0	66.6	30.8	1.2	1.4
Arson	8,827	6,500	2,083	141	103	100.0	73.6	23.6	1.6	1.2
Violent crime[2]	402,470	236,394	155,088	5,198	5,790	100.0	58.7	38.5	1.3	1.4
Property crime[2]	1,275,315	866,802	373,963	17,804	16,746	100.0	68.0	29.3	1.4	1.3
Other assaults	924,839	606,048	294,678	13,898	10,215	100.0	65.5	31.9	1.5	1.3

(Continued)

Table 8.1 (Continued)

Offense charged	Total arrests					Percent distribution[1]				
	Total	White	Black	American Indian or Alaskan Native	Asian or Pacific Islander	Total	White	Black	American Indian or Alaskan native	Asian or Pacific Islander
Forgery and counterfeiting	51,759	33,950	16,900	239	670	100.0	65.6	32.7	0.5	1.1
Fraud	117,706	78,331	37,171	1,143	1,061	100.0	66.5	31.6	1.0	1.6
Embezzlement	12,371	7,994	4,103	74	200	100.0	66.6	31.5	0.8	1.3
Stolen property; buying, receiving, possessing	75,516	50,144	23,787	615	970	100.0	66.4	31.5	0.8	1.3
Vandalism	175,243	125,987	44,650	2,845	1,761	100.0	71.9	25.5	1.6	1.0
Weapons; carrying, possessing, etc.	114,979	66,909	45,842	764	1,464	100.0	58.2	39.9	0.7	1.3
Prostitution and commercialized vice	43,216	23,172	18,486	175	1,383	100.0	53.6	42.8	0.4	3.2
Sex offenses (except forcible rape and prostitution)	52,354	38,063	12,850	628	813	100.0	72.7	24.5	1.2	1.6
Drug abuse violation	1,194,956	801,198	372,914	8,299	12,545	100.0	67.0	31.2	0.7	1.0

Offense charged	Total arrests					Percent distribution[1]				
	Total	White	Black	American Indian or Alaskan Native	Asian or Pacific Islander	Total	White	Black	American Indian or Alaskan native	Asian or Pacific Islander
Gambling	5,951	1,707	4,008	22	214	100.0	28.7	67.4	0.4	3.6
Offenses against the family and children	81,762	53,760	25,698	1,740	564	100.0	65.8	31.4	2.1	0.7
Driving under the influence	981,110	830,498	118,557	13,314	18,313	100.0	84.6	12.1	1.4	1.9
Liquor laws	337,687	275,457	46,355	11,314	4,561	100.0	81.6	13.7	3.4	1.4
Drunkenness	398,600	324,209	62,944	7,218	4,229	100.0	81.3	15.8	1.8	1.1
Disorderly conduct	418,960	262,810	145,183	7,751	3,216	100.0	62.7	34.7	1.9	0.8
Vagrancy	20,698	13,034	7,080	389	195	100.0	63.0	34.2	1.9	0.9
All other offenses	2,649,909	1,773,792	808,609	41,206	26,302	100.0	66.9	30.5	1.6	1.0
Suspicion	1,160	610	535	4	11	100.0	52.6	46.1	0.3	0.9
Curfew and loitering law violations	53,912	32,050	20,666	526	670	100.0	59.4	38.3	1.0	1.2

Source: FBI UCR, *Crime in the United States 2012*, "Arrests," Table 43A, B, C (2012). Retrieved from http://www.fbi.gov/about-us/cjis/ucr/crime-in-the-u.s/2012/crime-in-the-u.s.-2012/tables/43tabledatadecoverviewpdf

[1]Because of rounding, the percentages may not add to 100.0.

[2]Violent crimes are offenses of murder and nonnegligent manslaughter, forcible rape, robbery, and aggravated assault. Property crimes are offenses of burglary, larceny-theft, motor vehicle theft, and arson.

The National Crime Victimization Survey (NCVS) described in the next section was designed and implemented as an alternative source of information on the extent of crime and victimization.

The National Crime Victimization Survey

The Bureau of Justice Statistics (BJS) publishes an annual bulletin titled *Criminal Victimization*. The NCVS is conducted annually and in 2012 included a sample of 92,390 households and about 162,940 persons over the age of 12. Participants are asked about their experiences as victims of personal and household crimes. The survey has been redesigned several times, most recently in 2006 to improve data collection. More recently, the size of the sample also was increased. In the 2012 bulletin, the reported victimization rate for violent crimes was 26.1 per 1,000 persons and 155.8 per 1,000 households for property crimes (Truman, Langton, & Planty, 2013). The overall rate of violent crime for Blacks was 34.2, Whites 25.2, Hispanics 24.5, and two or more races 42.8. Rates were highest for persons aged 12 to 17 (48.4) followed by those 18 to 24 (41.0). Compared to 2011 rates, there was an increase in the violent victimization rate (serious violent crime) for non-Hispanic Blacks although not for non-Hispanic Whites and Hispanics (see Table 8.2).

Like the UCR, the NCVS also has limitations:

- It includes persons only over the age of 12.
- Victimization data are based on the respondent's recall about the incident either she or someone in the household was involved in.
- Minorities are probably underrepresented since they are underrepresented in population statistics and may be reluctant to participate in the survey.

In spite of the limitations of both sources, they both seem to indicate that crime and victimization are important to any discussion of race and crime because both sources show patterns of arrests for crime, victimization, and race that require explanation. Some of these explanations found in the race and crime theoretical research are presented next.

THEORETICAL PERSPECTIVES ON RACE AND CRIME

Why do African Americans and some other minorities continue to be overrepresented in crime and victimization statistics? Why do we downplay the role of criminal justice system professionals, especially police and prosecutors and their discretionary decisions concerning arrest, making charges, and negotiating pleas? The first question has perplexed criminologists and other scholars for decades. Both criminological and criminal justice theories offer explanations. In the criminological research, explanations include biological, sociological, and psychological explanations that focus on either the individual, the environment, or both. Although criminal justice theoretical research is more limited, it focuses on the fairness of the criminal justice system raised

Table 8.2	Rates of Violent Crime and Serious Violent Crime by Gender, Race, Hispanic Origin, and Age, 2003, 2011, 2012

Demographic characteristics of victims	Violent crime[a]			Serious violent crime[b]		
	2003	2011	2012	2003	2011	2012
Total	32.1	22.6	26.1	10.0	7.2	8.0
Sex						
Male	34.6	25.5	29.1	10.2	7.7	9.4
Female	29.7	19.8	23.3	9.9	6.7	6.6
Race/Hispanic origin						
White[c]	32.3	21.6	25.2	9.4	6.5	6.8
Black/African American[c]	35.9	26.4	34.2[‡]	12.8	10.8	11.3
Hispanic/Latino	26.6	23.6	24.5	9.7	7.2	9.3
American Indian/ Alaska Native[c]	85.2	45.4	46.9	35.2	12.6[!]	26.2[!]
Asian/Native Hawalian/Pacific Islander[c]	9.9	11.2	16.4	5.1	2.5[!]	9.1[†]
Two or more races[c]	140.7	65.0	42.8	47.8	26.2	9.5[†]
Age						
12-17	78.3	37.7	48.4[‡]	22.7	8.8	9.9
18-24	63.8	49.1	41.0	23.7	16.3	14.7
25 -35	39.0	26.5	34.2[‡]	11.9	9.6	10.9
35-49	23.1	21.9	29.1[†]	7.1	7.0	9.5
50-64	16.3	13.1	15.0	4.2	4.3	4.6
65 or older	3.1	4.4	5.7	0.9	1.7	1.6
Marital status						
Never married	57.7	35.5	40.7	18.2	11.7	11.9
Married	14.2	11.0	13.5	3.2	3.7	3.9
Widowed	7.8	3.8	8.3[†]	1.2	0.7[!]	2.6[‡]
Divorced	44.6	37.8	37.0	17.0	9.2	10.9
Separated	100.9	73.0	83.1	47.8	26.4	39.5

Source: Bureau of Justice Statistics, National Crime Victimization Survey, 2003, 2011, and 2012.

Note: Victimization rates per 1,000 persons age 12 or older. See appendix table 11 for standard errors.

[†]Significant change from 2011 to 2012 at the 95% confidence level.

[‡]Significant change from 2011 to 2012 at the 90% confidence level.

[!]Interpret with caution. Estimate based on 10 or fewer sample cases, or coefficient of variation is greater than 50%.

[a]Includes rape or sexual assault, robbery, aggravated assault, and simple assault.

[b]Includes rape or sexual robbery, and aggravated assault.

[c]Excludes pesons of Hispanic or Latino orgin.

| Table 8.3 | Percent of Victimization Reported to Police, by Type of Crime, 2003, 2011, and 2012 |

Type of crime	2003	2011	2012
Violent crime[a]	48%	49%	44%
Rape/sexual assault	56	27	28
Robbery	64	66	56
Assault	45	48	44
Aggravated assault	56	67	62
Simple assault	43	43	40
Domestic violence[b]	57	59	55
Intimate partner violence[c]	60	60	53
Violent crime involving injury	56	61	59
Serious violent crime[d]	58%	61%	54%
Serious domestic violence[b]	61	58	61
Serious intimate partner violence[c]	63	59	55
Serious violent crime involving weapons	59	67	56[†]
Serious violent crime involving injury	64	66	56
Property crime[e]	38%	37%	34%[†]
Burglary	54	52	55
Motor vehicle theft	77	83	79
Theft	31	30	26[†]

Source: Bureau of Justice Statistics, National Crime Victimization Survey, 2003, 2011, and 2012.

Note: See appendix table 6 for standard errors.

[†]Significant change from 2011 to 2012 at the 95% confidence level.

[a]Includes rape or sexual assault, robbery, aggravated assault, and simple assault.

[b]Includes victimization committed by intimate partners (current or former spouses, boyfriends, or girlfriends) and family members.

[c]Includes victimization committed by current or former spouses, boyfriends, or girlfriends.

[d]Includes rape or sexual assault, robbery, and aggravated assault.

[e]Includes household burglary, motor vehicle theft, and theft.

by the second question. According to Duffee and Allan (2007), "Theories of criminal justice raise questions about why the government is doing what it is doing" (p. 18). Justice including just processes, outcomes, and the just use of state power is central to criminal justice theory (Castellano & Gould, 2007).

Few contemporary criminology/criminal justice theories examine how religion influenced explanations of race and crime in the United States even though it was an important source of beliefs about evil and sin. Gabbidon (2007) points to the story of Noah's son Ham in the Bible as a possible source of the (Hamatic) myth that Black people were "evil" and criminal (p. 6). The role of religion in the United States and the acceptance of this myth during the colonial and antebellum eras is important to understanding prevailing beliefs about the criminality and inferiority of not only Blacks but also Native Americans, Asian Americans, and Latino Americans. It is still unclear how much of an influence religion has in American criminology. Some criminology/criminal justice texts include discussions of the contributions of religion to penal philosophy and the corrections movement, but few discuss the interconnectedness of religion, race ideology, and the administration of justice.

Classical and positivist criminological theories have predominated in the study of criminology for hundreds of years. Classical and neoclassical theories focus on several key concepts including utilitarianism, hedonism, free will, and rational choice. These theories did not address race and crime specifically. Positivists believe that criminal behavior is determined by biological, psychological, and/or sociological factors. Cesare Lombroso's research on physical characteristics was influential in the United States where beliefs about the inferiority of Blacks and Native Americans already existed. Though less popular, biological research continues in the United States today (Moffitt, 1993; Rowe, 2007; Rushton, 1995; Walsh & Beaver, 2008; Wilson & Herrnstein, 1985).

W. E. B. Du Bois, Monroe N. Work, Clifford R. Shaw, and Henry D. McKay were among the earliest group of scholars to refute the biological approach and its fixation on the individual. Instead, they focused on the role of one's environment and social disorganization on crime (Du Bois, 1899/1973; Work, 1900; Shaw & McKay, 1942). Du Bois (1899/1973) and Work (1900) noted the impact of slavery, discrimination, and segregation on Black criminality and pointed to social, economic, and political conditions that contributed to Blacks' involvement in crime. Du Bois conducted a study of Negroes in Philadelphia for the University of Pennsylvania that was published in 1899 and titled *The Philadelphia Negro: A Social Study.* One of his conclusions was that "crime is a phenomenon of organized social life, and is the open rebellion of an individual against his social environment" (Du Bois, 1899/1973, p. 235). Work, who studied at the University of Chicago and later worked at Tuskegee Institute, emphasized how historically the law was used against Blacks rather than to protect them. As a result, many Blacks not only feared the law but also evaded and had little respect for it (Greene & Gabbidon, 2000).

Although the research of Du Bois and Work was not widely known, other scholars in the early 20th century also pointed to the deleterious effect of social conditions on criminality. Shaw and McKay (1942), researchers affiliated with the Chicago School of Sociology, examined delinquency areas in Chicago and concluded that "within similar areas, each group, whether foreign-born or native, recent immigrant or older immigrant, black or white, had a delinquency rate that was proportional to the rate of the overall area" (as cited in Vold & Bernard, 1986, p. 170).

Unlike other immigrants that found themselves in "delinquency areas" and eventually were able to move out of them, many Blacks seem to be trapped there creating the "truly disadvantaged," a term coined by William Julius Wilson (1987). These areas experience concentrated indicators of social disorganization including poverty, crime, school dropouts, drug use and sales, inadequate housing, high incarceration rates, teen pregnancies, and unemployment. Over time, several factors including housing inequality and socially isolated residents, foster cultural adaptations that undermine both social organization and the control of crime (Sampson & Wilson, 1995).

One criticism of social disorganization theory is that all minorities in socially disorganized communities are not involved in criminal behavior (Gabbidon and Greene, 2009). Several researchers have examined social capital and/or collective efficacy to explain variations in levels of crime. Social capital refers to social ties, levels of trust, and the ability of individuals to work together for the good of the community. Communities with low levels of positive social capital and cohesion are more apt to succumb to negative social networks that value criminal behavior (Poteyeva, 2009).

Many other sociological explanations of criminality and delinquency, such as subcultural theories, the colonial model, conflict theory, critical race theory, the general theory of crime, social control, strain theory, and social inequality, are useful to understanding race and crime. Theoretical research on Latinos, Native Americans, and Asian Americans is still limited and more is needed. Is social disorganization theory applicable to these groups? Does another theory provide a better explanation for crimes (and arrests) committed by minorities? What about White Americans? What is the best theory to explain corporate crimes, serial killings, human trafficking, and selling drugs? All theories have their strengths and weaknesses and none fully explain patterns of race, crime, and victimization. Another explanation for the disproportionate representation of Blacks and other minorities in the criminal justice system is discriminatory practices. Discretion, that is, decisional latitude, permits justice practitioners to be guided by not only the official policies of their agencies but also their own values and perhaps biases as well. As a result, even though discrimination and injustices that existed in the past are less prevalent today, vestiges of racial and ethnic disparities still exist in criminal justice (Walker, Spohn, & DeLone, 2012). The next section examines research on contemporary race and crime issues.

CONTEMPORARY RACE AND CRIME ISSUES

What are the five most important issues in the study of race and crime today? Issues related to aspects of race and policing (racial profiling, police use of force), race and corrections and sentencing (the war on drugs, disparities, mass incarceration, prisoner reentry), and race and juvenile justice (disproportionate minority confinement, gangs, violent juvenile offenders) are often identified. In the next section, research is presented on three race, crime, and justice issues: racial profiling, prisoner reentry, and disproportionate minority contact.

Racial Profiling

According to the Institute on Race and Justice at Northeastern University, racial profiling has been defined in many ways. It usually refers to targeting individuals by using race and ethnicity as indicators of criminality (del Carmen, 2009). This can occur whether or not those targeted are actually engaged in any crimes. Today, racial and ethnic profiling is believed to occur in several situations including traffic stops (Harris, 2002; Withrow, 2006), ethnic profiling related to perceived terrorist threats (Abu-Lughod, 2009), and consumer racial profiling (Dabney, Dugan, Topalli, & Hollinger, 2006; Gabbidon & Higgins, 2007). According to del Carmen (2009), various forms of racial profiling existed in the United States during the Jim Crow and immigration eras in the 19th and 20th centuries (p. 666). More recently, drug courier profiles have been used by federal, state, and local law enforcement officials to identify suspected drug dealers. After several lawsuits, the existence of racial profiling was finally acknowledged by criminal justice practitioners. As a result, many states mandated data collection with varying methodological approaches (Higgins, Gabbidon, & Jordan, 2008). Profiling by private security officers in retail settings (consumer racial profiling) has received attention as well. Higgins et al. (2008) analyzed data from the 2004 Minority Rights and Relations/Black and White Social Audit (Gallup) poll and found that Blacks were more likely than Whites to believe that racial profiling is widespread.

Prisoner Reentry

Jeremy Travis, a former director of the National Institute of Justice and president of John Jay College of Criminal Justice in New York City was instrumental in drawing attention to the issue of prisoner reentry when he published his book in 2005 titled *But They All Come Back: Facing the Challenges of Prisoner Reentry.* According to Travis, the growth of the prison population (mass incarceration) during the past two decades has resulted in large numbers of ex-offenders returning to families, communities, and often crime. The most recent reentry data indicate that almost 750,000 prisoners were released in 2006. The overrepresentation of racial and ethnic groups in prison means that their communities will be burdened more by returning ex-offenders. Unfortunately, institutional and community corrections agents had not prepared for "mass reentry" and suddenly thousands of ex-offenders were returning with neither resources to assist them nor employment opportunities. During the past 5 years, there have been efforts to smooth the transition back into society in some jurisdictions that involve corrections officials (in facilities and in the community), law enforcement, faith organizations, families, and communities. The challenges of reentry include not only the lack of resources and limited employment but also family issues, transportation, health, and housing issues. The current sentencing policies including mandatory sentencing and three-strikes law guarantee that prisoner reentry will continue to be a problem that requires innovative solutions for decades.

Disproportionate Minority Contact and Confinement

Disproportionate minority contact and confinement (DMC) refers to the overrepresentation of minorities at various stages in adult and juvenile justice systems, especially confinement. The U.S. Congress has legislated core requirements in revisions to the Juvenile Justice and Delinquency Prevention Act's DMC since 1988. States are required to identify and address the problem in order to receive federal funding through formula grants (Gabbidon & Greene, 2009). The Office of Juvenile Justice and Delinquency Prevention (OJJDP) is responsible for monitoring DMC progress and providing technical assistance to the states. Unfortunately, progress in this area has been limited, and DMC continues to exist at many stages and in several states.

FUTURE ISSUES IN THE STUDY OF RACE AND CRIME

The next decade will present traditional crime and justice problems as well as new ones. If the historical relationship between economics and crime hold true, we should expect more crime in the coming years, especially if unemployment continues to rise. Unlike in the past, more attention will be paid to white-collar crime and fraud as a result of massive business failures in the banking, security, and housing industries. The race and crime conundrum may become less important as crime and victimization data reflect increases in other types of crime. As long as social and economic disparities exist, "street crime" will occur. It is important to continue to invest in crime and delinquency prevention, youth development, restorative justice, and other strategies that offer a more holistic approach to reducing crime and victimization. Justice agencies must also develop cultural competencies of employees in a continued effort to overcome hidden biases.

Another future issue is the changing demographic trends in the United States. Today, Latinos are the largest minority and compose the majority in many cities and counties in the United States. Researchers should resolve the dilemma of counting this group so that we have a better understanding of ethnic trends in criminal justice. Relatedly, the victimization trends for mixed races require more research since rates of victimization are high in this group. Two other important issues in the future study of race and crime are DNA analysis and human trafficking. The role of DNA in solving crimes, uncovering wrongful convictions, and maintaining DNA databanks is of great import although not without limitations. Last, human trafficking requires greater emphasis on how this global problem relates to race, ethnicity, crime, and justice. Banks and Kyckelhahn (2011) found that the majority of human trafficking victims were minorities.

DISCUSSION QUESTIONS

1. Explain why the historical context of the problem of race and crime in the United States is important.

2. Explain what crime and victimization statistics tell us about race and crime.

3. What is the best explanation of the overrepresentation of some minorities as crime perpetrators and victims?

4. Discuss the implications for the shift in population characteristics on the study of race and crime.

5. What do you think is the most important emerging research or policy issue related to the study of race and crime? Explain your answer.

REFERENCES

Abu-Lughod, R. (2009). Arab Americans. In H. T. Greene & S. L. Gabbidon (Eds.), *Encyclopedia of race and crime* (pp. 27–30). Thousand Oaks, CA: SAGE.

Aguirre, A., Jr., & Turner, J. H. (2011). *American ethnicity: The dynamics and consequences of discrimination* (7th ed.). New York, NY: McGraw-Hill Higher Education.

American Anthropological Association (1997). *AAA's statement on race.* Retrieved February 7, 2009, from http://www.understandingrace.org/about/statement.html

Banks, D., & Kyckelhahn, T. (2011). *Characteristics of suspected human trafficking incidents, 2008–2010.* Retrieved March 18, 2014, from http://www.bjs.gov/content/pub/pdf/cshti0810.pdf

Barack Obama's speech on race (Transcript). (2008, March 18). *The New York Times.* Retrieved June 29, 2009, from http://nytimes.com/2008/03/18/us/politics/18text-obama.html

Castellano, T. C., & Gould, J. B. (2007). Neglect of justice in criminal justice theory: Causes, consequences and alternatives. In D. E. Duffee & E. R. Maguire (Eds.), *Criminal justice theory: Explaining the nature and behavior of criminal justice* (pp. 71–92). New York, NY: Routledge Taylor & Francis.

Covington, J. (1995). Racial classification in criminology: The reproduction of racialized crime. *Sociological Forum, 10*(4), 547–568.

Dabney, D. A., Dugan, L., Topalli, V., & Hollinger, R. C. (2006). The impact of implicit stereotyping on offender profiling: Unexpected results from an observational study of shoplifting. *Criminal Justice and Behavior, 33*(5), 646–674.

del Carmen, A. (2009). Profiling, racial: Historical and contemporary perspectives. In H. T. Greene & S. L. Gabbidon (Eds.), *Encyclopedia of race and crime* (pp. 666–668). Thousand Oaks, CA: SAGE.

Du Bois, W. E. B. (1973). *The Philadelphia Negro.* Millwood, NY: Kraus-Thomson. (Original work published 1899)

Duffee, D. E., & Allan, E. (2007). Criminal justice, criminology and criminal justice theory. In D. E. Duffee & E. R. Maguire (Eds.), *Criminal justice theory: Explaining the nature and behavior of criminal justice* (pp. 1–26). New York, NY: Routledge Taylor & Francis.

Federal Bureau of Investigation (FBI). (2013). *Crime in the United States, 2012*. Retrieved March 18, 2014, from http://www. fbi.gov

Gabbidon, S. L. (2007). *Criminological perspectives on race and crime*. New York, NY: Routledge.

Gabbidon, S. L., & Greene, H. T. (2009). *Race and crime* (2nd ed.). Thousand Oaks, CA: SAGE.

Gabbidon, S. L., & Greene, H. T. (2013*)*. *Race and crime* (3rd ed.). Thousand Oaks, CA: SAGE.

Gabbidon, S. L., & Higgins, G. E. (2007). Consumer racial profiling and perceived victimization: A phone survey of Philadelphia area residents. *American Journal of Criminal Justice*, 32(1–2), 1–11.

Greene, H. T., & Gabbidon, S. L. (2000). *African American criminological thought*. Albany: State University of New York Press.

Harris, D. (2002). *Profiles in injustice*. New York, NY: The New Press.

Higgins, G. E., Gabbidon, S. L., & Jordan, K. (2008). Examining the generality of citizens' views on racial profiling in diverse situational contexts. *Criminal Justice & Behavior*, 35(12), 1527–1541.

Kennedy, R. (1997). *Race, crime, and the law*. New York, NY: Vintage Books/Random House, Inc.

Moffitt, T. E. (1993). Adolescence-limited and life-course-persistent antisocial behavior. A developmental taxonomy. *Psychological Review, 100*(4), 674–401.

Poteyeva, M. (2009). Social capital. In H. T. Greene & S. L. Gabbidon (Eds.). *Encyclopedia of race and crime* (pp. 756–757). Thousand Oaks, CA: SAGE.

Rowe, D. C. (2007). *Race and Crime*. New York, NY: Oxford University Press.

Rushton, J. P. (1995). Race and crime: International data for 1989–1990. *Psychological Reports*, 76, 3607–3612.

Sampson, R. J., & Wilson, W. J. (1995). Toward a theory of race, crime, and urban inequality. In J. Hagan & R. D. Peterson (Eds.), *Crime and inequality* (pp. 37–54). Stanford, CA: Stanford University Press.

Shaw, C., & McKay, H. D. (1942). *Juvenile delinquency and urban areas: A study of rates of delinquents in relation to different characteristics of local communities in American cities*. Chicago, IL: University of Chicago Press.

Tappan, P. (1947). Who is the criminal? *American Sociological Review, 12*(10), 96–112.

Travis, J. (2005). *But they all come back: Facing the challenges of prisoner reentry*. Washington, DC: The Urban Institute Press.

Truman, J., Langton, L., & Planty, M. (2013, October). *Criminal victimization, 2012* (Report NCJ 243389). Washington, DC: U.S. Department of Justice, Office of Justice Programs, Bureau of Justice Statistics.

Vold, G. B., & Bernard, T. J. (1986). *Theoretical criminology* (3rd ed.). New York, NY: Oxford University Press.

Walker, S., Spohn, C., & DeLone, M. (2012). *The color of justice* (5th ed.). Belmont, CA: Wadsworth.

Walsh, A., & Beaver, K. (2008). (eds.). *Contemporary biosocial criminology*. New York, NY: Routledge.

Wilson, J. Q., & Herrnstein, R. (1985). *Crime and human nature: Intelligence and crime construction*. Cambridge, MA: Harvard University Press.

Wilson, W. J. (1987). *The truly disadvantaged*. Chicago, IL: University of Chicago Press.

Withrow, B. L. (2006). *Racial profiling: From rhetoric to reason.* Upper Saddle River, NJ: Prentice-Hall.

Work, M. N. (1900). Crime among Negroes in Chicago. *American Journal of Sociology, 6*(2), 204–223.

Work, M. N. (1937). Problems of adjustment of the race and class in the South. *Social Forces, 16*(1), 108–117.

Young, V. D. (1996). The politics of disproportionality. (A. T. Sulton, Ed.). *African-American perspectives on crime causation, criminal justice administration and crime prevention.* Boston, MA: Butterworth-Heinemann.

CHAPTER 9

Popular Culture, Media, and Crime

Richelle S. Swan

INTRODUCTION

The interrelationship between popular culture, the media, and crime is complicated and can be approached from many angles. For years, interested scholars focused on a few different questions related to whether particular forms of popular culture influenced delinquency and crime and how the news media and other forms of mass media construct issues of crime, delinquency, and social control. These questions are still important and drive a great deal of research, but our contemporary social world requires us to ask contemporary questions as well. For example, do the popular television reality shows about crime issues impact viewers' behavior? What is the significance when people share examples of their own misbehavior or crime via the Internet or through social media? Although it is difficult to make any conclusive statements about the answers to these questions, one thing is clear when we consider the relationship between contemporary media, popular culture, and crime: The lines between fictional and nonfictional representations of crime are becoming less rigid. As a result, the need to interrogate existing social practices and mediated materials related to crime is more important than ever.

POPULAR THEORETICAL APPROACHES TO THE STUDY OF POPULAR CULTURE, MEDIA, AND CRIME

In order to study issues of popular culture, crime, and media, theoretical approaches that turn a critical eye toward issues of meaning making as they transpire within the larger institutions of the media, the criminal justice system, and overarching socio-political structures are often used. Insights from social constructionism (Berger & Luckmann, 1966), a theory that forwards the idea that people create reality based on their individual interpretation of symbols that are exchanged in processes of social interaction, are often central to such analyses. In the most recent edition of

141

Ray Surette's well-known book, *Media, Crime, and Criminal Justice: Images, Realities, and Policies* (2010), he explains that individuals make sense of the world by means of their personal experiences (i.e., their *experienced reality*) and from information obtained from significant others; social institutions, such as schools, government agencies, religious groups, and unions; and the mass media (i.e., our *symbolic reality*). The mass media can be especially powerful influences in terms of symbolic reality because they offer easy access to information that most of us are not privy to firsthand, and they have the ability to selectively shape, or *frame*, images and stories. Many of the insights from studies on the media, popular culture, and crime are based on analyses of these media frames and their impact (e.g., Chermak, 1995; Fishman & Cavender, 1998; McCormick, 2010). The social constructionist lens is often used in conjunction with conflict theory, feminist theory, and critical race theory in order to uncover the ways in which the mass media frame messages about socioeconomic class, gender, sexuality, race, and ethnicity and the media relationship to crime and social control (e.g., Bissler & Conners, 2012; Covington, 2010; Mann & Zatz, 2002; Rome, 2004; Russell-Brown, 2008).

Cultural criminology, a theoretical approach that first emerged in the 1990s, builds upon insights from earlier sociological and criminological theories, such as symbolic interactionism, labeling theory, and the work of British criminologists from the Birmingham School. According to Ferrell (2013), the social construction of meaning related to crime and social control is fundamental to its analysis,

> We see the power of meaning sometimes by its absence—when, for example, the harms wrought by powerful individuals or groups are allowed to remain meaning-less as regards to legal culpability or moral panic (Jenkins, 1999). We find meaning being made when we listen to the shared argot of marginal groups, or notice the stylistic codes around which illicit subcultures organized and define themselves. And every day, in newspaper headlines and television news feeds, we see meaningful accounts of crime and criminal justice assigned to certain stories, and differently to others. . . . meaning can be seen to be a constitutive element of human actions and a foundation of human culture—and ongoing, everyday process of sense-making, symbolic communication, and contested understanding. (p. 258)

Cultural criminological theory is used to examine the reasons behind people's engagement in popular cultural activities (e.g., street art or graffiti, raves and electronic music events) that are labeled as criminal, deviant, or socially problematic. It is also used to examine the meanings that risky and/or criminal behaviors have to individuals who participate in them as a means of better understanding their genesis. The various ways that people use popular culture and media outlets to resist stereotyping and criminalization by social control agents (through means such as the creation of music, written critiques on blogs and through social media, and the widespread dissemination of videos) are also facilitated by cultural criminological theory. When used in tandem with other theoretical approaches that generally come from a conflict or critical perspective, cultural criminology challenges the ways in which some meanings are legitimized in popular culture while others are delegitimized and the implications this has for crime, justice, and social control. Those using such critical frameworks often focus upon unveiling the structural factors that shape media production in our increasingly globalized world. Such scholarly examinations often consider the implications of the fact that less than 10 media corporations dominate the various communication formats (print, Internet, film, radio and music, and television and satellite) and the global media industry (CBS, NBC, Viacom, Time Warner, Disney, News Corporation, and Bertlesmann; see Arsenault & Castells, 2008; Potter & Kappeler, 2012).

Although works originating from a social constructionist or cultural criminological vein are arguably the most commonly employed by scholars analyzing issues of popular culture and crime today, it is important to note that a multitude of other criminological theories come into play when we consider the specific messages of crime communicated through news stories, books, songs, video games, and other media. In their book, *Criminology Goes to the Movies: Crime Theory and Popular Culture,* Nicole Rafter and Michelle Brown (2011) asserted that a number of traditional theories are apparent in popular cinema, and this is significant when we consider that most of the messages that people receive about crime and crime control are derived from popular culture as a whole. Thus, to understand what messages are being conveyed, a working knowledge of the range of criminological theories—from the individualistic to the sociological—is needed. Rafter and Brown label the space in which academic criminology and popular culture intersect "popular criminology" and claim that the consideration of the crime discourse found there can eventually enrich the development of academic criminological theory and popular culture. According to their perspective, students of criminology and seasoned scholars alike can benefit from turning a critical eye to the mass produced messages of crime and social control that we are subjected to on a daily basis. Although some criminological theories have fallen out of favor among criminologists, they tend to be recycled and reproduced by the media (Surette, 2010).

POPULAR METHODOLOGICAL APPROACHES USED IN THE STUDY OF POPULAR CULTURE, MEDIA, AND CRIME

An assortment of methods is used in studies of popular culture, media, and crime. Quantitative studies using experimental designs and surveys are commonly used alone or in conjunction with qualitative methods, such as interviews, content analysis, and ethnography. Statistical surveys that examine media consumption patterns and attitudes toward crime and/or past delinquent or criminal behavior are used to examine the nature of the relationship between them. Because the analysis of social constructions and meanings is a primary concern of many scholars in the field, qualitative methods, such as content analyses of media texts and discourse, the deconstruction of public messages about crime and justice in the news and entertainment media, and interviews with those who create mediated messages about crime and those who consume the messages, are commonly employed (Ferrell, 2013). Ethnography, which often employs long-term participant observation in a chosen setting, is also a popular method used by scholars who either want to understand the workings of individuals and groups who are engaging in popular culture to commit acts of crime and/or transgression or those who are resisting stereotyping and criminalization of their social group or others' groups. Sometimes, engaging in an ethnographic study translates into lawbreaking by researchers or otherwise risky behaviors as a means of better understanding a group's behavior or a cultural phenomenon (Ferrell & Hamm, 1998; Landry, 2013), but this is not commonly the case.

IMPORTANT RESEARCH THEMES IN STUDIES OF POPULAR CULTURE, MEDIA, AND CRIME

Painting a Punitive Picture: Traditional Media Frames of Crime Issues in Popular Culture and News

Studies of media, popular culture, and crime have often focused on an analysis of media frames, "the focus, a parameter or boundary for discussing a particular event" (Altheide, 1996, p. 45), and the ways in which frames are used to define social problems and then to implicitly or explicitly suggest solutions to those problems. Much research on the frames used to present information about crime, and justice issues show that they tend either to perpetuate a punitive crime control ideology and/or provide misleading or incomplete information about crime and criminal justice issues (Altheide, 1996, 1997; Barak, 1994; Sasson, 1995; Surette, 2010). This has been found to be true across a variety of forms of popular and news media.

For example, fictional and animated characters in cartoons, comic books, and films, are often shown to be crime fighters who are obsessed with obtaining some sort of punishment or retribution for wrongdoers. In Kort-Butler's (2013) examination of depictions of justice in superhero television cartoons (i.e., *Batman, Spider-Man,* and the *Justice League*) over a 15-year time period, she found that viewers were often presented with depictions of the criminal justice system and the actors within it as flawed and unequipped to properly address crime. The superheroes in the cartoons are often shown pursuing crime fighting themselves, claiming that it is their moral duty to do so and employing methods that usually involve breaking the very legal system's rules that they are defending. Ultimately, the messages that are conveyed by these cartoons is that harsh punishment of wrongdoers is uniformly necessary and that the criminal justice system has its limitations but should be respected by people who are not in possession of superpowers. There is no attention paid to the possibility of rehabilitation of wrongdoers or to the necessity of reforming or overhauling a flawed criminal justice system, which sends a message that it is futile to pursue such alternatives.

Mainstream constructions of crime and justice are often reinforced in media forms that focus upon the lives of nonfictional situations and characters as well (Fishman & Cavender, 1998). As a means of contextualizing the relevance of such work, Cecil (2010) explained that viewers of such media often believe them to be unblemished reflections of reality and accept them on face value. The editing behind the images presented may go unnoticed, and the message crafted through the presentation of material by those behind the scenes may go unquestioned. Her analysis of the social construction of crime and justice in reality-based television shows and documentaries about U.S. jails follows in the tradition of other such examinations of prisons and correctional institutions (e.g., Cecil, 2007; Cecil & Leitner, 2009). She finds that the vignettes pieced together in these forms of media tend to emphasize inmate violence, unpredictability, and the need to socially control them by any means available. By ignoring the more common activities of the jail day—such as watching television, reading, and exercising—in favor of showing scenes of violence and reality shows, documentaries tend to conflate jails with prisons and send a confusing message about what jails entail while paying little attention to underlying factors such as substance use problems and mental health challenges. Consequently, viewers are left with little information that might lead them to consider alternatives to punitive responses to inmates or reform of correctional institutions.

Similarly, studies of media frames used by various forms of news sources, including written forms, such as news magazines and newspapers, as well as television news and radio news, show that a skewed framing of crime and justice issues is the norm (e.g., Altheide, 1976, 2009a; Chermak, 1995; Cohen & Young, 1973). Collins, Farrell, McKee, Martin, and Monk-Turner's (2011) analysis of news magazines in both the United States and the United Kingdom demonstrates that the United States' sources tend to focus only upon state crime or governmental crime when the country itself is not involved. This focus on other nations shapes the U.S. public's perceptions of the acts of wrongdoing of those in power in the various levels of government. This is in keeping with the well-backed assertion that "a steady diet of sensationalist crimes hides more mundane and harder-to-detect crimes, just as a focus on street crime hides corporate crime" (McCormick, 2010, p. 11). For example, the typical characteristics of a given crime may be consistently ignored and/or misrepresented in news stories. This often happens in the case of rape, which gets a great deal more attention in the news media when it is perpetrated by a stranger than it does in the much more common case of being perpetrated by someone who is known to a rape victim (Carrabine, 2008; McCormick, 2010). The analysis of multiple forms of crime reporting has demonstrated that sensationalistic and/or partial crime reporting often works to stoke the fears of the general public (Altheide, 1996, 2009b; Chiricos, Padgett, & Gertz, 2000; Potter & Kappeler, 2012; Schlesinger & Tumber, 1994) and fuels other strong emotional reactions as well, including disgust and apathy (McCormick, 2010), which may increase support for punitive crime policies. By the same token, those crimes that are ignored, often crimes of those with some degree of social power, are more likely to go unaddressed in light of little public concern.

FRAMING GONE EXTREME: MORAL PANICS ABOUT CRIME, DELINQUENCY, AND POPULAR CULTURE

Social scientists have revealed that the framing of crime issues often results in a strong public reaction that can be analyzed as moral panic or scares about crime and delinquency (Cohen, 1972; Goode & Ben-Yehuda, 2009). These scares typically share a number of elements: The news and/or entertainment media spread exaggerated information about the prevalence and seriousness of crime and/or an alleged source of crime in the community, interested community members and politicians pick up on the information, and attempts are made to fuel some sort of change or reform to the system. Regardless of whether any meaningful change is accomplished, the particular characterization of the problem tends to fade away and subsequently reemerges in another form (Ferguson & Olson, 2010; Gauntlett, 1995).

These panics are fueled not only by the publicity generated by media sources, such as television shows, news stories, and print journalism, but also, often the very focus of the scares is the *consumption and/or use* of different means of communication and entertainment and how they allegedly lead to crime and delinquency. In the late 1700s, there was a burgeoning concern about the dangers of "explicit" songs as inspiration for lawbreaking (Bates & Swan, 2013). This was soon followed by panics related to the consumption of a number of different media forms and cultural practices and their hypothesized links to delinquency and/or crime. A few examples of these panics include the uproar over attending the theater and acting in the 1800s; listening to or playing jazz music (see McMahon, 1921), reading dime novels (Park, 2002), and watching talking films (Gilbert, 1986) in the early decades of the 1900s; and reading comic books (Goode & Ben-Yehuda, 2009) and listening to rock music in the 1950s. In the later decades of the 20th century, there were uproars about the connection between listening to psychedelic music in the late 1960s and early 1970s and crime, as well as with heavy metal and rap beginning in the 1980s and violent crime (Binder, 1993). In the 21st century, concerns about the dangers of some forms of cultural consumption, such as listening to electronic and other forms of music at raves, are not always characterized by moral outrage but, instead, are highly bureaucratized efforts at "quiet regulation" (Tepper, 2009). In spite of the different form of claims making present in these regulatory efforts, like moral panics, they ultimately facilitate the social control of media and cultural forms, as well as their consumers.

A contemporary moral panic that centers on a proposed link between popular culture, media consumption, and crime is related to playing video games, or *gaming*. Fears that playing violent and crime-ridden video games that are increasingly realistic (e.g., the *Grand Theft Auto* series) led to public discussions among politicians and community members in the early 2000s, following years of concerns that were voiced about gaming since the 1980s. News media and other forms of media were used to spread messages linking violence, crime, and gaming, and eventually, laws were passed prohibiting the sale of extremely violent video games in states, such as California. Later, the U.S. Supreme Court ruled that it was unconstitutional to pass such laws and cited the history of moral panics in their ruling (see *Brown v. Entertainment Merchants Association,* 2011 [vol. 564]).

EFFECTS OF POPULAR CULTURE AND MEDIA CONSUMPTION ON CRIME

An area of research that is related to the recognition of a moral panic is focused upon the effects of popular culture and media consumption. Studies on the possible effects of violent media have been the most prevalent, and they point to what has been labeled as the aggressor, victim, bystander, and appetite effects (Bickham, 2006). In sum, children who engage in violent media consumption are often found to have an increased likelihood to demonstrate aggressive forms of thought or behavior, to have an exaggerated fear of victimization and to experience the world as a scary place, to be desensitized to violence and less likely to care about victims or victimization, and to have an increased appetite for exposure to more violent media. Although many draw on insights from learning theory and assert that these effects will amount to an increase in violent delinquency or crime, there is no conclusive evidence in this regard. Given that most crime that is committed is nonviolent crime, even if media-influenced social aggression inspires some violent crime, it may not inspire a great deal of the crime that occurs today (Surette, 2010).

Current research on media and criminal behavior is hampered by a number of methodological challenges, including the fact that it is difficult to conduct experiments on media effects on crime; the media could be affecting crime in any number of different ways (e.g., influencing people who never committed crime to commit crime; influencing those who have committed crime to commit more crime, or to learn new techniques, or to become more violent in their acts; influencing media consumers to become more greedy and to engage in seemingly condoned acts of crime and violence, etc.); and effects of media consumption are likely intertwined with a number of other social factors affecting crime for only a small subset of people (Savage, 2008; Surette, 2010). Research on copycat crimes, crimes in which the offender mimics or imitates a criminal act, presented in a media portrayal is limited but generally demonstrates that they are committed by a subset of people who have previously committed an offense. These individuals tend to be primed to accept media-generated scripts and ideas about criminals and crimes more readily than most other media consumers (Gunter, 2008).

BEING FRAMED: THE SKEWED REPRESENTATION OF SOCIAL GROUPS IN CRIME, MEDIA, AND ENTERTAINMENT

The bulk of the research on media, popular culture, and crime indicates that the presentation of crime issues in either fictional, "reality," or nonfictional forms, tend to perpetuate the various social inequities and privileges that characterize a given society. The news stories that predominate are those that focus on lower income men of color, and they tend to exaggerate the likelihood of victimization of White, economically privileged members of society, elders, and children (Chiricos, Eschholz, & Gertz, 1997; Potter & Kappeler, 2012). The racialized and class-based messages of reality shows (Beckett & Sasson, 2000; Fishman & Cavendar, 1998; Mann & Zatz, 2002) and video games (Leonard, 2009) follow suit.

Rome (2004) found that Black men are often mistakenly linked to the perpetuation of violent crimes against White people and members of other racial and ethnic groups, due in part to racist stereotypes communicated in various types of crime media, which leads to unjust law enforcement practices, such as racial profiling. Other people of color tend to be met with a variety of problematic experiences as well: Latinos and Asian boys and men are commonly stereotyped as criminals who prey on others in their own ethnic and racial groups, and American Indians are faced with stereotypes related to drinking alcohol, gambling, and vice crimes. Other scholarly examinations of media representations of Black people find that the repeated perpetuation of images of Black men as violent criminals and Black women as irresponsible, oversexualized, and lazy works to further conservative political agendas within criminology and the larger society (Covington, 2010). Video games have been shown to teach players messages about race and racism by portraying youth of color as dangerous criminals or potential criminals (Leonard, 2009). Nationality and status also come into play in the replication of social inequities in the media as immigrants and refugees are often framed by media sources as potential terrorists and imminent threats (Esses, Medianu, & Lawson, 2013).

MEDIATING ONESELF: USING MEDIA AND POPULAR CULTURAL FORMS TO COMMUNICATE MESSAGES ABOUT CRIME AND JUSTICE

Although the framing of crime and justice issues in the mainstream media generally reinforces the need for punitive methods of crime control, fuels moral panics related to crime, and reinforces the marginalization of social groups, the creation of new media forms expand the possibilities for communicating messages about crime and justice. Yar (2012) explained that scholars have long assumed that to understand the relationship between media and crime, one needs to analyze the medias' production and dissemination of crime representations and the effects of exposure to those messages by their respective audiences. But unlike traditional forms of media (e.g., print, records or CDs, radio, film, and television) that involve the communication of messages of a few to many others with accompanying high-production costs, the various forms of new media (e.g., digital audiovisual recordings, computer-generated animation, desktop publishing, and image manipulation) are largely computerized communication technologies that allow many people to distribute their ideas to many others for little cost. For example, today there is widespread access to easily portable technologies, such as smartphones and video cameras, which allow people to record themselves in audio and/or video form with merely a touch of a finger and then to share their creations electronically with audiences big or small. As a result of these technological innovations, people have begun to publicize information about their own crimes and/or acts of misbehavior through the use of videos on YouTube and other online sites and social networking applications, such as Snapchat and Twitter.

The new dynamics of social media raise the question of whether the motivation to present a particular image to the world is increasingly serving as an impetus to commit crimes or acts of wrongdoing. As Yar (2012) noted, the examination of acts of people *mediating messages about themselves* is a necessary reversal of the assumption that the general public are acted upon by media and is a fruitful subject of inquiry for criminological research. He cites acts such as "happy slapping," youth recording themselves hitting or slapping their peers and then distributing the video via multimedia text messages; and "train surfing," people filming themselves or being filmed while standing on the outside of a moving train and jumping off of it, as transgressions that appear to be motivated by the desire to convey a particular image to the world. Once these images are widely disseminated through electronic social networks, the actor ostensibly feels some satisfaction and/or notoriety that may or may not inspire similar acts on the part of viewers. Similarly, researchers have studied other self-mediated framings, such as those related to gang involvement. New media forms are used to boast about gang activity and/or status (King, Walpole, & Lamon, 2007), communicate threats between gangs (Pyrooz, Decker, & Moule, 2013), and distribute videos showing violence between and within groups (Patton, Eschmann, & Butler, 2013).

Although popular media and cultural forms are often used to stoke long-standing stereotypes about the criminality of marginalized groups, they also serve as a means of communicating messages of societal resistance (Alvarez, 2009; Hall & Jefferson, 1976; Martinez, 1997; Negus, 1999; Tepper, 2009). As Ferrell, Hayward, Morrison, and Presdee (2004) explained, "Marginalization and criminalization certainly produce internecine predation, but they also produce, sometimes in the same tangled circumstances, moments in which outsiders collectively twist and shout against their own sorry situations" (p. 22). Saleh-Hanna (2010) finds that a variety of reggae, afrobeat, and hip-hop songs created by Black artists demonstrate such moments in their lyrical challenges to current U.S. criminal justice policies. Many hard-core fans of rap music have been found to view rap music as a form of protest music (Dyson, 2004; Kitwana, 2005; Quinn, 2005; Tanner, Ashbridge, & Wortley, 2009). Fans of acid house music have used alternative media, such as e-mail campaigns, gay focused media, mass mailings, and nonmainstream broadcasting to counter stereotypes about the dangers of raves and to stop measures to pass ordinances against raves (Tepper, 2009). Although girls and women who overtly stand up against gender oppression and victimization are often labeled delinquent or criminal, research has shown that they have persisted in using music and zines (self-published magazines) as a means of resistance (Leblanc, 1999; Schilt, 2003). In addition, social activist groups have used media tools in their campaigns against media messages about crime that they deem questionable, such as those supporting the use of shock incarceration methods for juveniles in the television show *Beyond Scared Straight* (Bates & Swan, 2013). All of these examples of resistance demonstrate that the relationship between popular culture, media, and crime continues to be a complex one that escapes simple characterizations and requires additional scholarly examination.

DISCUSSION QUESTIONS

1. Pick your favorite television show or film related to crime and consider how the issues of crime and social control are framed. What is/are the implied causes of crime? How are the "solutions" to the crime problem framed?

2. Analyze any experiences you may have had with the various forms of "new media" that allow for the easy dissemination of images and ideas about crime, criminalization, and social control to audiences of your choosing. How did you learn about these tools of communication? How have you used them in the past and to what effect/s?

3. When people make claims about the relationship between the consumption of violent media and crime, what factors do they need to take into consideration according to the existing research?

4. List and analyze at least three pieces of popular culture (e.g., songs, poems, books, blog posts, etc.) that have messages of resistance related to unjust stereotyping and/or injustice in the criminal justice system. Consider what audiences are generally exposed to these media forms and their messages and the related implications.

REFERENCES

Altheide, D. L. (1976). *Creating reality: How TV news distorts events.* Beverly Hills, CA: SAGE.

Altheide, D. L. (1996). *Qualitative media analysis.* Thousand Oaks, CA: SAGE.

Altheide, D. L. (1997). The news media, the problem frame, and the production of fear. *Sociological Quarterly, 38*(4), 647–668.

Altheide, D. L. (2009a). *Terror post 9/11 and the media.* New York, NY: Peter Lang.

Altheide, D. L. (2009b). The Columbine shootings and a discourse of fear. *American Behavioral Scientist, 52*(10), 1354–1370.

Alvarez, L. (2009). *The power of the zoot: Youth culture and resistance during World War II.* Berkeley: University of California Press.

Arsenault, A. H., & Castells, M. (2008). The structure and dynamics of global multimedia business networks. *International Journal of Communication, 2,* 707–748.

Barak, G. (Ed.). (1994). *Media, process, and the social construction of crime.* New York, NY: Garland Press.

Bates, K. A., & Swan, R. S. (2013). *Juvenile delinquency in a diverse society.* Thousand Oaks, CA: SAGE.

Beckett, K., & Sasson, T. (2000). *The politics of injustice.* Thousand Oaks, CA: Pine Forge.

Berger, P., & Luckmann, T. (1966). *The social construction of reality: A treatise in the sociology of knowledge.* New York, NY: Anchor Books.

Bickham, D. (2006, March 29). Testimony before the Senate *Judiciary Committee on the Constitution, civil rights and property rights.* Retrieved from http://www.judiciary.senate .gov/hearings/testimony.cfm?id=e655f9e2809e5476862f735da111ac22&wit_id=e655f9 e2809e5476862f735da111ac22-1-4

Binder, A. (1993). Constructing racial rhetoric: Media depictions of harm in heavy metal and rap music. *American Sociological Review, 58*(6), 753-767.

Bissler, D. L., & Conners, J. L. (2012). (Eds.). *The harms of crime media: Essays on the perpetuation of racism, sexism, and class stereotypes.* Jefferson, NC: McFarland.

Brown v. Entertainment Merchants Association, 2011, 564 U.S. 08-1448.

Carrabine, E. (2008). *Crime, culture and the media.* Cambridge, United Kingdom: Polity Press.

Cecil, D. K. (2007). Looking beyond "Caged heat": Media images of women in prison. *Feminist Criminology, 29*(4), 304-306.

Cecil, D. K. (2010). Televised images of jail: Lessons in controlling the unruly. *Sociology of Crime, Law & Deviance, 14,* 67-88.

Cecil, D. K., & Leitner, J. L. (2009). Unlocking the gates: An examination of MSNBC Investigates—Lockup. *Howard Journal of Criminal Justice, 48*(2), 184-199.

Chermak, S. (1995). *Victims in the news: Crime and the American news media.* Boulder, CO: Westview Press.

Chiricos, T., Eschholz, S., & Gertz, M. (1997). Crime, news, and fear of crime. *Social Problems, 44*(3), 342-357.

Chiricos, T., Padgett, K., & Gertz, M. (2000). Fear, TV news, and the reality of crime. *Criminology, 38*(3), 755-785.

Cohen, S. (1972). *Folk devils and moral panics.* London, United Kingdom: MacGibbon & Kee.

Cohen, S., & Young, J. (Eds.). (1973). *The manufacture of news: Deviance, social problems, and the mass media.* London, United Kingdom: Constable.

Collins, V. E., Farrell, A. L., McKee, J. R., Martin, F. A., & Monk-Turner, E. (2011). The state of coverage: The media's representation of international issues and state crime. *International Criminal Justice Review, 21*(1), 5-21.

Covington, J. (2010). *Crime and racial constructions: Cultural misinformation about African Americans in media and academia.* Lanham, MD: Lexington Books.

Dyson, M. E. (2004). *The Michael Dyson reader.* New York, NY: Basic Civitas Books.

Esses, V. M., Medianu, S., & Lawson, A. S. (2013). Uncertainty, threat, and the role of the media in promoting the dehumanization of immigrants and refugees. *Journal of Social Issues, 69*(3), 518-536.

Ferguson, C. J., & Olson, C. K. (2010). The Supreme Court and video game violence: Will regulation be worth the costs to the first amendment? *The Criminologist, 35*(4), 18-21.

Ferrell, J. (2013). Cultural criminology and the politics of meaning. *Critical Criminology, 21*(3), 257-271.

Ferrell, J., & Hamm, M. (1998). *Ethnography at the edge: Crime, deviance, and field research.* Chicago, IL: Northeastern University Press.

Ferrell, J., Hayward, K., Morrison, W., & Presdee, M. (Eds.). (2004). *Cultural criminology unleashed.* London, United Kingdom: Glasshouse Press.

Fishman, M., & Cavender, G. (Eds.). (1998). *Entertaining crime.* New York, NY: Aldine de Gruyter.

Gauntlett, D. (1995). *Moving experiences: Understanding television's influences and effects.* Luton, United Kingdom: John Libbey.

Gilbert, J. B. (1986). *A cycle of outrage: America's reaction to the juvenile delinquency in the 1950s.* New York, NY: Oxford University Press.

Goode, E., & Ben-Yehuda, N. (2009). *Moral panics: The social construction of deviance* (2nd ed.). Malden, MA: Wiley-Blackwell.

Gunter, B. (2008). Media violence: Is there a case for causality? *American Behavioral Scientist, 51*(8), 1061–1122.

Hall, S., & Jefferson, T. (1976). *Resistance through rituals.* London, United Kingdom: Hutchinson.

King, J. E., Walpole, C. E., & Lamon, K. (2007). Surf and turf wars online: Growing implications of Internet gang violence. *Journal of Adolescent Health, 41*(6), S66–S68.

Kitwana, B. (2005). *Why White kids love hip hop: Wankstas, wiggers, wannabes, and the new reality of race in America.* New York, NY: Basic Civitas Books.

Kort-Butler, L. (2013). Justice league?: Depictions of justice in children's superhero cartoons. *Criminal Justice Review, 38*(1), 50–69.

Landry, D. (2013). Are we human? Edgework in defiance of the mundane and measurable. *Critical Criminology, 21*(1), 1–14.

LeBlanc, L. (1999). *Pretty in punk: Girl's gender resistance in a boy's subculture.* New Brunswick, NJ: Rutgers University Press.

Leonard, D. (2009). Young, Black (& Brown) and don't give a fuck: Virtual gangstas in the era of state violence. *Cultural Studies-Critical Methodologies, 9*(2), 248–272.

Mann, C. R., & Zatz, M. S. (Eds.). (2002). *Images of color, images of crime* (2nd ed.). Los Angeles, CA: Roxbury.

Martinez, T. A. (1997). Popular culture as oppositional culture: Rap as resistance. *Sociological Perspectives, 40*(2), 265–286.

McCormick, C. (2010). *Constructing danger: Emotions and the mis/representation of crime in the news.* Black Point, Nova Scotia, Canada: Fernwood Press.

McMahon, J. R. (1921, December). Unspeakable jazz must go. *Ladies Home Journal, 38,* pp. 115–116.

Negus, K. (1999). *Music genres and corporate cultures.* London, United Kingdom: Routledge.

Park, D. (2002). The Kefauver comic book hearings as show trial: Decency, authority, and the dominated expert. *Cultural Studies, 16*(2), 259–288.

Patton, D. U., Eschmann, R. D., & Butler, D. A. (2013). Internet banging: New trends in social media, gang violence, masculinity and hip-hop. *Computers in Human Behavior, 29*(5), A54–A59.

Potter, W. J., & Kappeler, V. E. (2012). Introduction: Media, crime and hegemony. In D. L. Bissler & J. L. Conners (Eds.), *The harms of crime media: Essays on the perpetuation of racism, sexism, and class stereotypes* (pp. 3–17). Jefferson, NC: McFarland.

Pyrooz, D. C., Decker, S. H., & Moule, R. K. (2013). Crime and routine activities in online settings: Gangs, offenders and the Internet. *Justice Quarterly, 30*(3), 1–29.

Quinn, E. (2005). *Nuthin' but a "G" thang.* New York, NY: Columbia University Press.

Rafter, N., & Brown, M. (2011). *Criminology goes to the movies: Crime theory and popular culture.* New York: New York University Press.

Rome, D. (2004). *Black demons: The media's depiction of the Black male criminal stereotype.* Westport, CT: Praeger.

Russell-Brown, K. (2008). *The color of crime: Racial hoaxes, White fear, Black protectionism, police harassment, and other microaggressions* (2nd ed.). New York: New York University Press.

Saleh-Hanna, V. (2010). Crime, resistance and song: Black musicianship's Black criminology. *Sociology of Crime, Law & Deviance, 14*, 145–171.

Sasson, T. (1995). *Crime talk: How citizens construct a social problem.* Hawthorne, NY: Aldine de Gruyter.

Savage, J. (2008). The role of exposure to media violence in the etiology of violent behavior: A criminologist weighs in. *American Behavioral Scientist, 51*(8), 1123–1136.

Schilt, K. (2003). "I'll resist with every breath": Girls and zine making as a form of resistance. *Youth and Society, 35*(1), 71–97.

Schlesinger, P., & Tumber, H. (1994). *Reporting crime: The media politics of criminal justice.* Oxford, United Kingdom: Oxford University Press.

Surette, R. (2010). *Media, crime, and criminal justice: Images, realities, and policies* (4th ed.). Belmont, CA: Wadsworth.

Tanner, J., Ashbridge, M., & Wortley, S. (2009). Listening to rap: Cultures of crime, cultures of resistance. *Social Forces, 88*(2), 693–722.

Tepper, S. J. (2009). Stop the beat: Quiet regulation and cultural conflict. *Sociological Forum, 24*(2), 276–306.

Yar, M. (2012). Crime, media and the will-to-representation: Reconsidering relationships in the new media age. *Crime, Media, Culture, 8*(3), 245–260.

CHAPTER 10

Crime and Economics

Consumer Culture, Criminology, and the Politics of Exclusion

Stephen L. Muzzatti[1]

W hat does the American Dream mean today? For Niko Bellic, fresh off the boat from Europe, it is the hope he can escape his past. For his cousin, Roman, it is the vision that together they can find fortune in Liberty City, gateway to the land of opportunity. As they slip into debt and are dragged into a criminal underworld by a series of shysters, thieves, and sociopaths, they discover that the reality is very different from the dream in a city that worships money and status and is heaven for those who have them and a living nightmare for those who do not.[2]

INTRODUCTION: A SPECTRE IS HAUNTING CRIMINOLOGY . . .

The connection between crime and economics is complex and multifaceted. Perhaps because of this density, thorough coverage of the topic of crime and economics has proved to be so elusive to mainstream or administrative criminology, particularly in the United States, despite some ostensibly elaborate and occasionally very high-profile attempts to address it. In some respects, the topic is anathema to criminology. While such an assertion may read as sacrilegious to orthodox criminologists, it is not anywhere near as wildly unsubstantiated as some of orthodoxy's high priests might retort. As any devoted reader of the indecipherable articles that fill such journals as *Criminology* and *Justice Quarterly* (to say nothing of moribund textbooks and stale government reports) can undoubtedly attest, a plethora of criminological studies purport to address the matter of crime and economics. However, many (dare I suggest most) of these studies, if they address economics at all, do so in a disjointed, limited, and myopic way. In various degrees, these studies attempt to account for the impact of economics on crime rates, ethnoracial or subcultural variations in offending, policing practices, criminogenic age cohorts, victimization risks, incarceration, recidivism, and a host of other issues. They do so in a sophisticated and nuanced fashion, symbolically representing crime's factors with *lambda* and *chi,* employing elaborate multiple-regression models and the latest statistical alchemy (see Ferrell, Hayward, & Young, 2008; Muzzatti, 2006, 2010). They ultimately tell us very little about crime and economics. While I do not mean to cast any aspersions upon the researchers involved or question the countless hours of work and effort they devote to these projects, most fall victim to a fatal ontological flaw: They fail to address capitalism.

It seems that *capitalism* is a bad word in criminology. It is not something to be discussed in polite company (such as at the American Society of Criminology's annual meetings) lest you be labeled a leftist ideologue or, worse, a reductionist; and it is certainly not something to be committed to print (except occasionally, in esoteric, European-based criminology journals). Academic criminology's gatekeepers have long been aware of the potential consequences associated with allowing an unbridled thrashing of the "C-word" and work diligently to prevent it from sullying the good name of the discipline.[3] Aside from a few serpentine flashes, any emancipatory potential to be found in criminology is met with the Marcusian repressive tolerance of program committees, blind reviewers, institutional ethics boards, tenure and promotion committees, and outside funding sources like the National Institute of Justice (NIJ). It is far easier and more respectable to facilitate work on "nuts, sluts, and perverts" and "the exotic, the erotic, and the neurotic" under the aegis of "value-free" voodoo criminology and the numbers game than to risk the ire of editors, publishers, and granting agencies, to say nothing of the grief that one will undoubtedly suffer at the hands of orthodox criminology's high priests and most of the lesser clergy who totter along in ideological lockstep (Muzzatti, 2003; Young, 1999, 2007).

I am fortunate that editors Mary Maguire and Dan Okada were not only open to but also enthusiastic about including in this collection an ontological and epistemological challenge to the crime and economics canon. For that I am grateful. Of course, readers should note that any shortcomings or foibles are mine alone. Readers should also be aware that, in addition to the term *capitalism,* they will encounter throughout this chapter a number of other profanities well outside criminology's polite lexicon (e.g., *political economy, late modernity,* etc.) as I attempt to historically and genealogically reconstruct a criminology of capitalism.

READING THE PROFANE: THEORIZING CRIME AND CAPITALISM

While it is true that many contemporary American criminologists fail to address the role of capitalism in matters of crime (whether causation, creation, reification, or commodification), some late 19th- and early 20th-century European scholars paid it considerable attention. In the following section, I briefly address the work of two often-overlooked criminological theorists, Germany's Karl Marx and Holland's Willem Bonger, as a means of contextualizing extant issues of crime and capitalism in 21st-century America.

Karl Marx (1818–1883)

Considering his vast corpus of work, it is perhaps not surprising that many criminologists overlook Karl Marx's writing on crime. With the exception of his article "Debates on the Law on the Thefts of Wood" in 1842[4] and a few pieces for the *New York Daily Tribune*[5] in the 1850s, Marx rarely addressed the topic of crime specifically. However, he wrote extensively about capitalism as an economic and political system and the way this system essentially produced two classes of people: *capitalists* and *proletarians*. Because capitalists owned the means of production, they also were able to exert almost total control over social institutions (including but not limited to what we today understand as the criminal justice system) and were able to entrench their beliefs and values as *the* beliefs and values of society. In contrast, the proletarians owned and controlled nothing and hence were obliged to exchange their ability to work for a wage at the discretion of the capitalists. For Marx, the social production of concrete material relations—relations by which people secured their material existence—permeated all aspects of life. Because of this, the capitalist ruling class was able to translate its economic power into political and ideological power. Through his endeavor to illustrate that the material basis for systemic inequality produced conflict (which can manifest itself as crime), Marx provided the requisite conceptual tools for answering questions about crime.

At the risk of oversimplifying, Marx theorized that the criminal and criminal law are inextricably bound to the larger economic order. In *The German Ideology* (1846/1976), Marx and his coauthor, Friedrich Engels, described crime as the struggle of the isolated individual against the prevailing conditions. In other words, it was the economy, specifically industrial capitalism, that determined crime's incarnations. The creation and enforcement of law were at the discretion of the capitalist class. Though this thesis was ignored by most American criminologists, these correlates of crime and inequality are certainly no less true today than when Marx and Engels first described them.

Willem Adriaan Bonger (1876–1940)

Between the time of Marx's death and the first decade of the 20th century, a criminology of the capitalist economic system was emerging in several European nations, notably France, Germany, and Italy.[6] The late 1880s, in particular, saw a proliferation of these works by Italian criminologists, such as Bruno Battaglia, Napoleone Colajanni, and Filippo Turati. However, to the considerable detriment of Anglo-American criminology, few of these stellar contributions were ever translated into English.[7] A notable and instructive exception was the translation of Dutch criminologist Willem Bonger's book, *Criminalite et Conditions Economiques* (1905).

As a young man, Bonger studied law at the University of Amsterdam. It was here that he became well acquainted with the work of Marx and was inspired to study the political economy of crime by G. A. van Hamel, a renowned penologist who was his criminal-law professor. While Bonger made several major contributions to criminology in the areas of racism and criminal justice, suicide, penal philosophy, and militarism and war, it was the English translation of *Criminality and Economic Conditions* (1905/1916) that proved to be his most enduring and the one most relevant to this chapter.

According to Bonger, capitalism is criminogenic. Put simply, capitalism's brutality creates conditions under which crime is not only produced but also flourishes. For Bonger, crime and capitalism are connected in three fundamental ways. Bonger employed the historical materialism of Marx and Engels in illustrating the first of these connections: the development of criminal law in unison with the aggrandizement of property rights. Hence, for Bonger, the history of theft is the history of private property. Much of criminal law was created to protect the property of the haves from the have-nots. Connected to this was Bonger's second major assertion: that crime is engendered by the miserable conditions forced upon the working class in the emergence of industrial capitalism. Finally, and most prescient for the consideration of crime under late modernity, Bonger theorizes that the economic logic of capitalism promotes endless greed and fosters crime.

Both Marx and Bonger addressed the myriad ways capitalism produces crime, including the miserable conditions under which the majority of the population languished, the biased creation and application of law, and the destructive values of avarice and individualism that permeated industrial society. However, with the notable exception of what came to be known as the conflict criminology[8] of William Chambliss, Elliot Currie (1997), Julia and Herman Schwendinger, Steven Spitzer, Tony Platt, and Richard Quinney in the 1970s and 1980s, few American criminologists took up these themes with vigor.[9]

BANALITY AND VICIOUSNESS IN LATE MODERNITY

While the conditions of 21st-century America are very different from the early and high industrialism of Marx's and Bonger's Europe, capitalism rages on, leaving a broad swath of destruction and human suffering, including but not limited to what is narrowly defined as crime. Contrary to the vociferous pronouncements of capitalist running dogs, market-order cheerleaders, and neoliberal apologists, globalization and the concomitant postindustrialization have not made the American landscape a better, safer, or more humane environment. Massive transnational corporations the size and scope of which the authors of the Sherman Antitrust Act could nary imagine continue to steal and murder with impunity, street crime is evermore racialized, minor transgressions increasingly come to be addressed through the criminal justice system's formal and punitive mechanisms, and living-wage jobs are nearly impossible to find and even more difficult to keep.

Under such conditions, it is little wonder that people are adrift and cling desperately to anything that promises more stability than late modernism's liquidity (see Bauman, 2000). Unfortunately, there is relatively little available on which people, particularly young people, can moor themselves. As Hall, Winlow, and Ancrum (2008) illustrated with great aplomb, because the global capitalist project is increasingly reliant upon *finance* capital rather than *productive* capital, material reality has readily been displaced by a fictitious realm of fleeting visceral pleasure and ephemeral amelioration. Hence, unlike pre-deindustrialized generations, in which social worth was determined through the relationship to the means of production and other stratified forms of social meaning, under late modernity ourselves and our subjectivities are increasingly determined through our consumption practices (Ewen, 1977, 1988; Hayward & Yar, 2006; Muzzatti, 2010, 2013). In his seminal work on crime and consumer culture, Hayward (2004) illustrated that the products and services we acquire and access through our consumer exercises are the primary indices of identity. While there is nothing inherently new about capitalism's unapologetic promotion of consumerism as a gateway to social integration, the process has accelerated rapidly over the past decade, reaching gargantuan proportions. Today, the creation and expression of identities via the celebration of consumer goods have all but supplanted other, more traditional forms of identity expression. This, in combination with the aforementioned withdrawal of meaningful, living-wage employment opportunities, seriously undermines the life world, moral codes, and habitus of ordinary people (Bourdieu, 1984; Hall et al., 2008).

YOUTH AND THE VICISSITUDES OF LATE MODERNITY

Commenting on his experiences living and working in 1830s Manchester, Engels (1845/1973) wrote of the English working class's children,

> And children growing up in this savage way, amidst the demoralizing influences, are expected to turn out good-goody and moral in the end! Verily the requirements are naive, which the self satisfied bourgeois makes upon the working man! (p. 168)

Again, although he was writing about a place very different from 21st-century America, Engels's insight should not be lost on those of us who strive to better understand the contemporary workings of consumer capitalism and its impact on the every day and night lived experiences of young people. Although it is not my intention to demonize America's youth (that is the purview of the corporately owned news media), it behooves us to realize that the 18- to 25-year-old demographic is responsible for a not insignificant portion of traditional street crime, particularly violent street crime. So too, and perhaps equally as telling, young people disproportionately find themselves the subjects of the orthodox criminological lens. Historically, orthodox criminology's treatment of youth delinquency and crime has been no better than, and in some respects worse than, its "efforts" to address capitalism. However well intentioned, the canon—from "inverted values" and "generating milieus of gang delinquency" through "subcultures of violence" and "elements of bonding"—has provided little insight into youth involvement in criminality and has reified class bias both within academic criminological discourse and, more disturbingly, among criminal justice policy makers and practitioners.[10]

The criminalization of youth and class is itself part of the ideological work of capitalism. By suggesting that a particular working-class or underclass age cohort holds a monopoly on crime, orthodox criminology transmits a political economy of values that serves the interests of global capital while positioning the marginalized subject group for optimal regulation and control. It does so in part by atomizing or individualizing social problems and furtively sheathing late capitalism's destructive values beneath a veneer of spectacle and the *carnivalesque* (see Presdee, 2000).

CONSUMING CRIME AND CULTURE

Scything through capitalism's veneer, it is evident that lives of late-modern subjects have been so thoroughly colonized by consumerism that the goals–means discrepancy (i.e., "strain") Merton (1938) described over 70 years ago seems almost benign in comparison. Indeed, living in a world where work, if it exists at all, is increasingly deskilled, wages are pitifully low, and growing segments of the former middle classes slip into a vortex of unsecured debt, it is little wonder that consumption itself is now *the* strategy employed to demarcate, compartmentalize, and control the general public (see, relatedly, Bauman, 2000, 2007; Wilson, 1987). This transformation has served only to intensify capitalism's inequality. According to Bauman, late-modern consumer society is now polarized between indemnified, privileged, and dutiful consumers on the one hand and, on the other, the increasingly swollen ranks of the marginalized and criminalized classes, who, as a result of either inability or unwillingness, have failed to acquiesce to the hegemonic dictates of consumerism. The first of these groups, the "Seduced," comprises individuals who exhibit the requisite desire and fixation required by unmediated consumer societies. More important, though, they are in a position to satisfy their desire through continual cycles of unreflexive hyperconsumption. Standing in stark contrast to the Seduced are the "Repressed," a group that embodies what one might describe as the *collateral damage* of consumerism. This throng of uncommoditized or failed consumers represent an ever-growing, marginalized mass who, through negligence or willfulness, fail to adequately acquit themselves of their consumer "duties." The Repressed's insufficient and/or disreputable consumption patterns do not satisfactorily integrate them into the acceptable echelons of consumer society (Muzzatti, 2004, 2010). Though highly stylized, the opening soliloquy by Mark Renton, the heroin-addicted antihero from the film *Trainspotting*, sardonically captures the nihilism that is both the predictable and not unreasonable consequence of such a vicious bifurcation:

> Choose Life. Choose a job. Choose a career. Choose a family. Choose a fucking big television, choose washing machines, cars, compact disc players and electrical tin openers. Choose good health, low cholesterol, and dental insurance.

Choose fixed interest mortgage repayments. Choose a starter home. Choose your friends. Choose leisurewear and matching luggage. Choose a three-piece suit on hire purchase in a range of fucking fabrics. Choose DIY and wondering who the fuck you are on a Sunday morning. Choose sitting on that couch watching mind-numbing, spirit-crushing game shows, stuffing fucking junk food into your mouth. Choose rotting away at the end of it all, pishing your last in a miserable home, nothing more than an embarrassment to the selfish, fucked up brats you spawned to replace yourself. Choose your future. Choose life.[11]

LATE MODERNITY, CRIME, AND PSEUDO-PACIFICATION

What is of importance in terms of this chapter (and something overlooked by Bauman) is the way in which late modernity's ideological work serves not only to incessantly remind us of this bifurcation but also acts to control and manipulate us by illustrating the consequences of lax or ineffectual consumption work (Muzzatti, 2010, 2013). As Hall and his colleagues poignantly illustrated, late capitalism systematically organizes conditions of social insecurity while simultaneously lauding aggressive competition and individual hubris (Hall et al., 2008). Unlike the "norms" of the Mertonian framework, late modernity's norms are created in the fantasy world of venture capitalism, hyperwealth, and unlimited personal and natural resources. Such arrangements are potentially criminogenic, as they detach people from reality, breed frustration, and undermine any true sense of community and solidarity by fostering irresponsible and wholly instrumental attitudes toward other people (Hall et al., 2008). A rank, dog-eat-dog individualism and fortress mentality are vital components of late modernity's depoliticalization process, which lulls the populace into a state of false insecurity. Alternately described as *anelpis* (Taylor as cited in Hall & Winlow, 2004, p. 277) and *vertigo* (Young, 2007, p. 12), this malaise of late modernity is characterized by total cynicism, no opinions (except as they relate to the incontrovertibly mundane), no hope, a sense of entitlement, unrealistic expectations, giddiness, unsteadiness, uncertainty, and insecurity. Perhaps most significantly, it is evidenced by misplaced fear—not a legitimate fear of government, corporations, or other authority, but a misplaced and unrealistic fear of other people.

Capitalism produces numerous contradictions. In late modernity, we live in isolation from our neighbors and cut ourselves off from all but a small number of intimates, yet we pay high monthly fees to have cable companies and satellite providers pump mediated images of the outside world into our homes. We distrust strangers and move briskly to maintain our physical distance from those we do not recognize on the street, but we loudly discuss our most intimate personal details on mobile phones in shopping malls and post the prosaic intricacies of our lives on social networking sites for anyone to see. We are suspicious of those who migrate to our shores, because they may take our jobs or not work and live off our tax dollars. We fear terrorism but fail to scrutinize the foreign policy of our own government lest we be labeled un-American. Perhaps capitalism's greatest obfuscation is found in the fact that we continually feed our cravings for inexpensive consumer goods but fail to consider the real costs—economic, social, and environmental, at home and abroad—of doing so.[12]

SELLING CRIME, MARKETING TRANSGRESSION, AND COMMODIFYING VIOLENCE

Even in their most surreal nightmares, it is unlikely that either Marx or Bonger could have envisaged the leviathan proportions and seemingly infinite tentacles of 21st-century capitalism. However, given their respective historical contexts, both offered some discerning commentary on the salability of crime. In the first volume of *Theories of Surplus Value* (1861), Marx's insights into the marketability of crime are perhaps even more poignant under today's conditions of late modernity than when it was first written. According to him (as cited in Greenberg, 1981),

> The criminal produces not only crime but also criminal law, and even the inevitable text-book in which the professor presents his lectures as a commodity for sale in the market . . . but also art, literature, novels and the tragic drama, as *Oedipus* and *Richard III*. . . . (pp. 52–53)

In a similar vein and in stark contrast to most contemporary criminology textbooks, Bonger begins *Criminality and Economic Conditions* (1905/1916) not with the conventional hyperbolic pieties about the current state of crime and justice but instead with several pages devoted to Thomas More's (1516/1965) fictional account of the traveler Raphael Hythloday.[13] Although these examples focus on suffering under petty mercantilism and other precapitalist economic formations, they do address the narcissistic individualism that capitalism has exacerbated under late modernity.

While several early British conflict criminologists examined the way the news media used crime to sell (see Cohen, 1972; Cohen & Young, 1973; Hall, Critcher, Jefferson, Clarke, & Roberts, 1978), only in the last decade or so have criminologists seriously investigated the connection between crime and the entertainment media. A new wave of cultural criminologists has applied the contributions of such Frankfurt School theorists as Max Horkheimer and Theodor Adorno (1946/1972) to an understanding of the role played by the culture industries in transmitting corporate consumerism's destructive values. Ferrell and Sanders were among the first of this new wave to examine how mass, or common, culture is recast as crime. They theorized that the criminalization of everyday life is a cultural enterprise of the powerful and must be investigated as such (Ferrell & Sanders, 1995, p. 7). Similarly, Presdee's (2000) analysis of carnal desire and the sensuality of wickedness demonstrates how our everyday and night responses to late modernity come to be defined as criminal. Analogizing mediated crime to the board game Monopoly, Presdee examined the way in which crime, like monopoly capitalism, is dehistoricized, whitewashed, and transmogrified into mass-marketed pleasure. Citing a range of examples, from Internet bondage sites and arson to stolen-car racing and weapon bazaars, Presdee explored the contradictions and irrationality of a commodity-oriented society from which criminalized culture emanates.

More recently, cultural criminologists have been attentive to the processes and products associated with what they have variously described as the "marketing of transgression" (Hayward, 2004) and the "commodification of violence" (Ferrell et al., 2008). This visual representation of crime and transgression, they argued, is not only central to the production of news but now also a vital component of the entertainment media—gripping the collective imagination of television viewers, moviegoers, Internet browsers, video gamers, and other audiences. To a certain extent, of course, there is nothing intrinsically new about the use of this type of imagery in the service of consumerism; certainly, crime and violence have been used to sell movie tickets, TV programs, video games, and music for decades. However, what is new, as Ferrell, Hayward, and Young illustrated, is the force and range of these "illicit" messages (2008, p. 140) and the effect it has had on the tectonic landscape of the late-modern entertainment media. In particular, there appears to be a far greater willingness among *mainstream corporations* to utilize allusions to crime and transgression to give their products edgy appeal while still serving the conservative interests of consumer capitalism and its control functions. Considering late capitalism's oligopolistic media ownership patterns, it is perhaps not surprising that the same racialized and class-biased images of the new "dangerous classes" (i.e., chavs and hoodies in Canada and the United Kingdom; ghetto-fabulous bangers in the United States) that are meant to frighten the public on the news are also now employed to entertain us and sell us a host of products and services.

CONCLUSION: NOTHING TO LOSE BUT OUR CHAINS

This chapter's epigram from the enormously popular video/PC-game *Grand Theft Auto IV* poignantly illustrates the harsh and unforgiving landscape of late modernity. While the narrative framing of the Bellic cousins is fictional, the brutality of capitalism that undergirds the story-bound Liberty City is all too real in 21st-century America. Inexplicably, orthodox criminology continually fails to address this crimogenesis.

Irrespective of whether we conceptualize such a paucity of attention as obstinacy or as benign neglect, the end result differs little; the material conditions that influence our lives—and, indeed, the single most influential factor not only in the production, distribution, and consumption of crime but as well a driving force that has transformed human existence more in the last 200 years than anything in the previous millennia—remain unstudied by our discipline.

If there is a silver lining to this cloud, it is that late-modern capitalism's multiple appendages, coupled with orthodox criminology's inability and/or unwillingness to address it, leaves many openings available to those inclined to challenge the hegemony of these twin sacred cows. Certainly, from environmental racism and the prison industrial complex through the disappearance of work and crimes of globalization, the fissures are legion.

The intention of this chapter, as astute readers likely surmised several pages back, was to provide neither a comprehensive assessment nor, for that matter, a general overview of the literature on crime and economics. In fact, some readers may be uncomfortable with this chapter's leap from Marx and Bonger to a 21st-century criminology of capitalism. I am among them.[14] However, my intention here was to produce not a definitive piece but rather a heuristic tool through which readers can intellectually and politically confront the intersecting convenient fictions of late capitalism and orthodox criminology. As such, perhaps much of this chapter was superfluous; perhaps all that was required was the epigram.

DISCUSSION QUESTIONS

1. Other than the specific disciplinary constraints intimated by the author, why has American criminology failed to adequately address capitalism?

2. The author cites *Grand Theft Auto IV* as a crime–capitalism narrative. Draw on your own experiences with popular culture texts to provide another example.

3. Make a list of several street crimes and white-collar, corporate, or state crimes, and illustrate their connections to capitalism.

4. The author enumerates several examples of how capitalism fosters contradictory forms of human behavior. Provide examples of other such contradictions.

NOTES

1. The author gratefully acknowledges the research assistance of Brandon Rigato in the preparation of this chapter.
2. *Grand Theft Auto IV,* www.gta4.net
3. See, for example, William Chambliss (1989).
4. The article was the third of three that Marx was commissioned to write on the Proceedings of the Sixth Rhine Province Assembly for *The Rheinische Zeitung.* The paper published only the first and the third.
5. "Capital Punishment" (February 18, 1853) and "Population Crime and Pauperism" (September 16, 1859).
6. See Bonger (1905/1916, pp. 673–700).
7. Sadly, instead of translations of these, English language criminology was introduced to the racist, misogynistic, and bigoted work of Lombroso and other biodeterminist European criminologists. The seeding of this "pathological" theory to the American criminological canon was certainly fueled by, and served as an accelerant for, the eugenics movement and facilitated the growth of a homegrown pathological school (e.g., Henry Goddard, Ernest Hooton, Eleanor and Sheldon Glueck).

8. In the intervening years, the paradigm alternately came to be known as *radical* or *Marxist criminology*. Today, it is generally referred to as *critical criminology* and encompasses a variety of traditions, including left realist, peacemaking, social justice, anarchist, convict, state, feminist, and cultural criminologies.

9. A parallel but perhaps slightly more effervescent trajectory also emerged in the United Kingdom at this time, including the work of Stanley Cohen, Stuart Hall, Carol Smart, Ian Taylor (1983, 1999), Paul Walton, and Jock Young.

10. See Selke, Corsaros, & Selke (2002).

11. *Trainspotting* (1996), a screenplay by John Hodge based on Irvine Welsh's novel.

12. Many of the same structural conditions that facilitate the crimes by the capitalist state abroad also contribute to the social harms it inflicts on people in America (see Tifft & Sullivan, 1980).

13. Published as a novel in 1516, St. Thomas More's *Utopia* described a land of economic equality.

14. Among my most egregious offenses herein is relegating the rich, vibrant work of many of America's founding conflict criminologists to passing references and footnotes. It was a conscious decision made in keeping with space limitations. I hope that readers can take more from the chapter than a redundant and woefully incomplete history lesson.

REFERENCES

Bauman, Z. (2000). *Liquid modernity*. Cambridge, United Kingdom: Polity Press.

Bauman, Z. (2007). Collateral casualties of consumerism. *Journal of Consumer Culture, 7*(1), 25–56.

Bonger, W. A. (1905). *Criminalite et Conditions Economiques*. Amsterdam, Netherlands: G. P. Tierie.

Bonger, W. A. (1916). *Criminality and economic conditions* (H. P. Horton, Trans.). Boston, MA: Little, Brown. (Original work published 1905)

Bourdieu, P. (1984). *Distinction: A social critique of the judgment of taste*. Cambridge, MA: Harvard University Press.

Chambliss, W. (1989). On trashing Marxist criminology. *Criminology, 27*(2), 231–238.

Cohen, S. (1972). *Folk devils and moral panics: The creation of the mods and rockers*. Oxford, United Kingdom: Blackwell.

Cohen, S., & Young, J. (Eds.). (1973). *The manufacture of news*. Beverly Hills, CA: SAGE.

Currie, E. (1997). Market, crime and community: Toward a mid-range theory of post-industrial violence. *Theoretical Criminology, 1*(2), 147–172.

Engels, F. (1973). *The condition of the working-class in England*. Moscow, Russia: Progress. (Original work published 1845)

Ewen, S. (1977). *Captains of consciousness: Advertising and the social roots of consumer culture*. Toronto, Ontario, Canada: McGraw-Hill.

Ewen, S. (1988). *All consuming images: The politics of style in contemporary culture*. New York, NY: Basic Books.

Ferrell, J., Hayward, K., & Young, J. (2008). *Cultural criminology: An invitation*. London, United Kingdom: SAGE.

Ferrell, J., & Sanders, C. (Eds.). (1995). *Cultural criminology*. Boston, MA: Northeastern University Press.

Greenberg, D. (Ed.). (1981). *Crime and capitalism*. Palo Alto, CA: Mayfield.

Hall, S., Critcher, C., Jefferson, T., Clarke, J., & Roberts, B. (1978). *Policing the crisis: Mugging, the state, and law and order*. London, United Kingdom: Macmillan.

Hall, S., & Winlow, S. (2004). "Barbarians at the gate": Crime and violence in the breakdown of the pseudo-pacification process. In J. Ferrell, K. Hayward, W. Morrison, & M. Presdee (Eds.), *Cultural criminology unleashed* (pp. 275–286). London, United Kingdom: Glass House Press.

Hall, S., Winlow, S., & Ancrum, C. (2008). *Criminal identities and consumer culture: Crime, exclusion, and the new culture of narcissism*. Devon, United Kingdom: Willan.

Hayward, K. (2004). *City limits: Crime, consumer culture, and the urban experience*. London, United Kingdom: Glass House Press.

Hayward, K., & Presdee, M. (2010). *Framing crime: Cultural criminology and the image*. London, United Kingdom: Routledge.

Hayward, K., & Yar, M. (2006). The "chav" phenomenon: Consumption, media, and the construction of a new underclass. *Crime, Media, Culture, 2*(1), 9–28.

Horkheimer, M., & Adorno, T. (1972). *The dialectic of enlightenment*. New York, NY: Herder and Herder. (Original work published 1946)

Marx, K., & Engels, F. (1976). *The German ideology*. Moscow, Russia: Progress. (Original work published 1846)

Merton, R. (1938). Social structure and anomie. *American Sociological Review, 3*(5), 672–682.

More, T. (1965). *Utopia* (P. Turner, Trans.). Harmondsworth, United Kingdom: Penguin Books. (Original work published 1516)

Muzzatti, S. (2003). Anarchy against the curriculum. In M. Schwartz & M. Maume (Eds.), *Teaching the sociology of deviance* (5th ed., pp. 9–14). Washington, DC: American Sociological Association.

Muzzatti, S. (2004). Criminalizing marginality and resistance: Marilyn Manson, Columbine, and cultural criminology. In J. Ferrell, K. Hayward, W. Morrison, & M. Presdee (Eds.), *Cultural criminology unleashed* (pp. 143–153). London, United Kingdom: Glass House Press.

Muzzatti, S. (2006). Cultural criminology: A decade and counting of criminological chaos. In W. DeKeseredy & B. Perry (Eds.), *Advancing critical criminology: Theory and application* (pp. 63–81). Lanham, MD: Lexington Books.

Muzzatti, S. (2010). Drive it like you stole it: Imagery and automobile advertisements. In K. Hayward & M. Presdee (Eds.), *Framing crime: Cultural criminology and the image* (pp. 138–156). London, United Kingdom: Routledge.

Muzzatti, S. (2013). They sing the body ecstatic: Television commercials and captured music. In M. Pomerance & J. Sakeris (Eds.), *Popping culture* (7th ed., pp. 191–201). Toronto, Ontario, Canada: Pearson.

Presdee, M. (2000). *Cultural criminology and the carnival of crime*. London, United Kingdom: Routledge.

Selke, W., Corsaros, N., & Selke, H. (2002). A working class critique of criminological theory. *Critical Criminology, 11*(2), 93–112.

Taylor, I. (1983). *Crime, capitalism, and community*. Toronto, Ontario, Canada: Butterworths.

Taylor, I. (1999). *Crime in context: A critical criminology of market societies*. Boulder, CO: Westview Press.

Tifft, L., & Sullivan, D. (1980). *The struggle to be human: Crime, criminology, and anarchism*. Orkney, United Kingdom: Cienfuegos Press.

Wilson, W. J. (1987). *The truly disadvantaged: The inner city, the underclass, and public policy*. Chicago, IL: Chicago University Press.

Young, J. (1999). *The exclusive society*. London, United Kingdom: SAGE.

Young, J. (2007). *The vertigo of late modernity*. London, United Kingdom: SAGE.

CHAPTER 11

Gangs, Serious Gang Problems, and Criminal Justice: What to Do?

James C. Howell and Megan Q. Howell

INTRODUCTION

The history of street gangs in the United States begins with their emergence on the East Coast, in New York City in the 1820s. Gang emergence in the Northeast was fueled by immigration and poverty, first by two waves of largely White and poor families from Europe. City social services were overwhelmed and large groups of immigrants were isolated in slums (Riis, 1902/1969). Conflict was therefore imminent, and gangs grew in these environments as groups of adolescents and young adults fought one another over scarce resources, while striving to create a wedge of safety in squalor, social disorder, and chaos. Subsequent migrations of Europeans to the United States led to even greater social disorganization and subsequent gang formation, first in the Northeast cities then in Chicago. In many respects, gang emergence in Chicago replicated the Eastern region process following immigrant invasion and conflict, though one-half century later because of the delayed influx of large migrant groups into the U.S. heartland.

The Great Migration of Blacks from the rural South northward between 1910 and 1930 was a major contributing factor to White on Black conflict and gang formation and expansion among Black youth. In contrast, gangs grew out of the preexisting Mexican culture in the Western region, and their growth was fueled by subsequent Mexican American migrations. Gangs emerged in the southern states a generation later following steady Mexican American immigration and large-scale return migration of Blacks from northern cities after decades of disappointment from presumed opportunities to better their lives in those urban areas. There is little doubt that clashes among Black, White, and Mexican American groups was the predominant precipitating factor to gang growth in the southern states in the 1970s.

In time, New York, Chicago, and Los Angeles served as springboards for diffusion of the gang culture via adolescent subcultures. Youth groups, gangs included—comprising mostly unemployed persons approximately aged 17 to 26—came to play a central role in various social disorders, especially in riots, in a number of U.S. cities. These events served to popularize gang culture and give adolescents much sought-after personal identities. Next, two social policies boosted gang growth and expansion. First, the establishment of high-rise public housing complexes in many large cities isolated poor Black and Mexican American families. This policy provided gangs an operational base, a virtual kingdom, as these buildings became gang strongholds. In Chicago, at least one enormous public housing project consisting of 28 sixteen-floor buildings was deemed too dangerous for police to enter (Venkatesh, 2002). Hence, gangs policed several of these buildings on an everyday basis.

Second, "wars on gangs" led by federal law enforcement put many gang leaders and members in prisons, which led to the further development of prison gangs, and these steadily became formidable criminal operations once enormous growth in prison populations commenced in the 1960s (Schlosser, 1998). As prison gang members began returning to neighborhoods from whence they came, this inadvertently strengthened local gangs and led to multiple gang alliances, creating what some called "supergangs" (Chicago Crime Commission, 1995; Venkatesh, 2002). This continuing massive flow of returning inmates remains a major contributor to local gang violence and this factor has become more prominent in recent years (Egley & Howell, 2013).

Particular attention is paid here to the most serious gang activity in the United States. Key issues addressed are (a) key gang magnitude indicators of serious gang violence—the number of gangs, gang members, and homicides; (b) the distinguishing features of the most violent gangs; and (c) possible solutions to serious gang activity. Before proceeding, gang definitions are presented that guide our focus in this chapter.

GANG DEFINITIONS

There is no single, universally accepted definition of a *gang*. Federal, state, and local jurisdictions in the United States tend to develop their own definitions.[1] Presently, most states (42) and the District of Columbia have legislation that defines the term *gang*. Of these, 33 states and the District of Columbia define a gang as consisting of three or more persons; 26 states include a common name, identifying sign, or symbol as identifiers of gangs in their definitions; and 35 states refer to a gang as an "organization, association, or group."

Moore (1998) outlines four community conditions that facilitated permanent institutionalization of gangs. First, key conventional socializing agents, such as families and schools, must be largely ineffective and alienating. Second, the adolescents must have a great deal of free time that is not consumed by other prosocial roles. Third, members must have limited access to appealing conventional career lines, that is, good adult jobs. Finally, the young people must have a place to congregate—usually in a well-defined neighborhood. Some gangs have been known to regenerate themselves under these conditions across several decades. For example, two of the original gangs in that area of Los Angeles, Cuatro Flats and White Fence, are now nearly 80 years of age.

The following is a practical definition that has been recognized by the National Centers for Disease Control and Prevention and the National Institute of Justice as a reliable youth gang definition (J. C. Howell, 2013):

- The group has at least five members, generally aged 11 to 24.
- Members share an identity, typically linked to a name.
- Members view themselves as a gang and are recognized by others as a gang.
- The group has some permanence (at least 6 months).
- The group has a degree of organization (for example, with initiation rites, established leaders, symbols or colors).
- The group is involved in an elevated level of criminal activity.

| Figure 11.1 | Percentage of Law Enforcement Agencies Reporting Youth Gang Problems, 1996–2006 |

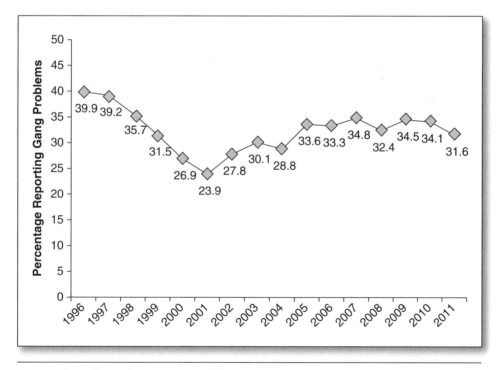

Source: Egley and Howell (2013, p. 2), modified.

Another gang definition applies more specifically to urban gangs whose members more often act together in committing crimes: "A youth gang is a self-formed association of peers united by mutual interests with identifiable leadership and internal organization who act collectively or as individuals to achieve specific purposes, including the conduct of illegal activity and control of a particular territory, facility, or enterprise" (Miller, 1992, p. 21). The term, *street gang,* is often used to reference gangs comprising older members to underscore their active involvement in murder, robbery, aggravated assault, and firearm offenses in street settings where most such offenses occur. In cities with populations of 50,000 or more, two thirds of the gang members are over the age of 18.

National Youth Gang Survey (NYGS)[2] results (Figure 11.1) show that in 2011, gangs were active in nearly one third (32%) of cities, towns, and counties across the United States. (Egley & Howell, 2013). This national estimate has remained fairly stable since 2005, fluctuating by only 3 percentage points during that time.

KEY INDICATORS OF SERIOUS GANG ACTIVITY

Little change in the level of gang violence in large cities has been observed over the past decade (J. C. Howell, Egley, Tita, & Griffiths, 2011) despite the large drop in violent crimes in the U.S. during this period (Federal Bureau of Investigation, 2013; Truman & Planty, 2012). The number of gang members, number of gangs, and occurrence of gang-related homicides are key indicators of the magnitude of serious gang activity in large cities. NYGS data for 2011 indicate that more than half (56%) of all gangs and three fourths (75%) of all gang members are located in metropolitan areas[3] and almost 9 out of 10 (87%) gang-related homicides occur in these areas (Egley & Howell, 2013). Over the past several years, increases have been observed in each of these gang-magnitude indicators in metropolitan areas in the NYGS. From 2002 to 2011, the number of gangs in these more heavily populated areas increased by 36%, while the number of gang members increased by 5%, and the number of gang-related homicides increased by almost 6%. A brief summary of important research on each of these indicators follows.

Number of gang members. It goes without saying that gang members are far more numerous in more densely populated cities that report a persistent gang problem. The number of gang members reported in the NYGS is a strong correlate of nationwide gang homicides (Decker & Pyrooz, 2010b). To illustrate the importance of the number of gang members, in the early 1990s, the Chicago Police Department estimated that membership in four very large gangs numbered about 19,000 (the Black Gangster Disciples Nation, the Latin Disciples, the Latin Kings, and the Vice Lords), and from 1987 to 1990 they accounted for 69% of all street gang-motivated crimes and for 56% of all street gang-motivated homicides, although they represented just 10% of the "major" Chicago gangs and 51% of the city's gang members (Block & Block, 1993).

Number of gangs. As noted earlier, more than half of all gangs are located in metropolitan areas. The number of gangs present in an area is significantly related to the area's overall level of violence and, particularly, nationwide gang homicides (Decker & Pyrooz, 2010b). As a case in point, Block's (2000) citywide Chicago research on the spatial distribution of gang violence found that "the relationship between the number of gangs that are active in an area and the levels of assaults and drug-related incidents is remarkably high" (p. 379).[4] To be sure, numerous other gang studies support this pattern (J. C. Howell, 2012).

Number of homicides. Of course, gang homicides characterize serious gang problem cities along with the number of gangs and gang members. Overall, approximately one quarter of all homicides in cities with populations greater than 100,000 are gang related each year (J. C. Howell et al., 2011). More than two thirds (70%) of these large cities consistently report that between 20% and 40% of their homicides are gang related. By the 1980s, gangs had considerably more firearms, including semiautomatic weapons, of greater lethality than ever before (J. C. Howell, 1999). Therefore, it is important to consider the history and dangerousness of gangs in these cities in crafting strategies for reducing their violence.

CONTEXTS OF SERIOUS GANG VIOLENCE

Four contexts of serious gang violence are important for understanding gang violence: gang hot spots, drug trafficking, gang territory or turf, and juvenile and criminal justice systems.

Established gangs in major gang cities, such as Chicago and Los Angeles, typically have long histories of gang violence. Block and Block (1993) first discovered "peaks and valleys" in homicides and other violence. Decker (1996) documented a series of escalating and de-escalating stages that create a feedback loop where each killing requires a new killing. Papachristos (2009) observed that murders spread in the neighborhood through a process of "social contagion" as gangs respond to threats from other gangs. Specific murders, particularly those in public view, have the intended effect of threatening the social status and ranking of groups within the neighborhood. Thus, in order to avoid subjugation themselves, other gangs "must constantly (re)establish their social status through displays of solidarity—in this case, acts of violence—which, in turn, merely strengthen these murder networks" (p. 76). Hence, Papachristos observed that while gang members come and go, their patterns of behavior create a network structure that persists over time and may very well provide the conduit through which gang values, norms, and culture are transmitted to future generations.

Owing to these well-established networks, violent hot spots and gang turf often co-occur, and these neighborhood places are said to have criminal *trajectories* in their own right (Griffiths & Chavez, 2004; Tita & Cohen, 2004). Block (2000) discovered that a large volume of violent Chicago gang crimes occur in very small "grid squares" (consisting of 150 square meters). Less than 5% of the total grid squares citywide accounted for 23% of the assaults and 44% of all drug-related incidents recorded by Chicago police in a single year. Based on interviews with gang members, Tita, Cohen, and Endberg (2005) mapped places where gangs came together as a sociological group, that is, their *set space*. This study indicates that the location of a gang set space is usually a very small geographic area, much smaller than neighborhoods or even census tracts. Tita and Ridgeway (2007) explained, "One might expect set space to serve as a sort of lightning rod for intergang violence" (p. 217).

Eight out of 10 law enforcement agencies nationwide contend that drug trafficking is the most predominant influence on local gang violence (Egley & Howell, 2013). The dynamics of this relationship are not straightforward, however. The so-called "crack cocaine epidemic" said to have occurred in the late 1980s and early 1990s was overstated and was most prevalent in only a few cities (J. C. Howell, 2007, 2012; Reeves & Campbell, 1994). Most street gangs—largely made up of adolescents—lack the necessary organizational characteristics to effectively manage drug distribution operations (Decker, 2007). Still, violence is most likely to occur where gang activity, drug trafficking, and firearm ownership or use intersects (Gordon et al., 2014). Another reality is that gun availability fuels gang violence. Lizotte, Krohn, Howell, Tobin, and Howard (2000) explained, "If one travels in a dangerous world of youth armed illegally and defensively with firearms, it only makes sense to carry a gun. Therefore, peer gun ownership for protection increases the probability of gun violence" (p. 830). In turn, during late adolescence, "involvement in serious drug trafficking, independent of gang involvement, is a much stronger factor explaining hidden gun carrying—typically after gang involvement has ended" (p. 829). In other words, many gang members who do not desist from gang involvement continue to carry guns and move on to drug trafficking.

The claiming and defense of turf or territory is a key characteristic of street gangs in serious gang problem cities. From the point of their origin in the United States, control over turf has been the basis of street gangs' social honor (Adamson, 1998). In these areas, the gang's very existence sometimes depended upon its capacity to stand its ground and ward off incursions from hostile groups. An East Los Angeles study found that violence strongly clusters along the boundaries between gangs (Brantingham, Tita, Short, & Reid, 2012). This research project catalogued 563 between-gang shootings involving 13 rival street gangs during a 3-year period.

Gang members are very prevalent in both juvenile and adult criminal justice systems. Youth gang involvement at least doubles the odds of being arrested (Curry, 2000); thus, probation and correctional caseloads is another context in which criminal involvement of gang members is quite evident. For example, statewide North Carolina data showed that youth gang members represent

- 7% of all juveniles on whom delinquent complaints are filed,
- 13% of juveniles adjudicated,

- 21% of juveniles admitted to short-term detention, and
- 38% of juveniles committed to secure residential facilities. (M.Q. Howell & Lassiter, 2011)

Adult prisons are also home to many gang members and prison gangs. A 2009 survey of federal and state prison systems estimated that 19% of all inmates were gang members (Winterdyk & Ruddell, 2010). Research has established that prison gangs are responsible for a disproportionate amount of prison violence (Griffin & Hepburn, 2006). Unfortunately, the number of prison gangs cannot be established at the present time because these are included in the overall category of security threat groups (American Correctional Association, 2009). In the mid-1980s, a national survey of prison systems identified 112 individual prison gangs with a total membership of 12,634 (Camp & Camp, 1985).

DISCUSSION OF PROGRAM IMPLICATIONS

This chapter concludes with some discussion of program implications of the foregoing research and data on gang crime. In this exercise, readers are encouraged to imagine themselves in governmental crime control positions before giving consideration to responses that you might make in the course of strategic planning to protect the public from serious gang problems. In other words, assume that you have some responsibility for public safety.

The leading program approach for addressing youth gang problems is the federal Office of Juvenile Justice and Delinquency Prevention's Comprehensive Gang Prevention, Intervention, and Suppression Program Model (commonly known as the Comprehensive Gang Program Model).[5] This three-pronged model guides jurisdictions of any size (communities, counties, cities, and states) in forming a continuum of gang prevention, intervention, and suppression programs and strategies. Prevention programs target youth at risk for gang involvement and reduce the number of youth who join gangs. Intervention programs and strategies provide sanctions and services for younger youth who are actively involved in gangs. Law enforcement suppression strategies target the most violent gangs and older, criminally active gang members. When it is implemented with fidelity, the Comprehensive Gang Program Model demonstrated effectiveness in reducing gang violence in multiple cities (National Gang Center, 2010; Spergel, Wa, & Sosa, 2006). It is the sole gang program model that has demonstrated effectiveness in both Chicago and Los Angeles—the widely recognized gang capitals in our nation—although other comprehensive community gang programs have proved effective in the United States (Hodgkinson et al., 2009).

Nevertheless, successfully engaging states, cities, and counties in gang prevention and control is not an easy thing to do. Despite the compelling evidence presented in this chapter on its seriousness, there is much resistance to the formidable task of addressing gang activity (Gebo & Bond, 2012). In St. Louis, juvenile justice and social service providers adamantly refused to collaborate in addressing gang activity, prompting researchers to title their report "I'm Down for My Organization" (Decker & Curry, 2002). Mayors, school administrators, and other public officials sometimes deny the obvious existence of gang problems because doing so may not be deemed in their best interest in the near term (Huff, 1990; Weisel & Howell, 2007).

In time, reliable comprehensive data and local gang studies can persuade public officials to act in addressing gang problems. A statewide North Carolina gang problem assessment revealed an elevated level of gang activity in schools across the state (North Carolina Department of Juvenile Justice and Delinquency Prevention and Department of Public Instruction, 2008). Gang activity was reported in two thirds (64%) of high schools and half (49%) of the state's middle schools. Almost one in five schools experienced gang activity daily. Assume that you are head of a state juvenile justice agency in North Carolina. How would you act upon these data to reduce gang activity statewide?

In response to these findings, the second author was instrumental in developing a statewide Community-Based Youth Gang Violence Prevention Project with the goal of preventing and reducing gang involvement and high-risk behavior statewide in North Carolina (M. Q. Howell & Lassiter, 2011). Awards were made to more than half of the state's 100 counties to support research partnerships for conducting comprehensive community gang assessments and to support implementation of evidence-based programs to address gang problems. Eligible applicants for awards under this $5 million program were restricted to the state Juvenile Crime Prevention Councils (JCPCs). These legislatively mandated JCPCs are charged with preparing county-wide comprehensive delinquency prevention plans, developing a continuum of programs based on a county-wide gang problem assessment, and developing individual offenders' risk and needs assessments. This initiative demonstrates the feasibility of undertaking statewide Comprehensive Gang Program Model programming by integrating gang prevention with delinquency prevention programming.

Assume that you are lead analyst or head of a state crime control agency and are considering options for addressing gang problems at the city level. In NYGS data on nearly 600 cities with populations greater than 50,000, some cities reported a consistent presence of gangs, while others experienced none, rapid increases over time, rapid decreases, fluctuating presence of gang activity, or inconsistent trends over a 14-year period between 1996 and 2009 (J. C. Howell et al., 2011). These patterns are seen in Figure 11.2, which shows "yes" or "no" annual responses to the question of whether they had experienced gang activity in the past year. Specifically, three main patterns are seen in the six trajectory groups of cities: first, no change (T5 group); second, increasing gang activity (T1, T2, and T3 groups); and third, decreasing gang activity (T4 and T6 groups). The largest group of cities (T1, 69.9%) reported gang activity almost every year across the 14-year period, indicating that gang activity is rather stable in the majority of cities with populations of more than 50,000 persons. These cities present a unique opportunity to impact gang activity because nearly two thirds of all gangs and eight out of 10 gang members nationwide

Trajectory Model: Presence of Gang Activity in Cities With Populations Greater Than 50,000

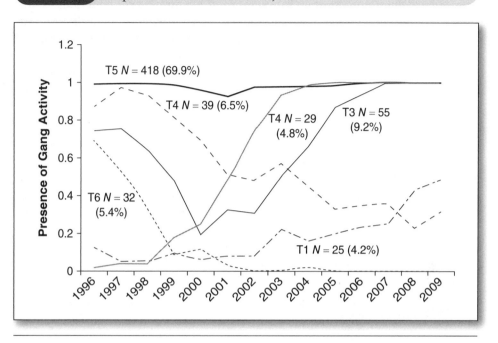

Source: Howell, J. C., Egley, A., Jr., Moore, J. P., Tita, G., & Griffiths, E. (2011). *U.S. gang problem trends and seriousness*. Tallahassee, FL: Institute for Intergovernmental Research, National Gang Center.

are found within these cities. Which of these trajectory groups of cities would you target? What is your rationale?

The Shannon Community Safety Initiative (Shannon CSI) was first funded in 2006 by the Massachusetts legislature to implement the Comprehensive Gang Program Model statewide. To qualify for participation, applicants were required to have a metropolitan population of at least 100,000, have high levels of youth violence and gang problems, commit to coordinated prevention and intervention strategies, and develop a comprehensive plan to work with multidisciplinary partners. Initially, 15 sites were funded, encompassing 37 communities. In the fourth year, funding was expanded to 17 sites, composed of 41 municipalities. In 2013, the Shannon CSI entered its seventh year of funding, having made awards totaling more than $56 million to date. A complete description of the initiative, along with several useful reports and other resources, can be found at Mass.gov/eopss/funding-and-training/justice-and-prev/grants/shannon-csi/.

What if you had reliable data on gang-related homicides within large cities within your state? Would you then consider a more targeted strategy to reduce those homicides? In the above 14-year analysis of gang activity in 600 cities, researchers examined homicide rates among a subgroup of 167 cities with populations of 100,000 or more. Among this subgroup, the overwhelming majority consistently reported that between 20% and 40% of their homicides were gang related across the 14-year period (J. C. Howell et al., 2011). Therefore, more populated cities are prime candidates for targeted interventions to reduce gang homicides. Other research has suggested that gang members in large cities have homicide rates 100 times higher than the national average (Decker & Pyrooz, 2010a). Which groups of cities would you select for intervention? What might your gang prevention and intervention strategy include? How would you integrate intervention with suppression?

Be aware that your public agency may be predisposed to take a heavy-handed approach. A tough-on-crime response to gang problems is often the first response, after which—usually several years later—officials typically recognize the shortcomings of singular suppression strategies and take a more balanced approach (Weisel & Painter, 1997). Boston Ceasefire is a strong deterrence-based approach that involves identification of active gang members and threatening them in community meetings ("call-ins") with extended prison sentences for any subsequent law violation. Although this individual-focused model has demonstrated good short-term results in a few cities (Braga & Weisburd, 2012), it could be coupled with the Comprehensive Gang Program Model (Braga & Hureau, 2012), with the potential for longer term impacts across multiple communities and cities.

How could you achieve a balance among prevention, intervention, and suppression strategies? Thus far, we have focused only on prevention and suppression strategies. For intervention purposes, consider including juvenile and criminal justice system components. Another benefit of the Comprehensive Gang Program Model is that it promotes intervention teams that should give priority attention to reducing violence among gang-involved probationers. These multidisciplinary teams manage cases for the coordinated delivery of targeted services to gang members who have been identified through screening criteria drawn from the assessment (Arciaga & Gonzalez, 2012). Once the intervention team has been convened, street outreach workers play an active role in connecting gang members to necessary services. Outreach workers are not only the primary source of program referrals, but also they often play an active role in delivering services and working closely with community service providers. Correctional and reentry gang interventions should also be developed (see American Probation and Parole Association and Institute for Intergovernmental Research, 2011).

Knowing that "gangs occupy stable territories does not necessarily imply that rival gangs exist in a constant, extreme state of war" (Brantingham et al., 2012, p. 878). But reducing the intensity of gang rivalries may well be a useful approach to reducing gang violence. The Cure Violence program approaches violence as an infectious disease. Thus, the program aims to identify, engage, and promote change among those gang members most likely to be involved in shootings or killings; detect and interrupt events that could lead to violence or retaliation; and change norms about the acceptance and use of violence. Consistent with the public health model, founder Gary Slutkin explained the attempt to *interrupt* the next violent event. Rather than aiming to directly change the behaviors of a large number of individuals, Cure Violence outreach workers concentrate on changing the behavior and risky activities of a small number of selected members of the community who have a high chance of either *being shot* or *being a shooter* in the immediate future. To stem the cycle of retaliatory violence, violence interrupters (mostly former gang members) work alone or in pairs mediating conflicts between gangs and high-risk individuals on the streets and in hospital emergency rooms. With reality therapy, they interject themselves into on-the-spot decision making by individuals at risk of shooting others, helping potential shooters weigh the likely disastrous, life-changing outcomes against perceived short-term gains. Long-term change agents (outreach workers) address key immediate causes of violence, including norms regarding violence, and serve as positive role models for young people, steering them to resources such as job or educational training and needed services.

Those states and cities that have a large volume of homicides could benefit from a recommendation that Tita and Abrahamse (2010) made to California officials, to implement a gang homicide surveillance system. These analysts suggested that it should be designed much like systems used by the public health community to monitor disease threats. The proposed system would provide an early warning of a rise in gang homicide victimization within particular communities. But Tita and Abrahamse stressed that such a homicide surveillance system needs to work fast enough to provide a warning of gang homicide onset. Furthermore, it also needs to be fine-grained with respect to geography and gang participants. However, reporting should not be delayed until a homicide is "solved," they argue, because early intervention opportunities could be lost. In addition, Tita and Abrahamse noted that such a system should capture and publish essential diagnostic information (including age, race, sex, circumstance, and census tract) about suspected gang homicides at least within a month of the event, which would support early detection of upswings in gang violence in the city or state and timely responses.

To sum up, several potentially effective programs and strategies are now available for responding to gang violence on a city, county, or statewide basis. The choice of particular options must be based on a thorough assessment of the key features of gang violence in those contexts. Recent research suggests that long-term trajectories of gangs and city gang problem histories can be modified, thereby, producing potentially important public safety benefits.

DISCUSSION QUESTIONS

1. What factors mainly account for gang emergence in the United States?

2. What are the key indicators of serious gang activity?

3. How could wars on gangs have strengthened them?

4. How does gang violence resemble a contagious disease?

5. How can a balance be achieved among prevention, intervention, and suppression strategies?

NOTES

1. http://www.nationalgangcenter.gov/Legislation/
2. For a description of the NYGS study population and sample methodology, see http://www.nationalgangcenter.gov/Survey-Analysis/Methodology. Independent evaluations have confirmed and demonstrated the validity and reliability of the NYGS data.
3. Cities with populations greater than 100,000 and suburban county sheriffs' and police departments.
4. Squares with no gang activity had an average of 2.88 assaults. Those with one active gang averaged 13.5 assaults. Those squares with four gangs averaged 42.7 assaults in 1996 (p. 379).
5. Access at http://www.nationalgangcenter.gov/Comprehensive-Gang-Model/About

REFERENCES

Adamson, C. (1998). Tribute, turf, honor, and the American street gang: Patterns of continuity and change since 1820. *Theoretical Criminology, 2*(1), 57–84.

American Correctional Association. (2009, Spring). Gangs/security threat groups in the U.S.A. and Canada. *Corrections Compendium,* pp. 22–37.

American Probation and Parole Association and Institute for Intergovernmental Research. (2011). *Guidelines to gang reentry.* Lexington, KY: American Probation and Parole Association.

Arciaga, M., & Gonzalez, V. (2012, June). Street outreach and the Comprehensive Gang Model. *National Gang Center Bulletin No. 7.* U.S. Department of Justice, Office of Juvenile Justice and Delinquency Prevention. Tallahassee, FL: National Gang Center. Retrieved from http://ncfy.acf.hhs.gov/library/2012/street-outreach-and-ojjdp-comprehensive-gang-model

Block, C. R., & Block, R. (1993). *Street gang crime in Chicago: Research in brief.* Washington, DC: U.S. Department of Justice, National Institute of Justice.

Block, R. (2000). Gang activity and overall levels of crime: A new mapping tool for defining areas of gang activity using police records. *Journal of Quantitative Criminology, 16*(3), 369–383.

Braga, A. A., & Hureau, D. M. (2012). Strategic problem analysis to guide comprehensive gang violence reduction strategies. In E. Gebo & B. J. Bond (Eds.), *Beyond suppression: Community strategies to reduce gang violence* (pp. 129–151). Lanham, MD: Lexington Books.

Braga, A. A., & Weisburd, D. L. (2012). The effects of focused deterrence strategies on crime: A systematic review and meta-analysis of the empirical evidence. *Journal of Research in Crime and Delinquency, 49(3),* 323–358.

Brantingham, P. J., Tita, G. E., Short, M. B., & Reid, S. (2012). The ecology of gang territorial boundaries. *Criminology, 50*(3), 851–885.

Camp, G. M., & Camp, C. G. (Eds.). (1985). *Prison gangs: Their extent, nature and impact on prisons.* Washington, DC: U.S. Department of Justice.

Chicago Crime Commission. (1995). *Gangs: Public enemy number one, 75 years of fighting crime in Chicago.* Chicago, IL: Chicago Crime Commission.

Curry, G. D. (2000). Self-reported gang involvement and officially recorded delinquency. *Criminology, 38*(4), 1253–1274.

Decker, S. H. (1996). Collective and normative features of gang violence. *Justice Quarterly,* 13, 243–264.

Decker, S. H. (2007). Youth gangs and violent behavior. In D. J. Flannery, A. T. Vazsonyi, & I. D. Waldman (Eds.), *The Cambridge handbook of violent behavior and aggression* (pp. 388–402). Cambridge, MA: Cambridge University Press.

Decker, S. H., & Curry, G. D. (2002). "I'm down for my organization": The rationality of responses to delinquency, youth crime and gangs. In A. R. Piquero & S. G. Tibbits (Eds.), *Rational choice and criminal behavior* (pp. 197–218). New York, NY: Routledge.

Decker, S. H., & Pyrooz, D. C. (2010a). Gang violence worldwide: Context, culture, and country. In *Small Arms Survey 2010: Gangs, groups, and guns* (pp. 128–155). Cambridge, United Kingdom: Cambridge University Press.

Decker, S. H., & Pyrooz, D. C. (2010b). On the validity and reliability of gang homicide: A comparison of disparate sources. *Homicide Studies, 14*(4), 359–376.

Egley, A. E., & Howell, J. C. (2013, September). Highlights of the 2011 National Youth Gang Survey (*OJJDP Fact Sheet*). Washington, DC: Office of Juvenile Justice and Delinquency Prevention.

Federal Bureau of Investigation. (2013). *Crime in the United States, 2012.* Washington, DC: U.S. Department of Justice, Federal Bureau of Investigation.

Gebo, E., & Bond, B. J. E. (2012). *Beyond suppression: Community strategies to reduce gang violence.* Lanham, MD: Lexington Books.

Gordon, R. A., Rowe, H. L., Pardini, D., Loeber, R., White, H. R., & Farrington, D. (2014, June). Serious delinquency and gang participation: Combining and specializing in drug selling, theft and violence. *Journal of Research on Adolescence, 24*(2), 201–409.

Griffin, M. L., & Hepburn, J. R. (2006). The effect of gang affiliation on violent misconduct among inmates during the early years of confinement. *Criminal Justice and Behavior, 33,* 419–448.

Griffiths, E., & Chavez, J. M. (2004). Communities, street guns and homicide trajectories in Chicago, 1980–1995: Merging methods for examining homicide trends across space and time. *Criminology, 42*(4), 941–977.

Hodgkinson, J., Marshall, S., Berry, G., Reynolds, P., Newman, M., Burton, E., . . . Anderson, J. (2009). *Reducing gang related crime: A systematic review of "comprehensive" interventions* [Summary report]. London, United Kingdom: EPPI-Centre, Social Science Research Unit, Institute of Education, University of London.

Howell, J. C. (1999). Youth gang homicides: A literature review. *Crime and Delinquency, 45*(2), 208–241.

Howell, J. C. (2007). Menacing or mimicking? Realities of youth gangs. *The Juvenile and Family Court Journal, 58*(2), 9–20.

Howell, J. C. (2012). *Gangs in America's communities.* Thousand Oaks, CA: SAGE.

Howell, J. C. (2013). Why is gang membership prevention important? In T. R. Simon, N. M. Ritter, & R. R. Mahendra (Eds.), *Changing course: Preventing gang membership* (pp. 7–18). Washington, DC: U.S. Department of Justice, U.S. Department of Health and Human Services.

Howell, J. C., Egley, A., Jr., Tita, G., & Griffiths, E. (2011). *U.S. gang problem trends and seriousness.* Tallahassee, FL: Institute for Intergovernmental Research, National Gang Center.

Howell, M. Q., & Lassiter, W. (2011). *Prevalence of gang-involved youth in NC.* Raleigh, NC: North Carolina Department of Juvenile Justice and Delinquency Prevention.

Huff, C. R. (1990). Denial, overreaction, and misidentification: A postscript on public policy. In C. R. Huff (Ed.). *Gangs in America* (pp. 310–317). Newbury Park, CA: SAGE.

Lizotte, A. J., Krohn, M. D., Howell, J. C., Tobin, K., & Howard, G. J. (2000). Factors influencing gun carrying among young urban males over the adolescent-young adult life course. *Criminology, 38*(3), 811–834.

Miller, W. B. (1992). *Crime by youth gangs and groups in the United States* (Rev. ed.; NCJ 156221). Washington, DC: U.S. Department of Justice, Office of Juvenile Justice and Delinquency Prevention.

Moore, J. W. (1998). Understanding youth street gangs: Economic restructuring and the urban underclass. In M. W. Watts (Ed.), *Cross-cultural perspectives on youth and violence* (pp. 65–78). Stamford, CT: JAI.

National Gang Center. (2010). *Best practices to address community gang problems: OJJDP's Comprehensive Gang Model.* Washington, DC: Author.

North Carolina Department of Juvenile Justice and Delinquency Prevention and Department of Public Instruction. (2008). *School violence/gang activity study* (S.L. 2008–56). Raleigh, NC: North Carolina Department of Juvenile Justice and Delinquency Prevention.

Papachristos, A. V. (2009). Murder by structure: Dominance relations and the social structure of gang homicide. *American Journal of Sociology, 115*(1), 74–128.

Reeves, J. L., & Campbell, R. (1994). *Cracked coverage: Television news, the anti-cocaine crusade, and the Reagan legacy.* Durham, NC: Duke University Press.

Riis, J. A. (1969). *The battle with the slum.* Montclair, NJ: Paterson Smith. (Reprinted from 1902 edition)

Schlosser, E. (1998, December). The prison-industrial complex. *The Atlantic Monthly, 282*(6), pp. 51–77.

Spergel, I. A., Wa, K. M., & Sosa, R. V. (2006). The comprehensive, community-wide, gang program model: Success and failure. In J. F. Short & L. A. Hughes (Eds.), *Studying youth gangs* (pp. 203–224). Lanham, MD: AltaMira Press.

Tita, G. E., & Abrahamse, A. (2010). *Homicide in California, 1981–2008: Measuring the impact of Los Angeles and gangs on overall homicide patterns.* Sacramento, CA: Governor's Office of Gang and Youth Violence Policy.

Tita, G. E., & Cohen, J. (2004). Measuring spatial diffusion of shots fired activity across city neighborhoods. In M. F. Goodchild & D. G. Janelle (Eds.), *Spatially integrated social science* (pp. 171–204). New York, NY: Oxford Press.

Tita, G., Cohen, J., & Endberg, J. (2005). An ecological study of the location of gang "set space." *Social Problems, 52*(2), 272–299.

Tita, G., & Ridgeway, G. (2007). The impact of gang formation on local patterns of crime. *Journal of Research in Crime and Delinquency, 44*(2), 208–237.

Truman, J. L., & Planty, M. (2012). *Criminal victimization, 2011* (NCJ 239437). Washington, DC: U.S. Department of Justice, Office of Justice Programs, Bureau of Justice Statistics.

Venkatesh, S. A., (2002). *American project: The rise and fall of a modern ghetto* (2nd ed.). Cambridge, MA: Harvard University Press.

Weisel, D. L., & Howell, J. C. (2007). *Comprehensive gang assessment: A report to the Durham Police Department and Durham County Sheriff's Office.* Durham, NC: Durham Police Department.

Weisel, D. L., & Painter, E. (1997). *The police response to gangs: Case studies of five cities.* Washington, DC: Police Executive Research Forum.

Winterdyk, J., & Ruddell, R. (2010). Managing prison gangs: Results from a survey of U.S. prison systems. *Journal of Criminal Justice, 38*(4), 730–736.

CHAPTER 12

Sex Crimes

Mary Maguire

John and Sage were only 14 years old when they met. Like many adolescents, they responded to hormones and their need for attention by engaging in a sexual relationship. Their relationship was short lived, and unfortunately for John, methamphetamine was his method of choice for soothing loneliness and depression. After several encounters with law enforcement through his teens and 20s, John eventually entered a rehabilitation center and became clean and sober by his 29th birthday. He was working his twelve-step program and enjoying his work in construction when he received an unexpected call from Sage, his childhood girlfriend of 15 years past. Their sexual relationship had resulted in a daughter, of whom John was unaware. Sage reported that their daughter, Carissa, now aged 14 herself, was out of control and too much for Sage to handle. Under duress, John agreed to help by allowing Carissa to live with him. The transition was difficult; although Carissa was John's biological daughter, they were strangers to each other. Carissa used drugs and regularly skipped school. The stress of responsibility for a child whom he could not control was more than John could manage with new sobriety, and he soon relapsed into methamphetamine use. With both John and Carissa using drugs and often home together, their relationship did not resemble a typical parent-child union. Carissa felt like she was falling in love with John and began to make sexual advances toward him. Eventually, the two entered into a full sexual relationship, which continued for over a year. Today, Carissa is in foster care, and John is serving time in prison for his sex crime.

Unlike John, Mark does not have a history of drug use. His family owns a successful business in the community, and Mark worked for his father. Uncomfortable with confrontation, Mark was a passive adolescent who grew into a passive man. In his everyday life, Mark was overly conciliatory and found maintaining relationships with women difficult. As a result, he began to use prostitutes to meet his sexual needs. The anonymity of the prostitutes allowed Mark to show emotions in a way that he could not with friends and family. As a result, his encounters with pros-titutes became dangerous. After securely locking the women he chose in his spare warehouse, he would rape, humiliate, assault, and terrorize his victims. Wanting to believe that his victims enjoyed the act, Mark sent them to the bathroom to wash their faces and "clean up" if they cried too much. Fearing for their lives or safety, as chain saws were always within reach, Mark's victims complied. Mark served time in prison for his sex crimes and is now in the community on parole.

Stories like John's and Mark's are only a part of what we regularly ingest through multiple media venues regarding sexuality and sex crimes. As consumers, we are inundated with sexual images. Whether it is the prepubescent children, like Carissa, in the Calvin Klein advertisements, the cleavage displayed on the covers of magazines sold in grocery stores, or the senior adult couples in the TV commercials for any number of pharmaceuticals, we are fed a steady diet of sexual images. We are equally intrigued by the steady narrative of sexual missteps of the power elite. Presidents, senators, congressmen, governors, and mayors alike are guilty; we listen to a seemingly never-ending stream of stories, from dalliances to misdemeanor sex crimes. Our interest in sexual deviance, however, has not informed our understanding of it. One might wonder if it is our ingestion of media spin regarding sexual deviance or our general lack of understanding of sex crimes that has allowed sweeping sex-crime legislation to proliferate in the past 10 years. Ironically, more stringent sex-offender management policies, such as residency restrictions, public notification laws, chemical castration, and GPS monitoring (Levenson, 2007), are being implemented as the rates of sex crimes are declining. Data from the Federal Bureau of Investigation's report, *Crime in the United States, 2005* (FBI, 2005, Table 1, data 1985–2005), show that sexual offenses against adolescents dropped by 79%, and the number of cleared cases against children of all ages declined by 39%.

It is unclear to what extent stringent post-prison management techniques keep communities safe by helping offenders reintegrate as responsible, contributing members of society. Considerable work has been done on identifying types of offenders, on understanding motivations and drives of offenders, and on the effects of the justice system response to offenders. This chapter discusses each of these areas and then asks readers to consider the implications of our present-day understanding of sex offenders.

SEX CRIMES DEFINED

Statutory definitions of sexual assault vary from state to state. A *sexual assault* is a statutory offense that occurs when one person, either by force or by threat, causes another person to engage in any form of sexual act. Sexual assault often occurs when one person touches another in a sexual way; however, touching does not have to occur for an act to be considered a sexual offense. Simply to offend or annoy another person sexually is considered a sexual offense. For example, exhibitionism—an act wherein a person exposes him- or herself in a sexual way to another person, who is unwilling—is a sex crime with no physical contact.

Did You Know?

- Convicted rape and sexual assault offenders serving time in state prisons report that two thirds of their victims were under the age of 18, and 58%—or nearly 4 in 10 imprisoned violent sex offenders—said their victims were aged 12 or younger.
- In 90% of the rapes of children under 12 years old, the child knew the offender, according to police-recorded incident data.
- Among victims 18 to 29 years old, two thirds had a prior relationship with the rapist.
- Four data sets (the FBI's *Uniform Crime Reports* arrests, state felony court convictions, prison admissions, and the National Crime Victimization Survey) indicate that most sex offenders are older than other violent offenders, generally in their early 30s, and more likely to be White than other violent offenders.

Source: Data provided by the Bureau of Justice Statistics (BJS, 2009).

There is no single profile for perpetrators. Sexual assault takes many forms and definitions, which may vary from state to state. Several researchers have created typologies of sexual offenders and sex crimes (Groth, 1979; Hale, 1997; Knight & Prentky, 1990). Sex offenders are largely categorized as rapists, child molesters, female offenders, juvenile offenders, and cyber offenders. This chapter focuses primarily on rapists, child molesters, and cyber offenders.

Rape

The U.S. Department of Justice defines *rape* as "unlawful sexual intercourse with a female, by force or without legal or factual consent" (FBI, 2002, p. 29). Although researchers' categorizations of rape have provided useful explanatory power, standard definitions follow the statutes and are outlined by the *Uniform Crime Reports*. They are (a) forcible rape, (b) statutory rape, and (c) rape by fraud. *Forcible rape* is the carnal knowledge of a female by force and against her will. This includes assaults as well as attempts to commit rape by force or threat of force. *Statutory rape* is the carnal knowledge of a girl under statutory age (usually between 16 and 18 years of age, depending on the state of residence) with or without her consent. This pertains exclusively to sexual intercourse and not to other types of sexual contact. *Rape by fraud* is engagement in a sexual act or relationship with a consenting adult female under fraudulent conditions or false pretenses.

While an understanding of statutory definitions is imperative, an understanding of the nuances of offenders is vital for assessing future risks of individuals. The Massachusetts Treatment Center (MTC) has a unique ability to increase our understanding of sex crimes, for it houses exclusively those who are civilly committed subsequent to being identified as sexually dangerous, as well as state inmates who are sex offenders. After extensive work with these offenders, researchers at the MTC have developed an empirically based model of rape typologies that has been tested both inside the MTC (Knight & Prentky, 1987) and by outside researchers (Barbaree, Seto, Serin, Amos, & Preston, 1994; Harris, Rice, & Quinsey, 1994). The model, called the Massachusetts Treatment Center rapist typology version 3 (MTC:R3), places rapists in four categories according to motivation (opportunistic, pervasively angry, sexual, and vindictive). The model further separates these four groups into nine subtypes. The subtypes are differentiated by six temperamental or cognitive dimensions (aggression, impulsivity, social competence, sexual fantasies, sadism, and naive cognitions or beliefs). These categories provide rough profiles and insight into offender motivation.

The *vindictive rapist* is an individual who directs his anger toward an undeserving target. His offenses are motivated not by sexual feelings but by anger; therefore, he is violent and aggressive in his attack. In the absence of any sexual feelings, this offender rapes to harm, humiliate, or degrade women. He usually rapes strangers; however, his victims might possess particular traits that either trigger or appeal to the offender (for example, Asian women, blonde women, or victims with a particular body type). Additionally, simply due to his own affect, he is more likely to behave violently toward women in his everyday life.

Similarly, the *pervasively angry rapist* is marked by anger that pervades each area of his life and is not gender specific. These individuals often have a long history of childhood and adult antisocial behavior and exercise random violence in their lives. Their attacks are often unplanned and without premeditation. Their offenses are characterized by extreme violence, and they cause significant injury to their victims.

Unlike the vindictive rapist and the pervasively angry rapist, the *nonsadistic sexually motivated rapist* is motivated not by anger but by feelings of inadequacy. His ability to overpower and gain control of a victim helps him compensate for various feelings of impotence. The sexually motivated rapist is often shy and lacks social skills. Through rape, he can "prove" not only sexual adequacy but also his own self-importance. His assaults are committed in response to sexual arousal produced by stimuli in the environment. The sexually motivated rapist, sometimes referred to as the "gentleman rapist," is likely to fantasize that the victim will enjoy the sex and return to him for more, even if she resisted the first time. We see these offender characteristics in the case study of Mark at the beginning of the chapter. Mark allowed his unexpressed anger and feelings of powerlessness to motivate him. His assaults had characteristics of the pervasively angry rapist and later escalated to resemble sadistic behavior.

The *sadistic sexually motivated rapist* combines sexual arousal with pain and violence in order to commit the act. This offender often believes that women enjoy being controlled and dominated by men. He is more likely to beat, violate, and possibly kill his victims. He is more likely to be involved in domestic disputes and has difficulty being loyal in committed relationships.

Last, the *opportunistic rapist* engages in spontaneous rape when the opportunity presents itself. Marked by impulsivity, he views the victim strictly as a sexual object. Although he does not necessarily employ overt aggression, he has no concern for his victim's fear or pain. Motivated only by his own desire, he will use no more force than necessary to gain control of the victim. With this type of offender, the rape is usually secondary to another crime, such as burglary or robbery.

Pedophilia

The clearest distinction between the rapist and the pedophile is the targeted victim. Unlike the rapist, who chooses adult women or men as victims, the pedophile is attracted to or assaults children. The term *pedophilia* encompasses acts of child molestation and sexual abuse. The American Psychiatric Association (2000) defines *pedophilia* as having recurrent and intense sexual urges toward children or experiencing sexual fantasies about children that cause distress or interpersonal problems.

The MTC has also grouped pedophiles into four categories according to their behavioral patterns: fixated pedophile, regressed pedophile, exploitative pedophile, and aggressive pedophile.

The *fixated pedophile* is exclusively attracted to children, or "fixated" on a particular developmental stage. Generally, victims are between the ages of 1 and 13, and the victim is at least 5 years younger than the offender. The fixated pedophile is more likely to be socially awkward, shy, and timid toward adults. He feels more comfortable associating with children and prefers children as both sexual and social objects. Sexual contact does not occur until the child and the pedophile have become well acquainted. The fixated pedophile does not use aggression to manipulate children and generally focuses on caressing and fondling, as opposed to sexual intercourse.

The *regressed pedophile* may not be primarily interested in children at all. For this offender, the interest in children is usually sparked by rejection or humiliation from a peer. Feelings of inadequacy related to finding a psychosexually equal partner lead this offender to target a child as a sexual partner. The offender regresses to a younger developmental stage himself to feel comfortable sexually with a child victim. He prefers female victims who do not live near him and usually seeks intercourse with his victim.

The *exploitative pedophile* takes advantage of a child's developmental weaknesses in order to receive sexual pleasure. He is less concerned about the child as an individual and is solely motivated by a desire for sexual dominance. He is more likely to molest stranger victims and will use aggression and physical force. Due to his impulsive nature, this offender is more likely to have a prior criminal record.

The *sadistic pedophile* uses the infliction of pain and violence on his victims to become sexually aroused. This offender generally has a long history of violence beginning in early adolescence. He may prefer same-sex relationships and is often responsible for child abductions and murders.

Cyber Offenders

The cyber offender is an individual who uses the Internet in the commission of a sexual offense. In some cases, Internet offenders exhibit a more addictive personality than the so-called classic offender (Young, 2005). However, just as with classic sex offenders, there is considerable variation in cyber offenders, who range from the online stalker to the child porn website operator. They are typically well versed in the use of the Internet.

The majority of cyber sex crimes involve adolescent victims, not younger children, and only about 5% of offenders use deception to manipulate their victims. About 80% are honest and direct about their intent to engage in sexual activity. Most of the victims in these cases are at-risk teens who crave romance and affection or sexual information and understanding (Mitchell, Finkelhor, & Wolak, 2003).

Cyber offenders might be individuals with no criminal record or indication of an interest in children (Young, 2005). Some have occupations that provide opportunities to work with children (Robertiello & Terry, 2007), but the Internet provides an anonymous forum for exploration of a range of fantasies. Cyber sex offender typologies are not as well studied, but there have been some significant attempts to increase understanding. The police department in Keene, New Hampshire, completed a 3-year law enforcement project in 2000 that resulted in the arrest of 200 cyber offenders and developed a typology for Internet sex offenders. The Keene project delineated four categories of online offenders: the chatter, the manufacturer, the traveler, and the collector.

The *chatter,* or *dialogue,* concerns chats online with an end goal of "cyber sex." This contact often escalates from contact online to phone contact and can lead to a face-to-face meeting.

Unlike the chatter, the *manufacturer* makes child pornography. He takes photos of children in public or in his own home and posts them online. He may collect child erotica instead of pornography.

The *collector* is often single and socially isolated. He collects and trades sexually explicit photos and child pornography. He looks for specific characteristics in his victims and often has a job with access to children.

The *traveler* often fits the MTC fixated typology and is most often thought of when cyber offenders are discussed. He targets adolescents and engages in extensive "grooming" behavior to build a relationship through online chat. He will travel to his target or pay for the child to travel, which usually culminates in a face-to-face meeting. This offender is often a collector of pornography.

THEORETICAL EXPLANATIONS

Understanding the differences between sex offenders helps us to develop more targeted treatment strategies and community safety procedures. These typologies also point to differences in motivation and drive of offenders, and their distinct characteristics also contribute to our theoretical understanding of sexual offending.

Multiple single-factor theories exist to aid our understanding of sexual offending. *Developmental theories* illuminate the difficulties with age-appropriate attachment and with adult intimacy experienced by sex offenders. Caregiver inconsistency at early developmental stages has been found to be a predictor of the degree of sexual violence perpetrated in adulthood (Prentky, Knight, & Lee, 1997). Resultant attachment disorders can include severe anxiety, distrust of others, insecurity and lack of ego strength, dysfunctional anger, and an inability to develop healthy adult relationships. Individuals who lack normal adult social skills are more likely than healthy adults to use children to fulfill psychosexual needs.

The *biosocial theory* also provides an explanation for inappropriate sexual activity. Hormonal levels, in particular an increase in testosterone, are associated with increased sex drive as well as with aggression (Walsh, 2002). Some argue that a biosocial explanation points to a predisposition of some offenders toward unusual sexual preferences.

Due to the nature and variance of sex crimes, *multifactor theories* provide a more robust explanation of the complexity of sexual offending. The *integrated theory* (Marshall & Barbaree, 1990) provides a comprehensive model for understanding sexual offending. This theory asserts that negative early life influences, such as poor or violent parenting, negatively affect one's self-esteem and the ability to manage emotions, to solve problems, and to form meaningful relationships. Consequently, normal adolescent developmental milestones cannot be successfully met, and individuals experience peer rejection and social isolation. This, in turn, exacerbates their existing vulnerabilities at a time when they are experiencing heightened hormonal changes and developing sexual feelings. The inability to successfully learn the skills to manage new sexual feelings and to develop adult relationships leaves socially compromised individuals to resort to unhealthy ways to meet their needs and manage their impulses.

Other theorists (Malamuth, 1996; Malamuth, Heavey, & Linz, 1996) have developed the confluence model, which also provides significant explanatory power regarding sexual offending. This model is based on three primary components: motivators, disinhibitors, and opportunities. Like the integrated theory, the confluence model asserts that individuals who are exposed to childhood physical and sexual abuse will be more vulnerable to developing antisocial coping skills and will be challenged to form healthy adult relationships. The confluence model asserts that individuals who suffer severe and persistent abuse are more likely to develop a delinquent orientation that leads either to the use of sexual power to elevate their peer status or to aggression toward women as a means of domination, control, and humiliation.

CRIMINAL JUSTICE RESPONSE TO SEX CRIMES

In some cases, laws that direct sexual contact between adults are useful in protecting human dignity and community safety. For example, in *Lawrence v. Texas* (2003), the Supreme Court ruled that sodomy among consenting same-sex adults is not a criminal act and sanctions the notion that consenting adults should be free to engage in nonharmful acts together in the privacy of their own homes. The utility of sex-crime legislation can also be seen in the states' removal of the marital rape exemption. Amendments to state marital rape laws that make it a crime to rape one's wife are a result of advocacy in the 1970s, and they add to a body of legal safeguards around sexual conduct. Unfortunately, not all legislation that intends to ensure public safety necessarily does so. It is yet to be determined whether the criminal justice response to sex crimes in general provides effective legal safeguards or merely exacerbates issues surrounding sex offenders and compromises community safety.

Sex-offender registration and notification laws are examples of laws of unknown utility and questionable constitutionality. Registration laws require sex offenders to register their addresses with local law enforcement. This is essentially a private exchange between the offender and law enforcement that is meant to aid law enforcement in tracking offenders. Notification laws require the offender to be listed in a community notification system that provides multiple forms of identifying information (address, demographics, a photo, and specific sex crimes committed) to the general public. These laws are intended to deter offenders from committing new sex offenses, to increase community awareness of possible danger, and to assist law enforcement in finding sex offenders if needed.

Although California implemented the nation's first sex-offender registry in 1947, it was not until the high-profile rapes and murders of Polly Klaas, Megan Kanka, and Jessica Lunsford that heightened public awareness and subsequent national registration laws were enacted. The offenders in these crimes had each served prison time for a sex offense. The Kanka family heightened attention to recidivism and lobbied to have communities notified of sex offenders living nearby; Megan's Law was passed in 1994. In 1996, it was added as an amendment to the Jacob Wetterling Crimes Against Children and Sexually Violent Offender Registration Act. Through a clause in The Jacob Wetterling Act, states that do not implement a community notification program can lose 10% of their funding under the Omnibus Crime Control and Safe Streets Act of 1968.

On the 25th anniversary of the abduction and subsequent murder of Adam Walsh, son of John Walsh (host of the television program *America's Most Wanted*), President George W. Bush signed the Adam Walsh Child Protection and Safety Act of 2006. This law creates three tiers of sex offenders, representing increasing risk of dangerousness and reoffense. Tier 1 offenders must register their addresses annually for 15 years. Tier 2 offenders must register their home addresses every 6 months for 25 years; and Tier 3 offenders must register their addresses every 90 days for life. The Adam Walsh Act provides for a national registry, and failure to register is a felony.

Effects of Sex-Offender Management Legislation

In the social science community, it is widely believed that sex-offender legislation is not meeting its intended goals. The laws are not based on empirical evidence and were instituted without analysis of the long-term consequences to the offender or the community; they provide little evidence of true community safety (Levenson, Brannon, Fortney, & Baker, 2007; Sample, 2006; Tewksbury, 2002). In particular, there have been many challenges to the Adam Walsh Act. The registry portion of the act was ruled unconstitutional by a federal judge in Florida, and the American Civil Liberties Union (ACLU) argues that this change constitutes cruel and unusual punishment by punishing sex offenders for crimes for which they have already paid.

Aside from constitutionality issues, it is not clear how the public safety is ensured. Prescott and Rockoff (2008) found that although there is a small decrease in crime when a notification system is in place, the benefit is lost with an increased number of offenders on the registry. In other words, convicted sex offenders can become more likely to commit crime because of the associated social costs of being publicly registered. Additionally, the information provided by sex-offender notification is not always accurate (Lees & Tewksbury, 2006); but even if one assumes that it is, most scholars do not believe there is a strong link between notification and a reduction in offending (Lovell, 2007; Tewksbury, 2002; Zevitz, 2006).

Similarly, Anderson and Sample (2008) found that although people are generally aware of the registry, most people do not access the sex-offender registration site to get information; the few who did took preventative measures as a result. This finding lends credence to the argument that the notification laws are not serving their ultimate goals of increasing public awareness and subsequent public self-protection.

Others, however, have found that notification laws cause considerable stress to offenders as they attempt to reintegrate into the community (Lees & Tewksbury, 2006; Levenson & Cotter, 2005). Sex offenders report harassment, social isolation, and severe social and occupational loss as a result of public notification. Residents of Long Beach, California, mobilized in 2008 to force out a group of sex offenders who had moved into their community. Similarly, the manager of a hotel in Hayward, California, forced seven sex offenders placed there by the California Department of Corrections and Rehabilitation to leave following angry calls from the community (Graham, 2006).

Another common sex-offender management tool is restricted residency of offenders. Residency restrictions are sometimes referred to as *sex-offender zoning laws* or *exclusionary zones* and often encompass approximately 2,000 feet to 2,500 feet around places where children regularly gather (such as schools and parks). Many local communities have instituted their own, sometimes stricter, residency restrictions that have forced offenders to move out of the community. In some densely populated urban areas like San Francisco, when boundaries are drawn around all schools and parks, there is virtually no room left where an offender may live.

California's Proposition 83 expanded restrictions to all sex offenders (not just those who offend against children) and passed with over 70% voter approval. Availability of housing for offenders released from California's prisons has plummeted. With a one-size-fits-all policy, a person who has been released from prison for adult rape also cannot live near a place where children regularly gather. A report by the California Sex Offender Management Board found that, since the passage of Proposition 83, the number of sex offenders registered as transient had increased by 60%.

This leads not only to problems with tracking paroled sex offenders, but also it reduces the social stability of the offender. Factors such as employment instability and reckless behavior are known risk factors for reoffending (Hanson & Bussiere, 1998) in general. So, it behooves those entrusted with developing policy that ensures community safety to consider the total impact of their decisions. Unfortunately, residency restrictions, although popular, have not proved to be effective.

CONCLUSION

People are inclined to think that a sex offender is a sex offender—that he commits one type of crime. This is a myth. Sex offenders vary widely in type and motivation; some respond well to treatment, others do not. Due to significant differences in motivation and type of offender and in type and severity of offense, sex offenders pose a challenge for categorization. Public policy cannot always effectively incorporate such nuances in a way that strengthens policy. In the case of sex-offender policy, public panic and legislators struggling to find solutions have led to legislation that offers limited success at best and in some cases exacerbates the problem it aims to solve.

Current policies that have led to new problems such as the contribution of residency restrictions to sex-offender homelessness, can be reevaluated in light of the empirical evidence. Informed legislation is that which is based on evidence of efficiency. With community safety in mind, legislators have an obligation to consider new reentry schemes for sex offenders. Darwin noted that it is not the strong who survive but those who are most adaptive to change. Change is needed with sex-offender community management. With an increasing number of convicted sex offenders being released from prisons, communities need reformed policy that provides appropriate housing, treatment, and supervision for offenders; this is what will change a false sense of security to a viable and meaningful effort toward community safety.

DISCUSSION QUESTIONS

1. Using the information in the chapter, provide a possible theoretical explanation for an offender who is classified as a regressed pedophile.

2. Given the theoretical model you developed in question 1, develop a policy that would assist law enforcement and/or corrections in appropriately managing someone with this type of drive and motivation.

3. Discuss where communities might be in 5 years if nothing changes in the realm of sex-offender management.

4. With your understanding of sex-offender typologies and unique motivations, how should the criminal justice system have responded differently to the behavior of John and Mark? What would you recommend as an appropriate course of action regarding each of them?

REFERENCES

American Psychiatric Association. (2000). *Diagnostic and statistical manual of mental disorders* (4th ed., Text revision, *DSM-IV-TR*). Washington, DC: American Psychiatric Association.

Anderson, A., & Sample, L. (2008, April). Public awareness and action resulting from sex offender community notification laws. *Criminal Justice Policy Review, 19,* 371–396.

Barbaree, H., Seto, M., Serin, R., Amos, N., & Preston, D. (1994). Comparisons between sexual and nonsexual rapist subtype: Sexual arousals to rape, offense precursors, and offense characteristics. *Criminal Justice and Behavior, 21*(1), 95–114.

Bureau of Justice Statistics (BJS). (2009). *Criminal offender statistics: Summary findings.* Retrieved from http://www.ojp.usdoj.gov/bjs

Federal Bureau of Investigation. (2002). *Uniform Crime Reports—2001.* Washington, DC: U.S. Department of Justice, Federal Bureau of Investigation.

Federal Bureau of Investigation. (2005). *Crime in the United States, 2005.* Washington, DC: U.S. Department of Justice, Federal Bureau of Investigation.

Graham, R. (2006, June 3). Sex offender forced out of Island Motel. *Oakland Tribune.* Retrieved July 14, 2008, from http://www.oaklandtribune.com

Groth, A. (1979). *Men who rape: The psychology of the offender.* New York, NY: Plenum.

Hale, R. (1997). Motives of reward among men who rape. *American Journal of Criminal Justice, 22*(1), 101–119.

Hanson, R. K., & Bussiere, M. T. (1998). Predicting relapse: A meta-analysis of sexual offender recidivism studies. *Journal of Consulting and Clinical Psychology, 66*(2), 348–362.

Harris, G., Rice, M., & Quinsey, V. (1994). Psychopathy as a taxon: Evidence that psychopaths are a discrete class. *Journal of Consulting and Clinical Psychology, 62,* 387–397.

Knight, R., & Prentky, R. (1987). The development antecedents and adult adaptations of rapist subtypes. *Criminal Justice and Behavior, 14,* 403–426.

Knight, R., & Prentky, R. (1990). Classifying sexual offenders: The development and corroboration of taxonomic models. In W. Marshall, D. Laws, & H. Barbaree (Eds.), *The handbook of sexual assault: Issues, theories, and treatment of the offender.* New York, NY: Plenum.

Lawrence v. Texas, 539 U.S. 558 (2003).

Lees, M., & Tewksbury, R. (2006). Understanding policy and programmatic issues regarding sex offender registries. *Corrections Today, 68*(1), 54–57.

Levenson, J. S. (2007). The new scarlet letter: Sex offender policies in the 21st century. In D. Prescott (Ed.), *Applying knowledge to practice: Challenges in the treatment and supervision of sexual abusers.* Oklahoma City, OK: Wood 'N' Barnes.

Levenson, J. S., Brannon, Y. N., Fortney, T., & Baker, J. (2007). Public perceptions and community protection policies. *Analyses of Social Issues and Public Policy, 7*(1), 137–161.

Levenson, J. S., & Cotter, L. P. (2005). The effect of Megan's Law on sex offender reintegration. *Journal of Contemporary Criminal Justice, 21*(1), 49–66.

Lovell, E. (2007). *Megan's Law: Does it protect children?* London, United Kingdom: Policy and Public Affairs, NSPCC.

Malamuth, N. (1996). Sexually explicit media, gender differences, and evolutionary theory. *Journal of Communication, 46*(3), 8–31.

Malamuth, N., Heavey, C., & Linz, D. (1996). The confluence model of sexual aggression: Combining hostile masculinity and impersonal sex. *Journal of Offender Rehabilitation, 23*(3), 13–37.

Marshall, W., & Barbaree, H. (Eds.). (1990). An integrated theory of the etiology of sexual offending. *The handbook of sexual assault: Issues, theories, and treatment of the offender.* New York, NY: Plenum.

Mitchell, K. J., Finkelhor, D., & Wolak, J. (2003). The exposure of youth to unwanted sexual material on the Internet: A national survey of risk, impact, and prevention. *Youth & Society, 34*(3), 330–358.

Prentky, R., Knight, R., & Lee, A. (1997). *Child sexual molestation: Research issues* (NIJ Research Report). Rockville, MD: National Criminal Justice Reference Service.

Prescott, J., & Rockoff, J. (2008, September 12–13). *Do sex offender registration and notification laws affect criminal behavior?* Paper presented at The Third Annual Conference on Empirical Legal Studies held at the Cornell Law School in Ithaca, New York. Retrieved from http://ssrn.com/abstract=1100663

Robertiello, G., & Terry, K. J. (2007). Can we profile sex offenders? A review of sex offender typologies. *Aggression and Violent Behavior, 12*(5), 508–518.

Sample, L. L. (2006). An examination of the degree to which sex offenders kill. *Criminal Justice Review, 31*(3), 230–250.

Tewksbury, R. (2002). Validity and utility of the Kentucky sex offender registry. *Federal Probation, 66*(1), 21–26.

Walsh, A. (2002). *Biosocial criminology: Introduction and integration.* Cincinnati, OH: Anderson.

Young, K. (2005). Profiling online sex offenders, cyber predators, and pedophiles. *Journal of Behavioral Profiling, 5*(1), 1–19.

Zevitz, R. G. (2006). Sex offender community notification: Its role in recidivism and offender reintegration. *Criminal Justice Studies, 19*(2), 193–208.

CHAPTER 13

Terrorism and the Criminal Justice System

Questions, Issues, and Current Applicable Law

Sharla J. "Kris" Cook and
Timothy A. Capron

INTRODUCTION

The attacks on September 11, 2001, brought the problem of al Qaeda-based terrorism to the attention of the American public. However, the U.S. government and its allies have been dealing with a Middle Eastern-based terrorist threat for many years. The United States battled jihadist terrorists motivated by their visions of Islam. There are two strains, the Shia, from Iran, and the Sunni, growing out of offshoots of the Muslim Brotherhood in Egypt. The Shia and Sunni split occurred after the death of the Prophet Mohammed in 632 AD over the successor to the Prophet. The Sunnis wanted to elect their leaders, or caliphs, while the Shia thought the caliphate should pass to a relative of the Prophet (Wright, 2011). Shia and Sunni jihadists both really began about the same time, around 1979. For the Shia, the overthrow of the Shah of Iran and subsequent takeover by Ayatollah Khomeini birthed Shia jihadists, giving rise to Hezbollah, designated as a Foreign Terrorist Organization (FTO) by the United States Department of State (The Bureau of Counterterrorism, 2012). Iran soon engaged in taking over the U.S. embassy in Tehran and holding hostages for some 444 days. This outrage was followed by the bombings of the American embassy and the U.S. Marine barracks in Lebanon in 1983 by Hezbollah with support from Iran's Revolutionary Guard and the Quds force.

Outraging the Sunnis in Egypt was the fact that the Camp David Accords resulted in a peace treaty between Egypt and Israel, predictably dooming President Sadat of Egypt. He was assassinated after much plotting by Ayman al-Zawahiri's al-Jihad organization. Al-Zawahiri ended up in prison as a result, realizing that violence and only violence would lead to change. Zawahiri soon joined the newly formed al Qaeda in Afghanistan, the United States getting a reprieve as it became involved in fighting the Soviet Union following its invasion of Afghanistan. Following a successful defeat of the Soviet Union in Afghanistan in 1988 by al Qaeda and the Taliban, al Qaeda would now focus on the United States.

The first attack on the World Trade Center in New York City occurred in 1993, and America and its citizens have been targets of terrorists at home and abroad since then. For example, the 1996 attack on Khobar Towers in Saudi Arabia (in which 19 Americans were killed and hundreds of others wounded), the nearly simultaneous 1998 attacks on U.S. embassies in Kenya and Tanzania, and the 2000 suicide bombing of the *USS Cole* in Yemen demonstrated a consistent and determined pattern of attack on American interests and its citizens (McCarthy & Velshi, n.d.; Yungher, 2008).

The response of the United States to these earlier terrorist attacks has been widely criticized as disjointed, ineffective, uncoordinated, and unfocused (Poland, 2004; White, 2008; Yungher, 2008) and as having "neither a common response nor the resources or equipment to counter terrorism" (Poland, 2004, p. 234).

The *9/11 Commission Report* (National Commission on Terrorist Attacks Upon the United States, 2004) described multiple mistakes in the U.S. counterterrorism efforts. These failures included inadequate gathering and sharing of intelligence by the Department of Defense (DOD), the Central Intelligence Agency (CIA), the Department of Justice (DOJ), and the Federal Bureau of Investigation (FBI). The report also faulted the Immigration and Naturalization Service (INS), the Federal Aviation Administration (FAA), the State Department, and Congress for underestimating or ignoring the terrorist threat and for failing to adequately develop and deploy defensive measures to detect and counter terrorism.

After the September 11 attack, the Bush administration determined it would not make similar mistakes. It asked Congress for the authority to take aggressive measures to detect and deter the terrorist threat by "break[ing] down barriers to information sharing, enabling law enforcement and intelligence personnel to share information that is needed to help connect the dots and disrupt potential terror . . . activity" (Department of Homeland Security [DHS], 2005, para. 2). Congress responded by passing Public Law 107–56, the Uniting and Strengthening America by Providing Appropriate Tools Required to Intercept and Obstruct Terrorism (USA PATRIOT) Act of 2001. The administration also quickly obtained from Congress a joint resolution Authorization for Use of Military Forces (AUMF; Public Law 107–40, 2001), which stated that

> the President is authorized to use all necessary and appropriate force against those nations, organizations, or persons he determines planned, authorized, committed, or aided the terrorist attacks that occurred on September 11, 2001, or harbored such organizations or persons, in order to prevent any future acts of international terrorism against the United States by such nations, organizations or persons. (Sec. 2a)

The sweeping authority found in the AUMF and in legal opinions based in part on the AUMF and issued by the Department of Justice's Office of Legal Counsel (Johnsen, 2008) were subsequently used by the president to issue multiple "military order(s) regarding the detention, treatment, and trial of individuals detained in the war on terrorism . . . and . . . (to set) the minimum standards of treatment for detainees" (Meier, 2007, p. 29). Moving beyond those who had attacked the United States on September 11, the Bush administration declared a comprehensive Global War on Terrorism (GWOT) that was virtually without limits and seemingly interminable. The president stated,

> Our enemy is a radical network of terrorists, and every government that supports them. Our war on terror begins with al-Qaeda, but it does not end there. It will not end until every terrorist group of global reach has been found, stopped and defeated. (Bradley & Goldsmith, 2005, p. 37)

The Bush administration argued that the president's authority as commander-in-chief and the authority in the AUMF gives him a virtually unlimited range of powers to prosecute the GWOT. Johnsen (2008) suggested it was the expanded interpretation of the GWOT that

> provided the context for [the Bush administration's] most controversial claims of unilateral authority: to override legal prohibitions on the use of torture and cruel, inhuman and degrading treatment; to hold "enemy combatants" indefinitely without access to counsel or any opportunity to challenge their detention; and to engage in domestic electronic surveillance without a court order. (p. 395)

The focus here is on the Bush administration's (circa 2001–2008) actions to detect terrorist plans through increased and enhanced surveillance, especially electronic surveillance methods and on how the Obama administration continues the controversial practices. Additionally, an examination is made of the Bush administration's policies on detention, treatment, and interrogation of suspected captured and detained terrorists and of how the Obama administration continued to deal with these issues, including opting for the widespread use of drones to kill suspected terrorists, even American citizens.

Researchers in various academic disciplines and government agencies, along with private think tanks have studied the motivation and actions of terrorists. But they have yet to develop a universally accepted definition of terrorism (White, 2008; Yungher, 2008). As Combs (2012) noted, "[T]errorism is a political as well as legal and a military issue . . . its definitions in modern terms has been slow to evolve" (p. 9).

The level of complexity in modern international terrorism is significant and makes a single definition and counterterrorism approach difficult. Whittaker (2002) noted, "The contemporary world presents terrorism in astonishing complexity and diversity" (p. 20). Badey (2002) commented on that diversity, noting that "after more than thirty years of inter-governmental discourse there is still no commonly accepted definition of international terrorism" (p. 2). He suggests that governmental definitions are written to provide maximum individual agency flexibility when dealing with politically sensitive issues.

As one might expect, various federal agencies have tailored their definitions of terrorism to provide the maximum flexibility Badey mentioned. The State Department (U.S. Department of State, 2004) defined terrorism:

> The term terrorism means premeditated, politically motivated violence perpetrated against noncombatant targets by subnational groups or clandestine agents, usually intended to influence an audience.
>
> The term international terrorism means terrorism involving citizens or the territory of more than one country.
>
> The term terrorist group means any group practicing, or that has significant subgroups that practice, international terrorism. (p. xii)

According to a statement of FBI policy on its Jackson Division website (FBI, 2001, p. iii),

> The FBI defines terrorism as "the unlawful use of force or violence against persons or property to intimidate or coerce a Government, the civilian population, or any segment thereof, in furtherance of political or social objectives." The FBI further describes terrorism as either domestic or international, depending on the origin, base, and objectives of the terrorist organization. (paras. 4–5)

The DOD, the CIA, and the Defense Intelligence Agency all have different definitions of terrorism (White, 2008). There are some common themes: the threat and/or calculated use of *violence against innocents*, civilians, or noncombatants and suggestions that the violence is *politically motivated* or used *to intimidate and to create fear* for political purposes (Combs, 2012; Yungher, 2008). Whatever the formal definition, there is no disagreement that terrorism is a threat that must be fought aggressively and effectively.

It is also worth noting that some critical terrorist academics suggest that common definitions of terrorism are flawed as they fail to include the possibility that the state may engage in terror against its citizens (Blakely, 2007). After watching 2014 events in Syria where its dictator has slaughtered over 100,000 of his nation's people—they may have a point.

FIGHTING TERRORISM EFFECTIVELY IN A CONSTITUTIONAL DEMOCRACY

How does one best balance the interests of national security with the interests of liberty? Royce C. Lamberth, a former presiding judge of the Foreign Intelligence Surveillance Court (FISC; Lamberth, as cited in Kris & Wilson, 2007), stated,

Like many competing American values, liberty and security converge in law. We strike the balance between them not only in the many particular statutes, orders, and policies of the government, but also in the ongoing process of Legislative, Executive, and Judicial action—and reaction—within the framework prescribed by the Constitution. Our national security is therefore cast, and continually recast, in the crucible of our legal system. (p. xxxiv)

The process Lamberth described is exactly what has happened since September 11. The Bush administration, sometimes working with Congress, implemented a number of statutes, executive orders, and policies designed to protect and enhance American security. Some who are concerned about American values and liberty have mounted challenges to those statutes, orders, and policies in both Congress and the courts (Bazen, 2008). Candidate Barack Obama was critical of virtually all of the Bush administration terrorism policies, but President Obama's record is largely indistinguishable from his predecessor's.

SURVEILLANCE AND DETECTION

As noted, immediately after the 9/11 attacks, Congress and the American public appeared to give the executive branch of government broad leeway to prosecute the Global War on Terror (Johnsen, 2008). In one of the most visible measures of that support, Congress passed the USA PATRIOT Act of 2001 (Public Law 107–56, 2001).

In passing the USA PATRIOT Act, Congress clearly sought to promote the interests of national security by liberalizing intelligence gathering and sharing, and by expanding the surveillance authority of government agencies. The USA PATRIOT Act consists of more than 1,000 antiterrorism measures. It expanded the government's authority to investigate terror-related threats, search premises, conduct expanded surveillance, detain suspects, and examine suspicious activities in such areas as immigration and banking. Regarding surveillance, Section 215 permits "roving wiretaps," as well as a wide range of surveillance activities, including the capability to obtain business records via warrant to include personal library records, e-mail records, medical treatment, websites visited, political events attended, church membership, and mental health records (Public Law 107–56, 2001).

A major change allowed sharing of investigative information between law enforcement agencies (like the FBI) and intelligence agencies (like the CIA). Section 203 of the USA PATRIOT Act (Public Law 107–56, 2001) permits

any investigative or law enforcement officer, to disclose . . . wire, oral, or electronic communication, or evidence derived . . . to any other Federal law enforcement, intelligence, protective, immigration, national defense, or national security official . . . foreign intelligence or counterintelligence, . . . or foreign intelligence information . . . to assist the official who is to receive that information in the performance of his official duties. (p. 280)

The Obama Administration and the PATRIOT Act

Fact One: Despite expressing grave misgivings about the PATRIOT Act as both a senator and when running for president, President Obama signed a 4-year extension of the PATRIOT Act, much to the chagrin of his critics, in 2011, with virtually no changes ("Obama Signs Last-Minute," 2011).

Fact Two: The PATRIOT Act must seem an effective tool for President Obama after receiving intelligence briefings on the terrorist threat and realizing the grave danger they posed (Lee, 2013).

Fact Three: Ironically, President Obama and his Justice Department have been spending a great deal of time in court, defending the very practices authorized by the PATRIOT Act. The American Civil Liberties Union (ACLU) managed to effectively challenge the PATRIOT Act in the case of *Al Haramain v. Obama* (Cohn, 2012). However, Congress passed legislation negating what looked like a defeat by crafting new legislation that resulted in the case ultimately being dismissed by the Ninth Circuit Court of Appeals on the grounds of sovereign immunity (Cohn, 2012).

In summary, the PATRIOT Act remains intact and is likely to remain intact under the current administration, despite calls for change.

Foreign Intelligence Surveillance Courts

The most current modernization of the Foreign Intelligence Surveillance Act (FISA) is the FISA Amendments Act of 2008. This new law expanded surveillance of persons located outside the United States who are not U.S. citizens or legal residents of the United States. No "probable cause" is required, and the government is not required to suggest that the target is a terrorist or a spy. The program does not allow the government to target American citizens directly; however, if the foreign target calls or e-mails an American citizen, that communication may be monitored (Harris, 1998, p. 28). The original FISA Act of 1978 created a special court located in Washington, D.C., to review applications for wiretapping and data mining of suspected spies or terrorists operating in the United States. In 2012, there were 1,856 requests for surveillance with 40 modified and one withdrawn (Mears & Abdullah, 2014).

In what has been a continuing pattern, on the same day the details of the law became publicly known in 2008, the American Civil Liberties Union (ACLU) filed a lawsuit challenging the constitutionality of the new law (ACLU, 2008). The ACLU was disappointed. The case, *Amnesty v. Clapper*, was initially rejected by a federal judge for plaintiffs failing to prove their communications would be monitored under the new FISA (aka FIS), but a federal appeals court reversed that in 2011; the U.S. Supreme Court in a 5–4 decision in 2013 ruled that ACLU plaintiffs lacked standing (the right to sue; ACLU, n.d.).

Proponents of both security and liberty have also focused on other issues in the Global War on Terrorism, including detention, interrogation, and treatment of prisoners. Their actions in "the ongoing process of Legislative, Executive, and Judicial action—and reaction—within the framework prescribed by the Constitution" (Lamberth, as cited in Kris & Wilson, 2007, p. xxxiv) are detailed in the next section.

FISA Court Facts

Fact One: Senator and then candidate Obama had serious reservations about FISA courts and said so on numerous occasions, noting in a campaign stop in 2008 that

> for one thing, under an Obama presidency, Americans will be able to leave behind the era of George W. Bush, Dick Cheney and "wiretaps without warrants," he said. (He was referring to the lingering legal fallout over reports that the National Security Agency scooped up Americans' phone and Internet activities without court orders, ostensibly to monitor terrorist plots, in the years after the September 11 attacks.)
>
> It is hardly a new stance for Obama, who has made similar statements in previous campaign speeches, but mention of the issue in a stump speech, alongside more frequently discussed topics like Iraq and education, may give some clue to his priorities. In our own Technology Voters' Guide, when asked whether he supports shielding telecommunications and Internet companies from lawsuits accusing them of illegal spying, Obama gave us a one-word response: "No." (Broache, 2008, paras. 4–5)

Fact Two: Senator and candidate Obama argued against awarding telecommunication companies immunity from lawsuits when they cooperate with the National Surveillance Agency (NSA; see Fact One above) but then, in 2008 as a senator, voted for a bill that would grant immunity (Kravets, 2012).

Fact Three: President Obama has been much more active than President Bush when it comes to opposing safeguards to FISA in Congress. President Obama has squelched any attempts to take legislative action against it. His Justice Department challenges any lawsuit questioning FISA court actions or NSA actions dismissed on the grounds of sovereign immunity or state secrets, usually successfully, something candidate Obama criticized the Bush administration for routinely doing (Timm, 2012).

Fact Four: President Obama, following revelations about the massive extent of NSA eavesdropping by Edward Snowden in 2013 and earlier, agreed, after much criticism to require the NSA to obtain a court order each time it searched its database of information about American phone calls. It would also move many of these data out of the hands of the federal government (Gorman, 2014).

Fact Five: President Obama in the last months appointed a commission to examine the surveillance program and make recommendations about changing, curtailing, and improving it. He has received the recommendations and will implement modest changes, including taking the metadata out of the hands of the NSA and require they file a request from the FISC to access the data (Kaplan, 2014).

In summary, despite changes by the Obama administration, numerous lawsuits have been filed following Snowden's leaks. Lawsuits seeking to stop the surveillance program caused government lawyers to propose that federal court rules would require the NSA to stop routinely destroying older phone records (Barrett & Gorman, 2014).

DETENTION AND TREATMENT OF SUSPECTED TERRORISTS

President Obama wasted little time ensuring a clean break from the Bush administration when it came to the treatment of detainees. In 2009, he signed executive orders ending the use of torture, which the Bush administration justified under the executive power of the commander-in-chief; a second executive order required that detainees be treated humanely under the Geneva Conventions, which prohibited humiliating and degrading treatment of prisoners; and a third order made interrogations subject to procedures of the *Army Field Manual* (Isikoff, 2009). These were controversial decisions, not without criticisms, primarily from the intelligence community.

Extraordinary Rendition of Suspected Terrorists

During the Bush administration, detention and treatment of suspected terrorists was controversial. President Obama pledged an end to harsh interrogations and extraordinary rendition, a practice of moving suspects to a location or country where they could be interrogated and tortured. The latter program, run by the CIA, had been utilized since the Reagan administration and routinely used by all administrations since (Benjamin, 2007). In 2009, a White House Task Force recommended maintaining its use, but with greater oversight. In the meantime, the Obama administration won a major victory when the Ninth Circuit Court of Appeals ruled in 2010 that former victims of rendition could not sue the CIA; the Supreme Court later refused to hear the case, ending the legal issue (Savage, 2010).

Does the Obama administration engage in the practice of extraordinary renditions? The answer apparently is yes, with a unique twist. Its current utilization seems to be that individuals of interest are arrested abroad by local authorities, in, say, Dijbouti (a small country in Africa), at the request of the CIA, and then are held in place while American interrogators show up and ask questions, building a case and then asking the country to extradite them to the United States.

This is even more complex as Congress and the president remain at odds over this and other issues:

> Renditions are taking on renewed significance because the administration and Congress have not reached agreement on a consistent legal pathway for apprehending terrorism suspects overseas and bringing them to justice.
>
> Congress has thwarted President Obama's pledge to close the military prison at Guantanamo Bay, Cuba, and has created barriers against trying al Qaeda suspects in civilian courts, including new restrictions in a defense authorization bill passed last month. The White House, meanwhile, has resisted lawmakers' efforts to hold suspects in military custody and try them before military commissions.

The impasse and lack of detention options, critics say, have led to a de facto policy under which the administration finds it easier to kill terrorism suspects, a key reason for the surge of U.S. drone strikes in Pakistan, Yemen, and Somalia. Renditions, though controversial and complex, represent one of the few alternatives. (Whitlock, 2013, paras. 4, 5)

Facts About Extraordinary Rendition

Fact One: The Obama administration continues the practice of extraordinary rendition though it has ended the practice of harsh interrogations (Whitlock, 2013).

Fact Two: The Obama administration, despite 5 years of calling for the closure of Guantanamo (a U.S. Navy prison on leased land in Cuba), has not been able to do so. It has, at various times, tried some recent cases in federal court and scheduled hearings for some detainees for a review of their case to see if they can be released; Congress continues to put roadblocks in place to allow trying terrorists in federal criminal courts (Bravin, 2014; Whitlock, 2013). The entire process is glacial. For example, Kahleed Sheik Mohammed, the alleged mastermind behind 9/11 and the admitted killer of *Wall Street Journal* reporter Daniel Pearl, has been in custody since 2003, and he has not even been tried for his role in 9/11 (Seib, 2014). Only 155 detainees remain there, with 75 designated for transfer, 20 others who are charged awaiting trial, and the remaining 60 or so able to ask for a review seeking release (Bravin, 2014).

Fact Three: The Obama administration obviously preferred trying suspected terrorists in federal courts and hoped to try the mastermind behind the 9/11 attacks in a federal court in New York. This provoked outrage from both parties; however, to its credit, over 125 suspected terrorists since 2009, a much better record than the military commissions in Cuba, have been successfully tried and convicted (Sullivan, 2013).

In summary, the current administration made a significant break from the Bush administration when it comes to treatment of detainees, including ending torture and adhering to the Geneva Conventions.

DRONE STRIKES

The United States has used drones as weapons since 2004, and by the end of the Bush Administration, there had been some 45 drone strikes (International Human Rights and Conflict Resolution Clinic [IHRCRC] & Global Justice Clinic [GJC], 2012). The use of drones by the Obama administration escalated with over 2,400 individuals killed by the fifth anniversary of the administration (IHRCRC & GJC, 2012; Serle, 2014). The administration claims there have been no civilian casualties or few civilian casualties (IHRCRC & GJC, 2012). This is clearly not the case as a report in *The New York Times* made clear in 2012:

The very first strike under his watch in Yemen, on Dec. 17, 2009, offered a stark example of the difficulties of operating in what General Jones described as an "embryonic theater that we weren't really familiar with." It killed not only its intended target, but also two neighboring families, and left behind a trail of cluster bombs that subsequently killed more innocents. It was hardly the kind of precise operation that Mr. Obama favored. Videos of children's bodies and angry tribesmen holding up American missile parts flooded YouTube, fueling a ferocious backlash that Yemeni officials said bolstered al Qaeda.

The sloppy strike shook Mr. Obama and Mr. Brennan, officials said, and once again they tried to impose some discipline. In Pakistan, Mr. Obama had approved not only "personality" strikes aimed at named, high-value terrorists, but "signature" strikes that targeted training camps and suspicious compounds in areas controlled by militants.

But some State Department officials have complained to the White House that the criteria used by the C.I.A. for identifying a terrorist "signature" were too lax. The joke was that when the C.I.A. sees "three guys doing jumping jacks," the agency thinks it is a terrorist training camp, said one senior official. Men loading a truck with fertilizer could be bomb makers—but they might also be farmers, skeptics argued. (Becker & Scott, 2012, p. Al)

Perhaps even more shocking but not surprising is the fact that President Obama has also authorized the use of drone strikes to kill American citizens at least four times, including Anwar al-Awlaki in 2011, using a military drone placed under CIA control at the last minute; it is now considering striking again, using a military drone (Barnes & Gorman, 2014).

Facts About Drone Strikes

Fact One: The Obama administration uses drone strikes freely in many areas of Pakistan, Yemen, and Afghanistan, at will, disputing that there are large numbers of civilian casualties or collateral damage (IHRCRC & GJC, 2012).

Fact Two: The Obama administration uses drone strikes to kill American citizens (Barnes & Gorman, 2014; Serle, 2014).

Fact Three: The Obama administration is now being sued for violating the rights of American citizens killed by drone strikes (Reilly, 2013).

The current administration has greatly expanded the use of drones. This is clearly controversial, and the killing of Americans using drones is at minimum questionable if not blatantly unconstitutional. It is interesting that the Obama administration's legal justification for using drones is the 2001 Authorization for Use Of Military Force, obtained by the Bush administration (Sorcher, 2013).

COURT CHALLENGES

There have been numerous court challenges to the detention and military commission tribunal policies of the Bush administration. Several of the most important cases decided in the U.S. Supreme Court are briefly summarized here.

In 2004, the U.S. Supreme Court held in *Hamdi v. Rumsfeld* that it was the role of Congress, not the president, to authorize the detention of combatants. The Court also held that the Constitution guaranteed Hamdi (a U.S. citizen) due process rights in a military tribunal. The Bush administration argued that Hamdi was an enemy combatant and could be detained indefinitely, without trial or other judicial hearings, until the war on terror ended (Perkins, 2005).

Also in 2004, the U.S. Supreme Court ruled in *Rasul v. Bush* that U.S. courts have jurisdiction to hear appeals from Guantanamo Bay detainees challenging their status as enemy combatants. The Court overturned a lower court's ruling that no U.S. court has jurisdiction to hear petitions for habeas corpus on behalf of the detainees because they are aliens detained abroad (Roosevelt, 2005). As noted earlier, in reaction to the *Rasul v. Bush* ruling and at the Bush administration's urging, Congress passed the Detainee Treatment Act (DTA) with a provision that denied detainees access to federal courts to file habeas corpus petitions (Suleman, 2005).

In 2006, in *Hamdan v. Rumsfeld,* the U.S. Supreme Court found that President Bush did not have the power, independent of congressional action, to unilaterally establish military tribunals to try detainees. Additionally, they found that the Geneva Convention protections for POWs applied to all detainees at Guantanamo and other "foreign" prisons (Spiro, 2006). In response, the DOD issued policies ordering the U.S. military to comply with Common Article 3 of the Geneva Convention Relative to the Treatment of Prisoners of War (GPW) in all aspects of its treatment of detainees. DOD Directive 2310.01E "provided a baseline standard of treatment for all detainees . . . and . . . was widely perceived as a repudiation of the harsh interrogation tactics and treatment standards approved subsequent to the attacks of September 11" (White, 2006, cited in Meier, 2007, p. 34).

In response to *Hamdan v. Rumsfeld,* the Bush administration sought congressional approval for its proposed military commission tribunal system to try suspected terrorists. In 2006, Congress approved the Military Commissions Act (MCA). The MCA authorized military commissions to prosecute detainees for war crimes. The MCA also stripped U.S. courts of jurisdiction to hear or consider habeas corpus appeals from anyone held as an enemy combatant. The MCA also prohibited detainees from invoking the GPW as a source of rights in U.S. Courts.

In 2008, the U.S. Supreme Court heard another challenge to the restrictions on habeas corpus in the case of *Boumediene et al. v. Bush.* The Court looked at four questions:

1. Should the MCA of 2006 be interpreted to strip federal courts of jurisdiction over habeas petitions filed by foreign citizens detained at the U.S. Naval Base at Guantanamo Bay, Cuba?

2. If so, is the MCA of 2006 a violation of the Suspension Clause of the Constitution?

3. Are the detainees at Guantanamo Bay entitled to the protection of the Fifth Amendment right not to be deprived of liberty without due process of law and of the Geneva Conventions?

4. Can the detainees challenge the adequacy of judicial review provisions of the MCA before they have sought to invoke that review? (*Boumediene et al. v. Bush*, 2007)

In a 5–4 majority opinion, the Court held

that because the procedures laid out in the Detainee Treatment Act are not adequate substitutes for the habeas writ, the MCA operates as an *unconstitutional suspension* [italics added] of that writ. The detainees were not barred from seeking habeas . . . merely because they had been designated as enemy combatants or held at Guantanamo Bay. (*Boumediene et al. v. Bush*, 2007)

THE LATEST DEVELOPMENTS

President Obama has replaced President Bush. It appears his approach to fighting the terrorist threat will vary significantly from that of the previous administration. Within days of taking office, President Obama signed executive orders "to close the U.S. detention facility at Guantanamo Bay, Cuba, within a year and end harsh interrogation techniques previously used on terrorist suspects, saying America will wage war on terrorism 'in a manner consistent with our values and ideals'" (Wilson & Fletcher, 2009, para 5).

President Obama also ordered the suspension of all judicial proceedings at Guantanamo Bay under the Bush administration's military commissions system. The new administration will have to determine what to do with the more than 200 prisoners, perhaps including trials in U.S. civilian courts or in military court-martial proceedings (Wilson & Fletcher, 2009). In what probably seemed an ironic twist to former Bush officials, a military judge at Guantanamo rejected Obama's request to suspend a hearing for a *USS Cole* bombing suspect (Associated Press, 2009). Thus, in that process that Lamberth described so eloquently, "We strike the balance between [liberty and security] . . . in the ongoing process of Legislative, Executive, and Judicial action—and reaction—within the framework prescribed by the Constitution" (as cited in Kris & Wilson, 2007, p. xxxiv). Whatever its challenges, seeking that balance is how democracy works.

Military trials are slowly underway again at Guantanamo, after President Obama ordered they begin in 2011, though lawsuits, questions, and controversy continue to lengthen the process. (CNN Wire Staff, 2011). As an example, following a hunger strike last year, inmates challenged conditions and a recent appellate court decision did find that federal judges do have the authority to oversee complaints about conditions by detainees; this was a major defeat for the administration and no doubt will result in more lawsuits (Savage, 2014).

DISCUSSION QUESTIONS

1. Do you believe the USA PATRIOT Act encroaches on such constitutionally guaranteed freedoms as protection against illegal search and seizure?

2. What is the proper balance between violation of detainees' rights and aggressive interrogation in the interests of national security?

3. What is the proper balance between national security and the national values of fairness, justice, due process, and rule of law? The Fourteenth Amendment ensures American citizens due process if they are suspects in a criminal case.

4. Should Fourteenth Amendment rights be extended to terrorist suspects who may not be American citizens?

5. Can we detain, interrogate, and hold enough terrorists to win the Global War on Terrorism?

6. Do our methods stand up to the scrutiny of a skeptical world (especially the Muslim world), which may doubt our commitment to fairness, justice, due process, and the rule of law?

7. Can we afford not to take the measure we have taken to protect our security?

8. Suppose you had just been elected president of the United States; what would you do about the war on terror, and what would you do to balance the competing concepts of security and liberty?

9. Does the president have the authority to kill American citizens using drones?

REFERENCES

American Civil Liberties Union (ACLU). (2008). *The Foreign Intelligence Surveillance Act.* Retrieved March 20, 2014, from https://www.aclu.org/blog/tag/fisa/

American Civil Liberties Union (ACLU). (n.d.). *Amnesty et al. v. Clapper: FISA Amendments Act challenge.* Retrieved February 19, 2014, from https://www.aclu.org/national-security/amnesty-et-al-v-clapper

Associated Press. (2009, January 29). *Judge refuses to delay Gitmo detainee's trial.* Retrieved February 1, 2009, from http://msnbc.msn.com/id/28914869

Badey, T. J. (2002). Defining international terrorism: A pragmatic approach. In T. J. Badey (Ed.). *Annual editions: Violence and terrorism* (pp. 32–35). Guilford, CT: McGraw-Hill/Duskin.

Barnes, J. E., & Gorman, S. (2014, February 10). *U.S. looks to target American with drone.* Retrieved February 21, 2014, from http://online.wsj.com/news/articles/SB10001424052702304104504579375443531873238

Barrett, D., & Gorman, S. (2014, February 20). NSA weighs retaining data for suits. *Wall Street Journal,* p. A4.

Bazen, E. B. (2008). *The Foreign Intelligence Surveillance Act: An overview of selected issues.* Washington, DC: Congressional Research Service.

Becker, J., & Scott, S. (2012, May 29). Secret "Kill list" proves a test of Obama's principles and will. *The New York Times,* p. A1.

Benjamin, D. (2007, October 20). 5 Myths about rendition (and that new movie). The *Washington Post.* Retrieved February 20, 2014, from http://www.washingtonpost.com/wp-dyn/content/article/2007/10/19/AR2007101900835.html

Blakely, R. (2007). Bringing the state back into terrorism studies. *European Political Science,* 6(3), 228.

Boumediene et al. v. Bush, 553 U.S., 128 S. Ct. 2229 (2007). Retrieved January 29, 2009, from http://oyez.org/cases/2000–2009/2007/2007/2007_06_1195/

Bradley, C. A., & Goldsmith, J. L. (2005). Congressional authorization and the war on terrorism. *Duke Law Magazine, 23*(1), pp. 36–37. Retrieved January 22, 2009, from http://www,law.duke.edu/magazine/2005spring/features/bradley.html?linker=2

Bravin, J. (2014, January 29). Hearing offers peek at Guantanamo. *Wall Street Journal,* p. A6.

Broache, A. (2008, January 8). *Obama: No warrantless wiretaps if you elect me.* Retrieved February 20, 2014, from http://news.cnet.com/8301–10784_3–9845595–7.html

CNN Wire Staff. (2011, March 8). *Obama orders resumption of military commissions at Guantanamo.* Retrieved February 21, 2014, from http://www.cnn.com/2011/POLITICS/03/07/obama.guantanamo/

Cohn, C. (2012, August 7). *9th Circuit dismisses Al Haramain case.* Retrieved February 20, 2014, from https://www.eff.org/deeplinks/2012/08/9th-circuit-dismisses-al-haramain-case

Combs, C. C. (2012). *Terrorism in the twenty-first century* (7th ed.). Upper Saddle River, NJ: Pearson, Prentice Hall.

Department of Homeland Security. (2005). *Fact sheet: The USA PATRIOT ACT—A proven homeland security tool.* Retrieved January 17, 2009, from www.dhs.gov: http://dhs.gov/news/releases/press_release_0815.shtm

Department of State. (2004, April). *Patterns of global terrorism, 2003.* Retrieved January 11, 2009, from http://www.state.gov/documents/organization/31912.pdf

Federal Bureau of Investigation (FBI). (2001). *Terrorism, 2000/2001.* Washington, DC: U.S. Department of Justice, Federal Bureau of Investigation. Retrieved from http://www.fbi.gov/stats-services/publications/terror/terror00_01.pdf

Gorman, S. (2014, February 1–2). NSA curbs added on eve of speech. *Wall Street Journal,* p. A4.

Harris, S. (1998, July 18). Explaining the FISA. *National Journal, 28.*

International Human Rights and Conflict Resolution Clinic (IHRCRC) of Stanford Law School (Stanford Clinic) & Global Justice Clinic (GJC) at New York University School of Law (NYU Clinic). (2012, September 25). *Living under drones: Death, injury and trauma to civilians from US drone practices in Pakistan.* Retrieved February 25, 2014, from http://www.livingunderdrones.org/report/

Isikoff, M. (2009, January 21). Obama's order ends Bush-era interrogation tactics. *Newsweek.* Retrieved February 28, 2014, from http://www.newsweek.com/obamas-order-ends-bush-era-interrogation-tactics-77965

Johnsen, D. E. (2008). What's a president to do? Interpreting the Constitution in the wake of Bush administration abuses. *Boston University Law Review, 88,* 395–419.

Kaplan, F. (2014, January 17). Pretty good privacy. *Slate.com.* Retrieved February 28, 2014, from http://www.slate.com/articles/news_and_politics/war_stories/2014/01/obama_s_nsa_reforms_the_president_s_proposals_for_metadata_and_the_fisa.html

Kravets, D. (2012, October 9). Supreme Court terminates warrantless electronic spying case. *Wired.com.* Retrieved February 20, 2014, from http://www.wired.com/threatlevel/2012/10/scotus-electronic-spying-case/

Kris, D., & Wilson, J. D. (2007). *National security investigations and prosecutions.* Eagan, MN: Thomson/West.

Lee, T. B. (2013, August 2). Sen. Obama warned about Patriot Act abuses. President Obama proved him right. *The Washington Post.* Retrieved February 20, 2014, from http://www.washingtonpost.com/blogs/the-switch/wp/2013/08/02/sen-obama-warned-about-patriot-act-abuses-president-obama-proved-him-right/

McCarthy, A., & Velshi, A. (n.d.). *Outsourcing American law: We need a national security court* (American Enterprise Institute working paper no.156). Retrieved from http://www.aei.org/files/2009/08/20/20090820-Chapter6.pdf

Mears, B., & Abdullah, H. (2014, January 17). *What is the FISA court?* CNN.com. Retrieved February 20, 2014, from http://www.cnn.com/2014/01/17/politics/surveillance-court/

Meier, M. W. (2007). A treaty we can live with: The overlooked strategic value of Protocol II. *The Army Lawyer,* pp. 28–41.

National Commission on Terrorist Attacks Upon the United States. (2004). *9/11 Commission Report* (Chap. 8). Retrieved June 26, 2013, from http://govinfo.library.unt.edu/911/report/911Report_Ch8.htm

Obama signs last-minute Patriot Act Extension. (2011, May 27). *Fox News*. Retrieved February 19, 2014, from http://www.foxnews.com/politics/2011/05/27/senate-clearing-way-extend-patriot-act/date

Perkins, J. (2005). Habeus Corpus in the war against terrorism: Hamdi v. Rumsfeld and citizen enemy combatants. *BYU Journal of Public Law, 19*(2). Retrieved from http://www.law2.byu.edu/jpl/Vol%2019.2/6Perkins.pdf

Poland, J. (2004). *Understanding terrorism: Groups, strategies, and responses* (2nd ed.). Upper Saddle River, NJ: Pearson Education.

Reilly, R. J. (2013, June 11). ACLU drones lawsuit slams Obama for asserting right to kill Americans without oversight. *The Huffington Post*. Retrieved February 21, 2014, from http://www.huffingtonpost.com/2013/06/11/aclu-drones-obama_n_3423419.html

Roosevelt, K., III. (2005). Application of the Constitution to Guantanamo Bay: Guantanamo and the conflict of laws: Rasul and beyond. *University of Pennsylvania Law Review, 153*, 2017–2071. Retrieved February 21, 2014, https://www.law.upenn.edu/cf/faculty/krooseve/workingpapers/153UPaLRev2017(2005).pdf

Savage, C. (2010, September 9). Court dismisses a case asserting torture by C.I.A. *The New York Times*. Retrieved February 20, 2014, from http://www.nytimes.com/2010/09/09/us/09secrets.html?pagewanted=all&_r=0

Savage, C. (2014, February 12). Appeals court allows challenges by detainees at Guantánamo Prison. *The New York Times*. Retrieved February 21, 2014, from http://www.nytimes.com/2014/02/12/us/appeals-court-clears-way-for-guantanamo-challenges.html

Seib, G. F. (2014, February 4). In war on terror, wheels of justice grind slowly. *Wall Street Journal,* p. A4.

Serle, J. (2014, January 23). *More than 2,400 dead as Obama's drone campaign marks five years*. Retrieved from http://www.thebureauinvestigates.com/2014/01/23/more-than-2400-dead-as-obamas-drone-campaign-marks-five-years/

Sorcher, S. (2013, February 14). Is Obama's drone policy really morally superior to torture? *National Journal*. Retrieved February 21, 2014, from http://www.nationaljournal.com/magazine/is-obama-s-drone-policy-really-morally-superior-to-torture-20130214

Spiro, P. J. (2006). Hamdan v Rumsfeld. 125 S. Ct. 2749. *The American Journal of International Law, 100*(4), 888–895.

Suleman, A. M. (2005). Detainee Treatment Act of 2005. *Harvard Human Rights Journal, 19*, 257–265.

Sullivan, E. (2013, October 15). Federal courts prosecute suspected terrorists as Guantanamo Bay remains open. *The Huffington Post*. Retrieved February 28, 2014, from http://www.huffingtonpost.com/2013/10/15/federal-courts-guantanamo_n_4100138.html

The Bureau of Counterterrorism. (2012, September 28). *Foreign Terrorist Organizations.* State Department. Retrieved from http://www.state.gov/j/ct/rls/other/des/123085.htm

Timm, T. (2012, October 24). Fact checking Obama's misleading answer about warrantless wiretapping on *The Daily Show.* Retrieved February 20, 2014, from https://www.eff.org/deeplinks/2012/10/fact-check-obamas-misleading-answer-about-warrantless-wiretapping-daily-show

Uniting and Strengthening America by Providing Appropriate Tools Required to Intercept and Obstruct Terrorism (USA PATRIOT). Pub. L. 107–56 (H. R. 3162). (2001). Retrieved December 22, 2008, from http://frwebgate.access.gpo.gov/cgi-bin/getdoc.cgi?dbname=107_cong_public_laws&docid=f:pub1056.107.pdf

White, J. R. (2008). *Terrorism and homeland security* (6th ed.). Belmont, CA: Wadsworth Cengage Learning.

Whitlock, C. (2013, January 1). Renditions continue under Obama, despite due-process concerns. *The Washington Post.* Retrieved February 20, 2014, from http://www.washingtonpost.com/world/national-security/renditions-continue-under-obama-despite-due-process-concerns/2013/01/01/4e593aa0–5102–11e2–984e-f1de82a7c98a_story.html

Whittaker, D. J. (2002). *Terrorism: Understanding the global threat.* London, United Kingdom: Pearson Education.

Wilson, S., & Fletcher, M. A. (2009, May 22). Obama and Cheney deliver dueling speeches on national security. *The Washington Post.* Retrieved February 20, 2014, from http://www.washingtonpost.com/wp-dyn/content/article/2009/05/21/AR2009052101748.html

Wright, L. (2011). *The looming tower: Al-Qaeda and the road to 9/11.* New York, NY: Vintage Books.

Yungher, N. I. (2008). *Terrorism: The bottom line.* Upper Sadddle River, NJ: Pearson.

CHAPTER 14

Developments in Cyber Criminology

Johnny Nhan and Michael Bachmann

THE EMERGENCE OF CYBER CRIMINOLOGY

Due to pronounced increases in the scale and scope of victimization and an omnipresence of news reporting, cybercrime issues have garnered considerable public attention in recent years. The reports span a wide array of issues, events, and activities, ranging from large chain retailers having been electronically robbed of millions of consumer credit cards by nefarious hackers to illicit mass surveillance of electronic communications by clandestine governmental agencies. Growing societal concerns over increased victimization,[1] escalating damages,[2] the protection of critical infrastructures related to national security,[3] and the arising conflicts between security and privacy have sparked considerable interest in cybercrime-related issues within the social and the computer sciences. Despite the heightened societal and academic awareness of the problem, the young discipline of cyber criminology still suffers from several fundamental issues other disciplines have long overcome, among them the lack of a clear identity as a criminological subdiscipline, standardized research methodologies and definitions, and a paucity of consistent theoretical frameworks. Nevertheless, several central areas are discernable as essential within this criminological subfield. This chapter explores four of the central themes: (a) definitional issues in cybercrime, (b) meanings and demarcations of Internet space, (c) policing and social control in cyberspace, and (d) theoretical explanations. Due to the difficulty of defining and understanding exactly what constitutes a cybercrime—a problem that is reflected in the first theme—these classifications are not mutually exclusive. A comprehensive categorization and explanation of the various types of cybercrime is not the intent here but rather an assessment of the progress and challenges in some main areas of cyber-criminological research.

Efforts to police and control the online environment are examined; hacking is used as an example to highlight the inherent conflicts between security and privacy issues that will be discussed, along with the debate surrounding the applicability of traditional criminological theories to cybercrime phenomena or whether formulating adequate explanations of cybercrime requires new or hybrid models. Finally, we are not presenting a comprehensive examination; instead, we discuss the challenges of researching cybercrime in the developing field of cyber criminology.

The Case of Target: Can We Really Protect Ourselves From Cybercrime?

The festive 2013 holiday shopping season was interrupted by the victimization of millions of customers of U.S. retail giant Target, who fell victim to one of the largest security breaches in U.S. history. Approximately 40 million credit and debit card account numbers, expiration dates, and card verification value (CVV) codes were stolen by hackers, who then sold this information in chunks on black carding markets to third party criminals to print fraudulent replica cards. While the case is still under investigation as of the time of this writing, network security experts believe customer information was stolen from the Target stores' point-of-sale (POS) database where credit and debit cards are swiped. Some security experts believe POS servers were compromised by attackers who installed malicious software through a periodic system firmware update, which could have been accomplished through finding a tiny vulnerability in the system or with insider knowledge obtained from an unlawful employee.

Investigators immediately combed through notorious online black market sites for stolen credit card information and found that Target's stolen cards were indeed sold in batches of one million cards, with prices ranging from $20 to $100 per card, according to security blogger Brian Krebs.[4] Krebs uncovered evidence that alleges the perpetrator is a high-level Ukranian hacker, Andrey Hodirevski, who goes by the nickname of Rescator on several online crime forums. Target and the U.S. Secret Service have not released any details of the investigation as of the time of this writing.

The high-profile Target hack occurred despite a growing number of Americans and companies being cognizant of and actively taking precautions to protect against cyber victimization and identity theft. For instance, individuals are increasingly using encryption technologies and firewalls to protect security home wireless networks, guarding their social security numbers, shredding documents, installing antivirus software on home computers, and taking other security measures. In addition, most online organizations today require strong passwords that are not commonly found in the dictionary and personal identification numbers (PINs), with some institutions requiring several levels of authentication. Despite such precautions, the Target hacking incident shows that you can fall victim to financial cybercrimes even if you do not shop online and that, unfortunately, you as the consumer lose the ability to safeguard your personal financial information every time you use it to make any purchase.

DEFINING AND CLASSIFYING CYBERCRIMES

The development of a generally accepted definition of cybercrime is obscured by substantive problems similar to white-collar crime, whose definition has been debated for over half a century. Sociologist Edwin Sutherland's address to the 1939 annual meeting of the American Sociological Association, white-collar criminality, sparked controversy by using a class-based orientation of crime "in the upper or white-collar class, composed of respectable or at least respected business and professional men" (Sutherland, 1940, p. 1). Many contemporary scholars of white-collar crime have expanded Sutherland's original orientation to include individuals of nonelite status (Edelhertz, 1970) and a wider range of activities. Geis (1991) considered the ramifications of broadening Sutherland's definition, questioning whether a television scam should be regarded as a white-collar crime or merely a petty consumer crime. The blurred distinction between white-collar and conventional crime makes a common definition difficult to establish. Likewise, the emerging field of cybercrime does not have a widely agreed-upon criminological definition and consequently suffers from similar problems.

The broad scope of different types of cybercrime lends itself to substantive definitional debate. The term *cybercrime* denotes a wide range of phenomena, encompassing such disparate activities as attacks on national critical infrastructures and online auction fraud. The vast scale of multifaceted phenomena comprised by the term *cybercrime* renders formulation of a precise general definition extremely difficult (Bachmann, 2008). However, three defining categories have emerged as essential elements of a broad conception of cybercrime: (a) its commission within electronic networks, (b) the role of technology, and (c) the various legal statutes that can be applied.

First, cybercrime is commonly understood as signifying a range of illegal acts that share commission through electronic information and communication networks. For example, Thomas and Loader (2000) defined cybercrime as "computer-mediated activities which are either illegal or considered illicit by certain parties and which can be conducted through global electronic networks" (p. 3). This definition distinguishes cybercrime from other crime types by limiting the term to crimes that occur in the "virtual space" of worldwide information networks, particularly the Internet (Castells, 2002).

Second, cybercrimes can also be categorized by the function of technology in their commission. Furnell (2002) differentiated between "computer-assisted crimes," in which "the computer is used in a supporting capacity, but the underlying crime or offense either predates the emergence of computers or could be committed without them"—such as fraud, theft, and (child) pornography—and "computer-focused crimes . . . in which the category of crime has emerged as a direct result of computer technology and there is no direct parallel in other sectors" (p. 22). These crimes include such activities as hacking, website defacing, and virus and worm attacks. The recently founded "Cyber" division of the Federal Bureau of Investigation (FBI) also distinguishes between "computer enabled" crimes that are traditional crimes committed with computer technology and "cybercrimes" that would not be possible without computer technology. A similar distinction is proposed by Gordon and Ford (2006), who isolated three main dimensions of the term *cybercrime:* (a) involvement of computer and hardware devices—that is, the part played by technology; (b) the technology–human-element continuum, which ranges from primarily technological cybercrimes to those that have pronounced human elements; and (c) the "crimeware"—the malicious software that is used for the commission of the crime. Unfortunately, both Furnell's classification and Gordon and Ford's, although useful in analyzing interdependency processes in social and technological developments, are of limited criminological value (Yar, 2005).

Third, cybercrime can be defined legally. Wall (2001, pp. 3–7) suggested translating four existing criminal law classifications into their cybercrime equivalents: (a) "(cyber)-trespass," the unauthorized crossing of the boundaries of computer systems and/or the causation of damage to those systems or their owners; (b) "(cyber)-deceptions/theft," the stealing of money or property through, for example, identity thefts, credit card frauds, phishing e-mails or pharming websites, or violations of intellectual property through online piracy; (c) "(cyber)-pornography/obscenity," the display of obscene or pedophile pornography or racist or otherwise offensive statements; and (4) "(cyber)-violence," inflicting psychological harm or threatening physical harm through, for example, hate speech, harassment, or the dissemination of information assisting in dangerous activities like bomb building.

Brenner (2001) classified cybercrime into four legal categories: (a) prohibited conduct (*actus reus*), (b) culpable mental state (mens rea), (c) attendant circumstances, and (d) forbidden result or harm. Using a legal orientation, Brenner considers all cybercrime materially indistinguishable from street crime thereby raising the question (which is also the title of her article), Is there such a thing as virtual crime? (Brenner, 2001). For example, when comparing theft or embezzlement by a cyber criminal to physical theft, "(the) perpetrators may use different methods to accomplish their thefts, but their conduct, their mental states, the pertinent circumstances and the ultimate result are conceptually indistinguishable" (Brenner, 2001, para. 85).

Beyond the various proponents and opponents who argue for or against certain aspects as essential to an overarching academic definition of cybercrime, a third faction of scholars is forming. These scholars see the definitional debate over cybercrime—and white-collar crime as well—as a mere distraction from meaningful, solution-oriented research. Grabosky (2001, p. 243) questioned whether the concept of cybercrime warrants a separate definition or has instead to be considered merely "old wines in new bottles." However, Clifford (2006) offered a more sensible solution. He questioned the practicality of attempting to subsume the vast scale of multifaceted phenomena encompassed by the term *cybercrime* under one legal definition. Instead, Clifford suggested focusing our attention on the rational implications of the various cybercrime-related statutes for investigators, prosecutors, and defense attorneys. Despite Clifford's suggestion to end the debate for an overarching definition, this discussion will likely continue as the line between cyber and crime becomes further obscured by a greater infusion of computers into society and by demarcation lines that will have to be established between the partially overlapping concepts of cybercrime, cyberterror, and cyberwarfare.

THE INTERNET SPACE AND JURISDICTION

Some criminologists and social scientists are seeking to understand the Internet structurally. These researchers are primarily concerned with the inherently "borderless" nature of the cyber environment and the resulting difficulties regarding the defining, demarcating, understanding, and ultimately controlling of crime on the Internet. The disembodied nature of cyberspace challenges the politically and legally defined borders that govern our physical world. This is not to suggest that cyberspace is entirely disconnected and independent from physical spaces. However, Internet borders are defined by other means. Wilson and Corey (2000) conceptualized electronic space by three distinctions: (a) the physical infrastructure, such as servers, switches, routers, and cables; (b) virtual disparities, or the power relations derived from the digital divide between those who have greater access to the Internet and those who do not; and (c) the demarcation of interaction of places, such as online communities that have informal regulations for interactions and restrictions for membership.

Many legal scholars have attempted to define Internet borders in terms of jurisdiction. Brenner and Schwerha (2004) examined jurisdictional difficulties in policing international cybercrime. They concluded that persisting legal discrepancies between sovereign countries often hinder investigations; they also found that formal processes governing transnational evidence gathering are "cumbersome" (p. 112). Kumar (2006) examined the decentralized nature of cyberspace as problematic for determining which court has jurisdiction over civil e-commerce cases. Reidenberg (2005) suggested considering certain types of cybercrime—such as hate, drugs, sex, gambling, and stolen music use—as "denial of service" attacks on the legal system because they pose "technologically based arguments to deny the applicability of rules of law interdicting their behavior" (p. 1953).

As is the case with white-collar crime, jurisdictional difficulties and the complexity of cybercrime have also affected prosecutorial strategies. Smith, Grabosky, and Urbas (2004) have found that, like white-collar crime, cybercrime is treated no differently from conventional crime under the court system. However, cross border jurisdictional legal difficulties, evidence-collection issues, and case complexities often affect the practicality of deciding which cases to prosecute. Nhan (2009) found that the strategies ensuing from these difficulties often result in heavy use of plea bargaining and minimal threshold requirements, which often create "free zones" in which lawbreakers are not subject to policing and regulation.

Criminologists and legal scholars are still grappling with the difficulties of fitting geographically defined rules, based on legal and politically defined borders, to the abstract nature of cyberspace. Political and legal institutions have been historically grounded in geographically defined notions of territory. The emergence and growing societal relevance of the Internet poses an unprecedented disruption to this long-established order of power and control. Similarly, institutions of formal social control, namely, law enforcement, also experience great difficulties in policing this new, "antispatial" environment.

POLICING AND SOCIAL CONTROL ON THE INTERNET

A growing number of criminologists and legal scholars have investigated the fit between law enforcement and cyberspace. Huey (2002) has examined the conceptual difficulties of fitting geographically based law enforcement (which historically has been tied to geographically limited, territorial arrangements in controlling assigned public spaces) to the complex and "abstract" environment of the Internet. She argued that the Internet is not fundamentally different from the physical world; rather, law enforcement's perception of cyberspace is shaped by cultural habits that "bar them from seeing their role as operating outside of geographic space" (p. 250). This perception of the Internet by police is further skewed by the general lack of understanding of computers and telecommunications technology and the tendency to interpret them as "magic boxes that mysteriously obey commands upon direction" (p. 244).

A number of criminologists and legal scholars have questioned whether the digital environment demands new policing strategies based on public–private collaborations. Brenner (2004) expounded on the inadequacy of the established policing model to control the vast scale of border-spanning cybercrime. Wall (2007) suggested a similar collaborative model, arguing that the public policing role must adapt to the Internet environment by establishing partnerships with nonstate institutions to create security networks. These concepts are derived from Ericson and Haggerty's (1997) proposed shift in the police paradigm from strict crime control to managing dangers and risks in an information society. The new policing paradigm is derived from Castells's (2000) network theory, which holds that security is produced from interconnected "nodes" (institutional actors) that require the diffusion of policing power to nonstate and hybrid entities (Burris, Drahos, & Shearing, 2005; Dupont, 2006; Wood & Shearing, 2007).

It remains to be determined whether it is even possible to implement entirely new models of policing, given the required larger structural changes to the policing and legal paradigms. The current model of policing cybercrime is still confronted with the restraints of the established criminal justice and legal systems. The primary functions of law enforcement agencies are still to detain suspects and prepare paperwork for court, regardless of the type of crime. In the case of cybercrime, this translates into computer forensics work and issues related to admissibility of digital evidence in court (Moore, 2007).

Current models of forensics employed by law enforcement are challenged by the cyber environment and by increasingly savvy criminals. The volatility and intangibility of evidence associated with these types of offenses holds significant difficulties for law enforcement, owing to the lack of such traditional forensic artifacts as fingerprints, DNA, and eyewitness accounts (Bachmann, 2008; Shinder & Tittel, 2002). Moreover, cyber criminals often employ anonymizing strategies and services, such as encryption algorithms, "spoofing" tools, and public wireless networks and access points to further complicate forensic cyber investigations.[5] The many technical obstacles and time constraints involved in the pursuit of cyber cases serve as additional disincentives for state and local prosecutors and investigators. To face these challenges, law enforcement has increasingly turned to partnership models of policing.

Law enforcement has embraced collaborative efforts to a limited degree, primarily through interagency task forces that partner with the private sector. Nhan and Huey (2008) in their study of high-tech crimes task forces in California have found this public–private model effective. Nevertheless, significant cultural and structural frictions still hinder more robust collaborations. Moreover, certain types of cybercrimes that fit well with the current policing model of apprehending offenders (such as illegal piracy and child predators—more traditional crimes in a different medium) are favored by state and local agencies over more transnational and/or decentralized and technical cybercrimes (such as hacking). Addressing this issue, Gros (2003) has questioned the notion of sovereignty and emphasized a greater role of collaborative international institutions, such as Interpol and the United Nations, in policing global cybercrime.

SECURITY VERSUS PRIVACY

One major complication in policing cybercrime that has been making headlines is the dichotomy between security and privacy, particularly the use of electronic surveillance. The question of whether the Internet represents a separate domain that operates by different rules is debated between law enforcement circles, whose members desire greater flexibility in monitoring cyberspace, and citizens' rights groups, which fight for extending privacy rights to the online environment.

Since the September 11, 2001, terrorist attacks, the federal government has drastically changed their terrorism security operations to include greater Internet monitoring. Several pieces of legislation allowed for "warrantless wiretapping" by federal agencies. Shortly after the 9/11 attacks, the Foreign Intelligence Surveillance Act of 1977 (FISA), which allowed for electronic and physical surveillance of foreign threats without a court-issued warrant, was amended by the USA PATRIOT Act of 2001 to include terrorist entities not affiliated with a foreign nation. A special court (the Foreign Intelligence Surveillance Court—FISC) was created as oversight to ensure the secrecy of antiterrorist operations. Several other pieces of legislation have been proposed to expand surveillance powers.

The abuse of foreign surveillance powers has come to light. The National Security Agency (NSA), in particular, has drawn sharp criticism for secret surveillance programs that gather mass data from Americans. According to an Internet rights advocacy group, the Electronic Frontier Foundation (EFF),[6] the NSA has been conducting illegal "dragnet" surveillance of Americans' e-mails, searches, and other Internet activities. Moreover, former CIA employee and NSA contractor Edward Snowden, exposed several mass surveillance programs, such as "PRISM," "Bullrun," and "XKeyScore," which decrypted and stored popular Internet e-mail, video, social media, and other communications applications and rendered all kinds of private communications searchable in extremely large databases. The colossal amounts of information that is intercepted by unwarranted wiretapping from the NSA alone necessitated this agency to build a $2 billion data center facility in Utah capable of storing exabytes of data. Despite its harsh criticism, the federal government is not the only entity collecting data on citizens. In principle, the dragnet fishing techniques employed by these agencies are the same as the data mining operations of private marketing corporations. The inputs, algorithms, and machine learning techniques are the same; solely the search terms differ.

Corporations have been collecting user information for storage, analysis, sharing, and sale. The term *big data* is used to describe a massive amount of data that cannot be stored and handled using traditional software and analytic tools (Snijders, Matzat, & Reips, 2012). Online companies, such Google, Facebook, Amazon, Apple, and Yahoo, collect data for targeted advertising, which includes search queries, physical location, IP address, Internet service provider, e-mail address and phone number, and sometimes even the user's face (Kelly, 2013). The abuse of data collection has raised concerns, as in the case of Facebook, where it continued to surreptitiously track Internet browsing habits of users even after they have logged out of the service (Acohido, 2011). Sociologist Amitai Etzioni (2010) warned that the fear of government surveillance, "Big Brother," may be taking attention away from corporations, "Little Brothers," who make large profits from indiscriminately collecting and selling all users information. Aside from large Internet corporations utilizing our personal data to increase profits, there are several other potential uses of such information that users should be concerned about. For instance, much of our digitized personal information can be subpoenaed without a warrant, enabling a range of persons and professions from private investigators to divorce attorneys to access our information and potentially reveal damaging insights into our most private activities. Moreover, governmental data mining aside, one cannot discount the impact of the many breaches of data security that wash all of this personal information into the welcoming hands of cyber criminals and fraudsters.

While online surveillance has gained international attention from the leaked information on clandestine programs, social scientists have studied the effects of surveillance in society. Contemporary scholars draw from Jeremy Bentham's panoptic prison design, where the physical cruelties of prisons during the Dark Ages were replaced by a more humane treatment more aligned with Enlightenment principles of rehabilitation and restoration. Bentham's circular "apparatus of surveillance" featured hegemonic self-surveillance through solitary confinement with a central observation tower whose occupants cannot be seen by each prisoner, who therefore must assume they are being watched at all times (Miller & Miller, 1987, p. 3). Foucault (1977) furthers these prison concepts in examining institutions of power in society, including schools and hospitals, which extend social control beyond prisons.

Cyber criminologists have adopted and adapted these classic scholars' concepts to issues of Internet surveillance. Dupont (2008) asserted that the nature of the Internet creates conditions for an "electronic panopticon," pointing to two trends underemphasized by scholars: (a) the increasing ubiquity and distributed nature of surveillance that blurs the distinction between those who are watching and those being watched and (b) the deployment of resistive antisurveillance cryptographic technologies by users. Brown and Korff (2009) discussed the balance between terrorism and the proportionality of Internet surveillance. They argued that the overuse of Internet surveillance under the name of terrorism undermines democratic rule of law and cross border collaborative law enforcement efforts that require transparency. The authors most likely did not know the timeliness of their foretelling article on the current state of cyber surveillance.

Edward Snowden: Traitor or Patriot?

In 2013, 29-year-old computer analyst Edward Snowden released classified information from a global network of mass surveillance programs headed by the NSA to two news outlets, *The Washington Post* and British newspaper *The Guardian*. Snowden, a former CIA employee and NSA contractor, was motivated to inform the public of Orwellian-like surveillance programs conducted indiscriminately on members of the public. For instance, Snowden has made claims that the NSA indiscriminately collects billions of pieces of information, ranging from the location and content of domestic and international phone calls and text messages to online services, such as the content of e-mails, social networking activities, and web searches.

Snowden asserted that the NSA has illegally gained backdoor access by exploiting technology companies, such as Microsoft, Cisco, Yahoo, and others. According to Snowden, people should care about surveillance "because even if you're not doing anything wrong you're being watched and recorded. And the storage capability of these systems increases every year consistently by orders of magnitude to where it's getting to the point where you don't have to have done anything wrong."[7]

Many others, however, feel Snowden's actions were an act of treason that threatens national security and Western intelligence operations as a whole. One can conclude that Snowden is not only a law breaker but also broke the national security oath he took. A federal judge, however, rejected the government's assertion that its activities are based on legal precedent of collecting public phone metadata and ruled in a preliminary hearing that the government's bulk collection of metadata is most likely a violation of privacy rights. Despite this legal opinion, no action as of this writing has been taken to halt these programs.

Public opinion is split over Snowden's actions. A 2013 poll showed 51% of Americans viewed Snowden as a commendable "hero" while 49% felt he was a "traitor" who should be punished.[8]

CYBER RIGHTS AND CYBERCRIME: THE CASE OF HACKING

The Internet was originally conceived with a set of principles in mind. It developed from the Advanced Research Projects Agency (ARPA) net,[9] a primarily research-oriented network designed to create a global infrastructure based on open and decentralized information sharing. Leonard Kleinrock (2004, pp. 199–200), computer scientist and one of the original architects of the Internet, explained that much of the perception of the Internet as a distinct, disembodied space with separate rules manifests from a set of initial norms. Among those norms are the notions that it serves everyone, that it is an "open" environment, that it is a means to share ideas and works, and that it is empowering, noncentralized, and owned by no one. These mentalities have manifested in various justifications for cybercrime.

Computer hacking is one form of cybercrime that has straddled the dichotomy between the open principles of the Internet and malicious behavior. The hacker subculture materialized in the genesis of computers in the 1960s and 1970s. Rather than simply using existing computer technology, original hacker enthusiasts were united in their passion for technological innovations and by their playful and individualistic quest to satisfy their intellectual curiosity (Hafner & Markoff, 1991; Jordan, 2008). All early contributors who pioneered the "computer revolution" (Naughton, 2000, p. 313) and all those who paved the way for today's superhighways of the Internet were considered prototypical hackers in this original understanding of the term (Levy, 1984).

The early hacking community was characterized by a fundamental distrust of governmental and military monopolies, power, and authority. Early hackers were characterized by their defiance of corporate domination of culture and by their rejection of traditional and conservative values and lifestyles (Yar, 2005). Instead, they advocated the idealistic notions of unrestricted distribution of information, knowledge, and intellectual thought (Lasica, 2005; Thomas, 2002) and the use of computer technology for the higher goals of intellectual discovery, the creation of art and beauty, and improvement of the overall quality of life (Levy, 1984). Furthermore, they challenged the status quo of closed models of software development produced by companies like Microsoft by creating a Free Software/Open Source (FOSS) countermovement dedicated to developing open and free software alternatives (Jordan, 2008).

However, this positive connotation of the word changed during the 1980s, as more malicious hackers drew the attention of the press. The increasingly mission-critical nature of computer networks for many industries and the expanding popularity of electronic financial transactions began to attract people who sought not to understand the systems but to abuse, disrupt, sabotage, and exploit them. Today, the hacker scene can be largely divided into *penetration testers*, who, following the spirit of the original hacker scene, hack legally and under contract to improve the security of systems and networks, and *black-hat hackers*, who attempt to illegally break into and exploit computers. Holt and Kilger (2008) further distinguished between computer experts who learn how to hack while in institutional settings, such as universities, whom they term "makecraft hackers," and hackers "in the wild," whom they call "techcraft hackers" (p. 76). Holt and Kilger showed that techcraft hackers, while exhibiting no differences in their knowledge of ethical conduct, have significantly fewer concerns about breaching the law and compensate for the lack of institutional support with a greater number of hacker peers (cf. Holt, 2007). Consequently, Holt and Kilger (2008) concluded that social learning mechanisms contribute to the greater rejection of ethical norms among techcraft hackers.

The primary focus of criminological research on hackers concerns their attitudes, ethics, social backgrounds, and behaviors (Bachmann, 2008; Holt, 2007; Holt & Kilger, 2008; Jordan, 2008; Jordan & Taylor, 1998; Thomas, 2002). Bachmann (2008) showed that the common hacker stereotype of the clever, lonesome, deviant male adolescent whose computer proficiency compensates for social shortcomings barely begins to tell the whole story of who hackers are. A significant inadequacy of this stereotype is the misperception that hackers are socially inept and invariably young (Bachmann, 2008; Holt, 2007; Holt & Kilger, 2008). More important, Bachmann (2008) also revealed that hackers undergo a maturation process over the course of their hacking careers and that the more experienced and seasoned black-hat hackers tend to be the most dangerous. They are more likely to attack higher profile targets, and many engage in illegal hacking activities with the stronger criminal intent to profit financially. The studies of hackers and the hacking subculture, while gathering important insights into the social dimensions of technical crimes, face several practical methodological challenges, as do the rest of the cyber-criminological studies. These challenges are addressed in the following section.

The 21st-Century Silk Road

The Internet you access, browse, and search daily is not the entire World Wide Web. Hidden from search engines and inaccessible to Google and Bing crawlers exists a different Internet, referred to as the deep web or the dark net. It consists of websites, chat rooms, and databases hidden behind cryptic and inaccessible code, layers of split and rerouted packages, ever-changing addresses, and accessible only with specialized anonymizing browsers. It is this underbelly of the Internet that most of the illegal black market sites call their home, including trading places for illegal drugs and weapons, stolen and forged goods, identities, and credit cards and other financial information; or even children, organs, human slaves, and contract killer services. One of the most well-known and notorious marketplaces during the last 2 years was the site The Silk Road. While it specialized in the large-scale distribution of illegal substances and was hence oftentimes called the Amazon.com or eBay of illegal drugs, the site also offered a cornucopia of other goods and services, ranging from fake identities to all the equipment necessary to produce your own fake credit cards with stolen information. The market became so successful because its owner Ross Ulbricht, known then only under his online handle Dread Pirate Roberts, had implemented a clever working principle that at the same time minimized the potential risk for buyers and sellers while also protecting their anonymity—a difficult problem to solve when you think about it. To accomplish this task, Ulbricht used the Tor network, an anonymizing network that uses encryption to conceal the user's location and ensures the communication is inaccessible to all parties except the intended recipient. Second, he conducted all financial transactions in the digital currency bitcoin. Known as the "hacker currency" because of its reliance on encryption algorithms, bitcoins have no association with any national government, are difficult to track, and are easy to move online. The site itself served as the mutual reassurance between buyers and sellers. The money was collected upon ordering, but it was paid to the seller only after the goods had actually been shipped. When he was arrested by the FBI in October 2013, Ulbricht had amassed a considerable personal fortune by charging sellers site registration and transaction fees. Upon closing the site, the FBI was able to freeze 26,000 Bitcoins (roughly $3.5 million at the time) and Ulbricht's encrypted personal wallet (his Bitcoin account), which is estimated to contain 600,000 Bitcoins (or

(Continued)

(Continued)

approximately $80 million). This case is exemplary for the cybercrime problem at large in many ways. It shows that—despite considerable law enforcement efforts today—the Internet, especially the dark net, is still very much the 21st century equivalent of the gold rush that brought with it the lawlessness of the Wild West. It further shows how much the unprecedented anonymity online hinders law enforcement efforts. The site had long been undercut by undercover agents, but an arrest of Mr. Ulbricht was not possible until investigators had a lucky break with intercepted drugs in mailed packages that could be traced and succeeded in foiling a staged murder plot Mr. Ulbricht had tasked undercover agents to commit. Last, the site itself was re-spawned in less than a month after the FBI seizure as Silk Road 2.0. Despite the mistrust the arrest has caused in the community and the uncertainty whether the new site was set up by undercover law enforcement, the trade on the new site, fueled by all the publicity of the high-profile arrest, is flourishing again.

METHODOLOGICAL CHALLENGES IN RESEARCHING CYBERCRIME

The developing field of cyber criminology has yet to overcome a series of distinct methodological and theoretical problems. As discussed, the foremost methodological problem stems from the lack of a general definition of cybercrime. This problem is fundamental because of its implications for the second problem, the operationalization and measurement of cybercrime.

To obtain an accurate assessment of the scope and severity of cybercrimes is a difficult undertaking. Official crime data, often used for criminological studies, are rare for cybercrime, and the few existing data sets are plagued by serious underreporting problems. To begin with, the two most important official crime data sources, the Uniform Crime Report (UCR) and the National Incident Based Reporting System (NIBRS), contain hardly any useful information. The UCR records no cybercrime, and the NIBRS contains only one, highly ambiguous computer-crime variable. Additionally, official crime statistics do not measure incident trends and distributions objectively but are socially constructed; particularly for the measurement of cybercrime, this circumstance poses a significant problem. An accumulation of various compounding factors leads to severe underreporting of cybercrime in official statistics. The most common of these factors are perceptions of the offense as private or trivial. Most people do not know exactly what constitutes a cybercrime and are therefore often confused about the appropriateness of reporting a particular incident (Howell, 2007). The intangibility of evidence and the lack of traditional forensic artifacts make online offenses more difficult to detect than terrestrial crimes. Moreover, the global nature of cybercrimes and the high level of offender anonymity in the online environment are two additional aspects that discourage both victims and law enforcement from reporting such crimes, because they decrease the perceived chance of apprehending the offender. As a result, many police stations prioritize reporting of local problems (Wall, 2001) occurring on their "patch" (Lenk, 1997, p. 129). One can only conclude that underreporting continues to be a serious problem in cybercrime victimization surveys and official statistics.

Victimization surveys are often used by criminologists because they can encompass offenses that are typically underreported in official statistics. However, these surveys cannot completely eliminate all difficulties faced by official measurements. First, undetected crime cannot be reported. Second, systematic errors can result from the survey process, such as various interviewer effects and other sources of bias. Survey researchers have long recognized that even the highest possible optimization of survey instruments will never completely eliminate survey errors (cf. Groves et al., 2004). However, many of the aforementioned problems of official statistics also plague cybercrime victimization surveys, thus rendering them particularly prone to bias. To make matters worse, most surveys measure only corporate or organizational victimization and exclude private computer users systematically. Wall (2001) also hints at various existing intersurvey inconsistencies regarding methodologies and classifications that complicate meaningful comparative analyses and aggregations. Yar (2006, p. 14) specifies three reasons for underreporting by corporations: (a) fear of embarrassment, (b) loss of public or customer confidence (as in the case of breaches relating to supposedly secure e-shopping and e-banking facilities), and (c) potential legal liability relating to the violation of data protection responsibilities. In addition to all of these problems of cross-sectional data, longitudinal measures of cybercrime often also must resolve issues resulting from rapidly changing legal classifications. All these problematic factors continue to affect quantitative criminological studies of cybercrime.

To overcome the limitations of using traditional criminological methodologies in studying cybercrime, some criminologists have resorted to more innovative means to obtain and analyze data that have yielded insightful results. Dupont (2013) examined the contents of a hacker Internet relay chat (IRC) chat room communications log among hackers from seized computer hard drives. Using these data, he was able to examine and map social and monetary structures of very illusive and ephemeral hacker networks. Fortin (2013) analyzed 45 days of text-based communications of known Usenet online discussion channels of cyber pedophiles to examine their community, ranging from moral support, conflict resolution, and technical assistance to promotion of illegal content.

Aside from measurement issues, cyber criminologists face certain theoretical problems. Differences in the cyberspace environment with regard to structural and social features call into question the transferability of traditional criminological theories to cybercrimes.

THEORETICAL CHALLENGES IN CYBERCRIME RESEARCH

Many criminologists have applied existing criminological theory to explain cybercrime. Some criminologists have applied Felson's (2000) routine activities theory to the subject, explaining that crime occurs out of everyday opportunity (Cox, Johnson, &

Richards, 2009; Grabosky, 2001). Yar (2005), however, raised some theoretical concerns regarding the applicability of this theory, principally that some of the theory's core elements lose their relevance when they are transposed from "terrestrial" to "virtual" worlds (Yar, 2005). Although cybercrimes certainly do exhibit many of the characteristics of traditional crimes, the qualitatively new environment in which they are committed is likely to invalidate some of the core components of traditional theories. Criminological theories rely in varying degrees on ecological and environmental propositions. Some of them explain crimes as occurring within particular settings that exhibit specific social, cultural, and economic characteristics. For example, routine activities theories focus on the time-space convergence of motivated offenders with suitable targets and the absence of capable guardians thereby implying certain environmental settings in which offenses can occur (Cohen & Felson, 1979; Felson, 2000). Disorganization theory and others that focus on ecological factors have initiated crime-mapping projects as well as several measurement and prevention programs aimed at the removal of criminogenic factors from the environment (Akers & Sellers, 2004). The problem regarding the applicability of these theories is that the cyberspace environment has no equivalent to easily distinguishable terrestrial locations. For the explanation of cybercrimes, the irrelevance of spatial distances within cyberspace handicaps criminological theories that rely on assumptions specific to terrestrial environments.

A different group of criminological theories examines the reasons some individuals repeatedly involve themselves in criminal activity while others abstain. These theories correlate categories of crime with certain social characteristics of the offender. For example, a significant amount of empirical evidence in the criminological literature substantiates a correlation between economic disadvantage and engagement in property crime or violent crime. This correlation is reversed with regard to computing skills and Internet access; the more disadvantaged segments of the economic and educational distribution possess them least (Yar, 2006). Conversely, Internet offenders typically have greater economic and intellectual resources and exhibit characteristics substantially different from the attributes of the majority of other criminals (Wall, 2001).

Some cyber criminologists suggest that the appearance of cybercrimes and the inability to simply transpose traditional empirical assumptions and explanatory concepts may require considerable theoretical innovation and new analytical tools (Yar, 2006). Clarke suggested a radical solution: to completely suspend criminological inquiries into the motivations of cyber offenders and instead focus solely on the crime reduction strategies provided by the "crime science" approach (Clarke, 2004). This interdisciplinary approach applies statistics, environmental design, psychology, forensics, policing, economics, and geography to the study of the characteristics of crime incidents and ignores the traits and motivations of criminal actors. Such methods as crime patterning, hot-spot analyses, and crime-mapping studies are substituted for the analytical and statistical tools of traditional criminology. Clarke demands that criminologists focus on concrete and manipulable factors of crime events and accept the remainder as immutable facts. Given the broad spectrum of opinions represented in the debate over whether and to what extent traditional criminological theories can and should be applied to cybercrimes, this debate is likely to continue in the future.

As a result of the debate surrounding the applicability of traditional theories, new and hybrid theoretical models have been developed to better explain certain types of cybercrime. Jaishankar (2007) underscores the deficiency of theory in explaining cybercrime. He proposed space transition theory to explain cybercrime behavior: The anonymous and unsupervised environment releases repressed propensities for crime in general (Jaishankar, 2008). This theory, although currently still untested, seems to be effective in explaining types of child-victimization-based cybercrimes, such as cyber bullying, pedophilia, pornography, stalking, and other online translations of terrestrial crime (Jaishankar & Halder, 2008).

Theoretical models have been applied to cyberspace security. Wall (2007) applied the nodal governance theoretical model, which stresses diffused policing power to nonstate security stakeholders for the policing of cyberspace. Nhan and Huey (2008) used this nodal framework to create *digital defensible spaces,* an online translation of Newman's (1973) theory on neighborhood-level self-efficacy. However, this model, too, is currently untested. Clearly, more research in the area of cyber criminology is needed to validate new theoretical approaches.

Despite the growth in both cybercrime and cybercrime research, cyber criminology faces challenges as a new paradigm of study in search of a clear definition, generally accepted methods, and theoretical models. A look at some of the shortcomings of the current research reveals good progress but a much greater need for empirical research and methods. Cyber criminology is slow to emerge from a niche area that is often marginalized by mainstream criminology to occupy a position of high importance.

CONCLUSION: TOWARD A CONCEPTUAL MODEL OF CYBER CRIMINOLOGY

The increased social relevance of cybercrime has finally drawn the attention of mainstream criminology, and criminologists are beginning to recognize the scope of the problem. The challenges to the criminal justice system, which arise primarily from the global dimensions and the complexity of cybercrime, warrant specialized research. Disparate criminal laws and geographical boundaries of jurisdictions pose important limitations for law enforcement efforts because they have no direct equivalent in cyberspace (Koops & Brenner, 2006). An increasing number of cyber criminologists are using these circumstances to justify establishing the discipline as a legitimate subsection of criminology, like white-collar crime.

Like white-collar crime, the development of cyber criminology is hindered by several fundamental problems that stem from the lack of a general definition. The blurred distinction between cyber-enabled crime and conventional, terrestrially based crime occurring online has made measuring and establishing standard research methodologies difficult.

Empirical research is vital to understand these phenomena and to guide the development of effective policies and practical strategies to combat cyber criminals. Much of our knowledge of cybercrime stems from very limited exploratory studies with small samples of cases. Qualitative interviews have greatly increased our knowledge of cybercrime phenomena, but the generalizability of their findings to any larger populations remains questionable. More empirical and cross-cultural studies must be pursued to guide the development of adequate theoretical frameworks and policies.

A patchwork of research is emerging from workers in the cyber-criminological field who range from criminologists to lawyers. Like the model of policing proposed by nodal governance researchers, collaboration in the research world is necessary. This way, shortcomings in one field can be supplemented by other non-criminological fields, from computer science to informatics to economics and the humanities.

DISCUSSION QUESTIONS

1. With more computers and Internet technology integrated into everyday life, will most crimes eventually become a form of cybercrime? Which ones will, and which ones never will? Why?

2. How would you change our current criminal justice and legal systems to deal with the lack of traditional borders on the Internet?

3. Why is it important to have a single definition of cybercrime? Why is it so difficult to establish one?

4. What type of police force is necessary to effectively police cyberspace? What changes would have to be made, and how would you describe the ideal "cyber officer"?

5. How would you design a study to measure cybercrime? What are some difficulties you might encounter, and how would you attempt to contact cyber criminals?

6. What should cyber criminologists do to overcome the problems currently facing the developing discipline?

7. How would you balance national security and privacy among government, corporations, and the general public?

NOTES

1. According to the National White-Collar Crime Center (NW3C), the Bureau of Justice Assistance, and the FBI's Internet Crime Complaint Center (IC3) *2007 Internet crime report,* 206,884 complaints were received in 2007, compared to 124,515 in 2003. See http://www.ic3.gov/media/annualreport/2007_IC3Report.pdf

2. The Computer Security Institute's *CSI 2008 Computer crime and security survey* (Richardson, 2008).

3. According to a 2003 White House report, *The national strategy to secure cyberspace,* cyberspace is considered the "control system" that interconnects critical infrastructures, such as agriculture, food, water, commerce, emergency services, energy, and communications. See http://www.dhs.gov/xlibrary/assets/National_Cyberspace_Strategy.pdf

4. See Krebs on Security blog at http://krebsonsecurity.com/2013/12/whos-selling-credit-cards-from-target/

5. U.S. Department of Justice (2002). *Searching and seizing computers and obtaining electronic evidence in criminal investigations.* Computer crime and intellectual property section. See http://www.usdoj.gov/criminal/cybercrime/searching.html

6. See https://www.eff.org/nsa-spying for a detailed history of NSA spying.

7. Watch the full Edward Snowden interview with *The Guardian* at http://www.theguardian .com/world/video/2013/jun/09/nsa-whistleblower-edward-snowden-interview-video

8. Angus Reid Global poll. See http://www.angusreidglobal.com/wp-content/uploads/2013/10/Snowden-Survey-October-20131.pdf for detailed results.

9. Acronym for the Advanced Research Projects Agency, the lead funding agency.

REFERENCES

Acohido, B. (2011, December 29). Consumers turn to do-not-track software to maintain privacy. *USA Today*. Retrieved from http://usatoday30.usatoday.com/tech/news/story/2011–12–29/internet-privacy/52274608/1

Akers, R. L., & Sellers, C. S. (2004). *Criminological theories: Introduction, evaluation, and application* (4th ed.). Los Angeles, CA: Roxbury.

Bachmann, M. (2008). *What makes them click? Applying the rational choice perspective to the hacking underground* [Electronic resource]. Orlando: University of Central Florida.

Brenner, S. W. (2001). Is there such a thing as virtual crime? *California Criminal Law Review, 4*(1). Retrieved from http://www.boalt.org/CCLR/v4/v4brenner.htm

Brenner, S. W. (2004). Toward a criminal law for cyberspace: A new model of law enforcement? *Rutgers Computer and Technology Law Journal, 30*, p. 1.

Brenner, S. W., & Schwerha, J. J., IV. (2004). Cybercrime: A note on international issues. *Information Systems Frontiers, 6*(2), 111–114.

Brown, I., & Korff, D. (2009). Terrorism and the proportionality of Internet surveillance. *European Journal of Criminology, 6*(2), 119–134.

Burris, S., Drahos, P., & Shearing, C. (2005, July). Nodal governance. *Australian Journal of Legal Philosophy, 30*, 30–58.

Castells, M. (2000). *The rise of the network society* (2nd ed.). Malden, MA: Blackwell.

Castells, M. (2002). *The Internet galaxy: Reflections on the Internet, business, and society.* Oxford, United Kingdom: Oxford University Press.

Clarke, R. V. (2004). New challenges for research: Technology, criminology, and crime science. In E. U. Savona (Ed.), *Crime and technology: New frontiers for regulation, law enforcement and research* (pp. 97–104). Dordrecht, Netherlands: Springer.

Clifford, R. D. (2006). Introduction. In R. D. Clifford (Ed.), *Cybercrime: The investigation, prosecution, and defense of a computer-related crime* (2nd ed., pp. 3–14). Durham, NC: Carolina Academic Press.

Cohen, L. E., & Felson, M. K. (1979). Social change and crime rate trends: A routine activity approach. *American Sociological Review, 44*(4), 588–608.

Cox, R. W., III, Johnson, T. A., & Richards, G. E. (2009). Routine activity theory and Internet crime. In F. Schmalleger and M. Pittaro (Eds.), *Crimes of the Internet* (pp. 302–316). Upper Saddle River, NJ: Pearson.

Dupont, B. (2006). Power struggles in the field of security: Implications for democratic transformation. In J. Wood & B. Dupont (Eds.), *Democracy, society, and the governance of security* (pp. 86–110). New York, NY: Cambridge University Press.

Dupont, B. (2008). Hacking the panopticon: Distributed online surveillance and resistance. In M. Deflem (Ed.), *Surveillance and governance: Sociology of crime law and deviance* (Vol. 10, pp. 257–278). Bingley, United Kingdom: Emerald.

Dupont, B. (2013). Skills and trust: A tour inside the hard drives of computer hackers. In C. Morselli (Ed.), *Crime and networks* (pp. 195–217). New York, NY: Routledge.

Edelhertz, H. (1970). *The nature, impact, and prosecution of white-collar crime.* Washington, DC: Law Enforcement Administration, U.S. Department of Justice.

Ericson, R. V., & Haggerty, K. D. (1997). *Policing the risk society.* Buffalo, NY: University of Toronto Press.

Etzioni, A. (2010). Who is really stealing your privacy? *CNN.* Retrieved from http://www.cnn.com/2010/OPINION/12/01/etzioni.privacy/

Felson, M. K. (2000). The routine activity approach as a general social theory. In S. Simpson (Ed.), *Of crime and criminality: The use of theory in everyday life.* Thousand Oaks, CA: SAGE.

Fortin, F. (2013). Usenet newsgroups, child pornography, and the role of participants. In C. Morselli (Ed.), *Crime and networks* (pp. 231–248). New York, NY: Routledge.

Foucault, M. (1977). *Discipline & punish: The birth of the prison.* New York, NY: Pantheon Books.

Furnell, S. (2002). *Cybercrime: Vandalizing the information society.* London, United Kingdom: Addison Wesley.

Geis, G. (1991). White-collar crime: What is it? *Current Issues in Criminal Justice, 3*(1), 9–24.

Gordon, S., & Ford, R. (2006). On the definition and classification of cybercrime. *Journal in Computer Virology, 2*(1), 13–20.

Grabosky, P. N. (2001). Virtual criminality: Old wine in new bottles? *Social and Legal Studies, 10*(2), 243–249.

Gros, J. G. (2003). Trouble in paradise: Crime and collapsed states in the age of globalization. *The British Journal of Criminology, 43*(1), 63–80.

Groves, R. M., Fowler, F. J., Couper, M. P., Lepkowski, J. M., Singer, E., & Tourangeau, R. (2004). *Survey methodology.* Hoboken, NJ: Wiley.

Hafner, K., & Markoff, J. (1991). *Cyberpunk: Outlaws and hackers on the computer frontier.* New York, NY: Simon & Schuster.

Holt, T. J. (2007). Subcultural evolution? Examining the influence of on- and off-line experiences on deviant subcultures. *Deviant Behavior, 28*(2), 171–198.

Holt, T. J., & Kilger, M. (2008, April). Techcrafters and makecrafters: A comparison of two populations of hackers. In *Information security threats data collection and sharing, 2008. WOMBAT Workshop on Information Security Threats Data Collection and Sharing, 2008* (pp. 67–78). Amsterdam, The Netherlands: IEEE.

Howell, B. A. (2007). Real-world problems of virtual crime. In J. M. Balkin, J. Grimmelmann, E. Katz, N. Kozlovski, S. Wagman, & T. Zarsky (Eds.), *Cybercrime: Digital cops in a networked environment.* New York: New York University Press.

Huey, L. J. (2002). Policing the abstract: Some observations on policing cyberspace. *Canadian Journal of Criminology, 44*(3), 248–249.

Jaishankar, K. (2007). Cyber criminology: Evolving a novel discipline with a new journal. *International Journal of Cyber Criminology, 1*(1), 1–6.

Jaishankar, K. (2008). Space transition theory of cyber crimes. In F. Schmalleger & M. Pittaro (Eds.), *Crimes of the Internet* (pp. 283–301). Upper Saddle River, NJ: Pearson.

Jaishankar, K., & Halder, D. (2008). Pedophilia, pornography, and stalking: Analyzing child victimization on the Internet. In F. Schmalleger & M. Pittaro (Eds.), *Crimes of the Internet* (pp. 28–65). Upper Saddle River, NJ: Pearson.

Jordan, T. (2008). *Hacking: Digital media and technological determinism.* Malden, MA: Polity Press.

Jordan, T., & Taylor, P. (1998). A sociology of hackers. *Sociological Review, 46*(4), 757–780.

Kelly, M. (2013, June 25). How Google, Yahoo, Apple, Facebook, and Amazon track you. *Venture Beat.* Retrieved from http://venturebeat.com/2013/06/25/every-day-tracking/

Kleinrock, L. (2004). The Internet rules of engagement. *Technology in Society, 26*(2), 193–207.

Koops, B.-J., & Brenner, S. (2006). Cybercrime jurisdiction—An introduction. In B.-J. Koops & S. Brenner (Eds.), *Cybercrime and jurisdiction* (pp. 1–9). The Hague, Netherlands: TMC Asser Press.

Kumar, J. (2006). Determining jurisdiction in cyberspace. *Social Science Research Network.* Retrieved November 15, 2008, from http://ssrn.com/abstract=919261

Lasica, J. D. (2005). *Darknet: Hollywood's war against the digital generation.* Hoboken, NJ: Wiley.

Lenk, K. (1997). The challenge of cyberspatial forms of human interaction to territorial governance and policing. In B. D. Loader (Ed.), *The governance of cyberspace: Politics, technology and global restructuring* (pp. 126–135). London, United Kingdom: Routledge.

Levy, S. (1984). *Hackers: Heroes of the computer revolution.* Garden City, NY: Doubleday.

Miller, J-A., & Miller, R. (1987, Summer). Jeremy Bentham's panoptic device. *October, 41,* 3–29.

Moore, R. (2007). The role of computer forensics in criminal investigations. In Y. Jewkes (Ed.), *Crime online* (pp. 81–108). Portland, OR: Willan.

National White-Collar Crime Center, Bureau of Justice Assistance, & Federal Bureau of Investigation. (2007). *2007 Internet crime report.* Internet Complaint Center. Retrieved October 12, 2009, from http://www.ic3.gov/media/annualreport/2007_IC3Report.pdf

Naughton, J. (2000). *A brief history of the future: The origins of the Internet* (2nd ed.). London, United Kingdom: Phoenix/Orion Books.

Newman, O. (1973). *Defensible space: Crime prevention through urban design.* New York, NY: Macmillan.

Nhan, J. (2009). Criminal justice firewalls: Prosecutorial decision-making in cyber and high-tech crime cases. In K. Jaishankar (Ed.), *International perspectives on crime and justice.* New Castle, United Kingdom: Cambridge Scholars.

Nhan, J., & Huey, L. J. (2008). Policing through nodes, clusters, and bandwidth. In S. Leman-Langlois (Ed.), *Technocrime: Technology, crime and social control* (pp. 66–87). Portland, OR: Willan.

Reidenberg, J. (2005, June). Technology and Internet jurisdiction. *University of Pennsylvania Law Review, 153,* 1951–1974.

Richardson, R. (2008). *CSI computer crime and security survey.* Computer Security Institute. Retrieved November 25, 2008, from http://www.gocsi.com/forms/csi_survey.jhtml;jsessionid=JQEWDNHGFHE4AQSNDLOSKHSCJUNN2JVN

Shinder, D. L., & Tittel, E. (2002). *Scene of the cybercrime: Computer forensics handbook.* Rockland, MA: Syngress.

Smith, R. G., Grabosky, P. N., & Urbas, G. (2004). *Cyber criminals on trial.* New York, NY: Cambridge University Press.

Snijders, C., Matzat, U., & Reips, U. (2012). "Big data": Big gaps of knowledge in the field of Internet science. *International Journal of Internet Science, 7*(1), 1–5.

Sutherland, E. H. (1940). White-collar criminality. *American Sociological Review, 5*(1), 1–12.

Thomas, D. (2002). *Hacker culture.* Minneapolis: Regents of the University of Minnesota.

Thomas, D., & Loader, B. D. (2000). Introduction—Cybercrime: Law enforcement, security and surveillance in the information age. In D. Thomas & B. Loader (Eds.), *Cybercrime: Law enforcement, security, and surveillance in the information age* (pp. 1–13). London, United Kingdom: Routledge.

U.S. Department of Justice (2002). *Searching and seizing computers and obtaining electronic evidence in criminal investigations.* Computer crime and intellectual property section. Retrieved October 12, 2009, from http://www.usdoj.gov/criminal/cybercrime/searching .html

Wall, D. S. (2001). Cybercrimes and the Internet. In D. S. Wall (Ed.), *Crime and the Internet* (pp. 1–17). London, United Kingdom: Routledge.

Wall, D. S. (2007). Policing cybercrimes: Situating the public police in networks of security within cyberspace. *Police Practice and Research, 8*(2), 183–205.

White House. (2003). *The National strategy to secure cyberspace.* Retrieved October 12, 2009, from http://www.dhs.gov/xlibrary/assets/National_Cyberspace_Strategy.pdf

Wilson, M. I., & Corey, K. E. (2000). *Information tectonics: Space, place, and technology in an electronic age.* New York, NY: Wiley.

Wood, J., & Shearing, C. (2007). *Imagining security.* Portland, OR: Willan.

Yar, M. (2005). The novelty of "cybercrime": An assessment in light of routine activity theory. *European Journal of Criminology, 2*(4), 407–427.

Yar, M. (2006). *Cybercrime and society.* London, United Kingdom: SAGE.

CHAPTER 15

Comparative Criminology and Criminal Justice

Philip L. Reichel

Does the United States have the best criminal justice system in the world? The question, of course, is more provocative than one for which an answer is expected—or can even be given. Since there are state, federal, and military justice systems to consider, a simple yes or no isn't even possible. But even if a simple answer were possible, how would "best" be judged? And, more important for this chapter, what are the other justice systems against which the United States is to be compared?

Public opinion polls show that among 16 national institutions, Americans have the most confidence in the military and the least in Congress. Falling in the middle, along with public schools and newspapers, is the criminal justice system with 29% of Americans expressing either "quite a lot" or a "great deal" of confidence. Unfortunately, the same percentage has either "very little" or "no" confidence in the criminal justice system (Jones, 2012). Interestingly, another poll found that 80% of all respondents agreed that "in spite of its problems, the American justice system is still the best in the world" (American Bar Association, 1999, p. 1). So while Americans seem to be critical of their criminal justice system, they cannot imagine that another system would be any better.

The goal of this chapter is not to argue that America's criminal justice system is either the best or the worst. Instead, the objective is to provide information that might allow you to make informed comparisons on your own. The primary concern is that determining whether something is good or bad cannot be accomplished fairly without understanding what alternatives are available.

WHY COMPARE?

The comparative method is popular in essentially every academic discipline and, for several of those disciplines, has been used since ancient times. In the fields of criminology and criminal justice, on the other hand, the comparative method is a relatively new technique. Its origins can be traced to Cesare Beccaria's 1764 essay on crime and punishment, which called for changes in Western European criminal justice. Soon thereafter, others such as Jeremy Bentham (1748–1832), Adolph Quetelet (1796–1874), Alexis de Tocqueville (1805–1859), and Émile Durkheim (1858–1917) conducted cross-national studies of crime.

During the 20th century and into the 21st century, interest in applying the comparative method to studying criminal justice systems continued, and today criminologists, governmental agencies, and international organizations have come to find value in the study and dissemination of information on issues of international and comparative criminal justice.

Of the many reasons to study and compare issues of crime and justice, three are highlighted here: (a) to benefit from the experience of others, (b) to expand our understanding of different cultures, and (c) to help deal with the transnational crime problems plaguing today's world (see Dammer, Reichel, & He, 2014).

Benefiting From Others' Experience

After the Casey Anthony jury in Florida acquitted her of first-degree murder charges in her daughter's death, 61% of persons polled still believed Anthony was actually guilty. Even so, the majority (58%) of Americans trust a jury over a judge to determine a defendant's guilt or innocence (Rasmussen Reports, 2011a, 2011b). Is that because the American public has carefully considered alternatives to the jury system and decided that other ways in which laypeople might be used to determine guilt are undesirable options? Or do we simply assume that if it is not American it is not for us? Comparative studies allow us to learn about, and from, others.

In all areas of the criminal justice system—police, courts, and corrections—there are examples of how countries have adapted procedures from each other. For example, people wonder why Japan has a much lower crime rate than the United States or, indeed, most other Western nations. The Japanese themselves give some of the credit for their low crime rates to their police methods—most notably, community policing and the use of small neighborhood police stations called *kobans*. In the area of courts and criminal procedure, countries have adapted entire criminal codes at one extreme and very specific aspects, such as the right to legal counsel, at the other extreme. Corrections strategies also tend to spill over borders. For example, the idea of day fines, which was first developed in Scandinavian countries, has been adapted by Germany, Great Britain, and the United States. And New Zealand, Belgium, Australia, Canada, and the United States all have implemented different kinds of restorative justice programs based on procedures rooted in the justice practices of many indigenous cultures.

The point is that a technique used in one country to combat crime might be successfully adapted for use in another country. Of course, no society can incorporate another culture's legal system in its entirety and expect it to work. Yet certain aspects of another system—modified to account for cultural differences—may operate successfully in a new setting. Comparative studies help us identify areas where we might benefit from things that have already been tried elsewhere.

Expanding Our Understanding of the World

As mentioned earlier, Americans tend to believe that their criminal justice system is the best; but many other countries have a great deal of confidence in their judicial system as well. Britons, for example, view the British justice system as fundamentally fair, and in Rwanda, public confidence in the judicial system and courts is remarkably high at 92% (Rheault & Tortora, 2008; Van de Walle, 2009). Of course, citizens do not always express confidence simply because something is their own—for example, almost 60% of Mexicans lack confidence in their judicial system and courts (Ray, 2008). However, ethnocentrism—or the belief that one's own way of doing something is the best—is typically a well-entrenched value among a country's citizens.

Ethnocentrism has some positive aspects. It encourages pride, confidence, and group identification. When ethnocentrism is attached to one's country, it is a key ingredient in what we call patriotism. Because feelings of patriotism and cultural identity are generally positive attributes that help make a nation strong, it is desirable for citizens to be somewhat ethnocentric about their own social institutions. However, as with many other cultural traits, ethnocentrism has negative aspects as well. When ethnocentrism makes people in one group unwilling to understand and appreciate differences with people from other groups, prejudice and discrimination can result. When ethnocentrism makes it difficult, or even impossible, to be critical about the status quo, society may not experience positive change. If people believe that no other way of doing something can be useful, desirable, or even better than the current way, opportunities for improvement are missed. Preferably, citizens should balance their cultural pride and confidence with a willingness to appreciate and learn from others—even when the "others" are culturally different and geographically separate (Reichel, 2013).

A goal of comparative studies is to extend a person's knowledge of people and cultures beyond his or her own group. After seeing the similarities and differences among countries and their citizens, comparative scholars have a better understanding of their own society and of ways that society might be improved. As important, that can be accomplished without loss of pride in one's own country or social institutions.

Responding to Transnational Crime

A third reason to study crime and justice from a comparative perspective is the increasing need to address transnational and international crime problems. As the world experiences increased international integration, or globalization, crime is also becoming more transnational in nature. Transnational crimes are occurring with increasing frequency as opportunities expand for the global movement of people, products, technology, and communications. In some regions of the world, it appears that garden variety thefts, robberies, and assaults have become less troublesome than offenses such as transnational organized crime, corruption, terrorism, and the trafficking of humans.

Using human trafficking as one transnational crime example, Dammer et al. (2014) described a young woman from an Eastern European country who answered an online advertisement for the position of "live-in baby sitter" in Canada. She was told that she would receive free transportation to Canada, so she could begin work. After her arrival at the airport, she was put on the plane and told to meet a contact in Frankfurt, Germany. In Frankfurt, she met a man who included her with a group of other recently arrived young women from a variety of countries. He put them all on a plane to Toronto. In Toronto, the women were met at the airport by an older woman who told them that they must all give the older women their passports for safekeeping. After being taken to a small apartment, the older woman tells all the young women that they will now become dancers and "escorts" at a local adult establishment. If they resist, they will be beaten, maybe killed, and their families back home will also suffer. The women now have no passport, little money, likely speak little English to ask for help, and have no freedom of movement.

Just as this example of human trafficking involved criminal activity across several countries, so will transnational crimes, such as drug trafficking, money laundering, and trade in human body parts. Other transnational crimes occur without obvious boundaries (for example, cybercrime) or where clear boundaries are not established (for example, sea piracy). In all those examples, however, international cooperation among countries has provided some success in preventing and combating transnational crime. Without that international cooperation, we cannot find, extradite, or serve justice on those who violate laws and cause pain, suffering, and loss throughout the world. To that end, a comparative approach is needed today more than ever.

Now that we understand why comparison is important, we can turn to two particular examples of comparative study in operation: comparative criminology and comparative criminal justice. Each has its own topics to cover and each helps us accomplish the goals of benefiting from the experience of others, expanding our understanding of the world, and combating transnational crime.

COMPARATIVE CRIMINOLOGY

Criminologists study crime as a social phenomenon (the focus is more on the crime) and as social behavior (the focus is more on the offender). Comparative criminologists are interested in the same things, but on a broader scale. Johnson and Barak-Glantz (1983) suggested that comparative criminologists seek to locate commonalities and differences in crime patterns among divergent cultures—here the focus is on the crime. Beirne and Nelken (1997) added that it is also important to have the analysis involve a systematic and theoretically informed comparison in two or more cultures—here the focus is more typically on the offender. Dammer and his colleagues (2014) agreed but believed it is important to include countries as well as cultures. Bringing these points together, we can define comparative criminology as a systematic and theoretically informed comparison of crime and criminal behavior in two or more cultures or across two or more countries.

Crime as Social Phenomenon

When studying crime as social phenomenon, comparative criminologists use a variety of variables in order to identify any similarities and differences. Dammer et al. (2014) noted that variables associated with economic conditions and urbanization have been especially popular with comparative criminologists. Economic development and industrialization are among the most common variables used—with homicide and theft often being the crimes of research choice. Most studies have shown that neither economic development nor industrialization is significantly related to homicide rate (for example, He, 1999; LaFree, 1999). However, the majority of researchers comparing theft rates among countries have found a significant positive effect of economic development and industrialization (for example, Hartnagel, 1982; He, 1999; Stack, 1984).

The availability and improvement in cross-national crime data sources, analytic techniques, and theoretical perspectives has encouraged more and more researchers to conduct comparative studies. For example, as Reichel (2013, p. 31) explained, data from the International Crime Victim Survey (ICVS) show that overall victimization rates in industrialized countries are relatively high (above 20% of the respondents in each country) in England and Wales, Iceland, Ireland, and New Zealand. Countries with relatively low counts (10% and less) included Hungary, Japan, and Spain. Australia, Canada, Sweden, and the United States show rates near the average of 16% (Van Dijk, Van Kesteren, & Smit, 2007). Further, when analyzing trends from the ICVS sweeps, there is a general consistency in country positions over the years. England and Wales, Estonia, the Netherlands, and New Zealand have consistently ranked high relative to others, whereas Austria, Japan, and Portugal consistently show low overall victimization. Information such as that can be quite useful as criminologists expand their understanding of crime in society.

Crime as Social Behavior

When looking at crime as social behavior, criminologists develop and test theories about crime's causes, origins, and distribution. Comparative criminologists, therefore, develop and test theories about crime across two or more countries.

Howard, Newman, and Pridemore (2000) identify three general frameworks that are commonly employed as comparative criminologists attempt to explain the variation of crime rates among nations: grand theories, structural theories, and theories relying on demographic characteristics. Because they have played a greater role in cross-national research to date, some examples of grand theory explanations are considered here (see Dammer et al., 2014; Reichel, 2013).

Modernization theories. Grand theories typically assume that a single theoretical concept has significant impact on a nation's crime level. Shelley's *Crime and Modernization* is an early example of this methodology (1981). As the book's title indicates, Shelley used empirical evidence to argue that modernization provides the best theoretical explanation for crime's contemporary evolution. Specifically, she suggested that social processes accompanying industrial development resulted in conditions conducive to increased criminality, such as loosened family ties, family instability, and lack of supervision of youthful members of a family. More recent versions of this approach are exemplified by Durkheimian-modernization theory. This perspective uses society as the unit of analysis, and it suggests that all nations develop through similar stages. Variables such as industrialization, population growth, urbanization, the division of labor, social disorganization, and cultural heterogeneity are used to explain variation in crime rates.

Civilization theory. Another type of grand theory uses a comparative historical approach to show a link between crime and civility. For example, these civilization theorists note that murder was more common in the Middle Ages than it is now and that it dropped dramatically in the 17th, 18th, and 19th centuries. This seems to directly contradict modernization theory because it suggests that violent crime decreased rather than increased as modernization undid traditional family and community bonds. Elias attributed the decline to the gradual introduction of courtly manners (for example, eating with a knife and fork, refraining from urinating in public) that transformed a violent medieval society into a more peaceful modern one (Elias, 1982). Modernization and civilization theories are not necessarily contradictory, however. Shelley, for example, modified her initial reliance on modernization as the key explanatory variable in favor of a synthesized modernization-civilization perspective, which suggests that a more civilized society has lower volumes of violent crimes because people exercise more internal control over their behavior as others increasingly depend on them (Heiland & Shelley, 1992). Interestingly, the modernization-civilization proponents argue that violence directed against the self (for example, suicide, drug abuse) will occur more often as civility increases.

Ecological-opportunity theory. The ecological-opportunity perspective takes a microlevel approach by concentrating on the criminal act itself. This theory argues that crime occurs where environmental conditions are favorable. For example, LaFree and Birkbeck (1991) studied victimization data in Venezuela and in the United States and found that in both countries, robbery typically involves public domains, lone victims, strangers, and incidents taking place outside buildings. Neuman and Berger (1988) saw this ability to identify the specific situations that immediately precede in space and time the actual execution of a crime as a strength of the ecological-opportunity perspective. Should comparative criminologists continue to find that crimes occur in similar situations, regardless of country, we will have valuable information about criminal acts—although our knowledge about motivation to commit those acts will not necessarily be advanced.

Howard and his colleagues noted that tests of grand theories have produced quite interesting, if conflicting, results (see Howard et al., 2000). For example, Bouley and Vaughn studied violent crime in Colombia and found support for grand theories with respect to the crimes of theft and robbery but not for the more violent crimes of assault and homicide. Gillis believed that civilization theory is supported by a climbing literacy rate in France from 1852 to 1914 and the associated decrease in the rate of crimes of passion and an increase in the suicide rate. Opportunity theory seems supported in studies such as that by LaFree and Birkbeck (1991).

COMPARATIVE CRIMINAL JUSTICE

While comparative criminologists examine crime patterns cross-nationally, comparative justice scholars are looking at the similarities and differences in how countries set up their criminal justice system. The result is a rich collection of research on such topics as how police organizations are structured (Bayley, 1985; Haberfeld & Cerrah, 2008), levels of public support for policing (Kutnjak Ivkovic, 2008; Van Craen, 2013), how laypeople can be used during adjudication proceedings (Kutnjak Ivkovic, 2007; Malsch, 2009; Vidmar, 2000), variations in the harshness of punishment (Cavadino & Dignan, 2006; Hood & Hoyle, 2008; Miethe & Lu, 2005; Whitman, 2003, 2005), how countries respond to misbehavior by juveniles (Friday & Ren, 2006; Hartjen & Priyadarsini, 2004; Junger-Tas, 2008; Winterdyk, 1997), and many other interesting and important topics. As an example of how comparative criminal justice scholars study one aspect of the justice system, consider the adjudication process—that is, how do countries go about determining whether an accused person actually committed the crime?

There are two primary ways by which a defendant's guilt is determined. Some countries rely on an adversarial process in which two sides (defense and prosecution) present evidence and arguments supporting their position. Other countries use the inquisitorial process wherein all parties work together to determine what happened. Of course, there are some countries that follow procedures best described as a mixture of these two; but the goal in this chapter is to simply distinguish between the two systems so we concentrate on them alone.

The Adversarial Process

Believing that truth results from a free and open competition over which side has the correct facts, the adversarial process matches the prosecution and defense as opponents in a contest. Each side plays an active role by calling witnesses and asking them questions. Cross-examination is used by each side to challenge or destroy a witness's testimony. Each side has a chance to question the honesty of witnesses, search for biases, and figure out what witnesses actually know instead of what they think they know. The judge serves as a referee in this contest by ensuring that the players abide by the rules. Observing the contest are laypeople who were selected as jurors and charged with deciding whether the prosecution has proved its claims against the defendant or if the defense has placed sufficient doubt in the jurors' minds regarding the prosecution's claims (Reichel, 2002, 2010). In this way, the prosecution and defense propose their version of the "truth," and the judge or jury determines which side has the most accurate portrayal.

The adversarial process is used primarily in countries that were influenced by the common law tradition as developed in England and spread among the British colonies. Each of those countries may implement the process a bit differently—for example, potential jurors in the United States are subjected to a voir dire process that is more stringent than is used in England—but generally speaking, the proceedings in those countries are clearly more adversarial than inquisitorial. Consider Canada as an example of a country that relies on the adversarial process when determining whether an accused person is guilty (see Dammer et al., 2014, p. 35).

Canada's 10 provinces and three territories generally have a three-tiered court system going from provincial and territorial courts at the lowest level through superior courts (with name variation by province or territory), to the provincial and territorial courts of appeal at the highest level (Department of Justice, 2013). The provincial and territorial courts carry the greatest workload of any court level because all cases start at this level. The majority will also be tried and disposed of in the provincial and territorial courts; but others (the most serious indictable offenses) will be sent to the superior court for trial.

Provincial courts may have separate divisions to handle family matters, cases of young offenders, traffic cases, and criminal cases. Most of the criminal cases have been charged as summary conviction offenses (that is, the least serious offenses and ones getting minimal punishment). In general, such offenses may be tried only before a provincial court judge sitting without a jury. The accused may appear in person at the trial or may send their lawyer to represent them—unless the judge has issued a warrant requiring their attendance. The term *summary conviction* implies that casual and concise justice is handed out.

Indictable offenses (the most serious crimes, bringing the harshest penalties) can be heard at either the superior or provincial court level. The most serious indictable offenses (for example, murder, treason, piracy) may be tried only by a judge of the superior court sitting with a jury, unless the judge and the attorney general consent to forgo the jury. The least serious indictable offenses (such as theft, fraud, or possession of stolen goods) may be tried by only a provincial court judge. If the charge is on an indictable offense not falling into either of those categories, the accused can choose the mode of trial. Robbery, dangerous driving, assault, and breaking and entering are examples of these "electable" offenses. The choices available to the accused are to have a trial by a provincial court judge, a superior court judge and jury, or a superior court judge. Failure to make a choice sends the case to a judge and jury. At the federal court level, and standing as the country's court of last resort, is the Supreme Court of Canada. The Supreme Court justices are appointed by the federal government from lists prepared by the provinces (Dammer et al., 2014; Department of Justice, 2013)

The Inquisitorial Process

Rather than a competition between opposing sides, the inquisitorial process is more like a continuing investigation. This is an important distinction because it means that public officials (whether the defense or the prosecution) are not engaged in a contest. Instead, they are all involved in an investigation that tries to determine what transpired. All parties in the case are expected to provide all relevant evidence to the court. Rather than being minimally involved referees monitoring the activities of two competitors, judges in the inquisitorial process take a much more active role. For example, inquisitorial judges, not the prosecution or defense, determine who will be called as witnesses and what questions will be asked. Should the prosecution or defense wish to hear from other witnesses or to ask questions of the witnesses called, they may do so only with the judge's permission. In other words, unlike the passive judges and active lawyers found in the adversarial systems, the inquisitorial process has a procedurally active judge and rather passive lawyers (Dammer et al., 2014; Reichel, 2010).

The inquisitorial process is used primarily in countries that were influenced by the Roman legal tradition as developed through the early Roman codes (for example, the *Corpus Juris Civilis*) and the codes of other European countries (for example, France's *Code Napoleon*). As England's influence and colonial practices resulted in the spread of common law and the adversarial process, colonial actions by such countries as France and Spain spread the Roman legal tradition and the inquisitorial process. Similarly, just as common law countries implement adversarial procedures differently; inquisitorial procedures vary among countries influenced by Roman law. However, Germany provides a good example of typical inquisitorial proceedings (see Dammer et al., 2014, p. 33).

The German states are responsible for administering federal law, so all trials are conducted at the state level. Federal courts exist primarily to handle appeals from the state courts. Germany's criminal courts are organized in three tiers (Council of Europe, 2000; Jehle, 2009). At the bottom are the *local courts* that hear minor criminal cases where the punishment is not likely to be more than four years imprisonment. Above them are the *regional courts* where major criminal cases are tried and the punishment is likely to be more than four years imprisonment. The *higher regional court* hears appeals from the lower state courts and will also try some exceptional cases (for example, treason). Appeals on points of law from the state courts may eventually reach the Federal Court of Justice, which is Germany's highest court (Dammer & Albanese, 2011; Federal Court of Justice, 2014).

Legal systems following the inquisitorial process seldom use a jury as Americans know the term. Instead, participation from the public is in the form of lay judges serving alongside professional judges on what is termed a "mixed bench." Working together, the professional and lay judges consider evidence, question defendants and witnesses, and then decide the punishment in cases where they find the defendant guilty. In Germany's version of the mixed bench, trials for the less serious crimes are heard by a panel of one professional judge and two lay judges. When the trial is for a more serious offense, it will be heard by three professional judges and two lay judges (Dammer & Albanese, 2011; Jehle, 2009). The verdict is by majority vote, so it is possible that the lay judges have a significant say in the outcome. However, since the professional judge or judges typically dominate the questioning and the deliberation, lay judges have to be especially assertive to have significant influence (Dammer et al., 2014).

COMPARATIVE STUDIES IN THE COMING YEARS

Although comparative criminology and comparative criminal justice have long and significant histories, each has had substantial growth and recognition during the last few decades. This is due in part to the increase in such transnational crimes as terrorism, human trafficking, and sea piracy; but it is also the result of more general globalization of world economies and politics. As important, there is every reason to believe that comparative criminology and criminal justice will have continued importance in the future.

One of the more interesting developments anticipated by several scholars in this field is the belief that entities other than national governments will play an increasingly important role in preventing and combating global crime. Transnational organizations, such as the United Nations, will play key roles for decades to come, as will more criminal justice-specific organizations, such as Interpol and Europol. But there is also likely to be more involvement by the private sphere and by civil society. The role of government and supranational organizations is not expected to diminish, but we are likely to see an increased role for non-governmental organizations (NGOs), nonprofit groups, and private companies (for example, ships increasingly use private security forces as they travel through areas at high risk for sea piracy).

Using the specific example of human trafficking, we see the involvement of supranational organizations, such as the UN's Global Initiative to Fight Human Trafficking (www.ungift.org); national-level government agencies like the U.S. State Department's Office to Monitor and Combat Trafficking in Persons (www.state.gov/j/tip/); major NGOs similar to the Organization for Security and Cooperation in Europe that are working to combat human trafficking (www.osce.org/cthb); and private foundations such at the International Cocoa Initiative (www.cocoainitiative.org) that works with labor unions and the chocolate industry to eliminate child labor and forced labor in cocoa farming and chocolate production.

These developments, as well as the likelihood of continued interest by politicians, policy makers, and the general public regarding global crime, suggest that scholars interested in comparative criminology and comparative criminal justice will have plenty to keep them busy in the coming years.

CONCLUSION

As the world continues to shrink in the sense of easier access to information, people, and places, there is increased interest in—and need for—an understanding and appreciation of other countries and their citizens. This is just as true for the topics of crime and justice as it is for business, technology, sports, entertainment, or any other area. Specifically, it is important to compare crime and justice across countries in order to (a) benefit from the experience of others, (b) expand our understanding of different cultures, and (c) help deal with the transnational crime problems plaguing today's world.

By looking at the way comparative criminologists study crime patterns and how comparative justice scholars study the procedures used to respond to criminal behavior, we are better able to understand the role of crime in the global community and how nations respond once crime is committed. The goal here was to encourage examination beyond your home country and to consider what other people, procedures, and agencies can be used both domestically and transnationally to combat the increasingly global nature of crime.

DISCUSSION QUESTIONS

1. Public opinion polls show that about 29% of Americans have either "quite a lot" or a "great deal" of confidence in the criminal justice system. A similar percentage has either "very little" or "no" confidence. Why do you think this is the case? What variables might explain one choice over the other (for example, gender, race, age, education, experience with police, etc.)? What might be done to move the "very little" or "no" people into the "quite a lot" or "great deal" categories?

2. Three criminology theories were highlighted to provide a basic overview of how comparative criminologists might explain crime's causes, origins, and distribution in countries around the world. How important do you think it is for a theory that might explain crime in one county to also be able to explain the same behavior in another country? Can criminological theories be useful if they are country- or region- or even city-specific? Are the variables that influence human behavior similar enough around the world to warrant or expect a macrotheory that "works" everywhere?

3. As an example of comparative criminal justice, this chapter reviews how two countries go about determining whether an accused person actually committed the crime. What other topics do you think comparative criminal justice scholars would find interesting? What differences do you think might be found when studying, for example, how policing differs around the world? How about punishment of convicted offenders?

4. Of the two primary ways by which a defendant's guilt is determined, people in the United States are most familiar with the adversarial process wherein truth is

believed to come about through two sides competing. The inquisitorial process, on the other hand, is based in the belief that truth is best achieved when everyone (prosecution, defense, judge) are working together to determine what happened. What are some of the pros and cons that you can see for both positions?

REFERENCES

American Bar Association. (1999). *Perceptions of the U.S. justice system, 1999*. Retrieved September 25, 2011, from www.abanow.org/wordpress/wp-content/files_flutter/1269460858_20_1_1_7_Upload_File.pdf

Bayley, D. H. (1985). *Patterns of policing: A comparative international analysis*. New Brunswick, NJ: Rutgers University Press.

Beirne, P., & Nelken, D. (Eds.). (1997). *Issues in comparative criminology*. Aldershot, United Kingdom: Ashgate/Dartmouth.

Cavadino, M., & Dignan, J. (2006). *Penal systems: A comparative approach*. London, United Kingdom: SAGE.

Council of Europe. (2000). Germany. In Council of Europe (Ed.), *Judicial organization in Europe* (pp. 135–150). Strasbourg, France: Council of Europe.

Dammer, H. R., & Albanese, J. S. (2011). *Comparative criminal justice systems* (4th ed.). Belmont, CA: Wadsworth Cengage Learning.

Dammer, H. R., Reichel, P. L., & He, N. (2014). Comparing crime and justice. In P. L. Reichel & J. S. Albanese (Eds.), *Handbook of transnational crime and justice* (2nd ed., pp. 23–46). Los Angeles, CA: SAGE.

Department of Justice. (2013). *How the courts are organized*. Retrieved from Canada's court system website: www.justice.gc.ca/eng/csj-sjc/ccs-ajc/page3.html

Elias, N. (1982). *The civilizing process: Power and incivility* (Vol. 2). New York, NY: Pantheon Books.

Federal Court of Justice. (2014). *The federal court of justice*. Retrieved from Der Bundesgerichtshof website: www.bundesgerichtshof.de/EN/Home/home_node.html

Friday, P. C., & Ren, X. (Eds.). (2006). *Delinquency and juvenile justice systems in the non-Western world*. Monsey, NY: Criminal Justice Press.

Haberfeld, M. R., & Cerrah, I. (Eds.). (2008). *Comparative policing: The struggle for democratization*. Los Angeles, CA: SAGE.

Hartjen, C. A., & Priyadarsini, S. (2004). *Delinquency and juvenile justice: An international bibliography*. Westport, CT: Praeger.

Hartnagel, T. F. (1982). Modernization, female social roles, and female crime: A cross-national investigation. *Sociological Quarterly, 23*(4), 477–490.

He, N. (1999). *Marx, Durkheim, and comparative criminology*. Lanham, MD: Austin and Winfield.

Heiland, H.-G., & Shelley, L. I. (1992). Civilization, modernization and the development of crime and control. In H.-G. Heiland, L. I. Shelley, & H. Katoh (Eds.), *Crime and control in comparative perspectives*. New York, NY: Walter de Gruyter.

Hood, R. G., & Hoyle, C. (2008). *The death penalty: A worldwide perspective* (4th ed., rev. and expanded). New York, NY: Oxford University Press.

Howard, G. J., Newman, G., & Pridemore, W. A. (2000). *Theory, method, and data in comparative criminology: Vol. 4. Measurement and analysis of crime and justice*. Washington, DC: National Institute of Justice.

Jehle, J.-M. (2009). *Criminal justice in Germany: Facts and figures.* Retrieved from www.bmj .de/SharedDocs/Downloads/EN/StudienUntersuchungenFachbuecher/Criminal_Justice_ in_Germany_Numbers_and_Facts.html

Johnson, E. H., & Barak-Glantz, I. L. (1983). Introduction. In I. L. Barak-Glantz & E. H. Johnson (Eds.), *Comparative criminology* (pp. 7–17). Beverly Hills, CA: SAGE.

Jones, J. M. (2012, June 20). Confidence in U.S. public schools at new low. *Gallup Politics.* Retrieved from Gallup website: www.gallup.com

Junger-Tas, J. (2008). *International handbook of juvenile justice.* New York, NY: Springer.

Kutnjak Ivkovic, S. (2007). Exploring lay participation in legal decision-making: Lessons from mixed tribunals. *Cornell International Law Journal, 40*(2), 429–453.

Kutnjak Ivkovic, S. (2008). A comparative study of public support for the police. *International Criminal Justice Review, 18*(4), 406–434.

LaFree, G. (1999). A summary and review of comparative cross-national studies of homicide. In M. D. Smith & M. A. Zahn (Eds.), *Homicide: A sourcebook of social research* (pp. 125–148). Thousand Oaks, CA: SAGE.

LaFree, G., & Birkbeck, C. (1991). The neglected situation: A cross-national study of the situational characteristics of crime. *Criminology, 29*(1), 73–98.

Malsch, M. (2009). *Democracy in the courts: Lay participation in European criminal justice systems.* Burlington, VT: Ashgate.

Miethe, T. D., & Lu, H. (2005). *Punishment: A comparative historical perspective.* Cambridge, United Kingdom: Cambridge University Press.

Neuman, W. L., & Berger, R. J. (1988). Competing perspectives on cross-national crime: An evaluation of theory and evidence. *The Sociological Quarterly, 29*(2), 281–313.

Rasmussen Reports. (2011a). *58% trust jury more to determine guilt or innocence, 27% trust judge.* Retrieved from www.rasmussenreports.com/

Rasmussen Reports. (2011b). *61% believe Casey Anthony is guilty of murder.* Retrieved from www.rasmussenreports.com/

Ray, J. (2008, February 20). *Mexico's citizens ready for improved justice system.* Retrieved from Gallup website: www.gallup.com

Reichel, P. L. (2002). Common law legal traditions. In D. Levinson (Ed.), *Encyclopedia of crime and punishment* (Vol. 1, pp. 257–262). Thousand Oaks, CA: SAGE.

Reichel, P. L. (2010). Justice systems in selected countries. In S. Kethineni (Ed.), *Comparative and international policing, justice, and transnational crime* (pp. 79–104). Durham, NC: Carolina Academic Press.

Reichel, P. L. (2013). *Comparative criminal justice systems: A topical approach* (6th ed.). Boston, MA: Pearson.

Rheault, M., & Tortora, B. (2008, October 6). *In South Africa, high level of confidence in judiciary.* Retrieved from Gallup website: www.gallup.com

Shelley, L. I. (1981). *Crime and modernization: The impact of industrialization and urbanization on crime.* Carbondale, IL: Southern Illinois University Press.

Stack, S. (1984). Income inequality and property crime. *Criminology, 22*(2), 229–258.

Van Craen, M. (2013). Explaining majority and minority trust in the police. *Justice Quarterly, 30*(6), 1042–1067.

Van de Walle, S. (2009). Trust in the justice system: A comparative view across Europe. *Prison Service Journal, 183,* 22–26.

Van Dijk, J., Van Kesteren, J., & Smit, P. (2007). *Criminal victimisation in international perspective: Key findings from the 2004–2005 ICVS and EU ICS.* Retrieved from http:// english.wodc.nl/onderzoeksdatabase/icvs-2005-survey.aspx?cp=45&cs=6796

Vidmar, N. (2000). *World jury systems*. New York, NY: Oxford University Press.

Whitman, J. Q. (2003). *Harsh justice: Criminal punishment and the widening divide between America and Europe*. New York, NY: Oxford University Press.

Whitman, J. Q. (2005). The comparative study of criminal punishment. *Annual Review of Law and Social Science, 1*(1), 17–34. doi:10.1146/annurev.lawsocsci.1.041604.115833

Winterdyk, J. (1997). *Juvenile justice systems: International perspectives*. Toronto, Ontario: Canadian Scholars' Press.

Part III

Policing and Law Enforcement

CHAPTER 16

A History of American Policing

Craig D. Uchida

American policing traces its roots in law enforcement and crime prevention to its English heritage and to the birth and growth of cities throughout the nation. Historians have documented these developments through comparative histories of the New York and London police (Miller, 1977; Richardson, 1970), through individual histories of specific departments (Lane, 1967; Schneider, 1980), and through specific issues in policing (Fogelson, 1977; Monkkonen 1981; Walker, 1977, 1998). These histories illustrate the way policing has evolved over time. Historical analyses also show the roots of problems in policing, such as corruption, brutality, and inefficiency.

THE ROOTS OF MODERN POLICING

In the 17th and 18th centuries, the English colonies followed the English policing system, adopting the sheriff, the constable, and the town watch. The county sheriff, who was appointed by the governor, became that jurisdiction's most important law enforcement agent, particularly when the colonies remained small and primarily rural. The sheriff's duties included apprehending criminals, serving subpoenas, appearing in court, and collecting taxes. The sheriff was paid a fixed amount for each task he performed. As sheriffs received higher fees, that is, income, based on the taxes collected, apprehending criminals was not a primary concern. In fact, law enforcement was a low priority.

In New York, Boston, and Philadelphia, constables and the night watch conducted a wide variety of tasks. The night watch reported fires, maintained street lamps, arrested or detained suspicious persons, raised the hue and cry when they needed assistance in apprehending criminals, and walked the rounds or beats. Constables engaged in similarly broad tasks: taking suspects to court, eliminating health hazards, and bringing witnesses to court.

LAW ENFORCEMENT IN THE WEST

At the same time that the English were colonizing the Eastern Seaboard, the Spanish were exerting their influence, culture, and religion in the areas that became Texas and California in the 1800s. For example, in 1718, the Royal Presidio of San Antonio de Bexar was established by the viceroy of New Spain, who also founded the Mission San Antonio de Valero (more famously known as the Alamo). The missions were home to Franciscan missionaries and local Native Americans from various tribes. Security and law enforcement in the area were handled by soldiers posted to the presidio, most of whom were Mexican frontiersmen from the northern territories of New Spain. In 1731, the king of Spain granted settlers a charter and permission to organize a town council, which included the first official law officer in San Antonio, the *alguacil* (constable or sheriff), Vicente Alvarez Traviesco, then 26 years of age (Mission Basilica, n.d.).

Farther west, in 1769, Franciscan friar, Junipero Serra, established the first mission in California, Mission Basilica San Diego de Alcala (Mission Basilica, n.d.), which eventually grew into the larger community of San Diego. The first of 21 missions in California, the San Diego mission relied upon soldiers and the tenets of the Catholic religion for security and enforcement of rules and laws. Converting American Indians to Catholicism was one of Father Serra's primary goals, and to do so, he relied on the military for support and security. According to the PBS film project *The West*,

> By law, all baptized Indians subjected themselves completely to the authority of the Franciscans; they could be whipped, shackled, or imprisoned for disobedience and were hunted down if they fled the mission grounds. Indian recruits, who were often forced to convert nearly at gunpoint, could be expected to survive mission life for only about 10 years. (West Film Project, 2001, para. 10)

FORMING THE NEW POLICE IN ENGLAND

During the mid- to late 1700s, European cities grew rapidly because of the Industrial Revolution. London, in particular, expanded at an unprecedented rate. From 1750 to 1820, the population nearly doubled (Miller, 1977), and the urban economy became more complex and specialized. With industrial growth came crime, disorder, riots, and public health problems. Food riots, wage protests, poor sewage control, pickpockets, burglars, and vandals created difficulties for city dwellers. The upper and middle classes, concerned about these issues, sought more protection and preventive measures. The constable-watch system of law enforcement could no longer deal successfully with the problems of the day, and alternative solutions were devised.

Suggestions were made to replace the constable-watch system with a stronger, more centralized police force. Prevention and deterrence became the focus of the police. Magistrates Henry Fielding, John Fielding, and Patrick Colquhoun, as well as philosopher Jeremy Bentham and his followers, advocated this new policing philosophy. A preventive police force would act as a deterrent to criminals and would serve the best interests of society. The idea of uniformed police officers, however, was opposed by many citizens and politicians in England because it resembled a standing army. In spite of this opposition, proponents of a police force eventually won out, and after much debate, the London Metropolitan Police Act was approved by Parliament in 1829 (Critchley, 1967).

The London Police Act established a full-time, uniformed police force having the primary purpose of patrolling the city. Sir Robert Peel is credited with the formation of the police, for he synthesized the ideas of the Fieldings, Colquhoun, and Bentham into law; convinced Parliament of the need for police; and guided the force's early development.

Through Peel, the role of the London police was formulated. Crime prevention became the primary function, but to enforce the laws and to exert its authority, the police first had to gain legitimacy in the eyes of the public. To earn acceptance, Peel and his associates chose a simple navy blue uniform, insisted that officers be restrained and polite, meted out appropriate discipline, did not allow officers to carry guns, and specifically identified select men who were even tempered and reserved. Overall, the London police emphasized its legitimacy based on *institutional* authority—that their power was grounded in the English Constitution and their behavior determined by rules of law. In essence, the power of the London "Bobby" or "Peeler" (so-called in deference to Robert Peel) was based on the institution of the government.

AMERICAN POLICE SYSTEMS

American cities and towns encountered problems like those in England. Eastern cities grew quickly, civil disorders swept the nation, and crime was perceived to increase. The population of New York, for example, grew from 33,000 in 1790 to 150,000 in 1830. Foreign immigrants, particularly Irish and Germans, accounted for a significant portion of the increase. Traveling to America in search of employment and better lifestyles, the immigrants competed with native-born Americans for both skilled and unskilled positions and were seen as social and economic threats. Other tensions existed in the city as well. Race became a factor, as those who opposed slavery were met with violence in both the North and the South.

Between the 1830s and 1870s, numerous confrontations occurred because of ethnic and racial differences, economic failures, and moral questions and during elections of public officials. In New York, 1834 was designated the "Year of the Riots" because so many took place (Miller, 1977). At the same time that the riots occurred, citizens perceived that crime was increasing. Homicides, robberies, and thefts were thought to be on the rise. In addition, vagrancy, prostitution, gambling, and other vices were more observable on the streets. Yet in spite of the apparent immediacy of these problems, replacements for the constable-watch police system did not appear overnight.

The political forces in the large industrial cities, like New York, Philadelphia, and Boston, hindered the immediate acceptance of a London-style police department.

City councils, mayors, state legislatures, and governors debated over a number of questions and could not come to an immediate agreement over the type of police they wanted. In New York City, for example, although riots occurred in 1834, the movement to form a preventive police department did not take shape until 1841. Four years later, in 1845, the New York Police Department was created, but officers did not begin wearing uniforms until 1853.

Eventually, American police departments borrowed selectively rather than exactly from the London model. The most notable carryover was the adoption of the preventive patrol idea. A police presence would alter the behavior of individuals and would be available to maintain order in an efficient manner. Differences, however, between the London and American police abounded. The London Metropolitan Police Department was a highly centralized agency. An extension of the national government, the police department was purposely removed from the direct political influence of the people. Furthermore, Peel recruited specific individuals—polite, aloof officers who were trained and followed strict guidelines. In addition, the Bobbies were encouraged to look upon police work as a career, not just a job.

American police systems followed the style of local and municipal governments, which were highly decentralized. Mayors were largely figureheads; real power lay in the wards and neighborhoods. City councilmen or aldermen ran the government and used political patronage freely. Police departments shared this style of participation and decentralization. The police were an extension of different political factions rather than an extension of city government. Police officers were recruited and selected by political leaders in a particular ward or precinct. As a result of the democratic nature of government, legal intervention by the police was limited, unlike the London police, which relied on formal control. That is, instead of drawing on institutional legitimacy (i.e., parliamentary laws), each American police officer had to establish his own authority among the citizens he patrolled. The personal, informal police officer could win the respect of the citizenry by knowing local standards and expectations. This meant that different police behavior would occur in different neighborhoods. In New York, for example, the officer was free to act as he chose within the context of broad public expectations. He was less limited by institutional and legal restraints than his London counterpart, entrusted with less formal power but given broader personal discretion.

POLICING IN THE 19TH CENTURY

Beginning around the Civil War and throughout the 20th century, American police departments appeared almost overnight in eastern cities (Monkkonen, 1981). Once New York, Philadelphia, Boston, and Cincinnati adopted the English model, the new version of policing spread from larger cities to smaller ones rather quickly.

Unlike eastern cities, however, the development of policing in the West varied, depending in large part on the way in which the city was formed. For example, San Antonio originated as a Spanish mission and presidio in 1718. According to the San Antonio Police Department's website,

In the earliest years of [the city's development], (1718–1800), the major law enforcement concerns were with problems related to settling residents' disputes over land and livestock, as well as protecting the settlements from Indian attacks. During the first half of the 19th century, according to most published histories on this period, law enforcement concerns were with the protection of the residents of San Antonio from the constant threat of attack by "marauding Indians and Mexican bandits" as well as other intruders. (San Antonio Police Department [SAPD], 2004, para. 2)

The city of Houston was established after Texas won its independence from Mexico in 1836. Although a constable was selected to serve as the first law enforcement official in 1837, it was not until 4 years later that an official police department was established and a city marshal appointed.

In Wichita, Kansas, and Fort Worth, Texas, the development of law enforcement was tied to the problems associated with cattle towns: all-night saloons, gambling houses, and gunfights. In the 1870s, Wichita, located on the Chisholm Trail, was known for its raucus and sometimes violent nights. Wyatt Earp was appointed to the force as a policeman in 1875, his second stop (Lamar, Missouri, was the first) in a law enforcement career that would lead him to Dodge City, Pima (AZ) County, and Tombstone, Arizona. To curb the violence that was occurring in Wichita, the city appointed a special police force to serve as toll keepers on the Chisholm Trail Bridge, which crossed the Arkansas River into Wichita. This special force also removed firearms from anyone coming into the city and held them for safekeeping until they departed. To curtail drunken behavior, the state passed a prohibition law in 1880 (City of Wichita, 2009).

In 1873, Fort Worth was incorporated; the city appointed a marshal with a force of four policemen to reduce levels of crime, gambling, and drunken behavior. Unlike Wichita, the local businesses in Fort Worth abolished the police force after 6 months for economic reasons. The cowboys who passed through the area needed supplies and recreation before taking their cattle onto Kansas and were a financial boon to the saloons and gambling houses. Not until 1876, when Jim Courtright became marshal, did violence abate. Courtright, a well-known gunfighter, hired two policemen to assist him and through his reputation reduced the number of killings while maintaining the flow of money and liquor in the city. For Courtright, legitimization came in the form of his ability to outgun his opponents.

POLICE WORK

Officers

The 19th-century patrolman was basically a political operative rather than a London-style professional committed to public service (Walker, 1998). Primarily selected for his political connections, the police officer in urban centers owed his allegiance to the ward boss and police captain who chose him. Similarly, in the West, the city marshal was an elected official who chose his subordinates.

Police officers were paid well, as salaries compared favorably with other occupations, but had poor job security. On average, in 1880, most major cities paid policemen in the neighborhood of $900 a year. Walker (1998) reported that a skilled tradesman in the building industry earned about $770 a year, while those in manufacturing could expect about $450 a year. In Wichita, Wyatt Earp earned $60 per month as policeman, or $720 per year; the marshal made $91.66 per month, or $1,100 per year; and the assistant marshal made $75 per month, or $900 per year (City of Wichita, 2009). In San Diego in 1889, the starting salary for a police officer was $80 per month, although he worked 12-hour shifts, 7 days a week (San Diego Police Historical Association, 2009).

Walking the Beat

Police officers walked a patrol route, or beat, in all types of weather for 2 to 6 hours of a 12-hour day. The remaining time was spent at the station house on reserve. During actual patrol duty, police officers were required to maintain order and make arrests, but they often circumvented their responsibilities. Supervision was extremely limited once an officer was beyond the station house. Sergeants and captains had no way of contacting their men while they were on patrol, as communications technology was limited. Telegraph lines linked district stations to headquarters in the 1850s, but call boxes on the beat were not introduced until late in the 19th century, and the radio and motorized communications did not appear until the 1900s. Police officers acted alone and used their own initiative.

Crime Control and Arrests

Monkkonen (1981) found that from 1860 to 1920 arrests declined in 23 of the largest cities in the United States. Crimes without victims (vice, disturbances, drunkenness, and other public order offenses) fell dramatically. Overall, Monkkonen estimated that arrests declined by more than 33% during the 60-year period. Further analysis showed that the decline occurred because the police role shifted from controlling the "dangerous class" to controlling criminal behavior only. From 1860 to 1890, the police were involved in assisting the poor, in taking in overnight lodgers, and in returning lost children to their parents or orphanages. In the period 1890 to 1920, however, the police changed their role, structure, and behavior because of external demands placed upon them.

Police Corruption and Lawlessness

One of the major themes of 19th-century policing is the prevalence of wide-spread corruption that was evidenced in numerous departments across the country. The lawlessness of the police—their systematic impropriety and nonenforcement of the laws—was one of the paramount issues in municipal politics during the late 1800s.

Because police officers worked alone or in small groups, there were ample opportunities to shake down peddlers and small businesses. Detectives allowed con artists, pickpockets, and thieves to go about their business in return for a share of their proceeds. Captains often established regular payment schedules for houses of prostitution according to the number of girls in the house and the rates charged. The monthly total for police protection ranged from $25 to $75 per house plus $500 to open or reopen after a raid (Richardson, 1970).

Officers who did not go along with the nonenforcement of laws or who did not approve of the graft and corruption of others found themselves transferred to less-than-desirable areas and beats. Promotions were also denied, as they were reserved for the politically astute and wealthy officer (promotions could cost $10,000 to $15,000).

REFORMING THE POLICE

A broad reform effort began to emerge toward the end of the 19th century. Stimulated mainly by the Progressives, attempts were made to create a truly professional police force. The Progressives were upper-middle-class, educated Protestants who opposed the political machines, sought improvements in government, and desired a change in American morality. By eliminating machine politics from government, all facets of social services, including the police, would improve.

These reformers found that the police lacked discipline, strong leadership, and qualified personnel. To improve conditions, the Progressives recommended three changes: (a) centralization of departments, (b) upgrading of personnel, and (c) narrowing of the police function (Fogelson, 1977). Centralization of the police meant that more power and authority would be placed in the hands of the chief. Autonomy from politicians was crucial to centralization. Upgrading the rank and file meant better training, discipline, and selection. Finally, these reformers urged that police give up all activities unrelated to crime, including operating ambulances, issuing licenses for businesses, and sheltering the poor.

From 1890 to 1920, the Progressives struggled to implement their reform ideology across the country. Some inroads were made during this period, including the establishment of police commissions, civil service examinations, and legislative reforms. In spite of their efforts, the Progressives still did not manage to change urban departments drastically. Chiefs continued to lack power and authority, most officers had little or no education, training was limited, and the police role continued to include a wide variety of nonenforcement tasks.

Walker (1977) gives several reasons for the failure of reform. First, political machines were too difficult to break. Despite the efforts by the Progressives, politicians could still count on individual supporters to undermine their reforms. Second, rank-and-file police officers resented the Progressives' interventions. Reformers were viewed by officers as knowing little about police work; therefore, officers saw their proposals for change as ill conceived. Finally, the reforms failed because the idea and culture of policing could not be divorced from politics.

BECOMING PROFESSIONALS

With the failure of the Progressives to change policing, a second reform effort emerged. A small cadre of chiefs sought and implemented a variety of innovations intended to improve policing generally. From about 1910 to 1960, police chiefs advocated for the adoption of the *professional model*.

The professional department included a number of characteristics: Officers were experts in the field of policing, police departments were autonomous, and police departments were efficient, using modern technology and businesslike practices to control crime and enforce the law. These reforms were similar to those of the Progressives, but because they came from within the police organizations themselves, they met with greater success.

The major innovator among the chiefs was August Vollmer. Serving first as the elected marshal of Berkeley, California, in 1905 and then appointed chief in 1909, Vollmer brought new ideas and science to policing. He is credited with a number of firsts: the first records system; the first use of the modus operandi investigation system; the first to use forensic science to analyze blood, soil, and fiber; the first to establish a motorcycle patrol unit; and the first to encourage college education for his officers.

Vollmer emphasized improvement of the quality of police personnel, believing that this would lead to professional officers. He initiated the use of intelligence, psychiatric, and neurological tests in the selection of applicants and was the first police chief to actively recruit college students. In addition, he was instrumental in linking the police department with the University of California at Berkeley, where in 1916, officers began to take summer courses. By 1931, a criminology program had been formally created at Berkeley, and in 1950 the School of Criminology was established, with Vollmer and his protégé, O. W. Wilson, as instructors (Berkeley Police Department, n.d.).

O. W. Wilson followed in his mentor's footsteps by advocating efficiency within the police bureaucracy through scientific techniques. From 1928 to 1939, Wilson served as police chief in Wichita, Kansas, where he conducted the first systematic study of one-officer squad cars. He argued that one-officer cars were efficient, effective, and economical. Despite arguments from patrol officers that their safety was at risk, Wilson claimed that the public received better service with single-officer cars.

TECHNOLOGY DEVELOPMENT

Technological changes enabled the police to move toward professionalism. The patrol car, the two-way radio, and the telephone altered the way in which the police operated and the manner in which citizens made use of the police. Motorized patrols meant more efficient coverage of the city and quicker response to calls for service. The two-way radio dramatically increased the supervisory capacity of police administrators, as continuous contact between sergeant and police officer could be maintained. Finally, the telephone provided the link between the public and the police.

Overall, the second reform movement met with more success than the Progressives' attempt, though it did not achieve its goal of total professionalization. On the other hand, the quality of police officers greatly improved during this period. Police reformers and others were able to reduce the influence of political parties in departmental affairs. Chiefs secured greater power and authority over their management abilities but continued to receive input from political leaders and remained political appointees. In terms of efficiency, the police moved forward in serving the public more quickly and competently. Technological innovations clearly assisted the police in this area, as did streamlining the organizations themselves.

TURBULENT TIMES: AMERICA IN THE 1960s

Policing in America encountered its most serious crisis in the 1960s. The rise in crime, the civil rights movement, anti-Vietnam War sentiment, and riots in virtually every major American city brought the police into the center of controversy.

During the decade of the 1960s, instances of crime increased phenomenally with the crime rate per 100,000 persons doubling in this 10-year period. As crime increased, so, too, did the demands for its reduction. The police, in emphasizing its crime-fighting ability, created a false expectation on the part of the public. As a result, the public image of the police became tarnished.

The civil rights movement created new demands from the police. The movement, begun in the 1950s, sought equality for Black Americans in all facets of life. Sit-ins at segregated lunch counters, boycotts of bus services, attempts at integrating schools, and demonstrations in the streets led to direct confrontations with law enforcement officers. The police became the symbol of a society that denied Blacks equal justice under the law.

Eventually, the frustrations of Black Americans erupted into violence in cities across the country. Most of these disorders were initiated by a routine police-citizen encounter, including the New York City riot of 1964 and the Watts riot in Los Angeles in 1965. By 1966, 43 more riots had broken out across the country. Disorders engulfed Newark for 5 days, leaving 23 dead, while the Detroit riot a week later lasted nearly 7 days and resulted in 43 deaths with $40 million in property damages.

On the final day of the Detroit riot, President Lyndon Johnson appointed a special commission to investigate the problem of civil disorder. The National Advisory Commission on Civil Disorders (aka the Kerner Commission) identified institutional racism as the underlying cause of the rioting. Police actions were also cited as contributing to the disorders. Direct police intervention had sparked the riots in Harlem, Watts, Newark, and Detroit. In Watts and Newark, the riots had been set off by routine traffic stops. In Detroit, a police raid of an after-hours bar touched off the disorders there. The police thus became the focus of national attention.

The Kerner Commission identified several problems in U.S. police departments. First, police officers were found to be brutal and abused their power. Second, training and supervision were inadequate. Third, police–community relations were poor.

And fourth, the employment of Black officers lagged far behind the growth of the Black population.

To partially remedy these problems, President Johnson created a crime commission (The President's Commission on Law Enforcement and the Administration of Justice), and Congress authorized federal assistance to criminal justice. The president's commission produced a final report that emphasized the need for more research, higher qualifications for criminal justice personnel, and greater coordination of a national crime-control effort. The federal aid program to justice agencies resulted in the creation of the Office of Law Enforcement Assistance, a forerunner of the Law Enforcement Assistance Administration (LEAA).

THE LEGACY OF THE 1960s

The events of the 1960s forced police, politicians, and policy makers to reassess the state of law enforcement in the United States. Academicians began to study the police in an effort to explain their problems and crises. With federal funding from LEAA and private organizations like the Police Foundation, researchers studied the police from a number of perspectives. Traditional methods of patrol development, officer selection, and training were questioned. Racial discrimination in employment practices, in arrests, and officer use of deadly force were among the issues most closely and often examined.

In addition, the professional movement itself came into question, for it created two unintended consequences. The first involved the development of the police subculture. The second was the problem of police–community relations. In terms of the subculture, police officers felt alienated from their administrators, the media, and the public and turned inward and to themselves as a result. Patrol officers resented the police hierarchy because of its emphasis on following orders and regulations. Officers saw the media and the public as foes because of the criticism and disrespect cast their way. As the crime rate increased, newspaper accounts criticized the police for their inability to curtail crime. As the riots persisted, some citizens cried for more order, while others demanded less oppression by the police on the streets. The conflicting message given to officers by these groups led to distrust, alienation, and frustration. Only by standing together did officers feel comfortable in their working environment.

The second unintended consequence of professionalism was the problems it generated for police–community relations. Modern technology (like the patrol car), removed the officer from the street and eliminated routine contact with citizens. The impersonal style of professionalism often exacerbated police–community problems. Tactics such as aggressive patrol in Black neighborhoods, designed to suppress crime efficiently, created more racial tensions.

These problems raised questions for the need and effectiveness of professionalism. Some police administrators suggested abandoning the movement altogether. Others sought to continue the effort while adjusting for and solving the difficulties it created. In spite of these misgivings, for the most part, the goal of professionalization has remained operative.

COMMUNITY POLICING

As a result of the problems of the 1960s and 1970s, a third wave of reform of police operations and strategies began to emerge: community-oriented policing.

Community policing came to light as a response to the communication gap between police and community and because of research that questioned police tactics and strategies. A new paradigm incorporating a "broken windows theory," proactive policing, and problem-oriented policing emerged and provided the foundation for the community policing reform era.

Police strategists recognized that simply reacting to calls for service limited the ability of law enforcement to control crime and maintain order. Police on patrol could not see enough to control crime effectively—they did not know how to intervene to improve the quality of life in the community. The reactive strategy used during the professional era no longer was effective in dealing with complex problems in the 1980s and 1990s. Instead, Herman Goldstein (1990) and James Q. Wilson and George Kelling (1982) called for police to engage in proactive work and problem-oriented policing. A whole body of work from police researchers, strategists, and reformers laid the groundwork for the community policing movement.

In its ideal sense, community policing promised to fundamentally transform the way police do business. Reformers argued that police should not be so obsessed with routine "people-processing" activities (e.g., making arrests, filling out reports) but should focus instead on "people-changing" activities (Mastrofski, Worden, & Snipes, 2006). These included building up neighborhoods, designing custom solutions to local problems, forging partnerships with other community agencies, and a variety of other non-routine police activities.

Since the 1990s, the implementation of community policing has been inconsistent. Federal funding from 1994 to 1999 enabled police departments to hire community policing officers, purchase new technologies for problem solving, and implement different programs (Roth et al., 2000). With the new millennium and the terrorist events of September 11, 2001, however, emphasis on community policing has waned. It remains to be seen how and in what way community policing will reemerge in the coming years.

CONCLUSION

This has been a brief look at the development of American police systems from its English heritage through the early years of the 21st century. Major emphasis has been placed on the police role, though important events that have shaped the development of the police have also been discussed. A number of present-day issues are seen to have their roots in different epochs of American history. For example, the idea of community policing can be traced to the colonial period. Preventive patrol, legitimacy, authority, and professionalism are 18th- and 19th-century concepts. Riots, disorders, and corruption are not new to American policing; similar events occurred in the 19th century. Thus, we can give contextual meaning to current police problems, ideas, and situations. By looking at the past, present-day events can be better understood.

DISCUSSION QUESTIONS

1. What are the differences and similarities between the London model and the American model of policing in the 19th century?

2. How does the democratic form of government in American cities influence the way police departments operate and function?

3. Throughout history, reform movements have tried to change policing. How have they succeeded or failed?

4. Describe and discuss the components of professionalism in American policing.

5. The 1960s posed problems for American police. What were those problems, and how were they resolved?

6. What are the historical roots of community policing?

REFERENCES

Berkeley Police Department (n.d.). *Our history.* Retrieved October 13, 2009, from http://www.ci.berkeley.ca.us/police/History/history.html

City of Wichita. (2009). *The beginnings: Excerpts from "Wichita Police Department 1871–2000."* Retrieved October 13, 2009, from http://www.wichita.gov/City Offices/Police/History/History

Critchley, T. A. (1967). *A history of police in England and Wales.* Montclair, NJ: Patterson Smith.

Fogelson, R. (1977). *Big-city police.* Cambridge, MA: Harvard University Press.

Goldstein, H. (1990). *Problem-oriented policing.* New York, NY: McGraw-Hill.

Lane, R. (1967). *Policing the city: Boston, 1822–1885.* Cambridge, MA: Harvard University Press.

Mastrofski, S. D., Worden, R. E., & Snipes, J. B. (2006). Law enforcement in a time of community policing. *Criminology, 33*(4), pp. 539–553.

Miller, W. R. (1977). *Cops and Bobbies: Police authority in New York and London, 1830–1870.* Chicago, IL: University of Chicago Press.

Mission Basilica San Diego de Alcala. (n.d.). *Mission history.* Retrieved October 13, 2009, from http://www.missionsandiego.com/mission_history.htm

Monkkonen, E. H. (1981). *Police in urban America, 1860–1920.* Cambridge, United Kingdom: Cambridge University Press.

Richardson, J. F. (1970). *The New York police: Colonial times to 1901*. New York, NY: Oxford University Press.

Roth, J. A., Ryan, J. F., Gaffigan, S. F., Koper, C. S., Moore, M. H., Roehl, J. A., . . . Thacher, D. (2000). *National evaluation of the COPS program—Title I of the 1994 Crime Act*. Washington, DC: National Institute of Justice.

San Antonio Police Department (SAPD). (1998–2004). *History of SAPD: Part one: The early years: 1718–1900*. Retrieved October 13, 2009, from http://sanantonio.gov/sapd/history1.htm

San Diego Police Historical Association. (2009). *History*. Retrieved October 13, 2009, from http://www.sandiegopolicemuseum.com/HistorySet.htm

Schneider, J. C. (1980). *Detroit and the problems of order, 1830–1880*. Lincoln: University of Nebraska Press.

Walker, S. (1977). *A critical history of police reform: The emergence of professionalism*. Lexington, MA: D. C. Heath.

Walker, S. (1998). *Popular justice: A history of American criminal justice* (2nd ed.). New York, NY: Oxford University Press.

West Film Project. (2001). *New perspectives on the West: Junipero Serra (1713–1784)*. PBS. Retrieved October 13, 2009, from http://www.pbs.org/weta/thewest/people/s_z/serra.htm

Wilson, J. Q., & Kelling, G. (1982). Broken windows: The police and neighborhood safety. *Atlantic Monthly, 249*, pp. 29–38.

CHAPTER 17

Police Theory

John Crank, Dawn M. Irlbeck,
and Connie M. Koski

W e review four ways of looking at theory: normative-rational, institutional, conflict and critical, and postmodern. Each of these has something to offer the police scholar, and each has its limitations. As important, each provides us a way to begin to organize this field called police scholarship and think about where we go next.

NORMATIVE-RATIONAL THEORY

Most people, when they think of the police, think of them reactively. That is, there is crime, and the police respond. Why do we need police theory? It is obvious that the police exist to do something about crime—if not, then one heck of a lot of us have been duped. It is not obvious that we need to know much more about them especially if we are looking for a job and want to become police officers.

Normative-rational perspectives look at police organizations as independent actors and ask what they can do to achieve their mission. *Normative* means that their work is defined in broad societal norms, in this case those norms that formally sanction behavior. *Rational* means that they can make reasonable decisions and act on them based on a reasonable, logical assessment of their environment.

Two ways of looking at normative perspectives are presented here. The first way is through the assessment of contingency theory, which is aimed at explaining the behavior of police organizations in terms of their fit with their environmental settings. The second is an overview of contemporary crime interdiction practices, those that represent the state of the art in police work today.

Contingency Theory

Contingency theory is a rational approach to theory building, but it is different from traditional notions of organizational rationality. The characteristic feature of

259

contingency theory is that organizations adapt to the contingencies they face. Their efforts to achieve particular goals will consequently depend on the nature of the community they service and the organizational circumstances in which they find themselves.

Donaldson (2001, p. 1) defined *contingency theory* as follows: "[O]rganizational effectiveness results from fitting characteristics of the organization, such as its structure, to contingencies that reflect the situation of the organization." *Structural contingency theory* refers to those theories or efforts that attempt to explain or change organizational structure and to perspectives that locate structure in terms of the three contingencies of environment, size, and strategy. Change in any of these contingencies tends to produce changes in organizational structure.

Contingency theory is not universalistic, or in today's jargon, it does not lend itself to best practices. Donaldson (2001) noted that contingency refers to adaptive processes: The relationship between any element of structure and its performance is mediated by contingencies that have to be recognized and addressed. "[A] contingency is any variable that moderates the effect of an organizational characteristic on organizational performance" (p. 7). Consequently, when we seek to understand organizational structure or the behavior of those structures, we take into consideration three issues:

1. There is a relationship between the contingency and the structure.

2. If the contingency changes, the structure changes.

3. The fit between the contingency and the organization determines organizational performance. The better the fit, the more effective the organizational performance.

Contingency theory can be traced to Langworthy (1986), who presaged it by noting that what works for organizations in some communities will not always work in others. Much of the work of empirically assessing contingency theory is traced to Mastrofski, whose work is considered later in this chapter in institutional theory, and to Maguire (see, e.g., Maguire, 2003; Mastrofski, Ritti, & Hoffmaster, 1987). Kuhns, Maguire, and Cox (2007), for example, in an application of contingency theory, showed how organizational emphases with regard to a variety of public safety concerns were related to environmental characteristics, particularly regional factors and levels of violent and property crime.

The three separate interactions of police-community-political environments and their relationship to the greater community's political environment research is a good example of structural contingency theory where the contingency is located in the environment. Since the seminal work of Wilson (1968), researchers have been interested in the relationship between characteristics of the community and the policing structure (see Klinger, 2004; Maguire, 2003; Stucky, 2005).

To illustrate what is and what is not contingency theory, we consider Morabito's (2008) paper on the role of the community environment on police innovation. (Please note that the authors make no claims that this is contingency theory.)

Morabito hypothesized that particular community political structures would facilitate the adoption of community policing practices. She identified three political structures: (a) jurisdictions with city managers, (b) those with partisan elections, and (c) community characteristics such as residential stability, diversity, and income that she used as a proxy for variations in district-based elections. She also included the contingencies of organizational size and formalization of structure. Her findings showed that form of government and district-based elections, as well as organizational formalization, emerged as significant predictors of innovation.

Morabito's work is on community theory, which can be considered a category of contingency theory. However, from a contingency theory perspective, there is an unasked question: What is the environment-organizational misfit those structural innovations of community policing addresses? That is, what is the policing problem that community policing addresses and that extant forms of policing do not address? In terms of effectiveness, what is the inefficiency that organizational change toward community policing makes effective?

This three-part question—What is it that (a) community policing addresses, that (b) represents a change in the environment, that (c) resulted from a misfit between community policing and the environment?—is not simply a research question. It is an organizational issue that has haunted community policing since its inception and may account for what appears to be the disestablishment of the community policing movement in the current era. One can argue, from a contingency theory perspective, that the rapid rise and institutionalization of data-driven computer statistics (CompStat), with its focus on effectiveness in terms of arrest-driven results, is a result of the misfit in community and policing created by the community policing movement, visibly indicated by public perceptions that crime was inadequately addressed (although see Willis, Mastrofski, & Weisburd, 2007).

Contingency theory does not seem to work well for understanding police organizations. Maguire (2003) noted that because departments have unclear outputs and survive from public need despite their performance, changes in environmental contingencies will have minimal affect on them. However, contemporary trends in policing, with their focus on the production of arrest statistics, may increase the importance of such outputs. That is, the relative unimportance of contingency theory may be passing.

Police Criminology

Police criminology refers specifically to police efforts to do something about crime. Most criminal justice research is police criminology. This area also represents the most applied area of police theory today, in that a great deal of research focuses on the effectiveness of police practices in a wide variety of crime and disorder settings.

The signature work on police criminology is the tome *Preventing Crime: What Works, What Doesn't, and What's Promising* (Sherman et al., 1997). This work represented a comprehensive evaluation of the effectiveness of Bureau of Justice grants to assist state and local law enforcement and communities in preventing crime. It is the most thorough overview of police practices yet undertaken. The work focuses on institutional settings, including labor markets, places, families, and schools and asks whether research carried out in these settings has had any significant effects on crime. Findings are organized according to two factors: (a) Did the interventions show success, and (b) was the methodology adequate for confidence in the conclusions of the research? A discussion of the principal findings are beyond the scope of this chapter, but any reader interested in police criminology is advised to spend some time in this work.

Police criminology today can be separated into two branches. The first assesses existing practices, and the second looks at innovations. The difference between the two branches is subtle and mostly depends on whether any given practice is part of the regular budget.

Existing Practices: Murder

Murder is perhaps the most important crime police deal with—it is the central focus of a great deal of media attention, and it carries the heaviest penal sanction. Yet the clearance rate for murder has gone sharply down over the past 50 years. In 1965, the average clearance rate for homicide was 91%. By 2002, it had dropped to 64%. Why?

The work of Cronin and his colleagues (Cronin, Murphy, Spahr, Toliver, & Weger, 2007) represents a solid review and analysis of the many facets of police work related to homicide clearance rates. The authors tracked current organizational practices for homicide: the management of homicide units, the identification of eyewitnesses, interrogation practices, the use of crime labs, and ways of dealing with cold cases in the age of DNA. This research did not identify a single causative agent—police work by all accounts has substantially improved over the past 50 years—but provided a range of suggestions in each of these areas. For example, the authors, noting that as many as 75% of eyewitnesses misidentify suspects, provided a series of recommendations with regard to the use of eyewitness testimony and for the management and organization of lineups. This is an excellent review of many aspects of police work central to contemporary routine police practices.

New Directions: The Return to the Professional Model

Researchers interested in new directions in policing have voluminous materials from which they can select. All the practices in the following list represent different ways the police have developed new directions in the past 30 years, and all focus on the mission of crime control.

CompStat: Crime control through managerial oversight and command responsibility

Lever pulling: Crime control through using all available prosecutorial and police tools to threaten (and carry out) apprehension conviction

Problem-oriented crime control: Identifying and gaining control of underlying problems

Broken windows: Crime control through aggressive order-maintenance activity

Zero tolerance: Nondiscretionary enforcement of all laws, sometimes focusing specifically on minor offenses

Crime mapping: Crime control by visual representation of high-crime areas and real-time response

Third-party policing: Crime control through pressure on third parties who in some way facilitate crime

Intelligence-led crime control: Crime control through higher quality intelligence and information in real-time policing

Hot-spot policing: Crime control through greater presence/visibility in high-crime areas

Crackdowns: Heavy use of arrest in areas associated with specific crimes or problems

Interestingly, these changes all have been frequently labeled as community policing, yet none of them involve activities in which the police reach out to the community in some pragmatic way, the sine qua non of community policing. To the contrary, all represent a rejection of mission that is not meaningfully tied to crime suppression and prevention. They appear to have piggybacked on community policing's legitimacy and today are emerging as the functional center of a new police professionalism, with the community policing movement in decline. From a historical point of view, we witness in these practices two features: (a) the emergence of police criminology as a strong area of academic research, and (b) the return of the field of policing to its professional roots, a neoprofessionalism movement with a central focus on the law enforcement mission but with a stronger scientific and intelligence-based foundation for its work.

INSTITUTIONAL THEORY

Institutional theory of policing is traceable to the writings of Mastrofski et al. (1987) and theoretically elaborated by Crank and Langworthy (1992; see also Crank, 1994). Briefly stated, *institutional theory* is the idea that organizational structure and policy are concerned with satisfying values carried by important constituencies in their environments. It represents a sharp challenge to contingency theories of police organizations. Put simply, organizations in highly institutionalized environments are concerned with constituent values, not technical efficiency. Police organizations, instead of focusing on clear-cut outputs around specific outcomes such as arrests or traffic stops, for example, turn outward to their institutional environments to determine appropriate organizational structures. This has several meanings:

1. Police departments loosely couple their structures to the technical core so that they can satisfy legitimacy concerns without being held accountable for what they actually do.

2. Departments operate under a logic of good faith, according to which members support each other and believe in the organization as a matter of faith rather than reliance on measurable outputs.

3. Organizational structures mirror turbulence in the external environment by becoming internally complex. Similarly, organizational complexity is a reflection of environmental conflict. For example, hiring processes tend to have built into their policy practices broad controversies regarding civil service, gender and race equality, and merit.

4. Organizations respond to environmental change by adding layers of complexity. Hence, departments tend to respond to community policing. This can be seen as departments adding community policing units with specialized police activities and trained officers rather than restructuring or streamlining organizational structures and processes.

Institutional theory itself is in the process of institutionalization in police theory today. Yet it faces a broad set of issues.

Issue 1: Transmission of Institutional Expectations

How are institutional values transmitted to organizations? If an institution is a causal agent, the specification of that cause agent is critical. Giblin (2006), adapting DiMaggio and Powell's (1983) model, identified three means of institutional transmission: mimetic, normative, and coercive pressures. *Mimetic pressures* are those by which organizations borrow items and strategies from member organizations in the organizational sector. *Normative pressures* relate to training, accreditation, and education and refer to pressures to conform to broad normative expectations in the institutional environment. *Coercive pressures* refer to compulsory pressures on organizations to conform to their environments. The law is an example of such a coercive pressure.

Crank (2003), adapting Scott's (1992) model of institutional transmission, identified six ways in which environmental elements are received by police organizations. The first, *imposition*, is the same as coercive pressure, noted above. *Authorization*, the second, is similar to normative pressure in that it refers to the way in which broad norms are defined and enforced. However, it refers to more formalistic sources of authority than the general normative category. Third, structure and policy may be *induced* in that they are accompanied with rewards for the organization.

Crank and Langworthy (1996) described the adoption of community policing as a process of institutional inducement, by which community policing was induced into police organizations through large grants that helped pay for programs and for officer salaries. *Acquisition,* the fourth, is about how organizations deliberately choose elements from their institutional environment. It recognizes that organizations are autonomous actors. The transmission of CompStat across the institutional settings of police organizations can be described as a process of acquisition. *Imprinting,* fifth, occurs when organizations are first formed. For example, one could argue that a militaristic rank structure was imprinted on police organizations in that most of the early departments were post–Civil War and were staffed by Civil War veterans who brought a military posture to the newly minted field of urban policing. Finally, *incorporation* refers to the tendency of multipurpose organizations, such as the police, to internally map their external environments. Conflicts in that environment will be elaborated in terms of broad policy statements, as in the example of personnel policies mentioned earlier.

Issue 2: Legitimating Processes

How is it that the process of legitimacy occurs in concrete settings? Vitale (2005) argued that the adoption of quality-of-life policing in New York should be understood in terms of institutional processes. Bratton and Giuliani came to power in New York in an environment in which the New York Police Department (NYPD) was seen as ineffectual in crime suppression. These two administrators had a legitimizing mandate: a "quality-of-life" philosophy focusing on zero tolerance, frequent use of stop-and-frisk strategy, broad use of civil enforcement practices, and the creation of other laws and regulations that aimed at controlling disorderly behavior. Through the ongoing commitments and very public support for quality-of-life policing, the mayor and the chief led the NYPD through broad and profound changes. Quality-of-life policing, with its intense law enforcement focus on arrest practices through command responsibility, was institutionalized across the organization. Vitale noted the unique historical circumstances behind the NYPD's transition, including the recognition that many elements of the new policing were already under way when Giuliani was elected. This is an excellent study of legitimacy lost and regained and of the transformation of a department to ultimately lead the transformation of policing across the United States.

Others have noted the importance of legitimacy for organizational well-being. Crank and Langworthy (1996) argued that the legitimacy of police organizations was carried out as a ceremonial function. The loss of legitimacy was indicated by the firing of the chief and restored only after the selection of a new chief with a new legitimizing mandate. Katz (2001) discussed how a specialized gang unit emerged from constituency pressure and consequently placed greater stock on ceremonial aspects aimed at satisfying environmental "sovereigns" than on substantive efforts to actually do something about gangs.

Issue 3: Empirical Testing Against Contingency Theory

A small number of authors have taken on what might be called the institutional–contingency debate. This debate is whether police practices and organizational changes are better understood in terms of contingency theory or institutional theory. Two works are noted in this regard.

Willis, Mastrofski, and Weisburd provided a qualitative assessment of three police organizations that adopted CompStat practices. All three organizations took technical issues into consideration, but the speed and pattern of acceptance of CompStat elements suggested that CompStat was adopted in response to "institutional pressures to appear progressive and successful" (2007, p. 148). Although it did not use the term, this study provided an excellent example of *loose coupling* in that actual crime-control practices remained fundamentally unchanged despite a broad administrative refocusing on crime control. Organizational structures are neither institutional nor technical but invariably carry some of each in their developments and practices. This has important theoretical implications that deserve further consideration. The theoretical study of organizations should not posit institutional and technical perspectives as contradictory or categorical but should consider each as part of the overall contribution to organizational success. It may be that organizational well-being requires both. That is, it must attend to technical requirements in its work on its product core, formalized in the public sector in terms of the mission or charter of the organization, and also ceremonially dress up its product to impress audiences who would like to know why the public should continue to fund it.

Giblin (2006), looking at the expansion of crime analysis units nationally, used measures derived from both perspectives. Unfortunately, his findings provided little support for either perspective; none of his predictors were significant at the .05 level. However, his data moved or tended in the direction of support for institutional predictors, an interpretation he indicated was justifiable based on relatively small sample sizes.

Issue 4: Understanding the Sweep of Police History

Institutional theory reminds us that there was not a "catechism" of police, as McEwen (1996) once noted, but that changes in police structure and practices are a consequence of broad changes in the environment of policing. Crank and Langworthy (1992) noted how the emergence of community policing, responsive to the urban conflicts of the 1960s, was initially aimed at building bridges between the African American community and police. Yet with an increasingly conservative electorate in the 1980s, community policing had shifted to aggressive, public order-oriented practices based on "broken windows" justifications for harsh treatment of minor crimes, despite its alienating effects on minority communities.

Ritti and Mastrofski (2002), in what is likely the exemplar of empirical analysis of institutional research, described the spread of community policing across the

American landscape as a three-phase institutional process. The first phase, "growing dissatisfaction with a problem," reflected the concerns about policing that emerged from the 1960s and early 1970s. The second phase, called "consensus about what to do about the problem," reflected the spread of community policing as an umbrella term and its creative adaptation in many departments outside those associated with its emergence. The third phase, "effective transmission of practices," was a period of intense assessment of community policing practices in a few large departments across the country. The fourth, "institutional transmission of practices," marked the period in which community policing practices were adopted, not because they were critically assessed but because they were "the right thing to do." They represented the new symbolic face of policing for the public, and they carried with them the appropriate discourse legitimizing the uncritical adoption of practices. Particularly useful was the way in which the authors operationalized their analysis. Ritti and Mastrofski's work is particularly helpful for researchers looking for ways of measuring institutional-level variables.

Institutional theory has been around in policing for 15 to 20 years, depending on where one locates its first efforts in policing. It has the support of a small but strong body of theorists and researchers. Its success today is due largely to the works of Mastrofski, who, working alone and with others, has provided a body of research aimed at the empirical measurement of institutional theory. The reader is recommended to look at the body of this work (Mastrofski et al., 1987; Mastrofski & Ritti, 1996, 2000; Mastrofski & Uchida, 1993; Uchida, Maguire, Parks, Mastrofski, & Solomon, 2002; Willis et al., 2007) to examine efforts to quantify institutional theory as well as to empirically compare institutional and contingency theory. This body of work has set the standard for the empirical assessment of institutional theory in policing in the current era.

CONFLICT THEORY

The Traditions of Conflict Theory

Conflict theory refers to a multifaceted set of perspectives loosely organized around the idea that strategies of crime control serve the interests of dominant groups (Holmes, 2000). Contemporary conflict theory can be traced to Blalock's (1967) work on the relationship between minority group presence and various social control efforts by the majority group. Turk (1969) extended Blalock's work by suggesting that culturally and racially dissimilar subordinate groups are perceived as threatening to the social and political order and are therefore disproportionally subject to arrest and punishment by the criminal justice system. Quinney (1970) expanded this notion when he argued that law is the primary means of establishing order in heterogeneous communities in order to compensate for the declining significance of informal control mechanisms therein. Liska, Chamlin, and Reed (1985) drew upon Blalock's threat hypothesis to further argue that an increase in the percentage of non-Whites increases the threat of crime perceived by authorities, thereby leading to increases in both the size of the crime-control apparatus and the pressure on that apparatus to control crime.

Law enforcement activities, from a conflict perspective, are a reaction to the threat that minority groups pose to the racial majority. As Jacobs (1979, p. 913) explained, "[C]onflict theorists maintain that the control of crime and deviance proceeds in accord with the wishes of those with power who use this control to further their own narrow interests." For instance, conflict theorists have demonstrated strong relationships between the size of minority populations and police resources and expenditures (Jackson & Carroll, 1981), as well as the size of police forces (Jacobs, 1979).

Three primary variations of conflict theory have emerged, all of which affect police research: the racial threat thesis, the inequality thesis, and the racial disturbance thesis. The racial threat thesis, initially advanced by Blalock (1967) suggests that minority group threat increases with the size of the minority population. This relationship may be curvilinear; that is, threat increases until minority groups reach a certain level, beyond which it diminishes. Results historically demonstrated that relative strength of police forces in the early 1970s was positively impacted by the size of the jurisdiction's Black population. The inequality thesis, on the other hand, is a slightly different version of conflict theory that focuses primarily on economic inequalities in a community rather than on the presence of racial minorities as the source of the threat that generates such social control efforts as heightened policing. From this perspective, places where economic resources are substantially unequal are places where the advantaged have the resources and desire to defend them against those who do not. Additionally, since the police constitute the primary governmental institution responsible for "the coercive maintenance of stability and order," enhanced police strength may be expected in areas where greater economic inequality is found (Jacobs, 1979, p. 914). Finally, the racial disturbance thesis asserts that potential threats influenced by minority group mobilizations, such as significant racial uprisings or riots, may directly affect the amount of resources devoted to policing. It is this facet of conflict theory that has been the least empirically supported in the literature (Jackson & Carroll, 1981; Sharp, 2006).

Overview: Research on Conflict Theory and the Police

Rational Choice and Conflict

Holmes, Smith, Freng, and Munoz (2008) provided an empirical analysis of police department expenditures and size, drawing on conflict and rational choice perspectives to construct contrasting hypotheses. The strengths of their analysis are that it comparatively analyzes two important and competing theoretical traditions and that it recognizes that the specification of minority group—in this case, Latinos—requires a greater degree of specificity than is usually given.

Rational choice theory maintains that resources are distributed in accordance with the *need* for crime control. Conflict theory counters that resources are allocated with the aim of controlling racial and ethnic minorities. In other words, for rational theorists, the police are the principle agents of action, whereas for conflict theorists, the police serve as the principal agents of domestic coercion (Bittner, 1970), and resource allocations to police departments largely determine the crime-control capacity of states (Liska, 1992). From rational choice, then, the distribution of resources to policing is tied to community crime rates. The central focus of the minority threat perspective, on the other hand, looks at distribution in terms of *percent minority* (most often White to Black).

The authors noted that the effects of minority threat "may depend on factors such as region and the degree of racial and ethnic tension" (Holmes et al., 2008, p. 137). Previous research on the Hispanic minority threat has found that percent Hispanic is related positively and strongly to the incidence of civil rights criminal complaints of police brutality in large southwestern cities. Additionally, it has been found that the dominant group, whose anxieties are fueled by media portrayals and political rhetoric, would marshal their superior political power to ensure allocations of public resources to policing. From conflict theory, then, Holmes et al. (2008) hypothesized that the perceived threat potential of Hispanics in the Southwest should result in greater allocations of fiscal and personnel resources to policing in southwestern cities with relatively large and relatively poor Hispanic populations, particularly those close to the border with Mexico.

The key contribution of this study's analysis, beyond providing support for conflict perspectives, is the identification of within-group class distinctions as potentially more important indicators of minority threat, at least in the Southwest, than percent Hispanic. Allocations of police resources appear to be tied to the presence of poor Hispanics on both sides of the border, pointing to the relevance of the intersection of class and ethnicity to public policy decisions in the region.

Agency Size and Race Conflict

Sharp (2006) presented hypotheses from racial threat, inequality, and racial disturbance theses to assess the growth of police organizations. It is a creative use of conflict theory to assess police organizational size, more typically studied in contingency theories of the police. The author particularly focuses on the historical legacy of police-force growth in the 1960s to 1970s era of racial turmoil and the playing out of racial threat dynamics in that era. The latter may have led to a shift in the base levels of department size.

Findings indicate the following:

1. The baseline or legacy effect of the department's relative force size as of 1980 appeared consistently to be the most important predictor of contemporary organizational size.

2. A city's more contemporary experience with racial disturbances is consistently the next most important predictor of contemporary force size (in other words, more significant than the legacy effect).

3. Although the racial threat thesis is unsupported when it is assessed in terms of the prevalence of Blacks in the population, there is evidence for this thesis when all minority groups are included in the analysis.

Findings suggest that contemporary racial threat and racial insurgency, more than historical and legacy influences, are the key predictors of enhanced contemporary police strength (i.e., cities that encountered recent race riots, from 1980 to 2000). This alone, we acknowledge, does not explain the actual processes by which local policy makers react to race riots; a qualitative, case-study approach is needed to possibly uncover what she described as the "veiled discourse" (Sharp, 2006, p. 303) that may be at play. She also argued that future research needs to focus on minorities more broadly and move away from the White or non-Black versus Black dichotomies that have historically been analyzed.

The staffing of U.S. police agencies, the author concluded, appears to be an artifact of the "social control phenomenon of subduing a population perceived to be rebellious" (Sharp, 2006, p. 305). This research also showed that crime rates, though most often studied in terms of functionalism, could be incorporated into conflict perspectives. That is, police-force size is an important part of the material frequently shaped and used by public officials in marketing the fear of crime (see Chambliss, 1999).

Drug Arrests and Conflict

Mosher (2001) argued that "spatial differences in rates of drug arrests are particularly relevant to the central tenets of conflict theory" (p. 88). Narcotics legislation in the United States, he noted, has been used to control minority populations, especially since the intensity of the war on drugs increased in the 1980s. He also points out that social disorganization and conflict theories posit that numerous measures of inequality will be related to higher drug arrest rates. Social disorganization, however, generally predicts that the effect of a population's ethnic and racial composition is mediated through structural indicators of the relative disadvantage of minority groups when compared to Whites. Contrarily, conflict theory (especially the variation focused on minority threat—e.g., Blalock, 1967) predicts that racial and ethnic composition will have an independent positive effect on drug arrest rates that will hold true even when relative economic disadvantage is controlled for. Finally, conflict theory predicts that police strength would exert a strong independent effect on the drug-arrest rate across cities.

Mosher (2001) found that percent African American is a statistically significant predictor of variation in possession arrest rates across cities, even when race-specific economic deprivation is controlled for. And when he looked at trafficking arrests, he found that percentage African American was the strongest predictor of arrest rates. Additionally, cities with more police per square mile had higher trafficking arrest rates. In sum, Mosher's findings provide strong support for the predictions developed from conflict theory.

Conflict and Racial Profiling

One of the more controversial issues in the current era is racial profiling, which refers to the perception that police make decisions to act based on the race of an individual. Petrocelli, Piquero, and Smith (2003) carried out microlevel analysis of police practices using census tract data from a single city to examine how neighborhood context may influence police behavior. This research examined the extent to which police stop, search, and arrest decisions are a function of neighborhood demographic and socioeconomic characteristics, in this particular city. Findings indicated that the percentage of population that was African American was significantly related to the percent of stops resulting in a search, and this was especially the case in Black neighborhoods. In addition, the number of police stops were significantly higher in neighborhoods with higher rates of Part I crime. Notably, however, in areas where a higher percentage of the population was Black, the chance of stops involving at least one arrest and summons is lower. Similarly, in high crime-rate areas, the chance of stops involving at least one arrest and summons is lower.

These findings suggest a *hurdle effect*. The likelihood of being stopped seems to be more a function of the crime rate in the area than of the demographic and/or socioeconomic characteristics. After the initial stop, however, searches appear to be more prevalent in neighborhoods with higher percentages of Black residents. They assert that this could be the result of one or two things: *ecological bias* (officer responses tied to neighborhood characteristics) or that officers are more likely to search African American residents based on general perceptions or stereotypes.

Hence, although they support a race effect, the findings overall do not tend to support a conflict explanation. Such an explanation would hold that officers are more likely to profile poor, minority areas and to make more stops in such areas. Instead, the crime rate appears to be a more important factor in the decision to stop.

Conflict and Communicative Action

Schneider's (1999) research study is based in grounded theory and looks at conflict and communication among residents of Vancouver, British Columbia (as cited in Maguire & Okada, 2011, p. 210). This study represents an effort to look at Habermas's ideas of communicative action as a recipe for conflicts between the police and community groups. Schneider argued that police officers, despite their advocacy of community policing, might be undermining their policing programs through communication problems with residents of socially disadvantaged neighborhoods (SDNs). Schneider's definition of communication is broad, ranging from interpersonal, verbal, or nonverbal personal communications to mass communication such as the promotion of a crime-prevention program by a police department.

Schneider (1999) found that police officers in this jurisdiction engaged in "unilingual" communication, demonstrated a limited range of understanding of different cultures, showed a lack of empathy with special needs groups, and overused offensive or overtly authoritative technical jargon. These communication practices perpetuated "the ongoing asymmetrical power relations" (p. 354) between the police and residents of these neighborhoods, ultimately undermining community policing efforts. Community policing programs, Schneider suggested, typically began with the broad assumption that society was pluralistic and that all communities had similar problems, needs, and access to political and economic resources. That assumption resulted in a law enforcement mind-set that approached crime prevention and community policing programs with a language geared toward "stable, ethnically homogeneous (i.e., white) middle and upper income neighborhoods" (p. 362). In SDNs, however, this type of approach inevitably failed to address the unique, specific needs and demands of poorer, less empowered neighborhoods.

Schneider (1999) concluded that community oriented policing (COP) principles and practices required a revised theoretical framework oriented toward (a) reducing power relations between the police and SDNs and (b) avoiding the technical, authoritative approaches characteristic of community policing. A more effective approach would be an "affective-emotional model that places community safety in the broader context of community and social development" (p. 362), rather than the rational, detached, and objective approach typically followed in contemporary law enforcement. The adoption of Habermas's theory of communicative action would facilitate "undistorted communication as a means to reduce asymmetrical power relations between social groups, address[ing] the epistemological weaknesses inherent in liberal community policing theory" (Schneider, 1999, p. 362; see also Forester, 1989, 1993). Shifts in the power differential between SDNs and the police, however, will not be accomplished by improving communication alone. An effective critical approach of community policing must include contributions to the social, economic, and political development of SDNs, as well as sharing of control of crime-prevention decision making and resources with SDNs by law enforcement agents.

POSTMODERNISM

Postmodernism carries several meanings, one as a philosophy that rejects modernism and postmodernism as a time period. It is also sometimes called late modernity. Postmodernism can represent the rejection of modernism or the fulfillment of it, depending on whom one reads and the perspective being advanced.

The Philosophy of Postmodernism

Postmodern theory, which gained prominence in the mid-1970s, is sometimes located under the umbrella of critical theory. However, though postmodernism continues to look at social class as one of the major causes of crime, it adds other dimensions of inequality, such as race and gender, which together are linked as the conditions of crime. Like critical criminology, postmodernism is less a theory of crime causation than an attempt to develop a more profound policy response to or deeper understanding of the causes of crime. In addition, postmodernism is interested in how structured inequalities (social class, race and ethnicity, and gender) contribute to and are reinforced by a culture that makes these divisions seem real. These social divisions, while faced as real and substantive, are socially constructed and, if subjected to critical analysis, can be deconstructed or dissolved (Lanier & Henry, 1998).

Postmodernism as a philosophy looks at the symbolic, everyday, and formal uses of language that underpin the socially constructed nature of various societies' rules, norms, and values. These languages represent discourses and are central to what is defined as criminal and to the way in which society is a source of crime (Lanier & Henry, 1998). Consequently, postmodernism highlights the significance of language and signs in the arena of crime and criminal justice and offers a source of concepts that capture elements of an emerging reality in the new context and set of conditions in which crime occurs, the current postmodern period (Schwartz & Friedrichs, 1994).

Postmodernism is often questioned for its failure to provide answers to the questions it raises. Yet that expectation reveals a misunderstanding of much of postmodernism. One can look at the brooding works of Cesar Vallejo and Jean-Paul Sartre—who are not normally considered postmodernists—and see a great deal of postmodernism in their dark existentialism. Postmodernism is a rejection—once discourse is shattered, it is unclear that anything remains underneath. Take away the meaning of a word, and sometimes all that is left is the jarring sound of mismatched consonants, conveying nothing. Only the most optimistic wing of postmodernism sees qualities of the human condition that somehow prevail with the deconstruction of the taken for granted.

Postmodernism as Historical Epoch

As explained by postmodern theorist T. R. Young (1997), premodern understanding of law and justice was based on the idea of "natural" laws given by God. The existing social hierarchy and its corresponding system of rights and privileges were right and proper, natural. Modernism, carried in Enlightenment ideals, replaced the good of God with the good of the individual. The American justice system, for example, was founded upon a statement of natural law in its Declaration of Independence, which moved the basis of lawmaking from the gods and/or nature to human beings acting in democratic concert. The priest was replaced by the research scientist, and modern criminology pays homage to the data gatherer rather than to the scriptural message. Postmodernism represents the dismantling or rejection of modern discourses. The legacy of modernism and its vanities of progress, far from being a democratic peace, is the firebombing of Dresden and the annihilation of the citizens of Hiroshima in thermonuclear fire.

Some writers recognize the interplay between both the philosophy and the historical sweep of postmodernism. In this regard, T. R. Young noted,

Whereas modern science privileges objectivity, rationality, power, control, inequality, and hierarchy, postmodernists deconstruct each theory and each social practice by locating it in its larger socio-historical context in order to reveal that human hand and the group interests which shape the course of self-understanding. (Young, 1995, pp. 578–579)

Police and Postmodernism

Postmodernism literature on the police tends to view them in terms of adaptation to a postmodernist landscape. Whereas in the modern period, policing was dictated by a militaristic, hierarchical, technical-rational, bureaucratic model of authority, in the postmodern (sometimes called the late-modern) era, the role of the police is seen as more fluid and multilateral. Policing becomes much more complex, characterized by (a) the fragmentation of values and moralities; (b) globalization; (c) a rise in consumerism, including private policing; (d) a hollowing out of the nation-state (Reiner, 1992; Sheptycki, 1995); (e) the emergence of a "risk society" (see, for example, Beck, 1986/1992; DeLint, 1999); and (f) adaptive risk-based policing strategies (see Ericson & Haggerty, 1997). One of the key implications for postmodern policing is the shift to a focus on discourse and mode of consumerism, where the community and community policing become coauthored in the same discourse (Reiner, 1992; see Clark, 2005).

Here, we recommend several papers. Waters (2007) discussed how the rhetoric of police reform is consistent with postmodern notions of discourse. Official discourse about police reform and policing developments, he argued, is overwhelmingly couched in terms consistent with postmodern discourse. Waters reviews the terminology of that discourse.

Sheptycki (2002) discussed contradictions between the modernist police setting and a postmodern one. The fragmented terrain of the policing field poses accountability problems not easily answered by the traditional model of constitutional control in a militaristic hierarchy.

Ericson and Haggerty (1997) focused on the communication systems that institutions develop to identify and manage risks and on how the police become involved in these systems. The police are seen as being in a complex, ambiguous, shifting, and contradictory field of risk management in relation to other institutions. This excellent work provides a sense of the fluid systems in which police find themselves and how they are adapting to those systems.

Manning and Singh (1997) focused on symbolic violence in the rhetoric of community policing. Using a case study of community policing in one western U.S. city, based on interviews with police, observations, and focus groups, they found that COP rhetoric is used as a public discourse. Yet the daily interdiction practices of patrol officers are relatively unchanged. Moreover, the absence of a crime-control emphasis alters public perceptions of the police while undercutting police morale.

Miller (2007) argued that data collection, the primary response to concerns over racial profiling, is ineffective, largely because it is driven primarily by police concerns about developing and maintaining the perception of responsiveness to public desires. That is, profiling is a symbolic response to public perceptions of crime and hence difficult to eradicate in view of contradictions between public and legal expectations of police behavior. Using Law Enforcement Management and Administrative Statistics, or LEMAS, data, Miller assessed the extent to which "antiracial profiling policies" are implemented.

CONCLUSION

Through this tour of police theory, one can see that police provide an amazingly colorful and richly detailed palette with which to paint a theory. They provide substantive analysis for policy theory, from institutions to individuals, and encompass us in the sweep of history. We have looked at only a few of the many writings on the police; we leave it to the reader to explore from here. There is much to enjoy on that journey—and an unfair share of pain and suffering as well. Of one thing you can be sure: You will be engaged in a study of people as they really are, sometimes without benefit of social custom and often layered in controversy, and in the end, you may learn much about yourself.

DISCUSSION QUESTIONS

1. What is police criminology? Is it scientific criminology?

2. What is institutional theory? Why is legitimacy central to understanding institutional theory?

3. Are the police shifting from the community policing model to a different model, to neoprofessionalism? Justify your answer from the book and from personal experience.

4. According to this chapter, what is the relationship between race and the police?

5. What is the link between conflict theory and profiling?

6. Identify three implications of postmodernism for the police.

REFERENCES

Beck, U. (1992). *Risk society: Toward a new modernity* (M. Ritter, Trans.). Newbury Park, CA: SAGE. (Original work published 1986)

Bittner, E. (1970). *The functions of police in modern society.* Washington, DC: Government Printing Office.

Blalock, H. (1967). *Toward a theory of minority group relations.* New York, NY: Wiley.

Chambliss, W. J. (1999). *Power, politics, and crime.* Boulder, CO: Westview.

Clark, M. (2005). The importance of a new philosophy to the postmodern policing environment. *Policing, 28*(4), 642–653.

Crank, J. (2003). *Understanding police culture* (2nd ed.). Cincinnati, OH: Anderson Press.

Crank, J., & Langworthy, R. (1996). Fragmented centralization and the organization of the police. *Police and Society, 6,* 213–229.

Crank, J. P. (1994). Watchman and community: Myth and institutionalization in policing. *Law and Society Review, 28*(2), 325–351.

Crank, J. P., & Langworthy, R. H. (1992). An institutional perspective of policing. *The Journal of Criminal Law and Criminology, 83,* 338–363.

Cronin, J., Murphy, G., Spahr, L., Toliver, J., & Weger, R. (2007). *Promoting effective homicide investigations.* Washington, DC: Office of COPS, Police Executive Research Forum.

DeLint, W. (1999). A postmodern turn in policing: Policing as pastiche? *International Journal of the Sociology of Law, 27*(2), 127–152.

DiMaggio, P., & Powell, W. W. (1983). The iron cage revisited: Institutionalized isomorphism and collective rationality in organizational fields. *American Sociological Review, 48,* 147–160.

Donaldson, L. (2001). *The contingency theory of organizations.* Thousand Oaks, CA: SAGE.

Ericson, R., & Haggerty, K. (1997). *Policing the risk society.* Oxford, United Kingdom: Clarendon Press.

Forester, J. (1989). *Planning in the face of power.* Berkeley: University of California Press.

Forester, J. (1993). *Critical theory, public policy and planning practice: Toward a critical pragmatism.* Albany: State University of New York Press.

Giblin, M. (2006). Structural elaboration and institutional isomorphism: The case of crime analysis units. *Policing, 29*(4), 643–664.

Holmes, M. (2000). Minority threat and police brutality: Determinants of civil rights complaints in U.S. municipalities. *Criminology, 38*(2), 343–368.

Holmes, M., Smith, B. W., Freng, A. B., & Munoz, E. A. (2008). Minority threat, crime control, and police resources allocation in the southwestern United States. *Crime and Delinquency, 54*(1), 128–152.

Jackson, P., & Carroll, L. (1981). Race and the war on crime: The sociopolitical determinants of municipal police expenditures in 90 non-southern U.S. cities. *American Sociological Review, 46*(3), 290–305.

Jacobs, D. (1979). Inequality and police strength: Conflict theory and coercive control in metropolitan areas. *American Sociological Review, 44*(6), 913–925.

Katz, C. (2001). The establishment of a police gang movement: An examination of organizational and environmental factors. *Criminology, 39*(2), 37–74.

Klinger, D. (2004). Environment and organization: Reviving a perspective on the police. *Annals of the American Academy of Political and Social Science, 593*(1), 119–136.

Kuhns, J., Maguire, E., & Cox, S. (2007). Public safety concerns among law enforcement agencies in suburban and rural America. *Police Quarterly, 10*(4), 429–454.

Langworthy, R. H. (1986). *The structure of police organizations.* New York, NY: Praeger.

Lanier, M. M., & Henry, S. (1998). *Essential criminology.* Boulder, CO: Westview Press.

Liska, A. E. (1992). Introduction to the study of social control. In A. E. Liska (Ed.), *Social threat and social control* (pp. 1–32). Albany: State University of New York Press.

Liska, A. E., Chamlin, M., & Reed, M. (1985). Testing the economic production and conflict models of crime control. *Social Forces, 64*(1), 118–1238.

Maguire, E. (2003). *Organizational structure in American police agencies.* Albany: State University of New York Press.

Maguire, M., & Okada, D. (2011). *Critical issues in crime and justice: Thought, policy, and practice.* Thousand Oaks, CA: SAGE.

Manning, P. K., & Singh, M. P. (1997). Violence and hyperviolence: The rhetoric and practice of community policing. *Sociological Spectrum, 17*(3), 339–361.

Mastrofski, S. D., & Ritti, R. (1996). Police training and the effects of organization on drunk driving enforcement. *Justice Quarterly, 13*(2), 291–320.

Mastrofski, S. D., & Ritti, R. R. (2000). Making sense of community policing: A theoretical perspective. *Police Practice and Research, 1*(2), 183–210.

Mastrofski, S. D., Ritti, R. R., & Hoffmaster, D. (1987). Organizational determinants of police discretion: The case of drinking-driving. *Journal of Criminal Justice, 15*(5), 387–402.

Mastrofski, S. D., & Uchida, C. D. (1993). Transforming the police. *Journal of Research in Crime and Delinquency, 30*(3), 330–358.

McEwen, T. (1996). *National data collection on police use of force* (Joint publication with National Institute of Justice). Washington, DC: Office of Justice Programs.

Miller, K. (2007). Racial profiling and postmodern society: Police responsiveness, image maintenance, and the left flank of police legitimacy. *Journal of Contemporary Criminal Justice, 23*(3), 248–262.

Morabito, M. (2008). The adoption of police innovation: The role of the political environment. *Policing, 31*(3), 466–484.

Mosher, C. (2001). Predicting drug arrest rates: Conflict theory and social disorganization perspectives. *Crime and Delinquency, 47*(1), 84–104.

Petrocelli, M., Piquero, A. R., & Smith, M. R. (2003). Conflict theory and racial profiling: An empirical analysis of police traffic stop data. *Journal of Criminal Justice, 31*(1), 1–11.

Quinney, R. (1970). *The social reality of crime*. Boston, MA: Little Brown.

Reiner, R. (1992). Policing a postmodern society. *Modern Law Review, 55*(6), 761–781.

Ritti, R., & Mastrofski, S. (2002). *The institutionalization of community policing*. Unpublished manuscript.

Schneider, S. R. (1999). Overcoming barriers to communication between police and socially disadvantaged neighbourhoods. *Crime, Law & Social Change, 30*, 347–377.

Schwartz, M., & Friedrichs, D. (1994). Postmodern thought and criminological discontent: New metaphors for understanding violence. *Criminology, 32*(2), 221–246.

Scott, R. (1992). Unpacking institutional arguments. In W. Powell & P. DiMaggio (Eds.), *The new institutionalism in organizational analysis* (pp. 164–183). Chicago, IL: University of Chicago Press.

Sharp, E. B. (2006). Policing urban America: A new look at the politics of agency size. *Social Science Quarterly, 87*(2), 291–307.

Sheptycki, J. (1995). Transnational policing and the makings of a postmodern state. *British Journal of Criminology, 35*(4), 613–631.

Sheptycki, J. (2002). Accountability across the policing field: Toward a general cartography of accountability for postmodern policing. *Policing and Society, 12*(4), 323–338.

Sherman, L., Gottfredson, D., Mackensie, D., Eck, J., Reuter, P., Bushway, S., & the Members of the Graduate Program. (1997). *Preventing crime: What works, what doesn't, and what's promising*. Washington, DC: U.S. Department of Justice.

Stucky, T. (2005). Local politics and police strength. *Justice Quarterly, 22*(2), 139–169.

Turk, A. (1969). *Criminality and legal order*. Chicago, IL: Rand McNally

Uchida, C. D., Maguire, E., Parks, R., Mastrofski, S. E., & Solomon, S. (2002). *Implementing community policing: A view from the top* (Report to National Institute of Justice). Silver Spring, MD: 21st Century Solutions.

Vitale, A. (2005). Innovation and institutionalization: Factors in the development of "quality of life" policing in New York. *Policing and Society, 15*(2), 99–124.

Waters, I. (2007). Policing, modernity and postmodernity. *Policing and Society, 17*(3), 257–278.

Willis, J., Mastrofski, S., & Weisburd, D. (2007). Making sense of COMPSTAT: A theory-based analysis of organizational change in three police departments. *Law and Society Review, 41*(1), 147–178.

Wilson, J. (1968). *Varieties of police behavior.* Cambridge, MA: Harvard University Press.

Young, T. R. (1995). *The Red Feather dictionary of critical social science.* Boulder, CO: The Red Feather Institute.

Young, T. R. (1997). *A constitutive theory of justice: Architecture and content* (No. 004; Distributed as part of the Red Feather Institute Postmodern Criminology Series). Weidman, MI: The Red Feather Institute.

CHAPTER 18

Contemporary Police and Society

Gennaro F. Vito

INTRODUCTION

In this volume, you will read chapters on police history (Uchida, Chapter 16) and police theory (Crank et al., Chapter 17). My mission here is to examine present police practices, use them to predict what policing will focus upon in the future, and get you to think about what you may be doing in law enforcement. In order to accomplish these tasks, let us begin by describing the dominant innovations in police operations in recent years in order to see where we may be going.

Paradigms in Policing

A paradigm is defined as "a mental screen or cognitive filter through which information must pass before it can be integrated into human thought processes and behaviors" (More, Vito, & Walsh, 2012, p. 139). While paradigms explain and guide operations, they also can impede progress by limiting our ability to recognize and develop new ways of doing things by restraining our thought processes to existing methods that have proved to be successful in the past (Covey, 2004, p. 26; More et al., 2012). In recent years, there has been a paradigm shift in police operations—innovative changes in practice that have shaken traditional organizational methods and tactics.

THE BRITISH PARADIGM: BALANCING DEMOCRATIC PRINCIPLES AND THE MILITARY MODEL

For the most part, modern police agencies developed in the 18th and 19th centuries as a response to the rise of industrialized, urban societies. In large cities, policing could no longer be the responsibility of its citizens. Urban policing is largely a modern phenomenon that evolved to deal with urban crime and disorder. In 1829,

279

the Home Secretary, Sir Robert Peel, established and organized the first metropolitan police force in London. These actions were undertaken because of the passage of the Metropolitan Police Act—An Act for Improving the Police in and Near the Metropolis. There were 10 essential elements of "Peelian Reform" (Johnson, 1981, pp. 59–60):

1. The police must be stable, efficient, and organized along military lines. Their policies must be independent of social and political influence.

2. The police must be under governmental control. Their basic mission is to prevent crime. The only alternative is the use of military force and severe legal punishments.

3. The police must secure and maintain the respect of the public to effectively maintain law and order. The best way to achieve this goal is to provide impartial service to all members of the community regardless of their wealth or social standing. Public support makes the exercise of force unnecessary.

4. The police should be ready to protect and preserve life while sacrificing their own. The police are also members of the community and should act in its best interests. In a sense, the police are paid to perform tasks that are the duty of every member of the community.

5. The police must refrain from seeming to act as agents of revenge, usurping the powers of the judiciary, judging guilt and punishing the guilty.

6. Physical force should be used only as a last resort when persuasion, advice, and warning have failed to result in cooperation. When force is exercised, it should be the minimum degree that is necessary to maintain order.

7. The test of police efficiency is the absence of crime and disorder, not the visible evidence of police action in dealing with them.

8. The distribution of crime news is essential.

9. The deployment of police strength both by time and area is essential.

10. The securing and training of proper persons is at the root of efficiency.

These themes have greatly influenced the evolution of policing—especially the community policing paradigm. Many of them serve as guidelines today.

The London police were called "Bobbies" in reference to their founder. Peel introduced the idea that the main mission of the police was crime prevention through patrol. His officers occupied the streets and patrolled their beats. Unlike the watchmen they replaced, their visibility was designed to discourage law breaking through deterrence. Structured along military lines, these 1,000 officers wore uniforms but were unarmed. Their administrative structure was modeled after the military. Although ultimately responsible to the Home Secretary and Parliament, two administrative heads were in charge of the police force.

The first two police commissioners were Colonel Charles Rowan and Richard Mayne. Naturally, the greatest fear among the public was that the police would become a "secret police" that would be used to enforce political views. Therefore, it was crucial that the police obtained the support of the public. Rowan and Mayne insisted that the police force obtained its authority from the English Constitution and that their behavior was determined by rules of law (Uchida, 2010, p 18). This approach tied the police to accepted and firmly established societal institutions that ensured their acceptance (Klockars, 1985, p. 49). They also developed a strong administrative structure with centralized authority. In addition, police officers were selected, retained, and promoted on the basis of merit. In 1856, Parliament passed a law that permitted justices of the peace to form police forces.

The newly established police force soon ran into serious problems. There was a threefold turnover of the officer population. Dismissals for corruption and drinking on duty were common (Klockars, 1985, p. 42). Despite these initial difficulties, the London policing experiment was adopted across the country and on the continent. Their development also profoundly influenced the structure and nature of policing in America.

This review of the British police paradigm reveals several basic themes. To be effective in a democratic society, the police must represent society in all its segments. Policing began as a responsibility of citizens to keep the peace and respect the rights of others. Even when a police force is established, this responsibility cannot be shirked and simply passed on to government. In fact, Peel took pains to demonstrate that the police force was not an agency of the government and not a political force commanded by the party in power. To be accepted and effective, the police must be tied to the norms and institutions of the country. The police cannot fight crime without community aid and support. Ultimately, the police represent and are accountable to the people they serve.

While Peel's reforms led to development of a "professional" police force, they had a number of unintended consequences. The strong administrative structure and recognition of the police as specialized workers led to the cutting of the close community ties necessary to do the job. This image led to the feeling that only the police know how to do their job or at least the best way to do it. In addition to abuse of authority, the police face problems with corruption due to the nature of their work. Substance abuse (in this case alcohol) was related to many of the crimes that the police commonly dealt with. Despite these limitations, the development of British police forces greatly influenced how this institution was formed in the colonies.

Early American Police Paradigms

As in Britain, the key law enforcement agent in rural, colonial America was the county sheriff. The crux of the sheriff's job was tax collection, rather than law enforcement. Sheriffs were paid under a fee system for every arrest made or other action taken. Patrol was not a function of the sheriff. Instead, sheriffs responded to calls or complaints from the public when a crime occurred. Thus, the sheriff was a reactive force—responding only when called upon. They often used citizens to assist them but did not act upon their own.

However, there was one critical difference between England and colonial America. While Britain was an island, America was a vast landmass with an ever-present frontier. When the population was scattered, the sheriff's system of law enforcement was effective. When people began concentrating in towns and cities, the nature of policing had to adapt. In the 1600s, colonists adopted the constable and watch system from Britain. Again, the watch was considered to be the duty of every male citizen. The watch performed many functions such as reporting fires, raising the "hue and cry," and maintaining street lamps (Uchida, 2010, p. 18).

In 1631, Boston formed a night watch to protect its citizens. They were called the rattlewatch because they used rattles to communicate with each other and announce their presence (Germann, Day, & Gallati, 1978, p. 64). As in England, these watchmen proved unreliable and unpredictable as colonial Americans evaded their duty. In 1658, New York replaced the rattlewatch with eight paid watchmen. In 1693, the first uniformed police officer was appointed, and the mayor of New York selected a 12-man watch (Law Enforcement Assistance Administration [LEAA], 1976, p. 15).

On the frontier, vigilantes assumed control of crime duties. In Virginia, Charles Lynch led a band of men that took the law into their own hands against criminals, British sympathizers, and Indians. They were so notorious that unlawful hanging became known as lynching. In the Wild West, officials who interpreted the law in their own fashion were commonplace. Men such as Judge Roy Bean fought crime using their own methods (LEAA, 1976, p. 15). However, Western law enforcement took a more traditional form with the establishment of the Texas Rangers in 1840.

The Political Era Paradigm

Kelling and Moore (1988) offer a precise description of American police reform efforts across the centuries. A number of American cities developed police departments following the British system in the 1800s. Beginning with organized watches, cities like New York (1844), Chicago (1851), Cincinnati and New Orleans (1852), Philadelphia (1854), Boston (1855), Newark and Baltimore (1857), and Kansas City and St. Louis (1861) established formal law enforcement agencies to deal with the dual trends of urbanization and industrialization. Factory owners wanted temperance—sober workers to operate machinery. Urbanization promoted unrest by bringing together people from diverse class, ethnic, and racial backgrounds that resented each other. What was needed now was crime prevention and order maintenance. Watchmen and constables became obsolete (Johnson, 1981, p. 17).

Although American cities faced similar pressures to London's, they tended to copy the London Police force selectively, rather than literally. Both police departments attempted to maintain the support of the public—maintaining order under the rule of law. However, their officers were recruited and trained in different ways. London's police were carefully selected and trained, exercised little discretion, maintained strict discipline, and remained aloof from the public. Police in New York were selected from the masses and received only rudimentary training, exercised great discretion in enforcing the law, exhibited lax discipline, and were close to their fellow citizens. The "most notable carryover" from London was the adoption of the preventive patrol (Uchida, 2010, p. 21).

One of the major differences in the development of the police between Britain and the United States was the Americans' inability to remove the negative impact of political influence from policing. In New York (and other U.S. cities), local government controlled the police. Their membership, management, and organizational structure reflected the patterns of city politics and administration. As a political operative, the police officer owed his allegiance to the ward boss and the police captain that chose him. They were largely under the control of the ward bosses—a continuous source of corruption (Kelling & Stewart, 1981). Political domination was problematic. It controlled who was hired and undermined departmental discipline. New York State attempted to seize control of the department and run it through a board appointed by the governor. This system held for 13 years and was attempted by other states (Germann et al., 1978, p. 66; LEAA, 1976, p. 18). The passage of the Pendleton Act in 1833 ended the "spoils system" and led to civil service examinations to select police officers and other public servants. It was the first of several attempts to remove the hand of political influence from police forces.

Other difficulties hampered the development of the police. By the late 1800s, corruption was commonplace. The police were also routinely involved in gambling and the drug trade in large cities. Naturally, they failed to command respect. Badges and uniforms became targets for gangs of ruffians who routinely beat up officers (Germann et al., 1978, p. 66; LEAA, 1976, p. 18).

America became the land of opportunity for both legitimate and illegitimate enterprises. The cities created an environment that both promoted crime and made it more difficult to control. The size of cities made it impossible for the police to establish a presence on the streets to deter criminal behavior. Land use was specialized, and thousands of strangers were thrown into close contact with one another (Johnson, 1981, pp. 34–36). The police officer was alone on the street and left to solve problems alone. This lack of direct supervision led not only to corruption but also to misuse of deadly force, ignorance of the law, and direct contact with victims.

The Reform Era Paradigm

In the 1890s, a reform movement swept America. The Progressive movement sought to eliminate corruption and return government to the hands of the people. Its advocates believed in the power of the state to serve all its members. In policing, progressive reformers sought to eliminate the influence of political machines upon departments and end corruption. Civil service appointments and the establishment of a rational, bureaucratic, and military organizational structure would improve the efficiency and effectiveness of policing. Police administrative boards would isolate departments from the negative influences of politics. The introduction of technology would both improve the quality of police services and establish a line of supervision between the street cop and his supervisor. The aims were to centralize authority in the chief, provide better training, discipline, and selection. In short, policing would be "professionalized."

For example, the Wickersham Commission (1931) determined that police forces lacked the expertise and equipment to deal with large American cities. It concluded that Prohibition was unenforceable. Prohibition made corruption a continual threat and sponsored the rise of criminal organizations. It made a number of pronouncements on police administration. Officers should be hired on the basis of competence, including intelligence tests and physical requirements. It also advocated the formation of state police forces and bureaus of investigation. The commission noted that police officers needed both training and discipline to carry out their job (Uchida, 2010, p. 24).

Professionalism was viewed as the result of expertise and training that provided the ability to deal with a set of problems. It led to a redefinition of the primary mission of policing—crime fighting. This ideology also made organizational change a priority. Departments should have centralized bureaucratic authority and strict control over its members. Political influence should be minimized. Without it, reform would be impossible. Educational and physical standards should be coupled with effective training. In sum, policing should be seen as a profession that requires specialized knowledge (Johnson, 1981, pp. 67–71). The professional police department was one (a) where police officers were experts—the only ones who knew how to do their job, (b) that was autonomous from external influences—made its own rules and regulated their personnel, (c) that was administratively efficient—carried out its mandate through modern technology and businesslike practices (Uchida, 2010 p. 26). A cadre of police chiefs led this movement.

These law enforcement leaders included August Vollmer—the Chief of Police of Berkeley, California, from 1905 to 1932. He was the first to suggest that police officers should have college training and become well rounded. As a result, Vollmer helped develop the School of Criminology at the University of California at Berkeley in 1916 (LEAA, 1976, p. 22). He emphasized the application of "scientific management" to the police organization. His principles of criminal investigation, deployment of personnel, and crime prevention were widely emulated. In 1914, his entire patrol force was operating out of automobiles (Douthit, 1975, p. 121). By 1921, these police cars were outfitted with radios. He advocated the use of psychological testing to hire officers and promotion based upon the evaluation of objective measures of performance, such as clearance rate (by arrest) statistics. He also promoted the development of specialized police units (e.g., juvenile units). Vollmer felt that police officers should develop crime prevention programs that attack the social causes of crime since they had more direct contact with social problems than any other governmental agency. In sum, he promoted the ideal that police officers were professional crime fighters who enforced the criminal law (Kelling & Stewart, 1981).

A protégé of Vollmer, O. W. Wilson's ideas on the professional administration of police departments has influenced a generation of administrators and scholars. His career as a police chief began in Fullerton, California (1925), continued in Wichita,

Kansas (1928—1935), and culminated as superintendent of the Chicago Police Department (1960—1967). In the academic world, he was a professor and dean of the University of California's School of Criminology at Berkeley from 1939 to 1960.

He believed that scientific principles of management could be applied to police departments, and he applied them to such problems as manpower deployment, crime analysis, and the functional division of the department (Carte & Carte, 1977, p. 213). Recognizing that organizational principles could be applied to policing, Wilson tied organizational theory, personnel administration, and technology to police work. Wilson believed that the police officer was subject to efficient and centralized control. For this reason, he sponsored the development of motorized (rather than foot) patrol with single-man squad cars, and improved methods of communication, such as the radio dispatch of police calls. These methods were central to Wilson's belief that the police could establish crime control through preventive patrol. Their dominant presence on the streets of the city would be a deterrent to crime.

J. Edgar Hoover, the director of the Federal Bureau of Investigation (FBI), introduced several innovations to law enforcement. He emphasized the scientific investigation of crime, the creation of the federal crime laboratory (1932), and the use of fingerprint technology in crime analysis. He raised the eligibility standards of his agents and founded the FBI National Academy in 1935 to train officers from local police departments around the country. In addition, he established the Uniform Crime Reports (UCR) as the dominant source of information about crime and the National Crime Information Center (NCIC)—a computerized record bank of offenders and offenses that could be accessed by police agencies across the country. Although his long tenure led to abuses of power and authority, particularly in the area of surveillance of citizens, Hoover's early reforms were clear examples of "enlightened, progressive law enforcement administration" (Murphy, 1977, p. 263).

The "reform era" sponsored by these leaders of the professionalism movement had many consequences (Kelling & Moore, 1988). Together, reformers and progressives wrestled the control of police departments from ward politicians. Leaders like Vollmer brought scientific principles of management to police departments in the deployment of forces, techniques of investigation, and crime prevention. Personnel were screened and hired only after they had successfully completed a battery of psychological tests. Promotion was based upon ratings achieved through the use of such objective measures as crime, arrest, and clearance rate statistics. Management authority was centralized and police services were tailored to meet specific functions (e.g., juvenile units). Together with the bureaucratic command structure, civil service examinations isolated departments from the corrupting influence of politicians.

Technology also made a significant impact upon police operations. Motorized patrol connected officers to their supervisors and simultaneously separated them from the improper influence of citizens and politicians. The telephone and the two-way radio made it possible for the police to respond to citizens without direct contact with them. Such technology "represented mobility, power, conspicuous presence, control of officers, and professional distance from citizens" (Kelling & Moore, 1988, p. 8).

The police rallied around their new, carefully crafted image of professional crime fighters—the impartial enforcers of the criminal law. This "thin blue line" metaphor was acceptable to the public and attractive to their peers. From 1940 to 1960, police executives built and maintained strong boundaries around their departments. Yet the creation of such "closed systems" had unintended, negative consequences as well. The community was not just a potential source of corruption. It was also the source of police legitimacy. The police became separated from the very people they were supposed to serve. This isolation led to difficulties with communities that still affect policing.

Throughout this period, the idea of professionalization became the dominant rationale in police departments. By the end of the 1930s, the central features of modern American police administration had taken shape. Police organizations conformed to a single model: large bureaucratic structures organized along hierarchical, quasi-military lines. For the rank and file, police work was a life-long career and the officers themselves were increasingly drawn into a tight-knit subculture. Almost no new ideas or techniques were introduced in police administration from the 1940s through the mid-1960s. The national crisis over the role of the police that erupted in the 1960s, then, was a direct consequence of several decades of police reform. As Walker states, the history of the police professionalization movement sheds new light on the origins of our contemporary police problems (Walker, 1977).

Minorities and the Police

By its very nature, the history of policing in America must consider the relationship between the police and minority groups. Here, we will focus on African Americans. Indeed, slavery, segregation, and racism have affected the development of police departments (Williams & Murphy, 1990, p. 1). As agents of the state, the police were charged with the enforcement of laws that were wholly discriminatory and were eventually recognized as unconstitutional. As a result, the police in America have been alienated from minority groups.

Although police in the South emerged from night watchmen, the history of policing in the South was much different from in the North (Curry, 1974, p. 53). Police in the South were typically organized along military lines. The controls placed upon private behavior led to the creation of a "new kind of police—consolidated, specialized, with a public mandate to enforce the laws, uphold certain standards of morality, and to ensure the security of persons and property" (Jordan, 1979, p. 123). For example, police in Charleston, South Carolina, evolved from the "city guard." This quasi-military force was founded on the notion that Blacks were "domestic enemies" who had to be kept constantly under surveillance and subordinate. The perception was "that Negroes could be awed into tractability by military display" (Jordan, 1979, p. 123). Often, these "slave patrols" were instruments of oppression, designed to prevent slaves from running away. They had the authority to track down and punish runaway slaves with impunity. Reichel (1977) noted that these patrols were common in the South and represented a "transitional" force led by citizens before cities developed professional police departments.

The repression of African Americans did not cease with the Civil War. In response to the abolition of slavery, Southern states passed legislation to suppress free Blacks. To defend their slave property interests, individual states passed the Slave Codes, a notion of the African slave as property that was later reinforced [by] the U.S. Supreme Court in the Dred Scott decision (Barlow & Barlow, 2000). Despite specific legislation and several constitutional amendments, the legal status of African Americans was less than that of their White counterparts. The U.S. Supreme Court declared civil rights legislation unconstitutional and upheld laws that established segregation. For example, in the case of *Plessy v. Ferguson* (1896), the Court supported a Louisiana railroad law that required "separate but equal" accommodations for African and Euro-Americans. This decision led to the passage of "Jim Crow" laws that set up separate facilities for African Americans in all arenas of public life, including education and public facilities of all types (Mann, 1993, p. 124). Of course, the police were charged with the enforcement of these laws.

Thus, the history of policing is one of alienation from minority communities. The police were viewed as the agents of a tyrannical system of racism and injustice. As Mann (1993, p. 165) said, this is an *indelible impression,* rooted in a long and bloody history of minority oppression. As a result, police departments now find it difficult to find and develop the level of support necessary to institute reforms (like community policing) in urban areas. Despite official measures to eliminate police brutality, resentment still exists.

Throughout the 1960s and 1970s, the public and the police were brought into conflict under the civil rights and anti-Vietnam War movements. As a result, the professional model of policing was questioned for several reasons. First of all, the police failed to meet the promise of crime control and prevention. Crime rose dramatically during the 1960s. Accordingly, the fear of crime also soared. Citizens abandoned parks, public transportation, and ultimately fled cities for the suburbs.

Racial and ethnic minorities felt that the police discriminated against them and made them the target of deadly force. Riots erupted in minority communities: New York City (1964), Los Angeles (1965), Detroit (1967), and Miami and Newark (1968). As a result, President Lyndon B. Johnson established the National Advisory Commission on Civil Disorders (The Kerner Commission) to investigate the causes of these disturbances. This commission uncovered several problems in police-community relations: (a) police conduct included brutality, harassment, and abuse of power against minorities; (b) training and supervision were inadequate; (c) police-community relations were poor; and (d) the employment of Black police officers lagged behind the growth of the population. The "disconnected, impersonal style" dictated by the professional model help create these problems (Uchida, 2010, pp. 29–30).

The civil rights and anti-war movements challenged the legitimacy of the police. A national television audience watched as students and minorities physically confronted the police and were shocked at what they saw (e.g., the "police riot" at the National Democratic Convention in Chicago, 1968). The use of force against the public, coupled with mass arrests, gave credence to the belief that the police were agents of repression.

Internal weaknesses of the professional model were exposed. Research revealed that the use of discretion characterized policing at all levels and that law enforcement activity was only a small part of the police officer's job. These conclusions ran counter to conventional wisdom about policing and attacked the basis of such bulwarks as preventive patrol and rapid response to calls from citizens (Kelling & Stewart, 1981, p. 15). The model also failed to rally line officers who were treated as "grunts" rather than professionals in the department. As a result of their low status, their work was routinized, standardized, and governed by rules aimed at their personal appearance and off-duty behavior. They were given few opportunities to make suggestions about their work and how it should be conducted. Clearly, the hierarchy failed to promote officers who thought for themselves. Instead, the organizational atmosphere fostered the creation of a police subculture directed against citizens and their supervisors (Uchida, 2010, p. 30).

The police lost financial support with the fiscal crisis faced by the cities as departments were forced to do more with less. Competitors in the business of protecting the public arose in the form of private security and the community crime control movement (Johnston, 1992). Clearly, the reform strategy promoted by the professional model was unable to adjust to the changing social circumstances of the 1960s and 1970s.

Several remedies were attempted during this period. In 1967, President Johnson's Commission on Law Enforcement and the Administration of Justice stated that the police needed to develop closer relations with citizens in all communities. As a part of the "war on crime," President Johnson also sponsored the development of the Law Enforcement Assistance Administration (LEAA) to improve and support police departments through training and equipment. One element of this program, the Law Enforcement Education Program (LEEP), was designed to help send police officers to college in the hope that education would benefit departments. However, these reforms did not address the structural changes that the reform of the professional model would require.

The Community and Problem-Oriented Policing Paradigms (POP)

During the early 1980s, experts in policing began to look for solutions to these problems and issues. Research on foot patrol programs in Flint, Michigan, and other cities proved promising. The research results led to the conclusion that the police could not "solve" the crime problem or even manage it effectively without active involvement and support from the community. The basic argument was that the police must get out of their cars and spend more time in public spaces, confronting and assisting citizens with their private troubles instead of driving around in cars waiting for a radio call (Moore & Kelling, 1983, p. 65).

Such sentiments became the basis for community policing. This concept was defined as both a philosophy and an organizational strategy that allowed the police and community residents to work closely together in new ways to solve the problems of crime, fear of crime, physical and social disorder, and neighborhood decay. Law-abiding citizens deserve input into the police process. Solutions to contemporary community problems demand freeing both people and the police to explore creative, new ways to address neighborhood concerns beyond a narrow focus on individual crime incidents (Trojanowicz & Bucqueroux, 1990, p. xii).

Basically, community policing involves two interrelated concepts—problem solving and community involvement. Problem-solving policing focuses upon the identification of chronic incidents in the community (Goldstein, 1990). The concept aims at the elimination of the problem to halt the calls for service that surround it. This organizational strategy requires a partnership between the police and the people they serve. The community helps the police identify, prioritize, and solve problems. The aim is to improve the quality of life in the area through the introduction of strategies designed to enhance neighborhood safety.

Problem-solving and community policing are strategic concepts that seek to redefine the ends and the means of policing. Problem-solving policing directs police attention to the problems that cause incidents, rather than to the incidents themselves. Community policing emphasizes the establishment of working partnerships between police and communities to reduce crime and enhance security (Moore, 1992).

Specifically, problem-oriented policing requires officers and crime analysts to identify the underlying conditions that produce crime and disorder problems and that seek a thorough and detailed analysis of a problem before determining a possible long-term resolution to it that eventually does not involve arrests. POP stresses that greater decision-making freedom should be given to line officers and that evaluation of the outcome of a solution is required in order to determine its success. POP outlines the use of the scanning, analysis, response, assessment (SARA) model:

- Scanning: Identify recurring problems and how they affect community safety
- Analysis: Determine the causes of the problem
- Response: Seek out, select, and implement activities to solve the problem
- Assessment: Determine if the response was effective or identify new strategies

Thus, the use of evidence-based information to guide operations is the key component of this process.

An analysis of the effect of community policing on crime indicated that one jurisdiction registered a significant decline in the level of violent and property crimes in the area served by the program (Connell, Miggans, & McGloin, 2008). A similar study determined that community policing had an indirect effect on crime and that citizens' fear of crime and perceived quality of life were significant predictors of the level of citizens' satisfaction with police performance (Xu, Fiedler, & Flaming, 2005). Of course, these goals are a key part of the community policing paradigm—meeting the demands of citizens for police services and promoting feelings of safety in the community. The core idea of community policing encourages individual agencies to adapt it to meet the circumstances that they face.

The CompStat Paradigm

Developed and implemented by the New York City Police Commissioner William Bratton in 1994, CompStat is a goal-oriented, strategic management process that aims to control crime by holding police officials accountable for organizational performance. It has been recognized as a revolutionary police management paradigm (Henry, 2002; McDonald, 2002; Walsh, 2001).

CompStat was designed to enforce administrative responsibility to reduce the incidence of crime. Basically, it consists of a four-step process:

1. Accurate and timely intelligence: To reduce crime, you must know about it.

   - What type of crime is it (i.e., drug sales, robbery, burglary)?
   - Where crime is occurring (areas, types of location)?
   - When crime is happening (day of week, hour of day)?
   - Why crime is happening (motive, i.e., drug-related shootings)?

2. Rapid deployment: By providing weekly crime statistics, the CompStat process allows administrators to assess this intelligence. Commanders can then deploy their resources as rapidly as possible to address crime conditions.

3. Effective tactics: Focusing specific resources on specific problems.

4. Relentless follow-up and assessment: The first three steps are effective only if commanders constantly follow up on what is being done and assess their results. If results are not what they should be, something needs to change.

Operational managers are held accountable for addressing the crime and disorder issues and trends associated with the CompStat data for their areas. They are empowered to focus, manage, and direct their unit's problem-solving process. Traditional, community, and problem-oriented policing strategies are integral parts of their operational tactics. A principle objective of the CompStat process is not to just displace crime but also to reduce it and create a permanent change in the community. CompStat is not just about crime statistics but also crime control (Safir, 1997).

The underlying concept of CompStat is that police officers and police agencies can have a substantial positive impact on crime and quality of life problems facing the communities they serve if managed strategically. It presents police executives and managers with a new way of looking at police organizations and police activities. It is radically different from the accepted concepts and practices that have guided police administration through most of its existence, and it points to new methods and strategies similar to those used by business managers that police agencies can use to fulfill their mission (Henry, 2002). CompStat emphasizes the vital link between information, operational decision-making, and crime-control objectives (McDonald, 2002). However, as a management tool, its impact extends way beyond crime fighting and can be applied to any organizational setting. Its strength is that it is a management process that can adapt to constantly changing conditions.

Operational managers are held accountable for addressing the crime and disorder issues and trends associated with the CompStat data for their areas. Under CompStat, operational managers are empowered to focus, manage, and direct their unit's problem-solving process. Traditional, community, and problem-oriented policing strategies are integral parts of their operational tactics. A principle objective of the CompStat process is not to just displace crime but also to reduce it and create a permanent change in the community. CompStat is not just about crime statistics but also crime control (Safir, 1997).

An exhaustive analysis of the effectiveness of the CompStat program by Zimring (2012, p. 134) reveals that New York City experienced a decline in seven major crime categories (homicide, rape, robbery, assault, burglary, larceny, auto theft) that was greater than the nine other largest U.S. cities during the period 1990–2009). For these crimes, the average decline in New York was 63% during the 1990s and 45% after 2000 (Zimring, 2012, p. 139). Specifically, Zimring (2012) attributed this crime drop to the effective use of hot spots emphases and tactics—"the most important of these is a data driven crime mapping and control strategy management program with many of the elements of Compstat" (p. 147). The use of a CompStat system in the White Plains (New York) Police Department between 2002 and 2005 led to a 69% increase in arrests that resulted in a 32% decrease in crimes against the person and a 33% decrease in property crime. In addition, vehicle and traffic summonses rose by 81% although a 6.4% reduction in motor vehicle accidents occurred (despite an increase in traffic flow) (O'Connell & Straub, 2007, p. 19).

Other studies of CompStat have been less conclusive. In particular, the Committee to Review Research on Police Policy and Practices (2004, p. 185) noted in its literature review that the effectiveness of CompStat would be difficult to scientifically ascertain. Recent research on the impact of CompStat and its strategies in New York City have been mixed and qualified in its assessment of effectiveness (Rosenfeld & Fornango, 2014; Weisburd, Telep, & Lawton, 2014).

The Intelligence Led Policing Paradigm (ILP)

Another data driven information system to guide police operations is known as intelligence led policing (Ratcliffe, 2008). Basically, it is designed to target prolific and serious criminals to combat a specific crime problem and "triage out" most other crime from further investigation. It features the strategic use of surveillance and informants to make intelligence central to operational decision making. In sum, ILP is a managerial model of evidence-based, police resource allocation decisions through prioritization of problems. ILP components feature investigation to determine the existence and management of linked series of crime incidents (hot spots), the targeting of specific offenders, and the application of preventative measures to combat the crime problem.

Over the past decade, intelligence led policing activities have been implemented in several cities. David Kennedy (2011) and his colleagues have helped police departments in Boston, Cincinnati, and other cities create and evaluate programs designed to deter specific criminal activity (e.g., gang violence, drug markets) without alienating the law-abiding residents in those areas. This program, now operating under the name National Network for Safe Communities, was adopted effectively in Boston (Operation Ceasefire—the Boston "Miracle"), Minneapolis, Stockton (CA), Indianapolis, Memphis, New Haven, Portland (OR), Baltimore, High Point (NC), and Cincinnati. Consistent with the premises of deterrence theory, drug market thugs are viewed as rational actors who will respond to the threat of imminent punishment. They are scared and carry guns for protection. Thus, heavy enforcement is announced ahead of time, showing the offenders that they are under police surveillance and demonstrating the prison terms given to their convicted peers while asserting the necessity of punishment that is immediate and forthcoming (through the use of Federal enforcement and sentencing). It is a plan of "focused deterrence" on one problem—strictly aimed at stopping the violence associated with the illegal drug trade.

In Cincinnati, homicides declined almost 20% overall and 36% among Black males using handguns (University of Cincinnati Policing Institute, 2009). While previous crackdowns in Cincinnati had resulted in a backlash from law-abiding residents who felt harassed by police, this targeted crackdown was praised by community members. In High Point, North Carolina, an evaluation of the drug market policing strategy in that city found a statistically significant reduction in violent crime within the targeted neighborhoods compared to other High Point neighborhoods although the violent crime rate actually increased after the interventions were implemented (Corsaro, Hunt, Hipple, & McGarrell, 2012). Implemented in this fashion, ILP has the potential to disrupt, enforce, and prevent crime problems previously believed to be intractable.

The Smart Policing Initiative (SPI)

This initiative melds the methods of previous paradigms (POP, CompStat, and ILP) together by emphasizing the use of data analysis to effectively improve police operations and use of evaluation research to assess the effectiveness of innovative approaches. According to the SPI website (http://www.smartpolicinginitiative.com), the Bureau of Justice Assistance has sponsored a number of Smart Policing Initiatives (SPI) in several cities. These initiatives feature approaches based upon hot-spot policing and focused deterrence, offender-based strategies (Coldren, Huntoon, & Medaris, 2013, p. 281).

The hot-spot policing tactic is an example of the SPI paradigm. Research evidence on hot-spot policing has been positive. For example, a problem-oriented approach to convenience store crime in Glendale, Arizona, resulted in a 42% decrease in crime at targeted stores (White & Katz, 2013, p. 305). In Boston, Safe Street Teams identified and targeted hot spots of violent crime resulting in a 17% reduction in violent crimes—particularly robbery and aggravated assault (Braga & Schnell, 2013, p. 351). In Lowell, Massachusetts, the police indentified hot spots of property crime. Increased survellience of these areas resulted in decreases in motor vehicle theft

(61%), larceny (43% and 50%), and shoplifting (42% and 41%; Bond & Hajjar, 2013, pp. 332–333). The Los Angeles Police Department (LAPD) targeted repeat violent offenders and gang members (Operation LASER) in its Newton Division—a hot spot of gun and gang-related, violent crime. The removal of the targeted offenders resulted in a 5.2% decrease in gun crime per month in the hot-spot area (Uchida & Swatt, 2013, p. 297). Braga and Weisburd (2010, p. 4) offered empirical evidence that "police can control crime hot spots without simply displacing crime problems to other places" by utilizing problem-oriented policing and situational crime-prevention techniques to address the "dynamics, situations and characteristics" of the location. To effectively implement and manage a hot-spot policing program, they specifically recommend that police departments utilize a "Compstat-like account-ability system that puts a premium on problem oriented policing and community policing" (Braga & Weisburd, 2010, p. 243).

In sum, these SPI efforts have demonstrated that evidence-based strategies can effectively reduce crime in areas that have had long-term crime problems (Joyce, Ramsey, & Stewart, 2013, pp. 366–367).

CONCLUSION

This review of police operational paradigms leads to a number of conclusions con-cerning where we have been and where we are going. The original purposes of polic-ing outlined by Sir Robert Peel have never lost their significance. To effectively prevent crime, the police must be tied to the community in a true democratic fash-ion. The reforms of the professional model were designed to prevent police corrup-tion and promote police independence from political influence. However, the focus of the professional model had the intended results of isolating the police from the community and promoting methods of patrolling that proved ineffective in combat-ing crime. Recent police paradigms have attempted to prevent these problems by reestablishing the vital linkage between the police and the communities they serve. They also use information to promote the implementation of operational methods to address identified crime problems.

What do these strategies have in common, and how do they differ from past policing paradigms? First of all, they use information to guide operations and meet the true purpose of policing—to prevent crime. Second, they also follow up to eval-uate and assess the effectiveness of these operations to determine whether or not they have been effective and, if not, determine how to alter operations so they can improve. Third, they seek the support of and input from the community and recog-nize that citizens are in partnership with the police in crime prevention efforts. The police departments of the future will be open and information driven operations that are based upon community support.

The problem that remains is the same caution that Peel identified in the first place: The police must use unobtrusive and democratic methods of crime prevention that respect the rights of citizens and their autonomy. For example, the major force behind the implementation of CompStat, William Bratton, has been named police commissioner of New York City for the second time. Bratton also served as chief of the Los Angeles Police Department. Under his leadership, the LAPD met the requirements of a federal consent decree that was designed to repair the relationship between the department and its communities in light of the Rodney King episode and subsequent riots. Although New York City has enjoyed a reduction in crime rates since the CompStat implementation, the use of stop and frisk tactics by the police have been denounced by community leaders and declared unconstitutional by the courts. Bratton has now been called in to solve the same problem that he faced in Los Angeles—to rebuild the department's relationship with the public (Rashbaum & Goldstein, 2013). These new paradigms place an emphasis upon the development of effective crime prevention tactics. However, they must be accompanied by an ethos that is consistent with the requirements of democracy. To do otherwise is to invite the abuses of an authoritarian police state that is directly contrary to the founding values of our country.

DISCUSSION QUESTIONS

1. Review Peel's 10 principles of policing, select the one you believe is most important and defend your selection.

2. American policing followed the British paradigm but discuss the ways in which they differ?

3. What are the elements of the "professional model," and how did they reform American policing?

4. Compare and contrast the elements of the community and problem-oriented policing models. How are they similar and how are they different?

5. What are the elements of the CompStat model? What is their relationship to crime control?

6. How can developing hot spots help the police prevent crime?

REFERENCES

Barlow, D. E., & Barlow, M. E. (2000). *Police in a multicultural society: An American story.* Long Grove, IL: Waveland Press.

Bond, B. J., & Hajjar, L. M. (2013). Measuring congruence between property crime problems and response strategies. *Police Quarterly, 16*(3), 323–338.

Braga, A. A., & Schnell, C. (2013). Evaluating place-based policing strategies: Lessons learned from the smart policing initiative in Boston. *Police Quarterly, 16*(3), 338–356.

Braga, A. A., & Weisburd, D. L. (2010). *Policing problem places: Crime hot spots and effective prevention.* New York, NY: Oxford University Press.

Carte, G. E., & Carte, E. (1977). O. W. Wilson: Police theory in action. In P. J. Stead (Ed.), *Pioneers in policing* (pp. 207–218). Montclair, NJ: Patterson Smith.

Coldren, J. R., Huntoon, A., & Medaris, M. (2013). Introducing smart policing: Foundations, principles, and practice. *Police Quarterly, 16*(3), 275–286.

Committee to Review Research on Police Policy and Practices. (2004). *Fairness and effectiveness in policing: The evidence*. Washington, DC: The National Academies Press.

Connell, N., Miggans, K., & McGloin, J. (2008). Can a community policing initiative reduce serious crime? *Police Quarterly, 11*(2), 127–150.

Corsaro, N., Hunt, E., Hipple, N., & McGarrell, E. (2012). The impact of drug market pulling levers policing on neighborhood violence: An evaluation of the High Point drug market intervention. *Criminology and Public Policy, 11*(2), 167–199.

Covey, S. R. (2004). *The 8th habit*. New York, NY: The Free Press.

Curry, L. P. (1974). Urbanization and urbanism in the old South: A comparative view. *Journal of Southern History, 40*(1), 43–60.

Douthit, N. (1975, Summer). August Vollmer, Berkeley's first police chief, and the emergence of police professionalism. *California Historical Review, 54,* 101–124.

Germann, A., Day, F., & Gallati, R. (1978). *Introduction to law enforcement*. Springfield, IL: Charles C Thomas.

Goldstein, H. (1990). *Problem-oriented policing*. New York, NY: McGraw Hill.

Henry, W. (2002). *The Compstat paradigm: Management accountability in policing*. New York, NY: Looseleaf Press.

Johnson, D. R. (1981). *American law enforcement: A history*. St. Louis, MO: Forum Press.

Johnston, L. (1992). *The rebirth of private policing*. London, United Kingdom: Routledge.

Jordan, L. W. (1979). Police power and public safety in antebellum Charleston: The emergence of a new police, 1800–1860. In J. Censer, N. S. Steinert, A. McCandless, S. Hines, & G. Hopkins (Eds.), *South Atlantic urban studies* (Vol. 3, pp. 122–140). Columbia: University of South Carolina Press.

Joyce, N. M., Ramsey, C. H., & Stewart, J. K. (2013). Commentary on smart policing. *Police Quarterly, 16*(3), 358–368.

Kelling, G. L., & Stewart, J. K. (1981). The evolution of contemporary police management. In W. A. Geller (Ed.), *Local government police management* (pp. 3–19). Washington, DC: International City Management Association.

Kelling, G., & Moore, M. (1988). *The evolving strategy of policing*. Washington, DC: U.S. Department of Justice.

Kennedy, D. M. (2011). *Don't shoot: One man, a street fellowship and the end of violence in inner-city America*. New York, NY: Bloomsbury.

Klockars, C. B. (1985). *The idea of police*. Beverly Hills, CA: SAGE.

Law Enforcement Assistance Administration (LEAA). (1976). *Two hundred years of American criminal justice*. Washington, DC: U.S. Department of Justice.

Mann, C. R. (1993). *Unequal justice: A question of color*. Bloomington: Indiana University Press.

McDonald, P. P. (2002). *Managing police operations: Implementing the New York crime control model—CompStat*. Stamford, CT: Thomson.

Moore, M. H. (1992). Problem-solving and community policing. In M. Tonry & N. Morris (Eds.), *Modern policing* (pp. 99–158). Chicago, IL: University of Chicago Press.

Moore, M. H., & Kelling, G. L. (1983, Winter). To serve and protect—Learning from police history. *The Public Interest, 70,* 49–65.

More, H. W., Vito, G. F., & Walsh, W. F. (2012). *Organizational behavior and management in law enforcement*. Upper Saddle River, NJ: Prentice Hall.

Murphy, P. V. (1977). John Edgar Hoover: The federal influence in American policing. In P. J. Stead (Ed.), *Pioneers in policing* (pp. 255–263). Montclair, NJ: Patterson Smith.

O'Connell, P. E., & Straub, F. (2007). *Performance-based management for police organizations*. Long Grove, IL: Waveland Press.

Rashbaum, W. K., & Goldstein, J. (2013, December 16). Bratton is expected to reshape police to rebuild relationship with the public. *The New York Times*, pp. A1, A7.

Ratcliffe, J. (2008). *Intellgence led policing*. Portland, OR: Willan.

Reichel, P. L. (1977). Southern slave patrols as a transitional police type. *American Journal of Police*, 7(2), 51–77.

Rosenfeld, R., & Fornango, R. (2014). The impact of police stops on precinct robbery and burglary rates in New York City, 2003–2010. *Justice Quarterly*, 31(1), 96–122.

Safir, H. (1997, December). Goal-oriented community policing: The NYPD approach. *The Police Chief*, 71(12), 31–58.

Trojanowicz, R., & Bucqueroux, B. (1990). *Community policing: A contemporary perspective.* Cincinnati, OH: Anderson.

Uchida, C. D. (2010). The development of the American Police: An historical overview. In R. G. Dunham & G. P. Alpert (Eds.), *Critical issues in policing: Contemporary readings* (6th ed., pp. 17–36). Long Grove, Il: Waveland Press.

Uchida, C. D., & Swatt, M. L. (2013). Operation LASER and the effectiveness of hotspot patrol: A panel analysis. *Police Quarterly*, 16(3), 287–304.

University of Cincinnati Policing Institute. (2009). *Implementation of the Cincinnati Initiative to Reduce Violence (CIRV): Year 2 report.* Cincinnati OH: University of Cincinnati.

Walker, S. (1977). *A critical history of police reform: The emergence of professionalism.* Lexington, MA: D.C. Heath.

Walsh, W. (2001). Compstat: An analysis of an emerging police managerial paradigm. *Policing*, 24(3), 347–362.

Weisburd, D., Telep, C. W., & Lawton, B. A. (2014). Could innovations in policing have contributed to the New York City crime drop even in a period of declining police strength?: The case of stop, question and frisk as a policing strategy. *Justice Quarterly*, 31(1), 129–153.

White, M. D., & Katz, C. M. (2013). Policing convenience store crime: Lessons from the Glendale, Arizona Smart Policing Initiative. *Police Quarterly*, 16(3), 305–322.

Williams, H., & Murphy, P. V. (1990). *The evolving strategy of police: A minority view.* Washington, DC: U.S. Department of Justice.

Xu, Y., Fiedler, M., & Flaming, K. (2005). Discovering the impact of community policing: The broken windows thesis, collective efficacy, and citizen's judgment. *Journal of Research in Crime and Delinquency*, 42(2), 147–186.

Zimring, F. E. (2012). *The city that became safe: New York's lessons for urban crime and its control.* New York, NY: Oxford University Press.

CHAPTER 19

Police Organization and Administration

Thomas W. Nolan

There are 17,985 state and local law enforcement agencies in the United States employing over 765,000 police officers of various types: state and local police, sheriff's departments, agents of the federal government, constables and marshals, and special jurisdiction police (such as campus and tribal police). Seven percent of police agencies employ 100 or more officers, and these accounted for 64% of sworn personnel nationwide; almost half of all law enforcement agencies employ fewer than 10 officers. "Among these smaller agencies, about 2100 (12%) had just one full-time officer or part-time officers only" (Reaves, 2011, p. 2). Additionally, 73 federal law enforcement agencies employ an additional 120,000 full-time law enforcement officers who carry firearms and who have the authority to make arrests, bringing the total number of law enforcement officers in the United States to approximately 885,000 (Reaves, 2011, para. 1).

Contemporary observers have used the metaphors "juggernaut" (Gordon, 1990; Websdale, 2001) and "monolith" (Maguire, 2008; Morash, 2005) to describe the criminal justice system generally and policing in particular, and any examination of the ways that law enforcement organizations are organized and administered ought to be conducted through these insightful and illuminating prisms.

When considering the topics of the administration and organization of police and other law enforcement agencies in the 21st century, an enlightened and progressive inquiry and analysis will necessarily eschew the traditional emphasis on organizational charts and structures, the span of control, unity of command, line and staff functions, the deployment of field forces, and the various organizational theories of Weber, Hammer, Katz, Maslow, Herzberg, McGregor, and others. Of more critical import (and more informed insight) in understanding how police departments are actually organized and administered (formally and informally) will be an examination of the organizational culture (or subculture) of contemporary law enforcement agencies.

ORIGINS OF THE STRUCTURAL MODEL
OF POLICE ORGANIZATIONS

What virtually all law enforcement agencies share, from the 561 departments consisting of but one officer to the New York (City) Police Department (NYPD) with over 37,000 officers, is an organizational model that is quasi-military, hierarchical, and rigidly structured along clearly delineated lines of authority and responsibility. This categorizes the *formal,* prescribed, and public organization of the police. The question arises as to how the organizational structure that we see present in virtually all police organizations came to assume its form, as the inchoate nature of urban policing during its dawn in the mid-19th century saw little, if any, "uniformity" (literally and metaphorically). "Police were involved in social service activities: they ran soup kitchens, provided lodging for indigents, and spurred moral reform movements against cigarettes and alcohol . . . [they] were union busters and political-machine enforcers" (Pollock, 2007, p. 191). Not yet established in the nascent days of policing were military ranks, uniforms, badges of office, or even the issuance and carrying of firearms. It is suggested here that the hierarchical and quasi-military structure of contemporary law enforcement agencies arose out of expediency and necessity when police departments, in their earlier incarnations, were confronted with rioting, looting, and hooliganism on a scale that was hitherto unprecedented.

The only organizational model available to those mid-19th century police administrative neophytes was that of the military: Easily recognized and identified, rapidly deployed, operating under a strict chain-of-command and span of control, trained in teamwork and coordination, the military structure seemed readily adaptable to the unprecedented exigencies confounding emerging police departments in New York, Boston, Philadelphia, and elsewhere. In London, the Metropolitan Police Act of 1829 created a police department founded on a military model that eventually met with a degree of success; thus, this proved to be the form that would be emulated in the United States.

This quasi-military model of police organization has been, throughout its history, a somewhat uneasy (if not unholy) alliance of philosophical underpinnings and operational strategies and policies. The contemporary emphases on community policing and problem-oriented policing philosophies, for example, have often proved to be inimical and incompatible with this model of police organization. The military emphasis on absolute deference and obedience to authority, rote conformity to group norms, the use of force and violence to overcome resistance, and closely monitored and orchestrated teamwork are all squarely at odds with the realities, practices, and expectations of policing in the 21st century, particularly as they relate to community and problem-oriented policing principles. These philosophies and principles privilege and endorse decision making at the lowest levels of the organizational hierarchy—the street-level police officer—in clear contraindication to military practice. Community policing and problem-oriented policing also place responsibility for the identification and resolution of police-related issues squarely in the hands of the individual officer(s) assigned to a particular area or beat. The model of policing in operational practice in the United States today sees the vast majority of what the police actually engage in conducted not only out of the public eye but also absent any scrutiny, inspection, or observation from police supervisors or managers (and this is especially so in the ±3% of U.S. police departments that comprise but a single officer), again clearly contrary to the military model (U.S. Department of Justice, Office of Justice Programs, 2003).

POLICE ORGANIZATION: THE MILITARIZATION OF THE POLICE

What police departments have adopted from the military, at least in part, is its hierarchical organizational rank structure. Consider this modified adaptation: officers of rank in most American police departments are referred to as "corporal," "sergeant," "lieutenant," and "captain." Some of the more highly militarized departments (such as many state police agencies) use the higher military ranks, such as "major" or "colonel," but chief executive officers of police departments in the United States are never referred to as "general," as they are in other countries where the organizational boundaries between the military and the police are somewhat blurred. Executive officers of American police departments typically use the title "chief," and the Western referent to this appellation lies in the Native American conception of the leader of a tribe or clan. Police chiefs often attire themselves in conspicuous displays of the trappings and symbols of their office: the hat (headdress) adorned with braided gold oak leaves, the number of gold stars (despite size of department, usually equivalent to the second highest general/admiral rank), the gold shield, the embroidered epaulets, the velvet stripes—all serve to set the chief above and apart from his or her subordinates, not unlike their earlier historical counterparts who were tribal leaders (see more on the "tribe" referent in the police subculture section below).

The police have also adopted many of the organizational designations employed by the military: Squads, platoons, units, task forces, and even battalions and regiments are commonly used in police organizational charts to describe function, lines of authority and accountability, numbers of sworn officers, duties, hours of work, and other identifying and organizationally pertinent information.

A more recent adaptation of military argot describing police organizational tactics is manifested in the (now) ubiquitous use of the term *operation*. Consider Operation Community Shield (Immigration and Customs Enforcement targeting violent gangs), Operation Would You Like Fries (sheriffs undercover in fast-food restaurants to spot impaired drivers), Operation Homefront (police working with clergy and troubled youths), Operation CARE (police warning motorists about safety belts), and Operation Falcon (or Federal and Local Cops Organized Nationally; to round up 30,000 petty criminals). In fact, in Boston, Massachusetts, the police department recently launched an incursion into that city's inner-city neighborhoods dubbed Operation Rolling Thunder (see http://www.cityof boston.gov/news/Default.aspx?id=2621) without any apparent awareness that its military counterpart and predecessor consisted of the aerial bombardment and "carpet bombing" of North Vietnam by the U.S. Air Force beginning in 1965 (see http://en.wikipedia.org/wiki/Operation_Rolling_Thunder). Even more recently, police in South Carolina have launched their own version of Operation Rolling Thunder in a law enforcement sledgehammer operation involving 21 different agencies and over 80 police officers.

The metaphor of the modern era police chief leading warriors into battle against criminals, gangbangers, terrorists, and drug dealers is telling in its irony. For it is here that the military analogy gains the most traction, while at serious risk of running aground. At the turn of the 21st century, the police in America had largely been organized as the first wave of shock troops on the urban battlefield that too many of our cities had become. Klockars (2005) sees three compelling themes in this analogy:

> First . . . the military analogy sought to confer some honor and respect on the occupation of policing. Second, the idea of a war on crime struck a note of emergency [and] . . . a moral urgency and a rhetorical tone that was difficult to resist. . . . Third, the military analogy sought to establish a relationship between local politicians and police chiefs that was analogous to the relationship between elected executives at the national level and the general of the U.S. military. (pp. 445–446)

In this role, the police were seen by many as an army of oppression and occupation (particularly in inner-city communities of color), and in large part, the police themselves did little to discourage this perception. That no small number of police departments initiated policies of arming the police with assault rifles and dressing them in military battle-dress uniforms (BDUs) drove a wedge into solid gains that had been made under community policing and problem-oriented policing initiatives dating from the late 1980s. Community partnerships and coproduction initiatives that had been the hallmarks of community policing risked being scuttled as police departments reorganized themselves to meet what they perceived to be the law enforcement exigencies of the 21st century. Thus, the so-called wars on drugs (declared in 1984), gangs, terrorists, and the like, saw the police at the turn of the 21st century morph into a military monolith, or juggernaut, whose mission may seem somewhat conflicted when community policing's "three core elements: citizen involvement, problem solving, and decentralization" (Skogan, 2006, p. 28) square off against the more recent mandate to meet violent crime (particularly when it is gang or potentially *terror* related) with a formidable and well-organized display of force—"In the words of one officer: 'We kick ass'" (Wilson & Kelling, 1982, p. 34).

Oliver (2007) has dubbed the epoch of policing that followed the terrorist attacks on the World Trade Center towers on September 11, 2001, the *Homeland Security era*, an approach to policing in the 21st century essentially characterized as the end of the *community policing era*. Community policing saw police agencies organized by partnerships and problem-solving engagement with communities where decision making could be accomplished at the lowest levels of law enforcement agencies. Policing in the Homeland Security era is focused on crime and terrorism-related crackdowns, using rules of engagement more effectively utilized and conceptualized for implementation on the battlefield in a war zone than in the neighborhoods of our cities and, more increasingly, small towns and rural areas. By the second decade of the 21st century, policing imperatives that privileged weaponry, firepower, technology, and surveillance over partnerships, problem solving, and crime prevention had largely superseded community policing mandates.

In furtherance of the escalating militarization of law enforcement agencies in the United States, the Department of Defense, through its Domestic Preparedness Support Initiative (known as the 1033 Program), distributes billions of dollars worth of surplus military weapons, vehicles, aircraft, technology, and other equipment to state, county, local, and even university police departments. "Equipping state and local law enforcement with military weapons and vehicles, military tactical training, and actual military assistance to conduct traditional law enforcement erodes civil liberties and encourages increasingly aggressive policing, particularly in poor neighborhoods and communities of color," said Kara Dansky (2013), senior counsel for the American Civil Liberties Union's (ACLU's) Center for Justice.

POLICE ORGANIZATION: SUBCULTURE, ETHOS, AND MILIEU

While the formal organization of contemporary police organizations is characterized by a quasi-military hierarchical structure that is governed by formalized rules, policies, procedures, and practices, it is perhaps an articulation and understanding of the *subculture* of policing that provides a richer and more elaborate understanding of the police organization and its membership, one not formally recognized and one rarely understood by the public.

Police and their organizations have been characterized as being insular, isolated, hidebound, conservative, masculinist, morally superior, autonomous, authoritarian, cynical, and ethnocentric (among other things). That the police subculture is insular owes much to the nature of the expectations that society has of its police: The police are organized in a fashion that clearly delineates them from other members of the communities that they police through their distinctive uniforms, badges of office, conspicuously marked modes of transport, and their being openly (and somewhat heavily) armed. The police are expected to maintain order, to prevent the occurrence of crime, and to ensure the safety of the public (among other duties) and as a result develop a self-image of a crime fighter engaged in a "noble cause." Waddington (1999) observed that the police, in the performance of their duties, do not confront an "enemy, but fellow citizens and that makes their position acutely marginal. . . . It is why the police are so insular: they find social encounters with non-police friends, acquaintances, neighbours and others fraught with difficulty" (p. 298).

The police are isolated largely owing to the environment in which they work and the significant degree of discretion that they exercise:

> Police officers often work alone or in pairs . . . there is no direct supervision. Also, a majority of police-citizen encounters occur in private places, with no other observers present . . . for this reason, policing has been described as low-visibility work. (Walker & Katz, 2007, p. 362)

Thus, the means by which the police "work product" is organized contributes directly toward physically isolating officers from their constituent communities and indirectly toward perpetuating a tangible sense of isolation (within the context of the police subculture) that the police themselves experience.

The police subculture is hidebound in its resistance to change, and there is perhaps nowhere in recent evidence a more convincing example of this than the arguably abysmal results of community policing initiatives from the early 1990s to the present. Mastrofski (2006) attributed these failures to the organizational subculture of the police and observed that efforts to change what some observers have dubbed a "monolithic" police culture through community policing and other likeminded innovations are likely to "die on the vine" (p. 53) owing to skepticism on the part of rank-and-file officers who are extremely resistant to change. He also suggested that "police socialization processes" are what influence officer behavior and the police subculture far more than hiring practices that emphasize diversity and cultural change (p. 51). These socialization processes are the mechanisms that serve to perpetuate, validate, and privilege the status quo. That status quo endorses behavioral practices that vehemently resist changes to the organizational subculture that would alter promotional practices, access to desirable assignments, the marginalization of women and minority officers, the tolerance of violence and brutality, and practices that turn a blind eye to minor acts of graft, corruption, and deceit (Nolan, 2009).

The police endorse and validate a conservative worldview in the execution of their duties, and this conservatism is a cornerstone of the organizational subculture of policing. In an environment permeated in gray, the police are habituated to see black and white:

> The police tend to view their occupational world as comprised [*sic*] exhaustively of three types of citizens. These ideal types are: (1) "suspicious persons"—those whom the police have reason to believe may have committed a serious offense; (2) "assholes"—those who do not accept the police definition of the situation; and (3) "know nothings"—those who are not either of the first two categories but are not police and therefore, according to the police, cannot know what the police are about. (Van Maanen, 2005, p. 281)

The police thus construct these conceptual categories as cognitive shorthand to deal with the myriad and occasionally overwhelming banalities and crises into which they are constantly being submerged. Under community policing initiatives, police organizational practice "privileges the law abider who cares for his home, his lawn, and his children, and the neighborhood merchant" (Harcourt, 2001, p. 127). The police are organized around a conservative ethic that "embraces an unmediated aesthetic of order, cleanliness, and sobriety" (p. 135) and one in which the "order or rules of civilian conduct . . . are geared toward producing a more harmonious social environment with strong moral bonds" (p. 140). The police organize their experiential practice into maintaining a conservative social agenda that embraces conformity and adherence to a middle-class ethic of adherence to tacitly understood canons of behavior and comportment. They value patriotism, religious practice, loyalty, respect for tradition and authority, duty to family, and the unquestioned righteousness of the rule of law, while they share distrust of the media.

ORGANIZATION AND SUBCULTURE: INITIATION AND MASCULINISM

Masculinism is a social construct that "justifies and naturalizes male domination. As such, it is the ideology of patriarchy. It sanctions the political and dominant role of men in the public and private spheres" (Brittan, 2001, p. 53). The police subculture is, for the most part, created, maintained, and structurally organized by the men who establish the discourse, enforce the formal and informal rules, and who maintain and assign group and member roles: the leaders, the cadre, the plebeians, the novitiates, and the outsiders. Even though women have been mainstreamed into the ranks of the police since the latter decades of the 20th century, the latest available Crime in the United States figures show that of the 706,866 full-time sworn personnel in all local and county police departments in 2009, approximately 11% were women (U.S. Department of Justice, 2010, Table 74, p. 1).

The training that police officers receive at the intake level is indoctrinary and instills in the initiate the language, the behaviors, the symbols, and the rituals that will ensure effective adaptation and assimilation for the novice. Ritualistic forms of voice, gait, posture, demeanor, language, and dress are all prescriptive and representative of a certain form of tribal initiation. Likewise, the ritualistic assembly in the "roll call" is a highly masculinized throwback to a secret military convocation that dates to the Roman Legions (roll calls are organizational rituals where officers are inspected and given their assignments). Outsiders are never allowed to watch or participate in a roll call, except on extremely rare occasions that are completely staged for the intrusion. The officers hardly see these assemblies as sites for bonding and reinforcing the subculture of policing; that what is said at roll call stays in the "guard room" (as the assembly point is referred to) seems only natural.

Revisit the particular form of masculinism that presents itself in the military representations of rank and vertical hierarchy. As in the military, those higher up in the vertical scale of rank, those bearing or wearing gold stars and bars, are accorded the respect and attention that the efficient operation of this masculinist enterprise mandates. Beyond that, officers of rank are viewed with mistrust, suspicion, and resentment, and a different construction of hierarchy emerges among the plebeians. For example, *street cops* (those who work more hazardous patrol duty) are depicted in the subculture as more masculine than officers who work in clerical positions or guarding prisoners. Likewise, police officers who work in what is (perhaps inaccurately) characterized as more dangerous duty in inner-city neighborhoods (i.e., communities of color) are held in higher masculine esteem than officers who work in the relative tranquility of a suburban or downtown community (Nolan, 2009).

A long held (and equally misguided) subcultural stereotype would have those who perform the more glamorous functions associated with plainclothes and undercover police work as more masculine than officers who must perform their duties conspicuously and publicly in uniform. Officers assigned to uniform duty are "in the bag," a pejorative reference to being unable to conceal oneself from public view and to wear the fashionable clothes of a "made" detective or the street clothes of an undercover officer. Those who work in drug investigations are perceived as *more male* than those who work with sexual assault victims (who are largely female). What emerges thus is a fraternity of those engaged in what they perceive as duty fraught with danger, a battle against the underworld, replete with the bonding, the secrecy, the faux loyalty, and the war metaphors that have historically accompanied those identified with the organizational subculture of policing (Nolan, 2009).

In an earlier writing (Nolan, 2001) was a description of how certain highly masculinized police organizations (perhaps unwittingly) routinely objectified, degraded, and sexualized female officers in coercing them into posing as decoy prostitutes during sting operations targeting "johns." So culturally ingrained are many masculinized organizational practices in police departments that they are often hardly recognized as such, even by progressive administrators.

ORGANIZATIONAL SUBCULTURE AND MORAL SUPERIORITY

The police see their mission as organized around a trope that is imbued with a sense of moral superiority and one in which the police have designated themselves the arbiters of the right/wrong or good/bad-dichotomies. Through the police use of discretion, they often decide in context-specific situations whether or not to invoke the provisions of the criminal law based on their assessment of the level of moral "injury" or offense present in a particular situation. This is particularly true in drug, gambling, prostitution, and other nonviolent and victimless crimes. The police believe themselves to be

> perpetually engaged in a struggle with those who would disobey, disrupt, do harm, agitate, or otherwise upset the order of the regime. And, that as policemen, they and they alone are the most capable of sensing right from wrong; determining who is and who is not respectable; and, most critically deciding what is to be done about it (if anything). Such heroic self-perceptions regarding moral superiority have been noted by numerous social scientists concerned with the study of the police. (Van Maanen, 2005, pp. 280–281)

In fact during the last two decades, the vast majority of police organizational strategy and policy has been driven by community policing and problem-oriented policing strategies, the nexus of which has been Kelling and Wilson's so-called broken windows theory. Foundational to this "theory" that drove so much of police practice was that the police themselves "defined 'order,'" and they themselves identified it, and they decided who had violated local moral norms: "Not necessarily violent people, nor, necessarily criminals, but disreputable or obstreperous or unpredictable people: panhandlers, drunks, addicts, rowdy teenagers, prostitutes, loiterers, the mentally disturbed" (Kelling & Wilson, 1982, p. 29). Thus, the police have assumed for themselves the role of identifying morality and immorality and have organized their mission at the local level in an effort to enforce standards of good and bad behavior, as they understand it.

Ethnocentrism is "the tendency to reject and malign other ethnic groups and their members while glorifying one's own group and its members" (American Psychological Association [APA], 2007, p. 345). Several observers have seen police organizations as akin to such groups whose members have a strong identification with a common history, culture, belief system, means of communicating, shared values, worldview, and designation of "out groups." It is suggested here that the ways in which the police are formally and informally organized are reflective of *in-group bias:*

> the tendency to favor one's own group, its characteristics, and its products, particularly in reference to other groups. The favoring of the ingroup tends to be more pronounced than the rejection of the outgroup, but both become more pronounced during periods of intergroup contact. (APA, 2007, p. 481)

Gendreau (2006) and Andrews and Bonta (2006) have described *theoreticism* as "the practice [that] involves accepting or rejecting knowledge on the basis of one's personal values and experiences" and one that "is a critical problem in the criminal justice field" (Gendreau, 2006, p. 226). In organizations (such as the police) that are insular and dogmatic, theoreticism can be especially pernicious in guiding organizational practice at the street level and organizational policy and philosophy at the administrative level. Police organizations collectively and the police themselves are very often skeptical of outsiders (*assholes*) and of "knowledge" that does not originate within and conform to the police's worldview and experience (and this is particularly true of academics and scholarly research).

POLICE ORGANIZATION: AUTONOMY AND AUTHORITARIANISM

That police organizations conduct the vast majority of their day-to-day operations out of the public eye and with little (if any) oversight by or input from the communities they serve has become routinized and normative as American law enforcement enters the second decade of the 21st century. The police are typically neither licensed nor controlled by any government or professional regulatory entity outside of the agency itself, unlike lawyers, doctors, haircutters, masseuses, acupuncturists, or even tattoo artists. For the most part, police organizations operate almost completely autonomously. For example, it was recently uncovered that in Massachusetts "some 82 local police departments have obtained more than 1000 weapons over the last

15 years under a federal program that distributes surplus guns from the U.S. military" (Slack, 2009, p. 1 of 3, para. 2) The weapons ranged from M-16 assault rifles to M-79 grenade launchers, and they were acquired by university police departments and some departments with fewer than 10 officers. No input was sought from affected communities, and the proposal to equip 200 police officers in the Boston police department with the assault rifles was shelved after it was leaked to the news media and the public backlash made the proposal politically untenable. One police official, when questioned about equipping officers with the assault rifles, stated, "That decision belongs with police officials, not the public" and "likened community involvement in arms decisions to public involvement in hospitals' decisions on what type and how many heart stents to buy" (Slack, 2009, p. 3 of 3).

In describing the work environment of policing, Skolnick observed that "police work constitutes the most secluded part of an already secluded system of criminal justice and therefore offers the greatest opportunity for arbitrary behavior" (1994, p. 13). Thus, it is the organizational autonomy of the police that sets them distinctly apart from other "individual practitioners of a craft" as Bittner has described them. In acting autonomously, "most of what a policeman needs to know to do his work he has to learn on his own" (2005, p. 169).

The perspective that it is the police who are the experts and the professionals in all matters pertaining to public safety and in the ensuing regulation of human behavior in the maintenance of public order assumes a standpoint that some have characterized as organizational authoritarianism and in police officers an

> authoritarian personality: a personality pattern characterized by (a) preoccupation with power and status, (b) strict adherence to highly simplified conventional values, (c) an attitude of great deference to authority figures while demanding subservience from those regarded as lower in status, and (d) hostility toward minorities and other outgroups and to people who deviate from conventional moral prescriptions. (APA, 2007, p. 89)

POLICE ADMINISTRATION AND THE CIVIL SERVICE

The vast majority of the over 17,000 police agencies in the United States operate under some type of civil service or tenured intake and promotion system that serves to severely restrict and delimit the discretion that an administrator or appointing authority has in hiring and promoting individuals within a particular police agency. In theory, the civil service system was instituted around the turn of the 20th century in an effort to abolish patronage appointments to local police departments. In practice, it has created and sustained a complicated and convoluted system that is often encumbered in cronyism adumbrated in administrivia. For example, preference provisions written into many civil service laws have given entry level and promotional preference to military veterans, survivors of police deemed to have died "in the line of duty," civilian "cadets," women, foreign language speakers, emergency medical technicians, and others. Further, tests and other instruments are administered to applicants that, to many observers, are in no way reflective or capable of measuring the skills necessary for the most qualified applicants for entry level and promotional positions. Police administrators often complain in being hamstrung by outdated legal requirements that hamper their efforts to place the most desirable and qualified applicants into open positions, as well as to terminate the employment of those proved to be unsuitable in the police service.

POLICE ADMINISTRATION AND UNIONS

Police unions and the collective bargaining process can prove vexing and frustrating for police administrators (full disclosure: this author was a long-time elected constitutional officer of a large police union). "Nationwide, 41% of local police departments, employing 71% of all officers, authorized collective bargaining for sworn personnel" (U.S. Department of Justice, Office of Justice Programs, 2003, p. 12). Contemporary police unions began forming in the 1960s and 1970s in response to oppressive working conditions for many police officers that included abysmal compensation, lack of overtime pay, poor equipment, work schedules that permitted few days off, no vacation, mandatory unpaid call outs, and draconian residency and travel notification requirements.

Many of today's police unions have negotiated generous compensation packages for their members and have proved to be formidable adversaries in often contentious and confrontational relationships with police administrators. Protracted and fractured contract negotiations between police unions and the City of Boston threatened to shut down the Democratic National Convention in 2004 until the city's police unions won a significant wage increase from the city in an unprecedented contract package that offered no concessions from the unions to the city (see http://www.nytimes.com/2004/07/23/us/convention-near-boston-police-win-raise.html).

CONCLUSION

Students of criminal justice are offered here a glimpse into the realm of the lived experience and worldview of the police from the perspective of one who has lived it for over 30 years. It is a dominion that is in many ways mired in a perspective on society jaded by constant exposure to a sliver of the polity that is hardly representative of the society in which most of us live; yet it is all too often for the police their only tangible grasp on the netherworld that is, for them, all too real, all too pervasive, all too unrelenting. Progressive police administrators (and enlightened students) understand that therein lay the value and sacrifice of what the police provide to the rest of us and the price that they pay in serving our communities.

DISCUSSION QUESTIONS

1. How does the formal organizational structure of contemporary police agencies contribute (if you believe that it does) to inconsistencies and difficulties in implementing community policing and problem-oriented policing philosophies and strategies?

2. Police organizations have been described as *masculinist* in nature and form. What are the manifestations of masculinism in contemporary police organizations? How has masculinism affected and informed the ways that police interact with their constituent communities? What are the implications of such masculinism for the future of police organizations?

3. The police are organized in a quasi-military form that employs military metaphors, such as war and operation (among others), in descriptions of its purpose and mission. What are the implications of using military terms to describe strategies, policies, and tactics that the police employ in our communities? Are these descriptions compatible with community policing initiatives?

4. The police are organized around the enforcement not only of the criminal law but also of moral behavior generally. How do the police engage in the identification and enforcement of morality? What are the implications of having the police enforce standards of behavior? Do the police in fact decide what appropriate moral behavior is?

REFERENCES

American Psychological Association (APA). (2007). *The American Psychological Association dictionary of psychology*. Washington, DC: American Psychological Association.

Andrews, D., & Bonta, J. (2006). *The psychology of criminal conduct* (4th ed.). Cincinnati, OH: Anderson.

Bittner, E. (2005). Florence Nightingale in pursuit of Willie Sutton: A theory of the police. In T. Newburn (Ed.), *Policing: Key readings* (pp. 150–172). Devon, United Kingdom: Willan.

Brittan, A. (2001). Masculinities and masculinism. In S. Whitehead & F. Barrett (Eds.), *The masculinities reader* (pp. 51–55). Cambridge, United Kingdom: Polity Press.

Dansky, K. (2013). *ACLU launches nationwide investigation into police use of military technology & tactics*. Retrieved from https://www.aclu.org/criminal-law-reform/aclu-launches-nationwide-investigation-police-use-military-technology-tactics

Gendreau, P. (2006). Offender rehabilitation: What we know and what needs to be done. In C. Bartol & A. Bartol (Eds.), *Current perspectives in forensic psychology and criminal justice* (pp. 223–229). Thousand Oaks, CA: SAGE.

Gordon, D. (1990). *The justice juggernaut: Fighting street crime and controlling citizens*. Piscataway, NJ: Rutgers University Press.

Harcourt, B. (2001). *Illusion of order: The false promise of broken windows policing*. Cambridge, MA: Harvard University Press.

Kelling, G., & Wilson, J. (1982). The police and neighborhood safety: Broken windows. *Atlantic Monthly, 127,* 29–38.

Klockars, C. (2005). The rhetoric of community policing. In T. Newburn (Ed.), *Policing: Key readings* (pp. 442–459). Devon, United Kingdom: Willan.

Maguire, M. (2008). Merry Morash: Understanding gender, crime, and justice. *Journal of Critical Criminology, 16*(3), 225–227.

Mastrofski, S. (2006). Community policing: A skeptical view. In D. Weisburd & A. Braga (Eds.), *Policing innovation: Contrasting perspectives* (pp. 44–76). Cambridge, United Kingdom: Cambridge University Press.

Morash, M. (2005). *Understanding gender, crime, and justice.* Thousand Oaks, CA: SAGE.

Nolan, T. (2001). Galateas in blue: Women police as decoy sex workers. *Criminal Justice Ethics, 20*(2), 63–67.

Nolan, T. (2009, August 13). Behind the blue wall of silence. *Journal of Men and Masculinities.* Advance preprint online publication. doi:10.1177/1097184X09334700

Oliver, W. (2007). *Homeland security for policing.* Upper Saddle River, NJ: Pearson Prentice Hall.

Pollock, J. (2007). *Ethical dilemmas and decisions in criminal justice* (5th ed.). Belmont, CA: Thomson Wadsworth.

Reaves, B. A. (2011). *Census of state and local law enforcement agencies, 2008.* Bureau of Justice Statistics. Retrieved from http://www.bjs.gov/content/pub/pdf/csllea08.pdf

Skogan, W. (2006). The promise of community policing. In D. Weisburd & A. Braga (Eds.), *Policing innovation: Contrasting perspectives* (pp. 27–43). Cambridge, United Kingdom: Cambridge University Press.

Skolnick, J. (1994). *Justice without trial* (3rd ed.). New York, NY: Macmillan.

Slack, D. (2009, June 15). Even small localities got big guns. *The Boston Globe.* Retrieved from http://www.boston.com/news/local/massachusetts/articles/2009/06/15/details_emerge_on_distribution_of_military_weapons_in_mass/?page=1

U.S. Department of Justice. (2010). *Crime in the United States, 2009: Table 74: Full-time law enforcement employees.* Retrieved from http://www2.fbi.gov/ucr/cius2009/data/table_74.html

U.S. Department of Justice, Office of Justice Programs. (2003). *Law enforcement management and administrative statistics: Local police departments, 2003.* Retrieved January 1, 2014 from http://www.bjs.gov/content/pub/pdf/lpd03.pdf

Van Maanen, J. (2005). The asshole. In T. Newburn (Ed.), *Policing: Key readings* (pp. 280–296). Devon, United Kingdom: Willan.

Waddington, P. (1999). Police (canteen) subculture: An appreciation. *British Journal of Criminology, 39*(2), 287–309.

Walker, S., & Katz, C. (2007). *The police in America: An introduction* (6th ed.). Boston, MA: McGraw-Hill.

Websdale, N. (2001). *Policing the poor: From slave plantation to public housing.* Boston, MA: Northeastern University Press.

Wilson, J. Q., & Kelling, G. L. (1982, March). Broken windows: The police and neighborhood safety. *Atlantic Monthly, 249,* 29–38.

Part IV

Policy and Jurisprudence

CHAPTER 20

Public Policy

Frank P. Williams III and Janice Ahmad

Public policy shapes our everyday life from the way we get to school and work (be it private or public transportation), to the breaks that employees are granted, to the degree of sanitary conditions of the restaurant where we eat lunch, to the taxes and fees we pay to maintain the schools, roads, police agencies, and correctional facilities. This short list indicates the extensive impact of public policy that is implemented at the federal, state, and local levels. This impact is particularly true for the criminal justice system in the United States.

Many will argue that there are two versions of public policy, the formal codified version and the daily way in which it is actually practiced. We first explain the formal version of public policy and law, after which we examine public policy as a practical matter, giving examples of recent use and misuse of public policy in law and criminal justice, followed by three contemporary influences on the creation of public policy and what we consider to be the future of public policy.

PUBLIC POLICY: THE FORMAL VERSION

Simply put, public policy is what the government chooses to do or not do (Dye, 2008). These actions or inactions are based on the social contract, that is, what society expects from government. The social contract evolves and changes based on the principles of the public and policy makers. Changes in the social contract occur due to reasons such as emerging problems (health epidemics, inflation or recession, natural disasters, acts of terrorism, etc.), principles held by new policy makers, or program evaluation results.

Public policy can be defined as purposive governmental courses of action or inaction. Choices are made and implementation takes place, resulting in outcomes that are subsequently evaluated to determine the policy's impact and effectiveness. This formal process of policy making follows a systems approach and is reviewed and revised to meet the social contract. Under this model, one would expect public policy to be the product of a carefully considered process.

313

Public policy is generally created when a problem has been identified and brought to the attention of policy makers. A critical influence is whether or not the problem is perceived as fitting the policy makers' agenda, in which case a public policy may be developed to resolve the problem. In criminal justice, policy agendas are generally based on one of the major goals of the criminal justice system—deterrence, incapacitation, punishment, rehabilitation, reintegration, and restoration (Marion & Oliver, 2006). However, before a policy is developed, the policy-making process must be enacted.

When developing public policy, we must keep in mind that it is not developed in a vacuum; rather, a policy can impact several systems and agencies as well as many people. Policy that does not account for this interconnectedness generally has unintended consequences and is ineffective. Recognizing this, Welsh and Harris (2008) separate the policy-making process into three components: defining and examining the problem, developing goals and objectives, and creating the policy.

The first step in developing public policy is to define and examine the problem. What may seem like a widespread problem when first presented may not, upon further examination, be as far reaching as first suggested. Thorough investigation into the problem will reveal its causes, impact, history, stakeholders, previous interventions and outcomes, agency interconnectivity, and the barriers to and support for change. This examination may reveal more than one approach for resolving the problem as well as the goals and objectives that need to be met by the public policy.

Stakeholders, those who will be positively and negatively affected and the agencies that will be impacted, must be identified and involved in the policy development process. Their involvement is critical in creating the most effective policy, gaining support for the policy, and having it implemented as intended. The cost, resources needed, and funding sources must also be determined. Finally, the process involves developing an evaluation component.

Evaluation of the public policy helps to determine if the goals and objectives are being met. During the past few years we have seen an evaluation component being included in public policies. For example, grant solicitations by the U. S. Department of Justice now require that performance measures be included in the grant application and for funding. Evaluations also guide the review and reassessment process to determine if the policy should be revised, continued, or discontinued.

Criminal justice is directly and indirectly impacted by public policies. Public policies that reduce fear of crime, punish or rehabilitate offenders, and fund 100,000 more police officers are easily identified as criminal justice policy initiatives and are created in consultation with criminal justice agencies. However, policies that involve other systems (mental health, education, the workplace) may also greatly impact criminal justice. For example, during the late 1960s and early 1970s, many mental health residential facilities were closed as it was deemed that their clients would be best served in their own communities using community resources. However, this public policy resulted in many mentally-ill persons becoming involved in a criminal justice system that was not equipped to handle them and subsequently treating them as criminals rather than as mentally ill. Had the policy-making process been more carefully assessed and criminal justice professionals included in the process, perhaps more community resources for treating the mentally ill would have been established thus reducing the number of mentally-ill people in jails and prisons. Therefore, thinking outside the proverbial box needs to be part of the policy-making process.

SOURCES OF CRIMINAL JUSTICE POLICY

Multiple sources create public policy that impacts criminal justice. These include the U.S. Constitution and court rulings, legislatures enacting statutes, administrative agencies issuing regulatory directives, and governmental agencies developing various procedures. In addition, all of these sources are duplicated at the federal, state, and local levels, increasing the number of criminal justice-related policies.

The U.S. Constitution outlines the rights of the people and the responsibility of government in our society. Ultimately, all public policies must conform to this doctrine. In the two-plus centuries since the Constitution was adopted, amendments have been added and its meaning has been debated and clarified. The U.S. Supreme Court in cases such as *Miranda v. Arizona* (1966; creating the now famous Miranda warnings), *In re Gault* (1967; which instituted due process for juveniles), *Furman v. Georgia* (1972; overturning the death penalty), *Gregg v. Georgia* (1976; reinstating the death penalty with required conditions), and *Roper v. Simmons* (2005; ending the death penalty for those under 18 years of age) has significantly impacted criminal justice public policy.

Federal and state statutes create criminal justice policy through the establishment of agencies (the California Commission on Peace Officer Standards and Training, Federal Bureau of Prisons, and departments of public safety); making certain behaviors illegal (speeding, taking property belonging to someone else, ingesting certain substances, white-collar crime); or providing funds for crime-related initiatives (crime victim compensation, new prisons, hiring of more police officers).

Regulatory agencies are created through federal and state statutes and are authorized to develop and enforce directives to meet the agency's goals and objectives. These directives in turn can impact criminal justice policy. Examples include the California's Corrections Standards Authority which regulates jail and prison standards, the U.S. Department of Agriculture which determines the type of vegetation and animals that can be brought into the country, and the Court Reporters' Board of California which sets standards for court reporters. Criminal justice agencies are then required to maintain the policies issued by these regulatory agencies.

Federal and state legislatures pass several bills each year, many of which change the law under which criminal justice agencies operate. These statutes are based on policy makers' agendas and are public policy in that they reflect what the government has chosen to do or not do—the basic definition of public policy. Laws making a substance illegal, establishing three-strikes legislation, or requiring police officers to have a 4-year college education are all criminal justice policies that involve making choices, having outputs, and impacting various constituencies. One of the most far-reaching of public policies for criminal justice was the federal decision to create a Department of Homeland Security. This legislative action and its subsequent administrative policies reconstituted federal criminal justice agencies and affected their duties and responsibilities. The affects filtered down to local levels, creating new positions and relationships. It still remains to be seen what its overall effects will be, but some have predicted that law enforcement might eventually become wrapped up in the umbrella of security (Williams, McShane, & Karson, 2007).

Agency-level policy in the criminal justice arena also reflects the policy makers' agenda and principles. While this public policy is generally specific to the agency and its employees, such policies affect those who are served by and interact with the agency. Some agency-level policies have produced their own problems, frequently because the policy-making process was not correctly implemented. These problems are then brought to the attention of other policy makers for remedy. Cases such as *Schmerber v. California* (1966; which permitted warrantless search and seizure of blood in DWI cases), *Gilbert v. California* (1967; establishing that handwriting samples were not protected under self-incrimination), *Chimel v. California* (1969; which permitted warrantless search incident to arrest), and *Pell v. Procunier* (1974; limiting media access to prisoners) are examples of agency policy being examined by other policy makers.

PUBLIC POLICY—AS IT IS IN PRACTICE

Public Policy and Law as a Practical Matter

Our description of public policy- and lawmaking in the formal sense is influenced, as usual, when it comes to actual practice in criminal justice matters, by elements inside and outside of the system. There are four primary groups of policy-influencing elements: moral entrepreneurs, or moral crusaders; lobbyists, think tanks, and those otherwise politically and financially connected to powerful people; vested interest groups; and the media.

Partisanship, Politicization, and Ideology

Any public policy is by definition a part of the political process because it can only be enacted through that process. However, certain parties both inside and outside of the political process attempt to exert power and influence so that the direction and content of public policy matches their interests. Within the political process itself, partisanship on certain issues results in setting aside the essential democratic conduct of our political system to ensure that issues near and dear to the hearts of political majorities (or at least those with substantial political power) are enacted into law. In some instances, it is sufficient that certain viewpoints hold sway thus becoming the preferred way of viewing issues of a similar type. In such cases, public policy is no longer a product of group consensus but instead a vehicle to force the values of a powerful group onto others. The recent history of partisan dealings and legislation in the U.S. Congress is a testament to the process of influence leading to politicization of issues. When issues can be politicized, values and sometimes influence itself become more important than the actual content or intent of policies and laws. In short, values embedded in policies are frequently used to direct far-reaching purposes that have little to do with the policies themselves.

These values are sometimes referred to as "ideologies" in social analysis. An ideology is a basic set of background assumptions controlling the way a phenomenon should be viewed and judged. It is "the way things are and should be." As a result, ideologies are rarely questioned by those who hold them. Indeed, to question an ideology would move it from the background to the foreground of ideas and therefore likely abort its power to control thought. In one sense, we all have ideologies, but it is when they are thrust into the political arena that they become most dangerous for public policy. The discussion of partisanship above suggests there are at least two opposing ideologies at work in the U. S. political world today. Each group of adherents is busy attempting to control how public realities are viewed. Public policy is used as an instrument to further that control. Thus, public policy by itself is not the important ingredient; the *control* of policy becomes a way to implement ideology, or core values.

Sources of Influence and Information

As noted earlier, there are several important policy-influencing elements. Moral entrepreneurs are among the most influential of these where the making of public policy and law are concerned. As described by Howard Becker (1963), moral entrepreneurs who are rule creators seek to influence and define social norms on a particular issue. They can do this for selfish reasons, but most likely their purpose is the result of a sense of moral outrage and evil to be fought, or as Becker puts it, a moral crusade (p. 148). In one of the more common criminal justice scenarios, usually as the product of a crime some relative of the victim finds abominable, the relative takes it upon him/herself to campaign for a new law or approach to the crime (for example, the killing of Candy Lightner's 12-year-old daughter by a drunken driver resulted in her campaign against Driving While Intoxicated [DWI] and the subsequent creation of Mothers Against Drunk Driving [MADD] in 1980). Even if the crime is statistically rare, the pursuit of "righting the wrong" results in artificially inflated numbers and a claim of common occurrence to justify policy change or a new law. Common characteristics among moral entrepreneurs are doggedly pursuing the issue, grandstanding, making out-of-proportion claims, and appealing to sympathy as a "victim." We would add that somewhere along the process, many of these people also begin to benefit from their cause, either financially or by the fame they gain. Some have become television personalities, and others have created foundations to disperse donated funds (and resulting in their own employment by the foundation). In this sense, they become vested participants in the public policy process, over and above their original interest.

These moral entrepreneurs are part of the process Stanley Cohen (1972) called "moral panics" and known more generally as *constructed social problems*. The process is virtually identical in all aspects for the recognition of social problems. Focusing on a real (or sometimes imagined) issue, the moral entrepreneur begins calling it to the attention of the public with exaggerated claims of its frequency. Those with a vested interest (for example, an agency handling such issues and thereby having a financial stake) pick up the public claims and begin to make media announcements designed to support the image of the problem as a relatively common occurrence. The media then circulate this information, again reporting the claims and the commonality of the problem. The claims tend to escalate the exaggeration, stressing the moral offensiveness of the problem. At this point, a group of politicians, sensing both publicity and political image to be gained, usually become involved and propose to become "saviors" by creating law and subsequent public policy against this heinous problem. Thus, law and public policy in the criminal justice arena is often a knee-jerk reaction to an exaggerated problem.

A factor in whether this reaction actually produces desired results is the timing with which others with actual knowledge of the extent of the problem begin to critique the exaggerations. If this happens fairly soon after the initial pronouncements, the creation of law and policy is less likely to occur. If the critique occurs later in the process, laws are frequently already passed, and the issue takes on a life of its own, regardless of the evidence against it. Once some organization or agency has gained responsibility for eliminating the issue, the financial incentives that go along with it almost ensure that the social problem will continue to exist. In fact, most documented cases have not only resulted in the survival of the *problem* but also actually resulted in its expansion. In other words, organizations use social problems to gain funding and expand; to the extent they can gain control over these problems, they can redefine problems in ways that best suit their own agendas.

Examples of this moral panic process have been documented time and again. In fact, it is hard to find a social problem, or moral panic, that has *not* undergone this process. Interesting criminal justice examples include the late-19th-century criminalization of oleomargarine (yes, the butter substitute—primarily because of the political strength of the dairy industry; Ball & Lilly, 1982), the creation of *juvenile delinquency* (by women engaged in the child-saving movement; Platt, 1969), the discovery of *child abuse* (by radiologists who increased their stature in the medical field by defining what constitutes child abuse; Pfohl, 1977), DWI (through the creation of a national organization dedicated to eradicating it; Jacobs, 1989), serial murder (a term originally invented by the Federal Bureau of Investigation [FBI] who defined it as multijurisdictional murders that only they could handle; Jenkins, 1994), missing children (by claims exaggerating the number by including parental abductions and runaways as if they were strangers' kidnappings; Best, 1987, 1990), and sex offenses (by false claims that it was widely perpetrated on children by strangers; Jenkins, 2004; Sutherland, 1950). Virtually every problem you can imagine was, at one point or another, exemplified by a moral panic with moral entrepreneurs at work (think about playing pool or baseball, watching movies, reading comic books, and listening to rock music—they were all defined as causes of delinquency).

Some of the characteristics associated with the ability of a moral panic to create law and public policy generally have emotional attributes and include such things as child victims, stranger offenders, and the *randomness* of the offense. Of course, the political power and degree of vested interest of both the claims makers and those potentially arrayed against the claims have to be factored in. But you may be asking, What's wrong with that? because, after all, most of the examples above are clear instances of offenses and problems. The problem is twofold. First, public policy should deal with common occurrences, not phenomena that have been exaggerated to make them seem more pervasive than they are. Second, they absorb limited criminal justice-system resources and distract attention from more frequent and serious issues.

Although we have focused on moral entrepreneurs, there are other common sources of people and organizations who push to have their agendas made into public policy. Included among them are lobbyists, think tanks and the power elite, many groups with a single focus, and, of course, the media. We leave you to consider the many ways these groups affect public policy through their efforts (usually, self-serving ones)—it won't be difficult to think of examples. Moreover, any of these can also serve as moral crusaders. The media, in particular, contribute to the agenda of other groups through their reporting on and coverage of emerging policy initiatives. Media are frequently seen as disinterested bystanders in all of this, but because they are businesses, media have an interest in selling themselves. Thus, any topic imbued with the essence of sensationalism and the right combination of images (the combination of a child, sex abuse, and an adult predator are ideal) will be given substantial coverage. As of late, some media sources have even given up the attempt to appear objective and simply push images of crime and victims as other businesses might push any high-profit item. Finally, it should be obvious that many criminal justice policy initiatives find most, if not all, of these influential sources coming together to push common agendas.

THE USE AND MISUSE OF PUBLIC POLICY

If all of this sounds as though public policy is frequently manipulated to benefit someone, you are correct. The use and misuse of criminal justice public policy is a virtual certainty. You can be sure that someone, or some group, has a vested interest in virtually every public policy created in the criminal justice arena. This fact, though, does not mean that policy is being misused; it just means that public policy has utility to people and groups.

One way to critically analyze any public policy is to think about its function. Robert K. Merton (1936; 1968, pp. 82–83) provided us with two types of functions: manifest and latent. *Manifest functions* are those that are intended. For example, in the public policy known as "three-strikes," the manifest function was to make sure that dangerous felons were removed from the streets and kept in prison for at least 25 years. *Latent functions* are the unanticipated consequences of social action, or those functions that are unintended. In the three-strikes example, these might include application of the law to criminals who are not dangerous, increased numbers of jury trials because of refusals to plead guilty or plea bargain, and increased number of inmates and costly new prison construction.

Another issue to look for in the proposed creation of public policy is a financial motive. Such motives do not usually surface in initial proposals and discussions because legislation rarely includes immediate funding for most social problems. Nonetheless, an agency can gain funding by showing that it has more to do than previously, thus, justifying a larger budget at a later date because of the need to add staff to deal with the new responsibilities for the problem. If an agency (or some other organization) can capture the ability to define the problem, then even more financial rewards accrue. Finally, there are cases of purposefully misleading the public to achieve other policy goals. These, too, are exemplified in the victims' movement and in the titles given to legislative bills and acts in general. Thus, while these titles are frequently misleading, they serve the purpose of generating policy statements on (usually) related issues.

Examples of California Public Policy Overreach

The victims' movement in California provides three good examples of the creation of social policy to benefit victims, while actually having another purpose. In 1984, the state legislature approved the Roberti-Imbrecht-Rains-Goggins Child Sexual Abuse Prevention Act. With children and sex abuse in the title, supporting the act was a "no brainer" for politicians, and they literally lined up to be associated with it. However, the fact was that the act did nothing to specifically support the prevention of child sexual abuse, and it was intentionally mislabeled to gain support (Inglehart, 1990). In truth, the act provided funds for police and prosecutors, instituted harsher punishments for child molesters, extended the statute of limitations for filing charges, and allowed judges and prosecutors (both elected officials) to reap political benefits as they claimed to get tough on crime in the new "get tough" atmosphere.

A second example of intentional mislabeling is the California Child Protection Act of 1984. Once again, there was nothing directly in the act leading to the protection of children, and the intended beneficiaries were prosecutors and legislators, both of whom could stake political claims of being protectors of children (Inglehart, 1990). The primary nonpolitical benefits were that prosecutors (a) no longer need to prove intent and (b) could confiscate property that was the fruit of child pornography profits, along with the equipment used in its production. The latter meant new money in the budgets of prosecutors as the confiscated property was auctioned off.

Finally, the California Crime Victims Justice Reform Initiative of 1990 (Proposition 115) was passed by voters as part of that state's proposition process. As with the other two acts, the title was intentionally misnamed (Inglehart, 1990). Victims gained little direct assistance with the passage of the proposition. On the other hand, judges, prosecutors, and politicians gained tremendously. Because the public at the time was caught up in a "crime wave" mentality and victims were a popular cause, the proposition provided political gains to its supporters and made it easier for judges and prosecutors to increase conviction rates. Even better for politicians faced with campaign spending caps, campaign money was transferred to support the proposition (along with mention of the candidate's largesse), and thus, candidates were able to avoid legal spending limitations and still gain media coverage by "campaigning" for a popular issue. In terms of latent functions, the main message disseminated to the public was that more crime was occurring than ever before and that they were almost certain to be victims, thus, pushing fear of crime to a new high (McShane & Williams, 1992).

An Example of Federal Public Policy Overreach

Turning to the federal level, a good example of time and resources being devoted to a continuing moral panic is exemplified by fears of pornography and child predators on the Internet. When the Internet was still rather young, a study of pornography on the Internet was published in the *Georgetown Law Review* by a Carnegie-Mellon University scholar. The author, Martin Rimm (1995), allegedly accessed, reviewed, and counted a sample of "obscene and pornographic" materials on the Internet and then constructed estimates that cyberporn represented as much as 83% of all Internet images. This study was given nationwide coverage by *Time* magazine even before it was published in the law journal. As Williams, McShane, and Hsieh (2007, pp. 149–151) reported, not only did this lead to an uproar over children being exposed to pornography on the Internet, but two prominent U.S. senators, Exon and Glade, sponsored a bill to eliminate this pornography and regulate such materials on the Internet as well (SB 314, Communications Decency Act). Another U.S. senator, Grassley, scheduled a hearing with the study author as the prime witness.

In reality, the Carnegie-Mellon "scholar" turned out to be an undergraduate student who accessed pay-only adult-oriented "bulletin boards" (dial-up subscription services not connected to the Internet) and accessed only one of the "newsgroups" on the Internet at that time. Thus, the "research" never actually sampled Internet content. A scandal erupted with Carnegie-Mellon University disowning the research and Senator Grassley pulling his star witness at the last moment, but the cyberporn issue was passed into law as an amendment to the Telecommuncations Decency Act (which was ultimately struck down by the federal courts). A 1995 study (Williams & McShane), using a random sample of all Internet sex-oriented newsgroups, estimated that sexual materials on the Internet represented no more than 2% of all materials and that specifically-pornographic sexual materials were much lower than that 2%. However, the initial claims and media coverage created a moral panic that has yet to die out.

The issue of predators stalking children over the Internet and arranging meetings was also a by-product of the cyberporn publicity. Parents were told time and again that children were vulnerable and to watch them carefully. Williams and McShane (1995) reviewed evidence on these claims in the early days of the moral panic (1994–1995). Examining those 2 years, using articles from three major newspapers, a total of seven articles were found dealing with actual cases or incidents involving children exposed to pornography or potential sex offenders or persons attempting to distribute pornographic stories and images. In regard to predators attempting to meet with children, three of the seven cases involved attempted contact. In sum, the evidence in those early panic days hardly pointed to a common problem, yet public policy was made in response (although most of it was ultimately discarded by the federal courts). The unanticipated consequences primarily restricted public Internet usage for all users, adults and children alike. More recently, a study by a Harvard University research center (Berkman Center for Internet & Society, 2008) and supported by the various states' attorneys general found that evidence of sexual predators using Myspace and Facebook was vastly overblown and reminiscent of a moral panic rather than reality. Regardless, legislating restrictions on social networking sites continues to attract attention.

THE POLICY IMPLICATIONS OF PUBLIC POLICY

The preceding discussion certainly suggests that formal versions of public policy formulation tend to identify the players and the process but not the actual motivations. There are ways by which this might be overcome, however. While it seems redundant to discuss the policy implications of public policy, it is possible to discuss some contemporary influences on the creation of public policy. Two of those we view as being favorable and one rather negative.

Evidence-Based Policy

Over the past few years, a new catchphrase has come into play when criminal justice decisions (and policies) are made. The phrase is *evidence-based decision making* and represents what criminal justice researchers have been arguing for decades. Instead of making decisions and policy based on many of the elements we have examined above (and including gut-level and instinctive decisions), the use of both research evidence and hard data from agency information systems provides a more objective, reality-based, and, certainly, more defensible way to determine what problems exist and what decisions might be made about them. Several criminal justice program-funding organizations, especially the Police Research Foundation, the Edna McConnell Clark Foundation, and the National Institute of Justice (NIJ), now require evidence-based program decisions when they are the funding sources.

The Obama administration has recently used *evidence based* as a mantra and insists that it be used to guide policy decisions. As a result of these requirements and the frequency by which the field is now using the phrase, evidence-based policy making is likely to be the approach of the future. This should result in better public policies and the laws to support them, particularly when compared to past examples of ideologically driven and gut-level policies. An example is a recent report from the National Academy of Sciences (Committee on Identifying the Needs of the Forensic Sciences Community, 2009). The scientific experts writing the report evaluated current forensic science practice, technology, and interpretation. They found that a substantial amount of the work of police crime labs was based on faulty, discredited, and/or imprecise science and procedures to match evidence to individuals, in particular non-DNA tests, such as fingerprint comparison, tool analysis, and hair analysis. NIJ will now be requesting research to determine what directions need to be pursued in developing policy for handling, testing, interpreting, and presenting criminal evidence.

The Politicization of Public Policy

Having said that evidence-based policy is likely to be the wave of the future, there is also little reason to believe that the informal elements and motivations involved in past policy making will disappear. Over the past two decades, a movement developed which essentially intended to subvert the use of scientific evidence in federal governmental agencies and congressional hearings. Using argumentative techniques developed by the tobacco industry after 1980, fringe "science" has been allowed to present itself as "sound science" (Mooney, 2006). While the term *sound science* sounds like a reasonable approach suggesting the use of the best available evidence and scientific positions, the opposite is true with antiscience pronouncements that all scientific opinion is equal. Science itself is highly skeptical, critical, and, above all, not a democratic process—quality and rigor are valued above all else. That very questioning and skepticism has been used to label real science as "uncertain" and fatally flawed and thus "junk science" (Mooney, 2006). Various vested interest groups and ideologues in the federal government have pushed *sound science* as a pseudonym, allowing fringe positions (those supportive of their positions) an equal voice with best available evidence in an effort to rig hearings and policy. Because real scientists are skeptical and critical, representatives of these interest groups or ideologies play up small disagreements and uncertainties in best available evidence as if there is actually no good evidence. Pseudoscientists asked to provide evidence in support of the vested interest position have no such qualms and critical stance; thus, they and their political supporters announce their fringe "evidence" as correct.

This process played out in criminal justice as political operatives were appointed to positions in various agencies within the Justice Department. Scientific research reports were suddenly required to be approved by a deputy director who knew very little about research. If the research findings did not match desired conclusions, the wording of the report was changed. Researchers who objected to this found their reports went unpublished. Even worse, the grant process was subverted to provide a substantial amount of money to those with business connections (criminal justice and homeland security technologies) and/or the correct political connections. Peer review of grants (the process of researcher experts being assigned to evaluate proposed research) was largely ignored, so that funded research was often poorly constructed and incapable of producing a defensible result. If this subversion of scientific research continues, then there is reason to doubt that evidence-based policy making will actually produce better informed and more objective policies.

The Contributions of Academic Criminal Justice

Another factor in the future of public policy development is the emerging majority of criminal justice agency personnel who have been educated in university criminal justice departments. This group is now developing into a critical mass in the field and is much more likely to ask for research results and related evidence before making decisions. As a result, better agency policy decisions will be made and better advice will be available to lawmakers and governmental agencies. Similarly, academic criminal justice professionals are now more likely to be asked to provide information for the development of legislation and public policy. This trend is a favorable one, but it is threatening to vested-interest groups, ideologues, lobbyists, and moral entrepreneurs. Because legislators and policy makers are ultimately public figures, loud public voices will continue to have a substantial say in criminal justice legislation and policy.

CONCLUSION

So what is the likely direction of public policy formulation? The use of evidence and research results in criminal justice decision making and the creation of agency policy has made great strides. Whether that will play out in the larger public policy realm is much more in doubt. Simply put, there is too much at stake among those with moral positions, ideological agendas, and political futures for public policy to be made in a true evidence-based, research-informed atmosphere. While there is reason to hope that future public policy will be made in a more objective fashion, perhaps the best we can do now is to ask for a voice in the process and offer information to those concerned. Time-sensitive and objective information can be provided to members of the media to counter exaggerated claims often made in the early stages of the policy process. Assuming the best public policy is based on objective reality rather than subjective versions of reality, any increase in the consumption of objective information can only serve to improve criminal justice policies.

DISCUSSION QUESTIONS

1. How should public policy making be accomplished in a democracy? How closely does that description fit with your experience?

2. How do you see public policy being made in your state? Do various checks and balances come into play, or is it a product of rather unfettered influence? Are there any other ways to make public policy that you might find preferable?

3. When federal mental health agencies deinstitutionalized the mentally ill in favor of community treatment, there was a profound effect on local criminal justice agencies. Thinking about such a policy, what would you have anticipated the effects to be?

4. What do you think of the concept of moral entrepreneurs and moral panics? Is it an overblown academic position, or does it represent reality? What would you say to someone who says that any moral panic still represents a real problem that must be dealt with? Finally, what examples of potential moral panics can you identify that would call for new criminal justice policies?

5. What do you view as the effect of ideology on the making of public policy? Is there anything wrong with the interplay of ideology and policy making? How would one create any particular focus to guide policy making if ideologies did not exist?

6. Rather than affect public policy by public outcry, as moral entrepreneurs do, others attempt to directly influence both the making and the direction of public policy. How would you describe the effect of lobbyists and think tanks on policy making? In a philosophical vein, what do you think about the fairness of their efforts and subsequent effects in a democratic society?

7. How do you react to the statement that the discipline of criminal justice may ultimately have an effect on the quality of public policy in the crime and justice area? If you agree, how do you see this happening? If you disagree, what are your reasons?

REFERENCES

Ball, R. A., & Lilly, J. R. (1982). The menace of margarine: The rise and fall of a social problem. *Social Problems, 29*(5), 488–498.

Becker, H. S. (1963). Moral entrepreneurs. In H. S. Becker, *Outsiders: Studies in the sociology of deviance* (pp. 147–163). New York, NY: The Free Press.

Berkman Center for Internet & Society at Harvard University. (2008, December 31). *Enhancing child safety and online technologies: Final report of the Internet safety technical task force to the multi-state working group on social networking of state attorneys general of the United States.* Cambridge, MA: Harvard Law School.

Best, J. (1987). Rhetoric in claims-making: Constructing the missing children problem. *Social Problems, 34*(2), 101–121.

Best, J. (1990). *Threatened children: Rhetoric and concern about child-victims.* Chicago, IL: University of Chicago Press

Cohen, S. (1972). *Folk devils and moral panics: The creation of the mods and rockers.* Oxford, United Kingdom: Basil.

Committee on Identifying the Needs of the Forensic Sciences Community, National Research Council, National Academy of Sciences. (2009). *Strengthening forensic science in the United States: A path forward.* Washington, DC: National Academies Press.

Dye, T. (2008). *Understanding public policy* (12th ed.). Upper Saddle River, NJ: Prentice Hall.

Inglehart, R. (1990, October). *The impact of Proposition 115: The Crime Victims Initiative.* Keynote speech delivered to the Association of Criminal Justice Researchers (CA), Claremont, CA.

Jacobs, J. B. (1989). *Drunk driving: An American dilemma.* Chicago, IL: University of Chicago Press.

Jenkins, P. (1994). *Using murder: The social construction of serial homicide.* New York, NY: Aldine de Gruyter.

Jenkins, P. (2004). *Moral panic: Changing concepts of the child molester in modern America.* New Haven, CT: Yale University Press.

Marion, N. E., & Oliver, W. M. (2006). *The public policy of crime and criminal justice.* Upper Saddle River, NJ: Pearson Prentice Hall.

McShane, M. D., & Williams, F. P., III. (1992). Radical victimology: A critique of the concept of victim in traditional victimology. *Crime & Delinquency, 38*(2), 258–271.

Merton, R. K. (1936). The unanticipated consequences of purposive social action. *American Sociological Review, 1*(6), 894–904.

Merton, R. K. (1968). Manifest and latent functions. In R. K. Merton, *Social theory and social structure* (3rd ed., Rev. and enlarged, pp. 73–91). New York, NY: Free Press.

Mooney, C. (2006). *The Republican war on science* (Rev. and updated ed.). New York, NY: Basic Books.

Pfohl, S. (1977). The "discovery" of child abuse. *Social Problems, 24*(3), 310–323.

Platt, A. (1969). *The child savers: The invention of juvenile delinquency.* Chicago, IL: University of Chicago Press.

Rimm, M. (1995). Marketing pornography on the information superhighway: A survey of 917,410 images, description, short stories and animations downloaded 8.5 million times by consumers in over 2000 cities in forty countries, provinces and territories. *Georgetown Law Journal, 83*(5), 1849–1915.

Sutherland, E. H. (1950). The sexual psychopath laws. *Journal of Criminal Law and Criminology, 40*(5), 543–554.

Welsh, W. N., & Harris, P. W. (2008). *Criminal justice policy and planning* (3rd ed.). Newark, NJ: LexisNexis.

Williams, F. P., III, & McShane, M. (1995, November). *Getting your kicks on cyberspace's Route 66: Erotica, the information highway, and constructed social problems.* Paper presented at the annual meeting of the American Society of Criminology, Boston, MA.

Williams, F. P., III, McShane, M. D., & Hsieh, M.-L. (2007). Juveniles in cyberspace: Risk and perceptions of victimizations. In M. McShane & F. Williams (Eds.), *Youth violence and delinquency: Monsters and myths* (Vol. 1, pp. 145–158). Westport, CT: Praeger.

Williams, F. P., III, McShane, M. D., & Karson, L. (2007). Security in the evolution of the criminal justice curriculum. *Criminal Justice Studies: A Critical Journal of Crime, Law and Society, 20*(2), 161–173.

CHAPTER 21

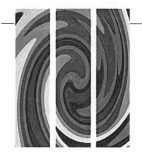

American Courts

Cassia Spohn

The past 50 years have witnessed significant changes in the structure of the American court system and the procedures that courts use to adjudicate criminal cases and sentence convicted offenders. Some of these changes resulted from Supreme Court decisions that interpreted constitutional provisions regarding right to counsel, selection of the jury, cruel and unusual punishment, due process of law, and equal protection under the law. Other changes resulted from legislative attempts to toughen criminal sentences and reduce sentence disparity, to provide alternatives to prison and probation, or to handle certain types of cases such as drug offenses or cases involving mentally-ill offenders more efficiently and effectively. Considered together, these changes have revolutionized the way American courts do business.

SUPREME COURT DECISIONS AND AMERICAN COURTS

The United States Supreme Court has played an important role in the development of the American court system, particularly with respect to such issues as right to counsel, jury selection, and sentencing. The decisions handed down by the Court in these areas have altered policy and practice and have led to fairer and less discriminatory court processing decisions.

The Right to Counsel

A series of court decisions broadened the interpretation of the Sixth Amendment's guarantee of the right to counsel and led to significant changes in requirements for provision of counsel for indigent defendants. The process began in 1932, when the Court ruled in *Powell v. Alabama* (287 U.S. 45 [1932]) that states must provide attorneys for indigent defendants charged with capital crimes. The Court's decision in a 1938 case, *Johnson v. Zerbst* (304 U.S. 458 [1938]), required the appointment of counsel for all indigent defendants in federal criminal cases, but the requirement was not extended to the states until *Gideon v. Wainwright* (372 U.S. 335 [1963]) was handed down in 1963. In subsequent decisions, the Court ruled that "no person may be imprisoned, for any offense, whether classified as petty, misdemeanor, or felony, unless he was represented by counsel"[1] and that the right to counsel is not limited to trial but applies to all "critical stages" in the criminal justice process.[2] As a result of these rulings, states must provide most indigent defendants with counsel, from arrest and interrogation through sentencing and the appellate process.

States moved quickly to implement the constitutional requirement articulated in *Gideon* and the subsequent cases, either by establishing public defender systems or by appropriating money for court-appointed attorneys. In 1951, there were only seven public defender organizations in the United States; in 1964, there were 136; by 1973, the total had risen to 573 (McIntyre, 1987). A national survey of indigent defense services among all U.S. prosecutorial districts found that 21% used a public defender program, 19% used an assigned counsel system, and 7% used a contract attorney system; the remaining districts (43%) reported that a combination of methods was used (Bureau of Justice Statistics, 2006). Although some critics have questioned the quality of legal services afforded indigent defendants (Casper, 1971; "Gideon's Promise," 2000), particularly in capital cases where the stakes are obviously very high (Bright, 1994), the findings of a number of methodologically sophisticated studies suggest that case outcomes for defendants represented by public defenders are not significantly different from those for defendants represented by private attorneys (Hanson & Ostrom, 2004; Williams, 2002). These results suggest that poor defendants are no longer "without a voice" (Myrdal, 1944, p. 547) in courts throughout the United States.

Jury Selection

Supreme Court decisions also have placed important restrictions on the jury selection process. The Court has consistently ruled against racial and ethnic bias in the selection of the jury pool and has made it more difficult for prosecutors and defense attorneys to use their peremptory challenges to exclude Black and Hispanic jurors. As the Court has repeatedly emphasized, the jury serves as "the criminal defendant's fundamental 'protection of life and liberty against race or color prejudice.'"[3] Reflecting this, in 1889, the Supreme Court ruled in the case of *Strauder v. West Virginia* (100 U.S. 303 [1880]) that a West Virginia statute limiting jury service to White males violated the equal protection clause of the 14th Amendment and therefore was unconstitutional.

The Court's ruling in *Strauder* made it clear that states could not pass laws excluding Blacks from jury service, but it did not prevent states, and particularly southern states, from developing techniques designed to preserve the all-White jury. In a series of decisions that began in the mid-1930s, the Supreme Court struck down these laws and practices, ruling, for example, that it was unconstitutional for a Georgia county to put the names of White potential jurors on white cards, the names of Black potential jurors on yellow cards, and then "randomly" draw cards to determine who would be summoned for jury service (*Avery v. Georgia,* 345 U.S. 559 [1953], at 562). As the Court stated in this case, "[T]he State may not draw up its jury lists pursuant to neutral procedures but then resort to discrimination at other stages in the selection process."

Critics contend that the Court's decisions regarding the peremptory challenge do, in fact, open the door to discrimination in jury selection (Kennedy, 1997; Serr & Maney, 1988). The Supreme Court's insistence that the jury be drawn from a representative cross section of the community and that race is not a valid qualification for jury service applies only to the selection of the jury pool. It does not apply to the selection of individual jurors for a particular case. As the Court has repeatedly stated, a defendant is *not* entitled to a jury "composed in whole or in part of persons of his own race."[4] Thus, prosecutors and defense attorneys can use their peremptory challenges—"challenges without cause, without explanation, and without judicial scrutiny"[5]—as they see fit. Critics of the process contend that, decisions handed down by the Supreme Court notwithstanding, prosecutors and defense attorneys can use their peremptory challenges to produce juries that contain few, if any, racial minorities.

The Supreme Court's rulings regarding racial discrimination in the use of peremptory challenges have evolved over time. The Court initially ruled that, although the prosecutor's use of peremptory challenges to strike all of the Black potential jurors in a jury pool did not violate the equal protection clause of the Constitution, a defendant could establish a prima facie case of purposeful racial discrimination by showing that the elimination of Blacks from a particular jury was part of a *pattern of discrimination* in that jurisdiction (*Swain v. Alabama,* 380 U.S. 202 [1965]). The problem, of course, was that the defendants in *Swain,* and in the cases that followed, could not meet this stringent test. As Wishman (1986, p. 115) observed, "A defense lawyer almost never has the statistics to prove a pattern of discrimination, and the state under the *Swain* decision is not required to keep them." The ruling, therefore, provided no protection to the individual Black or Hispanic defendant deprived of a jury of his peers by the prosecutor's use of racially discriminatory strikes.

It was not until 1986 that the Court, in *Batson v. Kentucky* (476 U.S. 79 [1986]), rejected *Swain's* systematic exclusion requirement and ruled "that a defendant may establish a *prima facie* case of purposeful discrimination in selection of the petit jury solely on evidence concerning the prosecutor's exercise of peremptory challenges at the defendant's trial." The justices added that once the defendant makes a prima facie case of racial discrimination, the burden shifts to the state to provide a racially neutral explanation for excluding Black jurors.

Although *Batson* seemed to offer hope that the goal of a representative jury was attainable, an examination of cases decided since 1986 suggests otherwise. State and federal appellate courts have ruled, for example, that leaving one or two Blacks on the jury precludes any inference of purposeful racial discrimination on the part of the prosecutor[6] and that striking only one or two jurors of the defendant's race does not constitute a "pattern" of strikes.[7] Trial and appellate courts have also been willing to accept virtually any explanation offered by the prosecutor to rebut the defendant's inference of purposeful discrimination (Serr & Maney, 1988, pp. 44–47). Decisions such as these led Kennedy (1997, p. 214) to characterize the peremptory challenge as "a creature of unbridled discretion that, in the hands of white prosecutors and white defendants, has often been used to sustain racial subordination in the courthouse." The Supreme Court's decisions notwithstanding, the peremptory challenge continues to be an obstacle to the creation of a racially neutral jury selection process.

Capital and Noncapital Sentencing

A third area that has been significantly reshaped by Supreme Court decisions is sentencing. The Court has handed down a series of important decisions on the capital sentencing process. Although the Court has never ruled that the death penalty per se is cruel and unusual punishment, it has said that the death penalty cannot be imposed on an offender convicted of the rape of an adult woman (*Coker v. Georgia*, 433 U.S. 584 [1977]) or child (*Kennedy v. Louisiana*, 554 U.S. 407___[2008]) and that the death penalty can be imposed on an offender convicted of felony murder if the offender played a major role in the crime and displayed "reckless indifference to the value of human life" (*Tison v. Arizona*, 481 U.S. 137 [1987], at 157). The Court also has ruled that the execution of someone who is mentally handicapped is cruel and unusual punishment in violation of the Eighth Amendment (*Atkins v. Virginia*, 536 U.S. 304 [2002]), that the Eighth and 14th Amendments forbid the imposition of the death penalty on offenders who were younger than age 18 when their crimes were committed (*Roper v. Simmons*, 543 U.S. 551 [2005]), and that the Constitution does not prohibit the use of lethal injection (*Baze v. Rees*, 553 U.S. _35__[2008]). With the exception of the felony murder and lethal injection rulings, these decisions all restrict the use of the death penalty by state and federal courts. In recent years, the Court also has overturned a number of death sentences due to ineffective assistance of counsel (see, for example, *Porter v. McCollum*, 130 S.C. 447 (2009) and *Sears v. Upton*, 130 S.C. 3,259 [2010]).

The Supreme Court also has addressed the issue of the role played by the jury at sentencing. The first case, *Apprendi v. New Jersey* (530 U.S. 466 [2000]), involved Charles Apprendi Jr., who fired several shots into the home of a Black family; made a number of statements, which he later retracted, suggesting that he had fired into the home because he did not want the family living in his neighborhood. Apprendi pleaded guilty to possession of a weapon for an unlawful purpose, a crime that carried a term of imprisonment of 5 to 10 years. The prosecutor then filed a motion for an enhanced sentence under the New Jersey hate-crime statute. The judge in the case found by a preponderance of the evidence that the shooting was racially motivated and sentenced Apprendi to 12 years in prison. Apprendi appealed, claiming that the due process clause of the Constitution required the state to prove the allegation of bias to the jury beyond a reasonable doubt. The Supreme Court ruled in Apprendi's favor, stating that any fact that increases the penalty for a crime beyond the prescribed statutory maximum, other than the fact of a prior conviction, must be submitted to a jury and proved beyond a reasonable doubt. In 2002, the justices similarly ruled that a jury—not a judge—must find the aggravating circumstances necessary for imposition of the death penalty (*Ring v. Arizona*, 536 U.S. 584 [2002]).

The Court reiterated this position in subsequent decisions involving defendants who were challenging sentences imposed under state and federal sentencing guidelines. In 2004, for example, the Court ruled in *Blakely v. Washington* (542 U.S. 296 [2004]) that the judge's decision to impose a sentence more severe than the statutory maximum allowed under the Washington sentencing guidelines violated the defendant's Sixth Amendment right to trial by jury. The Court revisited this issue 6 months later. This time, the issue was the power of federal judges to impose sentences more severe than called for under the U.S. sentencing guidelines. In *United States v. Booker* (543 U.S. 220 [2005]), the Court ruled, consistent with its decisions in *Apprendi* and *Blakely*, that the jury must determine beyond a reasonable doubt any fact that increases the defendant's sentence beyond the maximum sentence allowed under the sentencing guidelines.[8] The facts in this case were similar to those in *Blakely*. Booker was found guilty of a drug offense that, under the guidelines, carried a sentence of 210 to 262 months. At the sentencing hearing, however, the judge found additional facts that justified a harsher sentence; he sentenced Booker to 360 months in prison. The Court held that the 30-year sentence imposed by the judge violated the Sixth Amendment right to a jury trial and ordered the district court either to sentence Booker within the sentencing range supported by the jury's findings or to hold a separate sentencing hearing before a jury. The Court also ruled that the federal sentencing guidelines were advisory, not mandatory. In two cases decided in 2007,[9] the Court reiterated that the guidelines were advisory and ruled that the below-guidelines sentences imposed in each case were "reasonable" and that the judges who imposed the sentences had not abused their discretion. In the Gall decision, the Court noted, that although the guidelines are the starting point and initial benchmark, they are not the only factors to be taken into consideration.

The Supreme Court's decisions in these sentencing cases enhance the role played by the jury in both capital and noncapital cases. The decisions emphasize that the jury, not the judge, is to determine the facts in the case, that juries must determine the existence of aggravating factors that justify the imposition of the death penalty, and that sentences cannot exceed the maximum sentence based on the facts that were admitted in a guilty plea or found by the jury.

THE SENTENCING REFORM MOVEMENT

In 1972, Marvin Frankel, U.S. district judge for the Southern District of New York, issued an influential call for reform of the sentencing process (Frankel, 1972). The focus of Judge Frankel's critique was the indeterminate sentence, in which the judge imposed a minimum and maximum sentence, but the parole board determined the date of release based on its assessment of whether the offender had been rehabilitated or had served enough time for the particular offense. Judge Frankel characterized the indeterminate sentencing system as "a bizarre 'nonsystem' of extravagant powers confided to variable and essentially unregulated judges, keepers, and parole officials" (p. 1). Frankel (1972), who maintained that the degree of discretion given to judges led to "lawlessness" in sentencing, called for legislative reforms designed to regulate "the unchecked powers of the untutored judge" (p. 41).

Judge Frankel's calls for reform did not go unheeded. Reformers from both sides of the political spectrum joined in the attack on indeterminate sentencing and pushed for reforms designed to curtail judicial discretion and eliminate arbitrariness and disparity in sentencing. In response, state legislatures and Congress enacted a series of incremental structured sentencing reforms. A number of jurisdictions experimented with voluntary or advisory sentencing guidelines. Other states adopted determinate sentencing policies and abolished release on parole. Still other jurisdictions created sentencing commissions authorized to promulgate presumptive sentencing guidelines. Most states and the federal government also enacted mandatory minimum sentences for certain types of offenses (especially drug and weapons offenses), "three-strikes-and-you're-out" laws that mandated long prison sentences for repeat offenders, and truth-in-sentencing statutes that required offenders to serve a larger portion of the sentence before being released.

This process of experimentation and reform revolutionized sentencing in the United States. Thirty years ago, every state and the federal government had an indeterminate sentencing system, and "the word 'sentencing' generally signified a slightly mysterious process which . . . involved individualized decisions that judges were uniquely qualified to make" (Tonry, 1996, p. 3). The situation today is much more complex. Sentencing policies and practices vary enormously on a number of dimensions, and there is no longer anything that can be described as the American approach.

A discussion of each of the major reforms enacted during the sentencing reform movement is beyond the scope of this chapter. Instead, the chapter focuses on the movement away from the indeterminate sentence and toward a more structured sentencing process.

Determinate Sentencing

In the mid- to late 1970s, several states abolished release on parole and replaced the indeterminate sentence with a fixed (i.e., determinate) sentence. Under this system, the state legislature established a presumptive range of confinement for various categories of offenses. The judge imposed a fixed number of years from within this range, and the offender would serve this term minus time off for good behavior. Determinate sentencing, which was first adopted in California, Illinois, Indiana, and Maine, was seen as a way to restrain judicial discretion and thus to reduce disparity and (at least in the minds of conservative reformers) preclude judges from imposing overly lenient sentences. However, the degree to which the reforms constrain discretion varies. The California Uniform Determinate Sentencing Law, which took effect on July 1, 1977, provides that judges are to choose one of three specified sentences for persons convicted of particular offenses. The judge is to impose the middle term unless there are aggravating or mitigating circumstances that justify imposing the higher or lower term. Judges have considerably more discretion under the Illinois Determinate Sentencing Statute. Felonies are divided into six classifications, and the range of penalties is wide, especially for the more serious offenses. Murder and Class X offenses are nonprobationable, but judges can impose prison terms of 20 to 60 years or life for murder and 6 to 30 years for Class X offenses. If there are aggravating circumstances, the sentence range for Class X felonies increases to 30 to 60 years.

Although judges in jurisdictions with determinate sentencing retain control over the critical probation or prison decision, their overall discretion is reduced, particularly in states like California. Evaluations of the impact of the California law showed that judges complied with the law and imposed the middle term in a majority of the cases (Cohen & Tonry, 1983). Despite predictions that discretion would shift to the prosecutor and that plea bargaining would consequently increase, there were no changes in the rate or timing of guilty pleas that could be attributed to the determinate sentencing law. On the other hand, there was some evidence that prosecutors were increasingly likely to use provisions regarding sentence enhancements and probation ineligibility as bargaining chips. One study, for example, found that the sentence enhancement for use of a weapon was dropped in 40% of robbery cases and that the enhancement for serious bodily injury was struck in 65% to 70% of these cases (Casper, Brereton & Neal, 1982). As Walker (1993, p. 129) noted, "The net effect of the law seems to have been to narrow and focus the exercise of plea-bargaining discretion. Given the very restricted options on sentence length, the importance of the various enhancements and disqualifiers increased."

Partly as a result of research showing that determinate sentencing laws did not significantly constrain the discretion of judges, the determinate sentencing movement lost steam and eventually sputtered out. With the exception of the District of Columbia, no jurisdiction has adopted determinate sentencing since 1983. Moreover, in 2007, the Supreme Court addressed the validity of sentences imposed under California's determinate sentencing law. In the case of *Cunningham v. California* (127 S. Ct. 856 [2007]), the judge sentenced Cunningham to the higher term, based on six aggravating circumstances that the judge found by a preponderance of the evidence during a posttrial sentencing hearing. In striking down Cunningham's sentence, the Court reiterated that it had repeatedly held that facts that result in greater punishment for an offender must be found by a jury, not a judge, and using the standard of proof beyond a reasonable doubt. In response to this ruling, California changed its law and gave judges broad discretion to choose between the lower, middle, or upper term provided by the law for the particular crime; the judge does not need to show that there are aggravating factors that justify a sentence at the top of the range.

Presumptive Sentencing Guidelines and Mandatory Minimum Sentences

Since the late 1970s, presumptive sentencing guidelines developed by an independent sentencing commission have been the dominant approach to sentencing reform in the United States. About half of the states have adopted or are considering sentencing guidelines, and sentencing at the federal level has been structured by guidelines since 1987. In 1994, the American Bar Association (ABA) endorsed sentencing guidelines; it recommended that all jurisdictions create permanent sentencing commissions charged with drafting presumptive sentencing provisions that apply to both prison and nonprison sanctions and are tied to prison capacities (American Bar Association, 1994).

The guidelines systems adopted by Congress and by state legislatures have a number of common features (Stith & Cabranes, 1998). In each jurisdiction with presumptive guidelines, there is a permanent sentencing commission or committee composed of criminal justice officials and, sometimes, private citizens and legislators. The commission is charged with studying sentencing practices and formulating presumptive sentence recommendations. The commission is also authorized to monitor the implementation and impact of the guidelines and to recommend amendments. A second common feature is that the presumptive sentence is based primarily on two factors: the severity of the offense and the seriousness of the offender's prior criminal record. Typically, these two factors are arrayed on a two-dimensional grid; their intersection determines whether the offender should be sentenced to prison and, if so, for how long.

Jurisdictions with presumptive sentencing guidelines, as opposed to voluntary or advisory guidelines, require judges to follow them or provide reasons for failing to do so. Judges are allowed to depart from the guidelines and impose harsher or more lenient sentences if there are specified aggravating or mitigating circumstances. Some jurisdictions also list factors that should not be used to increase or decrease the presumptive sentence. For example, both the federal guidelines and the Minnesota guidelines state that the offender's race, gender, and employment status are not legitimate grounds for departure. In North Carolina, on the other hand, judges are allowed to consider the fact that the offender "has a positive employment history or is gainfully employed" (Bureau of Justice Assistance, 1996, pp. 79–80). In most states and in the federal system, a departure from the guidelines can be appealed to state appellate courts by either party. If, for example, the judge sentences the defendant to probation when the guidelines call for prison, the prosecuting attorney can appeal. If the judge imposes 60 months when the guidelines call for 36, the defendant can appeal.

Concomitant with the push toward sentencing guidelines, most jurisdictions enacted mandatory penalty statutes. These statutes, which require judges to impose minimum sentences on offenders convicted of certain types of crimes, proliferated during the war on crime that was waged during the 1970s, 1980s, and early 1990s. Candidates from both political parties campaigned on tough-on-crime and zero-tolerance-of-drug-use platforms and decried "lenient sentences" imposed by "soft" judges; they championed reforms designed to ensure that offenders "who do the crime will do the time." State and federal legislators responded enthusiastically (for a more detailed discussion of these laws see, Beckett & Sasson, 2000; Mauer, 2006; Tonry, 1995, 1996). Despite the fact that evaluations of these statutes revealed that they had not achieved their objectives, the mandatory penalty movement continued unabated. By the mid-1990s, mandatory penalties had been enacted in every state, and Congress had passed over 60 mandatory sentencing laws covering more than 100 federal offenses (Tonry, 1996, Chapter 5).

The Impact of Sentencing Guidelines

A detailed discussion of the impact of sentencing guidelines would consume many pages; there have been literally dozens of studies focusing on compliance with the guidelines and attempting to determine whether the guidelines (and mandatory minimum sentences) resulted in more punitive sentences and reduced disparity and discrimination in the sentencing process. Although the evidence is somewhat mixed, it does appear that sentences are more punitive today than in the past (Austin & Irwin, 2001; Engen & Steen, 2000; Frase, 1997; Kramer & Lubitz, 1985; Marvel & Moody, 1995; Moore & Miethe, 1986; Spohn, 2000; U.S. Sentencing Commission, 1991a, 1991b, 2004). The movement away from indeterminate sentencing and the rehabilitative ideal to determinate sentencing and an emphasis on just deserts—coupled with laws mandating long prison terms—have resulted in harsher sentences. As a result of these changes in sentencing policy, offenders convicted of felonies in state and federal courts face a greater likelihood of incarceration and longer prison sentences than they did in the pre-reform era. These changes, in turn, have led to dramatic increases in the nation's prison population.[10]

The evidence regarding the question of whether sentences today are fairer or more equitable than in the past also is mixed. Critics of sentencing reform contend that members of the courtroom workgroup have been able to circumvent—or even sabotage—the reforms enacted during the past 30 years; they argue that this makes it difficult to assess the impact of the reforms. Nonetheless, most studies of sentences imposed under federal and state guidelines conclude that guideline sentences are more uniform and less disparate (Anderson, Kling, & Stith, 1999; Ashford & Mosbaek, 1991; Hofer, Blackwell, & Ruback, 1999; Knapp, 1987; Kramer & Lubitz, 1985; Stolzenberg & D'Alessio, 1994; U.S. Sentencing Commission, 1991a; Washington State Sentencing Guidelines Commission, 1992; Wright, 1998). There is less interjudge disparity in jurisdictions with sentencing guidelines, and sentences are more tightly linked to the seriousness of the offense and the offender's prior criminal record.

The evidence regarding the effect of legally irrelevant offender characteristics—race, gender, age, education, and employment status—is less inconsistent and, unfortunately, more negative. There is a lack of longitudinal research comparing the effect of offender characteristics on sentence outcomes before and after the implementation of guidelines; this makes it difficult to assess the degree to which the guidelines have reduced unwarranted disparities in sentencing. Nonetheless, the studies of sentences imposed in federal and state jurisdictions operating under sentencing guidelines showed that racial minorities and women were sentenced differently from Whites and men (Albonetti, 1997, 2002; Demuth & Steffensmeier, 2004; Everett & Wojtkiewicz, 2002; Kramer & Steffensmeier, 1993; Kramer & Ulmer, 1996; LaFrentz & Spohn, 2006; Mustard, 2001; Spohn, 2000; Stacey & Spohn, 2006; Steen, Engen, & Gainey, 2005; Steffensmeier & Demuth, 2000, 2006; Steffensmeier & Hebert, 1999; Steffensmeier, Kramer, & Streifel, 1993; Steffensmeier, Ulmer, & Kramer, 1998). This suggests that attempts to constrain judicial discretion have not eliminated unwarranted disparities in sentencing. The guidelines notwithstanding, judges mete out harsher sentences to Black and Hispanic offenders than to similarly situated White offenders. They impose more lenient sentences on females than on males, and the unemployed and less educated receive harsher sentences than their counterparts.

These conclusions apply to sentences imposed under the more restrictive federal sentencing guidelines as well as the looser guidelines at the state level. They imply that judges and prosecutors are reluctant to place offenders into cells of sentencing grids defined only by crime seriousness and prior criminal record and, thus, that statutorily irrelevant factors such as race, gender, age, employment status, and social class may be factually relevant to criminal justice officials' assessments of dangerousness, threat, and culpability. In sum, these conclusions attest to the validity of Tonry's (1996, p. 180) assertion, "There is, unfortunately, no way around the dilemma that sentencing is inherently discretionary and that discretion leads to disparities."

SPECIALIZED OR PROBLEM-SOLVING COURTS: A FOCUS ON DRUG COURTS

The last three decades have witnessed another important change in the American court system: the development of specialized or problem-solving courts. These are limited-jurisdiction courts specializing in certain crime problems, such as drugs, guns, and domestic violence. These courts are like traffic courts in that they address a specific problem, but several factors set them apart (Berman & Feinblatt, 2001). The typical specialized court focuses on case outcomes—for example, getting offenders off drugs or protecting women from further intimate partner abuse— rather than case processing, and judges closely supervise offenders and monitor their progress. Specialized courts also are characterized by collaboration among criminal justice and social service agencies, nontraditional roles for participants, and a focus on systemic change.

The Drug Court Movement

The development of specialized courts is best illustrated by the drug court movement. Increases in the number of drug offenders appearing in state and federal courts—coupled with mounting evidence of both the linkages between drug use and crime and the efficacy of drug treatment programs—led a number of jurisdictions "to rethink their approach to handling defendants charged with drug and drug-related offenses" (Drug Court Clearinghouse and Technical Assistance Project, 1999, p. 3). Some jurisdictions, such as Cook County (Chicago), Illinois, established specialized dockets designed to manage the drug caseload more efficiently and to alleviate stress on the felony court system (Inciardi, McBride, & Rivers, 1996). Other jurisdictions, such as Dade County (Miami), Florida, created "drug treatment courts," which incorporated intensive judicial supervision of drug offenders, mandatory drug treatment, and rehabilitation programs providing vocational, educational, family, and medical services.

The drug treatment court concept spread rapidly during the 1990s. As of June 1999, there were 377 drug courts operating, and an additional 217 drug courts were in the planning stages in 49 of the 50 states, the District of Columbia, Puerto Rico, Guam, several Native American tribal courts, and two federal district courts (Drug Court Clearinghouse and Technical Assistance Project, 1999, p. 1). By December 2007, there were 1,786 adult and juvenile drug courts operating in jurisdictions throughout the United States; another 284 courts were in the planning stages (Bureau of Justice Assistance Drug Court, 2006). A 2005 report by the National Drug Court Institute (Huddleston, Freeman-Wilson, Marlowe, & Roussell, 2005) estimated that, at any one time, more than 70,000 drug offenders were participating in drug courts throughout the United States and its territories.

Although the nature and characteristics of drug courts throughout the United States vary widely, they share several key elements (National Association of Drug Court Professionals, 1997):

- Integration of substance abuse treatment with justice system case processing
- Use of a nonadversarial approach
- Early identification and prompt placement of eligible participants
- Access to a continuum of treatment, rehabilitation, and related services
- Frequent testing for alcohol and illicit drugs
- A coordinated strategy among judge, prosecutor, defense, and treatment providers to govern offender compliance
- Ongoing judicial interaction with each participant

In the typical preadjudication drug court, drug offenders who meet the eligibility criteria for the program are given a choice between participation in the drug court and traditional adjudication. Although the eligibility criteria vary, most programs exclude offenders who have prior convictions for violent offenses or whose current offense involved violence or use of a weapon. They target offenders whose involvement with the criminal justice system is due primarily to their substance abuse. The program may last 12 months, 18 months, or longer. Offenders who are accepted and agree to abide by the requirements of the program are immediately referred to a substance abuse treatment program for counseling, therapy, and education. They also are subject to random urinalysis and are required to appear frequently before the drug court judge. Offenders who do not show up for treatment sessions or drug court or who fail drug tests are subject to sanctions. Repeated violations may result in termination from the program and in adjudication and sentencing on the original charges. The charges against the offender are dismissed upon completion of the program.

The Effectiveness of Drug Courts

There is mounting evidence that drug courts reduce offender recidivism and prevent drug relapse. A report by the U.S. General Accounting Office (GAO, 1997) summarized the results of 20 evaluations of 16 drug courts that had been completed by early 1997. The GAO report indicated that these early evaluations generally concluded that drug courts were effective in reducing drug use and criminal behavior. A later review by Belenko (1998) summarized the results of 30 evaluations of 24 drug courts that had been completed by May 1998. Belenko (1998, p. 29) observed that most of these evaluations concluded "that criminal behavior was substantially reduced during participation in the program." For example, an evaluation of a Ventura County, California, drug court, which tracked recidivism over an 8-month period, found that only 12% of the drug court participants were rearrested, compared with 32% of those in a comparison group. A Jackson County, Missouri, evaluation similarly revealed 6-month rearrest rates of 4% for program participants and 13% for nonparticipants.

Belenko's review also included studies that assessed the impact of drug court participation on postprogram recidivism. Eight of the nine evaluations reported lower recidivism rates for the drug court group, compared with a group of similarly situated offenders who did not participate in the drug court program. An evaluation of the Multnomah County, Oregon, drug court, for example, found statistically significant differences between drug court participants (0.59 new arrests) and drug court-eligible nonparticipants (1.53 new arrests) over a 24-month tracking period. Belenko (1998, p. 18) concluded that "drug use and criminal behavior are substantially reduced while clients are participating in drug court, [and] criminal behavior is lower after program participation."

More recent and methodologically sophisticated studies also provide evidence that drug courts are effective in preventing recidivism. An evaluation of the Baltimore City Drug Treatment Court, for example, used an experimental design in which eligible offenders were randomly assigned either to the drug court or to traditional adjudication (Gottfredson & Exum, 2002). The results of the evaluation revealed that offenders assigned to the drug court were less likely than offenders placed in the traditional adjudication group to be rearrested during the 12-month follow-up period. A follow-up study using 3 years of recidivism data showed similar results; this study also showed that the positive effects of participation in the drug treatment court extended past the offenders' involvement in the drug court (Gottfredson, Najaka, Kearley, & Rocha, 2006).

CONCLUSION: POLICY IMPLICATIONS

The American court system has undergone significant changes over the past three decades. Criminal procedure has been reformed as a result of Supreme Court decisions that broadened the rights of criminal defendants, established rules for the selection of juries and the use of peremptory challenges, and placed restrictions on judges' sentencing discretion. Sentencing policies and practices in state and federal jurisdictions have undergone important modifications, and specialized or problem-solving courts have spread throughout the United States.

The question, of course, is whether these changes have produced a fairer and more equitable court system. It seems clear that the Supreme Court's decisions for broadening the right to counsel and restricting the use of race in the jury selection process have resulted in fairer treatment of poor defendants and defendants who are racial minorities and that the Court's decisions for limiting the use of the death penalty have made it more likely that capital punishment will be reserved for particularly heinous crimes. Less clear are the effects of the Court's decisions for enhancing the role of the jury in sentencing and making the federal sentencing guidelines voluntary. Although these decisions, which place significant restrictions on judicial discretion, may produce less disparity in sentencing, it also is possible that discretion will simply shift downstream to prosecutors. In other words, the source of disparity, including unwarranted disparity, in the new regime may be prosecutors' charging and plea-bargaining decisions.

The impact of specialized or problem-solving courts is also less evident. Research evaluating these courts is limited, and the research that does exist suffers from a number of methodological problems (Belenko, 1998). Nonetheless, there is mounting evidence that drug courts, domestic violence courts, and other specialized courts do reduce recidivism rates, and there is some evidence that these courts also lead to improvements in offenders' education and employment status, physical and mental health, and cognitive functioning. As research on problem-solving courts accumulates, our conclusions regarding their effectiveness will become less tentative.

DISCUSSION QUESTIONS

1. How have the Supreme Court's decisions regarding the right to counsel changed the American court system? In your opinion, have these been positive or negative changes?

2. Why would critics of the public defender system argue that criminal defendants "get what they pay for"? What are the problems inherent in the public defender system?

3. Evidence suggesting that prosecutors continue to use their peremptory challenges to preserve all-White juries in cases involving African American or

Hispanic defendants has led some commentators to call for the elimination of the peremptory challenge. What do you think is the strongest argument in favor of eliminating the peremptory challenge? In favor of retaining it? How would elimination of the peremptory challenge change the criminal trial?

4. What will be the impact of the Supreme Court's decision for making the federal sentencing guidelines voluntary and advisory rather than mandatory? Will these decisions lead to less uniformity and more disparity in sentencing, or will they enable judges to individualize justice in appropriate ways?

5. An important goal of sentencing guidelines was to eliminate unwarranted disparity in sentencing. Given this, how would you explain the fact that research reveals that both the offender's race and ethnicity and the offender's sex influence sentences imposed under state and federal sentencing guidelines?

6. How do specialized or problem-solving courts differ from traditional courts? Why have these courts become so popular in the United States?

NOTES

1. *Argersinger v. Hamlin,* 407 U.S. 25 (1972), at 37.
2. A defendant is entitled to counsel at every stage "where substantial rights of the accused may be affected" that require the "guiding hand of counsel" (*Mempa v. Rhay,* 389 U.S. 128 [1967], at 134). These critical stages include arraignment, preliminary hearing, entry of a plea, trial, sentencing, and the first appeal.
3. *McCleskey v. Kemp* (481 U.S. 279 [1987], at 310), quoting *Strauder v. West Virginia,* 100 U.S. 303 (1880).
4. *Strauder v. West Virginia,* 100 U.S. 303 (1880) at 305; *Batson v. Kentucky,* 476 U.S. 79 (1986) at 85.
5. *Swain v. Alabama,* 380 U.S. 202, 212 (1965) at 380.
6. *United States v. Montgomery,* 819 F.2d at 851. The Eleventh Circuit, however, rejected this line of reasoning in *Fleming v. Kemp* (794 F.2d 1478 [11th Cir. 1986]) and *United States v. David* (803 F.2d 1567 [11th Cir. 1986]).
7. *United States v. Vaccaro,* 816 F.2d 443, 457 (9th Cir. 1987); *Fields v. People,* 732 P.2d 1145, 1158 n.20 (Colo. 1987).
8. Also decided at the same time, and with the same result, was *United States v. Fanfan* (125 S. Ct. 12 [2004]).
9. *Gall v. United States,* No. 06–7949, decided December 10, 2007. *Kimbrough v. United States,* No. 06–6330, decided December 10, 2007.
10. Most scholars contend that this punitiveness has not produced the predicted reduction in crime. Conservative advocates of harsh crime control policies claim that locking up increasingly large numbers of felony offenders for increasingly long periods of time has caused the crime rate to fall; however, conceptual and methodological flaws in the "prison 'works'" argument call this conclusion into question. Critics suggest that a more careful examination of the evidence leads to the conclusion that increasing incarceration rates have little, if any, effect on crime rates (see, for example, Austin & Irwin, 2001; Tonry, 1995).

REFERENCES

Albonetti, C. A. (1997). Sentencing under the federal sentencing guidelines: Effects of defendant characteristics, guilty pleas, and departures on sentence outcomes for drug offenses, 1991–1992. *Law & Society Review, 31*(4), 789–822.

Albonetti, C. A. (2002). The joint conditioning effect of defendant's gender and ethnicity on length of imprisonment under the federal sentencing guidelines for drug trafficking/manufacturing offenders. *Journal of Gender, Race, and Justice, 6,* 39–60.

American Bar Association. (1994). *Standards for criminal justice—Sentencing alternatives and procedures* (3rd ed.). Boston, MA: Little, Brown.

Anderson, J. M., Kling, J. R., & Stith, K. (1999). Measuring interjudge sentencing disparity: Before and after the federal sentencing guidelines. *Journal of Law and Economics, 42*(S1), 271–307.

Ashford, K., & Mosbaek, C. (1991). *First year report on implementation of sentencing guidelines, November 1989 to January 1991.* Portland, OR: Oregon Criminal Justice Council.

Austin, J., & Irwin, J. (2001). *It's about time: America's imprisonment binge* (3rd ed.). Belmont, CA: Wadsworth.

Beckett, K., & Sasson, T. (2000). *The politics of injustice.* Thousand Oaks, CA: Pine Forge.

Belenko, S. (1998). Research on drug courts: A critical review. *National Drug Court Institute Review, 1*(1), 1–42.

Berman, G., & Feinblatt, J. (2001). *Problem-solving courts: A brief primer.* New York, NY: Center for Court Innovation.

Bright, S. B. (1994, May). Counsel for the poor: The death sentence not for the worst crime but for the worst lawyer. *The Yale Law Journal, 103,* 1835–1883.

Bureau of Justice Assistance. (1996). *National assessment of structured sentencing.* Washington, DC: U.S. Department of Justice, Bureau of Justice Assistance.

Bureau of Justice Assistance (BJA) Drug Court Clearinghouse. (2006, July 31). *Sentencing judges for Drug Court participants who are terminated.* Washington, DC: American University. Retrieved from http://www.ndcrc.org/sites/default/files/sentencingwithtermination.pdf

Bureau of Justice Statistics. (2006). *State court organization, 2004.* Washington, DC: United States Department of Justice, Bureau of Justice Statistics.

Casper, J. D. (1971). Did you have a lawyer when you went to court? No, I had a public defender. *Yale Review of Law and Social Action, 1,* 4–9.

Casper, J. D., Brereton, D., & Neal, D. (1982). *The implementation of the California determinate sentencing law: Executive summary.* Washington, DC: Government Printing Office.

Cohen, J., & Tonry, M. H. (1983). Sentencing reforms and their impacts. In A. Blumstein, J. Cohen, S. E. Martin, & M. H. Tonry (Eds.), *Research on sentencing: The search for reform* (Vol. 1, pp. 305–349). Washington, DC: National Academy Press.

Demuth, S., & Steffensmeier, D. (2004). Ethnicity effects on sentencing outcomes in large urban courts: Comparisons among White, Black, and Hispanic defendants. *Social Science Quarterly, 85*(4), 991–1011.

Drug Court Clearinghouse and Technical Assistance Project. (1999). *Looking at a decade of drug courts.* Washington, DC: U.S. Department of Justice.

Engen, R. L., & Steen, S. (2000). The power to punish: Discretion and sentencing reform in the war on drugs. *American Journal of Sociology, 105*(5), 1357–1395.

Everett, R. S., & Wojtkiewicz, R. A. (2002). Difference, disparity, and race/ethnic bias in federal sentencing. *Journal of Quantitative Criminology, 18*(2), 189–211.

Frankel, M. (1972). Lawlessness in sentencing. *University of Cincinnati Law Review, 41*(1), 1–54.

Frase, R. (1997). Prison population growing under Minnesota guidelines. In M. Tonry & K. Hatlestad (Eds.), *Sentencing reform in overcrowded times: A comparative perspective* (pp. 12–16). New York, NY: Oxford University Press.

Gideon's promise unfulfilled: The need for litigated reform of indigent defense. (2000). *Harvard Law Review, 113,* 2062–2079.

Gottfredson, D. C., & Exum, M. L. (2002). Baltimore City Drug Treatment Court: One-year results from a randomized study. *Journal of Research in Crime and Delinquency, 39*(3), 337–356.

Gottfredson, D. C., Najaka, S. S., Kearley, B. W., & Rocha, C. M. (2006). Long-term effects of participation in the Baltimore City Drug Treatment Court: Results from an experimental study. *Journal of Experimental Criminology, 2*(1), 67–98.

Hanson, R. A., & Ostrom, B. J. (2004). Indigent defenders get the job done and done well. In G. F. Cole, M. G. Gertz, & Bunger (Eds.), *The criminal justice system: Law and politics* (pp. 227–248). Belmont, CA: Wadsworth.

Hofer, P. J., Blackwell, K. R., & Ruback, B. (1999). The effect of the federal sentencing guidelines on interjudge sentencing disparity. *The Journal of Criminal Law & Criminology, 90*(1), 239–321.

Huddleston, C. W., III, Freeman-Wilson, K., Marlowe, D. B., & Roussell, A. (2005). *Painting the current picture: A national report card on drug courts and other problem solving court programs in the United States.* Washington, DC: National Drug Court Institute.

Inciardi, J. A., McBride, D. C., & Rivers, J. E. (1996). *Drug control and the courts.* Thousand Oaks, CA: SAGE.

Kennedy, R. (1997). *Race, crime, and the law.* New York, NY: Vintage Books.

Knapp, K. A. (1987). Implementation of the Minnesota guidelines: Can the innovative spirit be preserved? In A. von Hirsch, K. A. Knapp, & M. Tonry (Eds.), *The sentencing commission and its guidelines* (pp. 127–141). Boston, MA: Northeastern University Press.

Kramer, J. H., & Lubitz, R. L. (1985). Pennsylvania's sentencing reform: The impact of commission-established guidelines. *Crime & Delinquency, 31*(4), 481–500.

Kramer, J. H., & Steffensmeier, D. (1993). Race and imprisonment decisions. *The Sociological Quarterly, 34*(2), 357–376.

Kramer, J. H., & Ulmer, J. T. (1996). Sentencing disparity and departures from guidelines. *Justice Quarterly, 13*(1), 81–106.

LaFrentz, C., & Spohn, C. (2006). Who is punished more harshly? An examination of race/ethnicity, gender, age and employment status under the federal sentencing guidelines. *Justice Research & Policy, 8*(2), 25–56.

Marvel, T. B., & Moody, C. E. (1995). The impact of enhanced prison terms for felonies committed with guns. *Criminology, 33*(2), 247–281.

Mauer, M. (2006). *Race to incarcerate* (2nd ed.). New York, NY: The New Press.

McIntyre, L. (1987). *The public defender: The practice of law in the shadows of repute.* Chicago, IL: University of Chicago Press.

Moore, C. A., & Miethe, T. D. (1986). Regulated and unregulated sentencing decisions: An analysis of first-year practices under Minnesota's felony sentencing guidelines. *Law & Society Review, 20*(2), 253–277.

Mustard, D. (2001). Racial, ethnic and gender disparities in sentencing: Evidence from the U.S. federal courts. *Journal of Law and Economics, 44*(1), 285–314.

Myrdal, G. (1944). *An American dilemma: The Negro problem and modern democracy.* New York, NY: Harper.

National Association of Drug Court Professionals. (1997). *Defining drug courts: The key components.* Washington, DC: Bureau of Justice Assistance, U.S. Department of Justice.

Serr, B. J., & Maney, M. (1988). Racism, peremptory challenges and the democratic jury: The jurisprudence of a delicate balance. *Journal of Criminal Law & Criminology, 79*(1), 1–65.

Spohn, C. (2000). *Thirty years of sentencing reform: The quest for a racially neutral sentencing process.* Washington, DC: U.S. Department of Justice.

Stacey, A. M., & Spohn, C. (2006). Gender and the social costs of sentencing: An analysis of sentences imposed on male and female offenders in three U.S. District Courts. *Berkeley Journal of Criminal Law, 11*(1), 43–76.

Steen, S., Engen, R. L., & Gainey, R. R. (2005). Images of danger and culpability: Racial stereotyping, case processing, and criminal sentencing. *Criminology, 43*(2), 435–468.

Steffensmeier, D., & Demuth, S. (2000). Ethnicity and sentencing outcomes in U.S. federal courts: Who is punished more harshly? *American Sociological Review, 65*(5), 705–729.

Steffensmeier, D., & Demuth, S. (2006). Does gender modify the effects of race-ethnicity on criminal sanctioning? Sentences for male and female White, Black, and Hispanic defendants. *Journal of Quantitative Criminology, 22*(3), 241–261.

Steffensmeier, D., & Hebert, C. (1999). Women and men policymakers: Does the judge's gender affect the sentencing of criminal defendants? *Social Forces, 77*(3), 1163–1196.

Steffensmeier, D., Kramer, J., & Streifel, C. (1993). Gender and imprisonment decisions. *Criminology, 31*(3), 411–446.

Steffensmeier, D., Ulmer, J., & Kramer, J. (1998). The interaction of race, gender, and age in criminal sentencing: The punishment cost of being young, Black, and male. *Criminology, 36*(4), 763–797.

Stith, K., & Cabranes, J. A. (1998). *Fear of judging: Sentencing guidelines in the federal courts.* Chicago, IL: University of Chicago Press.

Stolzenberg, L., & D'Alessio, S. J. (1994). Sentencing and unwarranted disparity: An empirical assessment of the long-term impact of sentencing guidelines in Minnesota. *Criminology, 32*(2), 301–310.

Tonry, M. (1995). *Malign neglect: Race, crime, and punishment in America.* New York, NY: Oxford University Press.

Tonry, M. (1996). *Sentencing matters.* New York, NY: Oxford University Press.

U.S. General Accounting Office (GAO). (1997). *Drug courts: Overview of growth, characteristics, and results.* Washington, DC: U.S. General Accounting Office.

U.S. Sentencing Commission. (1991a). *The federal sentencing guidelines: A report on the operation of the guidelines system and short-term impacts on disparity in sentencing, use of incarceration, and prosecutorial discretion and plea bargaining.* Washington, DC: U.S. Sentencing Commission.

U.S. Sentencing Commission. (1991b). *Special report to Congress: Mandatory minimum penalties in the federal criminal justice system.* Washington, DC: U.S. Sentencing Commission.

U.S. Sentencing Commission. (2004). *Fifteen years of guidelines sentencing: An assessment of how well the federal criminal justice system is achieving the goals of sentencing reform.* Washington, DC: U.S. Sentencing Commission.

Walker, S. (1993). *Taming the system: The control of discretion in criminal justice, 1950–1990.* New York, NY: Oxford University Press.

Washington State Sentencing Guidelines Commission. (1992). *A decade of sentencing reform: Washington and its guidelines, 1981–1991*. Olympia, WA: Washington State Sentencing Guidelines Commission.

Williams, M. (2002, January). A comparison of sentencing outcomes for defendants with public defenders versus retained counsel in a Florida circuit court. *Justice Systems Journal, 23*, 249–257.

Wishman, S. (1986). *Anatomy of a jury: The system on trial*. New York, NY: Penguin Books.

Wright, R. F. (1998). *Managing prison growth in North Carolina through structured sentencing*. National Institute of Justice, Program Focus Series. Washington, DC: U.S. Department of Justice, National Institute of Justice.

CHAPTER 22

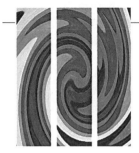

The Juvenile
Justice System

Randall G. Shelden

Founded in 1899 in Chicago and Denver, the juvenile court that initiated the juvenile justice system, promised that children's "best interest" would be served, as it was based upon the old English doctrine of parens patriae (for more detail, see Platt, 1977; Shelden, 2008, Chapter 5). New laws that defined delinquency and predelinquent behavior were broad in scope and quite vague, covering the following: (a) violations of laws also applicable to adults; (b) violations of local ordinances; (c) such catchalls as "vicious or immoral behavior," "incorrigibility," truancy, "profane or indecent behavior," "growing up in idleness," "living with any vicious or disreputable person," and many more. The third category would eventually be known as *status offenses* (Shelden, 2008, Chapter 5).

The juvenile court system rapidly spread throughout the country, following the lead of Chicago and Denver (both opened in 1899). Juvenile institutions, such as industrial and training schools and reform schools, continued to develop and expand. Until the 1960s, there were relatively few structural changes within the juvenile justice system. However, serious problems emerged from the very start, not the least of which was an obvious class, race, and gender bias. Indeed, the vast majority of youth brought to the juvenile court have been drawn from the ranks of the poor and racial and ethnic minorities (Shelden, 2008).

Although the most common disposition of cases processed through the juvenile court is probation, many young offenders end up placed somewhere other than within their own home. Most spend at least some time locked up in a secure facility, most commonly called a *detention center*.

Juvenile corrections include several different types of out-of-home placements of which the courts can make use. Some of these institutions are public (i.e., run by state or local governments), and others are privately funded. They can be further subdivided into short-term confinement (usually ranging from a few days to a couple of months) and long-term confinement (ranging from 3 or 4 months to 1 or 2 years).

DETENTION CENTERS

Detention is the most common temporary holding facility for juveniles. Here is where youth are placed pending a court hearing to determine whether or not they should be released. Despite the reforms of the past half century, conditions in many of the nation's detention centers remain horrible. This is especially true for the growing numbers of youth with serious mental health problems. Among the recent scandals surrounding detention centers, two Pennsylvania judges were convicted of sending more than 5,000 children to one of two privately operated detention centers in return for kickbacks that amounted to more than $2.6 million. These judges had helped the owners of these detention centers obtain county contracts worth $58 million. They then guaranteed the operators a steady income by providing a consistent stream of juveniles, mostly for very minor offenses (Chen, 2009; Ecenbarger, 2012; "Judges Sentenced Kids for Cash," 2009).

One of the most problematic features of detention centers is the large number of youth with serious mental health problems. The most recent estimates have found that from 67% to 70% of youth in all juvenile facilities (detention and juvenile prisons) "meet criteria for at least one mental health disorder" and that "79% of youth who met criteria for at least one mental health disorder actually met criteria for two or more diagnoses." Further, "over 60% of these youth were diagnosed with three or more mental health disorders" (Shufelt & Cocozza, 2006, p. 1).

Another survey found that more than one third of juveniles in detention and almost half of females "had felt hopeless or thought about death in the 6 months before detention," while about 10% had thought about suicide and the same percentage actually attempted suicide (Abram et al., 2008, p. 295). Another survey showed that about 11% of the males and 30% of the girls were diagnosed with major depression and just over half of both males and females were diagnosed with "conduct disorders" (Fazel, Doll, & Langstrom, 2008, p. 1010).

A 2004 report by the U.S. Senate's Governmental Affairs Committee concluded "thousands of children with mental illnesses await needed community mental health services in juvenile detention centers across the country" (Bazelon Center for Mental Health Law, 2004, para. 1). One expert testified, "Juvenile detention facilities lack the resources and staff to confront this problem; yet, corrections is being forced to shoulder the burden of the nation's failure to properly diagnose and care for children with mental or emotional disorders" (para. 1). The report identified 698 correctional facilities. Three quarters (524) responded to a survey in 2003, including facilities in every state except New Hampshire. In 33 states, juveniles with mental health problems were held even though there were no charges against them. Among the report's key findings was that the rate of suicide was 4 times higher than in the general juvenile population, that it is extremely expensive ($100 million per year to house youth waiting mental health placement), and that detention centers are overwhelmed, unable to cope with the situation (Associated Press, 2004). Writing in *The New York Times,* Solomon Moore said that "jails and juvenile justice facilities are the new asylums" (Moore, 2009, para. 6).

Additional reports continue to note the thousands of youth with mental health problems sitting in detention centers. Not surprisingly, the costs of keeping such youth in detention are greater than for other youth. A California study of 18 counties found that the cost per youth was $18,000 greater than for other youth; the study also noted that the costs of drugs administered to such youth amounted to an average of $4,387 per month (Justice Policy Institute, 2009).

One of the worst states (and there are many) in its treatment of juveniles is Mississippi. In March of 2010, the Southern Poverty Law Center filed suit against the state charging that

- Mississippi discriminates against children with mental illness by unlawfully separating them from their families and communities and by forcing them to cycle through psychiatric institutions that fail to provide adequate services.
- The state ignores the ongoing needs of children with mental illness by failing to provide federally mandated and medically necessary home- and community-based mental health services. (Southern Poverty Law Center, 2010, para. 3)

SPECIAL ISSUES FACING THE JUVENILE JUSTICE SYSTEM

The juvenile justice system cannot be discussed honestly without reference to two glaring problems: gender and race.

Status Offenses and the Double Standard

Since the beginning of the juvenile court, one of the most significant issues has been the vagueness of status offense treatment. Much of this vagueness stems from the differential application of such offenses, especially the use of a double standard for males and females who are brought within the juvenile court jurisdiction (Chesney-Lind & Shelden, 2014). Today, status offenses involve such behaviors as truancy, violating curfew, running away from home, and *incorrigibility* (often called by other names, such as *beyond control* and *unmanageable*). The ambiguity of such statutes gives those in authority a tremendous amount of discretionary power, which often leads to arbitrary decisions based on subjective value judgments imbued with class, race, and (of course) sexual bias.

From the very start of the juvenile court, girls particularly were victimized by the ambiguity of status offenses and the resulting double standard of treatment. Studies of early family court activity reveal that almost all the girls who appeared in these courts were charged with immorality or waywardness (Chesney-Lind, 1971; Schlossman & Wallach, 1978; Shelden, 1981).

The sanctions for such misbehavior were extremely severe. For example, the Chicago family court sent half the girl delinquents but only a fifth of the boys to reformatories between 1899 and 1909. In Milwaukee, twice as many girls as boys were committed to training schools, while in Memphis, females were twice as likely as males to be committed to training schools (Schlossman & Wallach, 1978; Shelden, 1981). In Honolulu between 1929 and 1930, more than half the girls referred to juvenile court were charged with *immorality*, which meant there was evidence of sexual intercourse; 30% were charged with waywardness. Evidence of immorality was vigorously pursued by arresting officers and social workers alike through lengthy questioning of the girls and, if possible, of males with whom they were suspected of having sex. Girls were twice as likely as boys to be detained for their offenses and spent 5 times as long in detention, on average, as their male counterparts. They were also nearly 3 times more likely to be sentenced to the training school. Well into the 1950s, half of those committed to training schools in Honolulu were girls (Chesney-Lind, 1971).

Subsequent studies of the juvenile justice system continued to produce evidence of this double standard continuing throughout the 20th century and into the current century (for a complete review, see Chesney-Lind & Shelden, 2014). For example, an investigation by the Southern Poverty Law Center showed that 75% of the girls at the Columbia Training School for Girls in Mississippi had been committed for status offenses, probation violations, or contempt of court (Southern Poverty Law Center, 2008). The suit "exposed brutal conditions at the prison, including the painful shackling of girls for weeks at a time. One girl was choked by a guard. Another girl was groped and fondled while in isolation" (para. 2). As a result, the institution was closed (para. 3).

The Human Rights Watch documented what is done to girls within the juvenile penal system of New York State. Their report, which focused on two training schools for girls, concluded,

> Far too often, girls experience abusive physical restraints and other forms of abuse and neglect, and are denied the mental health, educational, and other rehabilitative services they need. Because of the facilities' remote locations, confined girls are isolated from their families and communities. (Human Rights Watch, 2006, p. 3)

The Human Rights Watch report further noted,

> [A] disproportionate number of girls confined in New York are African-Americans from families who have lived in poverty for generations, with parents or other close relatives who themselves have been incarcerated. In many cases, these girls fall into juvenile facilities through vast holes in the social safety net, after child welfare institutions and schools have failed them. In the wake of legal reform in 1996, girls who commit "status offenses" such as disobedience and running away from home are no longer supposed to be placed in custody, but such offenses—and the related issue of involvement with child welfare agencies because of parental abuse and neglect—continue to function as gateways through which particularly vulnerable children are drawn into the juvenile justice system. (2006, p. 4)

The report was most critical of the agency responsible for overseeing these institutions, the New York State Office of Children and Family Services (OCFS). It tersely noted,

> Although OCFS is charged with rehabilitating children over whom it takes custody, it often fails to serve, and even to protect, confined girls, and this failure continues because there is little or no meaningful oversight of conditions in OCFS facilities. This last point is critical. Internal monitoring and oversight of the facility are, to put it charitably, dysfunctional, and independent outside monitoring is all but nonexistent. As a result, the conditions in the Tryon and Lansing facilities addressed in this report are shrouded in secrecy and girls who suffer abuse have little meaningful redress . . . we have found OCFS to be among the most hostile juvenile justice agencies we have ever encountered. (Human Rights Watch, 2006, pp. 3–4)

The report documented rampant abuse and the use of force on girls, including a

> forcible face-down "restraint" procedure intended for emergencies but in fact used far more often. In a restraint, staff seize a girl from behind and, in a face-down posture, push her head and entire body to the floor. They then pull her arms up behind her and hold or handcuff them. We found that the procedure is used against girls as young as 12 and that it frequently results in facial abrasions and other injuries, and even broken limbs. (Human Rights Watch, 2006, pp. 5–6)

Cases of sexual abuse by staff, including three cases of sexual intercourse with the girls were identified. Also, the girls "are bound in some combination of handcuffs, leg shackles, and leather restraint belts any time they leave the facility" (Human Rights Watch, 2006, pp. 5–6). They "are also subject to frequent strip-searches in which they must undress in front of a staff person and submit to a thorough visual inspection including their genitals" (pp. 5–6). Throughout the report there are documented incidents of human rights violations at both institutions, including violations of United Nations Standard Minimum Rules for the Treatment of Prisoners plus violations of New York State laws.

Race, the War on Drugs, and Referrals to Juvenile Court

It is impossible to talk about juvenile court processing without reference to race and, especially, regarding drug offenses. Race often plays an indirect role in that it relates to offense, which in turn affects the police decision to arrest. Race may also relate to the *visibility* of the offense. This is especially the case with regard to drugs. There is abundant evidence that the war on drugs has targeted African Americans on a scale unprecedented in U.S. history (Provine, 2007; Tonry, 1995; Walker, Spohn, & DeLone, 2007).

The juvenile arrest rate for both Whites and Blacks for heroin and cocaine possession was virtually the same in 1965. By the 1970s, the gap had begun to widen and continued to grow until the current era—a huge gap remains (Shelden, 2012), as noted below.

Regardless of whether race, class, or demeanor is statistically more relevant, one fact remains: growing numbers of African American youth are finding themselves within the juvenile justice system. They are more likely to be detained, more likely to have their cases petitioned to go before a judge, more likely to be waived to the adult system, and more likely to be institutionalized than their White counterparts (Walker et al., 2007, p. 144). On the bright side, there has been some progress in decreasing disproportionate minority representation within the juvenile justice system nationally (Davis & Sorensen, 2010).

One often overlooked source of racial bias is in child welfare case processing and how it relates to juvenile justice processing. Ryan, Herz, Hernandez, and Marshall (2007) examined data on child maltreatment cases over a 30-year period in Los Angeles and found that the child welfare system is a major source of African American overrepresentation in the juvenile justice system. Delinquency cases that began within the child welfare system were found to be far less likely to receive probation or other alternatives to incarceration.

Some believe that the overrepresentation of minority youth is a result of their committing more crimes than Whites. However, self-report surveys and surveys on drug use showing that Whites are more likely than minorities to use illegal drugs contradict that belief. The differential is more likely the result of police policies (e.g., targeting low-income, mostly minority neighborhoods) or the location of some offenses (especially drug use) in more visible places. Regardless of the reasons, studies have shown race is a very important indicator (Walker et al., 2007). A study conducted in Kentucky showed that at each stage of the process, Whites were treated more leniently than minorities. As cases move further and further into the system, the disadvantages of minority status increases (Colwell, Grieshop-Goodwin, & Swann, 2009).

Race and Detention

One of the most important decisions within the juvenile court is whether or not to detain a youth. Such decisions are usually based on written court policies. The three typical reasons for detention are: (a) the youth may harm self or others or may be subject to injury by others if not detained; (b) the youth is homeless or a runaway or has no parent, guardian, or other person able to provide adequate care and supervision; and (c) it is believed that, if not detained, the youth will leave the jurisdiction and not appear for court proceedings.

It could be argued that detention should be reserved for youth who are charged with serious crimes. This is not the case, however (Sickmund, Sladky, Kang, & Puzzanchera, 2013). The distribution according to offense is seen in Table 22.1. As shown here, about one fourth of those detained are charged with a serious violent

Table 22.1 Juveniles in Detention, by Offense, Sex, and Race 2011, (percent distribution)

	Detained								
	Sex			Race/Ethnicity					
Most serious offense	Total	Male	Female	White	Black	Hispanic	American Indian	Asian	Other
Total	100%	100%	100%	100%	100%	100%	100%	100%	100%
Delinquency	97%	98%	94%	96%	98%	99%	94%	97%	95%
Person	36%	37%	33%	31%	39%	36%	28%	50%	34%
Violent Crime Index*	24%	26%	15%	17%	29%	27%	13%	33%	16%
Other Person	12%	10%	18%	14%	11%	9%	14%	17%	17%
Property	22%	23%	16%	23%	22%	22%	20%	17%	21%
Property Crime Index**	18%	19%	13%	19%	19%	16%	16%	13%	18%
Other Property	4%	4%	3%	4%	3%	6%	4%	4%	3%
Drug	6%	6%	5%	7%	5%	7%	8%	6%	7%
Public order	12%	12%	10%	10%	12%	13%	8%	9%	9%
Technical violation	22%	20%	30%	25%	19%	21%	31%	16%	24%
Status offense	3%	2%	6%	4%	2%	1%	6%	3%	5%

Source: Sickmund, Melissa, Sladky, T. J., and Kang, Wei. (2008). "Census of Juveniles in Residential Placement Databook." Online. Available: http://www.ojjdp.ncjrs.gov/ojstatbb/cjrp/

* Includes criminal homicide, violent sexual assault, robbery, and aggravated assault.

** Includes burglary, theft, auto theft, and arson.

Notes: (a) U.S. total includes 2,325 juvenile offenders in private facilities for whom state of offense was not reported and a handful of youth who committed their offense in a U.S. territory but were being held in a U.S. mainland facility. (b) Detained juveniles include those held awaiting a court hearing, adjudication, disposition, or placement elsewhere. (c) The Hispanic category includes persons of Latin American or other Spanish culture or origin regardless of race. These persons are not included in the other race/ethnicity categories.

crime (24%), while technical violations (violation of a court order or violation of probation or parole, which does not include a new offense, as these are the most serious offenses) constitute 22%.

Race figures prominently in the decision to detain. The same data shown in Table 22.1 are presented in Table 22.2 but expressed as rate per 100,000 juveniles. Here, the racial discrepancies are clear. Regardless of offense, African American youths are far more likely to be detained than their White counterparts. Indeed, for all delinquent offenses, Black youth are about 5 times more likely to be detained, while for violent index crimes the ratio is almost 10:1.

The most severe disposition is commitment to an institution. Once again, race appears to be a big factor. Regardless of the offense, both African American and Hispanic youth have the highest rates of commitment. For all delinquent offenses, the ratio is about 5:1; for violent index crimes, the ratio 6.5:1. Hispanic youth have the second-highest rate in all offense categories, just ahead of Whites but far below Blacks. In the 1960s, the following phrase surfaced: "If you're white, you're all right; if you're brown, stick around; if you're black, stay back." This seems to apply to these data.

This is not to suggest that everyone connected with the juvenile justice system is racist and practices discrimination, although stereotypes about youth from certain race or class backgrounds definitely exist. Part of the problem is institutional in that such negative stereotypes are deeply embedded in our culture. Juvenile courts and police departments are largely staffed by Whites. The widespread poverty and joblessness affecting minority communities result in the lack of available resources (e.g., alternatives to formal court processing) to deal with crime-related issues and the general failure of schools.

Many studies have reported that prior record, instant offense, and previous sentences are among the most important factors in determining the final disposition (for a review, see Shelden, 2012).

THE RACIAL COMPOSITION OF JUVENILE INSTITUTIONS

The percentage of incarcerated youth who are racial minorities has risen steadily over the years. The national percentage of minorities in training schools was 23% in 1950, 32% in 1960, 40% in 1970, 60% in 1989, and 66% in 1997 then dropping to 63% in 2006 but increasing to 66% in 2011. One of the reasons White youth constitute the lowest percentage is that so many are confined in private facilities. This is no doubt because most of the costs are paid by family members, usually through their insurance (for details on these rates see Shelden, 2012, Chapter 12).

Not surprisingly, the overall *rate* of incarceration was considerably higher for minorities. Table 22.3 reveals stark contrasts. The rate for Blacks for all offenses (343) is almost double the rate for Hispanics (134) and is 4 times higher than Whites (79). For violent index crimes there is a huge difference, as the rate for Blacks (104) is 6.5:1 over Whites (16) and about 3 times greater than Hispanics (38).

Table 22.2 Juveniles in Detention, by Offense, Sex, and Race 2011, (rates per 100,000 juveniles)

Most serious offense	Detained							
	Sex			Race/Ethnicity				
	Total	Male	Female	White	Black	Hispanic	American Indian	Asian
Total	60	99	20	31	168	69	88	13
Delinquency	59	97	19	30	164	68	83	12
Person	22	36	7	10	66	25	24	6
Violent Crime Index*	15	26	3	5	48	18	12	4
Other Person	7	10	4	4	18	6	13	2
Property	13	23	3	7	37	15	18	2
Property Crime Index**	11	19	3	6	32	11	14	2
Other Property	2	4	1	1	5	4	4	0
Drug	4	6	1	2	8	5	7	1
Public order	7	12	2	3	20	9	7	1
Technical violation	13	20	6	8	33	15	27	2
Status offense	2	2	1	1	4	1	5	0

Source: Sickmund, Melissa, Sladky, T.J., and Kang, Wei. (2008) "Census of Juveniles in Residential Placement Databook." Online. Available: http://www.ojjdp.ncjrs .gov/ojstatbb/cjrp

* Includes criminal homicide, violent sexual assault, robbery, and aggravated assault.

** Includes burglary, theft, auto theft, and arson.

Notes: (a) The rate is the number of juvenile offenders in residential placement per 100,000 juveniles ages 10 through the upper age of original juvenile court jurisdiction in each State. (b) U.S. total includes 2,325 juvenile offenders in private facilities for whom State of offense was not reported and a handful of youth who committed their offense in a U.S. Territory but were being held in a U.S. mainland facility. (c) Rates for "All racial/ethnic groups" include juveniles identified in the Census of Juveniles in Residential Placement (CJRP) as "Other" race, most of whom were individuals with multiple race identification. Rates are not presented separately for these Other race juveniles because there is no comparable reference population available. (d) Detained juveniles include those held awaiting a court hearing, adjudication, disposition, or placement elsewhere. (e) The Hispanic category includes persons of Latin American or other Spanish culture or origin regardless of race. These persons are not included in the other race/ethnicity categories.

353

Table 22.3 Offense Profile of Committed Residents by Sex and Race/Ethnicity for United States, 2011 (rate per 100,000 juveniles)

| | | Committed | | | | | | |
| | | Sex | | | Race/Ethnicity | | | |
Most serious offense	Total	Male	Female	White	Black	Hispanic	American Indian	Asian
Total	133	228	34	79	343	134	264	23
Delinquency	128	222	29	74	332	132	241	22
Person	51	89	11	27	144	51	96	10
Violent Crime Index*	35	64	5	16	104	38	58	7
Other Person	16	25	6	10	40	14	39	2
Property	33	59	6	20	89	30	60	7
Property Crime Index**	28	50	5	17	78	24	49	6
Other Property	5	9	1	3	11	6	11	1
Drug	10	17	2	7	19	11	22	1
Public order	16	28	3	10	39	17	29	3
Technical violation	18	28	7	10	40	23	35	2
Status offense	5	6	4	5	11	2	23	1

Source: Sickmund, Melissa, Sladky, T. J., and Kang, Wei. (2008) "Census of Juveniles in Residential Placement Databook." Online. Available: http://www.ojjdp.ncjrs.gov/ojstatbb/cjrp/

Notes: (a) *The Hispanic category includes persons of Latin American or other Spanish culture or origin regardless of race. These persons are not included in the other race/ethnicity categories. (b) **U.S. total includes 2,325 juvenile offenders in private facilities for whom state of offense was not reported and a handful of youth who committed their offense in a U.S. territory but were being held in a U.S. mainland facility. (c) Rates for "All racial/ethnic groups" include juveniles identified in the CJRP as "Other" race, most of whom were individuals with multiple race identification. Rates are not presented separately for these Other race juveniles because there is no comparable reference population available. (d) Committed juveniles include those placed in the facility as part of a court ordered disposition.

A Notorious Example: The California Youth Authority

A large number of states have been plagued by scandals concerning their juvenile justice systems, especially their youth correctional institutions. Texas, Ohio, Florida, South Dakota, Oklahoma, Indiana, Maryland, Hawaii, Arizona, and Mississippi are among those states in which scandals have erupted and lawsuits have been filed (Dexheimer, 2007). Problems found in the California Youth Authority loom as some of the most significant.

The California Youth Authority (CYA) was created with the passage of The Youth Corrections Authority Act of 1941. The law created a three-person commission, mandated the acceptance of all youths under the age of 23 who had been committed to various prisons and already existing youth facilities, and appropriated $100,000 to run the CYA for 2 years. Until the early 2000s, this system consisted of 11 youth "correctional institutions," 11 forestry camps, 59 detention facilities, and several dozen "probation camps" scattered all over the state. At this time, there were about 10,000 youths housed within its 11 institutions.

Partly as a result of several publicized scandals (more about that shortly), there was a reorganization of the California Department of Corrections, and the CYA became the Division of Juvenile Justice (DJJ, or sometimes Department of Juvenile Justice Facilities [DJJF]) within the new Department of Corrections and Rehabilitation in 2005.[1] As of this writing (July 2014), there are fewer than 800 youth in three institutions. Part of the investigation into conditions within the CYA revealed the enormous costs of running these institutions. A detailed report noted that the yearly cost for one youth came to $234,029 (Buchen, 2013; Macallair, Males, & McCracken, 2009).

Beginning in the 1980s, a series of reports surfaced condemning practices within the CYA (DeMuro & DeMuro, 1988; Lerner, 1982, 1986). Each of these reports documented extreme brutality and the lack of meaningful treatment within these institutions. The third and final report showed that the CYA institutions "are seriously overcrowded, offer minimal treatment value despite their high expense, and are ineffective in long-term protection of public safety" (DeMuro & DeMuro, 1988, p. 11). Nothing significant was done about the problem.

In June, 1999, the Youth Law Center began investigating allegations that some CYA wards were being denied food as punishment. In December, the *Los Angeles Times* reported that wards at the Paso Robles Youth Correctional Facility were being handcuffed around the clock, sometimes for several days at a time. In May, 2000, the Youth Law Center filed a federal lawsuit (*Wilber v. Warner*) against the CYA for the failure of the CYA to license its inpatient medical and mental health. In September, the Inspector General of California released a report about "Friday Night Fights" (where correctional counselors forced wards to fight each other).

In 2002, another lawsuit was filed against CYA in *Farrell v. Harper,* alleging "inhumane conditions" and pointing out that "rehabilitation is impossible when the classroom is a cage and wards live in constant fear of physical and sexual violence

from CYA staff and other wards" (see http://www.clearinghouse.net/detail
.php?id=9466). A follow-up lawsuit (*Farrell v. Allen*) contended that the CYA is
inflicting "cruel and unusual punishment" on its wards, in violation of the Eighth
Amendment (see http://www.dralegal.org/impact/cases/farrell-v-allen). Meanwhile,
it was reported that there had been 13 suicides within CYA institutions since 1996,
and between 2001 and 2003 there were 56 attempted suicides.

A report by the Legislative Analyst's Office of California in 2004 stated,

> A significant amount of the educational program at various institutions is
> delivered in temporary buildings. These temporary buildings inherently have a
> rather limited useful life, and have functional deficiencies such as inadequate
> security and ineffective air conditioning at institutions located in warm cli-
> mates. The location of some of these temporary buildings is also an issue
> because they are often located a distance from housing units, requiring inten-
> sive staff supervision of ward movements. (California Legislative Analyst's
> Office, 2004, Mental Health Treatment and Education Program section)

Meanwhile, the press was getting involved. A series of reports in the *Los Angeles
Times* revealed cases of extreme brutality, suicides, horrible physical conditions, and
the CYA's almost total failure to live up to its mission statement. One report quoted
Dan Macallair, a 20-year veteran of juvenile justice work, who stated, "The California
Youth Authority is a dinosaur . . . based on a 19th century model. The institutions
need to be torn down" (as cited in Warren, 2004c, para. 5). Another report focused
on the cages used within some classrooms. The CYA called them "secure program
areas," ostensibly to protect both youth and teachers from violent acts. The *Los Angeles
Times* reported, "The cages essentially are large boxes in which wards are supplied
with a chair and desk, and teachers instruct them through a barrier of metal mesh or
chain link" (as cited in Leovy & Chong, 2004).

Bell and Stauring (2004) reported two other deaths within a CYA institution (Bell
& Stauring, 2004), saying,

> excessive rates of violence; inadequate mental health care and educational
> services; overuse of isolation cells; and deplorable conditions, including feces
> spread all over some of the cells. Some boys were being forced to sit or stand
> in cages while attending classes, a 'normal' situation in the state's Kafkaesque
> system. (para. 3)

The report further stated (para. 6) that "more than nine out of 10 CYA 'graduates' are back in trouble with the law within three years of their release."[2]

In December, 2004 the lawsuit was settled (now known as *Farrell v. Cate*[3]) and
the CYA was ordered to implement a plan to reduce violence and use-of-force. One
result of the suit was the changing of the name of the CYA to the Division of
Juvenile Justice (DJJ). In March 2006, the Safety and Welfare Planning Team, a
panel of state-approved correctional experts, found DJJ was "not a system that
needs tinkering around the edges, this is a system that is broken almost everywhere

you look." Moreover, the team concluded that the state's juvenile facilities had "[become] like adult prisons." Among its list of 17 significant problems, the team reported: "high levels of violence and fear," "antiquated facilities unsuited for any mission," "an adult corrections mentality," "hours on end when many youths have nothing to do," and "poor re-entry planning and too few services on parole" (Krisberg, 2009, p. 22).

Unfortunately, the agreement did not go far enough. As noted in a 2005 report (Anderson, Macallair, & Ramirez, 2005),

> What the agreement does not explicitly require, however, is that the CYA close any of its existing eight facilities as part of its new juvenile justice model for the state. These prison facilities are large, remote, outdated, dangerous, and cannot provide the right environment within which to conduct rehabilitative programming. (p. 1)

The CYA was ordered to develop what was called the Ward Safety and Welfare (S&W), Mental Health and Rehabilitation plan. In September 2007, Barry Krisberg (who was appointed as a "Special Master" to oversee the consent decree) filed a "DJJ Progress on the Standards and Criteria of the Safety and Welfare Remedial Plan." He wrote, "At this point, my judgment is that DJJ has not complied with the spirit and intent of the Safety and Welfare (S&W) standards and criteria. The current state of the custody classification process in DJJ does not meet nationally-accepted professional standards" (2009, p. 16).

Gradually the state began to order the closing of several CYA institutions, starting with two in July 2008; then, in August 2009, another one was closed. Finally, in 2011, two more were closed. Then, in September 2011, Krisberg issued his 19th report where he noted that there were "insufficient service provision for youth in restrictive programs" (2009, p. 16) and noted that there was frequent use-of-force (with chemical agents) toward youth with mental health problems.

The most recent developments include a proposal by Governor Jerry Brown to basically eliminate the youth prison system and transfer them to county-run facilities but as of this writing (July 2014). Nevertheless, the very idea of closing down the remaining institutions of the former CYA represents one of the most—if not the most—significant change in juvenile justice ever.

CONCLUSION: THE FUTURE OF THE JUVENILE COURT

In the years since the Supreme Court began reviewing issues related to juvenile justice (e.g., *In re Gault*), there has been a great deal of discussion concerning the role of the juvenile court. Should it be abolished, should it adhere strictly to a legalistic framework (e.g., due process considerations), or should it focus more on its original parens patriae principles? Many have challenged as counterproductive the movement toward treating young offenders as adults (Feld, 1999); besides, certification has not had very many positive results, which is one reason its use has declined in recent years (Shelden, 2012, pp. 385–388). The Supreme Court ruling in *Roper v. Simmons* demonstrated that young offenders need to be treated more leniently because there are significant differences between adolescent and adult reasoning processes (Shelden, 2012, pp. 360–362).

There is no question that there should be a separate system for young offenders, but it should be one that would adhere to principles consistent with that of restorative justice. Restorative justice is based on the idea that the only way to rid oneself of hurt and anger is through forgiveness. The object is to cease further objectification of those who have been involved in the crime—the victim, the offender, the families connected to these two individuals, and the community at large (Sullivan & Tifft, 2000). My position is summed up nicely in one of the classic critiques of the juvenile court by Supreme Court Justice Abe Fortas, when he wrote in *Kent v. United States* (383 U.S. 541, 1966) that "the child receives the worst of both worlds: that he gets neither the protection accorded to adults nor the solicitous care and regenerative treatment postulated for children" (as cited in Shelden, 2012, p. 354). Let us have a juvenile court that gives youth both the protection of the Bill of Rights *and* the care and treatment that should be available to all children.

DISCUSSION QUESTIONS

1. How do you explain the persistence of the double standard despite the many changes brought about by the women's movement of the past several decades?

2. Why do you think that race remains such a critical issue within the juvenile justice system?

3. Reports have consistently found little difference in drug usage among the different races, yet Blacks continue to be vastly overrepresented within the juvenile justice system for drug offenses. Explain this.

4. What do you think accounts for the persistent abuse within such juvenile institutions as the California Youth Authority?

5. Do a Google search of other states, and find some examples of other scandals centering on juvenile detention centers and correctional institutions.

6. Do you agree with the author's recommendation concerning the future of the juvenile court? Why or why not?

NOTES

1. Much of the information in this section has been obtained from the following: Center on Juvenile and Criminal Justice, (n.d.), "Juvenile Corrections Reform in California." Retrieved October 19, 2013, from http://www.cjcj.org/Education1/California-s-Farrell-Litigation.html

2. Numerous additional reports appeared in the *Los Angeles Times* and other newspapers in the state (Warren, 2004a, 2004b; Warren, Leovy, & Zamichow, 2004; Leovy & Chong, 2004, February 6). "Youth Authority to Review Use of Cages." *Los Angeles Times*. Retrieved from http://www.geocities.com/three_strikes_legal/lockup_blasted.html; de Sá, K. (2004, February 12). "Judge Orders Moratorium on Sending Juveniles to CYA Until Review." *San Jose Mercury News*, p. 1B.

3. *Kent v. United States* was the first juvenile court case heard by the U.S. Supreme Court; a minor's waiver from the jurisdiction of a juvenile court to that of an adult court was reviewed. For more detailed discussion, see Shelden (2012, Chapter 11).

REFERENCES

Abram, K. M., Choe, J. Y., Washburn, J. J., Teplin, L. A., King, D. C., & Dulcan, M. K. (2008). Suicidal ideation and behaviors among youths in juvenile detention. *Journal of the American Academy of Child and Adolescent Psychiatry, 47*(3), 291–300.

Anderson, C., Macallair, D., & Ramirez, C. (2005). *CYA warehouses: Failing kids, families, and public safety*. Oakland, CA: Books Not Bars. Retrieved October 19, 2013, from http://www.prisonpolicy.org/scans/cya_warehouses.pdf

Associated Press. (2004, July 7). *Report: Mentally ill teens "warehoused" in jails*. Retrieved October 17, 2013, from http://www.nbcnews.com/id/5387015

Bazelon Center for Mental Health Law. (2004, July 7). *Thousands of children with mental illness warehoused in juvenile detention centers awaiting mental health services*. Retrieved October 19, 2013, from http://www.bazelon.org/LinkClick.aspx?fileticket=sK FPwea2dVg%3D&tabid=328

Bell, J., & Stauring, J. (2004, May 2). Serious problems festering in juvenile justice system require serious reforms. *Los Angeles Times*. Retrieved October 19, 2013, from http://articles.latimes.com/2004/may/02/opinion/oe-bell2

Buchen, L. (2013). *California's Division of Juvenile Facilities: Nine years after Farrell*. San Francisco, CA: Center on Juvenile and Criminal Justice. Retrieved October 19, 2013, from: http://www.cjcj.org/uploads/cjcj/documents/state_of_djf.pdf

California Legislative Analyst's Office (2004, May). *A review of the California Youth Authority's infrastructure*. Retrieved from http://www.lao.ca.gov/2004/cya/052504_cya.htm

Chen, S. (2009, February 23). Pennsylvania rocked by "jailing kids for cash" scandal. *CNN*. Retrieved from http://www.cnn.com/2009/CRIME/02/23/pennsylvania.corrupt.judges/index.html

Chesney-Lind, M. (1971). *Female juvenile delinquency in Hawaii* (Unpublished master's thesis). University of Hawaii, Manoa.

Chesney-Lind, M., & Shelden, R. G. (2014). *Girls, delinquency, and juvenile justice* (4th ed.). New York, NY: Wiley-Blackwell.

Colwell, P., Grieshop-Goodwin, T., & Swann, A. (2009). *Opportunities lost: Racial disparities in juvenile justice in Kentucky and identified needs for system change*. Jeffersontown, KY: Kentucky Youth Advocates. Retrieved October 18, 2013, from http://www.louisvilleky.gov/NR/rdonlyres/52FB78DC-C5CC-4C3E-977E-99D65B79878D/0/KYAIssueBrief.pdf

Davis, J., & Sorensen, J. R. (2010). Disproportionate minority confinement of juveniles: A national examination of Black-White disparity in placements. *Crime & Delinquency*. Retrieved October 19, 2013, from http://cad.sagepub.com/cgi/rapidpdf/00111287 09359653v1.pdf de Sá, K. (2004, February 12). Judge orders moratorium on sending juveniles to CYA until review. *San Jose Mercury News*, p. 1B.

DeMuro, P., & DeMuro, A. (1988). *Reforming the California Youth Authority*. Bolinas, CA: Common Knowledge Press.

Dexheimer, E. (2007, April 29). Scandal and reform: A familiar cycle in agencies that deal with juvenile delinquents. *Austin American-Statesman*. Retrieved October 19, 2013, from http://www.texaspolicy.com/sites/default/files/documents/2007–04–29-AAS-ML.pdf

Ecenbarger, W. (2012). *Kids for cash: Two judges, thousands of children, and a $2.6 million kickback scheme*. New York, NY: The New Press.

Fazel, S., Doll, H., & Langstrom, N. (2008). Mental disorders among adolescents in juvenile detention and correctional facilities: A systematic review and meta regression analysis of 25 surveys. *Journal of the American Academy of Child & Adolescent Psychiatry, 47*(9), 1010–1019.

Feld, B. C. (1999). *Bad kids: Race and the transformation of the juvenile court*. New York, NY: Oxford University Press.

Human Rights Watch. (2006). *Custody and control conditions of confinement in New York's juvenile prisons for girls: Summary*. Retrieved October 18, 2013, from http://www.hrw.org/sites/default/files/reports/us0906webwcover.pdf

Judges sentenced kids for cash (Editorial). (2009, January 28). *Philadelphia Inquirer*. Retrieved from http://www.philly.com/philly/opinion/inquirer/20090128_Editorial__Judges_Sentenced.html

Justice Policy Institute. (2009, May). *The costs of confinement: Why good juvenile justice policies make good fiscal sense*. Retrieved October 17, 2013, from http://www.justicepolicy.org/images/upload/09_05_REP_CostsOfConfinement_JJ_PS.pdf

Krisberg, B. (2009, October 23). *Farrell v. Cate: Update on safety and welfare remedial plan progress*. Retrieved from http://www.prisonlaw.com/pdfs/OSM13,AppA.pdf

Leovy, J., & Chong, J. (2004, February 6). Youth Authority to review use of cages. *Los Angeles Times*. Retrieved October 19, 2013, from http://articles.latimes.com/2004/feb/06/local/me-cage6

Lerner, S. (1982). *The CYA report: Conditions of life at the California Youth Authority*. Bolinas, CA: Common Knowledge Press.

Lerner, S. (1986). *Bodily harm: The pattern of fear and violence at the California Youth Authority*. Bolinas, CA: Common Knowledge Press.

Macallair, D., Males, M., & McCracken, C. (2009). *Closing California's Division of Juvenile Facilities: An analysis of county institutional capacity*. San Francisco, CA: Center on Juvenile and Criminal Justice.

Moore, S. (2009, August 10). Mentally ill offenders strain juvenile system. *The New York Times*. Retrieved October 17, 2013, from http://www.nytimes.com/2009/08/10/us/10juvenile.html?pagewanted=all&_r=0

Platt, A. M. (1977). *The child savers: The invention of delinquency* (2nd ed.). Chicago, IL: University of Chicago Press.

Provine, D. M. (2007). *Unequal under law: Race in the war on drugs*. Chicago, IL: University of Chicago Press.

Ryan, J. P., Herz, D., Hernandez, P. M., & Marshall, J. M. (2007). Maltreatment and delinquency: Investigating child welfare bias in juvenile justice processing. *Children and Youth Services Review, 29*(8), 1035–1050.

Schlossman, S., & Wallach, S. (1978). The crime of precocious sexuality: Female delinquency in the progressive era. *Harvard Educational Review, 48*(1), 65–94.

Shelden, R. G. (1981). Sex discrimination in the juvenile justice system: Memphis, Tennessee, 1900–1917. In M. Q. Warren (Ed.), *Comparing male and female offenders* (pp. 55–72). Newbury Park, CA: SAGE.

Shelden, R. G. (2008). *Controlling the dangerous classes: A history of criminal justice in America* (2nd ed.). Boston, MA: Allyn and Bacon.

Shelden, R. G. (2012). *Delinquency and juvenile justice in American society* (2nd ed.). Long Grove, IL: Waveland Press.

Shufelt, J. L., & Cocozza, J. J. (2006). *Youth with mental health disorders in the juvenile justice system: Results from a multi-state prevalence study.* National Center for Mental Health and Juvenile Justice. Retrieved October 19, 2013, from http://ncmhjj.com/pdfs/publications/PrevalenceRPB.pdf

Sickmund, M., Sladky, T. J., and Kang, W. (2008) *Census of Juveniles in Residential Placement Databook.* Online. Available: http://www.ojjdp .ncjrs.gov/ojstatbb/cjrp/

Sickmund, M., Sladky, T. J., Kang, W., & Puzzanchera, C. (2013). *Easy access to the census of juveniles in residential placement.* Retrieved from http://www.ojjdp.gov/ojstatbb/ezacjrp/

Southern Poverty Law Center. (2008). J. A., et al. v. Barbour, et al. Retrieved October 18, 2013, from http://www.splcenter.org/get-informed/case-docket/ja-et-al-v-barbour-et-al

Southern Poverty Law Center. (2010, March 10). *SPLC sues Mississippi over mental health system for children on Medicaid.* Retrieved October 17, 2013, from http://www.splcenter .org/get-informed/news/splc-sues-mississippi-over-mental-health-system-for-children-on-medicaid

Sullivan, D., & Tifft, L. (2000). *Restorative justice as a transformative process.* Voorheesville, NY: Mutual Aid Press.

Tonry, M. (1995). *Malign neglect: Race, crime, and punishment in America.* New York, NY: Oxford University Press.

Walker, S., Spohn, C., & DeLone, M. (2007). *The color of justice: Race, ethnicity, and crime in America* (4th ed.). Belmont, CA: Cengage.

Warren, J. (2004a, February 3). Youth prison system unsafe, unhealthful, reports find. *Los Angeles Times.* Retrieved from http://articles.latimes.com/2004/feb/03/local/me-youth3

Warren, J. (2004b, February 4). Disarray in juvenile prisons jolts capital. *Los Angeles Times.* Retrieved from http://articles.latimes.com/2004/feb/04/local/me-cya4

Warren, J. (2004c, September 22). Shut down state youth prisons, experts say. *Los Angeles Times.* Retrieved from http://articles.latimes.com/2004/sep/22/local/me-cya22

Warren, J. (2005, February 1). For young offenders, a softer approach. *Los Angeles Times.* Retrieved from http://articles.latimes.com/2005/feb/01/local/me-cya1

Warren, J., Leovy, J., & Zamichow, N. (2004, February 17). A daily lesson in violence and despair. *Los Angeles Times.* Retrieved from http://articles.latimes.com/2004/feb/17/local/me-cya17

Part V

Corrections and Societal Response

CHAPTER 23

The Philosophical and Ideological Underpinnings of Corrections

Anthony Walsh and Ilhong Yun

WHAT IS CORRECTIONS?

Corrections is a generic term covering a wide variety of functions carried out by governmental agencies (and, increasingly, by private ones), having to do with the punishment, treatment, supervision, and management of individuals who have been convicted of crime. These functions are implemented in prisons, jails, and other secure institutions, as well as in community-based agencies, such as probation and parole departments. As the term implies, the whole correctional enterprise exists to correct, amend, or put right the criminal behavior of its clientele. This is a difficult task because that which must be corrected has festered for many years, and offenders often have a psychological, emotional, or financial investment in their current lifestyles (Andrews & Bonta, 2007).

THE THEORETICAL UNDERPINNINGS OF CORRECTIONS

Ever since humans have devised rules of conduct, they have wanted to break them. Most of us conform to the rules of our social groups most of the time and feel shamed and guilty when we violate them, but traveling the straight and narrow road does not always come naturally. Control theorists tell us that the real question is not why some people commit crimes but rather why most of us do not. After all, crime affords immediate gratification of desires with little effort: "money without work, sex without courtship, revenge without court delays" (Gottfredson & Hirschi, 2002, p. 210). We must learn to curb our appetites for immediate gratification and learn self-control as the social emotions—guilt, shame, embarrassment—merge with lessons taught to us to become our consciences.

In our earliest days, parents chastise us for doing things that we have an urge to do: throw temper tantrums, hit our siblings or steal their cookies, bite the cat's tail, and so on. Later on, teachers scold us, peers ostracize us, and employers fire us if we don't behave according to the rules. These chastisements are examples of informal social control used to achieve peace and predictability in our relationships with others. The more heavy-handed punishment handed out by the state is formal social control exercised against those who have not learned to behave well via informal control methods. In short, we have to learn to be good children and good citizens, and we learn that only when we realize that our wants and needs are inextricably bound up with the wants and needs of others and that they are best realized by cooperating with others who want the same things.

A SHORT HISTORY OF CORRECTIONAL PUNISHMENT

The earliest known written code of punishment is the Code of Hammurabi, created about 1780 BCE. This code expressed the concept of *lex talionis* (the law of equal retaliation, or "an eye for an eye, a tooth for a tooth"). These laws codified the natural inclination of individuals harmed by another to seek revenge, but they also recognize that personal revenge must be restrained if society is not to be fractured by a cycle of tit-for-tat blood feuds. To avoid this, the state took responsibility for punishing wrongdoers. Nevertheless, state-controlled punishment was typically as uncontrolled and vengeful as that which any grieving parent might inflict on the murderer of his or her child. Prior to the 18th century, human beings were considered born sinners because of the Christian legacy of original sin. Cruel tortures, used on criminals to literally "beat the devil out of them," were justified by the need to save sinners' souls.

The practice of brutal punishment began to wane in the late 18th century with the beginning of the Enlightenment, which was essentially a major shift in the way people viewed the world and their place in it. It was also marked by the narrowing of the mental and emotional distance between people. Enlightenment thinkers questioned traditional values and began to embrace humanism, rationalism, and science, values that ushered in the beginnings of a belief in the dignity and worth of all individuals. This view would eventually find expression in the law and in the treatment of criminal offenders.

The first person to apply Enlightenment thinking to crime and punishment was the English playwright and judge Henry Fielding (1707–1754). Fielding's book, *Inquiry Into the Causes of the Late Increase of Robbers* (1751/1967), set forth his thoughts on the causes of robbery, called for a "safety net" for the poor (free housing and food) as a crime prevention strategy, and campaigned for alternative punishments to hanging. Many of his suggestions were implemented and were apparently successful (Sherman, 2005).

THE EMERGENCE OF THE CLASSICAL SCHOOL

Enlightenment ideas led to a school of penology known as the *classical school*. More than a decade after Fielding's book, the Italian philosopher and politician Cesare Beccaria (1738–1794) published a manifesto for the reform of European judicial and penal systems titled *On Crimes and Punishment* (1764/1963). Beccaria did not question the need for punishment but believed that laws should be designed to preserve public order, not to avenge crime. Punishment should be proportionate to the harm done to society, should be identical for identical crimes, and should be applied without reference to the social status of offenders or victims. Punishment must be certain and swift to make a lasting impression on the criminal and to deter others. To ensure a rational and fair penal structure, punishments for specific crimes must be decreed by written criminal codes and the discretionary powers of judges curtailed.

Beccaria's work was so influential that many of his reforms were implemented in a number of European countries within his lifetime (Durant & Durant, 1967, p. 321). His reform ideas tapped into and broadened the scope of such emotions as sympathy and empathy among the intellectual elite of Europe. Alexis de Tocqueville (1838/1956, Book III, Chapter 1) noticed the diffusion of these emotions across the social classes, beginning in the Enlightenment with the spreading of egalitarian attitudes, and attributed the "mildness" of the American criminal justice system to the country's democratic spirit. Humans tend to feel empathy for those whom we view as being like us, and empathy often leads to sympathy, which may translate the vicarious experience of the pains of others into active concern for their welfare. With cognition and emotion blended into the Enlightenment ideal of the basic unity of humanity, justice became both more refined and more diffuse (Walsh & Hemmens, 2007).

Another prominent figure was the British lawyer and philosopher Jeremy Bentham (1748–1832). His major work, *A Fragment on Government and an Introduction to the Principles of Morals and Legislation* (1789/1948), is essentially a philosophy of social control based on the principle of utility, which prescribes "the greatest happiness for the greatest number." The proper function of the legislature is to promulgate laws aimed at maximizing the pleasure and minimizing the pain of the largest number in society. If legislators are to legislate according to this principle, they must understand human motivation, which for Bentham was easily summed up: "Nature has placed mankind under the governance of two sovereign masters, pain and pleasure. It is for them alone to point out what we ought to do, as well as to determine what we shall do" (1789/1948, p. 125). This was the Enlightenment concept of human nature: hedonistic, rational, and endowed with free will. Classical explanations of criminal behavior and how to prevent it are derived from these three assumptions.

Bentham devoted a great deal of energy (and his own money) to arguing for the development of prisons as substitutes for torture, execution, or transportation. He designed a prison in the 1790s called the *panopticon* ("all seeing"), which was to be a circular "inspection house" enabling guards to constantly see their charges, thus, requiring fewer staff. Because prisoners could always be seen without seeing by whom or when they were being watched, the belief was that the perception of constant scrutiny would develop into self-monitoring. Bentham felt that prisoners could be put to useful work to acquire the habit of honest labor.

THE EMERGENCE OF POSITIVISM

Classical thinkers were armchair philosophers, whereas positivist thinkers took upon themselves the methods of empirical science, from which more "positive" conclusions could be drawn. Positivists believe that human actions have causes and that these causes are to be found in the uniformities that precede those actions. Although early positivists were excessively deterministic, they slowly moved the criminal justice system away from a singular concentration on the criminal act as the sole determinant of punishment to an appraisal of the characteristics and circumstances of the offender as an additional determinant. Others such as Raffael Garofalo (1968) believed that, because human action is determined, the only things that should be considered at sentencing was offenders' "peculiarities" and the danger they posed to society. Garofalo's proposed sentences ranged from execution for *extreme criminals* (psychopaths), to transportation to penal colonies for *impulsive* criminals, to simply changing the law to deal with *endemic criminals* (those who commit "victimless crimes").

THE FUNCTION OF PUNISHMENT

The desire to punish those who have harmed us or otherwise cheated on the social contract is as old as the species itself. Punishment aimed at discouraging cheats is observed in every social species of animals, which leads biologists to conclude that punishment of cheats is an evolutionarily stable strategy designed by natural selection for the emergence and maintenance of cooperative behavior (Fehr & Gachter, 2002). Indeed, neuroimaging studies using positron-emission tomography (PET) and functional MRI (fMRI) scans provide hard evidence that positive feelings accompany the punishment of those who have wronged us and that negative feelings evoked when we are wronged are reduced. These studies showed that when subjects were able to punish cheats, they had significantly increased blood flow to areas of the brain that responded to reward, suggesting that punishing those who have wronged us provides emotional relief and reward for the punisher (de Quervain et al., 2004; Fehr & Gachter, 2002). Perhaps we are hardwired to get even, as suggested by the popular saying, vengeance is sweet.

Sociologist Émile Durkheim (1893/1964) also argued that crime and punishment are central to social life. Crime is socially useful, argued Durkheim, because by shocking the collective conscience it serves to clarify the boundaries of acceptable behavior, and punishing criminals maintains solidarity because the rituals of punishment reaffirm the justness of the social norms. Durkheim recognized the inborn nature of the punishment urge and that punishment serves an expiatory role, but he also recognized that we can temper the urge with sympathy. He observed that, over the course of social evolution, humankind had largely moved from retributive justice (characterized by cruel and vengeful punishments) to restitutive justice (characterized by reparation). Both forms of justice satisfy the human urge for social regularity by punishing those who violate the social contract, but repressive justice oversteps its adaptive usefulness and becomes socially destructive. Repressive justice is driven by the natural passion for punitive revenge that "ceases only when exhausted . . . only after it has destroyed" (Durkheim, 1893/1964, p. 86). Durkheim goes on to claim that restitutive justice is driven by simple deterrence and is more humanistic and tolerant, although it is still "at least in part, a work of vengeance" . . . since it is still "an expiation" (pp. 88–89).

THE OBJECTIVES OF CORRECTIONS

The five major objectives or justifications for the practice of punishing criminals are described next.

Retribution

Retribution is a *just deserts* model, which demands that criminals' punishments match the degree of harm they have inflicted on their victims. This is the most honestly stated justification for punishment because it both taps into our most primal urges and posits no secondary purpose for it, such as the reform of the criminal. California is among the states that have explicitly embraced this justification in their criminal codes (California Penal Code Sec. 1170a): "The Legislature finds and declares that the purpose of imprisonment for a crime is punishment" (cited in Barker, 2006, p. 12). This model of punishment avers that it is right to punish criminals, regardless of any secondary purpose that punishment may serve, simply because justice demands it.

Durkheim recognized that the urge to punish is inherent in human nature and that it serves to soothe, pacify, and even provide pleasant feelings for those witnessing it, vicariously or otherwise.

On a similar note, in his written opinion in *Furman vs. Georgia,* 408 U.S. 153 (1972) in which the U.S. Supreme Court invalidated Georgia's death penalty statute, Justice Stewart wrote the following about retribution (punishment that is justly deserved for its own sake):

> I cannot agree that retribution is a constitutionally impermissible ingredient in the imposition of punishment. The instinct for retribution is part of the nature of man, and channeling that instinct in the administration of criminal justice serves an important purpose in promoting the stability of a society governed by law. When people begin to believe that organized society is unwilling or unable

to impose upon criminal offenders the punishment they "deserve," then there are sown the seeds of anarchy—of self-help, vigilante justice, and lynch law.

Some of us may consider retribution to be primitive revenge and therefore morally wrong, but retribution as presently conceived is constrained revenge, curbed by proportionality and imposed by neutral parties bound by laws mandating respect for the rights of individuals against whom it is imposed. Logan and Gaes (1993) go so far as to claim that only retributive punishment "is an affirmation of the autonomy, responsibility, and dignity of the individual" (p. 252). By holding offenders responsible and blameworthy for their actions, we are treating them as free moral agents, not as mindless rag dolls blown around by the capricious winds of the environment.

Deterrence

Deterrence justifies punishment by assuming that it will prevent crime. The principle that people respond to incentives and are deterred by the threat of punishment is the philosophical foundation behind all systems of criminal law. Deterrence may be either specific or general.

Specific deterrence refers to the effect of punishment on the future behavior of people who experience the punishment. For specific deterrence to work, it is necessary that a person make a conscious connection between an intended criminal act and the punishment suffered as a result of similar acts committed in the past. If that person fails to make the connection, it is likely that he or she will continue to commit crimes. Committing further crimes after being punished is called *recidivism*, or "falling back" (into criminal behavior). Nationwide, about 33% of released prisoners recidivate within the first 6 months after release, 44% within the first year, 54% by the second year, and 67.5% by the third year (Robinson, 2005, p. 222).

The effect of punishment on future behavior depends on its certainty, celerity (swiftness), and severity. In other words, there must be a relatively high degree of certainty that punishment will follow a criminal act, the punishment must be administered soon after the act, and it must be harsh. Unfortunately, the wheels of justice grind excruciatingly slowly today, with many months passing between the criminal act and the imposition of punishment; so much for celerity. This leaves the law with severity as the only element it can realistically manipulate, but it is unfortunately the least effective element. Studies from the United States and the United Kingdom find substantial negative correlations (as one factor goes up, the other goes down) between the likelihood of conviction (a measure of certainty) and crime rates but much weaker ones (albeit in the same direction) for the severity of punishment (Langan & Farrington, 1998).

The effect of punishment on future behavior also depends on the *contrast effect*, which is the distinction between the circumstances of the possible punishment and the usual life experience of the person who may be punished. For people with little or nothing to lose, an arrest may be perceived as little more than an inconvenient occupational hazard, but for those who enjoy a loving family and the security of a valued career, the prospect of incarceration is a nightmarish contrast. Like so many other things in life, deterrence works least for those who need it most.

General deterrence refers to the preventive effect of the threat of punishment on the general population; it is thus aimed at *potential* offenders. The punishments meted out to offenders serve as examples to the rest of us of what may happen if we violate the law. The existence of a system of punishment for law violators deters a large but unknown number of individuals who might commit crimes if no such system existed.

What is the bottom line? Are we putting too much faith in the ability of criminals and would-be criminals to calculate the cost:benefit ratio of engaging in crime? Although many violent crimes are committed in the heat of passion or under the influence of mind-altering substances, there is evidence underscoring the classical notion that individuals do (subconsciously at least) calculate the ratio of expected pleasures to possible pains when contemplating a course of action. Gary Becker (1997) dismissed the idea that criminals lack the foresight to take punitive probabilities into consideration when deciding whether or not to continue committing crimes. He said, "Interviews of young people in high crime areas who do engage in crime show an amazing understanding of what punishments are, what young people can get away with, how to behave when going before a judge" (p. 20).

Some reviews of deterrence research indicate that legal sanctions do have "substantial deterrent effect" (Nagin, 1998, p. 16), and some have claimed that increased incarceration rates account for about 25% of the variance in the decline in violent crime over the last decade or so (Rosenfeld, 2000; Spelman, 2000). Paternoster cited a number of studies demonstrating that 20% to 30% of the crime drop from its peak in the early 1990s is attributable to the approximately 52% increase in the imprisonment rate in the United States. As he put it, "There is a general consensus that the decline in crime is, at least in part, due to more and longer prison sentences, with much of the controversy being over how much of an effect" (2010, p. 801). Of course, this leaves 70% to 80% to be explained by other factors. Unfortunately, we cannot determine if we are witnessing a *deterrent* effect (has violent crime declined because more would-be violent people have perceived a greater punitive threat?) or an *incapacitation* effect (has violent crime declined because more violent people are behind bars and thus not at liberty to commit violent crimes on the outside?). Paternoster concluded his review of the deterrence literature by stating,

> Finally, while there may be disagreement about the magnitude, there does seem to be a modest inverse relationship between the perceived certainty of punishment and crime [as certainty goes up, crime goes down], but no real evidence of a deterrent effect for severity, and no real knowledge base about the celerity [swiftness] of punishment. (2010, p. 818)

Incapacitation

Incapacitation refers to the inability of criminals, while incarcerated, to victimize people outside prison walls. Its rationale is aptly summarized in James Q. Wilson's (1976, p. 391) remark, "Wicked people exist. Nothing avails except to set them apart from innocent people." The incapacitation justification probably originated with Enrico Ferri's concept of social defense (1897/1917). To determine punishment, notions of culpability, moral responsibility, and intent were to be subordinate to an assessment of offenders' strength of resistance to criminal impulses, with the express purpose of averting future danger to society. Ferri reasoned that the characteristics of criminals prevented them from basing their behavior on rational principles, so they could be neither deterred nor rehabilitated; therefore, the only reasonable rationale for punishing offenders is to incapacitate them for as long as possible.

It goes without saying that incapacitation works, at least while criminals are incarcerated. Elliot Currie (1999) used robbery rates to illustrate this point. He stated that, in 1995, there were 135,000 inmates in state and federal institutions whose most serious crime was robbery, and that each robber on average commits five robberies per year. Had these robbers been left on the streets, they would have been responsible for an additional 135,000 x 5 or 675,000 robberies, on top of the 580,000 actual robberies reported to the police in 1995 (Home Truth Number Three section, para. 12). Similarly, Wright (1999) estimated that imprisonment averted almost 7 million offenses in 1990.

Rehabilitation

To *rehabilitate* means to restore or return to constructive or healthy activity. Whereas deterrence and incapacitation are primarily justified philosophically on classical grounds, rehabilitation is primarily a positivist concept. The rehabilitative goal is to change offenders' attitudes so that they come to accept that their behavior was wrong, not to deter them by the threat of further punishment. The difficulty with rehabilitation is that it asks criminals to return to a state which many (obviously, not all) of them have never been in (habilitation). But we keep on trying to rehabilitate criminals because what helps the offender helps the community. As former U.S. Supreme Court chief justice Warren Burger noted, "To put people behind walls and bars and do little or nothing to change them is to win a battle but lose a war. It is wrong. It is expensive. It is stupid" (as cited in Schmalleger, 2001, p. 439).

Correctional scholars are always mindful of the *nothing works* position of those who demand too much of rehabilitative efforts. Many correctional programs did not work in the past for a variety of reasons: They relied on nondirective methods that were inappropriate for offenders; they sought to change behaviors unrelated to crime; they used programs that were not intensive enough; and they used inadequately skilled staff to run them. Correctional scholars are somewhat more upbeat about rehabilitation today, given a range of new treatment modalities (Latessa, Cullen, & Gendreau, 2002; Walsh, 2006).

Reintegration

The goal of reintegration is to use the time criminals are under correctional supervision to prepare them to reenter the free community as well equipped as possible. In effect, reintegration is not much different from rehabilitation, but it is more pragmatic, focusing on concrete programs like job training rather than attitude change.

In 2004, there were 503,200 adult convicts who entered American prisons, and 483,000 left them (Glaze & Palla, 2005, p. 7, Table 4), and one in five will leave with no postrelease supervision, rendering parole "more a legal status than a systematic process of reintegrating returning prisoners" (Travis, 2000, p. 1). With the exception of convicts who max out, then, prisoners will be released under the supervision of a parole officer who is charged with monitoring offenders' behavior and helping them to readjust to the free world. The longer people remain in prison, the more difficult it is for them to readjust to the outside world.

Table 23.1 provides a summary of the key elements of the five punishment philosophies. Their common goal, of course, is the prevention of crime.

Table 23.1 Summary of Key Elements of Different Correctional Perspectives

	Retribution	Deterrence	Incapacitation	Rehabilitation	Reintegration
Justification	Moral; just deserts	Prevention of further crime	Risk control	Offenders have correctable deficiencies	Offenders have correctable deficiencies
Strategy	None; offenders simply deserve to be punished	Make punishment more certain, swift, and severe	Offenders cannot offend while in prison; reduce opportunity	Treatment to reduce offenders' inclination to reoffend	Concrete programming to make for successful reentry into society
Focus of Perspective	The offense and just deserts	Actual and potential offenders	Actual offenders	Needs of offenders	Needs of offenders
Image of Offenders	Free agents whose humanity we affirm by holding them accountable	Rational beings who engage in cost-benefit calculations	Not to be trusted but to be constrained	Good people who have gone astray; will respond to treatment	Ordinary folk who require and will respond to concrete help

Source: Anthony Walsh and Ilhong Yun

THE PAST, PRESENT, AND FUTURE OF CORRECTIONS

Many features of corrections' past still manifest themselves in the current correctional landscape, albeit in modified forms. Recent decades have seen an increase of a type of jail similar to Bentham's panopticon in terms of its design and efficiency (Tartaro, 2002). Frequently termed the *new generation jail*, the podular architecture permits continual surveillance with a minimal number of guards. In new generation jails, individual housing units are placed around an open area where a guard is permanently located. Inmates are allowed to move freely throughout the unit, but continual supervision of the movement is imposed by the centrally located guard. To maximize efficiency by reducing unnecessary movement and costs, all needed services—meals, phones, visits, counseling, showers, laundry, and so on—are directly offered within the unit.

The call for prison labor by early reformers as a way to reform criminals shaped the history of American corrections significantly, although the original rehabilitative rationale has largely been replaced by profits. In the United States, the Auburn system eventually outlasted the rival Pennsylvania system, largely due to the greater profits generated by the former's adoption of the congregate labor system, under which prisoners are able to pay for their own keep (Hawkins & Alpert, 1989).

Although inmate labor has been a central feature of prisons, it was not until the 20th century that prison industries flourished. During this period, the emerging *contract labor system* was implemented in many prisons nationwide. In this system, prison administrators contract with private firms, offering inmate labor in exchange for profits. The operation of prison industries was actively pursued, with the implicit notion of prisoner reform through disciplined work habits. This system hit a major roadblock during the Great Depression. Fearing the competition of inmate labor, labor unions successfully lobbied the legislature to curtail prison industries, and many of these legislative restrictions are still in force today. However, renewed emphasis on the rehabilitative merits of labor has recently brought about some regulatory relaxation. At the present time, goods produced in prison are mostly sold to public agencies, such as mental institutions or schools. Prison industries restore millions of dollars to state economies and contribute to rehabilitative relief from the boredom of prison life.

Diverse views still exist concerning what corrections is expected to accomplish, but the prevailing views of the public often become the basis for determining correctional objectives. With the advent of the Great Depression, the focus on retribution gave way to the goal of rehabilitation. The Great Depression drove many otherwise respectable people to poverty, suicide, and crime, owing to factors beyond their control. The age-old explanation of criminal behavior as a violation of free will did not seem to hold true anymore, and the time was ripe to look to what the positivists had to say about crime causation. The new *medical model* began to view inmates as individuals in need of help and treatment rather than moral failures. The old chain gangs and striped uniforms yielded to psychological diagnosis and counseling. Proof of rehabilitation became the basis of inmate release; therefore, indeterminate sentences and parole replaced determinate sentences.

Much to the dismay of supporters of the medical model, however, proof of rehabilitation was sparse. Instead, beginning in the tumultuous 1960s, the criminal justice landscape was painted by rising crime rates and unabated recidivism. Eventually, the public's disillusionment with the ideal of rehabilitation, and the general conservative mood of the 1980s, saw the return of the just deserts model. The public's mounting demand to "get tough" on criminals resulted in longer and mandatory sentences. Early releases through parole were increasingly supplanted by fixed sentences, and many institutions became "no-frills" prisons divested of TVs, recreational facilities, and educational and vocational opportunities (Finn, 1996). Chain gangs, lockstep marching, and striped uniforms reappeared in some localities. The dubious fame of the United States as the nation with the highest incarceration rate is the direct corollary of this correctional model.

SUMMARY

- Corrections is designed to punish, supervise, deter, and rehabilitate criminals. It is also the study of these functions.
- Although it is natural to want to exact revenge when people wrong us, to allow individuals to pursue this goal is to invite a series of tit-for-tat feuds that may fracture a community. The state has thus taken over responsibility for punishment. Over time, the state has moved to forms of punishment that are more restitutive than retributive, which, while serving to assuage the community's moral outrage, temper it with sympathy.
- Much of the credit for the shift away from retributive punishment must go to the great classical thinkers such as Fielding, Beccaria, and Bentham, all of whom were imbued with the humanistic spirit of the Enlightenment period. The view of human nature (hedonistic, rational, and possessing free will) held by these men led them to view punishment as primarily for deterrent purposes, that it should only just exceed the "pleasure" (gains) of crime.
- Opposing the classical notions of punishment are those of the positivists, who rose to prominence during the 19th century and who were influenced by the spirit of science. Positivists rejected the classicists' philosophical stance regarding human nature and declared that punishment should fit the offender rather than the crime.
- The objectives of punishment are retribution, deterrence, incapacitation, rehabilitation, and reintegration, all of which have come into and out of favor and back again over the years.
- Retribution is simply just deserts—getting the punishment you deserve, no other justification needed.
- Deterrence is the assumption that people are prevented from committing crimes by the threat of punishment.
- Incapacitation means that criminals cannot commit further crimes against the innocent while incarcerated.
- Rehabilitation centers on efforts to socialize offenders in prosocial directions while they are under correctional supervision so that they won't commit further crimes.

- Reintegration refers to efforts to provide offenders with concrete, usable skills that will provide them a stake in conformity.
- From the pursuit of correctional administrative efficiency emerged the construction of new generation jails and the wide use of sophisticated electronic devices. Traditionally, prison administrators made extensive use of inmate labor for monetary gain. Due to the opposition of labor unions and regulations imposed by the legislature, however, prison industry has been dwindling since the second half of the 20th century.
- The rehabilitation-oriented medical model of corrections largely gave way to the justice model during the 1980s. Instead of treatment and rehabilitation, the justice model emphasizes just deserts and being tough on criminals.

DISCUSSION QUESTIONS

1. Discuss the implications for a society that decides to eliminate all sorts of punishment in favor of forgiveness.

2. Is it good or bad that we take pleasure in punishment, and what evolutionary purpose does it serve?

3. Discuss the assumptions about human nature held by the classical thinkers. Are we rational beings, seekers of pleasure, and free moral agents?

4. Discuss the assumptions underlying positivism in terms of the treatment of offenders.

REFERENCES

Andrews, D., & Bonta, J. (2007). *The psychology of criminal conduct* (5th ed.). Cincinnati, OH: Anderson.

Barker, V. (2006). The politics of punishing: Building a state governance theory of American imprisonment variation. *Punishment & Society, 8*(1), 5–32.

Beccaria, C. (1963). *On crimes and punishment* (H. Paulucci, Trans.). Indianapolis, IN: Bobbs-Merrill. (Original work published 1764)

Becker, G. (1997). The economics of crime. In M. Fisch (Ed.), *Criminology 97/98* (pp. 15–20). Guilford, CT: Dusskin.

Bentham, J. (1948). *A fragment on government and an introduction to the principles of morals and legislation* (W. Harrison, Ed.). Oxford, United Kingdom: Basil Blackwell. (Original work published 1789)

Currie, E. (1999). Reflections on crime and criminology at the millennium. *Western Criminology Review, 2*(1). Retrieved October 20, 2009, from http://wcr.sonoma.edu/v2n1/currie.html

de Quervain, D., Fischbacher, U., Valerie, T., Schellhammer, M., Schnyder, U., Buch, A., & Fehr, E. (2004). The neural basis of altruistic punishment. *Science, 305*(5688), 1254–1259.

de Tocqueville, A. (1956). *Democracy in America* (H. Hefner, Ed.). New York, NY: Norton Books. (Original work published 1838)

Durant, W., & Durant, A. (1967). *Rousseau and revolution.* New York, NY: Simon and Schuster.

Durkheim, É. (1964). *The division of labor in society.* New York, NY: The Free Press. (Original work published 1893)

Fehr, E., & Gachter, S. (2002). Altruistic punishment in humans. *Nature, 415*(6868), 137–140.

Ferri, E. (1917). *Criminal sociology.* Boston, MA: Little, Brown. (Original work published 1897)

Fielding, H. (1967). *Inquiry into the causes of the late increase of robbers.* Oxford, United Kingdom: Oxford University Press. (Original work published 1751)

Finn, P. (1996). No-frills prisons and jails: A movement in flux. *Federal Probation, 60*(3), 35–44.

Furman v. Georgia, 408 U.S. 153 (1972).

Garofalo, R. (1968). *Criminology.* Montclair: NJ: Patterson Smith.

Glaze, L., & Palla, S. (2005, November). Probation and parole in the United States, 2004. *Bureau of Justice Statistics Bulletin.* Washington, DC: U.S. Department of Justice. Retrieved from http://149.101.16.41/content/pub/pdf/ppus04.pdf

Gottfredson, M., & Hirschi, T. (2002). The nature of criminality: Low self-control. In S. Cote (Ed.), *Criminological theories: Bridging the past to the future* (pp. 210–216). Thousand Oaks, CA: SAGE.

Hawkins, R., & Alpert, G. (1989). *American prison systems: Punishment and justice.* Englewood Cliffs, NJ: Prentice Hall.

Langan, P., & Farrington, D. (1998). *Crime and justice in the United States and England and Wales, 1981–1996.* Washington, DC: Bureau of Justice Statistics.

Latessa, W., Cullen, F., & Gendreau, P. (2002). Beyond correctional quackery—Professionalism and the possibility of effective treatment. *Federal Probation, 66*(2), 43–50.

Logan, C., & Gaes, G. (1993). Meta-analysis and the rehabilitation of punishment. *Justice Quarterly, 10*(2), 245–263.

Nagin, D. (1998). Criminal deterrence research at the onset of the twenty-first century. *Crime and Justice: A Review of Research, 23,* 1–42.

Paternoster, R. (2010). How much do we really know about criminal deterrence? *Journal of Criminal Law and Criminology, 100*(3), 765–823.

Robinson, M. (2005). *Justice blind: Ideals and realities of American criminal justice.* Upper Saddle River, NJ: Prentice Hall.

Rosenfeld, R. (2000). Patterns in adult homicide. In A. Blumstein & J. Wallman (Eds.), *The crime drop in America* (pp. 130–163). Cambridge, United Kingdom: Cambridge University Press.

Schmalleger, F. (2001). *Criminal justice today* (6th ed.). Upper Saddle River, NJ: Prentice Hall.

Sherman, L. (2005). The use and usefulness of criminology, 1751–2005: Enlightened justice and its failures. *Annals of the American Academy of Political and Social Science, 600*(1), 115–135.

Spelman, W. (2000). The limited importance of prison expansion. In A. Blumstein & J. Wallman (Eds.), *The crime drop in America* (pp. 97–129). Cambridge, United Kingdom: Cambridge University Press.

Tartaro, C. (2002). Examining implementation issues with new generation jails. *Criminal Justice Policy Review, 13*(3), 219–237.

Travis, J. (2000, May). *But they all come back: Rethinking prisoner reentry. Sentencing and Corrections: Issues for the 21st Century.* Washington, DC: U.S. Department of Justice, National Institute of Justice.

Walsh, A. (2006). *Correctional assessment, casework, and counseling* (4th ed.). Upper Marlboro, MD: American Correctional Association.

Walsh, A., & Hemmens, C. (2007). *Law, justice, and society: A sociolegal approach.* New York, NY: Oxford University Press.

Wilson, J. Q. (1976). *Thinking about crime.* New York, NY: Basic Books.

Wright, R. (1999). The evidence in favor of prisons. In F. Scarpitti & A. Nielson (Eds.), *Crime and criminals: Contemporary and classic readings in criminology* (pp. 483–493). Los Angeles, CA: Roxbury.

CHAPTER 24

Community Corrections, Rehabilitation, Reintegration, and Reentry

Traqina Emeka and Marilyn D. McShane

INTRODUCTION

Community corrections is undoubtedly the backbone of offender supervision in this country. Currently, the number of probationers and parolees in the United States is almost 5 million with one in every 50 adults in this country on correctional supervision. The most recent data indicate that the use of probation has decreased slightly over the last few years. However, the prevalence rates of community corrections sentences have been relatively stable for years, representing almost 70% of all who are under the supervision of the criminal justice system (Glaze & Parks, 2012). While community sentencing once may have represented a progressive reform in our justice system and an alternative to incarceration, it is now the primary form of punishment. Regardless of whether it is the most appropriate sanction, it appears to be the only one we can afford, given our limited resources.

The structure of community corrections operations reflects the inherent conflicts in managing local programs with significant state and even federal influence. While much of the day-to-day supervision of offenders takes place in a decentralized environment, there is always the coercive umbrella of legislation, regulation, and funding initiatives. Changes in the activities and priorities of law enforcement, court personnel, and prison and jail authorities mean that community corrections programs will be impacted and perhaps even undermined.

Realistically, the success of community corrections is likely to be determined by the ideological versions of one's goals and outcomes. Those who support a deterrence model will look for decreases in both self- and official reports of the offender's criminal activity. Evidence of rehabilitation would include abstaining from drug and alcohol use, steady employment, and consistent payments toward supervision and services. Retributive orientations, on the other hand, would expect the offender to have suffered for his or her offenses and, as with deterrence, to take steps to avoid more punitive sanctions in the future.

The concept of community corrections includes a broad array of legal alternatives to incarceration. Although most forms have traditionally involved monitoring the offender who resides at home, program options also include halfway houses, residential treatment, electronic tracking, and cyber monitoring. Today, advances in technology have changed the way community corrections officers perform their jobs, permitting more flexibility and remote supervision. In addition, contemporary public administration models rely more on networking and coordinating funded projects with schools, law enforcement, and civic leaders in the area. Both juvenile and adult justice systems employ these measures, and some do so as part of deferred adjudication, in which participants' records will be erased or expunged if the term of service under community supervision is successfully completed. The most common forms of community corrections are probation and parole.

Probation is usually administered by a local court, through the county or city, although separate systems are most often maintained for juveniles and adults. A probated sentence is the setting aside of a comparable prison term under a contract that includes a set of constraints and conditions the offender must meet in order to avoid incarceration. Conditions may include working; attending school; participating in treatment; paying various fines, restitution, and court costs; and avoiding high-risk people, places, and activities. Violations of the terms, as recorded by a supervising probation officer, may mean that the probation is revoked, and the offender will then serve the entire sentence in prison. Over the past few decades, almost two thirds of offenders have been arrested while on probation, although more than half will eventually complete their probation terms. However, recent efforts have created a continuum of punitive options as progressive or intermediate sanctions that might better control offenders' behavior on probation, reduce infractions, and perhaps eliminate the need to revoke probation of those who violate their terms and conditions.

Parole is a term used to mean a period of supervision in the community following early release from prison, during which the state continues to monitor the behavior of the parolee until the complete expiration of the defendant's full-sentence term. Thus, if a person with a 10-year sentence is released after 7 years, he or she will remain on parole, at least theoretically, for the remaining 3 years. Any violations that occur during the 3 years of release subject the parolee to revocation, whereby he or she would complete the entire remaining 3 years behind bars. Like probation, the offender agrees to follow conditions and rules enforced by a parole officer and may be subject to curfews, drug tests, and unannounced visits by the assigned case supervisor. Although more states are limiting the number of paroles and reducing the number of cases eligible to go before the parole board or increasing the time between parole hearings, more offenders are being released on a variation of parole called *mandatory release* or *mandatory supervision*. This is a legal status that usually reflects that inmates have served actual time and have accrued good time credit, the full length of their sentences. Release is then required by law; offenders remain under the jurisdiction of the state until the time by which they would have served the entire sentence without good time credit. This means that if a person has served 2 years in prison and has accumulated 2 years of good time credit through good behavior, he or she may be released from a 4-year-incarceration term. However, the offender will be supervised by a parole officer in the community until the remaining 2 years (the good time credit portion) has been served.

For newly released inmates, halfway houses are a popular option, as they provide a more gradual release from custody. This alternative allows offenders to remain in a more structured environment until their transition to independent living and working arrangements is functioning smoothly. Likewise, pre-revocation facilities, relapse centers for drug addicts, and state jails may provide structured support and intensive monitoring to avoid the need to return offenders to the more costly prison environment in order to control their activities.

PROBATION: PROGRESSIVE REFORM AND THE PROMISE OF REHABILITATION

While the concept of probation can be traced to the English corrections system, the term *probation* appears to have been coined by the American philanthropist John Augustus (Rothman, 1980). Augustus, who focused his efforts on helping the more undesirable elements of Boston society, created a system that allowed offenders, particularly alcoholics, to remain in the community under his strict supervision and to engage in work apprenticeships and mentoring. Probation as a sanction was also extended to juvenile offenders with the creation of the Juvenile Court in 1899.

The corruption of the original intent of this rehabilitative venture is seen in its widespread application to most offenders, not just those who appear motivated to reform. In addition, probation moved from providing a residential type of supervision to one that sends the offender back into a potentially high-risk environment. Today, only 40% of probationers have misdemeanor or petty offenses; the majority are convicted of felony crimes (Schloss & Alarid, 2007). What appear to be high failure rates may be explained by the attempt to make a very intensive sentence, constructed for a relatively select group, applicable to all at very low levels of programming.

It is not surprising that, in the process of moving more offenders toward community sanctions, and in our overreliance on the application of one-size-fits-all treatment programs, we grew more pessimistic about the effectiveness of a medical model in corrections. Martinson's controversial 1974 essay, "What Works?—Questions and Answers About Prison Reform" (better known as "Nothing Works"), reflected the public's concern that rehabilitation efforts were not effective enough and, consequently, resulted in the suspension of programming in favor of more conservative models of deterrence and harsh punishment. As a result, more offenders were released from prisons without any treatment, which undoubtedly diminished their prospects for success in society. Still, corrections officials persisted in finding ways to divert offenders and avoid building more prisons. In California, counties were offered state subsidies to keep fewer serious offenders within their jurisdictions. At local levels, corrections administrators struggled to find more effective community-based components and formulas that would prescribe how much treatment and supervision were needed at what point in time for each type of offender.

As part of the attempt to create new varieties of probation services, officials in the late 1970s and early 1980s experimented with shock probation and intensive supervision. For shock probation, offenders were sent to prisons for a short time, usually less than 180 days; then, judges would release them to a term of probation, believing that they had been "shocked" into good behavior by the harsh realities of prison, much like juveniles exposed to prisons in the Scared Straight programs. Efforts to provide intensive supervision were based on research that seemed to indicate that when offenders with the highest risk and needs levels receive the most intensive interventions, then reductions in recidivism were more likely to be realized (Lutze, Johnson, Clear, Latessa, & Slate, 2012). Still, in other studies, intensive supervision efforts seemed to yield higher levels of revocation, perhaps because probationers were being watched too closely or because supervising agencies were not able to sustain the surveillance efforts called for at this level. As one group of experts concluded (Lutze et al., 2012), alternative sanctions do not appear to be working and offenders recidivate because communities of reentry are unable to support the level of jobs and community-based services required by probationers. The lack of economic investments that would sponsor human capital and thus enhance community capacity can be cited as one of the most complex reasons for the failure of community supervision today.

PAROLE AS REWARD OR RELIEF

The earliest forms of parole were viewed as an indication that the offender was not only contrite and remorseful but also prepared to engage in productive citizenship. Inmates who best demonstrated literacy, discipline, job skills, and a deep appreciation of the habits of industry were carefully selected for the privilege of early release. This designation was not only a personal reward for conforming to American values but also a lesson to other inmates about the benefits of the assimilation of mainstream values. The period of postincarcerative supervision was considered an opportunity to ensure, under the watchful eye of the state, that the offender made a successful transition into the community. Ironically, Rothman's (1980) assessment of the public's perception of parole in the early 1900s is still relevant today. Then, as now, parole is criticized for its appearance of leniency and performance outcomes, in part, perhaps, because of unrealistic expectations about the criminal population. As Rothman explained,

Parole became the whipping boy for the failures of law enforcement agencies to control or reduce crime. Whenever fears of a 'crime wave' swept through the country, or whenever a particularly senseless or tragic crime occurred, parole invariably bore the brunt of attack. (p. 159)

Currently, it can be argued that the outside influence of legislators and political action groups makes it difficult for correctional systems to operate a cohesive and empirically driven program of risk assessment and release. The popularity of get-tough politicians has resulted in a wide range of increasingly harsh laws, restrictive parole policies, and barriers to release that seem to preclude officers and supervisors who work directly with inmates on a daily basis from utilizing their experience and expertise (DeMichele & Payne, 2012). Although validated assessments that can be objectively scored have become a major factor in the release decision, probation and parole officers fear that such generalized approaches do not allow them to include their instincts and experiences with specific offenders and offender populations. In places where there is almost exclusive reliance on these standardized risk and needs assessment tools to guide release decisions, caseworkers may attempt to subvert the outcomes. One study found that almost half of practitioners filling out prediction tools did so by either manipulating the data entered or reaching formal conclusions that were inconsistent with data included in the instrument (Miller & Maloney, 2013).

ASSESSMENT AND PREDICTION: RISK AND STAKES

One key to successful community corrections programming is making sure that proper mechanisms are in place not only for the rehabilitation of the offender but also for control measures to ensure the safety of the public. The latter would be accomplished by providing the most accurate assessment of the risk of each individual possible and then not only assigning offenders to levels of supervision that correspond to their different reoffending probabilities but also reviewing those classifications periodically to ensure their continued applicability. Part of a more sophisticated concept of risk is a realistic picture of the stakes involved in any one offender's release. These stakes represent the concept of harm: to the public, to the victims, and even to the supervising agency. For example, notorious offenders who have high public profiles seem to cause more political harm if they recidivate, as compared to lesser known and less serious offenders, because of the widespread anger and fear created by the publicity. Understandably, their cases must be weighed in terms of those stakes as well as according to the normal concept of risk (Williams, McShane, & Dolny, 2000). Stakes also include losses that may occur as a result of serious reoffending that remains undetected by the justice system.

There are typically two formal categories of risk assessments: clinical and actuarial (Gottfredson & Moriarty, 2006). Traditionally, clinical risk assessments have been used to determine the probability of offending based on professional judgments in the form of classification and prediction. Clinical assessments are more subjective and more individualized and take longer to complete than actuarial versions. Actuarial assessments, because they standardize prediction, are typically best for estimating future criminality for large groups of offenders. They involve statistical models and risk factor tools that predict behavior based on how others have acted in similar situations and/or an individual's similarity to various factor groupings. With an actuarial tool, offenders' characteristics are inventoried, and risk is determined by the extent to which he or she possesses various risk factors associated with recidivism (Zinger, 2004).

Risk prediction is traditionally based on static and dynamic factors that contribute to crime. Static variables are those which do not change (i.e., prior offense history, age at first offense). Dynamic factors represent issues or characteristics that may change, such as job stability and living arrangements. The importance of using risk assessment instruments involves matching needs with services, allocating resources efficaciously, preventing chronic offending, and increasing public safety.

WORSE THAN PRISON?

Public safety is a major concern any time offenders remain in the community. Conservative attacks by more punitive lawmakers often restrict the use of community supervision and narrow the potential pool served by these alternative sanctions. Truth-in-sentencing laws passed over the last decade have increased the proportion of actual sentences served in prison and have limited the accrual of good time credit toward early release. Realistically, however, the current capacity of prisons will not allow more significant portions of sentences to be served. This issue is often overlooked when more conservative, punitive laws are passed.

Underlying the fight against expanding the community corrections base is a perception that probation and parole are soft on criminals, easy to serve, and not painful enough to be a deterrent. However, studies now indicate that many offenders view longer and more intensive levels of community supervision as harsher than prison (Jones, 1996; Petersilia & Deschenes, 1994; Spelman, 1995). In *Profiles From Prison* (2003), Michael Santos described an offender who returned to prison to serve his final year rather than have his family suffer through the impositions and intrusions of constant surveillance. In this case, the parolee had to call for a recorded message each day to see if he was scheduled for a urinalysis, even though he had no prior drug use history or offenses. He also had to regularly attend anger management classes, Alcoholics Anonymous, and Narcotics Anonymous for 90 minutes each per week. He had to pay a fee for these meetings as well as miss work to attend them, which resulted in lower earnings. In addition, the offender reported to his parole officer monthly and filled out detailed records of all his finances and activities, including purchases made by his wife and children. His supervising officer made surprise weekly visits to his workplace and his home, sometimes at 5:30 in the morning when the family was asleep. The offender, Billy, describes the strain that parole put on his family. Billy told Santos that, for him and his wife, living under the parole officer's microscope for five years seemed worse than another six-to-twelve months of imprisonment. . . . Our marriage was strong. But the stress associated with supervised release was too much. . . . The stress threatened to break us up. I just wanted out. And if that meant going back to prison for a while, that's what I was willing to do. It was the only way I could get my life back. (p. 53)

REINTEGRATION AND REENTRY

Every year, more than 600,000 federal and state prisoners are released (Listwan, Jonson, Cullen, & Latessa, 2008), and another 9 million are released from jails (Yoon & Nickel, 2008). Although rates vary by state enforcement levels, caseloads, and revocation policies, close to one half will not complete their probation term, and two thirds will violate parole. These offenders will most likely be returned to prison within a relatively short period of time. Ironically, as conditions for community release become stricter and supervision becomes more punitive, revocations have increased and contributed to prison overcrowding. Thus, the mechanism used to relieve crowding becomes its major contributor. Fortunately, this is not inevitable; officials can reform and revise criteria to make success more probable through meaningful reentry programming. This is especially important, as some recent research has indicated that people who are granted a discretionary release from prison seem to have lower rates of recidivism than those who complete their entire term incarcerated and "max out" (Schlager & Robbins, 2008).

The goal of reentry programs is to rehabilitate offenders by equipping them with the necessary skills to become law-abiding, productive citizens. Officials agree, however, that high caseloads, limited resources, and the lack of specialized training on the part of criminal justice agents greatly impact the probability of a successful transition into society (Byrnes, Macallair, & Shorter, 2002). Adequately trained justice professionals are critical to ensuring that offenders in transition fully benefit from reentry programs. Offenders most likely to recidivate are those with low levels of education and a general lack of social support, including shelter, food, employment assistance, clothing, substance abuse, and mental health treatment. Because offenders exhibit mental health disabilities at a rate 3 times that of the general population, the demand for services often creates a strain on communities' already overburdened health-care systems (Skeem, Emke-Francis, & Louden, 2006).

Legislative barriers are also challenges that newly released offenders face. Certain crimes such as distribution of drugs may restrict someone with a felony record from accessing certain government services otherwise available for the needy. Federal education grants, welfare, food stamps, public housing, and certain types of jobs (i.e., child care, nursing, etc.) often exclude those with certain offense histories (Byrnes et al., 2002). Likewise, supplemental security income (SSI) recipients may lose benefits if they violate certain parole conditions. Offenders may also be excluded from jobs that require them to be bonded and to obtain driver's licenses (Travis, 2002).

Today, the most common reentry programs are those funded in part by faith-based and nonprofit community organizations (Yoon & Nickel, 2008). Civil liberties concerns about the potentially exclusive nature of religious programming and its implications for ideological coercion have generated parallel programs that are more secular. Both types utilize volunteers, donations, and local services as well as opportunities to integrate the offender back into the community with both physical and psychological support, mentoring, and gradual progression toward independent living.

FACTORS CORRELATED WITH COMMUNITY SUPERVISION SUCCESS AND FAILURE

Throughout the research literature and over time, there are several consistent correlates of community supervision success and failure, including offense history, substance use and abuse, age, marriage, employment status, and gender. Individuals with a history of criminality, particularly property offenders, have long been associated with probation and parole failure (Morgan, 1994; Petersilia, Turner, Kahan, & Peterson, 1985; Stahler et al., 2013; Sims & Jones, 1997; Whitehead, 1991). Alcohol and drug use also appear to predict recidivism. In addition, alcohol and drug treatment that is initiated but not completed may also result in a high rate of recidivism. Alcohol and drug treatment that addresses the motivation for committing crimes seems more likely to result in community supervision success (Gottfredson, Najaka, & Kearley, 2003).

Age appears to be a consistent predictor of probation success or failure, as younger offenders and those who begin their criminal activity at a younger age appear to be at greater risk for recidivism (Clarke, Yuan-Huei, & Wallace, 1988; Irish, 1989; Williams et al., 2000). The theoretical literature suggests that those more likely to reoffend typically have fewer social bonds than offenders who have more social bonds. Further, having a job and living with a spouse would influence criminality (Farrington, 1988). Carmichael, Gover, Koons-Witt, and Inabnit (2005) found that age, race, and the use of alcohol and drugs were predictors of parolee success in a sample of 503 female offenders. Also, Whites and older females were most likely to complete their sentences successfully. Females who did not indicate a history of drug or alcohol use and those who successfully addressed such problems were more likely to succeed on supervision.

Overall, it appears that most community supervision revocations are the result of technical violations, as opposed to a new offense (Carmichael et al., 2005). According to Sims and Jones (1997), technical violations surpass both major and minor violations. Gray, Fields, and Maxwell (2001) examined offenders who received probation violations, reasons for probation violation, and the time lapse till violation. The 30-month study of 1,500 probationers found that most technical probation violations occurred during the first 3 months of supervision.

One of the major difficulties in interpreting studies on community corrections outcomes is the different definitions of recidivism that are used. Events that trigger revocation vary in levels of seriousness or degrees of probability that a violation actually took place. Some researchers measure arrest, reconviction, incarceration, absconding, and any probation or parole violations, as well as probation suspension or revocation. While most use arrest records, this is often a subjective outcome that depends to some extent on law enforcement resources, probation and parole supervision policies, and court workloads.

Research at both the macro and micro levels has indicated that stereotypes about race and dangerousness may lead to harsher sentences (those that do not include community supervision) as well as to higher rates of probation and parole revocations (Huebner & Bynum, 2008). Awareness of disproportionate minority confinement has directed attention toward minimizing discretion in the community corrections process that might introduce bias and discriminate against segments of society. The U.S. Sentencing Commission's recent decision to address crack and powder cocaine-sentencing disparities by revising the sentencing guidelines and making those revisions retroactive may mean that many minority defendants are now eligible for parole or release. The development of a number of ethnically and culturally based programming initiatives has also created opportunities to meet the needs of minority youth in the community.

A recent New Mexico study found that although the law required all offenders to receive mandatory treatment for any DWI after the initial offense, few actually did. Findings indicated that, in many instances, judges were not putting the orders for treatment into sentences. Although some offenders may have been attending regular treatment, the system did not have the reporting mechanisms needed to track their progress (Woodall, 2008). This finding is consistent with research over the years indicating that the consistency with which mandated services are provided and the integrity of treatments offered explain much of the success and failure in community corrections programming.

ONGOING DEBATES AND POLICY IMPLICATIONS

Community corrections continues to be a controversial component of the justice system, perhaps because of its attempt to balance meaningful correctional measures with fair sentences, affordable policies and practices, and victims' rights. As we often see, sensationalized media accounts of some crimes feed panics that create assumptions about risk and violence that perpetuate harsher punishments. In some cases, youthful offenders are transferred from juvenile courts to adult criminal courts. As trends indicate, harsher sentencing strategies and more assertive victims' rights measures may make it more difficult for some offenders to be assigned community corrections options.

As the criminal justice system struggles to adapt to changing public views about appropriate conditions of supervision as well as the technologies available to enforce them, many questions are ultimately settled by the courts. As judges review cases, they continue to divide the priorities of the system into control and reform. Conditions in either category must be rationally related to a correctional goal and must be clear, reasonable, and constitutional. Recently, the courts have found that probationers could not be compelled to enroll in religiously oriented treatment programs like Alcoholics Anonymous (AA; *U. S. v. Myers,* 1994; *Warner v. Orange County Department of Probation,* 1994), nor can they be forced to participate in publicly humiliating displays of guilt (*People v. Hackler,* 1993). While there is agreement that a wider range of strategies must be available, authorities must be careful about the potentially damaging effects of any requirements.

Responding to scandals and abuses in the juvenile corrections system in Texas, the 2012 to 2013 legislative appropriations bill specifically set aside funding for new diversion programs for youthful offenders. The goal was to provide resources for juvenile probation services locally that would reduce the population of the trouble-plagued Youth Commission (Texas Juvenile Justice Department, 2012). In California, historic legislation signed by Governor Brown in 2011 already appears to have significantly reduced that state's prison population. California's Public Safety and Realignment Act of 2011 transferred the custody of low-level and nonserious offenders to the county for both jurisdiction and funding. Early reports seem to indicate that lower recidivism rates may reflect the greater reentry and reintegration potential in this arrangement (California Department of Corrections and Rehabilitation, 2013), and national prisoner statistics indicate that over half of the reductions in the U.S. prison population can be attributed to California's new mandates (Carson & Golinelli, 2013).

The reality of the revolving door between community and prison also has led Congress to pass several pieces of legislation aimed at increasing success in local corrections programming. First, the 2003 Serious and Violent Offender Reentry Initiative directed funds to programs nationwide that would develop best practices for dealing with high-risk juvenile and adult offenders at release. Second, in 2007, a $300 million federal spending package was passed to increase resources for reentry programs across the country under the Second Chance Act (Burke & Tonry, 2006). Funding focused on continued aftercare for those released after undergoing mental health or substance abuse treatments in prison. Programs were also developed around work readiness, family reunification, and mentoring services (Listwan et al., 2008). Still, though these new experimental programs and services appear to have significantly lowered recidivism rates, they reach only a fraction of the offenders in need. Much remains to be done to convince offenders that a true second chance really does exist.

DISCUSSION QUESTIONS

1. What is the purpose of community corrections in this country today, and what are the strengths and weaknesses of the concept in general?

2. What changes would you make in the operation of community supervision programs in your area, and how, specifically, would you engage the community in this process?

3. What are some of the barriers faced by offenders who have recently been released from prison? How can we address them effectively?

4. Many people seem to want to lock up more and more people for longer periods of time. How do we select offenders for community supervision programs so that we stay within our current budgets?

5. How realistic is the argument some offenders make that community supervision is worse than prison?

REFERENCES

Burke, P., & Tonry, M. (2006). *Successful transition and reentry for safe communities.* Silver Spring, MD: Center for Effective Public Policy.

Byrnes, M., Macallair, D., & Shorter, A. (2002). *Aftercare as afterthought: Reentry and the California Youth Authority.* San Francisco, CA: Center on Juvenile and Criminal Justice.

California Department of Corrections and Rehabilitation. (2013). *Realignment Report: A one-year examination of offenders released from state prison in the first six months of Public Safety Realignment.* Sacramento, CA: CDCR.

Carmichael, S., Gover, A., Koons-Witt, B., & Inabnit, B. (2005). The successful completion of probation and parole among female offenders. *Women & Criminal Justice, 17*(1), 75–97.

Carson, E. A., & Golinelli, D. (2013). *Prisoners in 2012.* Washington, DC: Bureau of Justice Statistics.

Clarke, S., Yuan-Huei, W. L., & Wallace, W. L. (1988). *Probationer recidivism in North Carolina.* Chapel Hill: University of North Carolina, Institute of Government.

DeMichele, M., & Payne, B. K. (2012). Measuring community corrections' officials perceptions of goals, strategies, and workload from a systems perspective. *The Prison Journal, 92*(3), 388–410.

Farrington, D. P. (1988). Studying changes within individuals: The causes of offending. In M. Rutter (Ed.), *Studies of psychosocial risk: The power of longitudinal data* (pp. 158–183). Cambridge, United Kingdom: Cambridge University Press.

Glaze, L. E., & Parks, E. (2012). *Correctional populations in the United States, 2011.* Washington, DC: Bureau of Justice Statistics.

Gottfredson, D., Najaka, S., & Kearley, B. (2003). Effectiveness of drug treatment courts: Evidence from a randomized trial. *Criminology and Public Policy, 2*(2), 171–196.

Gottfredson, S., & Moriarty, L. (2006). Statistical risk assessment: Old problems and new applications. *Crime and Delinquency, 52*(1), 178–200.

Gray, M., Fields, M., & Maxwell, S. (2001). Examining probation violations: Who, what, and when. *Crime and Delinquency, 47*(4), 537–557.

Huebner, B., & Bynum, T. (2008). The role of race and ethnicity in parole decisions. *Criminology, 46*(4), 907–937.

Irish, J. F. (1989). *Probation and recidivism: A study of probation adjustment and its relationship to post-probation outcome.* Mineola, NY: Nassau County Probation Department.

Jones, M. (1996). Voluntary revocations and the "elect-to-serve" option in North Carolina probation. *Crime and Delinquency, 42*(1), 36–49.

Listwan, S. J., Jonson, C. L., Cullen, F. T., & Latessa, E. (2008). Cracks in the penal harm movement: Evidence from the field. *Criminology and Public Policy, 7*(3), 423–465.

Lutze, F. E., Johnson, W., Clear, T., Latessa, E., & Slate, R. (2012). The future of community corrections is now: Stop dreaming and take action. *Journal of Contemporary Criminal Justice, 28*(1), 42–59.

Martinson, R. (1974). What works?—Questions and answers about prison reform. *The Public Interest, 35*(2), 22–54.

Miller, J., & Maloney C. (2013). Practitioner compliance with risk/needs assessment tools: A theoretical and empirical assessment. *Criminal Justice and Behavior, 40*(7), 716–736.

Morgan, K. D. (1994). Factors associated with probation outcome. *Journal of Criminal Justice, 22*(4), 341–353.

People v. Hackler, 13 Cal. App. 4th 1049 (1993).

Petersilia, J., & Deschenes, E. P. (1994). Perceptions of punishment: Inmates and staff rank the severity of prison versus intermediate sanctions. *The Prison Journal, 74*(3), 306–328.

Petersilia, J., Turner, S., Kahan, J., & Peterson, J. (1985). Executive summary of Rand's study, "Granting felons probation: Public risks and alternatives." *Crime and Delinquency, 31*(3), 379–392.

Rothman, D. (1980) *Conscience and convenience: The asylum and its alternatives in progressive America.* Boston, MA: Little, Brown.

Santos, M. (2003). *Profiles from prison: Adjusting to life behind bars.* Westport, CT: Praeger.

Schlager, M. D., & Robbins, K. (2008). Does parole work?—Revisited. *The Prison Journal, 88*(2), 234–251.

Schloss, C. S., & Alarid, L. (2007). Standards in the privatization of probation services. *Criminal Justice Review, 32*(3), 233–245.

Sims, B., & Jones, M. (1997). Predicting success or failure on probation: Factors associated with felony probation outcomes. *Crime and Delinquency, 43*(3), 314–327.

Skeem, J. L., Emke-Francis, P., & Louden, J. (2006). Probation, mental health, and mandatory treatment. *Criminal Justice and Behavior, 33*(2), 158–184.

Spelman, W. (1995). The severity of intermediate sanctions. *Journal of Research in Crime and Delinquency, 32*(2), 107–135.

Stahler, G., Mennis, J., Belenko, S., Welsh, W., Hiller, M., & Zajac, G. (2013). *Predicting recidivism for released state prison offenders: Examining the influence of individual and neighborhood characteristics and spatial contagion on the likelihood of reincarceration.* Bethesda, MD: National Institute on Drug Abuse.

Texas Juvenile Justice Department. (2012). *Community Juvenile Justice appropriations, riders and special diversion programs. Annual report to the governor and Legislative Budget Board.* Austin, TX. Retrieved December 14, 2013, from http://www.tjjd.texas.gov/publi cations/reports/AnnualReportFundingandRiders2012–12.pdf

Travis, J. (2002). Invisible punishment: An instrument of social exclusion. In M. Mauer & M. Chesney-Lind (Eds.), *Invisible punishment: The collateral consequences of mass imprisonment* (Chapter 1, pp. 15–36). New York, NY: W. W. Norton.

U. S. v. Myers, 864 F. Supp. 794 (1994).

Warner v. Orange County Department of Probation, 870 F. Supp. 69 (1994).

Whitehead, J. T. (1991). The effectiveness of felony probation: Results from an eastern state. *Justice Quarterly, 8*(4), 523–543.

Williams, F. P., McShane, M. D., & Dolny, M. (2000). Developing a parole classification instrument for use as a management tool. *Corrections Management Quarterly, 4*(4), 45–56.

Woodall, G. (2008). *Treating DWI offenders.* Albuquerque: University of New Mexico Center of Alcoholism, Substance Abuse and Addictions.

Yoon, J., & Nickel, J. (2008). *Reentry partnerships: A guide for states and faith-based and community organizations.* New York, NY: The Council of State Governments, Justice Center.

Zinger, I. (2004). Actuarial risk assessment and human rights: A commentary. *Canadian Journal of Criminology and Criminal Justice, 46*(5), 607–621.

CHAPTER 25

Restorative Justice in Theory

Lois Presser and Kyle Letteney

Wen we have been harmed by another, we respond by seeking justice. But what is justice? According to the restorative justice perspective, justice is repair of harms, with the offender as the main agent of repair. The harms requiring repair are considered both concretely and broadly. For example, restorative justice requires attention to the medical bills that an assault victim might have accumulated. But the victim's fears and self-doubt must also be addressed. Harm to *relationships* is taken especially seriously. Restorative justice stresses the victim's and the offender's relationships with each other and with other members of their communities. So in the restorative justice perspective, repair is seen as best facilitated by dialogue—the key tool of human relationship that it is.

In practice, restorative justice varies. Restorative justice programs include community service orders for offenders, school-based antibullying interventions, victim-offender dialogue, and meetings where representatives of Mothers Against Drunk Driving confront offenders who drive while intoxicated. Restorative justice clearly means different things to different people. The expression *restorative justice* gets pressed into the service of various goals, such as community building, rehabilitation of offenders, and victim healing. This wide interpretation is a boon if one's goal is to gain support for a restorative justice program. It is a problem, however, if one's goal is to design a *focused* program—one whose measures of performance are agreed upon by all stakeholders. The attempt here is to clarify what restorative justice is and how it is *supposed to* work—that is, to review theories of restorative justice. Along the way, we identify certain key controversies surrounding restorative justice in theory and in practice. These concerns ask whether restorative justice should ever intentionally harm offenders, whether participants should be forced to participate, whether certain interpersonal crimes are inappropriate for restorative justice practices, and whether restorative justice reproduces societal inequalities.

WHAT IS RESTORATIVE JUSTICE?

"So what are we actually here for today? Can I ask you?"[1]

A restorative justice program is any organized practice in which those in conflict, especially laypersons, talk with one another, focus on a specific (pattern of) harm, stand opposed to harm, and is based on an understanding of justice as harm reduction. According to Presser and Van Voorhis (2002), the core processes of restorative justice are dialogue, relationship building, and communication of moral values. A restorative justice program generally aims to facilitate all three processes.

Essential and Desirable Features

The expression restorative justice was first applied in the 1970s to interventions with low-level property offenders which entailed encounters between the offender and her/his victim (Zehr, 1995). Restorative justice is still frequently associated with face-to-face dialogue, but the latter must not be overstated. Dialogue may not occur, or it may occur via correspondence—as between incarcerated offenders and their victims. Expressions of apology and forgiveness are generally associated with restorative justice, but they are not essential, even as such expressions—if genuine—can be uniquely helpful in rebuilding relationship in the aftermath of harm.

Correctional treatment programs are designed to change offenders. But the potential targets of restorative justice are *all* those affected by crime: victims, offenders, and communities, whom Bazemore (1991) refers to as the "three clients" of restorative justice (p. 43). The healing of victims and communities is at least as important as any correctional impact that the intervention might have on the offender.

Is restorative justice simply a more traditional, premodern kind of justice? Ancient responses to crime were focused on the harms caused (Zehr, 1995). Dialogue, relationship building, and communication of moral values prevailed. Laypersons "ran the show": Governments had not yet codified and commandeered social conflicts (Christie, 1977; Weitekamp, 1996). Hence, restorative justice borrows from traditional responses to crime. However, restorative justice proponents are not necessarily opposed to state sponsorship of responses to crime. For example, Van Ness and Strong (2006) include in their vision of restorative justice a role for the state in ensuring order: It has "both the power and mandate" to do so (p. 47).

A Place for Retribution and Control?

Some ancient societies, while focused on harm and not law violation, nonetheless sought to *harm* the offender—to exact retribution, and the same is true for indigenous societies today (Daly, 2002). The intent to harm would seem inconsistent with today's restorative justice. But the incompatibility of restorative justice and retribution has been contested.

Both restorative justice and retribution focus on harms due to crime. They share the same end—to achieve justice—as opposed to the crime control sought by other rationales of punishment (i.e., deterrence, incapacitation, and rehabilitation). Zehr (2002) observed: "Both retributive and restorative theories of justice acknowledge a basic moral intuition that a balance has been thrown off by a wrongdoing" (p. 59). Yet whereas retributionists would correct the balance through imposition of pain, restorationists, or restorativists, would correct it through acknowledgment and repair of harms. In addition, restorationists consider the harms that the offender has experienced, which may or may not have instigated the offending behavior.

Bazemore and Schiff (2001, pp. 64–65) framed the difference another way: Retribution has the offender taking responsibility but passively and retrospectively, as s/he must pay in the same measure as her/his past action harmed the victim. Restorative justice looks both backward and forward, not only holding the offender responsible for what s/he did but also encouraging the active, future responsibility to make amends.

Whether or not restorative justice in *practice* precludes infliction of harm remains controversial. Some scholars contend that restorative justice is not incompatible with retribution. Based on her own careful research, Daly (2002) wrote:

> I have come to see that apparently contrary principles of retribution and reparation should be viewed as dependent on one another. Retributive censure should ideally occur before reparative gestures (or a victim's interest or movement to negotiate these) are possible in an ethical or psychological sense. Both censure and reparation may be experienced as "punishment" by offenders (even if this is not the intent of decision-makers), and both censure and reparation need to occur before a victim or community can "reintegrate" an offender into the community. (p. 60)

Duff (2002) likewise made a case for "restoration through punishment." He wrote, "The wrongdoer should be pained by the censure of his fellow citizens: if he is not pained, their censure has failed to achieve its intended result" (p. 96).

Restorative justice proponents specify that censure, however harsh, involve declarations that the offense *but not the offender* is bad (Barton, 2003, p. 23). The reasons for this principle mainly have to do with crime control and are discussed in the next section. At the same time, in the restorative justice ideal, victims are encouraged to express the full range of their thoughts and feelings. Thus, the "disciplining" of censure within restorative justice encounters is *potentially* at odds with its deference to victims. What victims might want to say does not always accord with restorative justice ideals or theories.

Arrigo and Schehr (1998) observed that the protocol and language of restorative justice constrain what participants can say: "Limiting potentially hostile outbursts from victims (and offenders) is essential to the reconciliation and restitution process" (p. 649). For Barton (2003), however, a high degree of structure during the victim-offender conference ensures that all participants speak (relatively) freely of intimidation: He believed that structure ultimately empowers. Braithwaite (2002) observed that "at least compared to courtroom processes, restorative justice does better in terms of recognition and empowerment" (p. 133). We believe that the disagreements over harm and control in restorative justice encounters reflect deep questions concerning the very nature of harm and control, and whether these are even avoidable in human interaction. To what extent can social control be avoided in human encounter? What is harm, and can we avoid doing harm as we attempt to change harmful ways?

Restorative justice is *not* a return to ancient justice practices, because it orients to an *ideal* of nonharm and usually works with or within a government-justice system. It follows that restorative justice seeks order *and* peace, crime control *and* healing experience (Van Ness & Strong, 2006).

How Is Restorative Justice Supposed to Work?

Sometimes it is like you are getting picked at. Like they are picking away at you but it is for the good. . . . And then other times it is like I have a whole circle, a whole network of people that are willing to help me and volunteer their time to come and do this, and I appreciate it.[2]

We turn now to theories of restorative justice.[3] What is restorative justice supposed to accomplish, and how? In an earlier essay, Presser (2004) suggested that restorative justice "works" by *being* an experience of justice). It need not achieve some other thing. Still, when people ask if restorative justice works, they are generally asking if it helps in reducing crime. The corresponding theoretical question is, How is restorative justice *supposed to* reduce crime? But equally important questions are, How is restorative justice *supposed to* help victims heal? and How is restorative justice *supposed to* help build communities?

These questions are equally important; as such, I depict the corresponding theories laterally and not hierarchically in Table 25.1. Yet it is certainly the case that theories of crime reduction receive the lion's share of attention, so I begin with these.

Theories of Crime Reduction

A restorative justice practice may reduce crime at either individual (micro) or societal (macro) levels. That is, individual participants might change in ways that reduce criminal behavior, *or* crime rates might fall because a restorative justice practice changes something about culture or social structure. What follows is a selective review of given explanations of how restorative justice practice might reduce crime.[4]

John Braithwaite's (1989) reintegrative shaming theory is most often cited as the explanation of how restorative justice practice might reduce reoffending. Reintegrative shaming involves affirming and insisting upon conventional standards of behavior

Table 25.1	Theories of Restorative Justice Effects

Theories of Crime Reduction	Theories of Victim Healing	Theories of Community Building

by the (would-be) offender. Reintegrative refers to the mode of communication—the "shamed" person is treated as a member of the collective—and to the practical reintegration that may follow from the shaming, including, for example, help finding or keeping a job. The offense, not the (would-be) offender, is condemned. In this way, s/he gets a lesson on how to behave without being and feeling alienated from those giving the lesson.

Reintegrative shaming theory is a macro, micro, and mesolevel theory of crime. On the macro level, cultures that engage in reintegrative shaming should have lower rates of crime. In other words, reintegrative shaming supposedly prevents crime. The same is said to hold true for groups (mesolevel): Group members are influenced by others' experiences with reintegrative shaming. On the micro level, offenders who are subject to reintegrative shaming should change their wayward patterns of behavior. That is, reintegrative shaming supposedly reduces recidivism. Commonly used restorative justice practices, especially those that convene community members *and* victims *and* offenders like family group conferencing and peacemaking circles, involve both practical and symbolic gestures of reintegrative shaming (Braithwaite, 2002).

Closely related to reintegrative shaming theory are Lawrence Sherman's (1993) defiance theory and Tom Tyler's (2006) legitimacy theory. Generally stated, these two theories propose that people obey the law to the extent that they view the law and its enforcers as legitimate. Sherman (1993) further specified that obedience to law is conditioned by bonds to its enforcers. To the extent that restorative justice practices involve affirmation of the law by those whom the offender respects, then according to these theories, we should expect greater conformity with law following such practices.

Barton (2003) proposed that restorative justice works by intervening in moral disengagement. In offending against another, a person "will tend to silence their conscience by means of various internal mechanisms of moral disengagement" (Barton, 2003, p. 50). Of course, the assumption here is that offenders have a conscience or sense of morality that proscribes doing what they did, an assumption not inconsistent with the optimistic attitude restorative justice proponents tend to hold concerning human nature. Barton referred to Bandura, Barbaranelli, Caprara, and Pastorelli's (1996) four mechanisms of moral disengagement by which the perpetrator of a harmful deed silences her/his conscience: morally justifying the deed, reducing one's personal responsibility, denying the harmfulness of the deed, and derogating the victim. These mechanisms are roughly comparable to Sykes and Matza's (1957) techniques of neutralization, and interventions to disable their use among known offenders are already featured in cognitively oriented correctional interventions (Andrews & Bonta, 2001). Barton's thinking is that encountering victims—and seeing and hearing what the crime did to them—is *uniquely* disabling to these means of disengaging. He proposed, "When victims tell offenders face-to-face about the harm the offenders' actions have caused, offenders' internal mechanisms of disengagement are seriously challenged and, in most cases, reversed" (Barton, 2003, p. 50).

Barton's theory of crime reduction based on moral engagement pertains exclusively to restorative justice programs that convene victim-offender encounters. Theories that emphasize strain (Agnew, 1992) and deficient social control (Hirschi, 1969) as the causes of offending pertain to those restorative justice programs that do not involve encounter but address offender needs. For example, a restorative justice program might intervene in offending patterns to the extent that the program contributes to the development of "competencies" among offenders (see Bazemore, 1991). A community member might offer job training and a job to the participant who perpetrated a property crime. This participant may thus gain the social capital that can serve as a hedge against future offending.

Finally, restorative justice practices may reduce reoffending by helping the offender to tell a new story about her/himself. The dialogue featured in many restorative justice practices invites a renarrating of the past and a redemptive script for the future, which Maruna (2001) identified as conducive to desistance from crime. Theories of narrative—in the social sciences and in literary studies—suggest that "one's story" is actually a collaborative production and that we act based on our stories (Bruner, 1990). As Braithwaite (2006) wrote, "In restorative justice conferences, after each individual has their stories listened to, new stories that allow new identities are coauthored by a plurality of stakeholders in the injustice" (p. 428).

Note that each of the foregoing theories engages with some or all of the concepts of the dominant criminological theories, such as strain, learning, control, and labeling theories. As suggested earlier in regard to strain and control theories, the dominant theories can thus also explain restorative justice effects on criminal behavior. In addition, restorative justice practices can be seen as reinforcing positive conduct (social learning theory) or undermining *criminal* labels (labeling theory). However, the theories previously reviewed (e.g., theories of reintegrative shaming or revised narratives) go beyond the mainline theories in explicitly assigning causal roles to dialogue, relationship building, and communication of moral values. They are in that sense more true to what restorative justice aims to do.

Theories of Victim Healing

Victim healing is central to restorative justice. The goals of crime reduction and control ought not overshadow the goal of healing (Presser, Gaarder, & Hesselton, 2007). It follows that theories of restorative justice must give pride of place to theories of victim healing.

How is restorative justice practice supposed to help victims heal? The answer depends on what healing is thought to consist in. In some cases, healing can be tangible, such as compensation for destroyed or stolen property, or recovery from broken bones sustained during a robbery. The restitution agreements made via a restorative justice practice, if kept, thus can help in healing. Restitution can be used to replace property or to pay medical bills.

Victims generally experience a need for *emotional* healing. This is as true for victims of many property crimes as it is for victims of violence (Deem, Nerenberg, & Titus, 2007). Restorative justice stands to promote victim healing far more than interventions associated with criminal justice, which are largely neglectful of victims (see Kelly & Erez, 1997) and may even revictimize them. Herman (1997) squarely made this argument: "If one set out by design to devise a system for provoking intrusive post-traumatic symptoms, one could do no better than a court of law" (p. 72). Some crime victims are especially ill-treated by police officers, prosecutors, and/or judges. These include victims of rape and battering—crimes that, by their threat, oppress all women. But Daly and Stubbs (2006) noted that use of restorative justice practices to address such crimes might provide the offender with a forum for further manipulation or abuse and possibly communicates that the crime is not serious enough to warrant punishment such as the formal system metes out. These scholars also consider the *potential* for restorative justice to give victims a voice and an opportunity for validation of harms, which formal justice systems, at their best, have not.

Bracketing these contrasting potentialities, we turn again to theories. Several theories can be advanced as to how restorative justice might emotionally heal victims. We identify three, which concern communication of the victim's worth, social reintegration of victims, and communication about moral order and disorder.

With acknowledgment of the crime and its effects and assurances that it was wrong, restorative justice participants would convey the basic worth of the victim. According to the late philosopher Jean Hampton (1988), the essential degradation of criminal victimization lies in its implicit or explicit message that the victim is less than the offender. The positive promise of retribution, she found, is that it degrades the offender and, thus, counters the message that the victim is less than the offender.

Hampton observed that punishment has come to signify the victim's worth to the punishing collective. But punishment need not be the signifier of the victim's worth. Instead of bringing the offender down to the level that s/he has brought the victim, we could do something to raise the victim up. It need not be the "ticker tape parade" that Hampton playfully suggested, but we could do far more to communicate, emphatically and publicly, that the victim should not have been hurt as s/he was. That message is clearest if the offender expresses remorse and apologizes. But even hearing an offender's relative or a neighbor say, "That should not have happened to you," can be restorative. Hampton's philosophy of retribution thus works as a theory of victim healing via restorative justice, especially those restorative justice programs that invite community members to participate.

Trouble lies in the possibility that restorative justice participants do not convey a message of victim worth—a message that they did not deserve to experience what they did. Rather, encounters might provide the offender or community members with a forum for reaffirming her/his/their disrespect toward the victim. Such a hazard gives us pause when considering the circumstances under which victims should meet with offenders and their supporters. The generally accepted guideline of *voluntary* participation, of both victims and offenders, is geared toward avoiding that hazard. Other guidelines pertaining to the order of speech in encounter programs (Barton, 2003), the screening of offenders (Presser & Lowenkamp, 1999) and victims, and the exclusion of certain crimes (e.g., battering) where disrespect is an entrenched feature of the victim-offender relationship are relevant here as well. In our view, however, because honest dialogue cannot be scripted in advance, the risk that dialogue will cause further trauma cannot be *completely* eliminated.

Crime can leave victims feeling alone, with isolation compounding the experience of degradation (Herman, 1997). Restorative justice programs that bring community members together, such as family group conferences and community circles, can assist victims in reconnecting with other people. Barton (2003) has been explicit about the restorative justice goal of victim reintegration. The victim's experience of reintegration relies not merely on *getting together* with other people. It relies also on telling one's story and having one's story taken as truth, discussing one's needs and getting help in meeting them, and expressing emotions and having those emotions acknowledged. As Herman (1997) wrote, "Recovery can take place only within the context of relationships; it cannot occur in isolation" (p. 133).

Finally, restorative justice programming may reaffirm a sense of moral order for the victim. Crime can undermine victims' erstwhile belief that the world makes sense and that they control what happens to them. As a result, many victims feel confused and helpless (Herman, 1997). A victim-offender conference, where one confronts and questions the wrongdoer (e.g., "Why me?"), can lead to the recovery of a sense of order and personal power. Alternatively, the conference may reveal that one actually had and has limited control over one's experiences (e.g., the victim was randomly chosen), and *this* might be a source of comfort (i.e., the victim did nothing wrong) or even spiritual enlightenment (Zehr, 2001). As spiritual writer Eckhart Tolle (2005) explained, "The irruption of disorder into a person's life, and the resultant collapse of a mentally defined meaning, can become the opening into a higher order" (p. 196).

Theories of Community Building

From some perspectives, the essence of restorative justice is in community building or change. The expression restorative community justice is common (e.g., Bazemore & Schiff, 2001; Young, 1995). Clear and Karp (1999) subsumed their discussion of restorative justice under that of community justice. And Sullivan and Tifft (2005) called for a restorative justice that transforms unjust social structures.

In the short run, a restorative justice conference brings people together to address a problem of common concern. As Nils Christie (1977) famously noted, interpersonal conflicts are the stuff with which healthy interpersonal relationships are forged. When governmental agents deal with citizens' conflicts for them, as is the case in developed societies, communities are weakened (see also McKnight, 1995).

In the long run, the values of restorative justice might infuse our society culturally (Harris, 1991). The restorative justice emphasis on harms and needs might influence public policies, including but not limited to criminal justice policies. If injustice is tolerance of unmet needs, then courtrooms might take more seriously the injustice of, say, constricted economic choice that causes poverty and despair. Yet some charge restorative justice with simply reproducing societal inequalities. How so? If a restorative justice program is an adjunct of the criminal justice system, it will usually take the state's designations of *victim* and *offender* as given and not question those (Presser & Hamilton, 2006). As discussed previously, unimpeded, a restorative justice conference might provide a new forum for the offender to bully or to show disrespect toward the victim. Or the scripting of restorative justice dialogue might adhere to institutionalized inequalities, as when young offenders must abase themselves before adult victims (Arrigo & Schehr, 1998).

Observing that generally held values may be oppressive and thus that "justice" often requires transformation and not just restoration, Hudson (2003) stated that restorative justice encounters can "not only perform the norm-affirming expressive role of adversarial criminal justice; it can also perform an additional, norm-creating role" (p. 444). Hudson saw the potential for restorative justice dialogues as resembling Habermas's "ideal speech situation," with all "participants expressing their viewpoints and needs" and being heard (p. 444). The restorative justice philosophy is compatible with Collins's (1981) view of social structures as aggregations of human encounters. Thus, restorative justice is indeed compatible with, and might further, change to societies.

CONCLUSION

The nature of restorative justice and theories of how restorative justice works was examined. Studies of restorative justice are usually concerned with restorative justice as a means to reducing the reoffense rates of participating offenders. In fact, restorative justice sets its sights on far more than recidivism reduction, because it serves victims *and* community members *and* offenders. As we have seen, several theories explain how restorative justice might achieve its goals. The next step is many careful program evaluations, both to discover what programs are accomplishing, if anything, and to discover how.

DISCUSSION QUESTIONS

1. Why is dialogue important to restorative justice?

2. What theories explain how restorative justice might help victims to heal?

3. What theories explain how restorative justice might help reduce crime?

4. What theories explain how restorative justice might help build communities?

5. Why should restorative justice planners take care in planning victim-offender encounters?

6. Could harming offenders be compatible with doing restorative justice? Explain.

7. How could restorative justice practices reproduce societal inequalities?

8. How could restorative justice practices transform societies?

NOTES

1. Question posed by father of young offender, during a victim-offender mediation session concerning vandalism. The excerpt is taken from Presser and Hamilton's (2006) study of a victim-offender mediation program with young offenders.
2. Comment by domestic violence offender concerning a sentencing circle in Minnesota (Gaarder, 2008).
3. The chapter focuses on theories that *explain* potential *effects* of restorative justice practice. However, theories, in general, do not merely explain; they also discern the nature of things (Abend, 2008). That is, a theory can outline what a thing *is*. Theories that speak to the nature of restorative justice include (but are not limited to) theories of justice and the state, social movements, dialogue and democracy, the nature of conflict, and the nature of power.
4. See Chapter 4 in Braithwaite (2002) for an excellent discussion.

REFERENCES

Abend, G. (2008). The meaning of "theory." *Sociological Theory, 26*(2), 173–199.

Agnew, R. (1992). Foundation for a general strain theory of crime and delinquency. *Criminology, 30*(1), 47–88.

Andrews, D. A., & Bonta, J. (2001). *The psychology of criminal conduct* (3rd ed.). Cincinnati, OH: Anderson.

Arrigo, B. A., & Schehr, R. C. (1998). Restoring justice for juveniles: A critical analysis of victim-offender mediation. *Justice Quarterly, 15*(4), 629–666.

Bandura, A., Barbaranelli, C., Caprara, G. V., & Pastorelli, C. (1996). Mechanisms of moral disengagement in the exercise of moral agency. *Journal of Personality and Social Psychology, 71*(2), 364–374.

Barton, C. K. B. (2003). *Restorative justice: The empowerment model.* Sydney, Australia: Hawkins Press.

Bazemore, G. (1991). New concepts and alternative practice in community supervision of juvenile offenders: Rediscovering work experience and competency development. *Journal of Crime and Justice, 14*(2), 27–52.

Bazemore, G., & Schiff, M. (2001). *Restorative community justice: Repairing harms and transforming communities.* Cincinnati, OH: Anderson.

Braithwaite, J. (1989). *Crime, shame, and reintegration.* Cambridge, United Kingdom: Cambridge University Press.

Braithwaite, J. (2002). *Restorative justice and responsive regulation.* New York, NY: Oxford University Press.

Braithwaite, J. (2006). Narrative and "compulsory compassion." *Law & Social Inquiry, 31*(2), 425–446.

Bruner, J. (1990). *Acts of meaning.* Cambridge, MA: Harvard University Press.

Christie, N. (1977). Conflicts as property. *The British Journal of Criminology, 17*(1), 1–15.

Clear, T. R., & Karp, D. R. (1999). *The community justice ideal: Preventing crime and achieving justice.* Boulder, CO: Westview.

Collins, R. (1981). On the microfoundations of macrosociology. *American Journal of Sociology, 86*(5), 984–1014.

Daly, K. (2002). Restorative justice: The real story. *Punishment & Society, 4*(1), 55–79.

Daly, K., & Stubbs, J. (2006). Feminist engagement with restorative justice. *Theoretical Criminology, 10*(1), 9–28.

Deem, D., Nerenberg, L., & Titus, R. (2007). Victims of financial crime. In R. C. Davis, A. J. Lurigio, & S. Herman (Eds.), *Victims of crime* (3rd ed., pp. 125-145). Thousand Oaks, CA: SAGE.

Duff, R. A. (2002). Restorative punishment and punitive restoration. In L. Walgrave (Ed.), *Restorative justice and the law* (pp. 82–100). Devon, United Kingdom: Willan.

Gaarder, E. (2008, June 6). *Sentencing circles and domestic violence: Examining a pilot project in Minnesota.* Paper presented at the Justice Studies Association Annual Meeting, Fairfax, VA.

Hampton, J. (1988). The retributive idea. In J. G. Murphy & J. Hampton (Eds.), *Forgiveness and mercy* (pp. 111–161). Cambridge, United Kingdom: Cambridge University Press.

Harris, M. K. (1991). Moving into the new millenium: Toward a feminist vision of justice. In H. E. Pepinsky & R. Quinney (Eds.), *Criminology as peacemaking* (pp. 83–97). Bloomington: Indiana University Press.

Herman, J. L. (1997). *Trauma and recovery: The aftermath of violence—From domestic abuse to political terror* (2nd ed.). New York, NY: Basic Books.

Hirschi, T. (1969). *Causes of delinquency.* Berkeley: University of California Press.

Hudson, B. (2003). Restorative justice: The challenge of sexual and racial violence. In G. Johnstone (Ed.), *A restorative justice reader: Texts, sources, context* (pp. 438–448). Devon, United Kingdom: Willan.

Kelly, D. P., & Erez, E. (1997). Victim participation in the criminal justice system. In R. C. Davis, A. J. Lurigio, & W. G. Skogan (Eds.), *Victims of crime* (2nd ed., pp. 231–244). Thousand Oaks, CA: SAGE.

Maruna, S. (2001). *Making good: How ex-convicts reform and rebuild their lives.* Washington, DC: American Psychological Association.

McKnight, J. (1995). *The careless society: Community and its counterfeits.* New York, NY: Basic Books.

Presser, L. (2004). Justice here and now: A personal reflection on the restorative and community justice paradigms. *Contemporary Justice Review, 7*(1), 101–106.

Presser, L., Gaarder, E., & Hesselton, D. (2007). Imagining restorative justice beyond recidivism. *Journal of Offender Rehabilitation, 46*(1/2), 163–176.

Presser, L., & Hamilton, C. A. (2006). The micro-politics of victim offender mediation. *Sociological Inquiry, 76*(3), 316–342.

Presser, L., & Lowenkamp, C. T. (1999). Restorative justice and offender screening. *Journal of Criminal Justice, 27*(4), 333–343.

Presser, L., & Van Voorhis, P. (2002). Values and evaluation: Assessing processes and outcomes of restorative justice programs. *Crime and Delinquency, 48*(1), 162–188.

Sherman, L. (1993). Defiance, deterrence, and irrelevance: A theory of the criminal sanction. *Journal of Research in Crime and Delinquency, 30*, 445–473.

Sullivan, D., & Tifft, L. (2005). *Restorative justice: Healing the foundations of our everyday lives* (2nd ed.). Monsey, NY: Willow Tree Press.

Sykes, G. M., & Matza, D. (1957, December). Techniques of neutralization: A theory of delinquency. *American Sociological Review, 22*, pp. 664–670.

Tolle, E. (2005). *A new Earth: Awakening to your life's purpose.* New York, NY: Plume.

Tyler, T. R. (2006). *Why people obey the law.* Princeton, NJ: Princeton University Press.

Van Ness, D., & Strong, K. H. (2006). *Restoring justice: An introduction to restorative justice* (3rd ed.). Cincinnati, OH: LexisNexis/Anderson.

Weitekamp, E. G. M. (1996). The history of restorative justice. In G. Bazemore & L. Walgrave (Eds.), *Restorative juvenile justice: Repairing the harm of youth crime* (pp. 75–102). Monsey, NY: Criminal Justice Press.

Young, M. A. (1995). *Restorative community justice: A call to action.* Washington, DC: National Organization for Victim Assistance.

Zehr, H. (1995). *Changing lenses: A new focus for crime and justice.* Scottdale, PA: Herald Press.

Zehr, H. (2001). *Transcending: Reflections of crime victims.* Intercourse, PA: Good Books.

Zehr, H. (2002). *The little book of restorative justice.* Intercourse, PA: Good Books.

CHAPTER 26

Garbage In, Garbage Out?

Convict Criminology, the
Convict Code, and
Participatory Prison Reform[1]

Alan Mobley

T he prison experience and its aftermath have been the subjects of much study and description. In different ways and with varying degrees of success, scholars (e.g., Clemmer, 1958; Jacobs, 1977; Johnson, 2002; Stern, 1998; and Sykes, 1958), journalists (e.g., Conover, 2000; Earley, 1992), and current and former prisoners (e.g., Abbott, 1981; Cleaver, 1968; Hassine, 1999; Irwin, 1970, 2005; and Jackson, 1970) have sought to chronicle the pain, degradation, and emotional devastation of incarceration. In spite of these efforts, the present authors are inclined to believe that much remains to be told. Although we hold confidence in the possibility that sensitive people can achieve a conceptual understanding of "doing time" without having to experience prison for themselves, we respectfully maintain that an intellectual understanding of prison is not enough.

Our task in this paper is to provide some sense of the many intangibles implicit in a prisoner perspective on incarceration. Someday, humans may have the ability to download sensate experience directly, but until that day, it seems that the best we can do for our readers is to analogize. Instead of laboring to induce empathy, we will try to convey some of the learning we have acquired as a result of occupying—indeed, embodying—the convict perspective. The named author has passed 10 years in prison and 5 more on parole. His collaborators tally decades more behind bars, and some remain there still. The analogy that presents itself as most like the psychological cesspool of prison is the locker room: a high school or college locker room for male athletes.

In your mind's eye, fill out the room, if you will, with damp and sweat, stench and soiled belongings. Now, put in place a large number—too large for the room—of opposing athletes. Watch some gamely strut and posture while others withdraw into the self-imposed isolation of daydreams and consuming, reflexive thought. Feel the hypermasculinity manifested in shouted expletives and grunting sexual innuendo. Observe the sophomoric humor and carelessly displayed bodily functions.

Think of those participating in the antics as World Wrestling performers. See their legendary menace and outrageous, provocative acts. Now consider, quite seriously, that they are not acting, that they see their individual performances as competitive, as vital to their integrity and personal safety. Consider that they view one another as lethal threats. Throw in one or two officials who are paid to keep an eye on things but who make going home safely every night their top priority. Now, finally, go ahead and step into the locker room yourself, and seal the door behind you. How do you feel? If you have conscientiously engaged in this exercise, you now have a reasonable approximation of prison. Enjoy your stay.

MASS INCARCERATION IN AMERICA

From 1970 to 1988, the prison population in the United States tripled (Bureau of Justice Statistics, 1989). In the next 12 years, it tripled again, threatening to fill prisons faster than states could build them (Lynch, 2000). The incarceration business is said to employ 747,000 people and involve over $37 billion in expenditures (Jacobson, 2005, pp. 67–70). California now spends more on prisons than on the state university system. The electoral passage of Proposition 21 in California, which allows prosecutors to try accused criminal perpetrators 14 years old and above as adults, has at least symbolically impacted the state's prisons by bringing children—disproportionate numbers of minority children—into the adult justice system.

Advocates for the rights of racial minorities are alarmed at this new development, since overcrowding and racial segregation may worsen prevailing conditions both in prisons and in mostly minority neighborhoods. The life chances of African American and Latino males are already diminished by their frequent interaction with the criminal justice system (Miller, 1996; Western, 2007). Across the country, they are overrepresented in the new cohorts of specially selected penal detainees (Mauer, 1999; Mauer & King, 2007). Critics of the expanding prison-industrial complex complain that offender incapacitation is just the latest punitive twist in the continuing legacy of America's hot and cold running fascination with race-based social engineering (Clear, 2007; Gordon, 1999).

Criticisms of penal expansion and its variations are not new. Auerhahn (1999) convincingly shows that the underlying rationales supporting incapacitation have been repeatedly challenged on conceptual, ethical, and methodological grounds. Even the chief architect of selective incapacitation, the Rand Corporation's Peter Greenwood (with colleague Susan Turner, 1987), later disputed the efficacy of profiling and targeting selected groups for incarceration.

Some proponents of penal incapacitation responded to criticism by crediting the policy with lowered crime rates in U.S. cities and towns. Officially compiled crime rates do show that some categories of major crimes are down 15% to 20% and more (Austin et al., 2007; Lichtblau, 1999). It is uncertain to what extent we can credit the decrease in crime to the increase in the number of the incarcerated.

The so-called war on drugs has brought other groups into prison besides the traditionally oppressed minorities. Among them are the middle class. These convicts have had some impact on the prison system, and the system has deeply affected them. Some have gone on to make the study of prison their lifework. Most of these are reformers. Their energy, it is said, comes from the poignant observation that "you can take the man out of prison, but it's hard to take the prison out of the man." Some of these folks, mostly male, mostly of European American extraction, have grouped together under the banner of convict criminology.

CONVICT CRIMINOLOGY

It is fair to say that convict criminology was brought into being by the war on drugs. Although the large majority of people swept into prisons by the wars on drugs and crime have been minority, poor, and poorly educated, another subgroup has been brought along, mostly for the ride, it seems. This group, mostly of European American extraction and middle class, found itself imported into a world of strange customs and moral codes. The prison experience itself, far from being routine and an accepted rite of passage, was bizarre. Some individuals within this group began to look upon the prison as an object of study and brought the culture of prison into their inquiry as well. They have become known, at least in their initial foray into research and publishing, as *convict criminologists*. The form and function of prisons in America was taken up as their first object of study.

Convict criminology began as an organizing effort to bring the human back into prison scholarship. In the mid-1990s, agitated by a curriculum void of any indication that those persons referred to as criminals, inmates, and offenders were also flesh-and-blood human beings, Chuck Terry and I—two University of California, Irvine, graduate students—met regularly to share strong coffee and even stronger opinions reflecting our convicted perspective.

Soon, Terry and I realized that what we saw in the course materials as the dehumanization of justice system clients existed at an even more profound level at professional conferences. As intense immersions in the thoughts, politics, and personalities of a profession, these professional conferences were both repulsive and alienating for Terry and me. From these intense experiences came our desire to step beyond conventional criminology and make our own way. I soon began to pursue social justice activism, prison reform, and fieldwork-based scholarship. Terry, however, sought out other academics who shared an incarcerated past. His research revealed several former prisoners teaching criminal justice and sociology at U.S. universities. As he began to share his misgivings over criminological study and practice, these new colleagues responded with a litany of their own concerns.

Sparked by the collective sentiment, Terry wanted change. Rather than continue to toil in relative isolation among the conventionally minded, he thought that the ex-con criminologists ought to take a tip from Narcotics Anonymous (a group to which he belonged) and form a mutual-aid support group. When one of his graduate school advisors suggested he organize a panel of ex-con academics for the upcoming American Society of Criminology (ASC) meeting, Terry did the legwork. As luck would have it, his advisor also happened to be on the conference organizing committee and could see to it that the panel was seated. So out of frustration, comradeship, and with logistical help from a sympathetic insider, *convict criminology* was born (Terry, 2003).

Convict criminology was announced as a "new school" in a 2001 issue of the journal *Social Justice* (Richards & Ross, 2001). An edited volume titled *Convict Criminology* was released in 2003 by Jeffrey Ross and Stephen Richards. As defined, "Convict Criminology represents the work of convicts or ex-convicts, in possession of a PhD or on their way to completing one, or enlightened academics and practitioners, who contribute to a new conversation about crime and corrections" (p. 6).

Several principles were declared as core to this new school. Among them were the failure of prisons, the value of taking an insider perspective, the centrality of ethnography, and the preeminence of noted penologist and ex-convict John Irwin.

Irwin is the author of several works of penology (Irwin, 1970; 1980; 1985; 2005; Irwin & Austin, 2000) that have achieved the status of classics in the field. His work combines social analysis with descriptive statistics and ethnography. For his latest book, *The Warehouse Prison,* Irwin gained access to California state prisons, where he assembled groups of convicts with whom he met over a two and one half year period. Irwin credits them with contributing significantly to the book. The group "shared ideas, descriptions, and analyses of prisoner behavior and relationships. These 'experts' read and critiqued drafts of most of the book's chapters. They [10 prisoners] have served a total of 207 years in prison" (Irwin, 2005, p. ix).

Following Irwin's lead, convict criminologists offer an often blistering critique of U.S. penal justice and mainstream criminology. Often, the two are lumped into one lucrative, self-perpetuating machine (see Ross & Richards, 2003). Convict criminologists use their academic credentials to argue for their own analytical abilities, if not their objectivity, and burnish their pasts as further validation of the insights and recommendations they offer. They challenge the standard bearers of the mainstream to let them in and heed their words, and to an extent, they have been successful. Since the first conference panel in 1997, convict criminology (as topic and group) has grown tremendously. The group now boasts three very well-attended panels at criminology's flagship conference and other national and regional meetings, dozens of journal articles and books, a website (see http://www.convictcriminology.org/index.html) that offers everything from consulting services to advice for prisoners wanting to attend college, and, most important, many new cohort members. In short, Convict Criminology is productive and growing.

As might be expected, countercriticism has come from the criminological mainstream. *The New York Times* quoted one prominent criminologist as implying that convict criminologists lack objectivity, asking, "What convict criminologist is going to say people are in prison because they have low self-control and lower I.Q.

scores?" (St. John, 2003, p. 7). The prominent mainstream criminologist goes on: "There's a tendency among convict criminologists to say, 'Because I've been there, I know and you don't. Being there gives you access to some information, but not all the information. It illuminates and it distorts" (p. 7).

A more subtle form of critique is the exclusion of convict criminology from the discipline's leading journals. This does not surprise the convict criminologists, however, as they see their exclusion as further proof of scholarly complicity with a negligent (and perhaps malign) government in furthering a mutually beneficial prison-industrial complex (see Ross & Richards, 2003, pp. 18, 41, 349). John Irwin set the tone in the preface to *Convict Criminology,* when he stated the need for a convict perspective within the larger, ill-informed discipline: "Not only do we have to push, we have to guide them" (as cited in Ross & Richards, 2003, p. xviii).

The prison is one place where all agree that convict criminologists can serve as useful guides. In what follows, we discuss the legendary convict code and its more recent variation (for the traditional treatment of the "inmate code," see Sykes and Messinger, 1960).

THE CONVICT CODE

Modern American prisons are largely self-contained establishments operating behind barbed wire-topped fences and razor wire rolls. Within the confines of penal institutions, prisoners live, work, and play, providing all manner of services necessary for the continued safety, security, and sanitation of their community. Off hours are passed in leisure activities not so different from those in the outside world. Prisoners read; watch television; engage in sports, games, and hobbies; eat junk food; and sleep. A prisoner's incarcerated life is lived in a compressed, communal lifestyle, no doubt much altered from whatever manner of living the imprisoned knew when free (see Wacquant, 2001, and Anderson, 1998, for different views on the exclusivity of the prison experience).

Prior to the introduction of congregate-style prisons, prisoners passed their days in silence and solitude. Meals were taken, labor performed, and all activities carried out within each individual prisoner's cell. No particularly new mode of living was imparted to prisoners; they were simply expected to utilize the time their sentences allowed to make peace with themselves and with God. Reaching the goal of inner peace was more than some prisoners could manage, however, and methods of incarceration were implemented that were essentially like those used today.

Adapting to limited personal autonomy, enforced material and heterosexual deprivation, and the rigors of communal living among strangers necessitated the development of norms, rules, and roles appropriate to the peculiar world of the prison. Solitary confinement had made for peacefully running prisons, and the shift to prisoners working together to perform institutional tasks was rough. Congregate living did ease high rates of suicide and insanity among prisoners, but it replaced those hazards with violence. Frustrated convicts spent their rage upon one another, finally settling into regular patterns of transactions, exchanges, and interactions that permitted each prisoner an opportunity to survive according to his strength and cunning. Two rules in particular emerged as conducive to peaceful, individualized communal living: "Do your own time" and "Don't snitch."

Both these rules mainly concern the effects of prisoner actions on other prisoners. Doing your own time entails not bothering others, while not snitching means not involving officials or other convicts in one's private affairs. Our contention here is that these two behavioral guidelines are not only obsolete and in disuse but also, through a lingering sense of their continuing validity, actually serve to undermine the ability of prisoners to rehabilitate themselves. A new basis for interaction between incarcerates, between prisoners and staff, and between prison society and the outside world can interrupt our prisons' current spiral toward stupefaction or anarchy and serve the best interests of all who participate in good faith.

Before explaining the fundamentals of a new *convict code*, however, we will review the original code, its current state, and some causes of its demise.

The Original Convict Code

The convict code is a short set of principles that serve as guidelines for interactions between convicts, convicts and jailers, and convicts and the outside world. The convict code recognizes that each prisoner has different goals and desires to fulfill within a highly circumscribed environment of scarce resources. The convict code also encourages each prisoner to acknowledge the commonality of circumstances all prisoners face. No matter what a prisoner chooses to do with his time, all are subjected to the same limitations that coerced, unisexual incarceration brings.

By explicitly identifying the predicaments of imprisonment as universal to all convicts, while simultaneously admitting the validity of diverse individual pursuits among the prisoner population, the convict code of conduct was intended to provide for peaceful, individualized, communal living.

Rule 1: Do Your Own Time

The vague but fundamental rule, do your own time, typifies the code. Do your own time implies the uncomfortable fact that each convict is essentially alone. Each was judged alone, sentenced alone, admitted to prison alone, and will be released completely alone. The criminal justice system places other individuals in extremely close proximity and in remarkably similar circumstances to each convicted individual, but the salient point of imprisonment, time to be served, belongs and applies to each individual alone. Because of this simple fact, that each prisoner's sentence (or "time") is his to serve alone, each individual in prison is separate from the start. The question is not, How and when do we get out? It is, How can I get out?

Obtaining release appears to be a main goal of nearly all prisoners. The actions in which a convict chooses to engage can often either speed or delay the release process, however. Participation in activities that can prolong a prisoner's sentence, such as fights, killings, escape attempts, or drug use, is therefore a highly personal decision affecting the decision maker, his confederates, and possibly victims. Being drawn into such situations unexpectedly is a convict's worst nightmare. As defense against this possibility, a high degree of external awareness is advisable at all times.

Doing your own time means one should mind one's own business so as not to become involved in the potentially dangerous escapades of others. Strengthening oneself as a preventative measure against possible victimization is a second goal of this rule. When a convict follows the suggestion, do your own time, don't let the time do you, he is careful not to let the deprivations of prison life get him down. When prisoners mope around in an attitude of self-pity, the chances of becoming entangled in confrontations with staff and other prisoners are greatly increased. A convict is a person who practices self-defense with the utmost vigilance. A convict can take a breather and relax when he goes home.

Safety

The issue of personal safety is the only issue that rivals obtaining release as a convict's priority. The convict code tries to restrict one's exposure to dangerous situations and to those situations one willingly enters. For example, if a prisoner enters into a gang relationship for personal safety, drug accessibility, or any other reason, certain obligations are acquired. If a gang member is peacefully walking down a hallway and happens to see a fellow gang member being physically assaulted by one or more assailants, he is obligated to immediately enter the fray on the side of the compatriot. Such an action could result in injury or death immediately or in the future, or in an increased sentence should injury or death occur to another involved in the conflict. A prisoner knowingly assumes this sort of obligatory risk when voluntarily entering into a gang relationship. A prisoner who is unaffiliated with the gang, who walks by and witnesses the same incident, is under no obligation to put himself at risk. In fact, the convict code demands that bystanders be totally detached and not even look toward any event outside each one's immediate personal interest.

The prohibition against rubbernecking, or looking at things or people beyond one's previously established parameters of legitimate interest, exists for two reasons. The first, essentially what you don't know can't hurt you, alludes to the precariousness of witnessing any illegal act. If a passerby witnesses illegal or improper actions, that person can be seen as a possible informant and therefore threatens the perpetrators by his very existence. Strong feelings of mistrust born of personal or vicarious experience involving the treachery of informants, or snitches, can build to the point of confrontations and preemptive violence. It is also standard procedure for the prison administration to segregate, or "lock up," witnesses to serious events in order to interrogate them more effectively. If one fails to witness the activities of others, however, one bypasses exposure to such unpleasant involvements.

Privacy

A second reason why rubbernecking is derided, is simple privacy. Prisons are designed so that most every prisoner action occurs in a public, or at least a visible, space. There are windows in every door, lights never go completely off, and even the toilet stalls are open to view, the doors having been removed. In such a potentially degrading environment, where a total lack of privacy for inhabitants is institutionalized, prisoners must look to one another for whatever bits of privacy there are to be had. After all, usually only one or two officers patrol each living unit at any one time. Nearly every eye observing any prisoner's actions, therefore, belongs to a fellow convict. If prisoners have the consideration and discipline not to allow their eyes to wander into areas outside their immediate, legitimate concern, some vestige of personal privacy is possible for each individual. Not surprisingly, having a greater degree of privacy is often considered a more pleasant, dignified, and safer manner of living.

Personal Responsibility

Surviving the prison experience as comfortably as possible and allowing others to do the same is basic to the code. Each imprisoned individual is granted the right to say and do as he pleases. With this right comes the further implication that one's actions, because they are freely chosen, are representative of one's intentions. Prisoners' words and actions are assumed to demonstrate their thoughts, and others form judgments accordingly. Failure to defend one's words or actions when challenged sends a message that one is weak and can be exploited easily.

Exploitation

The nature of communal living, as well as the administration's perceived need to force all actions and interactions of prisoners into open spaces, guarantees tension over utilization of scarce resources. This tension is often prevented from becoming hostile and potentially dangerous competition by the implicit threat of retaliation against aggression. Retaliation against aggressors can be carried out by the offended party or by someone acting as his proxy. The possibility of retaliation by the state may be just as deterring as unsanctioned violence. If a prisoner is caught engaging in overt aggression by an officer or through the use of informants, privileges can be taken away and sentences lengthened. Prisoners acting aggressively to hoard resources or intimidate others are looked upon as intentionally challenging those chosen as victims. The convict code holds the aggressor responsible for his actions and thus liable to retaliation for encroachment on the rights of others. The code also provides for victims to rightfully seek revenge.

Actually, the convict code stipulates that those acting as aggressors must themselves be victimized by their victims. The manner of such retaliation should be disproportionately greater than the original offense. Those who fail to defend themselves, their speech, or their property violate the code. Compliant victims unwilling to retaliate against aggressors forfeit their "respect," that is, their right to expect others to treat them in accordance with the code. Victims who do not stand up for themselves are seen as both weak and failing to abide by the code's directions. In short, the convict code condones the exploitation of people who are unwilling or unable to defend themselves.

Opportunities to exploit others without fear of retaliation are rare in prison, so those who seek victims are drawn to individuals who have revealed a willingness to be victimized. If the degradation inflicted by "wolves" upon a "mark" becomes too great, the mark often seeks protection in the formal structure, either by requesting to be segregated (locked up) or by informing on victimizers so that they are segregated.

Rule 2: Don't Snitch

The use of informants by police agencies is responsible for a majority of arrests. In exchange for lesser sentences, money, or other considerations, individuals with knowledge of others' criminal culpability often provide incriminating evidence to police. Nearly all prisoners serving time in prison were convicted with the aid of informants, often former friends. As the conviction and incarceration experience is perceived to be the wellspring of a prisoner's troubles, individuals responsible for incarcerating others are particularly despised by convicts. Police officials and officers of the court are usually viewed quite unfavorably, but governmental informants, people ostensibly acting as criminals but actually helping law enforcement build cases against outlaws, are generally hated.

Many convicts presume that one small benefit of imprisonment is separation from informants. Everyone in close-custody prisons (fenced and guarded facilities) is there for conviction of a felony considered serious, a conviction most often made possible by the cooperation of an informant. Prisoners thus feel they should have some things in common: an identity as convicts, similar deprivations, and status as victims of informants. When a prisoner is identified as an informant, therefore, it causes a fissure in the social bond of prisoner society.

Life outside frequently permits individuals to let their guard down and be themselves. Prison life does not. With essentially no privacy and surrounded by mostly hostile or apathetic strangers, prisoners have no "back stage" in which to relax. The assumed presence of snitches within prisons influences convicts to cloak their acts with respect to how they may appear to others. Even if a prisoner is not doing anything significantly deviant, chances are he could be set up as another's "fall guy." Additionally, each prisoner knows that hardly a day goes by when he does not commit some sort of infraction of prison rules, and most prisoners have personal property in violation of known statutes. Even if the nature of one's deviance falls short of provoking severe official sanctions, such as segregation or additional time, just the prospect of being hassled by guards and having one's lifestyle disrupted is bothersome and threatening.

To illustrate this point, prisoners who possess items considered "serious" contraband—knives, syringes, tattoo guns, and so forth—usually do not store such things in their designated personal territory. Contraband is routinely tucked into hidden spots in public places, territory over which no single prisoner has responsibility or control. This sort of precaution against prosecution presupposes the eventuality of detection. Though snitches ensure that no one gets away with anything for long, if one avoids being caught red-handed with illicit goods, disciplinary action by the prison administration cannot usually be taken.

Prisoners who do not routinely engage in serious deviance still check their living areas for signs of tampering. Intrusion by guards, thieves, or setup artists trying to plant evidence is not uncommon. In self-defense against loss of property or additional punishment, prisoners routinely police their primary personal territories. The fact that prisoners feel compelled to take precautions against theft or entrapment reveals the high level of mistrust present in captive society.

Thieves and snitches form an antisocial aggregate most responsible for the breakdown of community values in prison. Together, they create an atmosphere of defensiveness and suspicion that is perpetuated because each group feeds off the other. For example, thieves operate with near impunity because they know that snitches indirectly protect them. If a thief is caught by a prisoner and violence ensues, the victim of the theft will be punished by authorities as harshly as the thief. The convict code is supposed to protect the anonymity of both thieves and revenge-seeking victims of theft so that retribution against thievery can occur without official intervention. Snitches bring officials into privacy disputes and therefore undermine enforcement of the code.

Victims of thieves and snitches often see the wisdom of cutting their losses and simply writing off stolen articles and incidences of disrespect. Silent acceptance of ostensibly prohibited conduct has always occurred in prison. When, for example, the perpetrator of a proscribed act is an especially feared individual or one particularly well supported by a strong group, discretion on the victim's part becomes the wiser part of valor.

Snitches benefit from thieves in equal measure to the covert assistance given. When a rash of break-ins raises tensions and the administration needs an arrest to quiet things, snitches provide the information. Those apprehended often avoid serious punishment because actual physical evidence of their guilt is rarely discovered. Snitches, however, still get credit from officials for cooperating at significant personal risk.

The existence of informants on the outside and snitches inside works to absolve individuals of a measure of responsibility for their own actions. Where dealings between individuals are based on at least some level of trust and expectation of mutual profit, activities involving bureaucratized structures revolve around procedures, laws, and regulations. Individual responsibility is replaced by systematized expediency where benefit accrues to the bureaucracy. Snitches bring third parties—police agents—into private affairs. The power relationship of any interaction between prisoners is fundamentally altered by including the bureaucracy. Involving the formal prison structure in informal private dealings takes the responsibility for outcomes and consequences away from prisoners and places it in the hands of hostile administrators. Instead of trust and mutual benefit, prisoner interactions become forced, shaped by suspicion and fear.

Bringing the prospect of negative sanctions and lengthened incarceration to another's door is antithetical to the convict code. "Squealing" by prisoners compels officials to enter situations they could not otherwise involve themselves in. Since police agents dispense negative sanctions almost exclusively, little chance exists for prisoners to benefit from their inclusion in prisoner affairs. Snitching, squealing, and informing thus make a mockery of Rule 1, do your own time. For this fundamental reason, the proscription against snitching has always held a prominent position in the convict code. Snitching has traditionally been met with the most severe informal sanctions, including removal from the general population of prison society—one way or another.

FACTORS UNDERMINING THE CONVICT CODE/FORMAL STRUCTURE

As stated above, the two traditional premises underlying the convict code of conduct are don't squeal on other prisoners and do your own time (i.e., mind your own business). The second principle implies that it is forbidden to disturb anything other than oneself, one's relationships, and one's possessions. For example, bothering others by noisy or intrusive behavior is considered wrong. Listening in on, or "burglarizing," others' conversations or looking at what others are doing (rubbernecking) are likewise inappropriate. Taking or in any way upsetting others' possessions or modes of lifestyle, called "routines," is forbidden as well.

Previous studies and anecdotal evidence suggest that belief in the validity of these elements of the informal convict code are fairly universal in U.S. prisons, especially higher security prisons. Popular adherence to the code's dictates, however, has probably never been as consistent as hardcore convicts would like to believe. By and large, episodes of violence resulting from deviations from the code have kept alive the notion that the code is still a valid expression of prisoner ideals and a reliable guideline for prisoner action. The relative rarity of violent incidents in prison as compared with the generally high level of disrespectful behavior, however, illustrates how seldom the code is actually enforced.

Several factors have arisen in recent years to help break whatever real effectiveness the code once had. First, unprecedented growth in prison construction now enables authorities to more easily transfer prisoners between facilities and isolate prison leaders. Frequent transfers dilute prisoner solidarity, remove leaders from leadership positions, pacify prisoners by keeping them either farther from home or closer to it, and remove the threat of such negative social sanctions as ostracism and violent attacks, violations of conduct codes once promised. Authorities now have the luxury of rewarding informants and punishing the rebellious through facility designation.

A second factor leading to the code's demise is the professionalization of correctional occupations. Authorities' unwillingness to allow prisoners to enforce informal codes and police themselves has removed an important ingredient of power from prisoner groups. Enforcement of informal rules through violence is no longer tacitly or implicitly permitted. Enforcers are now themselves harshly punished through additional time incarcerated and segregation from general population. Code enforcers are also transferred to other facilities as punishment for their informal roles. Their sacrifices for the common good are then unknown, unrecognized, and therefore unrewarded in unfamiliar, far-flung facilities.

The growing number of institutions in most prison systems has enhanced the trend toward professionalization of increasingly sought-after careers in corrections, as well as exposing the presence of individual code enforcers and informal leadership structures. Informants who reveal the secrets of captive society to officials can be protected by the anonymity of submergence in an ocean of inmates at one of any number of prisons. Bureaucratic tendencies to centralize expanding prison systems and staff institutions with better trained personnel stem largely from the same causes that have boosted incidences of snitching. The criminalization of drug use and the prioritization of law enforcement resources against drugs criminals—known in recent years as the drug war—is the central factor influencing the prison industry and the dissolution of the convict code itself.

Self-Concept

The rise of drug sales and consumption in the 1980s and 1990s led certain individuals into criminality who otherwise possessed mainstream sensibilities. Stringent drug-law enforcement prompted by political pressures brought many of these users and dealers into contact with the criminal justice system. The experience of being taken from one's environment, stripped of possessions, separated from friends and family, and labeled a criminal often has a dramatic and apparently enlightening effect on offenders guilty of consensual crimes. Drug profiteers were often trying to reach approved societal goals but used inappropriate means to do so. (Criminology has long recognized this phenomenon. See Akers, 1997; Sykes & Messinger, 1960.) For individuals who have no real *outlaw mentality*, after feeling the power of negative social sanctions, the shift back to a more complete agreement with legal, socially approved norms is not difficult to envision.

Whether from upper-, middle-, or lower class backgrounds, offenders without genuine criminal self-concepts typically adapt to the incarceration experience by throwing themselves upon the mercy of the criminal justice system and begging for release. Their common strategy is to prove to law enforcement officials that a terrible mistake has been made and a valuable lesson learned. The convict code, therefore, has little force or meaning for prisoners without criminal self-concepts. This self-styled "noncriminal" tries to impress officials by cooperating in every way. He works hard for nominal pay, keeps his living area up to prescribed standards, acts respectfully toward staff, withdraws from illicit elements of prison life, and informs, either baldly or surreptitiously, on other prisoners.

In medium- and lower security institutions, these mostly Caucasian, noncriminal drug users and entrepreneurs compose a substantial aggregate. The presence of such a large segment of prisoners disinterested in adherence to the convict code calls into question the code's relevance as a functioning normative system. Following the code's prescriptions once guaranteed prisoners' personal safety. In today's largely nonviolent medium- and lower security institutions, however, adapting one's behavior to an existent prison subculture has become unnecessary. The threat to personal safety and the subculture itself have been invalidated by the introduction of relatively large numbers of uninitiated prisoners acting independently and unilaterally who are interested in only one thing: going home.

Gangbangers

Gangbangers are another large group of prisoners who fail to abide by the principles of the convict code. Interestingly, on the surface, gangbangers are almost exact opposites of the mostly Caucasian, noncriminal drug-user entrepreneur. Gangbangers are primarily African Americans from homogeneous inner-city social environments. They appear to have completely assimilated criminal identities and consider doing time just another part of the criminal lifestyle. Like noncriminals, however, gangbangers have no use for the convict code. They care little what members of the general population think or do. Their alliances and allegiance are uniformly tied to outside gangs operating inside prison walls. So many young inner-city African American males are incarcerated that one's homeboys can be found in any penal institution. Young gangsters, therefore, need not trouble themselves to adapt their behavior to a prison subculture.

With their homeboys, gangsters make up a distinct subculture themselves, whether on the streets or in prison. They look out for, or protect, their own, live an almost familial lifestyle, and rarely so much as speak to prisoners outside their own set. No loyalties exist toward prisoners in general or to the ideal of a united convict society. Gangbangers "run with" their "dogs" from "the 'hood" and meet up with each other in the joint then plan to reunite again on home turf. No involvement with outsiders is needed or apparently desired.

This fragmentation of incarcerated African Americans into distinct gangs, whether Crips, Bloods, or others, mirrors a similar move made by Chicanos in the 1960s. Racial and ethnic minorities have long tended to congregate in large prison gangs (for reflections on a firsthand examination of racial tensions in California prisons, see Irwin, 1980). Neighborhood economic and protection associations merged with others of the same race in prison in order to provide a larger membership, greater economic power, and individual security. Particularly in large state prison systems, the formation of race-based groups led to strict voluntary racial segregation. Incidences of personal differences often escalated into tit-for-tat warfare, with a seemingly endless supply of gang "soldiers" ready to avenge attacks on "brothers." In self-defense, Whites were forced to form similar associations, dropping in the name of survival the cliquishness typical of intra-Caucasian behavior.

Today, some state systems, such as California's, have had to adopt the extraordinary practice of designating certain prisons as the territory of certain gangs. Where once wings of particular prisons were segregated by race, now entire prisons are integrated racially but segregated according to gang affiliation. Internecine rivalries apparently arose around the struggle for control of prison groups. Leaders of smaller street gangs were reluctant to surrender their power and authority just because they were incarcerated. As more and more members of individual gangs were incarcerated, however, gang leaders saw less need to join larger, prison-based racial associations. Street gangs thus reformed within prison yards, with competition for traditional rackets soon flaring and then evolving into hostile and often violated truces.

Intraracial unity is no longer the norm in prison except in times of extreme interracial conflict. Prisoners brought into the penal system by increased law enforcement pressure on urban areas and mandatory prison terms for crack cocaine crimes look to alliances formed in neighborhoods for guidance, protection, and provision of material resources in prison.

The task of initiating prisoners into the prison subculture, once accomplished by means of a generalized code of conduct, is now successfully completed for a large number of prisoners by reliance on preprison affiliations. Whether they are Native Americans associating exclusively with members of their own tribe; voluntarily segregated gang members; old-timers, bank robbers, and dope fiends hanging out on the compound, telling lies; or noncriminal drug entrepreneurs reverting to precriminal behavior patterns and beliefs, a majority of today's prisoners no longer need to feel accepted by a generalized inmate subculture. The convict code of conduct, therefore, which exists for the explicit purpose of initiating prison neophytes into captive society, is functionally obsolete.

A NEW CODE

Today's convict would be well advised to admit several things and react accordingly. First, society has developed a habitual intolerance for deviance. Increased frustration with unsolved social problems has led politicians and the public to scapegoat societal out-groups as responsible. Political rhetoric that decried intolerance and punishment-laden responses to deviance born of inequality, although often heard during national election campaigns of past generations, has been dropped from public discourse. To pacify a frightened and worried public, policy makers continue to resort to higher levels of policing, criminalization of deviant behavior, and incarceration. Even though fiscal shortfalls will result in early releases for some prisoners and the elimination of parole supervision for others, this exercise in budgetary pragmatics should not be mistaken for a new, liberal wave in incarceration practices. In fact, reactionary measures and increased unpleasantness for prisoners should be anticipated. Budget cuts mean reduced programs and services for prisoners, and hard times tend to bequeath hard time.

Second, because policy makers have an apparent mandate to use whatever means are necessary to curb crime, factors contributing to the demise of the convict code will intensify in magnitude. More corrections infrastructure will be built, more professionalization of correctional occupations will occur, more noncriminal offenders and gang-oriented criminals will be incarcerated, and increased competition in overcrowded institutions for scarcer material resources will further splinter captive populations and promote the formation of antagonistic prison groups.

Third, due to these factors, prison officials now hold all the cards in their dealings with medium- and lower security prisoners. Penal administrators will only be strengthened by prisoner uprisings. Any show of protest against social or penal policies will be met by harsher conditions, justified by the public's unwillingness to face and deal with social problems or the offspring of those problems. America's problem children are to be incarcerated for the foreseeable future because no one sees any long-term solutions.

Fourth, the high level of mistrust in prisons will intensify between prisoners themselves and between prisoners and politicians. Harsher sentencing and mandatory minimum prison terms for drug crimes have taken the carrot from government's traditional carrot-and-stick program. Prisoners of past years have had a glimmer of hope for early release through the parole mechanism. Even if apprehended, convicted, and sentenced, felons knew that, with good behavior, time incarcerated could be cut drastically. The pressure to inform on colleagues in order to avoid prison was there, but it was not nearly as strong as it is today, when little hope exists for meaningful sentence reduction.

The fate of prisoners and prison society depends partly on prisoners themselves. If convicts insist on perpetuating antagonism among themselves and toward prison staff, they play right into the hands of custody-oriented penal administrators. The structural antagonism between incarcerates and staff has reached its intended goal and serves only the interests of career bureaucrats, politicians, and corrections unions. Individual prisoners are not well served by prisons filled with tension and removed from mainstream culture; nor are their families, communities, or victims, and surely not the public well served. Convict criminology suggests that all groups can best be served if each is permitted a meaningful voice in the justice reform process. We hope that this chapter has provided some evidence for the value of the convict perspective.

DISCUSSION QUESTIONS

1. Why do you think incarceration rates have continued to climb in spite of falling crime rates? Is this a reasonable state of affairs?

2. What might you consider to be the pros and cons of convict criminologists in the classroom? What value do you place on experience in your own education?

3. What do you see as the appropriate role (if any) for prisons in a free society?

4. Many commentators take note of the distinct racial composition of U.S. prisons and jails. To what do you attribute the overrepresentation of racial minorities? What, if anything, should be done about it?

NOTE

1. This paper was prepared with the assistance of many current and former prisoners, particularly my friend and colleague, Chuck Terry. The collaborative nature of the project suggests to the named author that he honor his unnamed colleagues through the use of "we" throughout the narrative. We also acknowledge the patient assistance of Paul Jesilow, William Granados, Michael Braun, and the editors and peer reviewers of this volume in the preparation of this paper.

REFERENCES

Abbott, J. H. (1981). *In the belly of the beast: Letters from prison.* New York, NY: Vintage Books.

Akers, R. (1997). *Criminological theories: Introduction and evaluation.* Los Angeles, CA: Roxbury.

Anderson, E. (1998). *Code of the street: Decency, violence, and the moral life of the inner city.* New York, NY: W. W. Norton.

Auerhahn, K. (1999). Selective incapacitation and the problem of prediction. *Criminology,* 37(4), 703–733.

Austin, J., Clear, T., Duster, T., Greenberg, D. F., Irwin, J., McCoy, C., . . . Page, J. (2007). *Unlocking America: Why and how to reduce America's prison population.* Washington, DC: JFA Institute.

Bureau of Justice Statistics. (1989). *Prisoners in 1988.* Washington, DC: U.S. Government Printing Office.

Clear, T. (2007). *Imprisoning communities.* London, United Kingdom: Oxford University Press.

Cleaver, E. (1968). *Soul on ice.* New York, NY: McGraw-Hill.

Clemmer, D. (1958). *The prison community.* New York, NY: Rinehart.

Conover, T. (2000). *Newjack: Guarding Sing Sing.* New York, NY: Random House.

Earley, P. (1992). *The hot house: Life inside Leavenworth Prison.* New York, NY: Bantam Books.

Gordon, A. F. (1999). Globalism and the prison industrial complex: An interview with Angela Davis. *Race and Class,* 40(2/3), 145–157.

Greenwood, P., & Turner, S. (1987). *Selective incapacitation revisited: Why the high-rate offenders are hard to predict.* Santa Monica, CA: Rand.

Hassine, V. (1999). *Life without parole: Living in prison today* (2nd ed.). Boston, MA: Roxbury.

Irwin, J. (1970). *The felon.* Englewood Cliffs, NJ: Prentice Hall.

Irwin, J. (1980). *Prisons in turmoil.* Boston, MA: Little, Brown.

Irwin, J. (1985). *The jail.* Berkeley: University of California Press.

Irwin, J. (2005). *The warehouse prison: Disposal of the new dangerous class.* Los Angeles, CA: Roxbury.

Irwin, J., & Austin, J. (2000). *It's about time: America's imprisonment binge.* Belmont, CA: Wadsworth.

Jackson, G. (1970). *Soledad brother.* New York, NY: Coward-McCann.

Jacobs, J. B. (1977). *Stateville.* Chicago, IL: University of Chicago Press.

Jacobson, M. (2005). *Downsizing prisons: How to reduce crime and end mass incarceration.* New York: New York University Press.

Johnson, R. (2002). *Hard time: Understanding and reforming the prison.* Belmont, CA: Wadsworth.

Lichtblau, E. (1999, May 17). Crime rates continue record 7-year plunge. *Los Angeles Times,* p. A1.

Lynch, T. (2000, February 20). All locked up. *The Washington Post,* p. B07.

Mauer, M. (1999). *Race to incarcerate.* New York, NY: New Press.

Mauer, M., & King, R. (2007). *A 25-year quagmire: The "War on drugs" and its impact on American society.* Washington, DC: The Sentencing Project.

Miller, J. (1996). *Search and destroy: African-American males in the criminal justice system.* Cambridge, MA: Cambridge University Press.

Richards, S. C., & Ross, J. I. (2001). The new school of convict criminology. *Social Justice, 28*(1), 177–190.

Ross, J. I., & Richards, S. C. (2003). *Convict criminology.* Belmont, CA: Wadsworth.

St. John, W. (2003, August 9). Professors with a past (Quoting University of Cincinnati criminal justice professor Francis Cullen). *The New York Times,* p. 7.

Stern, V. (1998). *A sin against the future.* Boston, MA: Northeastern University Press.

Sykes, G. (1958). *The society of captives.* Princeton, NJ: Princeton University Press.

Sykes, G., & Messinger, S. (1960). The inmate social system. In R. Cloward et al. (Eds.), *Theoretical studies in social organization of the prison* (pp. 6–9). New York, NY: Social Science Research Council.

Terry, C. M. (2003). From C-block to academia: You can't get there from here. In J. I. Ross & S. C. Richards (Eds.), *Convict criminology* (pp. 95–119). Belmont, CA: Wadsworth.

Wacquant, L. (2001). Deadly symbiosis. *Punishment and Society, 3*(1), 95–133.

Western, B. (2007). Mass imprisonment and economic inequality. *Social Research, 74*(2), 509–542.

Index

About the Editors

Mary Maguire is a Professor and the Chair of the Division of Criminal Justice at California State University Sacramento. Her research interests include moral panic and public policy, as well as issues related to the incarceration movement in the United States, including drugs, race, class, and management of those at risk for offending. Selected publications include: *A False Sense of Security: Moral Panic Driven Sex Offender Legislation, Corrections in California: The California Department of Corrections and Rehabilitation, and The Prevalence of Mental Illness in California Sex Offenders on Parole: A comparison of Those Who Recidivated With a New Sex Crime Versus Those Who Did Not*. In addition to *Critical Issues in Crime and Justice*, she has two editions of *Annual Editions: Drugs, Society, and Behavior*. Dr. Maguire served as the Book Review Editor for Contemporary Justice Review and is the past President of the Western Society of Criminology. Dr. Maguire is currently working on prevention measures for families at risk for violence.

Dan Okada is an associate professor in the Division of Criminal Justice at Sacramento State University. He has professed at California State University Long Beach and Marist College in Poughkeepsie, New York. His work centers on juvenile justice and the promotion and examination of restorative justice, and the search for peace. His play centers on Fender electrics and Ovation acoustics, and often acting his shoe size, not his age.

About the Contributing Authors

Janice Ahmad is an associate professor in the Department of Criminal Justice at the University of Houston-Downtown, where she also serves as graduate coordinator. Dr. Ahmad's research interests include police management, citizen involvement in policing, women in policing, crime victims, and program evaluation. Dr. Ahmad earned her PhD in criminal justice from Sam Houston State University.

Michael Bachmann is associate professor of Criminal Justice at Texas Christian University. He received his PhD in sociology from the University of Central Florida and his MA in social sciences from University of Mannheim, Germany. Dr. Bachmann specializes in the investigation of computer and high-tech crimes. His research focuses primarily on the social dimensions behind technology-driven crimes. He is the author of several book chapters and journal articles on cybercrime and cyber-criminals. His pioneering research on online offenders has won him several distinguished awards and grants.

Cyndi Banks is associate vice provost and associate dean of University College and professor of Criminology and Criminal Justice at Northern Arizona University. She teaches a range of subjects with a special focus on criminal justice ethics, juvenile justice, and human rights. As well as being an accomplished academic, Dr. Banks is an expert on overseas development projects in the justice sector and, in that capacity, has worked in Papua New Guinea, Bangladesh, Iraq, South Sudan, East Timor, Kurdistan, and Myanmar. She is the author of eight books including *Criminal Justice Ethics* (SAGE), *Youth Crime and Justice* (Routledge), and *Developing Cultural Criminology: Theory and Practice in Papua New Guinea* (University of Sydney). She is currently writing *International and Comparative Criminal Justice* (SAGE).

Timothy A. Capron graduated from Midwestern State University and cleverly avoided the draft by enlisting and graduating from Marine Corps Officer Candidate School at Quantico, Virginia. Upon leaving active duty, he completed his graduate studies in 1979 earning a PhD in criminal justice administration from Sam Houston State University. He returned to active duty with the Marine Corps in 1980, transferring to the Army later that year. He retired from the military as a lieutenant colonel, having served as a military police officer and a nuclear weapons officer, and attended the Command and General Staff College and the Army Management Staff College. He is professor of Criminal Justice at Sacramento State University. He is a lifetime member of the Academy of Criminal Justice Sciences and the Association for the Study of the Mideast and Africa. His latest textbook is *Deviant Behavior: Crime, Conflict and Interest Groups,* eighth edition (with Charles H. McCaghy, J. D. Jamieson, and Sandra Carey; Allyn & Bacon). He will coauthor a text on violence and terrorism (with Stephanie Mizrahi, SAGE) and was recently appointed to be a program advisor for the California State Mitigation Assessment Response Team.

Meda Chesney-Lind, PhD, teaches Women's Studies at the University of Hawaii. She is internationally recognized for her work on women and crime, and her testimony before Congress resulted in national support of gender responsive programming for girls in the juvenile justice system. Her most recent book on girls' use of violence, *Fighting for Girls* (coedited with Nikki Jones, State University of New York Press), won an award in 2012 from the National Council on Crime and Delinquency for "focusing America's attention on the complex problems of the criminal and juvenile justice systems."

Sharla "Kris" Cook is a retired U.S. Air Force general officer who studied and wrote policy on international terrorism at the U.S. Air Force's Air University, Maxwell AFB, Alabama; the National Defense University, Fort McNair, Washington D.C.; and at Sacramento State University. She holds master's degrees in management and criminal justice, has taught both live and online courses about violence and terror-ism, and was selected to teach in those areas in Israel by the Foundation for Defense of Democracies. Kris is a breast cancer survivor and a proud veteran. She has volun-tarily jumped out of perfectly good airplanes, paddled her own kayak down white water rapids, and has long carried her own backpack—believing every life should contain a little challenge and adventure.

John Crank, PhD, is professor of Criminology and Criminal Justice at University of Nebraska, Omaha. He is the author or coauthor of eight books and 56 articles in peer-reviewed journals. He most recently wrote *Global Warming, Violence, and Crime* (with Linda Jacoby, Lexis/Nexis, Spring 2014), and is currently writing its follow-up. He received the Academy of Criminal Justice Science's outstanding book award for *Imagining Justice* (Anderson Publishing) and was nominated for that same award for *Mission-Based Policing* (with Rebecca Murray, Mark Sundermeier, and Dawn Irlbeck, CRC Press).

Leah E. Daigle is associate professor in the Department of Criminal Justice in the Andrew Young School of Policy Studies at Georgia State University. She received her PhD in criminal justice from the University of Cincinnati. Her research has centered on repeat sexual victimization of college women and the development and continua-tion of victimization across the life course. She is coauthor of *Criminals in the Making: Criminality Across the Life Course,* second edition (with Bonnie Fisher and Francis Cullen, SAGE) and *Unsafe in the Ivory Tower: The Sexual Victimization of College Women* (with John Paul Wright and Stephen Tibbets, SAGE), which was awarded the 2011 Outstanding Book Award by the Academy of Criminal Justice Sciences, and author of *Victimology: A Text/Reader* (SAGE) and *Victimology: The Essentials* (SAGE). Her research has appeared in *Justice Quarterly, Victims and Offenders, The Journal of Quantitative Criminology,* and *The Journal of Interpersonal Violence.*

Traqina Emeka is associate professor of Criminal Justice at the University of Houston Downtown, having earned her doctorate at Prairie View A&M University. Her research interests include juvenile delinquency, victimology, recidivism, and community corrections. She is also the coauthor of *American Victimology* (LFB Scholarly Publishing) and has published in the areas of child abuse, juvenile recidivism, and community corrections.

Helen Taylor Greene, PhD (University of Maryland), is a professor in the Department of Administration of Justice in the Barbara Jordan-Mickey Leland School of Public Affairs at Texas Southern University in Houston, Texas. She is the author, coauthor, and coeditor with Dr. Shaun L. Gabbidon of *Race and Crime,* third edition (SAGE) and *Race and Crime: A Text Reader* (SAGE). She also served as lead coeditor of the *Encyclopedia of Race and Crime* (SAGE) with Dr. Gabbidon. Dr. Taylor Greene is the 2014 recipient of the 2014 W. E. B. Du Bois Award from the Western Society of Criminology. In 2011 she received the Academy of Criminal Justice Science's Outstanding Mentor Award.

James C. (Buddy) Howell, PhD, worked at the federal Office of Juvenile Justice and Delinquency Prevention for over 20 years where he mainly served as director of Research and Program Development. Dr. Howell presently is senior research associate at the National Gang Center. He has published more than 50 works on youth gangs, including a recent book, *Gangs in America's Communities* (SAGE). His research topics include gang history, gang homicides, drug trafficking, gangs in schools, myths about gangs, risk factors for gang involvement, and what works in preventing and reducing gang involvement and gang violence. He also consults with communities in assessing their gang problem and in strategic planning, using the OJJDP Comprehensive Gang Program Model.

Megan Qually Howell, MCJ, is a correctional research and evaluation analyst with the North Carolina Department of Public Safety. She has been an analyst in the North Carolina juvenile justice system and has carried out several statewide policy studies on topics including youth gang activity, youth violence prevention, school crime and violence, juvenile justice policies and practices, juvenile diversion, and disproportionate minority contact. In her role as an analyst, Ms. Howell assists with the development of statewide and local initiatives, legislative reports, grant programs, and collaborations with external researchers. She also has responsibility for data quality assurance and management information system (MIS) improvements.

Dawn M. Irlbeck is associate professor of Sociology at Creighton University where she facilitates the criminal justice policy track as well as the Nebraska State Victims Assistance Academy. Her primary research interests include policing and minority communities, racial profiling, and Latino police officers. She published (with John Crank, Rebecca Murray, and Mark Sundermeier) *Mission Based Policing* (CRC

Press), which was nominated for the Academy of Criminal Justice Sciences 2012 Outstanding Book Award.

Connie M. Koski received her PhD in criminology and criminal justice from the University of Nebraska at Omaha and is currently assistant professor of Criminology & Criminal Justice Studies at Longwood University in Farmville, Virginia. Her primary research interests focus on police-community relationships, neighborhood collective efficacy and informal social control, and qualitative research methods. Dr. Koski's work has been published in *Journal of Criminal Justice, Police Practice and Research: An International Journal, the Journal of Criminal Justice Education,* and *The Encyclopedia of Criminology & Criminal Justice* (Wiley-Blackwell).

Peter Kraska, PhD, is professor and chair of Graduate Studies and Research in the School of Justice Studies. He has distinguished himself as a leading scholar in the areas of criminal justice theory, police and criminal justice militarization, and research methods. He has published seven books including *Criminal Justice and Criminology Research Methods* (Prentice Hall), *Theorizing Criminal Justice: Eight Essential Orientations* (Waveland Press), *and Militarizing The American Criminal Justice System: The Changing Roles of the Armed Forces and Police* (Northeastern University Press). Dr. Kraska's research can be found in a number of leading journals, including the *British Journal of Criminology, Social Problems, Justice Quarterly,* and *Policing and Society.* His research interests include making theoretical sense of the emergence of underground cage fighting, the trend to legalize through medicalization the use of performance enhancing drugs, and a continuation of study into the blurring distinction between criminal justice and the military in the wars on drugs and terrorism.

Kyle Letteney received his BA degree in criminal justice with a minor in sociology at Rochester Institute of Technology. From 2011 to 2013 he worked with the Center for Public Safety Initiatives in Rochester, New York, conducting research on state-level narcotic laws and community empowerment projects. He is a graduate student in sociology at the University of Tennessee. His research interests include restorative justice in contemporary society, the social impacts of law, structural violence, and mass incarceration.

Mary Maguire is a Professor and the Chair of the Division of Criminal Justice at California State University Sacramento. Her research interests include moral panic and public policy, as well as issues related to the incarceration movement in the United States, including drugs, race, class, and management of those at risk for offending. Selected publications include: *A False Sense of Security: Moral Panic Driven Sex Offender Legislation, Corrections in California: The California Department of Corrections and Rehabilitation, and The Prevalence of Mental Illness in California Sex Offenders on Parole: A comparison of Those Who Recidivated With a New Sex Crime Versus Those Who Did Not.* In addition to *Critical Issues in Crime and Justice,* she has two editions of *Annual Editions: Drugs, Society, and Behavior.* Dr. Maguire served as the Book Review Editor for Contemporary Justice Review and is the past President of the Western Society of Criminology. Dr. Maguire is currently working on prevention measures for families at risk for violence.

Marilyn D. McShane is professor of Criminal Justice at the University of Houston, Downtown. She has been co-principal investigator on a number of correctional research grants and her published work includes journal articles, monographs, encyclopedias, and books on a wide range of criminological and criminal justice subjects. Recent materials include *Women and Criminal Justice* (Aspen Publishers); *Criminological Theory*, sixth edition, (with Frank P. Williams, III, Pearson); *A Thesis Resource Guide for Criminology and Criminal Justice* (with Frank P. Williams, III, Prentice Hall); the three-volume set *Youth Violence and Delinquency: Monsters and Myths* (Praeger); and the *Encyclopedia of Juvenile Justice* (SAGE).

Alan Mobley is associate professor of Criminal Justice and Public Affairs at San Diego State University. He teaches courses on restorative justice, community-based service learning, and law and society. His academic career began with sporadic attendance at several California community colleges. Later, while in federal prison for cocaine convictions, he earned a BS in economics from Regents College of the University of the State of New York and an MA in sociology from Vermont College. After a decade of incarceration, he was released to 5 years parole. He received a doctorate in criminology, law, and society from the School of Social Ecology at the University of California, Irvine. His work engages interdisciplinary convict criminology, including participatory action research on mass incarceration, shame and trauma, and restorative practices. His recent writing appears in *Contemporary Justice Review, Museums and Social Issues, Western Criminology Review, Eurovista, Peace Review,* and *Journal of Critical Animal Studies.*

Stephen L. Muzzatti is associate professor of Sociology at Ryerson University in Toronto, Canada, specializing in the areas of crime, media, and popular culture. He has published work on state crime and crimes of globalization, consumerism and violence, the news media, working class identities, and the motorcycle culture. He is also an expert in arson and demolition. Dr. Muzzatti has served as the vice-chair of the American Society of Criminology's Division on Critical Criminology and as editor of *The Critical Criminologist* and is a member of the editorial board of *Contemporary Justice Review.*

Johnny Nhan has a doctorate from the University of California, Irvine, and is associate professor of Criminal Justice at Texas Christian University. His research primarily focuses on issues of technology and crime. He has written on a variety of cybercrime related topics, ranging from online piracy to cyber vigilante groups. He is author of *Policing Cyberspace: A Structural and Cultural Analysis* (LFB Scholarly Publishing).

Thomas Nolan is an associate professor of criminology and the director of graduate programs in criminology at Merrimack College. A former senior policy analyst in the Office of Civil Rights and Civil Liberties at the Department of Homeland Security in Washington, DC, as well as a 27-year veteran (and former lieutenant) of the Boston Police Department, Nolan is consulted regularly by local, national, and international media outlets for his expertise in policing and civil rights and civil liberties issues, police practices and procedures, the police subculture, and crime trends and criminal behavior. Nolan's scholarly publications are in the areas of gender roles in policing, the police subculture, and the influence of the popular culture on criminal justice processes.

Daniel Okada earned his doctorate at the University of Maryland and his undergraduate degree at the University of California, Berkeley. He is associate professor of Criminal Justice at Sacramento State University. He is editor-in-chief of *Contemporary Justice Review,* the internationally recognized leading venue for work in the area of transformative, social, and restorative justice, and served as president of Justice Studies Association. His academic work is in the area of juvenile delinquency and juvenile justice, and restorative justice. He is also engaged in research, advocacy, and promotion of the Japanese American community.

David L. Parry is professor of Criminal Justice at Endicott College in Beverly, Massachusetts, where he has taught for over 18 years, offering courses in nearly all core criminal justice subject areas and mentoring hundreds of undergraduates through empirical senior thesis projects. The editor of *Essential Readings in Juvenile Justice* (Pearson Prentice Hall), he has directed research projects examining delinquent behavior, the operation of state and local juvenile justice systems, and the interaction of police, court, and correctional agencies with youth in numerous jurisdictions across the United States. After completing his undergraduate education at University of California, Los Angeles, Dr. Parry earned his PhD from the School of Criminal Justice at the University at Albany, State University of New York.

Lois Presser is professor of Sociology at the University of Tennessee. She holds a bachelor's degree in human development and family studies from Cornell University, an MBA from Yale University, and a doctorate in criminal justice/criminology from the University of Cincinnati. She studies cultural patterns that promote—and abate—harm to people and others, using a narrative approach. Dr. Presser is author of the books *Why We Harm* (Rutgers University Press) and *Been a Heavy Life: Stories of Violent Men* (University of Illinois Press), as well as articles in *Justice Quarterly, Signs, Social Justice,* and *Social Problems.*

Philip L. Reichel is professor emeritus of Sociology at the University of Northern Colorado. He has authored or coauthored more than 30 articles, book chapters, and encyclopedia entries and has lectured at universities in Austria, China, Germany, and Poland. He has also presented papers at side events during the UN Congress on Crime Prevention and Criminal Justice (Brazil) and the UN Commission on Crime Prevention and Criminal Justice (Vienna). Dr. Reichel is an active member of the American Society of Criminology and the Academy of Criminal Justice Sciences, serving as a trustee-at-large for the latter.

Randall G. Shelden is professor of Criminal Justice, University of Nevada-Las Vegas. He is also a senior research fellow with the Center on Juvenile and Criminal Justice in San Francisco. Dr. Shelden received his master's degree in sociology at Memphis

State University and PhD in sociology at Southern Illinois University. He is author or coauthor of the following books: *Criminal Justice in America: A Sociological Approach* (Little, Brown); *Girls, Delinquency and Juvenile Justice*, fourth edition (Thomson/Wadsworth), with Meda Chesney-Lind (which received the Michael Hindelang Award for outstanding contribution to Criminology in 1992); *Youth Gangs in American Society*, fourth edition (Wadsworth, Cengage), with Sharon Tracy and William B. Brown; *Crime and Criminal Justice in American Society*, second edition (with William Brown, Karen Miller, and Randall Fritzler, Waveland Press); *Controlling the Dangerous Classes: The History of Criminal Justice*, second edition (Allyn & Bacon); *Delinquency and Juvenile Justice in American Society*, second edition (Waveland Press); *Juvenile Justice in America: Problems and Prospects* (Waveland Press, coedited with Daniel Macallair); *Our Punitive Society* (Waveland Press). He is also the author of more than 50 journal articles and book chapters on the subject of crime and justice. He has also written more than 100 commentaries appearing in local and regional newspapers. He is the coeditor of the online *Justice Policy Journal*. His website is www.sheldensays.com.

Cassia Spohn is a foundation professor in the School of Criminology and Criminal Justice at Arizona State University (ASU). She is the author or coauthor of six books, including *Policing and Prosecuting Sexual Assault: Inside the Criminal Justice System* (with Katharine Tellis, Lynne Rienner Publishers), which was published in 2013. Her research interests include prosecutorial and judicial decision making, the intersections of race, ethnicity, crime and justice, and sexual assault case processing decisions. In 2013 she received ASU's Award for Leading Edge Research in the Social Sciences and was selected as a fellow of the American Society of Criminology.

Richelle Swan is associate professor of Sociology at California State University, San Marcos. She earned a PhD in criminology, law & society from the University of California, Irvine, and a MS in justice studies from Arizona State University. She teaches a number of classes related to crime, deviance, law, and social justice. Her current research includes popular culture and the social construction of crime and delinquency, gang injunction laws on Southern California communities, the socio-legal consciousness of deviantized populations, and the intersection of gender, race, class, and transformative justice programs and movements. She is the coauthor (with Kristin Bates) of *Juvenile Delinquency in a Diverse Society* (SAGE); coauthor and editor of *Through the Eye of Katrina: Social Justice in the United States*, second edition, and the *Instructor's Manual* (with Kristin Bates, Carolina Academic Press); and *Spicing Up Sociology: The Use of Films in Sociology Courses* (with Marisol Clark-Ibáñez, Wadsworth/Thomson Learning). In addition, she has published on topics such as problem-solving courts, welfare fraud diversion, restorative justice, and social justice movements.

Craig D. Uchida, PhD, is president and founder of Justice & Security Strategies, Inc. (JSS), a consulting firm that specializes in law enforcement, criminal justice, homeland security, children and youth violence, public health, and public policy. At JSS, he oversees contracts and grants with cities, counties, criminal justice agencies, foundations, and foreign nations. Dr. Uchida has been a member of the Senior Executive Service (SES) at the U.S. Department of Justice, and assistant director for Grants

Administration in the Office of Community Oriented Policing Services (COPS), which led to two major U.S. Department of Justice Awards—the Attorney General's Distinguished Service Award in 1995 and the JustWorks Award for innovation in government in 1997. JSS has conducted research, evaluations, and training in over 100 law-enforcement agencies in the United States, U.S. Virgin Islands, and Trinidad and Tobago. He is the author of numerous journal articles on policing and criminal justice, has coedited two books, and coauthored a National Academy of Sciences book on the security of America's dams. Dr. Uchida received his PhD in criminal justice from the University at Albany and holds two master's degrees, one in criminal justice and one in American history.

Gennaro F. Vito is professor of Justice Administration at the University of Louisville. He also serves as a faculty member in the Administrative Officer's Course at the Southern Police Institute. He holds a PhD in public administration from The Ohio State University. He is a past president and fellow of the Academy of Criminal Justice Sciences and a recipient of their Bruce Smith Award in recognition of his outstanding contributions to criminal justice as an academic or professional endeavor. He has published journal articles on capital sentencing, police consolidation, police traffic stops, policing strategies for drug problems in public housing, attitudes toward capital punishment, and the effectiveness of criminal justice programs, such as drug elimination programs, drug courts, and drug testing of probationers and parolees. He is the coauthor of nine textbooks in criminal justice and criminology including *Criminology: Theory, Research and Practice* (Jones & Bartlett) and *Organizational Behavior and Management in Law Enforcement* (Prentice Hall).

Anthony Walsh received his PhD from Bowling Green State University, Ohio. He is professor of Criminal Justice at Boise State University in Idaho, where he teaches criminology, statistics, law, and correctional casework and counseling. He has field experience in both law enforcement and corrections, and is the author or coauthor of 34 books and approximately 150 other publications. He also has a drop-dead gorgeous wife whom he has loved with all his being for at least 27 years.

Frank P. "Trey" Williams III is professor emeritus at California State University, San Bernardino. He has published well over a hundred articles, research monographs, and government reports and more than two dozen books in areas ranging from criminological theory to correctional management. He received the Fellow Award from the Academy of Criminal Justice Sciences. Recent works include *Statistical Concepts for Criminal Justice and Criminology* (Prentice Hall) and, with Marilyn D. McShane, *A Thesis Resource Guide for Criminology* (Prentice Hall) and *Criminological Theory*, sixth edition (Pearson).

Ilhong Yun is associate professor of Police Administration at Chosun University in South Korea. He earned his doctorate in criminal justice from Sam Houston State University. He has field experience as a police officer for 12 years in South Korea, and his 30 research articles have been published in *Journal of Interpersonal Violence, Journal of Criminal Justice, Policing,* and other academic journals. Currently, his research interests lie in the area of biosocial criminology, comparative criminal justice, and policing.

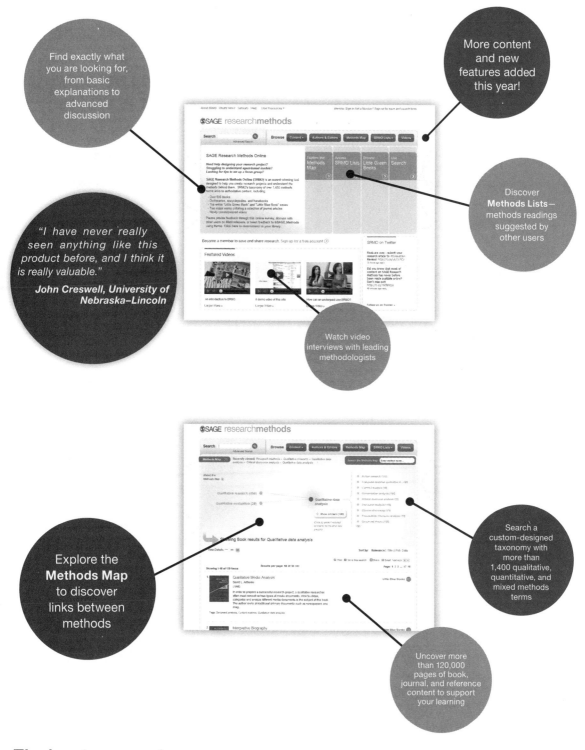

⑤SAGE researchmethods

The essential online tool for researchers from the world's leading methods publisher

Find exactly what you are looking for, from basic explanations to advanced discussion

More content and new features added this year!

"I have never really seen anything like this product before, and I think it is really valuable."

John Creswell, University of Nebraska–Lincoln

Discover **Methods Lists**— methods readings suggested by other users

Watch video interviews with leading methodologists

Explore the **Methods Map** to discover links between methods

Search a custom-designed taxonomy with more than 1,400 qualitative, quantitative, and mixed methods terms

Uncover more than 120,000 pages of book, journal, and reference content to support your learning

Find out more at
www.sageresearchmethods.com